The Reformation of Historical Thought

St Andrews Studies in Reformation History

Lead Editor

Bridget Heal (*University of St Andrews*)

Editorial Board

Amy Burnett (*University of Nebraska- Lincoln*)
Euan Cameron (*Columbia University*)
Bruce Gordon (*Yale University*)
Kaspar von Greyerz (*Universitat Basel*)
Felicity Heal (*Jesus College, Oxford*)
Karin Maag (*Calvin College, Grand Rapids*)
Roger Mason (*University of St Andrews*)
Andrew Pettegree (*University of St Andrews*)
Alec Ryrie (*Durham University*)
Jonathan Willis (*University of Birmingham*)

The titles published in this series are listed at *brill.com/sasrh*

The Reformation of Historical Thought

By

Mark A. Lotito

BRILL

LEIDEN | BOSTON

Cover illustration: Matthias Merian, *Topographia Germaniae* (Frankfurt a.M., 1650) – Wittenberg. Collection of the Author.

The Library of Congress Cataloging-in-Publication Data is available online at http://catalog.loc.gov

Typeface for the Latin, Greek, and Cyrillic scripts: "Brill". See and download: brill.com/brill-typeface.

ISSN 2468-4317
ISBN 978-90-04-34794-6 (hardback)
ISBN 978-90-04-34795-3 (e-book)

Copyright 2019 by Koninklijke Brill NV, Leiden, The Netherlands.
Koninklijke Brill NV incorporates the imprints Brill, Brill Hes & De Graaf, Brill Nijhoff, Brill Rodopi, Brill Sense, Hotei Publishing, mentis Verlag, Verlag Ferdinand Schöningh and Wilhelm Fink Verlag.
All rights reserved. No part of this publication may be reproduced, translated, stored in a retrieval system, or transmitted in any form or by any means, electronic, mechanical, photocopying, recording or otherwise, without prior written permission from the publisher.
Authorization to photocopy items for internal or personal use is granted by Koninklijke Brill NV provided that the appropriate fees are paid directly to The Copyright Clearance Center, 222 Rosewood Drive, Suite 910, Danvers, MA 01923, USA. Fees are subject to change.

This book is printed on acid-free paper and produced in a sustainable manner.

For my grandparents
†*William &* †*Lucille Lotito and Armin &* †*Esther Schuetze*

∴

Das liebe, heil'ge Röm'sche Reich,
Wie hält's nur noch zusammen?[1]

⁂

---
1 Johann Wolfgang von Goethe, *Faust Erster Teil, Auerbachs Keller in Leipzig* (*Frosch*); translated in Johann Wolfgang von Goethe, *Faust Part One*, trans. David Luke (New York: Oxford University Press, 1998), lines 2089-2092 ("The Holy Roman Empire, we all love it so; But how it holds together, that's what we don't know.").

Contents

Acknowledgements XI
Additional Acknowledgements XIII
List of Illustrations XV
Abbreviations XVIII

1 **Introduction** 1
  1 The Constitution of Europe 1
  2 Philipp Melanchthon 4
  3 Prior Research 7
  4 Reformation of Historical Thought 13
  5 Melanchthon's Historical Works 17
  6 *Carion's Chronicle* 25
  7 Chapter Summaries 31

2 **The Fourth Monarchy and the *Translatio Imperii*** 34
  1 Introduction 34
  2 Universal History and the Roman Empire 35
  3 Christian Historiography 37
  4 Late Antiquity and the Fourth Monarchy 42
  5 St. Augustine and the Six Ages 44
  6 Universal History in the Early Middle Ages 46
  7 The Four Monarchies in the High Middle Ages 48
  8 *Translationes Imperii* and the *Donation of Constantine* 53
  9 Papal-Imperial Chronicles 55
  10 Challenges to the Curial Theories 59
  11 Early Printed Chronicles 62
  12 The *Germania Illustrata* and *Nauclerus's Chronicle* 71
  13 Conclusion 82

3 **Johann Carion of Bietigheim: The Berlin Court Astronomer** 84
  1 Introduction 84
  2 Carion's Early Career 88
  3 *Sintflut* of 1524 91
  4 A Second Flood Prediction 99
  5 Natural Art of Astrology 101
  6 The Dispute with Andreas Perlach 104
  7 Carion and Königsberg 110
  8 Carion and Melanchthon 112

9	Melanchthon and Annius of Viterbo	117
10	Carion's 1532 Visit to Wittenberg	121
11	Seventy Weeks of Daniel	127
12	Celestial Signs and Portents	131
13	Carion's Career after 1532	136
14	Conclusion	140

4 Carion's Chronicle: A Wittenberg View of the Past   142

1	Introduction	142
2	The Reformation of Form and Structure	146
3	*Translationes Imperii*	149
4	The Holy Roman Empire	153
5	The Four Monarchies and the Turks	161
6	The Wittenberg World Map	166
7	The Turks in *Carion's Chronicle*	169
8	Ecclesiastical History	174
9	The Melanchthon-Peucer *Chronicle* of 1572	185
10	Melanchthon's Revisions	186
11	Caspar Peucer's Revisions	191
12	The Electoral College	195
13	The Medieval Papacy	197
14	Ecclesiastical History and Periodization	199
15	Conclusion	205

5 The Transmission and Reception of Carion's Chronicle   207

1	Introduction	207
2	The Early Transmission of *Carion's Chronicle*	210
3	The Latin Transmission of the Carion-Melanchthon *Chronicle*	213
4	Translations	218
5	*Carion's Chronicle* in the Catholic Context	223
6	Johann Funck and the 1542 Turkish Campaign	228
7	The 1546 Wittenberg Edition	236
8	The Schmalkaldic War	238
9	Unauthorized Editions of the *Chronicle*	239
10	Melanchthon's Revised *Chronicle*	242
11	Caspar Peucer	252
12	Peucer and the *Chronicle*	255
13	Wittenberg and Frankfurt	258
14	*Wittenberg Chronicle*	266
15	The Fall of the Philippists	271
16	Conclusion	278

6 **The Legacy of Wittenberg Historiography**   281
    1   Introduction   281
    2   Jean Bodin's Attack on German Political Thought   283
    3   The Initial German Response to Bodin   288
    4   The Fourth Monarchy and the Theologians   296
    5   The Fourth Monarchy and the Imperial Publicists   302
    6   The Fourth Monarchy and the Historians   307
    7   The Four Monarchies in the Graphic Arts   316
    8   The Last Days of the Fourth Monarchy   325

7 **Conclusion**   333

    Appendix A: Carion's Chronicle – Textual Transmission   337
    Appendix B: Carion's Chronicle – Manuscript Notes   352
    Appendix C: Carion's Chronicle – Stemma of Editions   354
    Appendix D: Carion's Chronicle – Indices to the Editions   359
    Appendix E: Carion's Chronicle – Census of Editions   374

    Bibliography   470
    Index   535

Acknowledgements

I wish to thank those who have presided over my studies and fostered my research these many years. Since I first entered his classroom, Tom Ziebell has remained a steadfast supporter, and he has made so much possible in the years that have followed. At the University of Chicago, Hanna H. Gray and Michael I. Allen encouraged my interests in the classical tradition and Renaissance learned culture, and I still fondly remember those early days of reading in the Regenstein. I undertook the initial research for this study at the Warburg Institute (University of London), and I am grateful for the supervision of my teachers there, especially Magnus Ryan, now of Cambridge (Peterhouse), and my Warburg advisor, Jill Kraye.

At the University of Michigan, I would like to acknowledge the kind mentoring of my dissertation committee: Tom Tentler, Michael I. Allen (University of Chicago), Gottfried Hagen, and Paolo Squatriti. I am indebted to them all for their encouragement and support over the years, as well as to Tom Green for his patient advice. I have learned much in the process, and any failings in the final product remain entirely my own. The law school community at Cornell University also provided much encouragement, and the reading room of Myron Taylor Hall served as a quiet refuge during my studies in Ithaca. During my time now as an attorney, I have appreciated the support of many colleagues, who amidst it all have kindly asked over the years when they would finally see this book in print. Perhaps, now, at long last, I too can say, "the doing has been worth the price."

This study is based primarily on the collections of two wonderful institutions: the British Library and the Herzog August Bibliothek. It was a pleasure to spend a year at each, first in London and later in Wolfenbüttel; and I am especially grateful to Dr. Jill Bepler at the Herzog August Bibliothek for her kindness during my many visits. I have likewise appreciated the opportunities to discuss Reformation research, and especially *Carion's Chronicle*, with Dr. Helmut Claus, retired director of the Gotha Forschungsbibliothek. In my younger days, †Dr. Ruth Roebke-Berens, Prof. Daniel M. Deutschlander, and †P. Dr. Wolfgang Renz all nurtured my training in European cultural history. More recently, I wish to thank Prof. Andrew Pettegree, Prof. Bridget Heal and Mrs. Francis Knikker for their support in adding this book to the St. Andrews Studies in Reformation History series at Brill.

Over the years, I have received encouragement from family and many friends, both in the States and in Europe, who always remained interested in my engagement with the distant past. The writing of this book has been a long journey and I have appreciated the kindness of all those who have helped along the way. Most of all, though, I am grateful to Annette, my dear wife, who has stayed by me through so much. I owe her more than I can ever express.

Even after all these years, there is still something magical about wandering through Europe from library to library and monastery to monastery in search of old manuscripts or long-forgotten books. From Hyde Park and the shores of Lake Michigan, these grand adventures have now extended to the far corners of the world. In looking back, I recall happy memories of those first train rides from Zürich along the lake and up to Einsiedeln, those morning walks from London House, past Coram's Fields, to the steps of the British Library, and those soothing words at the end of many a weary scholar's pilgrimage: "nächster Halt ist Wolfenbüttel." Traveling with *Carion's Chronicle* through this lost world has been the most improbable and enchanting of journeys, and if I only publish one book, I am glad that it will have been this one.

Mark A. Lotito
Milwaukee, Wisconsin
5 January 2019

Additional Acknowledgements

I wish to acknowledge the support I received from various sources in carrying out my research: the American Friends of the Warburg Institute, Goodenough College (London House), the University of Michigan, especially the Rackham School of Graduate Studies and the Department of History, the American Friends of the Herzog August Bibliothek, the Gesellschaft der Freunde der Herzog August Bibliothek, and the German Academic Exchange Service (DAAD).

I wish to thank the staff at the libraries of the Warburg Institute in London, the University of Michigan in Ann Arbor, and Cornell University in Ithaca. I also wish to thank the scholars, and especially the Wolfenbüttel community of researchers, who aided my search for Carion editions or otherwise provided support and encouragement over the years. In addition to the British Library and Herzog August Bibliothek, I have made use of the following collections, either in person or by proxy, or I received assistance from their members of staff. I am grateful to all concerned for the help with my research:

Queen Mother Library (Aberdeen), Bibliothèque Méjanes (Aix-en-Provence), Bibliothèque municipale (Amiens), Universiteitsbibliotheek (Amsterdam), Vrije Universiteit (Amsterdam), Bibliothèque municipale (Angers), Emory University Pitts Theology Library (Atlanta), Staats- und Stadtbibliothek (Augsburg), Bibliothèque municipale (Avignon), Universitätsbibliothek (Basel), University of California Bancroft Library (Berkeley), Staatsbibliothek zu Berlin Preußischer Kulturbesitz (Berlin), Bibliothèque Abbé Grégoire (Blois), University of Indiana Lilly Library (Bloomington), Universitäts- und Landesbibliothek (Bonn), Tufts University Library (Boston), Stadtbibliothek (Braunschweig), Harvard University Houghton Library (Cambridge), Emmanuel College (Cambridge), University Library (Cambridge), Bibliothèque municipale (Carcassonne), University of North Carolina Wilson Library (Chapel Hill), Center for Research Libraries (Chicago), Newberry Library (Chicago), University of Chicago Libraries (Chicago), Landesbibliothek (Coburg), University of Maryland Library (College Park), Det Kongelige Bibliotek (Copenhagen), Biblioteca civica De Gregoriana (Crescentino), Biblioteca civica (Cuneo), Ohio State University Library (Dayton), Lippische Landesbibliothek (Detmold), Bibliothèque Municipale (Dijon), Sächsische Landesbibliothek- Staats- und Universitätsbibliothek (Dresden), Duke University Library (Durham), Stiftsbibliothek (Einsiedeln), Universitätsbibliothek (Erlangen), Biblioteca Nazionale Centrale (Firenze), Universitätsbibliothek (Freiburg im Breisgau), Niedersächsische Staats- und Universitätsbibliothek (Göttingen), Forschungsbibliothek (Gotha), Bibliothèque municipale (Grenoble),

Koninklijke Bibliotheek (Den Haag), Universitäts- und Landesbibliothek Sachsen-Anhalt (Halle), Staats- und Universitätsbibliothek (Hamburg), Innerpeffray Library (Innerpeffray), Thüringer Universitäts- und Landesbibliothek (Jena), Badische Landesbibliothek (Karlsruhe), Universitätsbibliothek (Kiel), Erzbischöfliche Diözesan- und Dombibliothek (Köln), Universitäts- und Stadtbibliothek (Köln), Universiteitsbibliotheek (Leiden), Universitätsbibliothek (Leipzig), Médiathèque Louis Aragon (Le Mans), Institute for Historical Research (London), University of London Senate House Library (London), Wellcome Library (London), University of California Charles E. Young Research Library (Los Angeles), Bibliothèque municipale (Lunel), Bibliothèque municipale (Mâcon), Drew University Library (Madison), University of Wisconsin Memorial Library (Madison), University of Manchester John Rylands Library (Manchester), Universitätsbibliothek (Mannheim), University of Melbourne Libraries (Melbourne), Bibliothèque municipale (Metz), University of Wisconsin Golda Meir Library (Milwaukee), University of Minnesota Libraries (Minneapolis), Bibliothèque municipale Antonin Perbosc (Montauban), Médiathèque centrale d'agglomération Emile Zola (Montpellier), Russian State Library (Moscow), Bayerische Staatsbibliothek (München), Bibliothek der Ludwig-Maximilians-Universität (München), Bibliothèque municipale (Nancy), Yale University Beinecke Library (New Haven), Pierpont Morgan Library (New York), Martin Luther College Library (New Ulm), Bibliothèque Carré d'art (Nîmes), Médiathèque de la communauté d'agglomération (Niort), Germanisches Nationalmuseum Bibliothek (Nürnberg), Stadtbibliothek (Nürnberg), Bibliothèque municipale (Orléans), Nasjonalbiblioteket (Oslo), All Souls College Library (Oxford), Bodleian Library (Oxford), Taylor Institution Library (Oxford), Queen's College Library (Oxford), Bibliothèque Nationale (Paris), Bibliothèque Sainte-Geneviève (Paris), Bibliothèque municipal (Périgueux), Médiathèque François Mitterrand (Poitiers), Strahov Monastery Library (Prague), Staatliche Bibliothek (Regensburg), Bibliothèque Rennes Métropole Les Champs Libres (Rennes), Universitätsbibliothek (Rostock), Bibliothek des Franziskanerklosters (Salzburg), Huntington Library (San Marino), Stiftsbibliothek (Sankt Gallen), Biblioteca del Seminario Vescovile (Padova), National Library of Russia (St. Petersburg), Biblioteca comunale Giosue' Carducci (Spoleto), Württembergische Landesbibliothek (Stuttgart), University of Toronto Thomas Fisher Rare Book Library (Toronto), Universitätsbibliothek (Tübingen), Universitetsbibliotek (Uppsala), University of Illinois Library (Urbana), Universiteitsbibliotheek (Utrecht), Bibliothèque municipale (Valognes), Bibliothèque municipale (Versailles), Österreichische Nationalbibliothek (Vienna), Hessische Landesbibliothek (Wiesbaden), Lutherhalle (Wittenberg), Biblioteka Uniwersytecka (Wrocław), Stiftsbibliothek St. Viktor (Xanten), Zentralbibliothek (Zürich).

Illustrations

Figures

1 Werner Rolevinck, *Fasciculus Temporum* (Venice, 1484), fol. 5v–6r. Herzog August Bibliothek Wolfenbüttel: A: 274.1 Hist. 2° (1)   65
2 Werner Rolevinck, *Fasciculus Temporum* (Venice, 1484), fol. 61v–62r. Herzog August Bibliothek Wolfenbüttel: A: 274.1 Hist. 2° (1)   67
3 Hartmann Schedel, *Buch der Chroniken* (Nuremberg, 1493), fol. 75v. Bayerische Staatsbibliothek München: 2 Inc.c.a. 2922, urn:nbn:de:bvb:12-bsb00059084-6   69
4 Johann Carion, *Practica* ([Augsburg], 1518). Staats- und Stadtbibliothek Augsburg: 4 Kult 186-109, urn:nbn:de:bvb:12-bsb11216306-6   90
5 Leonhard Reynmann, *Practica* (Nuremberg, 1523). Herzog August Bibliothek Wolfenbüttel: A: 171.21 Quod. (51)   93
6 Alexander Seitz, *Ain Warnung* ([Augsburg], [1520]). Staats- und Stadtbibliothek Augsburg: 4 Kult 186-114, urn:nbn:de:bvb:12-bsb11216311-4   94
7 Johann Carion, *Prognosticatio* (Leipzig, 1521). Herzog August Bibliothek Wolfenbüttel: 57 Quod 4°   96
8 Johann Carion, *Bedeütnusz vnnd Offenbarung* (Augsburg, 1526). Herzog August Bibliothek Wolfenbüttel: A: 44.10 Astron. (15)   102
9 Lucas Cranach the Elder, *Johann Carion* (ca. 1530). Staatsbibliothek zu Berlin (on loan to Staatliche Museen zu Berlin, Gemäldegalerie). Photo Credit: The Warburg Institute, University of London, Photographic Collection   113
10 Carion, *Chronica* (Wittenberg, 1532), sig. Cij v. Herzog August Bibliothek Wolfenbüttel: Gb 56.   120
11 Carion, *Chronica* (Wittenberg, 1532). Herzog August Bibliothek Wolfenbüttel: Gb 56   126
12 Justus Jonas, *Das Siebend Capital Danielis* (Wittenberg, 1529), sig. [Aj] v. Herzog August Bibliothek Wolfenbüttel: H: T 454.4° Helmst. (4)   167
13 Martin Luther, *Eine Heerpredigt* (Wittenberg, 1542), sig. B r. Herzog August Bibliothek Wolfenbüttel: M: Li 5530 Slg. Hardt (58, 1172)   168
14 Carion, *Chronica* (Frankfurt a.M., 1546). Herzog August Bibliothek Wolfenbüttel: H: T 226.8° Helmst.   231
15 Carion, *Chronica* (Wittenberg, 1546). Herzog August Bibliothek Wolfenbüttel: H: T 224.8° Helmst.   231
16 Carion, *Chronica* (Frankfurt a.M., 1564). Herzog August Bibliothek Wolfenbüttel: H: T 232.8° Helmst.   241

17 Carion, *Chronica* (Frankfurt a.M., 1564), fol. 166r. Herzog August Bibliothek Wolfenbüttel: H: T 232.8° Helmst. 241

18 Melanchthon, *Chronicon Carionis* (Wittenberg, 1558). Herzog August Bibliothek Wolfenbüttel: H: YT 39.8° Helmst. 247

19 Melanchthon, *Chronicon Carionis* (Wittenberg, 1558). Herzog August Bibliothek Wolfenbüttel: S: Alv.: U 214 (1) 247

20 Peucer, *Chronicon Carionis* (Geneva, 1617), *Tabella*. Herzog August Bibliothek Wolfenbüttel: H: T 259.8° Helmst. 257

21 Melanchthon, *Neuwe vollkommene Chronica* (Frankfurt a.M., 1566). Herzog August Bibliothek Wolfenbüttel: H: T 365.2° Helmst. 262

22 Melanchthon, *Chronica Carionis* (Wittenberg, 1573). Herzog August Bibliothek Wolfenbüttel: A: 178 Hist. 2° 270

23 Johann Ludwig Gottfried, *Historische Chronica* (Frankfurt a.M., 1630). Basel University Library: Falk 1079:1 308

24 Johann Sleidanus, *De Quatuor Summis Imperiis* (Wittenberg, 1658). Basel University Library: EA VI 8b 312

25 Lorenz Faust, *Anatomia Statuae Danielis* (Leipzig, 1585 [1586]), chart opposite sig. Hiij r. Herzog August Bibliothek Wolfenbüttel: A: 91.1 Quod. (1) 318

26 Wolfgang Kilian, *Imago... Danielis 2.v.31* (Augsburg, 1623). National Library of Sweden: KoB Tr. B. 2014_B. 17. Photo Credit: Ann-Sofie Persson, National Library of Sweden 321

27 Anonymous, *Colossus* (Altdorf, 1667). Herzog August Bibliothek Wolfenbüttel: IH 2 322

28 Matthias Seutter, *Colossus Monarchicus* (Augsburg, ca. 1734). Basel University Library: Ew 397:2 Grossfolio 324

29 Matthias Seutter, *Pontificum Romanorum Series Chronologica* (Augsburg, ca. 1734). Basel University Library: Ew 397:2 Grossfolio 325

30 Matthias Seutter, *Statua Regum Europæorum* (Augsburg, ca. 1734). Basel University Library: Ew 397:2 Grossfolio 326

31 Matthias Seutter, *Icon Synoptica Sac. Rom. Imp. Electorum* (Augsburg, ca. 1734). Basel University Library: Ew 397:2 Grossfolio 327

32 Tobias Lotter, *Colossus Monarchicus* (Augsburg, ca. 1775). Bern University Library: MUE Ryh 8303 : 31 328

33 Anonymous, *Colossus Monarchicus* ([s.n.], ca. 1735). Photo Credit: Kestenbaum & Company, New York 329

34 Carion, *Chronica* (Wittenberg, 1532). Herzog August Bibliothek Wolfenbüttel: H: T 223.8° Helmst. (1) 347

35 Anonymous, *Chronica* (Wittenberg, 1532). Herzog August Bibliothek Wolfenbüttel: H: T 223.8° Helmst. (2) 347

ILLUSTRATIONS

Maps

1 Carion-Melanchthon *Chronica* (1532) Textual Transmission. Map Credit: University of Wisconsin-Milwaukee Cartography & GIS Center   357
2 Melanchthon-Peucer *Chronicon Carionis* (1558–1565) Textual Transmission. Map Credit: University of Wisconsin-Milwaukee Cartography & GIS Center   358

Stemmas

1 *Carion's Chronicle* (1532–1573)   354
2 *Carion's Chronicle* Latin Editions (1537–1565)   355
3 *Carion's Chronicle* (1558–1625)   356

Abbreviations

ADB	*Allgemeine Deutsche Biographie*. 56 vols. Leipzig: Duncker & Humblot, 1875–1912.
Bibliotheca Palatina	Mittler, Elmar, ed. *Bibliotheca Palatina: Druckschriften = Stampati Palatini = Printed Books: Katalog zur Mikrofiche-Ausgabe*. 4 vols. München: K.G. Saur, 1999.
Baudrier, Bibliographie Lyonnaise	Baudrier, Henri Louis. *Bibliographie Lyonnaise. Recherches sur les imprimeurs, libraires, relieurs et fondeurs de lettres de Lyon au XVIe siècle*. 12 vols. Paris: F. de Nobele, 1964.
Brunet	Brunet, Jacques-Charles. *Manuel du Libraire et de l'Amateur de Livres*. 9 vols. Paris: Firmin-Didot frères, 1860–80.
Brunet, Supplément	Deschamps, Pierre. *Manuel du Libraire et de l'Amateur de Livres Supplément*. 2 vols. Paris: Firmin-Didot, 1878–1880.
Cartier	Cartier, Alfred. *Bibliographie des Èditions des De Tournes Imprimeurs Lyonnais*. 2 vols. Paris: Editions des Bibliothèques Nationales de France, 1937.
CR	Melanchthon, Philipp. *Corpus Reformatorum*, vols. 1–28, *Philippi Melanthonis Opera quae supersunt omnia*. Edited by Carolus Gottlieb Bretschneider and Heinrich Bindseil. Halis Saxonum: apud C.A. Schwetschke et filium, 1834–60.
CRL	Center for Research Libraries (Chicago, IL)
Le Edizioni italiane del XVI secolo	*Le Edizioni italiane del XVI secolo: censimento nazionale*, vol. 3. Roma: Istituto centrale per il catalogo unico delle bibliotheche italiane e per le informazioni bibliografiche, 1993.
French Vernacular Books	Pettegree, Andrew, ed. *French Vernacular Books: Books Published in the French Language before 1601*. 2 vols. Leiden: Brill, 2007.
Imprimeurs & Libraires Parisiens du XVIe siècle	Renouard, Philippe. *Imprimeurs & Libraires Parisiens du XVIe siècle*. Paris: Paris musées, 1964-.
Iter Italicum	Paul Oskar Kristeller. *Iter Italicum: A Finding List of Uncatalogued or Incompletely Catalogued Humanistic Manuscripts of the Renaissance in Italian and Other Libraries*. 7 vols. London: Warburg Institute, 1963–1997.

ABBREVIATIONS

Knihopis českých a slovenských tisků	*Knihopis českých a slovenských tisků od doby nejstarší až do konce XVIII. století*, vol. 2. Prague: Druckerei des Protektorates Bohmen und Mähren in Prag, 1941.
MBW	Melanchthon, Philipp. *Melanchthons Briefwechsel: Kritische und Kommentierte Gesamtausgabe im Auftrag der Heidelberger Akademie der Wissenschaften.* Edited by Heinz Scheible. Stuttgart: Frommann-Holzboog, 1977-.
MGH	*Monumenta Germaniae Historica*
Moller	Moller, Daniel Wilhelm. *Disputationem Circularem De Joh. Carione, Sub Praesidio Dan. Guil. Molleri, Com. Palat. Caesar. & Prof. Publ. Facult. Philosoph. h.t. Decani, Iuventuti Karinophilus P.P. Joh. Leonhardus Kulmichius, Norimb. Altdorf. d. 13. Febr. A. MDCXCVII. H.L.Q.C.* [Altdorf]: Meyerus, 1697. VD17 12:136858G
Nielson	Nielsen, Lauritz. *Dansk Bibliografi*, vol. 2, *1551–1600*. København: Gyldendal, 1933.
NRSV	*The Bible. New Revised Standard Version.*
Oxford DNB	*Oxford Dictionary of National Biography*. Oxford: Oxford University Press, 2004. [On-line Edition]
RE	Hauck, Albert, ed. *Realencyklopädie für Protestantische Theologie und Kirche, begründet von J. J. Herzog.* 24 vols. Leipzig: J. C. Hinrichs, 1896–1913.
Reske	Reske, Christoph. *Die Buchdrucker des 16. und 17. Jahrhunderts im deutschen Sprachgebiet: Auf der Grundlage des gleichnamigen Werkes von Josef Benzing.* Wiesbaden: Harrassowitz, 2007.
Scherer	Scherer, Emil Clemens. *Geschichte und Kirchengeschichte an den deutschen Universitäten: Ihre Anfänge im Zeitalter des Humanismus und ihre Ausbildung zu selbständigen Disziplinen.* Freiburg i. B.: Herder, 1927.
STC (2nd ed.)	Pollard, Alfred W. *A Short-Title Catalogue of Books Printed in England, Scotland, & Ireland and of English Books Printed Abroad, 1475–1640*, 2nd ed. 3 vols. London: Bibliographical Society, 1976–1991.
Strobel	Strobel, Georg Theodor. "Von Carions Leben und Schriften." *Miscellaneen literarischen Innhalts, Sechste Sammlung* (Nürnberg, 1782): [139]–206.
TRE	Krause, Gerhard and Gerhard Müller, eds. *Theologische Realenzyklopädie.* Berlin: W. de Gruyter, 1976-.

USTC	*Universal Short Title Catalogue.*
VD16	*Verzeichnis der im deutschen Sprachbereich erschienenen Drucke des XVI. Jahrhunderts.*
VD17	*Verzeichnis der im deutschen Sprachraum erschienenen Drucke des 17. Jahrhunderts.*
WA	Luther, Martin. *D. Martin Luthers Werke: Kritische Gesamtausgabe.* Weimar: Böhlaus Nachfolger, 2003- [Unveränderter Nachdruck].
WA BR	Luther, Martin. *D. Martin Luthers Werke: Kritische Gesamtausgabe. Briefwechsel.* 18 vols. Weimar: Böhlaus Nachfolger, 2002 [Unveränderter Nachdruck].
WA DB	Luther, Martin. *D. Martin Luthers Werke: Kritische Gesamtausgabe. Die Deutsche Bibel.* 15 vols. Weimar: Böhlaus Nachfolger, 2001 [Unveränderter Nachdruck].
WA TR	Luther, Martin. *D. Martin Luthers Werke: Kritische Gesamtausgabe. Tischreden.* 6 vols. Weimar: Böhlaus Nachfolger, 2000 [Unveränderter Nachdruck].
Willems, Les Elzevier	Willems, Alphonse. *Les Elzevier: Histoire et Annales Typographiques.* 2 vols. Bruxelles: G.-A. van Trigt, 1880.

CHAPTER 1

Introduction

1 The Constitution of Europe

On a fateful Christmas Day in A.D. 800, Charlemagne, king of the Franks and the Lombards, entered St. Peter's in Rome. Through inheritance and conquest, he had created a European Empire that reached from northern Spain to modern Poland and from the English Channel to southern Italy. He ruled most of the old Western Roman Empire, which had splintered apart in the fifth century, and he had added to this the lands of the Germanic tribes beyond the Rhine, which the Romans sometimes defeated but ultimately failed to conquer and subdue. During the ceremonies that winter day, Pope Leo III crowned Charlemagne as "Roman Emperor," and he was acclaimed by the Roman people. According to Einhard, his earliest biographer, Charlemagne always regretted the events that Christmas, and he claimed the Emperor never would have entered the church if he had known what was to unfold.[1]

At his death in 814, Charlemagne's realm passed intact to his son, Louis the Pious, but the unity of the Carolingian Empire did not survive into the next generation. Louis had three sons who lived to inherit; and in 843, after years of intra-familial strife and open war, they finally divided the Empire into three kingdoms. Ludwig the German received the eastern lands, Charles the Bald, the son of Judith, Louis's second wife, received the western lands, and Lothar, the eldest son and holder of the Imperial title, received a middle territory from the North Sea to Italy, including Aachen, the Carolingian capital.[2]

The real and symbolic force of those early medieval events has reverberated across the centuries, and the legacy of the Carolingians has defined the political history of Europe to the present. Based on the precedent of Charlemagne's coronation, later popes asserted the right to crown the rulers of the West; and, like Charlemagne, later kings and Emperors often rued the significance of that Christmas Day in Rome. For generations, intellectual battles were joined and brutal wars were fought over claims to political supremacy in the West. Ultimately, hundreds of years would pass before the papacy was excluded from an

---

1 Pierre Riché, *The Carolingians: A Family who Forged Europe*, trans. Michael I. Allen (Philadelphia: University of Pennsylvania Press, 1993), 121–122; and Einhard, *The Life of Charlemagne*, with a foreword by Sidney Painter (Ann Arbor: University of Michigan Press, 1960), 56–57.
2 Riché, *The Carolingians*, 165–169.

official role in the high politics of Europe, and then only under virulent protest from Rome.[3]

The Treaty of Verdun in 843 likewise had lasting implications for the future of the West. The tripartite division of Charlemagne's Empire meant that as the eastern and western kingdoms developed into modern France and Germany, they were separated by a poorly defined middle ground (Lotharingia). This stretch of land, including the Low Countries, Alsace-Lorraine, and also northern Italy, witnessed centuries of intrigue and bloodshed as stronger neighbours asserted claims to ancient rights and "natural frontiers." France, for instance, waged a long, and ultimately futile, series of wars to extend its eastern border to the Rhine and to assert control over northern Italy.[4] Likewise, the Emperors repeatedly marched across the Alps to make real their claims to the peninsula and the riches of the Italian city-states.[5]

In many ways, the formation of the modern European Union embodies a conscious effort to end the bloody consequences of decisions made eleven hundred years ago. Indeed, from a historical perspective, the last seventy years of peaceful coexistence in Western Europe is a striking anomaly. The early idea of a post-WWII economic union was meant to align the fortunes of France and Germany, and thereby prevent the recurring conflicts that had at times engulfed all of Europe. Even if the European Economic Community, and its successor, the European Union, are no longer driven primarily by the need to prevent open war in Europe, they nevertheless began as a solution to the problems created by Charlemagne's bellicose grandsons.[6]

The European Union, however, is only the latest in a series of "constitutional" solutions implemented over time, and with varying degrees of success and permanence, to address the legacy of the Carolingians. After the Napoleonic Wars, for instance, the Great Powers decided to ensure peace by containing France, and they did so by placing a formidable obstacle on the French frontier: the Prussian army. The solution, of course, worked, in the sense that France has never again waged an aggressive war in Europe. At the same time, however, the

---

3   See Constantin Fasolt, "Sovereignty and Heresy," in *Infinite Boundaries: Order, Disorder, and Reorder in Early Modern German Culture*, ed. Max Reinhart (Kirksville: Sixteenth Century Journal Publishers, 1998), 381–391.
4   On Louis XIV's wars, for instance, see F.L. Carsten, ed., *The New Cambridge Modern History*, vol. V, *The Ascendancy of France 1648–88* (Cambridge: Cambridge University Press, 1961).
5   On the twelfth century wars, for example, see Benjamin Arnold, "The Western Empire, 1125–1197," in *The New Cambridge Medieval History*, vol. 4, *Part 1 c. 1024–c. 1198*, ed. David Luscombe and Jonathan Riley-Smith (Cambridge: Cambridge University Press, 2004), 384–421.
6   See generally, Desmond Dinan, ed., *Origins and Evolution of the European Union* (Oxford: Oxford University Press, 2006).

INTRODUCTION

decision at the Congress of Vienna allowed for what France had rightly feared and long sought to prevent – a strong, united Germany.[7]

Like the Congress of Vienna, earlier meetings and agreements have marked changes to the "European constitution." The Council of Constance (1414–1418) and the Peace of Westphalia (1648), for example, both redefined the European order by addressing the problems of European strife in their respective periods. In the early fifteenth century, the delegations at Constance rewove the torn fabric of the Christian West by ending the Great Schism, in which as many as three "popes" had claimed to rule as the heir of St. Peter. The European leaders at the council reestablished ecclesiastical unity by agreeing on a single pope, and they tried, with limited success, to create a system of ongoing dialogue to address the governance of the church.[8] Similarly, in the mid-seventeenth century, the meetings at Münster and Osnabrück were a recognition of the exhaustion after decades of turmoil caused by warring alliances in Europe. The Peace of Westphalia that emerged from those negotiations ended the Thirty Years' War, gave legal legitimacy to Calvinism and established the modern system of states in Europe.[9] It was the last great rewriting of the European constitution prior to the Napoleonic Wars.

As with Constance, Westphalia, and Vienna, the Europeans of the sixteenth century also engaged in a profound rewriting of the European constitution. The process was political, but it dovetailed with the religious Reformations of the sixteenth century; and although it involved all of Europe, the focus here is on the Holy Roman Empire.[10] By the early sixteenth century, Europeans had spent hundreds of years engaged in an intellectual, and often armed, struggle over the question of political supremacy in the Christian West, and especially

---

7   See E.V. Gulick, "The Final Coalition and the Congress of Vienna, 1813–15," in *The New Cambridge Modern History*, vol. IX, *War and Peace in an Age of Upheaval 1793–1830*, ed. C.W. Crawley (Cambridge: Cambridge University Press, 1965), esp. 650–651, 656.

8   See Anthony Black, "Popes and Councils," in *The New Cambridge Medieval History*, vol. VII, *c. 1415–c. 1500*, ed. Christopher Allmand (Cambridge: Cambridge University Press, 1998), 65–86.

9   See E.A. Beller, "The Thirty Years War," in *The New Cambridge Modern History*, vol. IV, *The Decline of Spain and the Thirty Years War 1609–48/59*, ed. J.P. Cooper (Cambridge: Cambridge University Press, 1970), 306–358.

10 See generally C. Scott Dixon, "The Politics of Law and Gospel: The Protestant Prince and the Holy Roman Empire," in *The Impact of the Reformation: Princes, Clergy and People*, ed. Bridget Heal and Ole Peter Grell (Burlington, VT: Ashgate, 2008), 37–62; Robert von Friedeburg, "The Making of Patriots: Love of Fatherland and Negotiating Monarchy in Seventeenth Century Germany," *The Journal of Modern History* 77 (December 2005): 881–916; and Robert Scribner, "Politics and the Institutionalisation of Reform in Germany," in *The New Cambridge Modern History*, vol. II, *The Reformation 1520–1559*, ed. G.R. Elton (Cambridge: Cambridge University Press, 1990), 172–197.

in the Empire. Within forty years of Martin Luther's entry onto the European stage, however, the great medieval question of supremacy had been answered, in the sense that the papacy had essentially been removed from Imperial political affairs. With the Peace of Augsburg (1555), Protestantism attained official recognition within the Empire; and from the mid-1550s, Catholic and Protestant princes were agreed that the legitimacy of the Emperor depended on the election of the seven Imperial Electors, rather than a papal coronation. In a matter of decades, the Protestant intellectual community had effectively rewritten the constitution of the Holy Roman Empire to strip the papacy of its role in German political life. On that basis, the Holy Roman Empire, freed of its medieval adversary, continued as an elected monarchy until the abdication of the last Emperor in 1806.

2   Philipp Melanchthon

The present study addresses an integral aspect of this struggle to rewrite the Imperial constitution, the sixteenth century reformation of historical thought, and specifically the perspective on the European past developed at Reformation Wittenberg. As a definitional matter, I have used the term "Wittenberg Historiography" because it captures the idea of Wittenberg as a centre of historiographical activity without confining the inquiry to a theological perspective or to "Lutheranism." Indeed, "Wittenberg" uniquely encompasses city, court and university, and reflects the Electoral Saxon residence's importance as a political, cultural, and intellectual centre of the sixteenth century world. The term likewise cuts across the traditional scholarly divide between the topographical-historical approach of German humanism and the more theologically oriented historiography of the Reformation itself. So too, it recognizes the diffusion of a Wittenberg perspective through print and through the generations of students who journeyed to the university on the banks of the Elbe. For that brief moment in time, Wittenberg was transformed into one of the most dynamic and innovative centres in all of Europe, and its intellectual influence stretched from the shores of Iceland all the way to Istanbul.

The specific subject here is the historiographical activity of the leading Wittenberg historian, Philipp Melanchthon (1497–1560), and especially his universal history, *Carion's Chronicle*.[11] Melanchthon was active as an historian from

---

11   The standard biographies of Melanchthon are Heinz Scheible, *Melanchthon: Eine Biographie* (München: Verlag C.H. Beck, 1997); Wilhelm Maurer, *Der junge Melanchthon*, 2 vols. (Göttingen: Vandenhoeck & Ruprecht, 1967–1969); and Karl Hartfelder, *Philipp*

the 1510s down to his death in 1560, so his career affords a unique perspective on the changing patterns of German historiography in the course of the sixteenth century. Many of the Wittenberg reformers, including Georg Spalatin and Nicolaus von Amsdorf, wrote historical works,[12] and even Luther composed a treatment of historical chronology, his *Reckoning of the Years of the World*.[13] Nevertheless, Melanchthon, more than any of his colleagues, was responsible for creating a coherent view of the past, and his perspective achieved wider dissemination, both through his students and through print, than any other historian of the sixteenth century.

During his studies in South Germany, Melanchthon was trained by the humanists of the Upper Rhine region, and by 1518, when he departed to join the faculty at Wittenberg, he had already established his reputation as the most promising young scholar in Germany. After his arrival in Saxony, Melanchthon's thought was refined in the crucible of the Wittenberg Reformation, and he was soon converted to Luther's movement. Following this initial euphoria, the experience of unrest in Germany during the 1520s, and especially the Peasants' War, left the young professor deeply scarred. He witnessed outbreaks of iconoclasm, religious fanaticism, and then open revolt by the peasants. Those tumultuous events left a lasting impression, and they conditioned Melanchthon's subsequent thinking about political, social and ecclesiastical order. From farther afield, he listened in dread as reports arrived in Wittenberg about the sack of Rome and the march of the Turks through the Balkans.[14] After the

---

Melanchthon als Praeceptor Germaniae (Berlin: A. Hofmann & comp., 1889). In English, nothing has yet replaced Clyde Manschreck, *Melanchthon: The Quiet Reformer* (New York: Abingdon Press, 1958).

12 See Christiane Andersson, "Die Spalatin-Chronik und ihre Illustrationen aus der Cranach-Werkstatt," in *Lucas Cranach: Ein Maler-Unternehmer aus Franken*, ed. Claus Grimm et al. (Regensburg: Verlag Friedrich Pustet, 1994), 208–217; Christina Meckelnborg and Anne-Beate Riecke, "Die 'Chronik der Sachsen und Thüringer' von Georg Spalatin," in *Fata Libellorum: Festschrift für Franzjosef Pensel zum 70. Geburtstag*, ed. Rudolf Bentzinger und Ulrich-Dieter Oppitz (Göppingen: Kümmerle Verlag, 1999), 131–162; and Wolf-Friedrich Schäufele, "Kirche Christi und Teufelskirche: Verfall und Kontinuität der Kirche bei Nikolaus von Amsdorf," in *Nikolaus von Amsdorf (1483–1565) zwischen Reformation und Politik*, ed. Irene Dingel (Leipzig: Evangelische Verlagsanstalt, 2008), 79–86.

13 On Luther as an historian, see generally John Headley, *Luther's View of Church History* (New Haven: Yale University Press, 1963); and Ernst Schäfer, *Luther als Kirchenhistoriker: Ein Beitrag zur Geschichte der Wissenschaft* (Gütersloh: C. Bertelsmann, 1897).

14 When the city of Rome was sacked in 1527, one of Melanchthon's greatest fears was the fate of the libraries. See MBW 556. On this point, see also Stefan Rhein, "Melanchthon und der italienische Humanismus," in *Humanismus und Wittenberger Reformation: Festgabe anläßlich des 500. Geburtstages des Praeceptor Germaniae Philipp Melanchthon am 16.*

Ottoman victory over the Hungarians at Mohács (1526), Melanchthon, like many Germans, lived in perpetual fear of the Turks.

For decades, Melanchthon frequented Imperial diets and regional meetings of the German princes. Indeed, since Luther, as an outlaw, was confined to Saxony after 1521, Melanchthon assumed a leading role as theological negotiator for the German Protestants. As a result, he had first-hand experience of the religious and political forces at play in the Empire, and although he never travelled outside of Germany, he was well informed about the international affairs of his day. During those years, the Turkish threat dominated German political life, and at the same time, the tensions created by the Reformation often brought the German princes to the brink of civil war. After years of failed negotiations, and then Luther's death in 1546, the Emperor finally marched against the Protestants. By the end of the brief Schmalkaldic War, he had invaded Saxony, defeated the Elector's army and captured Wittenberg.

The remaining years of Melanchthon's life were embittered by the upheavals of the war and the religious disputes that followed. After his victory, Charles V actively sought to reimpose religious uniformity on Germany, and Melanchthon acquiesced to several Imperial demands. The question of compromise divided the Protestant ranks, and many of Melanchthon's former students turned against him. Some remained Protestant and berated him as a traitor to Luther; others rejoined the Catholic fold and attacked him as a heretic. After the Princes' War in 1552 and the subsequent Peace of Augsburg (1555), the Protestants finally attained legitimacy within the Empire, which brought a measure of calm to German political life. Nevertheless, Melanchthon's final years were marked by the failure of the last Imperial religious colloquy at Worms (1557) and the continuing attacks by several of his former students. He had spent his life trying to preserve the unity of the Western Church through dialogue and compromise, and he watched with dismay as theological divisions became ever more entrenched. Melanchthon died at Wittenberg in 1560, and his followers buried him next to Luther in the Castle Church.

Melanchthon left a mixed legacy. Already in his own lifetime, his dual role as reformer and humanist scholar made him a difficult figure to characterize, particularly in comparison to Luther, the reformer, or Erasmus, the philologist. Despite his importance within Protestantism, Melanchthon's reputation was permanently damaged by the religious controversies of his later years, and to many he became a reminder of the dangers of compromise. Indeed, a mixture of admiration and alienation has persisted in some confessional circles to the

---

Februar 1997, ed. Michael Beyer (Leipzig: Evangelische Verlagsanstalt, 1996), 372–373; and Hartfelder, *Philipp Melanchthon*, 305–306.

present. By contrast, other aspects of Melanchthon's legacy are less clouded by lingering religious concerns. During his long career, he had moulded generations of students, and he had reformed many of the schools and universities in the Protestant lands. In recognition of his contributions to education, he became known as the *Praeceptor Germaniae*, or teacher of Germany. Through his written works, his years of teaching and his administrative activities, Melanchthon had a profound and enduring influence on German intellectual culture that finds no parallel in early modern Europe.

3   Prior Research

The study of early modern German historiography has traditionally been divided into three parts: the flourishing humanist historiography of the late fifteenth and early sixteenth century, the abrupt transition to Reformation concerns, and finally the static condition of the field at the end of the century. As an overarching concern, one body of literature has addressed questions of method and the development of history as an independent discipline, especially since German universities, often under Melanchthon's influence, established many of the first history professorships in Europe.[15] Indeed, the early institutional support for historical studies in Germany has no real equivalent in the rest of Europe. More commonly, however, within this chronological framework, two thematic realms have been carved out – the *Germania Illustrata* tradition and Reformation historiography – and these divisions have held fairly constant over the decades.

The *Germania Illustrata* tradition refers to the movement among German scholars from the late fifteenth century onwards to reclaim the German past through topographical-historical treatments of land and people.[16] The movement was clearly indebted to the *Italia Illustrata* tradition from south of the

---

15   See Emil Clemens Scherer, *Geschichte und Kirchengeschichte an den deutschen Universitäten: Ihre Anfänge im Zeitalter des Humanismus und ihre Ausbildung zu selbständigen Disziplinen* (Freiburg i. B.: Herder, 1927).

16   See generally, Paul Joachimsen, *Geschichtsauffassung und Geschichtsschreibung in Deutschland unter dem Einfluß des Humanismus* (Leipzig and Berlin: Teubner, 1910); Gerald Strauss, *Sixteenth Century Germany: Its Topography and Topographers* (Madison: University of Wisconsin Press, 1959); Ottavio Clavuot, *Biondos "Italia Illustrata" – Summa oder Neuschöpfung? Über die Arbeitsmethoden eines Humanisten* (Tübingen: Niemeyer, 1990); Larry Silver, "Germanic Patriotism in the Age of Dürer," in *Dürer and His Culture*, ed. Dagmar Eichberger and Charles Zika (New York: Cambridge University Press, 1998), 38–68; Gernot Müller, *Die "Germania generalis" des Conrad Celtis: Studien mit Edition, Übersetzung und Kommentar* (Tübingen: Niemeyer, 2001).

Alps, but in the German context, a driving concern was the desire to wrest German history and ethnography from intellectual colonization, primarily by Italian Renaissance scholars, such as Aeneas Silvius Piccolomini. The most notable contribution to this genre is Hartmann Schedel's *Nuremberg Chronicle* (1493), perhaps the most famous of all illustrated incunabular works.[17] Later examples include the *Cosmography* (1545) of Sebastian Münster, which was expanded several times and republished as late as 1628.[18] Although very German focused, Schedel and Münster tended to be less overtly patriotic than some of their contemporaries, such as Conrad Celtis, so both have remained well within the scholarly mainstream, particularly from a history-of-the-book perspective.

By contrast, the use of the German historical past in Reformation polemics has often disenchanted later generations of medieval and Renaissance historians,[19] and the general lack of illustrations in these works has sometimes made them less inviting. Although some historians have accordingly walled off Reformation historiography from the European mainstream, the same body of historical literature has often appealed to more theologically oriented scholars, who have focused on the wealth of content rather than the paucity of illustration.[20] Because of these distinctions, sixteenth century religious reformers, such as the Wittenbergers, are often put into separate categories from their contemporaries, both by those who study them closely and also by those who do not study them at all.[21] The segregation is not entirely arbitrary, but it can easily distort the picture of early modern German historiography, especially by concentrating attention on changes, rather than continuity, in intellectual perspective following the outbreak of the Reformation.

---

17 Hartmann Schedel, *Chronicle of the World: The Complete and Annotated Nuremberg Chronicle of 1493*, ed. Stephan Füssel (London: Taschen, 2001).

18 On Münster, see Jasper van Putter, *Networked Nation: Mapping German Cities in Sebastian Münster's 'Cosmographia'* (Leiden: Brill, 2018); Matthew McLean, *The Cosmographia of Sebastian Münster: Describing the World in the Reformation* (Aldershot, UK: Ashgate, 2007); and Karl Heinz Burmeister, *Sebastian Münster: Versuch eines biographischen Gesamtbildes* (Basel and Stuttgart: Helbing & Lichtenhahn, 1963).

19 See generally Frank Borchardt, *German Antiquity in Renaissance Myth* (Baltimore: The Johns Hopkins University Press, 1971).

20 See, for example, Ronald Diener, "The Magdeburg Centuries: A Bibliothecal and Historiographical Analysis" (Ph.D. diss., Harvard Divinity School, 1978).

21 See, for example, Borchardt, *German Antiquity*, 10: "By limiting this study to the period preceding the widest spread of the Reformation in Germany, I hope to avoid the problems involved in untangling polemic from the joy of invention, propaganda from what was considered real learning." For a similar perspective, see W. Bradford Smith, "Germanic Pagan Antiquity in Lutheran Historical Thought," *The Journal of the Historical Society* IV:3 (Fall 2004): 360–361.

Against this general background, in recent years, the study of early modern German historiography has experienced something of a revival, both in Germany and in England. The Reformation Institute at St. Andrews has sponsored dissertations on two leading sixteenth century German historians, Johann Sleidanus and Sebastian Münster, and both studies have now appeared as monographs in this same series.[22] Brill has likewise added a new English monograph on the study of Greek Antiquity and Byzantine history among sixteenth century German Lutherans.[23] Two recent German publications have addressed the historiography of sixteenth century Germany from the perspective of Lutheran confessional culture.[24] A detailed treatment of the *Magdeburg Centuries* has now also appeared in the Wolfenbütteler Forschungen series.[25] The renewed interest is not, however, limited to Protestantism, and a recent monograph has focused on the historiography of Baroque Catholicism.[26] Early German humanism is also experiencing a revival, and Conrad Celtis, the German "arch-humanist," has been the subject of a book length treatment for the first time in decades.[27] The *Nuremberg Chronicle* has similarly undergone a thorough re-examination.[28]

Within these broader developments, Melanchthon's historical works have also received more attention. Most of these new contributions have been limited to articles or book chapters;[29] but a recent German dissertation provides

---

22   Alexandra Kess, *Johann Sleidan and the Protestant Vision of History* (Burlington, VT: Ashgate, 2008); and McLean, *The Cosmographia of Sebastian Münster*.
23   Asaph Ben-Tov, *Lutheran Humanists and Greek Antiquity: Melanchthonian Scholarship between Universal History and Pedagogy* (Leiden: Brill, 2009).
24   Susanne Rau, *Geschichte und Konfession: Städtische Geschichtsschreibung und Erinnerungskultur im Zeitalter von Reformation und Konfessionalisierung in Bremen, Breslau, Hamburg und Köln* (Hamburg: Dölling und Galitz Verlag, 2002); and Matthias Pohlig, *Zwischen Gelehrsamkeit und konfessioneller Identitätsstiftung Lutherische Kirchen- und Universalgeschichtsschreibung 1546–1617* (Tübingen: Mohr Siebeck, 2007).
25   Harald Bollbuck, *Wahrheitszeugnis, Gottes Auftrag und Zeitkritik: Die Kirchengeschichte der Magdeburger Zenturien und ihre Arbeitstechniken* (Wiesbaden: Harrassowitz, 2014).
26   Stefan Benz, *Zwischen Tradition und Kritik: Katholische Geschichtsschreibung im barocken Heiligen Römischen Reich* (Husum: Matthiesen Verlag, 2003).
27   Gernot Müller, *Die "Germania generalis" des Conrad Celtis: Studien mit Edition, Übersetzung und Kommentar* (Tübingen: Niemeyer, 2001).
28   Bernd Posselt, *Konzeption und Kompilation der Schedelschen Weltchronik* (Wiesbaden: Harrassowitz Verlag, 2015).
29   See Harald Bollbuck, "Universalgeschichte, Kirchengeschichte und die Ordnung der Schöpfung. Philipp Melanchthon und die Anfänge der protestantischen Geschichtsschreibung," in *Fragmenta Melanchthoniana: Humanismus und Europäische Identität*, vol. 4, ed. Günter Frank (Ubstadt-Weiher: Verlag Regionalkultur, 2009), 125–152; Frank Prietz, "Geschichte und Reformation. Die deutsche Chronica des Johannes Carion als Erziehungsbuch und Fürstenspiegel," in *Universitas: Die mittelalterliche und frühneuzeitliche*

an extensive guide to the sources for *Carion's Chronicle*, and it offers a wealth of detail through a focused reading of the text.[30] Nevertheless, the problems of textual transmission, addressed below, have proven a difficult barrier to a new interpretation of Melanchthon's historical thought and his role within early modern intellectual culture.

The prior research on Melanchthon as an historian has generally centred on three related, but still very different, aspects of his historiographical activities. In the early twentieth century, Aby Warburg wrestled with the survival of ancient thought during the transition into the modern world through a series of studies on the tension between the pre-modern and modern. Along with his interest in Renaissance Italy, he turned to the Lutheran reformers and the "arcane survivals of paganism" in Wittenberg, i.e. the vast body of astrological and prophetic literature that circulated in Germany during the sixteenth century.[31] Luther mostly rejected astrology and he expressed doubts about contemporary prophecy, though he deployed it when it seemed useful. In contrast to this, Warburg focused on how Melanchthon, the leading humanist among the Reformers, actively sought the sublunar significance of astronomical events.

For Warburg, Melanchthon's textbook of universal history, *Carion's Chronicle* (1532), became one of the key texts in understanding Reformation thought on the intersection of history, prophecy and astrology, in part because the book was written as a joint project between Melanchthon and Johann Carion, the court astronomer in Berlin.[32] As such, it provided a striking example of the way that seemingly irrational ways of thinking about past, present and future could hold such a prominent place in the intellectual world of sixteenth

Universität im Schnittpunkt wissenschaftlicher Disziplinen. Festschrift für Georg Wieland zum 70. Geburtstag, ed. Oliver Auge and Cora Dietl (Tübingen: Francke, 2007), 153–165; Volker Leppin, "Humanistische Gelehrsamkeit und Zukunftsansage: Philipp Melanchthon und das 'Chronicon Carionis,'" in *Zukunftsvoraussagen in der Renaissance*, ed. Klaus Bergdolt, (Wiesbaden: Harrassowitz, 2005), 131–142; and Barbara Bauer, "Die *Chronica Carionis* von 1532, Melanchthons und Peucers Bearbeitung und ihre Wirkungsgeschichte," in *Himmelszeichen und Erdenwege: Johannes Carion (1499–1537) und Sebastian Hornmold (1500–1581) in ihrer Zeit*, ed. Elke Osterloh (Ubstadt-Weiher: Verlag Regionalkultur, 1999), 203–246.

30 Frank Prietz, *Das Mittelalter im Dienst der Reformation: Die* Chronica *Carions und Melanchthons von 1532. Zur Vermittlung mittelalterlicher Geschichtskonzeptionen in die protestantische Historiographie* (Stuttgart: W. Kohlhammer Verlag, 2014).

31 Aby Warburg, "Pagan-Antique Prophecy in Words and Images in the Age of Luther (1920)," in *The Renewal of Pagan Antiquity: Contributions to the Cultural History of the European Renaissance*, trans. David Britt (Los Angeles: Getty Research Institute for the History of Art and the Humanities, 1999), 603.

32 Johann Carion, *Chronica durch Magistru[m] Johan Carion / vleissig zusamen gezogen / meniglich nützlich zu lesen.* (Wittenberg: Rhau, [1532]). VD16 C 998.

century Wittenberg. Indeed, Warburg argued that "astrological method, for [Melanchthon], represented a practical survival of the harmonizing worldview of the ancients, which was the very foundation of his cosmologically oriented humanism."[33] Warburg's use of *Carion's Chronicle* as an illustrative text for the survival of prophetic traditions into the Renaissance meant that this collaborative endeavour came to be seen as an important case study for the interaction of prophecy and history in the sixteenth century.[34]

The second line of research on Melanchthon has dealt primarily with his use of historical argument in the context of theological controversy.[35] Here too a point of tension in sixteenth century thought has provided the framework for approaching Melanchthon's engagement with historical studies and his deployment of history as a normative force. In view of the Reformation emphasis on Scripture alone, the question has been posed: how is it possible to resolve the intellectual conflict between this basic tenet and the consistent recourse by the Reformers to ecclesiastical history, and especially patristic studies, in their arguments?[36] Since Melanchthon composed both the standard textbook of Reformation theology, his *Loci Communes*, and the *Augsburg Confession*, the official statement of Protestant belief, his use of history in those texts, and more broadly within his written corpus, has offered a test case for the transition from Catholic to Protestant views of ecclesiastical tradition. Amidst this body of texts, *Carion's Chronicle* has likewise held a privileged place within the research into questions of doctrine and practice, especially because the later version of the book, which Melanchthon revised shortly before his death in 1560, represented his final statement on the history of the early Church.

---

33   Warburg, "Pagan-Antique Prophecy," 602–603.
34   See, for example, Katharine Firth, *The Apocalyptic Tradition in Reformation Britain, 1530–1645* (Oxford: Oxford University Press, 1979), esp. 15–22; Robert Lerner, *The Powers of Prophecy: The Cedar of Lebanon vision from the Mongol Onslaught to the Dawn of the Enlightenment* (Berkeley: University of California Press, 1983), 157–182; Robin Bruce Barnes, *Prophecy and Gnosis: Apocalypticism in the Wake of the Lutheran Reformation* (Stanford: Stanford University Press, 1988), 264; Avihu Zakai, *Exile and Kingdom: History and Apocalypse in the Puritan Migration to America* (Cambridge: Cambridge University Press, 1992), 12–55, esp. 18–22; Volker Leppin, *Antichrist und Jüngster Tag: Das Profil apokalyptischer Flugschriftenpublizistik im deutschen Luthertum 1548–1618* (Gütersloh: Gütersloher Verlagshaus Mohn, 1999), esp. 130–139; and Claudia Brosseder, *Im Bann der Sterne: Caspar Peucer, Philipp Melanchthon und andere Wittenberger Astrologen* (Berlin: Akademie Verlag, 2004).
35   See especially Pierre Fraenkel, *Testimonia Patrum: The Function of the Patristic Argument in the Theology of Philip Melanchthon* (Geneva: Librairie E. Droz, 1961).
36   See Irena Backus, *Historical Method and Confessional Identity in the Era of the Reformation (1378–1615)* (Leiden: Brill, 2003); and Pontien Polman, *L'Élément Historique dans la Controverse religieuse du XVIe Siècle* (Gembloux: J. Duculot, 1932).

In both of these cases, the questions asked of Melanchthon's historical endeavours have led to a focused and select reading of his works to harness them in pursuit of broader inquiries, whether grounded in Reformation theology or Renaissance learned culture. The third major focus of research has been on Melanchthon's role in the transformation of history into an independent, secular discipline. Within Germany, Melanchthon is remembered as one of the earliest advocates for adding history to the university curriculum, and his lectures at Wittenberg have been seen as crucial to the promotion of historical studies within academic culture.[37] Melanchthon was able to place many of his students in the first chairs of history established at the Protestant universities; and they in turn taught from classical texts edited by Melanchthon or they lectured on *Carion's Chronicle*.[38] In essence, Melanchthon and his followers were the first university professors to do what many history professors still do – they lectured on a printed textbook of history, written by one of their own, and held by the students themselves sitting in the classroom.

---

37 See, above all, Scherer, *Geschichte und Kirchengeschichte*; see also Samuel Berger, "Melanchthons Vorlesungen über Weltgeschichte," *Theologische Studien und Kritiken: Beiträge zur Theologie und Religionswissenschaft* 70 (1897): 781–790; Emil Clemens Scherer, "Die letzten Vorlesungen Melanchthons über Universalgeschichte," *Historisches Jahrbuch* 47 (1927): 359–366; Manfred Müller, "Geschichte und allgemeine Bildungstheorie: Eine Untersuchung über die Auffassung des Geschichtsunterrichts bei Johann Ludwig Vives und Philipp Melanchthon," *Geschichte in Wissenschaft und Unterricht: Zeitschrift des Verbandes der Geschichtslehrer Deutschlands* 14 (1963): 418–428; Heinz Scheible, "Melanchthons Bildungsprogramm," in *Lebenslehren und Weltentwürfe im Übergang vom Mittelalter zur Neuzeit: Politik, Bildung, Naturkunde, Theologie*, ed. Hartmut Boockmann (Göttingen: Vandenhoeck & Ruprecht, 1989), 233–248; Kathi Petersen, "Melanchthon als Lehrer der Geschichte," in *Politik, Religion, Kunst: Beiträge zur Geschichte Schweinfurts, Festschrift Horst Ritzmann*, ed. Uwe Müller (Schweinfurt: Historischer Verein, 1998), 361–370.

38 See Gustav Kohfeldt, "Der akademische Geschichtsunterricht im Reformationszeitalter, mit besonderer Rücksicht auf David Chytraeus in Rostock," *Mitteilungen der Gesellschaft für deutsche Erziehungs- und Schulgeschichte* 13 (1902): 201–228; Viljo Adolf Nordman, *Victorinus Strigelius als Geschichtslehrer* (Abo Turku: Aura, 1930); Uwe Neddermeyer, "Kaspar Peucer (1525–1602). Melanchthons Universalgeschichtsschreibung," in *Melanchthon in Seinen Schülern*, ed. Heinz Scheible (Wiesbaden: Harrassowitz, 1997), 69–101; Inger Ekrem, "Melanchthon – Chytraeus – Gunarius: Der Einfluss des Geschichtsunterrichts und der Geschichtsschreibung in den deutschen Ländern und in Dänemark-Norwegen auf einen norwegischen Lektor (ca. 1550–1608)," in *Reformation and Latin Literature in Northern Europe*, ed. Inger Ekrem et al. (Oslo: Scandinavian University Press, 1996), 207–225; and Markus Völkel, "Theologische Heilanstalt und Erfahrungswissen: David Chytraeus' Auslegung der Universalhistorie zwischen Prophetie und Modernisierung (UB-Rostock, MSS. hist. 5)," in *David Chytraeus (1530–1600) Norddeutscher Humanismus in Europa: Beiträge zum Wirken des Kraichgauer Gelehrten*, ed. Karl-Heiz Glaser and Steffen Stuth (Ubstadt-Weiher: Verlag Regionalkultur, 2000), 121–141.

4 Reformation of Historical Thought

For my own research, I too have been guided by many of these overarching issues, and I contribute here to different areas of this scholarly discourse, even if at times only incidentally. In contrast to this literature, however, I have been primarily concerned with a different type of question, one both textual and interpretative. Turning away from the approaches that have used Melanchthon as exemplary of particular tendencies in sixteenth century thought, I have sought instead to engage with the specific arguments that he deployed in his historical works and the immediate context of his historiographical activities. Melanchthon was perhaps the most widely read historian of the sixteenth century; but within the current scholarly research on early modern historiography, his work is often referred to as "ubiquitous" and then treated only in passing.[39] Melanchthon's historical writings are, however, far more than unpretentious schoolbooks or printed editions. They are, rather, texts that contributed to a wider conversation about social, political and religious developments within Europe during the reign of Emperor Charles V.

From early on, the Wittenberg Reformers recognized that their survival depended on attaining legitimacy within the Imperial order, and they were keenly aware that the papacy would always oppose any compromise, political or religious, that sanctioned deviance from Rome.[40] Melanchthon and his colleagues knew that the traditional method for addressing religious schism was the convocation of a church council, whether regional or universal. Nevertheless, they feared that any council outside of Germany would be packed with pro-papal delegates, who would simply crush the Protestant attendees by outvoting them. As a result, the Wittenbergers were forced to confront the issue of ecclesiastical supremacy, not only with regard to the pope, but also more generally with regard to the authority of the Christian community and its right to stifle dissent. In these struggles, a sense of historical change became an

---

39   See, for example, Daniel Woolf's comments about the circulation of historical texts in early modern England: "In the mid-1540's there appear the first signs of interest in post-classical history, with editions of Higden's *Polychronicon* and – soon to be an ubiquitous favorite – Johannes Carion's *Chronicle*." Daniel R. Woolf, *Reading History in early modern England* (Cambridge: Cambridge University Press, 2000), 143. *The Oxford History of Historial Writing* even states: "The *Chronicon Carionis* may well be the most influential historical manual ever written." Markus Völkel, "German Historical Writing from the Reformation to the Enlightenment," in *The Oxford History of Historical Writing*, vol. 3, *1400–1800*, ed. José Rabasa et al. (Oxford: Oxford University Press, 2012), 330.

40   See generally Dixon, "The Politics of Law and Gospel;" and Scribner, "Politics and the Institutionalisation of Reform in Germany."

integral component of Protestant attacks because history demonstrated that the ecclesiastical order of the sixteenth century was the product of development rather than divine command.

Besides these religious arguments, the Wittenberg Reformers turned to history to validate their perspective that the papacy lacked any claim to political supremacy, or indeed, even to a legitimate role in Imperial affairs. The political philosophy of German Protestantism was soon grounded in a belief that the Holy Roman Empire could overcome the threats from its two hostile neighbours, the Turks and the French, only if the papacy were permanently excluded from Imperial political life. Along with this, the Wittenbergers sought to demonstrate the exclusive right of the Germans to hold the title of "Empire," and they forcefully argued that neither the French nor the Turks could ever claim the mantel of Imperial Rome. Indeed, Melanchthon rejected any effort to reunify the old Carolingian Empire on French terms.

Therefore, for both religious and political reasons, the Wittenberg Reformers, and much of the Protestant community, became hostile to real or presumptive claims of papal supremacy in the West. In this context, historical studies proved an effective way to erode rival arguments developed in the Middle Ages and advanced by sixteenth century Catholic controversialists. By rewriting the story of the past, Melanchthon and his followers transformed the contemporary understanding of the Imperial constitution, and they decisively influenced the political future of the Holy Roman Empire. In the process, they crafted a narrative and interpretative framework that became normative for much of Protestant Europe; and the underlying arguments of sixteenth century historical thought have animated much of Western historiography ever since.

Melanchthon was deeply conscious of the difference between his own historiographical view and that of his medieval German predecessors. According to his assessment, medieval historians had been monks who lacked experience in affairs of state; as such, they were unable to address, or even to pose, the questions necessary to formulate analytical history.[41] Indeed, monkish historians

---

41   "Wie sich aber die sachen weiter zugetragen haben / finde ich auch nicht Denn vnsere Deudschen Historici haben kein handel gruntlich beschreiben können / mit vrsachen vnd vmbstenden / denn es sind Mönche gewesen / vnd sind nicht zun hendeln gezogen worden / So haben sie so viel verstands nicht gehabt / das sie darnach gefraget hetten / odder bedacht / was zu eim Historico gehöret." Carion, *Chronica* (Wittenberg, 1532), fol. 125r. Melanchthon also made disparaging remarks about medieval historians, presumably as part of revising *Carion's Chronicle*, in a letter of 2 November 1531: "Fama huc affertur de pugna ad Turegum facta, in qua dicitur et Cinglius periisse, si quid habes comperti, totam historiam velim te mihi perscribere, non ut Germanorum scriptores solent, qui

had lacked the intellectual capacity to recognize what was of genuine importance among the events of their day. In their blindness, they even passed over landmark events – such as the formation of the Electoral College – in silence.

In contrast, Melanchthon appreciated, and his works reflect, an understanding of history as more than a narration of events. Melanchthon recognized, for instance, that the election of Emperor Charles V would determine the course of European history for decades, even centuries to come.[42] In fact, the Imperial Election of 1519 was the last serious discussion about reuniting the Carolingian Empire through dialogue, rather than conquest, prior to the formation of the European Union.[43] Melanchthon's pamphlet on the Imperial election of 1519 is generally considered the best description and sixteenth century analysis of that momentous event.[44] His view of the Imperial constitution underlies the text, and he used the formal process of the election to demonstrate that papal involvement in Imperial elections was unwanted and illegitimate. These general arguments about Imperial elections appear repeatedly in Melanchthon's historical and political thought, and they also inform the narrative in *Carion's Chronicle*.

With regard to sources, Melanchthon did not engage in extensive "archival" research, and he relied mostly, though not entirely, on printed materials. Nevertheless, he was a critical reader, and his success as an historian can undoubtedly be attributed, at least in part, to his ability to select reliable historians and synthesize them for classroom use. Concerning the more distant past, Melanchthon believed that he possessed a chain of sources from Creation to his own day. The Old Testament provided a narrative from the beginning of time to the point when Greek historians began to write; and instead of seeing biblical and classical sources as offering competing narratives, Melanchthon viewed them as complementary. Indeed, he stressed the importance of

---

nullas causas, nullas occasiones, nulla consilia, nullas περιστάσεις exponunt." CR II, 551 (MBW 1201 dates the letter as 6 November 1531).

42   See VD16 M 3089–3100. The text is found at CR XX, 473–514. See Richard Fester, "Sleidan, Sabinus, Melanchthon," *Historische Zeitschrift* 89 (1902), 1–16; and Bauer, "Die *Chronica Carionis*," 217–222.

43   See Ernst Laubach, "Wahlpropaganda im Wahlkampf um die deutsche Königswürde 1519," *Archiv für Kulturgeschichte* 53 (1971): 207–248.

44   See Horst Dreitzel, *Absolutismus und ständische Verfassung in Deutschland: Ein Beitrag zu Kontinuität und Diskontinuität der politischen Theorie in der frühen Neuzeit* (Mainz: Verlag Philipp von Zabern, 1992), 20–21, esp. n. 10; Friedrich Hermann Schubert, *Die deutschen Reichstage in der Staatslehre der frühen Neuzeit* (Göttingen: Vandenhoeck & Ruprecht, 1966), 209–211.

classical historians for shedding light on biblical narratives and the fulfilment of biblical prophecy.[45]

With regard to the Middle Ages, by the late 1520s, Melanchthon was the beneficiary of a vast amount of medieval source material discovered and published by his contemporaries. The manuscript searches of Melanchthon's student, Matthias Flacius Illyricus, are rightly famous for the role they played in the formulation of the *Magdeburg Centuries*, the most important Protestant historical work of the later sixteenth century.[46] In fact, much of Flacius's collection was absorbed into the Herzog August Bibliothek in Wolfenbüttel. Far less appreciated, however, is the important role that early printed texts played in Melanchthon's initial reframing of medieval history. Much of the early printed material about the Middle Ages had been pro-papal, but newly available sources, such as Sigebert of Gembloux, facilitated Melanchthon's rewriting of the struggles between the popes and the Emperors. The theological currents of the Reformation changed Melanchthon's historical perspective, but that transformation was itself part of a symbiotic relationship between medieval sources and Reformation arguments.[47]

Melanchthon's reformation of historical thought also extended to interpretive frameworks. In *Carion's Chronicle*, Melanchthon rejected one of the most important medieval patterns of historical narration, the Six Ages of the world (drawn from Augustine). In its place, Melanchthon turned to the Talmudic Prophecy of Elias, which divided history into three two-thousand year intervals, and to the Four Monarchies of the Prophet Daniel. Melanchthon did not explicitly separate history into ancient, medieval and modern; rather he was an intermediate figure in the transition from medieval paradigms to the tripartite division imposed by the Enlightenment.[48]

Melanchthon's use of the Four Monarchies and the Prophecy of Elias was not strictly new; nevertheless, the way he deployed these frameworks marked a

---

45 On Melanchthon's sources, see Gotthard Münch, "Das Chronicon Carionis Philippicum: ein Beitrag zur Würdigung Melanchthons als Historiker," *Sachsen und Anhalt* 1 (1925): 238–253.

46 See Robert Kolb, "Philipp's Foes, but Followers Nonetheless: Late Humanism among the Gnesio-Lutherans," in *The Harvest of Humanism in Central Europe: Essays in Honor of Lewis W. Spitz*, ed. Manfred P. Fleischer (St Louis: Concordia Publishing House, 1992), 163–164.

47 On the importance of the humanists for publishing medieval sources, see John D'Amico, "Ulrich von Hutten and Beatus Rhenanus as Medieval Historians and Religious Propagandists in the Early Reformation," in *Roman and German Humanism, 1450–1550*, ed. Paul F. Grendler (Brookfield, VT: Variorum, 1993), XII: 1–33.

48 See generally Wallace K. Ferguson, *The Renaissance in Historical Thought: Five Centuries of Interpretation* (Boston: Houghton Mifflin, 1948).

INTRODUCTION

conscious departure from his intellectual predecessors.[49] With regard to Daniel, Melanchthon achieved an interpretive fixity that ended centuries of inconsistency. For Melanchthon and his followers, the course of history hinged on the succession of the Four Monarchies: Assyria, Persia, Greece and Rome, with its successors. According to this perspective, the Holy Roman Empire existed as the final fulfilment of Daniel's prophecy, and its demise would usher in the last days of the world. Despite this prophetic sense, Melanchthon did not treat all of history after Christ as an undifferentiated march to the Last Judgment. Instead, he recognized the importance of political change over time. In this respect, three key issues marked the developments in Europe after the collapse of the Western Roman Empire: the formation of the medieval German Empire under the Carolingians, the entrance of the papacy into secular affairs, and the rise of the Turks.[50] Accordingly, within the confines of his narrative frameworks, Melanchthon traced specific themes to develop a view of Europe's past, present and future.

5 Melanchthon's Historical Works

Although the focus here is on *Carion's Chronicle*, an outline of Melanchthon's other historical works is useful for understanding his contribution to different areas of historical inquiry. Melanchthon's written corpus encompasses a broad array of historical material, and chance discoveries, along with frequent collaboration, involved him in projects that he never could have foreseen when he left Tübingen for Wittenberg. Some of Melanchthon's works established historiographical paradigms that lasted for centuries, others were ephemera

---

49   On periodization, see especially Roderich Schmidt, "Aetates mundi: Die Weltalter als Gliederungsprinzip der Geschichte," *Zeitschrift für Kirchengeschichte* LXVII (Vierte Folge V) (1955/56): 288–317. See also Michael I. Allen, "Universal History 300–1000: Origins and Western Developments," in *Historiography in the Middle Ages*, ed. Deborah Mauskopf Deliyannis (Leiden: Brill, 2003); and Joseph Swain, "The Theory of the Four Monarchies: Opposition History under the Roman Empire," *Classical Philology* 35 (1940): 1–21.

50   "Die letzte zeit / sind zwey tausent iar von Christus geburt an zu ende der welt / wiewol dabey angezeiget / das nicht gantz zwey tausent iar sein sollen / Vnd warlich dieser spruch begreifft viel nützlicher lere / vnd ist sonderlich wol zu mercken / das er von der zeit Christi / auch wenn der welt ende komen sol / weissaget / Derhalben / ich yhn gern hie forn angezogen habe / damit er meniglich bekant werde / Wie aber die Römisch Monarchi nach Christus geburt sich verendert / vnd auff die Deudschen komen / wie auch das Mahometisch reich entstanden / vnd wie das Bapstumb ynn weltlichem gewalt gestigen / wil ich jnn diesem dritten teil anzeigen." Carion, *Chronica* (Wittenberg, 1532), sig. Bij v - Biij r.

and quickly forgotten. Considered as a whole, Melanchthon's historiographical activities defy easy classification, especially because he often recycled material for use in different contexts. Many of Melanchthon's individual texts have received treatment in earlier scholarship, but no one has ever offered a comprehensive study of his historical corpus.

With regard to contemporary history (*Zeitgeschichte*), Melanchthon prepared: [1] epistolary reports, including accounts of the Leipzig Debate (1519),[51] the Marburg Colloquy (1529),[52] and the Diet of Augsburg (1530);[53] [2] letter prefaces, such as the introduction to Jacques Fontaine's *Three Books on the Rhodian War*,[54] and the introduction, really a capsule Reformation history, for Luther's collected works;[55] [3] document collections relating to important events, such as the Colloquies at Regensburg (1541)[56] and Worms (1557),[57] as well as the Schmalkaldic War;[58] [4] pamphlets (*Flugschriften*) on notable

---

51 For the Leipzig disputation, see MBW 59; VD16 M 3210. See also VD16 M 3205–3211, VD16 L 5791.
52 For the Marburg Colloquy, see MBW 777, 831, 832, with references to publication history, as well as MBW 775 and VD16 M 3188. The *Marburg Articles* are included in MBW 825.
53 For Augsburg, see VD16 M 3204; MBW 1093; and VD16 M 2384. See also VD16 C 4263.
54 For the Siege of Rhodes, see MBW 546; and VD16 F 1843. See also Arthur Freeman, "Editions of Fontanus, *De bello Rhodio*," *The Library* 5th series, 24 (1969): 336–339.
55 The text of Melanchthon's biography is found in CR VI, 155–170; MBW 4277; and a review of the printing history at CR XX, 429–438; see also VD16 M 3416–3440. On Melanchthon's prefaces to the Wittenberg edition of Luther's works, see Eike Wolgast, "Melanchthons Fürstenwidmungen in der Wittenberger Lutherausgabe," in *Humanismus und Wittenberger Reformation: Festgabe anläßlich des 500. Geburtstages des Praeceptor Germaniae Philipp Melanchthon am 16. Februar 1997*, ed. Michael Beyer (Leipzig: Evangelische Verlagsanstalt, 1996), 253–265.
56 See VD16 M 2385–2391, ZV 10687. See the introduction in CR IV, 119–123, and the discussion of the editions in Cornelis Augustijn, "Melanchthons Editionen der Akten von Worms und Regensburg 1540 und 1541," in *Dona Melanchthoniana: Festgabe für Heinz Scheible zum 70. Geburtstag*, ed. Johanna Loehr (Stuttgart-Bad Cannstatt: Frommann-Holzboog, 2001), 24–39. The text of Melanchthon's edition is found in CR IV, 664–668, MBW 2816; CR IV, 190–238; CR IV, 668–676, MBW 2817; CR IV, 348–376, MBW 2713; CR IV, 476–505 (i.e. 479–491), MBW 2749, 2751; CR IV, 559–561, MBW 2755. See also CR IV, 722–728, MBW 2863; CR IV, 33–78; CR IV, 530–541, MBW 2715; CR IV, 541–552, MBW 2752; CR IV, 455–456, 465–466, 509–512, 524–525, 526–529, 516–520; CR IV, 506, 554–555, 506–509. For the German edition, see VD16 M 2388, VD16 M 2736.
57 For Worms, see VD16 S 5142; and, in German, VD16 S 5152. See also VD16 S 5138–5153, ZV 14284, 14285, 17113, 22663; and the text in CR IX, 385–390, MBW 8441, 8442. See also CR IX, 393–395, MBW 8468; CR IX, 451–456 (only in manuscript), MBW 8539; and CR XI, 456–461, MBW 8540.
58 The collection was published under the name of the University of Wittenberg faculty, see VD16 W 3727. Melanchthon mentioned his intention to prepare a history of the war in his *Annals*: "Was aber für Ursachen des Krieges gewesen, so er mit Kaiser Carl geführt,

events, including *The Election and Coronation of Charles V*,[59] *The History of Thomas Müntzer*,[60] *The Martyrdom of Juan Diaz*,[61] *The History of the Death of Pier Luigi Farnese*,[62] *The History of Francesco Spiera*,[63] and *The History of Two Martyrs Burned at Mecheln*;[64] [5] biographical orations on contemporary

wie sich derselbe angesponnen, und was er für einen Ausgang gehabt, soll anderswo vollkömmlich und ausführlich vermeldet werden." CR VIII, 401; [1554].

59   The text is found at CR XX, 473–514; see the description of the editions there as well as VD16 M 3089–3100.

60   See VD 16 M 3431; the work is not included in CR. See Heinz Scheible, "Die Verfasserfrage der 'Histori Thome Muntzers,'" in *Flugschriften der Reformationszeit: Colloquium im Erfurter Augustinerkloster 1999*, ed. Ulman Weiß (Tübingen: Bibliotheca Academica Verlag, 2001), 201–213; Bo Andersson, "Melanchthons Polemik gegen Thomas Müntzer: Die Histori Thome Muntzers / des anfengers des Döringischen uffrur," in *Philipp Melanchthon und seine Rezeption in Skandinavien*, ed. Birgit Stolt (Stockholm: Distributed by Almqvist & Wiksell International, 1998), 25–50; and Abraham Friesen, "Philipp Melanchthon (1497–1560), Wilhelm Zimmermann (1807–1878) and the Dilemma of Muntzer Historiography," *Church History* 43, no. 2 (June 1974): 164–182.

61   See VD16 M 4415; as well as VD16 M 4413–4416, ZV 10656, ZV 20977; the text is found in CR VI, 112–114; and CR XX, 515–518; this account was also included in the editions of *Carion's Chronicle* published at Wittenberg and Leipzig between 1546 and 1554, see VD16 C 1004–1005, C 1007–1008, ZV 22534. On the Diaz brothers, see Kathrin Stegbauer, "Perspektivierungen des Mordfalles Diaz (1546) im Streit der Konfessionen : Publizistische Möglichkeiten im Spannungsfeld zwischen reichspolitischer Argumentation und heilsgeschichtlicher Einordnung," in *Wahrnehmungsgeschichte und Wissensdiskurs im illustrierten Flugblatt der Frühen Neuzeit (1450–1700)*, ed. Wolfgang Harms (Basel: Schwabe, 2002), 371–414.

62   See VD16 H 3902. Melanchthon learned of Farnese's death by 1 October 1547 (MBW 4911.2), and he in turn passed along the report on 6 October 1547 to Georg of Anhalt (CR VI, 692; MBW 4912.4). On 1 November 1547, he also commented on the seizure of Piacenza by Charles V (CR VI, 716; MBW 4943.6). The account of Farnese's death appeared anonymously in 1548, but Melanchthon refers to the pamphlet on 10 March 1548 – "Nescio an historia de filio pontificis antea ad te missa sit. Nunc mitto et quaeso ut scribas saepissime." CR VI, 824; MBW 5080.2.

63   See VD16 G 3304. The editors of *Corpus Reformatorum* included this history based on Strobel's authority at CR XX, 613–632. The attribution to Melanchthon rests on later editions, which designated him as the author of the *Additio* to the text (CR XX, 629–632). This *Additio* was at times treated separately, e.g. VD17 23:283822X. On Spiera see M.A. Overell, "The Exploitation of Francesco Spiera," *Sixteenth Century Journal* 26, no. 3 (Autumn 1995): 619–637, esp. 627–628; and Michael MacDonald, "The Fearefull Estate of Francis Spira: Narrative, Identity, and Emotion in Early Modern England," *The Journal of British Studies* 31, no. 1 (January 1992): 32–61.

64   See VD16 H 3956 and VD16 H 3958. The text was also published at Dresden in 1556 (VD16 H 3957), and in Low German at Lübeck (VD16 H 3959). The pamphlet was published anonymously, but Melanchthon refers to it in his correspondence in late March 1556 (CR VIII, 698–699, MBW 7763; MBW 7766 – see also the discussion of the pamphlet there). Melanchthon mentions receiving the report of the martyrdom on 12 March 1556 (CR VIII,

figures, such as Rudolph Agricola and Erasmus;[65] [6] funeral orations (*Leichenpredigten*), most importantly the oration at Luther's funeral;[66] [7] orations on contemporary events, such as the Sack of Rome in 1527;[67] [8] municipal histories (*Stadtgeschichte*), including histories of Wittenberg and Torgau;[68] and [9] a municipal chronicle (*Stadtchronik*) of Wittenberg, the *Wittenberg Annals*.[69]

691–692, MBW 7744), and again on the following day (CR VIII, 693–694, MBW 7746), so the pamphlet was prepared within days of when the news reached Wittenberg. The date on the title page "October 1555" refers to the start of the case against the Thiessen brothers rather than the execution itself. On this case and the pamphlets dealing with the Thiessen brothers, see especially Robert Foncke, *Duitse vlugschriften van de tijd over het proces en de terechtstelling van de protestanten Frans en Nikolaas Thys te Mechelen (1555) : met inleiding en aantekeningen opnieuw uitgegeven* (Antwerpen: De Sikkel, 1937), esp. 134–165, where Melanchthon's text is reproduced, and 166–185 for the Low German version. Variant spellings include of the brothers' name include Thiessen, Thys, Thiß, Thijs, Diessen.

65   See generally Horst Koehn, "Philipp Melanchthons Reden," *Archiv für Geschichte des Buchwesens* 25 (1984): 1277–1486; on form and content, see Heinz Scheible, "Melanchthons biographische Reden: Literarische Form und akademischer Unterricht," in *Biographie zwischen Renaissance und Barock: Zwölf Studien*, ed. Walter Berschin (Heidelberg: Matthes Verlag, 1993), 73–96; and Philipp Melanchthon, *Orations on Philosophy and Education*, ed. Sachiko Kusukawa (Cambridge: Cambridge University Press, 1999), xi–xxxi. Many of the orations are edited in CR X and CR XI, see the index in CR XXVIII, 367–374. See also Sachiko Kusukawa, "Melanchthon's life of Erasmus (1557)," *Erasmus of Rotterdam Society Yearbook* 23 (2003): 1–24; Quirinus Breen, "Melanchthon's Sources for a Life of Agricola: The Heidelberg Memories and the Writings," *Archiv für Reformationsgeschichte* 52 (1961): 49–74; and James Michael Weiss, "The Six Lives of Rudolph Agricola: Forms and Functions of the Humanist Biography," *Humanistica Lovaniensia* 30 (1981): 19–39.

66   See VD16 M 3854; and CR XI, 726–734. The various German and Latin versions are edited in Siegfried Bräuer, "Die Überlieferung von Melanchthons Leichenrede auf Luther," in *Humanismus und Wittenberger Reformation: Festgabe anläßlich des 500. Geburtstages des Praeceptor Germaniae Philipp Melanchthon am 16. Februar 1997*, ed. Michael Beyer (Leipzig: Evangelische Verlagsanstalt, 1996), 185–252. See also James Michael Weiss, "Erasmus at Luther's Funeral: Melanchthon's Commemorations of Luther in 1546," *Sixteenth Century Journal* 16 (Spring 1985): 91–114. See generally Cornelia Moore, *Patterned Lives: The Lutheran Funeral Biography in Early Modern Germany* (Wiesbaden: Harrassowitz, 2006).

67   Few of these orations have been examined more than in passing; but for the Sack of Rome, see Rhein, "Melanchthon und der italienische Humanismus," 372–373.

68   For the Wittenberg *Stadtgeschichte*, see VD16 M 2384; CR IX, 582–587 Nr. 6568; and MBW 8686. See also Nikolaus Müller, "Die Funde in den Turmknäufen der Stadtkirche zu Wittenberg," *Zeitschrift des Vereins für Kirchengeschichte in der Provinz Sachsen* 8 (1911): 94–118, 129–180. For Torgau, see CR X, 612–613 Nr. 260; and CR XX, 429–430; VD 16 M 3737. In 1537, Melanchthon also wrote a preface in praise of the city of Hamburg, see VD16 F 2500; MBW 1963.

69   See VD16 M 2383; VD17 3:600040W (1603); and in CR: 1552 = CR VII, 1170–1172 Nr. 5300; 1553 = CR VIII, 198–200 Nr. 5523; 1554 = CR VIII, 400–404 Nr. 5711; 1555 = CR VIII, 650–656 Nr. 5905; 1556 = CR VIII, 942–946 Nr. 6142; 1557 = CR IX, 416–420 Nr. 6432; 1558 = CR IX, 706–718 Nr. 6661; 1559 = CR IX, 1011–1029 Nr. 6899; 1560 = CR IX, 1103–1104 Nr. 6982 [Text

Although Melanchthon never wrote a comprehensive history of the sixteenth century, he had a decisive influence on later interpretations of the Reformation. His funeral oration[70] and biographical sketch[71] of Luther from 1546 became the point of departure for the entire tradition of Luther biography, as well as the early history of the Reformation. Indeed, the iconic image of Luther nailing the *Ninety-Five Theses* to the door of the Castle Church in Wittenberg derives principally from Melanchthon.[72] Likewise, many of Melanchthon's shorter works were incorporated into the official Protestant history of the Reformation, Johann Sleidanus's *Commentaries on Religion and Politics during the Reign of Charles V* (1555), which remained the standard account of the Reformation until the nineteenth century.[73] Several of Melanchthon's texts, such as *The History of Thomas Müntzer*, were also inserted into Luther's collected works, so by default they exercised a normative influence on the interpretation of key Reformation events.[74] Many of Melanchthon's texts did not circulate independently or even under his name; instead they took on a life of their own as they were absorbed into the broader traditions of Reformation historiography.

With regard to pre-sixteenth century history, Melanchthon's works and activities included: [1] print corrections for *Nauclerus's Chronicle* (1516) and Franciscus Irenicus's *Description of All Germany* (1518);[75] [2] student editions of classical historians, including Lucian and Sallust;[76] [3] letter prefaces to new

---

      given up to the death of Melanchthon]. The manuscript of the *Wittenberg Annals* is now in Detmold (Lippische Landesbibliothek: 10), and it contains material from the years after Melanchthon's death.

70   See VD16 M 3854; and CR XI, 726–734.

71   See CR VI, 155–170; MBW 4277; and a review of the printing history at CR XX, 429–438; see also VD16 M 3416–3440.

72   "In hoc cursu cum esset Lutherus, circumferuntur venales indulgentiae in his regionibus a Tecelio Dominicano, impudentissimo sycophanta, cuius impiis et nefariis concionibus irritatus Lutherus, studio pietatis ardens, edidit Propositiones de Indulgentiis, quae in primo Tomo monumentorum eius extant, Et has publice Templo, quod arci Witebergensi contiguum est, affixit pridie festi omnium Sanctorum anno 1517." CR VI, 161–162. See Ernest Schwiebert, *The Reformation*, vol. 2, *The Reformation as a University Movement* (Minneapolis: Fortress Press, 1996), 360; and Joachim Ott and Martin Treu, eds., *Luthers Thesenanschlag – Faktum oder Fiktion* (Leipzig: Evangelische Verlagsanstalt, 2008).

73   Johann Sleidanus, *Ioan. Sleidani, De Statv Religionis Et Reipvblicae, Carolo Qvinto, Caesare, Commentarij. Cvm indice luculentißimo* (Strasbourg: Rihel, 1555). VD16 S 6668. On Sleidanus, see Kess, *Johann Sleidan*.

74   See Eike Wolgast, "Die Wittenberger Luther-Ausgabe," *Archiv für Geschichte des Buchwesens* 11 (1970/1971): 1–336.

75   For Nauclerus, see VD16 N 167; and for Irenicus, see VD16 F 2815.

76   For Sallust, see VD16 S 1379; and CR XVII, 583–610. For Lucian, see VD16 L 2989; and MBW 79.

editions of classical historians, such as Xenophon;[77] [4] Latin translations of Greek historians, most notably Thucydides;[78] [5] letter prefaces to medieval historical works, including the *Ursberger Chronicle*[79] and the *Annals* of Lambert of Hersfeld;[80] [6] biographical orations on ancient and medieval figures;[81] [7] orations on historical events, such as the Fall of Constantinople;[82] [8] texts on Turkish history;[83] and [9] universal history, i.e. *Carion's Chronicle*. Over the years, Melanchthon also directed searches for important manuscripts; and most notably, one former Wittenberg student, acting on Melanchthon's advice, discovered the Fifth Decade of Livy at Lorsch.[84]

---

77 See VD16 X 2; CR III, 1113–1116; MBW 2341. See also VD16 ZV 23091; and VD16 X 3.

78 See VD16 T 1131; CR XVII, 1074–1080. See also Marianne Pade, "Thucydides," in *Catalogus Translationum et Commentariorum*, ed. Virginia Brown (Washington, D.C.: The Catholic University of America Press, 2003), 130–136, 164–166.

79 The 1537 Latin edition is VD16 B 9801, and Melanchthon's letter preface is MBW 1857. The 1539 edition is VD16 B 9804, and Melanchthon's letter preface is MBW 2138. See also MBW 1880.

80 See MBW 304; and VD16 L 161 (without Melanchthon's preface), and VD16 ZV 23175 (with preface). See Maurer, *Der junge Melanchthon*, vol. 1, 120–121; Hartfelder, *Philipp Melanchthon*, 295–296; and Lambert of Hersfeld, *The Annals of Lampert of Hersfeld*, trans. I.S. Robinson (Manchester: Manchester University Press, 2015), 34–36.

81 See Scheible, "Melanchthons biographische Reden," 84–85; see also Hartfelder, *Philipp Melanchthon*, 297–299; and the index in CR XXVIII, 367–374. The orations on Aristotle are discussed in Ralph Keen, "Melanchthon's Two Lives of Aristotle," *Wolfenbütteler Renaissance Mitteilungen* 8 (1984): 7–11; for St. Jerome, see Fidel Rädle, "Biographie als 'Declamatio': Zu Melanchthons 'Vita Hieronymi,'" in *Scripturus vitam: Lateinische Biographie von der Antike bis in die Gegenwart: Festgabe für Walter Berschin zum 65. Geburtstag*, ed. Dorothea Walz (Heidelberg: Mattes, 2002), 273–285.

82 See the listing in Koehn, "Philipp Melanchthons Reden," 1477–1482.

83 For Melanchthon's 1560 description of Turkish history, see VD16 D 3032 and VD16 D 3034. See also Otto Clemen, *Unbekannte Drucke, Briefe und Akten aus der Reformationszeit* (Leipzig: Harrassowitz, 1942), 74–84.

84 Simon Grynaeus (1493–1541), who discovered the manuscript, was a lifelong friend of Melanchthon. In the mid-1520s, Melanchthon had suggested that Grynaeus search for manuscripts associated with Bishop Johann von Dalberg (1445–1503), an important early German humanist. Melanchthon was aware of Dalberg's library, which was then in Ladenburg, and he also suspected that undiscovered treasures might be kept in the collections at the Abbey of Lorsch, near Worms, where Dalberg had been bishop. It was at Lorsch in 1527 that Grynaeus found the last major manuscript of Livy to have survived into the Renaissance (now Vienna Bibl. Nat. Lat. 15), and it contained Books 1–5 of the Fifth Decade, which were previously unknown. Grynaeus intended that his letter to Melanchthon announcing the find (MBW 587) would be printed as the dedicatory epistle to the new Livy edition based on Lorsch manuscript. See Otto Clemen, ed., *Supplementa Melanchthoniana* (1926), Abteilung 6, vol. 1, 380–383. Instead, when Froben published the new edition at Basel in March of 1531 (VD16 L 2094), Erasmus, rather than Grynaeus or Melanchthon, wrote the preface. Erasmus briefly explained how Grynaeus found the

INTRODUCTION 23

For centuries, the problem of classifying Melanchthon's historical works has had a direct effect on research concerning Melanchthon as an historian. Although the problem is particularly acute with regard to *Carion's Chronicle*, the interconnected issues of access, attribution and classification have long influenced general interpretations of Melanchthon's historical thought and activities. The critical edition of Melanchthon's works, in *Corpus Reformatorum* (CR), fills twenty-eight volumes, and it represents a monument to nineteenth century German scholarship. Despite the strengths of the edition, however, its age has begun to show, and the conventions of nineteenth century editorial practice have also resulted in serious limitations. Nevertheless, the scholarship of the last century and a half has been conditioned by the presentation of Melanchthon's texts in the volumes of CR, so a basic introduction to the edition is fundamental for understanding its influence on studies of Melanchthon's historiography.

The editors of *Corpus Reformatorum* sought to arrange Melanchthon's works in ways that would simplify access to his thought. Accordingly, they tended to extract texts from their context and insert them into volumes based on genre or subject matter and then by chronology. On many levels the approach makes perfect sense, but it was applied so rigidly that it has often caused confusion for uninitiated readers. The project of editing Melanchthon's letters took priority in *Corpus Reformatorum*, and the first ten volumes of the edition are devoted to them. In the later volumes, however, Melanchthon's letter prefaces were not reprinted to begin the works they were meant to introduce. Instead the editors directed the reader to the volumes of correspondence, as is the case for the dedicatory epistles to *Carion's Chronicle*. Furthermore, the historical material itself was split into two volumes – CR XII and CR XX – so these works do not appear together, and Melanchthon's commentaries are presented in isolation from the works they were meant to explicate.

---

manuscript at Lorsch, but he said nothing of Melanchthon's part in the discovery, thereby effectively (and probably intentionally) erasing Melanchthon's contribution to the discovery. On Livy in the Renaissance, see B.L. Ullman, "The Post-Mortem Adventures of Livy," in his *Studies in the Italian Renaissance* (Rome, 1973), 53–77; Joseph Trapp, "The image of Livy in the Middle Ages and the Renaissance," *Lecturas de Historia del Arte* 3 (1992): 211–238. For the textual transmission of Livy see L.D. Reynolds, *Texts and Transmission: a survey of the Latin classics* (Oxford: Clarendon Press, 1983), 205–214; as well as Livy, *Titi Livi Ab vrbe condita libri XLI–XLV*, ed. John Briscoe (Stuttgart: Teubner, 1986), III–XXIV; and the introduction to the facsimile: Livy, *Livius: Codex Vindobonensis Lat. 15 / Praefatus est Carolus Wessely* (Lugduni Batavorum: Sijthof, 1907). Erasmus's letter preface is printed in Desiderius Erasmus, *Opus epistolarum des Erasmi Roterdami*, ed. P.S. Allen (Oxford: Oxford University Press, 1992 [Reprint]), vol. 9, p. 143–145 Nr. 2435.

The shortcomings of these editorial practices are particularly noticeable in the case of Tacitus's *Germania*, a text that Melanchthon edited for publication three times in his career.[85] The prefaces to these editions and Melanchthon's commentary are printed separately and in different volumes. The text of the *Germania* itself is omitted, as well as the other works that Melanchthon had collected and bound together in his editions, including Ulrich von Hutten's *Arminius*, *Julius Excluded from Heaven* (formerly attributed to Erasmus),[86] and the *Germania Generalis* of Conrad Celtis.[87] Thus, the way *Corpus Reformatorum* presents the "text" divorces it from the context that Melanchthon created and imposed on the reading of these works. Likewise, the contemporary circumstances that influenced the changes to these editions are mostly obscured. In this way, Melanchthon's overall design and purpose are lost.

Nineteenth century views of authorship also influenced the selection of material for these volumes, and several of Melanchthon's more prominent collaborative projects were rejected, including Justus Jonas's *Commentary on the Seventh Chapter of Daniel*, which dealt with the Turkish threat of the late 1520s.[88] The editors also rejected *The History of Thomas Müntzer*, because it could not be attributed exclusively, or definitively, to Melanchthon.[89] Deciding questions of Melanchthonian authorship are sometimes as difficult as distinguishing between a painting by Cranach and his workshop. In these cases, the editors of *Corpus Reformatorum* mostly erred on the side of exclusion.

In other instances, historical works inserted amidst the letters often are not noticed by historians as what they properly are. These include the *Wittenberg Annals* and the *History of the City of Wittenberg*. Likewise, pamphlets that Melanchthon wrote anonymously have been attributed to him only more recently based on his correspondence, so they are not found at all in *Corpus*

---

85 See VD16 H 6281 (1538), there is also a second printing from 1538, VD16 H 6282. The other editions are VD16 H 6283 (1551), see MBW 6290; and VD16 T 37 (1557). For a description, with a reprinting of the text, see Gerhard Binder, "Der Praeceptor Germaniae und die 'Germania' des Tacitus: Über eine Tacitus-Ausgabe Philipp Melanchthons," in *Philipp Melanchthon: Exemplarische Aspekte seines Humanismus*, ed. Gerhard Binder (Trier: WFT Wissenschaftlicher Verlag, 1998), 103–140. Melanchthon's *Vocabulary* is also found in CR XVII, 611–638, see the additional notes at CR XVII, 1141–1146.

86 See Peter Fabisch, *Iulius exclusus e coelis: Motive und Tendenzen gallikanischer und bibelhumanistischer Papstkritik im Umfeld des Erasmus* (Münster: Aschendorff, 2008).

87 The 1557 edition is discussed in Kirsti Ohr, "Historiographie," in *Melanchthon und die Marburger Professoren (1527–1627)*, ed. Barbara Bauer (Marburg: [Universitätsbibliothek Marburg], 1999), vol. 1, 213–215. See also CR XIII, 162; MBW 8236.

88 See VD16 J 897. On the joint authorship, see Wilhelm Bonacker and Hans Volz, "Eine Wittenberger Weltkarte aus dem Jahr 1529," *Die Erde* 8, no. 2 (1956): 154–156.

89 The text is VD16 M 3431. See Scheible, "Die Verfasserfrage der 'Histori Thome Muntzers.'"

Reformatorum. These include his *History of the Death of Pier Luigi Farnese* (1548), which appeared anonymously and seems to have gone mostly unnoticed, even in the sixteenth century.[90] Modern editions, whether *Corpus Reformatorum* or the Weimar Edition of Luther's works, provide a sanitized view of the Reformers' writings, or at least one tied to a different set of contemporary concerns. Translation is an act of interpretation, and so is the production of an edition, critical or otherwise.

While the editors of *Corpus Reformatorum* explained all of this, and careful internal notation is made within the edition as a whole, these comments are given in Latin, and they easily go unread. *Corpus Reformatorum* is indeed difficult to navigate, and even later editors of Melanchthon's works recognized this problem. In one revealing case, Heinrich Bindseil, the second editor of *Corpus Reformatorum*, decided to include Melanchthon's account of the *Martyrdom of Juan Diaz* in CR XX with other historical works. Only when the volume was in page proofs did he realize that the previous editor, Karl Gottlieb Bretschneider, had already printed the text in CR VI, where it fit chronologically at 17 April 1546, and a footnote was accordingly added to indicate this.[91] In a similar way, Melanchthon's shorter works, such as his poems, were scattered about the twenty-eight volumes of *Corpus Reformatorum*; and when Otto Clemens began to publish a supplement of works missed by previous editors, he reprinted some material simply because it was almost impossible to find in *Corpus Reformatorum* itself.[92]

6 *Carion's Chronicle*

Interpretations of Melanchthon's historical thought have generally focused on *Carion's Chronicle*, his universal history that extends from Creation to the sixteenth century. The problem, however, is that *"Carion's Chronicle"* is not a single text, but rather a rubric for the various editions, adaptations and

---

90   See VD16 H 3902; CR VI, 824; and MBW 5080.2.

91   CR VI, 112–114; and CR XX, 515–518, where Bindseil added this note: "Nota. Postquam haec narratio typis exscripta erat, cognovi, eandem iam in huius Corporis Vol. VI. p. 113 sq. esse exhibitam."

92   "Da dies Erstlingsgedicht Melanchthons im C.R. erst nachträglich an ziemlich versteckter Stelle Aufnahme gefunden hat, drucken wir es hier als das erste uns erhaltene literarische Erzeugnis seiner Feder nochmals ab." Otto Clemen, ed., *Supplementa Melanchthoniana: Werke Philipp Melanchthons die im Corpus Refomatorum vermisst werden* (Leipzig: Haupt, 1926), Abteilung 6, vol. 1, 1. In discussing Melanchthon's first printed poem from 1510 (CR XX, 765 Nr. 1).

translations that derive from the original *Carion's Chronicle*, which was published at Wittenberg in 1532. The complexity of the *Chronicle's* transmission resembles, and in some respects surpasses, the most intricate textual history of a medieval manuscript. Hundreds of editions have survived in libraries scattered around the globe, and the printing history is so muddled that until recently no one could even say with certainty which was the *editio princeps*. Unravelling the *Chronicle's* textual transmission only had to be accomplished once; but once complete, its explication opens a new perspective on sixteenth century historiography.

The analysis of *Carion's Chronicle* is itself a foundational project for understanding the context, development and diffusion of Wittenberg historiography. Over the decades, the *Chronicle* was translated from the original German (1532) into *Plattdeutsch* (Low German) (1534), Latin (1537), Czech (1541/1584), Italian (1543), Dutch (1543/1586), French (1546/1579), Spanish (1549?/1553), English (1550), Danish (1554/1595), Swedish (1649), Turkish (1654), and Icelandic (1692). Both within and across these linguistic categories the *Chronicle* underwent a series of revisions that adapted the text to specific audiences or particular events. Indeed, some of these revisions are so extensive that by the later sixteenth century, Carion's name had become more a part of the title than an indication of actual authorship. The various editions and translations provide a guide to the *Chronicle's* dissemination across Europe, but the sheer number of extant copies has long presented a barrier to understanding Melanchthon's intervention in the traditions of Western historiography.

No critical edition of the entire *Chronicle* exists, and no one has previously accounted for its printing history.[93] The result is that any two studies of "*Carion's Chronicle*" might reflect engagement with very different texts. *Corpus Reformatorum* reproduces the narrative from Creation to Charlemagne, but only in the Latin version that Melanchthon revised at the end of his life. The history of the medieval German Empire is excluded, even though this section was the main focus of the original German *Chronicle*. As a result, *Corpus Reformatorum* shifts the emphasis, through omission, to the themes that Melanchthon developed in the early sections of the *Chronicle*, especially the parallels between the history of the early Church and the Reformation. By distilling *Carion's Chronicle* to the highest standards of authorial purity, *Corpus Reformatorum* removed the true sixteenth century flavour of the text.

Anglo-American scholars often use the 1550 English translation of the *Chronicle*, rather than, or in addition to, the text in *Corpus Reformatorum*.

---

93   The most detailed study of the text was Scherer, *Geschichte und Kirchengeschichte*, 468–474.

INTRODUCTION

The English edition is "complete," but it transmits a version of *Carion's Chronicle* that Melanchthon spent fifteen years trying to eradicate because of its anti-Hohenzollern treatment of the Turkish wars.[94] This version of the text also contains more prophetic material than the original *Chronicle*, none of it Melanchthon's work. Furthermore, the translator added material to appeal to an English audience, and he included an appendix, mostly on events in sixteenth century England. Both *Corpus Reformatorum* and the English translation present *"Carion's Chronicle"* to the reader, but neither does so in a form that reflects Melanchthon's actual design.

Because of this textual fluidity, it has been necessary to engage with Melanchthon's work in the forms presented to the early modern reader and to chart their circulation in print both within and beyond Germany. The repeated revisions during the sixteenth century offer a unique perspective on the continuing process of historical reflection among the Wittenbergers, as well as the relationship of history to contemporary events and changed contexts. The classic texts of confessional historiography – the *Magdeburg Centuries* (1559–1574), the *Ecclesiastical Annals* (1588–1607) of Cesare Baronio, and Foxe's *Book of Martyrs* (1563) – all appeared in the second half of the sixteenth century, forty years or more after the outbreak of the Reformation.[95] These works are explicitly, and at times virulently, partisan, and they served as self-legitimating critiques of incompatible theological positions. Focusing on these later texts has at times given a false impression that the transition to a distinctly Protestant perspective of the past was effortless and immediate. Indeed, because Luther turned the papacy into the Antichrist, it seems that once the *Ninety-Five Theses* were posted, every "Protestant historian" is expected to have written with as much anti-papal bitterness as Matthias Flacius Illyricus and the Centuriators of Magdeburg or John Foxe in his *Book of Martyrs*.[96]

---

94   Johann Carion, *The thre bokes of Cronicles* (London: Gwalter Lynne [by Steven Mierdman], 1550).

95   Matthias Flacius, et al., *Ecclesiastica Historia*, 13 vols. (Basel: Oporinus, 1559–1574). VD16 E 218–238. Cesare Baronio, *Annales ecclesiastici*, 37 vols. (Paris: Barri-Ducis, 1864–1883). John Foxe, *Actes and Monuments of These Latter and Perillous Dayes* (London: Iohn Day, 1563).

96   For example: "Indeed, it was their attempt to provide an historical basis for the break with the Church of Rome, and to demolish thoroughly the historical foundation upon which the Papacy built its claim to exclusive power, that led the Protestants to stress the study of history, an emphasis that became a major dimension of the Reformation itself and gave rise to a new form of historical consciousness – Protestant historiography based upon an apocalyptic interpretation of history, or upon an apocalyptic mode of historical thought." Avihu Zakai, "Reformation, History, and Eschatology in English Protestantism," *History and Theory* 26, no. 3 (October 1987): 301.

The history of *Carion's Chronicle* requires a much different explanation for the development of Protestant historiography. The *Chronicle* is alluring in many ways, but it is a deceptively difficult text. The contemporary audience immediately recognized it as a contribution to the *Germania Illustrata* movement, since it was imbued with a strong sense of German patriotism and a mildly Protestant perspective on religious matters. Even so, at first glance, the *Chronicle* seems unremarkable. The *editio princeps* was based almost entirely on printed sources, and it contains little of particular interest about sixteenth century events. The narrative is brief, so much so that it can feel terse; and chronological reckonings are frequently wrong. In spite of, but also because of, all this, the *Chronicle* became the most widely read sixteenth century historical work, and a foundational text for the European understanding of the past.

As the first Protestant universal history, the *Chronicle* set a basic script that historians have followed, or reacted to, ever since. *Carion's Chronicle* is a text in the "mirror of princes" (*Fürstenspiegel*) tradition, meaning that it was ostensibly intended as a tool in the moral upbringing of future rulers. Accordingly, the historical narrative stresses the lessons of exemplary figures, good and bad, for young Christian princes. Interwoven with its moralizing themes, the *Chronicle* also develops a forceful argument about the Imperial constitution, and it reflects what might be called Melanchthon's "constitutional patriotism."[97] No single event or particular episode separates *Carion's Chronicle* from other sixteenth century historical works; rather only in the aggregate does it reveal itself to be a distinctly Wittenberg text.

Through seemingly insignificant details, Melanchthon painstakingly constructed a view of European order rooted in the recent and distant historical past. The issue of papal authority within the Church is addressed, but only in passing, and from an ecclesiastical perspective, Melanchthon did not develop a strong anti-Catholic argument. Far more than the Reformation, the central concerns of the original 1532 edition were the Turkish wars and the question of political supremacy in the Empire. Melanchthon edited the text in the immediate aftermath of the 1529 Ottoman Siege of Vienna and in the expectation of the Imperial Turkish campaign of 1532. In this context, he used history to argue that the princes of Germany, both secular and ecclesiastical, and especially the Electors, could solve the problems of Church and state through dialogue and compromise within the confines of the Imperial constitution. The Electoral College itself represented a settlement of the competition between

---

97 On this point, see Michael Stolleis, "Public Law and Patriotism in the Holy Roman Empire," in *Infinite Boundaries: Order, Disorder, and Reorder in Early Modern German Culture*, ed. Max Reinhart (Kirksville: Sixteenth Century Journal Publishers, 1998), 11–33.

secular and ecclesiastical interests, and as Melanchthon demonstrated in the *Chronicle*, Germany had known peace when the pope and the Emperor agreed to cooperate for the good of Europe.

With *Carion's Chronicle*, Melanchthon sketched a historical argument for excluding the papacy from political affairs and for limiting the Emperor through the Imperial constitution. In doing so, he built on the traditions of medieval political thought and earlier German historiography, which had focused on the popes and the Emperors, but at the same time, he recognized, and fostered, the increasing importance of the Imperial princes. His emphasis on the Imperial constitution and the Electoral princes as the chief guarantors of German stability represented a decisive shift from the political perspective of the later Middle Ages and early German humanism. Thus, in its initial form, *Carion's Chronicle* addressed the political problems of the early 1530s, and especially from the perspective of the Imperial constitution. By contrast, the important questions of the Reformation hardly featured at all.

Twenty years later, in the mid-1550s, Melanchthon decided to revisit *Carion's Chronicle*, and the revised text reflects the changed circumstances of the intervening decades, especially the effects of the Schmalkaldic War and the ensuing theological strife.[98] In this later context, Melanchthon set greater emphasis on the question of where true doctrine and the true Church were to be found. Accordingly, he made lengthy and detailed revisions to the religious material in the *Chronicle*; and in the volumes he lived to write, he used the history of the early Church to address the pressing issues then facing the Wittenbergers. Nevertheless, as before, Melanchthon intended to develop three major themes in *Carion's Chronicle*: the formation of the medieval German Empire under the Carolingians, the entrance of the papacy into secular affairs, and the rise of the Turks. At his death, however, the material after Charlemagne, the most interesting period for German constitutional and religious history, was still unfinished.

The task of completing *Carion's Chronicle* fell to Melanchthon's son-in-law and heir, Caspar Peucer (1525–1602), who dominated Saxon intellectual life in the decade after Melanchthon's death.[99] Although Peucer was clearly indebted to Melanchthon, he nevertheless transformed *Carion's Chronicle* into a text of second generation Protestantism. At times, Peucer drew almost verbatim from

---

98 Philipp Melanchthon, *Chronicon Carionis* (Wittenberg, 1580). VD16 M 2718.
99 On Peucer generally, see Uwe Koch et al., *Zwischen Katheder, Thron und Kerker: Leben und Werk des Humanisten Caspar Peucer, 1525–1602* (Bautzen: Domowina-Verlag [Stadtmuseum Bautzen], 2002); and Hans-Peter Hasse and Günther Wartenberg, eds., *Caspar Peucer (1525–1602): Wissenschaft, Glaube und Politik im konfessionellen Zeitalter* (Leipzig: Evangelische Verlagsanstalt, 2004).

some of Melanchthon's works, including his later treatments of Charlemagne and the foundation of the Holy Roman Empire.[100] Even so, Peucer shifted the *Chronicle* away from its earlier political message, and through voluminous additions, he converted the text into a diatribe against medieval Catholicism. Melanchthon's death had marked the passing of a generation, and the revised *Chronicle* reflects this change in perspective. Through Peucer's intervention, the *Chronicle* was transformed into an overtly Protestant text, and it became a justification for the Reformation.

Nevertheless, even after Melanchthon's death, his ideas about political order continued to stimulate intense discussion in the learned communities of Europe. Indeed, his views about the Imperial constitution and the importance of elected monarchy stood in direct opposition to the French thinkers then favouring hereditary royal rule, and especially royal authority capable of crushing aristocratic interests, as the best way to achieve political stability. Because of Melanchthon's authority within this discourse, the French thinker Jean Bodin attacked the German Protestant perspective by concentrating on Melanchthon's arguments in *Carion's Chronicle*. Melanchthon's followers recognized the threat that Bodin's ideas posed to the constitutional structure of the Empire, and they immediately came to the defence of Melanchthon's position.[101] In the end, France realized the strong, hereditary monarchy favoured by Bodin, and it became the most predatory state within Europe before the nineteenth century. In contrast, the Holy Roman Empire remained a limited, elected monarchy until its dissolution, and it became incapable of waging wars of aggression.

By the early seventeenth century, Melanchthon's direct influence began to fade as a new generation arose that never understood what he had worked so hard to accomplish and to preserve. In the 1570s, Melanchthon's followers had been expelled from Saxony, and once they lost the University of Wittenberg to the ultra-conservative branch of Lutheranism, it was only a matter of time before Melanchthon too was abandoned. Because of the cohesive nature of

---

100 See Neddermeyer, "Kaspar Peucer (1525–1602)," 69–101.
101 See John Brown, *The Methodus ad facilem historiarum cognitionem of Jean Bodin: A Critical Study* (Washington, D.C.: The Catholic University of America Press, 1939), 67–85; Arno Seifert, *Der Rückzug der biblischen Prophetie von der neueren Geschichte: Studien zur Geschichte der Reichstheologie des frühneuzeitlichen deutschen Protestantismus* (Cologne: Böhlau Verlag, 1990), 65–69; Adalbert Klempt, *Die Säkularisierung der universalhistorischen Auffassung: zum Wandel des Geschichtsdenkens im 16. und 17. Jahrhundert* (Göttingen: Musterschmidt, 1960), 50–59; and Hanns Gross, *Empire and Sovereignty: A History of the Public Law Literature in the Holy Roman Empire, 1599–1804* (Chicago: University of Chicago Press, 1973).

INTRODUCTION   31

Melanchthon's thought, the rejection of his theology meant that all of his textbooks became suspect. In the early decades of the seventeenth century, some of the faculty at Wittenberg waged a campaign against Melanchthon's lingering influence, so that by the late 1630s, the *Loci Communes* were replaced and even *Carion's Chronicle* had fallen out of use.[102]

Despite this, Melanchthon's thought continued to animate the intellectual circles of Europe. Wittenberg historiography derived from a process of development over time and a dialogue with received traditions and contemporary context. With *Carion's Chronicle,* Melanchthon created a basic interpretative pattern for the European past that focused on the Imperial constitution and blamed the papacy for the decline of the medieval German Empire. While this seems self-evident now, at the time, the shift in perspective fundamentally transformed interpretations of the centuries between Charlemagne and the Reformation. Furthermore, Melanchthon developed a framework for understanding the complementary interaction of political and religious history that guided or challenged historians well into the nineteenth century. Ultimately, Melanchthon's reformation of historical thought became an integral aspect of European intellectual culture for the centuries that followed.

7   Chapter Summaries

This study analyzes the ways that Melanchthon reformed classical and Christian traditions of historical thought to project a Wittenberg vision of Europe. Within this overarching framework, the individual chapters address specific questions concerning Melanchthon's intervention in the annals of Western historiography. Each chapter in its own way engages with earlier scholarly discourses, and they all argue, sometimes explicitly but often tacitly, for a different perspective than "earlier literature" has presented on these topics.

Chapter 2 addresses the traditions of the "Four Monarchies" and the "transfer of empire" (*translatio imperii*) in historical thought. The Four Monarchies is found in both pagan and Christian traditions, and it refers to the idea that four "world-empires" would rule in a succession that most interpreters presented as culminating in the Roman Empire. In Late Antiquity, the Four Monarchies became especially important in discussions about the decline of Rome, but after the collapse of the Empire in the West, the interpretive scheme lost much of its relevance. The chapter shows how the idea of the Monarchies was slowly reintroduced during the Middle Ages, but it demonstrates that German historians

---

102   See Manschreck, *Melanchthon*, 15–16.

did not make strong associations between the Holy Roman Empire and the Fourth Monarchy on the eve of the Reformation. Instead, the chapter explains how medieval historians developed a pro-papal view of the past that was closely linked to papal claims of religious and political supremacy. Despite centuries of papal-Imperial conflict, Imperial controversialists never developed a comprehensive historical narrative to compete with this pro-papal historiography.

Chapter 3 is a biographical study of Johann Carion, the original co-author of *Carion's Chronicle*. Carion was a fellow student with Melanchthon in Tübingen, and they both left for northern Germany just as Luther was becoming a public figure. Carion officially served the Hohenzollern court at Berlin as court "astronomer," but in fact, he acted in a variety of capacities, including princely tutor and diplomat. Carion was an unlikely candidate for scholarly greatness, and the chapter shows how disputes over astrological method and accuracy endangered his professional reputation in the years leading up to the *Chronicle's* publication. In the 1520s, history had not yet entered the university curriculum as a standard subject, so Melanchthon had little need for a history textbook at Wittenberg. In contrast, Carion's position as a court tutor meant that he was not bound by the university structure, and he had greater flexibility to add lessons on history to his teaching. In its initial form, *Carion's Chronicle* met this need for a compendium of history that would be useful for instructing young princes.

Chapter 4 is devoted to the arguments that Melanchthon, Carion and Caspar Peucer incorporated into *Carion's Chronicle*. The original *Chronicle* of 1532 was very much a response to the Turkish threat, political upheaval in Germany and the early years of the Reformation. In this context, Melanchthon made forceful, but often subtle, arguments about the Imperial constitution to restore religious and political peace in Germany and to build a foundation for united resistance against continuing Turkish invasions. In doing so, Melanchthon effectively overturned the pro-papal narrative of the Middle Ages, and he presented a persuasive, though mostly tacit, argument for the legitimacy of the Wittenberg Reformation.

Between 1558 and 1565, Melanchthon and Caspar Peucer revised the original Melanchthon-Carion narrative. Their revisions involved both a vast expansion of the text and changes to the style of argument. Melanchthon set greater emphasis on religion than he had in 1532, but he died before completing the key sections on the Middle Ages. Peucer finished Melanchthon's work, but as he revised the text, he transformed the *Chronicle* into an attack on medieval Catholicism. With Peucer, "Wittenberg Historiography" became an argument against the legitimacy of the papal involvement in religion or politics, and a justification for the Reformation.

INTRODUCTION 33

Chapter 5 addresses the textual transmission and reception of *Carion's Chronicle* from its initial publication in 1532 down to the last editions in the seventeenth century. The printing history of the *Chronicle* has challenged generations of researchers, and the analysis provides an explanation for Melanchthon's concerns about protecting the text from unauthorized revision. Here again, the Turkish wars are fundamental for Melanchthon's engagement with the *Chronicle*, and the chapter shows that the disastrous 1542 Turkish campaign is the key to understanding later modifications of the text as well as the efforts to control its printed form. More generally, the chapter traces the dissemination of the *Chronicle* across Europe through reprintings, adaptations and translations to demonstrate the truly remarkable diffusion of Wittenberg historiography.

Through Melanchthon's intervention, the Four Monarchies became the point of departure for theologians, historians and jurists to debate the past, present and future of the Holy Roman Empire. Chapter 6 sketches the contours of these later debates, and it demonstrates the continuing importance of Melanchthon's views even as *Carion's Chronicle* fell out of use as a classroom text. During his long career, Melanchthon developed a compelling interpretation of the Empire's history and its constitution, and Wittenberg historiography provided a political and religious vision for a secure and peaceful Europe. Melanchthon's perspective remained an integral part of European intellectual culture down to the last days of the Empire.

> Nihil tam circumspecte dici potest, ut calumniam euitare queat.[103]
> PHILIPP MELANCHTHON

---

103 *Die Bekenntnisschriften der evangelisch-lutherischen Kirche* (Göttingen: Vandenhoeck & Ruprecht, 1998), 234 (*Apologie der Konfession*, VII.2) ("Nothing can be said so carefully such that it is possible to avoid [all] controversy.").

CHAPTER 2

The Fourth Monarchy and the *Translatio Imperii*

1   Introduction

In *Carion's Chronicle*, Melanchthon engaged with a venerable tradition of historical thought that reached back over a millennium.[1] Already in Late Antiquity, Christian historians created frameworks of interpretation that set important precedents for the Middle Ages. They confidently charted a teleological narrative that focused especially on lineages and chronology to unfold a divine story that progressed from Creation to the Last Day. Medieval historians built on this foundation, and for subsequent centuries they added the lineages of the Emperors and the popes, whose relationship defined the political and religious history of the Middle Ages. The historical narrative that emerged during those centuries was marked by claims of papal supremacy and the need to conform the past to the dictates of canon law. Despite intermittent currents of Imperial resistance, by the early sixteenth century, history had long been on the side of the papacy.

In the late seventeenth century, Christoph Cellarius (1638–1707), a professor at Halle an der Saale, popularized the tripartite division of universal history into ancient, medieval and modern.[2] It quickly became the standard frame of reference, and it has remained so to this day. Prior to Cellarius, historians had used several different interpretive schemes to structure narratives of universal history. Of these, the most important were the Six Ages of the world, based on key events in biblical history, and the sequence of world-empires, usually known as the Four Monarchies. Both of these frameworks entered the Christian tradition in Late Antiquity, and they remained normative down to the sixteenth century.

Historical periodization is an interpretive process, and the approaches developed in Antiquity were closely related to broader political and theological currents. Although they ostensibly framed the past, these schemes functioned

---

1 See generally Ernst Breisach, *Historiography: Ancient, Medieval, and Modern*, 2nd ed. (Chicago: University of Chicago Press, 1994); Denys Hay, *Annalists and Historians: Western Historiography from the VIIIth to the XVIIIth Century* (London: Meuthen & Co., 1977).

2 See generally Wallace K. Ferguson, *The Renaissance in Historical Thought: Five Centuries of Interpretation* (Boston: Houghton Mifflin, 1948), 73–77 for Cellarius; and Peter Schaeffer, "The Emergence of the Concept '*Medieval*' in Central European Humanism," *Sixteenth Century Journal* 7, no. 2 (October 1976): 21–30.

as commentaries on the present and they offered predictions about the future. Interpretations, however, changed over time, and during the Middle Ages, emphases shifted as historians enlisted the past to address new concerns, especially the issue of supremacy in the West. At first glance, *Carion's Chronicle* seems conventional, but when set against a thousand years of tradition, its subtle reconceptualization of form and argument become indicative of a seismic shift in intellectual perspective.

2   Universal History and the Roman Empire

Much of ancient universal history has been lost and must be reconstructed from fragmentary references, but a few important authors, such as Polybius and Pompeius Trogus (in Justin's *Epitome*), have survived more intact. As a general rule, Greco-Roman historians used four different schemes to frame universal history: [1] a progression of metals that paralleled a succession of peoples, [2] the stages of the life-cycle as applied to individuals, political entities or the world as a whole, [3] a narrative of progress from barbarism to cultural sophistication, or [4] a sequence of world-empires.[3] Of these, the most important for later centuries was the scheme of world-empires culminating in Rome, and the idea became a vehicle for both positive and negative commentary on the Roman Empire.[4]

In the second century B.C., the Greek historian Polybius traced Rome's rise to the status of a world-empire.[5] His *Histories* considered the reasons for Roman success, and he compared Rome to earlier empires, specifically Persia, Sparta and Macedonia. Rome had defeated Carthage, its great rival, and it now surpassed all other empires, because it had subdued almost the entire world.[6] Besides his comparative examples, Polybius also knew the tradition of an

---

3   Arnaldo Momigliano, "The Origins of Universal History," in *On Pagans, Jews, and Christians* (Middleton, CT: Wesleyan University Press, 1987), 32.
4   On periodization, see especially Roderich Schmidt, "Aetates mundi: Die Weltalter als Gliederungsprinzip der Geschichte," *Zeitschrift für Kirchengeschichte* LXVII (Vierte Folge V) (1955/56): 288–317. See also Momigliano, "The Origins of Universal History;" Wilhelm Schmidt-Biggemann, *Philosophia perennis: Historical Outlines of Western Spirituality in Ancient, Medieval and Early Modern Thought* (Dordrecht: Springer, 2004), 369–408; Michael I. Allen, "Universal History 300–1000: Origins and Western Developments," in *Historiography in the Middle Ages*, ed. Deborah Mauskopf Deliyannis (Leiden: Brill, 2003); and Joseph Swain, "The Theory of the Four Monarchies: Opposition History under the Roman Empire," *Classical Philology* 35 (1940): 1–21.
5   Breisach, 45–50; Momigliano, "The Origins of Universal History," 39–41.
6   Momigliano, "The Origins of Universal History," 39–40.

older succession of Eastern empires: Assyria, Media, Persia and Macedonia.[7] To these, Rome was easily added as a fifth, all conquering world-empire.

Polybius was only one of many conduits that transmitted the Eastern idea of a succession of empires, and by the first century B.C., it had become part of Roman tradition.[8] Latin writers, such as Vergil, fused Rome's mythic Trojan origins and destiny to rule the world with the expectation that Rome would endure, unlike earlier empires, as the "Eternal City" (*urbs aeterna*).[9] Through historians, such as Appian (fl. 140), and later poets, such as Claudian (fl. 400), the idea of Rome as the eternal empire continued as a fixture of Roman culture down to the waning days of the Western Empire.[10]

As Polybius composed his story of Roman ascendance, a countercurrent was developing in response to the conquests in Greece, Asia and Egypt. There, the imposition of Roman rule met continuing resistance, and prophecies sustained hope of a reversal in Roman fortunes and a return of power to the East.[11] As part of this cultural defiance, provincial authors began composing "opposition history" that contrasted the barbarism of the Romans with the sophistication of the kingdoms they had overthrown.[12] Many of these historians wrote in Greek, but at the time of Augustus, Pompeius Trogus, a Romanized Gaul, composed a Latin history of the Eastern empires from an anti-Roman perspective.[13] His *Philippic History* has survived only in the second or third century Latin *Epitome* by Justin, and in that form it became a particularly important source for later historians.

Trogus structured the *Philippic History* according to the four ancient empires: Babylon, Media, Persia and Greece;[14] he also included Carthage and Parthia.[15] Although he concluded briefly with Rome as the fifth world-empire, he mostly avoided Roman history in the rest of his narrative. Anti-imperial sympathies pervaded the *Histories*, and when Trogus did mention the Romans,

---

7 Momigliano, "The Origins of Universal History," 41.
8 Swain, "The Theory of the Four Monarchies," 13.
9 Samuel Kliger, "The Gothic Revival and the German *Translatio*," *Modern Philology* 45, no. 2 (November 1947): 73–74.
10 Swain, "The Theory of the Four Monarchies," 13–14.
11 Momigliano, "The Origins of Universal History," 43–44; Swain, "The Theory of the Four Monarchies," 14–16.
12 Momigliano, "The Origins of Universal History," 44–45.
13 For Trogus, I rely on Momigliano, "The Origins of Universal History," 44–56; Swain, "The Theory of the Four Monarchies," 16–18; and the English translation – Justin, *Epitome of the Philippic History of Pompeius Trogus*, trans. J.C. Yardley (Atlanta: Scholar's Press, 1994).
14 Momigliano, "The Origins of Universal History," 44–56; Swain, "The Theory of the Four Monarchies," 17–18.
15 Justin, *Epitome*, 7 (Introduction).

the implications were largely negative. As a final stab at the Empire, he presented the hated Parthians as co-rulers of the world with the Romans, thereby demonstrating that the East still resisted the legions.[16] Initially, the *Philippic History* seems to have been mostly ignored, but by the time of Justin's *Epitome*, the anti-Imperial perspective was less of an obstacle, even for a Latin speaking audience. Ultimately, Christian historians embraced the *Epitome*, and it became one of their most important sources for pre-Roman events.

3 Christian Historiography

The idea of a sequence of world-empires also permeated Christian historical thought in Antiquity.[17] Christian writers were heirs to pagan and Old Testament traditions, and they used both to interpret the past, assess the present and gaze into the future. The Eastern traditions inherited by the Romans had not definitively fixed the number of world-empires. Assyria, Babylon (the Chaldeans), Media, Persia, Greece (the Macedonians), Egypt, Carthage and Rome could all legitimately be included, and there was no limit on future candidates. Four or five was a common number, and the enumeration in the canon tables of ancient astronomers provided an important model, but ultimately no single list became universally accepted.[18] In contrast, the Christian tradition was limited to four world-empires because of the prophecies in the Book of Daniel. These were called the "Four Monarchies" or "chief empires," and according to many commentators, the Fourth Monarchy would be the last, and it would endure until Christ's return to rule. In Antiquity, Christian scholars, like

---

16   Justin, *Epitome*, 255–258 (Book 41); see Momigliano, "The Origins of Universal History," 44–56; Swain, "The Theory of the Four Monarchies," 17–18.
17   On the Four Monarchies and the *translatio imperii*, see generally H.H. Rowley, *Darius, the Mede and the Four World Empires in the Book of Daniel: A Historical Study of Contemporary Theories*, (Cardiff: University of Wales, 1959 [Reprint]); Kliger, "The Gothic Revival and the German *Translatio*;" Werner Goez, *Translatio imperii: Ein Beitrag zur Geschichte des Geschichtsdenkens und der politischen Theorien im Mittelalter und in der frühen Neuzeit* (Tübingen: Mohr, 1958); Edgar Marsch, *Biblische Prophetie und chronographische Dichtung: Stoff- und Wirkungsgeschichte der Vision des Propheten Daniel nach Dan. VII* (Berlin: Erich Schmidt Verlag, 1972); Hanns Gross, *Empire and Sovereignty: A History of the Public Law Literature in the Holy Roman Empire, 1599–1804* (Chicago: University of Chicago Press, 1973); and Arno Seifert, *Der Rückzug der biblischen Prophetie von der neueren Geschichte: Studien zur Geschichte der Reichstheologie des frühneuzeitlichen deutschen Protestantismus* (Cologne: Böhlau Verlag, 1990).
18   On the ancient astronomical canon tables (generally associated with Claudius Ptolemy), see James Evans, *History and Practice of Ancient Astronomy* (Oxford: Oxford University Press, 1998), 176–177.

their pagan counterparts, did not settle on a uniform pattern for the sequence of ancient empires. Biblical and non-biblical perspectives could overlap, but they were not always, or necessarily, congruent. Understanding this diversity of thought is important, because it created tensions within Christian patterns of interpretation that persisted into the sixteenth century.

The Christian reading of the Four Monarchies is based on two prophecies in the Book of Daniel: King Nebuchadnezzar of Babylon's dream (Daniel 2) and Daniel's own vision (Daniel 7).[19] In the dream of Daniel 2, Nebuchadnezzar saw a colossal statue with a head of gold, chest of silver, midsection of bronze, legs of iron, and feet made partly of clay and partly of iron. Daniel explained that the dream foretold a succession of great powers beginning with Babylon:

> [King Nebuchadnezzar], you are the head of gold. After you shall arise another kingdom inferior to yours, and yet a third kingdom of bronze, which shall rule over the whole earth. And there shall be a fourth kingdom, strong as iron; just as iron crushes and smashes everything, it shall crush and shatter all these. As you saw the feet and toes partly of potter's clay and partly of iron, it shall be a divided kingdom; but some of the strength of iron shall be in it, as you saw the iron mixed with the clay. As the toes of the feet were part iron and part clay, so the kingdom shall be partly strong and partly brittle.
> DANIEL 2:38–42 (NRSV)

In his own vision (recorded in Daniel 7), Daniel saw four ferocious beasts arise from the sea: a lion, a bear, a leopard and a terrifying fourth beast with ten horns:

> I, Daniel, saw in my vision by night the four winds of heaven stirring up the great sea, and four great beasts came up out of the sea, different from one another. The first was like a lion and had eagles' wings. Then as I watched, its wings were plucked off, and it was lifted up from the ground and made to stand on two feet like a human being; and a human mind was given to it. Another beast appeared, a second one, that looked like a bear. It was raised up on one side, had three tusks in its mouth among its teeth and was told, "Arise, devour many bodies!" After this, as I watched, another appeared, like a leopard. The beast had four wings of a bird on its back and four heads; and dominion was given to it. After this I saw in the

---

19   See Allen, "Universal History 300–1000," esp. 17–39; and Swain, "The Theory of the Four Monarchies," 1–21.

> visions by night a fourth beast, terrifying and dreadful and exceedingly strong. It had great iron teeth and was devouring, breaking in pieces, and stamping what was left with its feet. It was different from all the beasts that preceded it, and it had ten horns. I was considering the horns, when another horn appeared, a little one coming up from among them; to make room for it, three of the earlier horns were plucked up by the roots. There were eyes like human eyes in this horn, and a mouth speaking arrogantly.
>
> DANIEL 7:2–8 (NRSV)

As with the statue of Daniel 2, the beasts of Daniel 7 would correspond to four earthly monarchies; and Daniel received a more detailed explanation regarding the fourth, terrifying beast:

> As for the fourth beast, there shall be a fourth kingdom on earth that shall be different from all the other kingdoms; it shall devour the whole earth, and trample it down and break it to pieces. As for the ten horns, out of this kingdom ten kings shall arise, and another shall arise after them. This one shall be different from the former ones, and shall put down three kings. He shall speak words against the Most High, shall wear out the holy ones of the Most High, and shall attempt to change the sacred seasons and the law; and they shall be given into his power for a time, two times, and half a time. Then the court shall sit in judgment, and his dominion shall be taken away, to be consumed and totally destroyed.
>
> DANIEL 7:23–25 (NRSV)

In the third century, St. Hippolytus of Rome († ca. 236) interpreted the two prophecies in Daniel as referring to the same sequence of empires. In his *Commentary on Daniel*, he designated these Four Monarchies as Babylon, Persia (sometimes including the Medes), Greece, and Rome.[20] Hippolytus set an important exegetical precedent, and Eusebius of Caesarea († 339) adopted a similar, but not identical, interpretation in his *Demonstratio Evangelica*: Assyria, Persia, Macedonia, and Rome, with the weakened Rome of his day as the statue's feet of iron mixed with clay.[21] In his own *Commentary on Daniel* (A.D. 406), St. Jerome followed Eusebius, and through his influence, this particular sequence of Monarchies became mostly fixed among later interpreters of

---

20 See Swain, "The Theory of the Four Monarchies," 18.
21 Swain, "The Theory of the Four Monarchies," 19.

Daniel in the Latin West.[22] His interpretation was ultimately incorporated into the *Glossa Ordinaria*, the standard resource for biblical exegesis in the Middle Ages.[23]

Several decades before his Daniel commentary, Jerome had already tacitly endorsed the Four Monarchies as a framework for historical scholarship in his Latin translation of Eusebius's *Chronicle*.[24] Initially, Christian historians showed little concern for the political history of Rome.[25] Instead, they concentrated on sacred history, and especially the question of chronology. In this respect, the foundational work for later Christian historians was the *Chronographies* of Julius Africanus (fl. 220).[26] The *Chronographies*, originally five books in Greek, collated sacred and pagan chronology down to A.D. 221. It has survived only in fragments and quotations, but it was widely used in Antiquity, and Eusebius relied on it as an important source for his *Chronicle*.[27]

Although Eusebius is most famous for his *Ecclesiastical History*, his *Chronicle* was equally important within its field. The *Chronicle* consisted of two books. The first was a narrative account of ancient history, and the second traced parallel chronologies in a series of columns. The original Greek edition is lost, but Jerome preserved the second book by translating it into Latin and extending the chronology down to 380. In the Eusebius-Jerome *Chronicle,* one column, placed prominently on the far left of the page, was dedicated to the succession of world-empires culminating in Rome. The *Chronicle* did not mention Daniel, but the world-empires column corresponded to the interpretation of the Fourth Monarchies found later in Jerome's *Commentary on Daniel*. The idea was not unique to Jerome, and Sulpitius Severus used a sequence of Four Monarchies in his own *Chronicle* (A.D. 400) with explicit reference to Daniel 2.[28] Nevertheless, through the broad dissemination of his works, Jerome was largely responsible for aligning the Four Monarchies with the ancient

---

22 See Allen, "Universal History 300–1000," 20–23; Swain, "The Theory of the Four Monarchies," 19.
23 Schmidt-Biggemann, *Philosophia Perennis*, 396.
24 An English translation is available: Saint Jerome, *The Chronicle of St. Jerome* (2005), trans. Roger Pearse, http://www.ccel.org/ccel/pearse/morefathers/files/jerome_chronicle_00_eintro.htm.
25 Momigliano, "Pagan and Christian Historiography," 89.
26 Julius Africanus, *Chronographiae: The Extant Fragments*, ed. Martin Wallraff et al. (Berlin: Walter de Gruyter, 2007).
27 Momigliano, "Pagan and Christian Historiography," 83–88.
28 Sulpitius Severus, *The Sacred History*, trans. Alexander Roberts, in *A Select Library of Nicene and Post-Nicene Fathers of the Christian Church*, vol. XI, ed. Philip Schaff and Henry Wace (Grand Rapids: Eerdmans Publishing Co., 1986 [Reprint]), 98 (II.3).

world-empires, and the specific succession of Babylon (or Assyria), Persia (and Media), Greece, and Rome.

Old Testament traditions provided a primary frame of reference for the idea of world-empires, but some early Christian scholars were also influenced by older currents of anti-Imperial history and Eastern prophecy.[29] Prior to Emperor Constantine's conversion, Christian controversialists sometimes responded to outbreaks of persecution with virulent polemics against the Empire, and in that context, Eastern anti-Imperial prophecies could became a source of consolation. During the persecutions in the early fourth century, the Christian apologist Lactantius († ca. 320) began writing an extended defence of Christianity, his *Divine Institutes*, and he incorporated several anti-Roman prophecies.[30]

In a chapter entitled, "Of the Devastation of the World and Change of the Empires," he transmitted a prophecy attributed to the Eastern king Hystaspes concerning a future conqueror from the East and the inevitable fall of Rome:

> [T]he Roman name, by which the world is now ruled, will be taken away from the earth, and the government will return to Asia; and the East will bear rule, and the West be reduced to servitude.[31]

By drawing on traditions of opposition, Lactantius offered comfort to persecuted Christians, and he found hope in a continuing succession of empires. However, once the Roman Empire became Christian, the perspective changed dramatically, and the prophecies transmitted by Lactantius alarmed later generations of Christians when new invaders, such as the Turks, arose in the East.[32]

---

29 On these countercurrents, see Swain, "The Theory of the Four Monarchies," 15–16.
30 See Momigliano, "The Origins of Universal History," 44; Swain, "The Theory of the Four Monarchies," 15; and Oliver Nicholson, "Broadening the Roman Mind: Foreign Prophets in the Apologetic of Lactantius," in *Studia Patristica*, vol. XXXVI, ed. M.F. Wiles and E.J. Yarnold (Leuven: Peeters, 2001), 364–374.
31 Lactantius, *The Divine Institutes*, trans. William Fletcher, in *The Ante-Nicene Fathers*, vol. VII, ed. Alexander Roberts and James Donaldson (Grand Rapids: Eerdmans Publishing Co., 1989 [Reprint]), 212 (VII.15).
32 See Robin Barnes, *Prophecy and Gnosis: Apocalypticism in the Wake of the Lutheran Reformation* (Stanford: Stanford University Press, 1988), 79; and Pál Fodor, "The View of the Turk in Hungary: The Apocalyptic Tradition and the Legend of the Red Apple in Ottoman-Hungarian Context," in *In Quest of the Golden Apple: Imperial Ideology, Politics, and Military Administration in the Ottoman Empire* (Istanbul: Isis Press, 2000), 94.

4 Late Antiquity and the Fourth Monarchy

In the fourth century, the transformation of Christianity from a persecuted sect into a state sponsored religion lead to new perspectives on the history of the Empire and its purpose in the world.[33] After Emperor Constantine's conversion, Christianity had enjoyed a moment of triumph. By the end of the fourth century, however, the relative calm of Constantine's reign had been followed by internal turmoil and barbarian invasions. The declining political fortunes of the Empire brought renewed interest in Roman history, especially among pagans who blamed Rome's problems on the abandonment of the old state religion.[34] In A.D. 378, Emperor Valens was defeated and killed by the Goths at Adrianople. Then in A.D. 410 the unthinkable happened when Rome was sacked for the first time in centuries. The shock of those catastrophes forced Christian historians to confront the relationship of the Church to a political Empire that had ceased to be invincible.

The tradition of world-empires had been introduced to Rome at a moment of political ascendance. The anti-Imperial movements in the East, however, had reappropriated the idea, and eventually it became unpatriotic to speak of a succession, since it implied that Rome too would fall, as had all the earlier empires. The Jewish historian Josephus, for example, purposely avoided discussing the Four Monarchies, so as not offend his Roman audience.[35] In Late Antiquity, Christian scholars again reconfigured the traditions of the world-empires in response to the declining fortunes of Rome. In that moment of external threats and political decay, they deployed the "Four Monarchies" to demonstrate their patriotism and to provide consolation against a multitude of disasters.

St. Jerome had begun this process, both with his *Commentary on Daniel* and the Eusebius-Jerome *Chronicle*, but among historians, the chief exponent of the idea that Rome must endure was Paulus Orosius (fl. 415), a pupil of both Jerome and St. Augustine. Orosius, like Jerome, saw the culmination of ancient political history in the Christian Roman Empire, and he too wrote of "Four Monarchies," but in different ways than other Christian commentators. At Augustine's urging, Orosius composed his *Seven Books of History Against*

---

33 For the fourth century developments, see Arnaldo Momigliano, "Pagan and Christian Historiography in the Fourth Century A.D.," in *The Conflict Between Paganism and Christianity in the Fourth Century*, ed. Arnaldo Momigliano (Oxford: Oxford University Press, 1963), 79–87.

34 Momigliano, "Pagan and Christian Historiography," 81.

35 Swain, "The Theory of the Four Monarchies," 16 n. 40.

the Pagans as a companion volume to *The City of God*.[36] The specific directive from Augustine was to produce a chronicle of earlier calamities, which would demonstrate that recent misfortunes were hardly exceptional. As instructed, Orosius produced a massive catalogue of disasters – military defeats, political downfalls, earthquakes, etc. – and he used this vast reservoir of material to develop the ongoing historical theme of divine reward and punishment.[37]

Beyond this, however, Orosius seems to have misunderstood Augustine or simply disregarded him.[38] From a simple catalogue of disasters, the text swelled into a comprehensive narrative of ancient history. Within this, Orosius emphasized the Christian character of the Roman Empire, and he used the sequence of the Four Monarchies to demonstrate that Rome was destined to endure. He set particular emphasis on the intersection of Roman and Christian history in the reign of Augustus and the birth of Christ. Later, he stressed the foundation of Constantinople, the new Rome, as a distinctly Christian city, free of idols.[39]

Despite this Christian tone, Orosius did not draw on the Judeo-Christian tradition of Four Monarchies as found in Daniel. Indeed, he never mentioned, or even alluded to, the prophecies. The "Four Monarchies" in the *History against the Pagans* are not chronologically sequential, rather they are geographically oriented according to: East – Assyria, Babylon, Persia (Book I); North – Greece (Books II–III); South – Carthage (Book IV); West – Rome (Books V–VII). Of the four world-empires, for Orosius, Babylon in the East and Rome in the West were the most important. Greece and Carthage were both of comparatively short duration, only seven hundred years, while Babylon had lasted for fourteen hundred. Rome, the last empire, would similarly endure well beyond the limits fixed for the empires of North and South.[40] In this way, Orosius, one of the most widely read historians in the Middle Ages, deployed the Four Monarchies without specifically linking the organization of his history to Daniel's prophecies or to the standard Christian interpretations found in Jerome.[41] Orosius's inclusion of Carthage and his emphasis on geography may owe

---

36 Paulus Orosius, *The Seven Books of History Against the Pagans*, trans. Roy J. Deferrari (Washington, D.C.: The Catholic University of America Press, 1964). For Orosius, I rely on Allen, "Universal History," 26–32.
37 Allen, "Universal History," 29.
38 See Theodor E. Mommsen, "Orosius and Augustine," in *Medieval and Renaissance Studies*, ed. Eugene F. Rice, Jr. (Ithaca: Cornell University Press, 1959), 325–348.
39 Orosius, *History Against the Pagans*, 288–290 (VII.3), 331 (VII.28).
40 Orosius, *History Against the Pagans*, 285–287 (VII.2).
41 See Allen, "Universal History 300–1000," 26–32; Swain, "The Theory of the Four Monarchies," 20–21.

something to his roots in Iberia, but regardless, his approach was more in dialogue with Eastern traditions, whose anti-Roman perspective he neutralized, than with the Christian exegesis of Daniel.

5   St. Augustine and the Six Ages

Jerome and Orosius used the Four Monarchies to assert Christian-Roman patriotism and offer consolation that the Empire, despite its decline, would endure. St. Augustine offered a different perspective. In *The City of God*, he responded to the sack of Rome by arguing that Christianity was not linked to the political fortunes of the Empire.[42] For Augustine, Rome was not necessarily the "Eternal City." The Empire could fall or splinter apart, and the "City of God" would endure regardless. Augustine briefly referred to the Four Monarchies, and he cited Jerome's *Commentary on Daniel*, but he did not develop the idea of world-empires at any length.[43]

Instead, Augustine endorsed two different frameworks for understanding universal history: the Six Ages and the Three Ages. Both had a long after-life, but Augustine had greater influence on the interpretation of the Six Ages, which he revised to accord with his theological perspective.[44] Because God had created the world in seven days, some early Christians had proposed that the world itself would endure for a single "week," meaning it was to last for six thousand years. The seventh day of sabbath rest would then follow in the eternal rest at the end of time or in a millennial period during which Christ would reign on earth. The basis for this view lay in biblical passages that referred to a thousand years as being like a day in the sight of God (Psalm 89:4; II Peter 3:8). From this perspective, the Six Ages seemed to fall naturally into one thousand year intervals.

Augustine accepted the Six Ages, but he rejected the rigid pattern of millennial interpretation. Instead, he marked each age according to a decisive event or key figure in sacred history, thereby creating clearly defined, but uneven, intervals of time. As a result, the Sixth Age, which began with Christ, was not confined to a specific duration, but simply extended to the end of time.

---

42   Saint Augustine, *The City of God Against the Pagans*, trans. R.W. Dyson (Cambridge: Cambridge University Press, 1998). See R.A. Markus, *Saeculum: History and Society in the Theology of St. Augustine* (Cambridge: Cambridge University Press, 1988); Allen, "Universal History 300–1000," 31–39.
43   Augustine, *The City of God*, 1021–1024 (XX.23).
44   Allen, "Universal History," 31–39.

In addition, Augustine made each age correspond to a stage of the human life cycle, and each stage, with the exception of the Sixth (old age), included either ten or fourteen generations from the genealogy of Christ. The resulting framework defined the Six Ages as follows: [1st] from Adam to Noah, ten generations (infancy – *infantia*), [2nd] from Noah to Abraham, ten generations (childhood – *pueritia*), [3rd] from Abraham to David, fourteen generations (adolescence – *adolescentia*), [4th] from David to the Babylonian Captivity, fourteen generations (youth – *iuventus*), [5th] from the Babylonian Captivity to Christ, fourteen generations (maturity – *gravitas*), [6th] from Christ to the Last Days, unknown number of generations (old age – *senectus*), and [7th] Eternal Rest.[45] In this way, Augustine preserved the Six Ages, but he avoided the problem of a fixed six thousand year duration for the world. His approach became the standard interpretation of the Six Ages, and later historians who used the framework generally derived it directly or indirectly from his works.

In contrast to the Six Ages, Augustine had less influence over the interpretation of the Three Ages, but it too entered the framework of Christian historical thought, though it was less common. The scheme seems to derive from Talmudic traditions, specifically the so-called "Prophecy of Elias," or *Vaticinium Eliae*.[46] According to the prophecy, the world is to endure for six thousand years: two thousand years of void, two thousand years of the Torah, and two thousand years of the Messiah. Since Christians saw Christ as the fulfilment of the Messianic prophecies, they usually reconfigured the tripartite division as: two thousand years of natural law (*ante legem*), two thousand years of Mosaic law (*sub lege*), and two thousand years of the Gospel (*sub gratia*).[47] The Christianized interpretation then looked to Adam, Moses and Christ as the markers of each age. Even in Christian form, however, the scheme perpetuated the idea of a fixed duration for the world, not to exceed six thousand years.

Augustine had adopted the Six Ages specifically to avoid linking the survival of the Church with the Empire. In contrast, the perspective of Jerome and Orosius was to make the Roman Empire the culmination of political history and the fulfilment of biblical prophecy or typology. Thus, the difference in frameworks of interpretation was symptomatic of differences in perspective concerning the past, present and future of the Roman Empire. Ultimately, for Jerome and Orosius, history and Scripture demonstrated that the Empire must endure even to the end of time, whereas for Augustine there was no assurance

---

45 Augustine, *The City of God*, 1182 (XXII.30); Schmidt, "Aetates Mundi," 292–293; Allen, "Universal History," 31.
46 Schmidt, "Aetates Mundi," 299–301.
47 Schmidt, "Aetates Mundi," 299.

of divinely favoured political continuity. Later historians would attempt to reconcile the Six Ages and the Four Monarchies, but in the early fifth century these interpretive patterns represented diametrically opposed responses to external threats and internal political decline.

6 Universal History in the Early Middle Ages

After the collapse of the Western Roman Empire, many of the questions that had animated the historiography of Augustine, Jerome and Orosius faded into irrelevance. The leading historians of the early Middle Ages, Isidore of Seville († 636) and the Venerable Bede († 735), adopted the Six Ages as a pattern of historical interpretation, and they added chronological information to give precise, even if disputed, dates for the first five ages.[48] Like Eusebius before him, Isidore set an important precedent with the second edition of his *Greater Chronicle* and with his *Lesser Chronicle*, which was included in his *Etymologies*.[49] In both of these works, Isidore substituted the Six Ages for the Four Monarchies, and instead of aligning multiple columns, he traced a single timeline of events according to a "year of the world" (*anno mundi*) dating system. Within this streamlined format, he did not designate "world-empires" or even mention Daniel's Four Monarchies. Political history remained important, but its prophetic fulfilment no longer served as the primary frame of reference.

A century later, Bede followed Isidore's lead, and in a series of studies, he provided definitive answers for the Middle Ages concerning biblical chronology, a key aspect of universal history, and through his knowledge of dating systems, he also solved the vexing problem of Easter reckoning.[50] Other chronological innovations by Bede were less successful. In the sixth century, Dionysius Exiguus had pioneered the system of dating events "in the year of our Lord" (*anno domini*). Bede adopted this perspective in his *Ecclesiastical History of the English People*, and he also added the system of dating B.C. Despite its obvious utility, the latter failed to gain wide currency in the Middle Ages or even

---

48 For Isidore and Bede, I rely on Allen, "Universal History," 32–35; and Schmidt-Biggemann, *Philosophia Perennis*, 375–380.

49 On Isidore's *Chronicles*, see Sam Koon and Jamie Wood, "The Chronica Maiora of Isidore of Seville," *e-Spania* 6 (December 2008): 2–7, http://e-spania.revues.org/index15552.html; and Isidore of Seville, *The Etymologies of Isidore of Seville*, trans. Stephen A. Barney et al. (Cambridge: Cambridge University Press, 2006), 130–133 (V.XXXIX).

50 See the introduction in Bede, *The Reckoning of Time*, trans. Faith Wallis (Liverpool: Liverpool University Press, 1999).

in the Renaissance, and historians continued to use the *anno mundi* system, which remained problematic because of inconsistencies regarding the date of Creation.[51] Bede himself used the *anno mundi* system in his *Greater Chronicle*.

The changed perspective of early medieval historiography reflects the political collapse of the Western Roman Empire. Bede and Isidore lived in a fragmented political landscape, and Rome no longer defined their historical perspective. The revival of the Empire under the Carolingians would seem auspicious for a return to historiography based on the Four Monarchies, but such was not to be. The ninth century produced few examples of universal history, and the most important representative, Frechulf of Lisieux's *Histories*, tacitly rejected an extension of prophetic fulfilment into Roman politics.[52] Frechulf (fl. 830) relied heavily on Orosius and he knew Jerome's *Commentary on Daniel*, but he ignored the Four Monarchies paradigm. Even so, Frechulf, although influenced by Augustine, did not adopt the Six Ages. Instead, he developed his own narrative framework that focused on sacred history and Judeo-Christian cultus. For Old Testament history, Frechulf adopted a scheme that had been noted, but not used, in the Eusebius-Jerome *Chronicle*: [1] Adam to the Flood, [2] the Flood to Abraham, [3] Abraham to Moses, [4] Moses to the building of Solomon's Temple, [5] the building of Solomon's Temple to the rebuilding of the Temple, [6] the rebuilding of the Temple to the Advent of Christ.[53]

Unlike the early fifth century, the political circumstances of Frechulf's day did not dictate a view of history that would fortify the Empire against the shock of invasion and political collapse. As a result, Frechulf was not compelled to extend the history of the Roman Empire to its revival among the Franks. Instead, he continued to emphasize the locus of worship in his account of Christian times. Accordingly, he closed the *Histories* in the early seventh century with two events: the declaration by Emperor Phocas that the pope was the head of all the churches and the conversion of the Pantheon into a Christian church.[54] Frechulf presented these two developments as the triumphal capstone to the narrative he had unfolded from Creation.

---

51   C.A. Patrides, "Renaissance Estimates of the Year of Creation," *The Huntington Library Quarterly* 26, no. 4 (August 1963): 315–322.

52   On Frechulf, see Allen, "Universal History," 39–42; and Nikolaus Staubach, "*Christiana Tempora*: Augustin und das Ende der alten Geschichte in der Weltchronik Frechulfs von Lisieux," *Frühmittelalterliche Studien* 29 (1995): 167–206. The *Histories* are included in Frechulf of Lisieux, *Opera Omnia*, 2 vols., ed. Michael I. Allen (Turnhout: Brepols, 2002).

53   Allen, "Universal History," 40–41; Schmidt, "Aetates Mundi," 304–305.

54   Frechulf, *Historiae* II.5, 26.

Later Carolingian historians, such as Regino of Prüm († 915), were mostly silent about the Four Monarchies.[55] Notker Balbus († 912) briefly addressed the prophecy from Daniel 2 in the introduction to his *Life of Charlemagne*, but he presented the Franks as a new head of gold and a new Empire, rather than the continuation of Rome.[56] A century later, the Ottonian historian Liudprand of Cremona († ca. 972) alluded to the Monarchies in his *Embassy to Constantinople*, but he did so more in the context of prophecy than history.[57] The Carolingians knew and read both Orosius and the Eusebius-Jerome *Chronicle*, but in the end, the Four Monarchies never became central to their historical interests.[58]

7 The Four Monarchies in the High Middle Ages

After Charlemagne's grandsons divided the Carolingian realm, the idea of a renewed Roman Empire faded until its revival again in the tenth century under the Ottonians, who created the vast Empire in central Europe and Italy that became known as the Holy Roman Empire.[59] Although the dynasty died out in the early eleventh century, the reconstituted Empire proved enduring, and it continued as an elected monarchy, with the Imperial Prince-Electors selecting each new Emperor. By then the papacy was also in political ascendance, and successors to the Ottonians increasingly clashed with the popes over the right to appoint, or "invest," ecclesiastical officials, whose offices often included important secular powers and responsibilities. The resulting "Investiture Controversy" lead to decades of civil war in Germany, as the popes sought to undermine the Emperors by stirring up rebellions among the German princes.

---

55 See Regino of Prüm, *History and Politics in Late Carolingian and Ottonian Europe: The Chronicle of Regino of Prüm and Adalbert of Magdeburg*, trans. Simon MacLean (New York: Manchester University Press, 2009), 13–14 (Translator's Introduction).

56 Einhard and Notker the Stammerer, *Two Lives of Charlemagne*, trans. Lewis Thorpe (New York: Penguin Books, 1969), 93.

57 Liudprand of Cremona, *The Complete Works of Liudprand of Cremona*, trans. Paolo Squatriti (Washington, D.C.: The Catholic University of America Press, 2007), 262–264 (*Embassy of Liudprand*, Chapters 39–41).

58 Regino of Prüm, *History and Politics*, 11–12 (Translator's Introduction).

59 On the Holy Roman Empire, see the exhibition catalog: *Heiliges Römisches Reich Deutscher Nation 962–1806*, 4 vols. (Dresden: Sandstein Verlag, 2006); Joachim Whaley, *Germany and the Holy Roman Empire*, 2 vols. (Oxford: Oxford University Press, 2012); and Peter Wilson, *Heart of Europe: A History of the Holy Roman Empire* (Cambridge, M.A.: Harvard University Press, 2016).

An accord was finally reached in A.D. 1122 with the Concordat of Worms, but by then the strong Empire of the Ottonians had been permanently weakened.[60]

In the ninth century, the Carolingian Empire had unravelled rapidly and from internal dynastic quarrels, rather than external pressures.[61] In contrast, the late eleventh and early twelfth century were more akin to Late Antiquity on several levels. By that time, the Empire had become a fixture of the medieval world, and its permanence meant that there was no living memory of a pre-Imperial Europe. Nevertheless, the Empire, once strong and powerful, was now wavering under the stress of civil war and ecclesiastical strife. Not since Late Antiquity had the conditions been so similar to the turmoil in the Roman world that Jerome and Orosius had experienced.

In the eleventh century, for the first time in five hundred years, the tension between decline and permanence brought renewed application of the Four Monarchies to the prevailing political order. From the late antique historian Jordanes (fl. 550) to the chronicler Berthold of Reichenau († 1088), every surviving universal history had used the Six Ages rather than the Four Monarchies as a conceptual framework. In contrast, from the late eleventh century onwards, the Four Monarchies appeared with increasing frequency, often, but not always, in combination with the Six Ages. Specific interpretations varied, but the scheme never again fell out of use in the Middle Ages.[62]

Although historians from the twelfth century onwards began referring to a sequence of Empires, many used Daniel's vision as a frame of reference rather than an animating principle. They reflect an acceptance, but also general ambivalence, regarding the Holy Roman Empire as the Fourth Monarchy. The *Chronicle* of Frutolf-Ekkehard, for instance, used the Six Ages, with passing reference to the Four Monarchies.[63] Later, Burchard of Ursberg († ca. 1231)

---

60 On the Investiture Controversy generally, see I.S. Robinson, "Reform and the Church, 1073–1122," in *The New Cambridge Medieval History*, vol. 4, Part 1 c. 1024–c. 1198, ed. David Luscombe and Jonathan Riley-Smith (Cambridge: Cambridge University Press, 2004), 268–334.

61 See Pierre Riché, *The Carolingians: A Family who Forged Europe*, trans. Michael I. Allen (Philadelphia: University of Pennsylvania Press, 1993), 160–169.

62 For these statistics, I rely on the tables in Anna-Dorothee von den Brincken, "Die lateinische Weltchronistik," in *Mensch und Weltgeschichte: Zur Geschichte der Universalgeschichtsschreibung*, ed. Alexander Randa (Salzburg and Munich: Pustet, 1969), 77–86. The tables are reproduced in Karl Heinrich Krüger, *Die Universalchroniken* (Turnhout: Brepols, 1976), 37–45. On the Four Monarchies in Berthold of Reichenau, see I.S. Robinson, trans., *Eleventh-Century Germany: The Swabian Chronicles* (New York: Manchester University Press, 2008), 24, 50. Robinson's introduction explains the relationships between the chronicles of Herman of Reichenau, Berthold of Reichenau and Bernold of St. Blasien.

63 MGH *Scriptores* 6:90.

incorporated this material into his own *Chronicle* with stronger emphasis on the Four Monarchies, and he extended the narrative to his own day.[64] The resulting text, however, suffered from internal tensions because the Frutolf-Ekkehard *Chronicle* had a pro-papal perspective, while Burchard's additions were strongly Imperial. Sigebert of Gembloux († 1112), a strong Imperial supporter, presented the Roman Empire as the fulfilment of Daniel's Fourth Monarchy, but instead of composing a new narrative of the ancient empires, he simply continued from the fourth century where Eusebius-Jerome had ended.[65]

The History of the Two Cities by Otto of Freising († 1158) is the great exception to this general inconsistency or ambivalence.[66] Like many medieval historians, Otto was a well-educated cleric, but he was also a member of the Imperial family and the half-brother of Emperor Conrad III (r. 1138–1152). At the time he wrote *The Two Cities*, Otto believed that the Empire had entered into permanent decline, and that the end of the world was drawing near. The tone of *The Two Cities* is generally pessimistic, and despite his Imperial lineage, Otto inclined more toward the papacy than the Emperors. Although he drew on Augustine, not least for his title, Otto structured his history according to a series of *translationes imperii* rather than the Six Ages.[67] He was, however, not entirely consistent. Like Orosius, he concentrated on the geographic shift of political power from ancient Babylon in the East to the Roman Empire in the West;[68] but in the introductory remarks from his dedication, he inclined toward Daniel and Jerome:

> That there were from the beginning of the world four principal kingdoms which stood out above all the rest, and that they are to endure unto the world's end, succeeding one another in accordance with the law of the universe, can be gathered in various ways, in particular from the vision of Daniel. I have therefore set down the rulers of these kingdoms, listed in chronological sequence: first the Assyrians, next (omitting the Chaldeans, whom the writers of history do not deign to include among the others) the Medes and the Persians, finally the Greeks and the Romans, and I have recorded their names down to the present emperor, speaking

---

64 See the sixteenth century edition – Burchard of Ursberg, *Chronicvm Abbatis Vrspergensis* (Strasbourg: Mylius, 1537). VD16 B 9801.
65 MGH *Scriptores* 6:300. See Hay, *Annalists and Historians*, 46–49.
66 For Otto of Freising, I rely on the introductions by Charles Mierow and Karl Morrison in Otto of Freising, *The Two Cities*, trans. Charles Mierow (New York: Columbia University Press, 2002), xi–84.
67 Concerning Otto's various uses of the *translatio imperii* idea, see the comments by Mierow in Otto of Freising, *The Two Cities*, 27–32.
68 Otto of Freising, *The Two Cities*, 153 (II.Prologue).

of the other kingdoms only incidentally, to make manifest the fluctuations of events.[69]

Otto included multiple *translationes imperii*, rather than four specific transfers, that accounted for the shifts in political rule both in Antiquity and from the Carolingians down to the Hohenstaufens.[70] He also drew attention to the transfers of learned culture and religion, which were part of a general movement from the East to the West.[71] Despite this general language of "transfers," Otto resisted the idea that the Ottonians had formed a new Empire and that they were the first in a new line of Emperors. Instead, he presented a continuous, though shifting, succession from Charlemagne to his own day:

> From this point [the reign of Otto I] some reckon a kingdom of the Germans as supplanting that of the Franks. Hence they say that Pope Leo, in the decrees of the popes, called Henry's son Otto the first king of the Germans. For that Henry of whom we are speaking refused, it is said, an honor offered him by the supreme pontiff. But it seems to me that the kingdom of the Germans – which today, as we see, has possession of Rome – is a part of the kingdom of the Franks. For as is perfectly clear in what precedes, at the time of Charles the boundaries of the kingdom of the Franks included the whole of Gaul – that is, Gallia, Celtica, Gallia Belgica and Gallia Lugdunensis – and all Germany, from the Rhine to Illyricum. When the realm was divided between his son's sons, one part was called the eastern, the other the western, yet both together were called the Kingdom of the Franks. So then in the eastern part, which is called the Kingdom of the Germans, Henry was the first of the race of the Saxons to succeed to the throne when the line of Charles failed. In West Francia, on the other hand, Charles, a king of the stock of Charles still survived. Henry's son Otto, because he restored to the German East Franks the empire which had been usurped by the Lombards, is called the first king of the Germans – not, perhaps, because he was the first to reign among the Germans but because he first, after those who were named after Charles Carlings or Carolingians (as the Merovingians were named after Merovech), was born of another line (that is, the Saxon) and restored the empire to the German Franks. But just as, when the Merovingians failed and the

---

69 Otto of Freising, *The Two Cities*, 91 (Dedication).
70 Otto of Freising, *The Two Cities*, 91 (Dedication), see also 167–168 (II.13), 283 (IV.5), 317–218 (IV.31), 347 (V.22), 353–354 (V.31), 400–401 (VI.36).
71 Otto of Freising, *The Two Cities*, xxii, 28–33.

Carlings succeeded, the kingdom nevertheless remained Frankish – so also, when the Carlings ceased, the Ottos, though of another family and speech, yet came to the throne of a kingdom that kept its identity. Such changes, betraying the frailty of mortal estate, appear at intervals from the beginning of the world down to the present day.[72]

The issues that Otto addressed in this section would become a touchstone for later historians. Those who held to a continuous succession from Charlemagne presented Henry the Fowler (r. 919–936) as Emperor, even though he was not crowned by the pope. Others saw Henry's son, Emperor Otto I (r. 936–973), as the true founder of the Holy Roman Empire, rather than Charlemagne. (Indeed, this is the "official" modern view.)[73] The difference was important. If Otto was the first German Emperor, then the French could claim that Charlemagne himself had been French, rather than German, and they accordingly had a legitimate claim that the Imperial dignity should "return" to them. The issue resurfaced now and then in the Middle Ages, but it became a subject of intense debate in the late fifteenth century and for several decades thereafter, especially when the French presented King Francis I as a strong candidate for the Imperial throne.[74]

Unlike many medieval historians before and after, Otto made no real effort to reconcile the Four Monarchies with the Six Ages. Indeed, even the book divisions contributed to the general theme of translations, with the end of each marking an important change: Book I – End of the Assyrian Empire and rise of the Medes; Book II – End of the Roman Republic and beginning of the Roman Empire; Book III – Constantine and the establishment of the Christian-Roman Empire; Book IV – Odoacer and the end of the Western Roman Empire; Book V – Division of the Carolingian Empire among Charlemagne's grandsons; Book VI – Death of Pope Gregory VII (Hildebrand) in 1085; Book VII – Date of Composition (1146).[75] Ultimately, *The Two Cities* remained an anomaly within medieval German historiography, and much like Frechulf's *Histories*, it lacked imitators or continuators among later historians.

---

72 Otto of Freising, *The Two Cities*, 376–377 (VI.17).
73 The official exhibition to mark the anniversary of the end of Holy Roman Empire began with Otto I: *Heiliges Römisches Reich Deutscher Nation 962–1806*, 4 vols. (Dresden: Sandstein Verlag, 2006).
74 See Ernst Laubach, "Wahlpropaganda im Wahlkampf um die deutsche Königswürde 1519," *Archiv für Kulturgeschichte* 53 (1971): 207–248.
75 See Otto of Freising, *The Two Cities*, 27.

8 Translationes Imperii and the Donation of Constantine

Otto of Freising's use of Daniel in *The Two Cities* was part of a broader twelfth century revival of interest in the Four Monarchies among historians, theologians and poets.[76] The twelfth century also witnessed the revival of Roman law in the West and the codification of canon law, especially in Gratian's *Decretum*. These developments gave new significance to the Four Monarchies and more generally to the legal and scriptural bases for papal involvement in the high politics of Europe. In particular, refinements to the idea of the "*translatio imperii*" provided an intellectual forum for articulating claims to political supremacy.[77] Otto of Freising composed *The Two Cities* before the rise of Roman and canon lawyers as a major intellectual force, and his brief discussions of the *translatio imperii* lacked the sophistication of later historians, who wrote in dialogue with the canon law perspective. From the early thirteenth century onwards, the *translatio imperii* became an integral part of European political, and historical, thought.

Although the *translatio imperii* could be used in tandem with the Four Monarchies, the two concepts were not necessarily interdependent. Indeed, the way the two ideas were deployed tended to reflect partisan affiliations, with papal writers especially emphasizing the *translatio imperii*.[78] In its technical meaning, the *translatio imperii* refers to the foundational precedent for the assertion that the pope acted as the final arbiter of Imperial elections.[79] Based on Charlemagne's coronation, the popes claimed that they had transferred the Empire from the Greeks to the Germans, and they accordingly retained the right to approve or reject the candidate for the Imperial throne selected by the Electoral Princes. Pope Innocent III (r. 1198–1216) provided the defining statement of the *translatio imperii* in a decretal entitled *Venerabilem* (1202), which was, in effect, an assertion of supremacy over all secular rulers.[80]

Strictly speaking, the papal, or curial, *translatio imperii* theory was not dependent on Daniel and the Four Monarchies. Instead, it was grounded in a specific historical event, the coronation of Charlemagne. Furthermore, the theory was not necessarily associated with the other historical, and also legal, basis for

---

76 See Christian Gellinek, "Daniel's Vision of Four Beasts in Twelfth-Century German Literature," *Germanic Review* 41, no. 1 (January 1966): 5–26.
77 See generally Goez, *Translatio imperii*, 137–198.
78 See Goez, *Translatio imperii*, 137–198.
79 See Goez, *Translatio imperii*, 137–139; and J.A. Watt, "Spiritual and Temporal Powers," in *The Cambridge History of Medieval Political Thought, c. 450–c. 1450*, ed. J.H. Burns (Cambridge: Cambridge University Press, 1988), 367–387.
80 See Watt, "Spiritual and Temporal Powers," 381–383.

papal claims to political supremacy in the West, the *Donation of Constantine*.[81] The *Donation* was an early medieval forgery that purported to record the transfer of the Western Roman Empire to the papacy; and like the curial *translatio imperii* theory, its exact origins remain uncertain.[82] According to the legend it records, Pope Sylvester I cured Emperor Constantine the Great of leprosy, and out of gratitude for his healing, he ceded control of the Western Empire to the papacy when he removed to his new capital in Constantinople. On its face, the *Donation of Constantine* bestowed political supremacy in the West on the popes, but it did not include the right to transfer Roman rule from the Greeks to the Germans, since the Eastern Emperors had never ceded their rights to the papacy. Therefore, although the *Donation* presumed to give the papacy the right to crown or depose Western rulers, as had happened when the Carolingians received permission to remove the Merovingians, it did not grant rights outside of the old Western Empire.[83] In contrast, the *translatio imperii* theory made greater claims, because it gave the papacy the ability to transfer all political rule irrespective of geography.

In *Venerabilem*, Innocent did not mention, or even allude to, the Four Monarchies, but other writers combined the curial *translatio imperii* theory with Daniel's prophecies.[84] In the turmoil of the early fifth century, Jerome and Orosius had adopted an "imperial patriotism" that emphasized the permanence of the Roman Empire and the prophetic consolation that it would endure until the end of time. In contrast, medieval papal supporters stressed the *translatio* aspect in Daniel's sequence of Empires, and they deemphasized the finality and lasting duration of the Fourth Monarchy. Along with this, the pattern of argumentation shifted from prophecy to typology. Just as sacred figures from the Old Testament had presided over the transfer of kingdoms and empires, so now, it was argued, the papacy held, and could freely exercise, similar power.[85] Some papal writers went even further, maintaining that the Fourth Monarchy, the Roman Empire, had already fallen and the Fifth Monarchy, the Christian Church, was now reigning and would endure until the return of Christ.[86]

---

81 The *Donation* itself is included in Lorenzo Valla, *The Treatise of Lorenzo Valla on the Donation of Constantine*, trans. Christopher B. Coleman (Toronto: University of Toronto Press, 2000 [Reprint]), 10–19; and Lorenzo Valla, *On the Donation of Constantine*, trans. G.W. Bowersock (Cambridge, M.A.: Harvard University Press, 2007), 81–93.

82 See Goez, *Translatio imperii*, 137; Michael Wilks, *The Problem of Sovereignty in the Later Middle Ages: The Papal Monarchy with Augustinus Triumphus and the Publicists* (Cambridge: Cambridge University Press, 1964), 543–547.

83 Watt, "Spiritual and Temporal Powers," 377.

84 See the appendix on "The Hierocratic Interpretation of History" in Wilks, *The Problem of Sovereignty*, 538–547.

85 Wilks, *The Problem of Sovereignty*, 538–541.

86 Wilks, *The Problem of Sovereignty*, 542–543.

The *Donation of Constantine* and the *translatio imperii* were both aspects of a "hierocratic" worldview that subordinated Imperial, and indeed all secular power, to the papacy.[87] Based on an allegorical reading of the "two swords" in Luke 22:38, medieval political theory separated secular and spiritual power into two distinct realms. In the early Middle Ages, when the papacy was weak, papal apologists vigorously argued for a "dualist" interpretation of the two swords to protect ecclesiastical affairs from Imperial interference. By the High Middle Ages, the perspective had changed. The papacy, now strong and assertive, claimed that the secular sword was subordinate to the spiritual sword, thereby shifting from a dualist to a hierocratic perspective. The Old Testament also supported these claims to supremacy in the divine pronouncement to the Prophet Jeremiah: "See, today I appoint you over nations and over kingdoms, to pluck up and to pull down, to destroy and to overthrow, to build and to plant" (Jeremiah 1:10) (NRSV). In this context, the *Donation of Constantine* served as legal proof, and the *translatio imperii* as historical affirmation, of a supremacy that was ostensibly grounded in Scripture.

The weakness of these theories was that historical arguments could, and eventually did, undermine the assertion that the papacy had been necessary to effect transfers of secular rule. Until the fifteenth century, however, the curial interpretation of history remained the dominant view, and only in the sixteenth century did Protestant historians finally craft a coherent counternarrative.

9   Papal-Imperial Chronicles

In the thirteenth century, historians increasingly turned to a new historiographical framework, the papal-imperial chronicle (*Papst-Kaiser Chronik*), which presented parallel histories of the popes and the Emperors. Since it became relevant only after Augustus and the Incarnation, the format could be used independently, or in combination with the Four Monarchies and the Six Ages. Among these chronicles, the most important was the *Papal-Imperial Chronicle* by the Dominican Martin of Troppau, or Martinus Polonus († 1278).[88] Martin's *Chronicle*, which issued in three recensions, survives in hundreds of

---

87   For a concise summary, see Watt, "Spiritual and Temporal Powers," 367–374.
88   On Martin of Troppau and his *Chronicle*, see Anna-Dorothee von den Brincken, "Martin von Troppau," in *Geschichtsschreibung und Geschichtsbewusstsein im Späten Mittelalter*, ed. Hans Patze (Sigmaringen: Jan Thorbecke Verlag, 1987), 155–193; Wolfgang-Valentin Ikas, "Martinus Polonus' Chronicle of the Popes and Emperors: A Medieval Best-Seller and Its Neglected Influence on Medieval English Chroniclers," *The English Historical Review* 116, no. 466 (April 2001): 327–341; and Heike Johanna Mierau, "Das Reich, Politische Theorien und Die Heilsgeschichte: Zur Ausbildung eines Reichsbewußtseins durch die

manuscripts, many with continuations, and it was translated into several vernaculars. During the Late Middle Ages, no other historian was so widely read.[89]

Martin composed his *Chronicle* as a historical compendium for theologians and canon lawyers, and in it he concentrated on the history of Rome, both temporal and spiritual. In its final form (usually referred to as Recension C), the *Chronicle* was divided into three books: [1] from Ninus, first king of the Assyrians, to the expulsion of Tarquinius Superbus, the last king of Rome; [2] from the first Roman consuls to the end of the Republic; and [3] from Augustus and Christ to the thirteenth century. Martin did not use the Six Ages, instead he adopted the Four Monarchies (Assyria, Greece, Carthage, Rome) from Orosius. Furthermore, like Orosius, he used the scheme to emphasize geographic universality and the culmination of ancient history in the Roman Empire.

The first two books of the *Chronicle* focused entirely on the temporal history of Rome, only in the third book did Martin bifurcate his narrative into the temporal and spiritual history of the City. Beginning with Augustus and the Incarnation, he structured the *Chronicle* according to a precise graphic layout, so when the manuscript was opened the popes were on the left page (verso) with Emperors on the facing right page (recto). Each page had fifty lines and covered fifty years, so each book opening presented a half century of papal and Imperial history. By setting the popes before the Emperors, the page layout itself emphasized papal supremacy over the Emperors.[90]

With the *Chronicle*, Martin provided a compendium for understanding Roman history, and especially the historical context of the Imperial constitution and canon law. The *Chronicle* was not necessarily anti-Imperial, even in its description of the Investiture Controversy, but it unequivocally presented papal power as superior to Imperial.[91] At the time of Augustus, for instance, Martin inserted the standard curial interpretation of the "two swords,"[92] and in his description of Constantine, he provided the historical context for the *Donation*.[93] Later, in discussing the anointment of the young Charlemagne, he referred to *Venerabilem* and the *translatio imperii*, and instead of focusing on the Imperial

---

Papst-Kaiser-Chroniken des Spätmittelalters," *Zeitschrift für Historische Forschung* 32, no. 4 (2005): 543–573. The text of the *Chronicle* is found in MGH *Scriptores* 22:377–482.

89   See Anna-Dorothee von den Brincken, "Studien zur Überlieferung der Chronik des Martin von Troppau," *Deutsches Archiv für Erforschung des Mittelalters* 41 (1985): 460–531; and Anna-Dorothee von den Brincken, "Studien zur Überlieferung der Chronik des Martin von Troppau: Zweiter Teil," *Deutsches Archiv für Erforschung des Mittelalters* 45 (1989): 551–591.

90   von den Brincken, "Martin von Troppau," 168–169.

91   von den Brincken, "Martin von Troppau," 188; Mierau, "Das Reich, Politische Theorien und Die Heilsgeschichte," 548, 558.

92   MGH *Scriptores* 22:406–407.

93   MGH *Scriptores* 22:415, 450.

coronation in 800 as the key act, he presented this earlier ceremony as the official transfer of the Roman Empire from the Greeks to the Germans.[94] Nevertheless, according to Martin, the first "German" Emperor was Otto I, who began the line of Emperors that extended to the present.[95]

Despite Martin's interest in canon law, he did not develop a strong hierocratic argument in the *Chronicle*, and he sometimes included embarrassing material about the papacy (*Papstfabeln*), such as the legend of Pope Joan, supposedly a female pope of the ninth century.[96] More than polemics, Martin was interested in the problem of constitutional history, both secular and ecclesiastical. The *Chronicle* was a convenient reference for chronology and legal developments, but more importantly, it offered a historical interpretation of how the Imperial constitution had been formed through the struggles between the papacy and the Empire.[97] Martin composed the final recension of the *Chronicle* at the end of the Great Interregnum (1254–1273) between the last Staufer Emperor and Rudolph of Hapsburg. The election of a new Emperor may explain Martin's interest in providing a comprehensive history of Rome, as well as the general lack of hostility toward the Emperors in the *Chronicle*.[98]

Martin's *Chronicle* was immensely popular, but within the Empire, its propapal perspective met with resistance especially in South Germany. Around 1290, an anonymous Franciscan from Swabia prepared a competing papal-imperial chronicle, the *Flores Temporum*.[99] In contrast to Martin's *Chronicle*, the *Flores Temporum* followed the Six Ages rather than the Four Monarchies, and the text accordingly began with Creation instead of the Assyrian Empire. In the Sixth Age, the author inverted the usual papal-imperial layout by putting

---

94 "Stephanus II ... Hic ultimo anno pontificatus sui Romanum imperium a Grecis transtulit in Germanos in personam magnifici regis Karoli, tunc in iuvenili etate constitui. De qua translacione tangit decretalis: *Venerabilem*." MGH *Scriptores* 22:426. See Goez, *Translatio imperii*, 202–206.

95 "Otto I. imperavit annis 12. Hic fuit primus imperator Theontonicorum. Exempto enim imperio ab Ytalicis, soli Theotonici imperaverunt usque ad presens tempus." MGH *Scriptores* 22:465.

96 MGH *Scriptores* 22:428; see von den Brincken, "Martin von Troppau," 174–175; Mierau, "Das Reich, Politische Theorien und Die Heilsgeschichte," 562.

97 Mierau, "Das Reich, Politische Theorien und Die Heilsgeschichte," 562, 570–573.

98 Mierau argues that Martin's perspective was influenced by Bohemian efforts to gain the Imperial crown at the end of the Great Interregnum, see Mierau, "Das Reich, Politische Theorien und Die Heilsgeschichte," 563.

99 I rely on Anna-Dorothee von den Brincken, "Anniversaristische und chronikalische Geschichtsschreibung in den 'Flores Temporum' (um 1292)," in *Geschichtsschreibung und Geschichtsbewusstsein im Späten Mittelalter*, ed. Hans Patze (Sigmaringen: Jan Thorbecke Verlag, 1987), 195–214. The text of the *Flores Temporum* is found in MGH *Scriptores* 24:226–250.

the Emperors before the popes, a change that subtly countered papal claims to supremacy.

Martin had prepared his *Chronicle* for theologians and jurists, and it served as a useful historical guide to canon law. In contrast, the *Flores Temporum* was meant for preachers, and it can be seen as a companion piece to the medieval collection of anecdotes about the saints, the *Golden Legend* (*Legenda Aurea*).[100] Although the author of the *Flores Temporum* indicated that he used Orosius, Isidore and Martin of Troppau as his primary sources, he was more concerned with legends and humanizing details than with developing a grand vision of papal and Imperial history.[101] As a result, the *Flores Temporum* contain little information about constitutional issues, but with one important exception. Martin of Troppau had set the formation of the Electoral College during the reign of Otto III, which was not unreasonable, though it lacks a basis in surviving Ottonian sources.[102] In the *Flores Temporum*, Martin's discussion was copied almost verbatim, but the author moved the section forward to the Carolingians, and he designated Charlemagne as the founder of the Electoral College. Furthermore, although the author referred to *Venerabilem*,[103] he nevertheless asserted that Charlemagne, rather than the pope, had transferred the seat of Empire back to Rome.[104] In general, the *Flores Temporum* was hardly a compelling Imperial response to *Martin's Chronicle*; but by making Charlemagne himself responsible for the *translatio imperii*, it anticipated an approach that later anti-papal controversialists would adopt to preserve the *translatio imperii* while denying an active role to the papacy.

The papal-Imperial *Chronicles* of the thirteenth century became standard historical references, and until the late fifteenth century, historians were more inclined to write continuations to *Martin's Chronicle* or the *Flores Temporum* than to compose new narratives.[105] In these continuations, the style often shifted to an annalistic account for events from the author's own lifetime. Subsequent continuators might synthesize this information or simply continue with their own annals. The Late Middle Ages also produced a vast number of

---

100 von den Brincken, "Anniversaristische und chronikalische Geschichtsschreibung," 202–203.
101 von den Brincken, "Anniversaristische und chronikalische Geschichtsschreibung," 202–203, 205.
102 MGH *Scriptores* 22:426.
103 MGH *Scriptores* 24:242.
104 "Karolus autem sedem imperialem in Roman transtulit, et ius eligendi imperatorem Theutonicis acquisivit." MGH *Scriptores* 24:234.
105 For the late medieval continuations to Martin of Troppau, see Rolf Sprandel, "World Historiography in the Late Middle Ages," in *Historiography in the Middle Ages*, ed. Deborah Mauskopf Deliyannis (Leiden: Brill, 2003), 157–179.

municipal chronicles that sometimes reached deeper into the past,[106] but as a general introduction, Martin of Troppau set the standard with which later historians had to reckon.

Martin wrote at a particular moment in Imperial history, and as his *Chronicle* spread across Europe, copyists, translators and continuators adapted it to different political contexts, and in many ways, its transmission and reception provide a manuscript equivalent to the diffusion of *Carion's Chronicle* in the sixteenth century. In this respect, *Martin's Chronicle* can be seen as a contribution to the broader conversation about the European constitution. Even though the *Chronicle* did not vehemently defend a hierocratic view,[107] Martin of Troppau set the tone for German historiography down to the early sixteenth century, and as a result, the prevailing, though not unchallenged, perspective of late medieval German historiography remained strongly papal.

10   Challenges to the Curial Theories

Although the curial *translatio imperii* theory remained dominant until the Reformation, the Imperial controversialists of the Middle Ages developed arguments that anticipated its eventual overthrow. In times of papal-Imperial strife, they vehemently condemned the curial theory, and against papal claims of supremacy, they often, though not always, reasserted the dualist interpretation of the two swords.[108] Indeed, Gratian's *Decretum* transmitted earlier dualist arguments, meaning that canon law itself provided ammunition for Imperial controversialists.[109] In the early fourteenth century, Dante (1265–1321) entered the dispute on the side of the Emperors with his *Monarchy*,[110] but the most famous challenges to the curial view of the Imperial constitution came from the court of Emperor Ludwig IV of Bavaria (r. 1314–1346).

Ludwig IV and Pope John XXII (r. 1316–1334) engaged in the last great papal-Imperial struggle of the Middle Ages, and many of the most aggressive texts in the Imperial tradition were written by the intellectuals Ludwig sponsored,

---

106   On late medieval municipal chroniclers, see F.R.H. Du Boulay, "The German town chroniclers," in *The Writing of History in the Middle Ages: Essays Presented to Richard William Southern*, ed. R.H.C. Davis and J.M. Wallace-Hadrill (Oxford: Clarendon Press, 1981), 445–469.
107   Mierau, "Das Reich, Politische Theorien und Die Heilsgeschichte," 562.
108   Watt, "Spiritual and Temporal Powers," 383–387.
109   Watt, "Spiritual and Temporal Powers," 378.
110   Dante, *Monarchy*, trans. Prue Shaw (Cambridge: Cambridge University Press, 1996).

including Marsilius of Padua and William of Ockham.[111] Although the Imperial Prince-Electors had elected Ludwig, John XXII and his successors refused to approve the election and crown Ludwig Holy Roman Emperor, mostly to prevent the assertion of Imperial claims in Italy. In response, Ludwig marched to Rome, and he was acclaimed as Emperor by the Roman people in 1328. A group of bishops carried out the coronation ceremonies at St. Peter's; then a few months later, he was crowned in Rome again by an anti-pope.[112]

Ludwig's attempts to gain legitimacy through acclamation by the Roman people or coronation by an anti-pope proved unsuccessful. In July 1338, the Prince-Electors finally responded to the situation, both to support Ludwig and to protect their rights as Electors. At Rhens, they issued an official statement affirming the long tradition that a German king chosen by the Prince-Electors could immediately administer the Empire and use the royal title without papal approval or coronation.[113] At Frankfurt a month later, Ludwig himself declared that election by the Prince-Electors, rather than papal approval, determined the succession to the Imperial dignity.[114] The right of the "Emperor-elect" to use the Imperial title prior to a papal coronation remained an open question, but the ability to administer the Empire was clearly established.[115] In 1356, the requirements and procedures for Imperial Elections were finally reduced to written form in the Golden Bull of Emperor Charles IV.[116]

The Imperial controversialists of the fourteenth century used history in their texts, but they did not develop a comprehensive counter-narrative to compete with the curial perspective in Martin of Troppau and his continuators. Dante attacked the *Donation of Constantine* in his *Monarchy*, but the text did not circulate widely, and Flacius published the *editio princeps* only in 1559.[117] As a supplement to the more famous *Defensor Pacis*, Marsilius of Padua composed a brief tract, *De translatione Imperii*, specifically to undermine the curial *translatio imperii* theory.[118] He used an earlier pro-papal tract on the same subject by Landolfo Colonna as his primary source for historical information. By

---

111 See Peter Herde, "From Adolf of Nassau to Lewis of Bavaria, 1292–1347," in *The New Cambridge Medieval History*, vol. VI, c. 1300–c. 1415, ed. Michael Jones (Cambridge: Cambridge University Press, 2000), 537–550.
112 Herde, "From Adolf of Nassau to Lewis of Bavaria," 541–542.
113 Herde, "From Adolf of Nassau to Lewis of Bavaria," 545; Gross, *Empire and Sovereignty*, 15–16.
114 Herde, "From Adolf of Nassau to Lewis of Bavaria," 546.
115 Herde, "From Adolf of Nassau to Lewis of Bavaria," 546.
116 See the summary in Gross, *Empire and Sovereignty*, 16–20.
117 Dante, *Monarchy*, esp. 80–83 (III.10).
118 Marsilius of Padua, *Defensor minor and De translatione Imperii*, trans. Cary J. Nederman (Cambridge: Cambridge University Press, 1993).

adapting and reinterpreting the materials Landolfo had gathered, Marsilius wrote a brief historical sketch of Roman history with an emphasis on the transfers of Roman rule that had occurred over time. Within this, he presented the pope as a ceremonial actor rather than as the final arbiter of changes in secular rule.[119] The tract, however, was too short and topically focused to serve as a new papal-Imperial history.

After generations of conflict, the papal-Imperial relationship became less antagonistic in the mid-fifteenth century. The prestige of the papacy had declined dramatically during the Babylonian Captivity of the Church (1309–1376), when the popes resided in Avignon,[120] and even more so during the Great Schism (1378–1417), when multiple popes were elected.[121] The Council of Constance (1414–1418) restored unity to the fragmented ecclesiastical landscape, and the popes finally returned to Rome, where they concentrated on reestablishing their supremacy within the Church and on their political claims in Italy.[122] The generally peaceful co-existence continued through the long reign of Emperor Frederick III (r. 1440–1493), the last Emperor crowned by the pope in Rome, and it lasted until the Italian wars during Emperor Maximilian's reign.[123]

Even during the relative calm of the fifteenth century, the curial *translatio imperii* theory and the *Donation of Constantine* were subject to continued scrutiny. In *The Catholic Concordance* (ca. 1434), Nicolas of Cusa (1410–1464), who later became a German cardinal, rejected both on the basis of historical evidence, or rather lack thereof.[124] A few years later, the Italian humanist Lorenzo Valla wrote an oration, *On the Donation of Constantine* (1440), that used rhetoric and philology to dismiss the supposed grant of temporal power

---

119   Marsilius of Padua, *Defensor minor and De translatione Imperii*, xii–xiii (Introduction).
120   See generally P.N.R. Zutschi, "The Avignon Papacy," in *The New Cambridge Medieval History*, vol. VI, *c. 1300–c. 1415*, ed. Michael Jones (Cambridge: Cambridge University Press, 2000), 653–673.
121   See generally Howard Kaminsky, "The Great Schism," in *The New Cambridge Medieval History*, vol. VI, *c. 1300–c. 1415*, ed. Michael Jones (Cambridge: Cambridge University Press, 2000), 674–696.
122   See generally Anthony Black, "Popes and Councils," in *The New Cambridge Medieval History*, vol. VII, *c. 1415–c. 1500*, ed. Christopher Allmand (Cambridge: Cambridge University Press, 1998), 65–86.
123   See generally F.R.H. Du Boulay, *Germany in the Later Middle Ages* (London: Athlone Press, 1983), 54–63.
124   Nicolas of Cusa, *The Catholic Concordance*, trans. Paul E. Sigmund (Cambridge: Cambridge University Press, 1991), 216–227 (Book III, para. 294–324), see also the English introduction.

to the papacy.[125] Cusa wrote as a proponent of the "Conciliar Movement," a current of ecclesiastical reform that viewed councils as superior to popes. Valla composed his tract while in the service of the king of Naples, who was resisting papal political claims. Thus, their attacks on the *Donation* were driven by both ecclesiastical and political motives, and for purposes of reform as well as temporal rights. Both Cusa and Valla, however, abandoned the positions they held early in their careers, and each eventually entered the service of the papacy. Neither inspired a broader Imperial response to the *Donation*, and after an initial uproar, Valla's tract went mostly unnoticed until Ulrich von Hutten republished it in the sixteenth century.[126]

The Imperial response to the curial *translatio imperii* theories of the Middle Ages never developed into a comprehensive historiographical tradition. Marsilius of Padua, Nicolas of Cusa, and Lorenzo Valla all anticipated arguments that would be made during the Reformation, but no historian emerged to synthesize their ideas into a broader reinterpretation of the past. Like their papal adversaries, the Imperial controversialists concentrated on the *translatio imperii* rather than on Daniel and the fulfilment of the Four Monarchies. In their intellectual world, issues of canon law and biblical typology were far more relevant than pre-Christian chronology or the succession of the ancient world-empires. Furthermore, their interest in history was directed more at specific events, such as Charlemagne's coronation, than at a broader understanding of the past. Down to the advent of printing, German historians continued to adapt or extend Martin of Troppau rather than write something new.

11 Early Printed Chronicles

Once the animosity between the papacy and the Empire receded into the past, the learned circles of Germany became largely "ambivalent" about the papacy.[127] Reform movements festered, and anti-Italian sentiments were common, but Germans mostly refrained from vociferous attacks on the papacy. Early printed chronicles reflect this general ambivalence toward the papal-Imperial struggles of the past. Their authors concentrated more on harmony between

---

125 For the text and translation, as well as explanatory introduction, see Valla, *The Treatise of Lorenzo Valla on the Donation of Constantine* (2000); and Valla, *On the Donation of Constantine* (2007).
126 Valla, *On the Donation of Constantine* (2007), x–xi.
127 See Noel L. Brann, "Pre-Reformation humanism in Germany and the papal monarchy: a study in ambivalence," *Journal of Medieval and Renaissance Studies* 14, no. 2 (Fall 1984): 159–185.

pope and Emperor, and a pro-papal, though not necessarily anti-Imperial, perspective remained the dominant view. The Six Ages continued to act as the standard frame of reference, and mention of the Four Monarchies was mostly perfunctory.

Despite their popularity in the late Middle Ages, Martin of Troppau's *Chronicle* and the *Flores Temporum* were almost completely neglected by early printers. The *Flores Temporum* were published (in a revised German form) in 1473,[128] but *Martin's Chronicle* was not published until 1559, a century after the invention of printing, and it has appeared in Latin only five times since then, with the last edition in 1872.[129] As a general rule, fifteenth century printers showed little interest in the papal-Imperial chronicles that had been so popular in the late Middle Ages.[130] The historians of Late Antiquity fared well, and Eusebius-Jerome, Orosius and Isidore were all published in the Incunabular period (i.e. before 1501). In contrast, many of the most important medieval chronicles remained unpublished until the sixteenth century: Frutolf-Ekkehard and Otto of Freising did not appear until 1515, and Frechulf of Lisieux followed only in 1539.[131] Early publishers preferred historical texts that were very old or those that were freshly written, and it would be several decades before they demonstrated sustained interest in printing medieval historians.[132]

Among the new fifteenth century chronicles, the text reprinted most often was Werner Rolevinck's *Fasciculus Temporum*, first published at Cologne in the 1470s.[133] Rolevinck (1425–1502), a Carthusian monk, was directly involved in

---

128 See Anna-Dorothee von den Brincken, "Die Rezeption mittelalterlicher Historiographie durch den Inkunabeldruck," in *Geschichtsschreibung und Geschichtsbewusstsein im Späten Mittelalter*, ed. Hans Patze (Sigmaringen: Jan Thorbecke Verlag, 1987), 221; and Heike Johanna Mierau, Antje Sander-Berke and Birgit Stunt, *Studien zur Überlieferung der Flores Temporum* (Hannover: Hahnsche Buchhandlung, 1996), 44–48.

129 von den Brincken, "Studien zur Überlieferung der Chronik des Martin von Troppau," 494–497.

130 See von den Brincken, "Die Rezeption mittelalterlicher Historiographie," 230–233; and Peter Johanek, "Historiographie und Buchdruck im ausgehenden 15. Jahrhundert," in *Historiographie am Oberrhein im Späten Mittelalter und in der Frühen Neuzeit*, ed. Kurt Andermann (Sigmaringen: Jan Thorbecke Verlag, 1988), 110–111.

131 The editions are Frutolf-Ekkehard-Burchard of Ursberg (VD16 B 9800); Otto of Freising (VD16 O 1434); and Frechulf of Lisieux (VD16 F 2497).

132 See von den Brincken, "Die Rezeption mittelalterlicher Historiographie," 230–233; and generally Frank Borchardt, *German Antiquity in Renaissance Myth* (Baltimore: The Johns Hopkins University Press, 1971).

133 I have used a facsimile, with transcription, of the 1481 Venetian edition: Werner Rolevinck, *Fasciculus Temporum: Compendio Cronológico* (León: Universidad de León, 1993). See, with reference to earlier literature, Volker Honemann, "Theologen, Philosophe, Geschichtsschreiber, Dichter und Gelehrte im 'Fasciculus temporum' des Werner Rolevinck: Ein

converting his work from manuscript to printed form,[134] and over thirty editions in Latin and various vernaculars were published before 1501.[135] Even more so than Jerome or Martin of Troppau, Rolevinck used the layout of each page to structure his chronicle, which traced multiple timelines from Creation to his own day. Rolevinck adopted the Six Ages as his primary framework, but within that he traced several sequential patterns, including the Four Monarchies.

Instead of vertical columns, as in the Eusebius-Jerome *Chronicle*, the *Fasciculus Temporum* consists of horizontal lines that run continuously as each page is turned (Figure 1). In the centre, Rolevinck set two lines that provide the primary chronological references: an *anno mundi* timeline, and below that an *anno ante Christi nativitatem* timeline that changes to *anno Christi* after the Nativity. (Rolevinck was one of the first to make systematic use of B.C. dating.) For pre-Christian chronology, the timelines mark fifty-year intervals, but after Christ, this changes to ten-year intervals. Between the two timelines, Rolevinck set a lineage of Christ (*Linea Christi*) with the individual names in roundels. Before the Nativity, the lineage consists of Christ's biological ancestors, after Christ it contains his successors, the popes. The two timelines divide each page roughly in half. Before Christ, descriptions of secular material appear mostly in the upper half, and biblical and ecclesiastical material appears in the lower half. After Christ, this arrangement changes slightly. Secular material still appears in the upper half, but to this is added ecclesiastical history, with the exception of papal history, which is set below the timelines.

In the top half of the page, Rolevinck provided two additional succession lists, again with the names in roundels. The upper list gives all the rulers of Italy and Rome, from the first Italian kings to the Roman kings and consuls and then to the Emperors. In this way, Rolevinck, like Martin of Troppau, presented a continuous history of Rome from its earliest days to the time of composition. Below the Roman list, Rolevinck traced the history of the Four Monarchies (Assyria-Babylon, Persia, Greece, and Rome), until the two lines finally merge in Augustus. After Christ, a single line of Emperors runs across the page, which

---

Beitrag zur mittelalterlichen Literaturgeschichtsschreibung," in *Der weite Blick des Historikers: Einsichten in Kultur-, Landes- und Stadtgeschichte: Peter Johanek zum 65. Geburtstag*, ed. Wilfried Ehbrecht (Köln: Böhlau, 2002), 337–341; particularly useful for general themes is Laviece C. Ward, "A Carthusian View of the Holy Roman Empire: Werner Rolevinck's *Fasciculus Temporum*," in *Die Kartäuser und das Heilige Römische Reich* (Salzburg: Institut für Anglistik und Amerikanistik, 1999), 23–44.

134 See Johan Martens, "Arnold ther Hoernen and his Cologne competitors: of sheets, corrections, and variants," *Quaerendo* 24:1 (1994): 30–38.

135 von den Brincken, "Die Rezeption mittelalterlicher Historiographie," 222.

THE FOURTH MONARCHY AND THE TRANSLATIO IMPERII

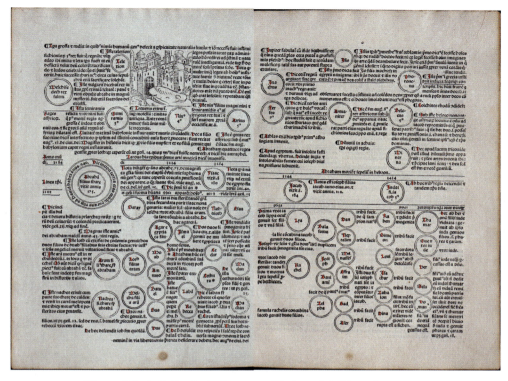

FIGURE 1   Werner Rolevinck, *Fasciculus Temporum* (Venice, 1484), fol. 5v–6r
HERZOG AUGUST BIBLIOTHEK WOLFENBÜTTEL: A: 274.1 HIST. 2° (1)

shifts from the Eastern Emperors to the Western Emperors at Charlemagne.[136] Between Abraham and Christ (the Third, Fourth and Fifth Ages), Rolevinck also included the spiritual and temporal succession of the Old Testament: the high priests beginning with Levi, the judges, and the kings of Israel and Judah followed by their political successors, the kings of Syria (*reges Syrie*) and the Roman procurators down to Pontius Pilate.

Within this overall framework, Rolevinck conveyed a wealth of political and ecclesiastical history in condensed, tightly organized form. He also inserted descriptions of important figures in intellectual and ecclesiastical history, and he noted the appearance of important texts, such as Gratian's *Decretum*, the decretals, and the *Sentences* of Peter Lombard.[137] The resulting product offered

---

136   On the organization in general, see Ward, "A Carthusian View of the Holy Roman Empire," 23–35; and Johan Martens, "The *Fasciculus Temporum* of 1474: On form and content of the incunable," *Quaerendo* 22:3 (1992): 197–204.

137   See Honemann, "Theologen, Philosophe, Geschichtsschreiber, Dichter und Gelehrte," 350–351.

a reference for understanding the development of the political and ecclesiastical structures, as well as the texts, that governed late medieval life.

Like Martin of Troppau, Rolevinck was pro-papal, even if not a virulent partisan. He inserted a hierocratic discussion of the "two swords" as background to the *Donation of Constantine*, and he was unwavering in his assertion of papal political supremacy.[138] Even so, Rolevinck wrote during a period of relative calm in papal-Imperial relations, and he was not interested in showcasing earlier antagonism between the papacy and the Empire.[139] Indeed, the format of the *Fasciculus Temporum* itself precluded extended discussions of specific events, and Rolevinck emphasized the struggles of the Investiture Controversy[140] no more than moments of harmonious interaction, such as the formation of the Electoral College under Otto III and Gregory V.[141]

Tracing lineages, however, forced Rolevinck to make tacit statements about the legitimate succession of both the Emperors and the popes, an issue central to the question of supremacy. During the reign of Henry the Fowler, for example, Rolevinck included both Henry and the Italian kings in the line of Emperors.[142] Nevertheless, he did not number Henry among the Emperors. In his roundel, Henry is called "Henricus Alemanus," and in the text he is designated "Dux Saxonum."[143] Likewise, during the Great Schism, when multiple popes were elected, Rolevinck represented them with half, rather than full, roundels (Figure 2).[144] The graphic layout of the *Fasciculus Temporum* meant that it was possible to "omit" narrative descriptions of controversial events; but ultimately, the lineage format restricted Rolevinck's freedom to avoid the explosive question of Imperial and papal succession.

Martin of Troppau's *Chronicle* and the *Fasciculus Temporum* were both relatively brief compendia, and their physical layout forced the narrative to remain focused and succinct. In contrast, the most famous chronicle of the fifteenth century, the *Nuremberg Chronicle* (1493) of Hartmann Schedel (1440–1514), is a thick, lavishly illustrated, folio volume.[145] Schedel was a doctor and

---

138   Ward, "A Carthusian View of the Holy Roman Empire," 36–40.
139   Ward, "A Carthusian View of the Holy Roman Empire," 23.
140   Rolevinck, *Fasciculus Temporum* (Venice, 1481), fol. 54v–55r.
141   "Electores imperii post Ottonem tertium instituti fuerunt non propter quam culpam saxonum, sed ad precauendum pericula futura." Rolevinck, *Fasciculus Temporum* (Venice, 1481), fol. 52v.
142   Rolevinck, *Fasciculus Temporum* (Venice, 1481), fol. 51r–51v.
143   "Iste Henricus dux saxonum fuit et totus inclytus, nec ipse inter imperatores computatur, quia tamen in Alemania regnauit." Rolevinck, *Fasciculus Temporum* (Venice, 1481), fol. 51r.
144   Rolevinck, *Fasciculus Temporum* (Venice, 1481), fol. 62r–63v.
145   I have used a facsimile of the German edition that includes an introduction to the text and its context – Hartmann Schedel, *Chronicle of the World: The Complete and Annotated Nuremberg Chronicle of 1493*, ed. Stephan Füssel (London: Taschen, 2001).

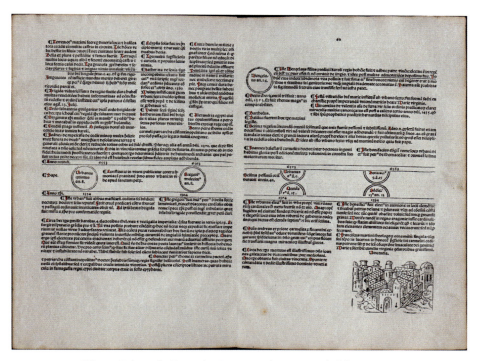

FIGURE 2   Werner Rolevinck, *Fasciculus Temporum* (Venice, 1484), fol. 61v–62r
HERZOG AUGUST BIBLIOTHEK WOLFENBÜTTEL: A: 274.1 HIST. 2° (1)

a humanist, rather than a cleric, and he was a patrician of the city of Nuremberg.[146] Much of the narrative content in the *Nuremberg Chronicle* is compiled from other sources, and Schedel's original contributions are found mostly in the transitional sections.[147] Key aspects of the layout are also derivative. Indeed, the overall framework is largely a reconfiguration, and vast expansion, of the *Fasciculus Temporum*.

In the *Nuremberg Chronicle*, Schedel used the Six Ages, and he integrated the lineages from the *Fasciculus Temporum*. Nevertheless, he abandoned the rigid chronological structure from the *Fasciculus Temporum*, and he did not incorporate the timelines that had provided the guiding thread from Creation to the fifteenth century. The *Nuremberg Chronicle* is arranged vertically, rather than horizontally, so Schedel reconfigured Rolevinck's continuous horizontal

---

146   Schedel, *Chronicle of the World* (London, 2001), 9–10.
147   Schedel, *Chronicle of the World* (London, 2001), 10–14, 634–635. See also Bernd Posselt, *Konzeption und Kompilation der Schedelschen Weltchronik* (Wiesbaden: Harrassowitz Verlag, 2015); and Klaus A. Vogel, "Hartmann Schedel als Kompilator. Notizen zu einem derzeit kaum bestellten Foschungsfeld," *Pirckheimer Jahrbuch* 9 (1994): 73–97. According to Vogel, Schedel's copy of the *Fasciculus Temporum* has been lost (78).

lineages into vertical chains of succession. Instead of roundels with names, he used names with images, and he arranged them in lined columns on the inner or outer margins (Figure 3). The voluminous amount of narrative text, as well as pages filled with "extra" material, such as the famous genealogies and cityscapes, lead to frequent interruptions in the lines that Rolevinck had carefully, and clearly, traced. Indeed, amidst the jumble of text and images, the debt to the *Fasciculus Temporum* is not immediately apparent, especially because of the change from horizontal to vertical, and the overall stress on Rolevinck's framework from Schedel's bulging mass of illustrations and information. For the Sixth Age, Schedel continued to follow Rolevinck, but he also adapted the format of the papal-Imperial chronicles, and similar to Martin of Troppau, he placed popes on the left (verso) and the Emperors on the right (recto). Schedel then added "extra" material on pages inserted between the matching papal-Imperial layout. By simply omitting the "extra" pages, the *Nuremberg Chronicle* could easily have been abridged into a conventional Six Ages/papal-Imperial chronicle, and in 1533, Christoph Egenolff (1502–1555) published a shorter *Chronicle* based largely on this approach.[148] In 1493, Conrad Celtis was hired to revise and supplement Schedel's text, but he never finished the project.[149]

Since Schedel followed the patterns he knew from the *Fasciculus Temporum*, the Four Monarchies were among the various lineages he incorporated. However, the line itself was fragmented, so it is not always clear that he was following Rolevinck's succession of ancient empires: Assyria-Babylon, Persia, Greece, and Rome. Indeed, in the text itself, Schedel adopted Orosius's perspective rather than Jerome's, and in a chapter on the "Origins of the Empire," he referred to the sequence of ancient empires as Assyria, Greece, Carthage and Rome, though without direct reference to Orosius.[150] Subsequently, he saw the Imperial dignity as passing from the Romans through Charlemagne to the Gauls, then to the Lombards, and finally through Otto I to the Germans.[151] Although Schedel referred to Charlemagne as "German born," he, like

---

148   Christian Egenolff, *Chronic von an vn[d] abgang aller Weltwesenn. Auß den glawbwirdigsten Historien / On alle Gloß vnnd Zůsatz / Nach Historischer warheyt beschriben. Künig / Keyser / vnnd fürneme Personen / nach warer fürbildung Controfeit*. (Frankfurt a.M.: Egenolff, 1533). VD16 E 573.
149   Schedel, *Chronicle of the World* (London, 2001), 24.
150   See Schedel, *Chronicle of the World* (London, 2001), fol. CLXXVIII r. The chapter is entitled, "Von vrsprung vnd herkomen des kaiserthumbs vnd wie dasselb an die teütschen nation gewendet worden ist."
151   "Von disem kaiser Karolo bis auff kaiser Ludwigen den sun Arnulphi hat das kaiserthumb in hundert vnd zehen iarn bey den galliern nit klaine zunemung gehabt. vnd darnach auff

FIGURE 3 Hartmann Schedel, *Buch der Chroniken* (Nuremberg, 1493), fol. 75v
BAYERISCHE STAATSBIBLIOTHEK MÜNCHEN: 2 INC.C.A. 2922,
URN:NBN:DE:BVB:12-BSB00059084-6

Rolevinck, nevertheless presented Otto I as the founder of the Holy Roman Empire.[152] Thus, Schedel conceived of Imperial history in terms of multiple *translationes imperii*, rather than a single defining renewal among the Germans through Charlemagne.

Because Schedel included the succession of the popes and the Emperors, he faced the same issue as Rolevinck concerning how to represent the legitimate holders of the Imperial title but still preserve an unbroken line from Augustus. To address the issue, all of the problematic Emperors are shown with the Imperial crown, while the questionable ones, such as the deposed "Emperor" Wenceslaus (1361–1419), have only a royal crown.[153] Similarly, although he wears an Imperial crown, Schedel was careful to distinguish "Emperor" Charles the Bald, the ruler of the West Franks, from the other Carolingian Emperors to preempt claims that his coronation had transferred the Empire to the French.[154]

With regard to papal-Imperial struggles, Schedel wrote during a period of good relations between the Emperor and the papacy, and he accordingly focused on the harmony between the two rather than confrontation. Indeed, one of the last images in the *Nuremberg Chronicle* portrays Pope Pius II and Frederick III enthroned together and surrounded by members of the temporal and spiritual hierarchy.[155] Concerning the Imperial constitution, Schedel included a strong argument for the importance of the Electoral College, and he credited it with preserving the Empire among the Germans.[156]

After bringing the narrative down to his own day, Schedel left black space to continue the history of the Sixth Age, then he skipped ahead to offer a description of the Seventh, and final, Age of the world.[157] The effect is to bookend the *Nuremberg Chronicle* with descriptions of Creation and the Last Judgment with space left for later chroniclers to fill in the rest. Schedel did not present

---

gie Lombardier gelangt. vnnd ist zu letst an die teütschen. an hertzog Otten könig Heinrich sun gewenndt worden." Schedel, *Chronicle of the World* (London, 2001), fol. CLXXVIII r.

152 "...Karl könig zu Franckreich den gepornen teütschen." Schedel, *Chronicle of the World* (London, 2001), fol. CLXXVIII r.

153 Schedel, *Chronicle of the World* (London, 2001), fol. CCXXXIII r.

154 "Vnd wiewol das ankomen des kaiserthumbs an disen Carolum nicht aigentlich angezaigt wirdet. so ist doch offenbar bey allen gschihtbschreibern das sich diser Carolus des kaiserlichen namens angenomen. gein rom gefüegt vnd daselbst von babst Johanne dem achten die kaiserlichen kron empfangen vnd alßpald wider in franckreich gekeret." Schedel, *Chronicle of the World* (London, 2001), fol. CLXXII r.

155 Schedel, *Chronicle of the World* (London, 2001), fol. CLXVIII v.

156 See the chapter on "Ordnung der churfursten des reichs" and the surrounding material at Schedel, *Chronicle of the World* (London, 2001), fol. CLXXXIII r–CLXXXV r.

157 "Zu beschreibung mer gschihten oder künftiger ding sinn hernach ettliche pletter lere gelassen." Schedel, *Chronicle of the World* (London, 2001), fol. CLVIII v.

the Holy Roman Empire as Daniel's Fourth Monarchy, and the end of the world is not linked to the political fortunes of the Empire or the Germans. The *Nuremberg Chronicle* incorporated a sense of the coming end, but in keeping with the tradition of the Six Ages, it did not fix definite chronological bounds or offer a specific fulfilment of Daniel's prophecies.

12   The *Germania Illustrata* and *Nauclerus's Chronicle*

During Emperor Maximilian's reign (r. 1493–1519), and the renewed conflicts with the papacy, German Imperial patriotism was reawakened, and the Emperor encouraged German humanists such as Conrad Celtis (1459–1508) and Jacob Wimpfeling (1450–1528) in their historical studies.[158] Celtis had grand plans, and Wimpfeling wrote several important tracts, but none of the humanists sponsored by Maximilian produced a new history from an Imperial perspective to compete with the pro-papal works already in circulation. The early German humanists did, however, begin the search for manuscripts about the medieval German past, and by publishing their findings, they began to build a foundation that Melanchthon would eventually use in *Carion's Chronicle*.[159]

In the late fifteenth century, the *Germania Illustrata* movement started to shape historical and geographical scholarship in Germany.[160] The Italian humanist Aeneas Silvius Piccolomini (1405–1464), later Pope Pius II, had kindled early interest in German history and geography by introducing the Germans to Tacitus's *Germania*.[161] The *Germania* offered a solid, classical source for the German past, since it provided a written record of ancient German culture and a description of the tribes from which the Germans descended. Aeneas also

---

158   See generally Kurt Stadtwald, *Roman Popes and German Patriots: Antipapalism in the Politics of the German Humanist Movement from Gregor Heimburg to Martin Luther* (Geneva: Librairie Droz, 1996).

159   See John D'Amico, "Ulrich von Hutten and Beatus Rhenanus as Medieval Historians and Religious Propagandists in the Early Reformation," in *Roman and German Humanism, 1450–1550*, ed. Paul F. Grendler (Brookfield, VT: Variorum, 1993), XII:1–33

160   See Paul Joachimsen, *Geschichtsauffassung und Geschichtsschreibung in Deutschland unter dem Einfluß des Humanismus* (Leipzig and Berlin: Teubner, 1910), 155–195; Larry Silver, "German Patriotism in the Age of Dürer," in *Dürer and His Culture*, ed. Dagmar Eichberger and Charles Zika (Cambridge: Cambridge University Press, 1998), 38–68; and Gernot Michael Müller, *Die "Germania generalis" des Conrad Celtis: Studien mit Edition, Übersetzung und Kommentar* (Tübingen: Niemeyer, 2001).

161   Donald Kelly, "Tacitus Noster: The *Germania* in the Renaissance and Reformation," in *Tacitus and the Tacitean Tradition*, ed. T.J. Luce and A.J. Woodman (Princeton: Princeton University Press, 1993), 156.

wrote the first "modern" description of Germany, his own *Germania*, which built on classical foundations as well as eyewitness experience from his travels in Germany.[162] Later writers relied heavily on Aeneas, but they also challenged his view of Germany as a land indebted to the papacy for its greatness.[163]

The idea of a *Germania Illustrata* was drawn from Italian models, especially the *Italia Illustrata* of Flavio Biondo,[164] and in the narrow sense, it refers to the grand, but unfinished, project of Conrad Celtis to write a comprehensive treatment of German history and geography. More broadly, however, it includes texts on those subjects written by other German humanists beginning in the late fifteenth century. Initially, the movement was largely a reaction against real and perceived Italian dominance in German historical-geographical studies. This anti-Italian perspective was especially noticeable in Celtis, and it persisted among later humanists such as Wimpfeling. Besides this, some humanists, and especially South Germans, were motivated by anti-French sentiments, since they feared, rightly, that the French would eventually try to seize Alsace from the Empire.[165]

Philipp Melanchthon (1497–1560) grew up in this world of South German humanism and the *Germania Illustrata* movement.[166] He was born in Swabia and attended the Latin school at Pforzheim, near Stuttgart, before leaving for Heidelberg and then Tübingen. During those early years, he came to know many of the leading German humanists, including Wimpfeling, Heinrich Bebel (1472–1518) and Johann Reuchlin (1455–1522), the great Hebrew scholar. Tübingen in particular was a magnet for talented students, and it produced many of the finest *Germania Illustrata* scholars of the next generation including Sebastian Münster (1488–1552), the famous cosmographer, Andreas Althamer († 1538/39), the Tacitean scholar, and Johann Carion (1499–1537), the Berlin court astronomer. During his stay in Tübingen, Melanchthon was involved in the two most comprehensive *Germania Illustrata* projects published prior to the Reformation, *Nauclerus's Chronicle* (1516) and the *Exegesis*, or *Description*

---

162 Aeneas Silvius Piccolomini, *Germania und Jakob Wimpfeling: "Responsa et Replicae ad Eneam Silvium,"* ed. Adolf Schmidt (Cologne: Böhlau Verlag, 1962).
163 See especially Jacob Wimpfeling's reply in Aeneas Silvius, *Germania und Jakob Wimpfeling*.
164 Ottavio Clavuot, *Biondos "Italia Illustrata" – Summa oder Neuschöpfung? Über die Arbeitsmethoden eines Humanisten* (Tübingen: Niemeyer, 1990), 18.
165 See Borchardt, *German Antiquity*, 98–100.
166 See generally Clyde Manschreck, *Melanchthon: The Quiet Reformer* (New York: Abingdon Press, 1958); Heinz Scheible, *Melanchthon: Eine Biographie* (München: Verlag C.H. Beck, 1997); Wilhelm Maurer, *Der junge Melanchthon*, 2 vols. (Göttingen: Vandenhoeck & Ruprecht, 1967–1969); and Karl Hartfelder, *Philipp Melanchthon als Praeceptor Germaniae* (Berlin: A. Hofmann & comp., 1889).

of Germany (1518), by Franciscus Irenicus. Of these two massive works, *Nauclerus's Chronicle* is particularly important because it typifies the late medieval view of history that Melanchthon sought to reform through *Carion's Chronicle*.

Johannes Vergenhans (1425–1510), or Nauclerus as he is usually known, was active at the University of Tübingen from its foundation in 1477 to the time of his death, first as rector and then as chancellor; he also taught law.[167] He was a cleric and close advisor to Eberhard im Bart (1445–1496), the ruler of Württemberg; he had travelled to Italy and knew Pope Pius II personally. *Nauclerus's Chronicle* was meant as a capstone work to his long career, but he died before its completion, so Nicolaus Basellius, a monk of Hirsau, prepared the final text for publication.[168] Leading Northern humanists, including Erasmus and Reuchlin endorsed the *Chronicle*, and introductions from both were included with the text.[169] Melanchthon later echoed the themes from Reuchlin's introduction in his own historical works,[170] especially the utility of historical examples and the importance of understanding chronology.[171]

---

167   The best discussions are Joachimsen, *Geschichtsauffassung und Geschichtsschreibung*, 91–104; Hermann Haering, "Johannes Vergenhans, gennant Nauclerus: Erster Rektor der Universität Tübingen und ihr langjahriger Kanzler, Verfasser einer Weltchronik 1425–1510," in *Schwäbische Lebensbilder*, vol. 5 (Stuttgart: Kohlhammer Verlag, 1950), 1–25; and Gerhard Theuerkauf, "Soziale Bedingungen humanistischer Weltchronistik: Systemtheoretische Skizzen zur Chronik Nauclerus," in *Landesgeschichte und Geistesgeschichte: Festschrift für Otto Herding zum 65. Geburtstag*, ed. Kaspar Elm, Eberhard Gönner and Eugen Hillenbrand (Stuttgart: W. Kohlhammer Verlag, 1977), 315–340.

168   Johannes Nauclerus, *Memorabilivm omnis aetatis et omnivm gentivm chronici commentarii A Ioanne Navclero I.V. Doctore Tubing. Praeposito, & Vniuersitatis Cancellario, digesti an annum Salutis M.D. Adiecta Germanorum rebus Historia de Svevorvm ortu, institutis ac Imperio. Compleuit opus F. Nicolavs Basellivs Hirsaugiensis annis XIIII. ad M.D. additis* (Tübingen: Anshelm, 1516). VD16 N 167.

169   Despite Erasmus's contribution to the *Chronicle*, Reuchlin's preface is the principal introductory piece. Erasmus's letter preface is printed in Desiderius Erasmus, *Opus epistolarum des Erasmi Roterdami*, ed. P.S. Allen (Oxford: Oxford University Press, 1992 [Reprint]), vol. 2, p. 221–222 Nr. 397.

170   See Heinz Scheible, "Reuchlins Einfluß auf Melanchthon," in *Reuchlin und die Juden*, ed. Arno Herzig (Sigmaringen: Thorbecke, 1993), 146; and Heinz Scheible, *Die Anfänge der reformatorischen Geschichtsschreibung: Melanchthon, Sleidan, Flacius und die Magdeburger Zenturien* (Gütersloh, [1966]), 27 n. 43.

171   "Etenim quando de argumento dicendum est, nulla plane uitae pars, neque publicis, neque priuatis, neque forensibus, neque domesticis in rebus, neque si tecum agas quid, neque si cum altero contrahas, magistra potest non uti. Age quae principum, quae ciuium, quae cuius aetatis caussae non hac complexae, quasi ante oculos dispiciuntur. Quae uero pars in studiis literarum consummata, si negligas historiam, et istos quidem doctorum peculiares συγχονισμοὺς id est temporum collationes. Rursum quoties exemplo futuros illa casus expendit, quare qui dicant ciuilis prudentiae partem, qui humanae vitae imaginem, viri sunt non pauci. Sic ad virtutem hominum animos excitat, sic ad honorem,

In Tübingen, Melanchthon worked as print corrector for the *editio princeps* of the *Chronicle*, but his involvement beyond that is uncertain. Melanchthon's followers later believed that he had extensively reworked the entire *Chronicle*, and Melanchthon's son-in-law, Caspar Peucer (1525–1602), was furious when Laurentius Surius (1523–1578), a Carthusian monk, published a new edition in 1564 as a competitor to *Carion's Chronicle*.[172] The title page of the *editio princeps* credited Basellius with writing the final sections, but the division of labour between Melanchthon and the long forgotten monk of Hirsau remains unclear.[173]

Nauclerus's Chronicle is a massive history in two volumes that cover events from Creation down to the sixteenth century; and although much less famous than the *Nuremberg Chronicle*, the book became a standard, factual reference

ad immortalitatis opinionem inflammat .... Diximus qui ortus historiae, quam gentibus omnibus diligens custodia memoriae. Modo id quantum authoritatis historiae praestet, nemo non agnoscit, ut omnis uita, omne studiorum genus indigeat historia, atque ist hac in primis quae certis temporum articulis rem digestam exponit, ea est Chronica, nolo enim putetis in omnibus esse Chronicam frugem, aut diligentiam, quae historiae nomen habent. Hac una prodesse uoluit hic noster Ioannes Nauclerus I.V. Doctor illustraturus & gesta & literas Germanorum, quae multos iam annos in tenebris & situ delituerant, uir literis & fide praestans, quorum alterum sua potuit industria & principum uirorum fauore, alterum, & si id quoque uere suum, quasi ex traduce accepisse uidetur a patre Ioanne Nauclero uiro equestris ordinis, qui monumenta probitatis suae apud Ludouicum Vracharium comitem egregia reliquit." Nauclerus, *Chronica* (1516), vol. 1, fol. ii r - iii r (emphasis added).

172 Laurentius Surius's edition includes a Catholic continuation with the events of the sixteenth century (VD16 N 169). See Peucer's comments in Peucer, *Chronicon Carionis* (Wittenberg, 1580), 488–489, where he refers to Surius as *scurrilous*. Surius also attacked Peucer's *Commentary on Divination* for its comments on transubstantiation, see Martin Roebel, "Humanistische Medizin und Kryptocalvinismus: Leben und medizinisches Werk des Wittenberger Medizinprofessors Caspar Peucer (1525–1602)" (Ph.D. diss., Ruprecht-Karls-Universität Heidelberg, 2004), 232 n. 815.

173 See Hermann Müller, "Nicht Melanchthon, sondern Nikolaus Basellius Urheber der Interpolationen in der Chronographie des Nauklerus," *Forschungen zur deutschen Geschichte* 23 (1882): 595–600. This point is discussed in Hartfelder, *Philipp Melanchthon*, 294–295; see also the brief comments in Scheible, *Melanchthon* (1997), 251. The view that Melanchthon, rather than Basellius, had prepared Nauclerus's work for publication is found in much of the older literature. It seems that this notion can be traced to the funeral oration for Melanchthon delivered by his Wittenberg colleague, Vitus Winsemius, where he remarked: "Praefuit et Typographicae officinae Anshelmi aliquandui. Excudebatur tunc illud grande historicum volumen Naucleri, in quo multa quae corrupta erant, ipse emendavit, mutila multa complevit, confusanea in ordinem redegit, obscuris lucem reddidit, supervacanea praecidit, effecitque ut is liber, qui antea erat farrago verius, quam integrum historiae corpus, postea a multis adpeteretur, et magna cum utilitate legeretur." CR X, 192; see also CR X, 260.

on German history for the rest of the century. In contrast to the vast number of cityscapes and woodcuts in Schedel's work, *Nauclerus's Chronicle* is unadorned, and the narrative is much more coherent than the rambling patchwork of material found in the *Nuremberg Chronicle*. The *Chronicle* itself has a pro-ecclesiastical tone, which is especially apparent in the lengthy discussion of the Investiture Controversy. Indeed, Nauclerus praised Pope Gregory VII (Hildebrand), the great adversary of Emperor Henry IV,[174] and he claimed that the available sources, with only a few dissenting voices, presented Gregory favourably.[175] Nevertheless, even among the patriotic South German humanists, the *Chronicle* became an extremely influential work. It later served as the principal source for the medieval sections of *Carion's Chronicle*.[176]

The *Fasciculus Temporum* and the *Nuremberg Chronicle* both used page layouts to convey a sense of linear progression, and to some extent, graphic form dictated the narrative content. *Nauclerus's Chronicle* was free of these constraints. Nauclerus used an innovative structure that traced a series of generations from the beginning of time to his own day. Augustine had associated the genealogy of Christ with the Six Ages, but Nauclerus inverted the emphasis, so the generational scheme, rather than the Six Ages, determined the organizational pattern. The first volume of the *Chronicle* covers sixty-three generations from Creation to the Incarnation; these are the direct, physical descendants of Adam down to Christ. The second volume changes this narrative pattern, because the descendants of Christ himself are spiritual rather than physical, and the subsequent generations are assigned strict thirty-year intervals, so there are fifty generations from Christ to 1500.[177] Nauclerus treated each generation

---

174   "[V]ir fuit certe Gregorius religiosus, timens Deum, iustitiae ac aequitatis amator, in aduersis constans, qui praeter deum in his quae ad iustitiam pertinebant nil timuisset perficere." Nauclerus, *Chronica* (1516), vol. 2, Generatio XXXVII, fol. CLXI v.

175   "Sub hoc pontifice ecclesia nouis & inauditis schismatum erroribus periclitari cepit, sunt etiam qui illum non canonice constitutum sed tyrannice papatum sibimet usurpasse referunt. Alii & fere omnes prorsus contrarium referunt, nos ea quae uarie scripta de eo inueniuntur fideliter annotabimus." Nauclerus, *Chronica* (1516), vol. 2, Generatio XXXVI, fol. CLVII v.

176   See Emil Menke-Glückert, *Die Geschichtschreibung der Reformation und Gegenreformation: Bodin und die Begründung der Geschichtsmethodologie durch Bartholomäus Keckermann* (Leipzig: J.C. Hinrichs, 1912), 136–152; Hildegard Ziegler, *Chronicon Carionis: ein Beitrag zur Geschichtschreibung des 16. Jahrhunderts* (Halle a. S: Niemeyer, 1898), 53–62; Gottfried Münch, "Das Chronicon Carionis Philippicum: ein Beitrag zur Würdigung Melanchthons als Historiker," *Sachsen und Anhalt* 1 (1925): 251.

177   "In primis itaque praemittendum duco, quod sicut ueteris testamenti caput est Adam primus homo, a quo per .63. generationes recta linea descendentes, peruenimus ad Christum filium Dei: ita noui testamenti caput est Christus, a quo conformiter de generatione in generationem descendendum erit, usquequo perueniamus ad finem mundi. Ita tamen

as self-contained, so although he was not confined by page size, he nevertheless established a fixed internal structure for the narrative. The approach gave flexibility to write as much, or as little, as wanted for each generation.

Nauclerus used the generational scheme as his primary framework, but he also thought in terms of the Six Ages.[178] Although he did not use a continuous timeline, he inserted chronological information throughout his work, and much of the narrative flows almost annalistically.[179] He also used the Four Monarchies, but unlike Martin of Troppau and Schedel, he did not invoke Orosius. Instead, he explicitly referred to Nebuchadnezzar's dream in Daniel 2[180] – though not to Daniel's vision from Daniel 7 – and he followed

quod sciamus generationes noui testamenti non esse carnales, cum Christus carnales filios non habuerit, sed spirituales, quales ex aqua & spiritu generauit, id est, regenerauit. Factus est enim, inquit Apostolus, primus Adam in animam uiuentem, nouissimus Adam, id est, Christus in spiritum uiuificantem, non enim primus erat spiritualis, nam primus homo de terra terrenus, secundus homo de caelo caelestis qualis terrenus tales terreni & qualis caelestis tales & caelestes. Erunt itaque generationes noui testamenti non inaequales duratione temporis ut carnales fuere, sed sicut Christus noui testamenti autor expleto tandem aetatis suae anno .30. incepit sibi filios generare & acquirere per euangelium, ita quaelibet generatio noui testamenti pariformiter consummabitur in sequentibus spatio .30. annorum, hanc ego supputationem annorum ea solum ratione intendo sequi, ut infra scripta facilius possint inueniri." Nauclerus, *Chronica* (1516), vol. 2, fol. 1 r. See Theuerkauf, "Soziale Bedingungen humanistischer Weltchronistik," 327 n. 37.

178 "Modus autem procedendi talis est. Quod in qualibet generatione primo loco caput generationis ponitur, & mox historiae canonicae, deinde quae durante generatione per nationes varias gesta sunt, pauca de multis celebriora scribentur. Et quia nonnulli catholici scriptores exemplo microcosmi macrocosmum, id est, maiorem mundum in sex aetates diuiserunt, & sua cuique aetati dicta gestaque attribuerunt. Cunque haec diuisio ab hac nostra non abhorreat partitione, curaui & aetates mundi annotare. Et cuique aetati generationes sub ea concurrentes attribuere, hoc modo. Prima aetas ab Adam usque ad diluuium, habet annos iuxta Hebraicam scripturam mille sexingentos quinquaginta sex. Sed iuxta Septuaginta interpretes, quos sequi intendo, annos bis mille ducentos quadraginta duos. Generationes uero decem, iuxta utranque editionem. Quamuis autem computatio Hebraeorum uideatur uerior, secundum Augustinum in libro de ciuitate Dei. Altera tamen nempe Septuaginta interpretum est nobis communior." Nauclerus, *Chronica* (1516), vol. 1, fol. II v. See Theuerkauf, "Soziale Bedingungen humanistischer Weltchronistik," 327 n. 37.

179 See for example: "Anno igitur ab exordio mundi secundum hebraicam veritatem .3962. Secundum septuaginta interpretes eorumque sectatores .5199. uel ut alii volunt .201. [i.e. 5201] Ab urbis uero romanae conditione .751. Olympiadis nonagesimae centesimae tertiae anno tertio imperante Augusto Octauiano Caesare anno imperii eius .42. Ab oriente in occidentem, a septentrione in meridiem, ac per totum Oceani circulum quo Romanum uenit imperium cunctis gentibus una pace compositis. Exiit edictum ab eodem caesare Augusto ut describeretur uniuersus orbis...." Nauclerus, *Chronica* (1516), vol. 2, fol. 1 r.

180 Nauclerus, *Chronica* (1516), vol. 1, Generatio LI, fol. CI r.

Jerome's interpretation (Assyria, Persia, Greece, and Rome).[181] Rolevinck and Schedel had treated the Four Monarchies mostly as a chronological matter, as in the Eusebius-Jerome *Chronicle*. In contrast, Nauclerus treated them as both a chronological marker and the unfolding of prophetic fulfilment. Although he did not place strong emphasis on the prophetic aspect, it was nevertheless present, and he explicitly used the term "world monarchy" (*monarchia mundi*) for the Fourth Monarchy, which God himself had bestowed on the Germans.[182]

In contrast to earlier historians, Nauclerus's interest in the Four Monarchies stemmed primarily from changes in available sources rather than specific political developments. In 1498, a papal official, Annius of Viterbo (1432–1502),[183] had published a collection of texts that purported to supplement classical and biblical sources.[184] Some scholars quickly, and correctly, recognized the

---

181 See Theuerkauf, "Soziale Bedingungen humanistischer Weltchronistik," 327 n. 37. The Four Monarchies are specifically addressed in Nauclerus, *Chronica* (1516), vol. 1, fol. XII r–XII v (Assyriorum regnum), LXXXVIII v (Finis ac translatio regni assyriorum), XCIX v–CI r (Explicatur a Daniele somnium regi), CIIII r (Cyrus), CVII r (Translatio monarchiae Babyloniorum ad Persas), CXXXVI v (De Alexandro), CXXXVIII r (Monarchiae diuisio), CLXXXV v (Quarta monarchia); vol. 2, fol. I v–II r, CXVI v (De imperii ad Germanos tralatione), CXVIII v–CXIX v (Imperii ad germanos tralatione).

182 "Post tam egregia maiorum uestrorum gesta o nobilissimi Germani quid aliud uobis faciundum restat, nisi eorum sequi uestigia, quorum foelicibus auspiciis tantopere exaltati estis. Vos prae omnibus elegit deus, ut dominaremini omni nationi, uobis data est monarchia mundi. Itaque quantum reliquis christianis censeri debeatis foeliciores ex hoc uno iudicari licet quod etsi sint aliae gentes fortitudine & cultu christiano non negligendae, uobis tamen dedit deus imperium, dedit gloriam & nomen excellentissimum." Nauclerus, *Chronica* (1516), vol. 2, Generatio XXVII, fol. CXXII r. The idea of "world-empire" is also present to some extent in Schedel: "[D]arzu sich alle völcker. alle nation. vnd alle könig vnd fürsten disem kayerthumb mit willigem gemüet ergeben sollen." Schedel, *Chronicle of the World* (London, 2001), fol. CLXXVIII r.

183 See, with reference to earlier literature, Wilhelm Schmidt-Biggemann, "Heilsgeschichtliche Inventionen. Annius von Viterbos 'Berosus' und die Geschichte der Sintflut," in *Sintflut und Gedächtnis: Erinnern und Vergessen des Ursprungs*, ed. Martin Mulsow and Jan Assmann (München: Fink, 2006), 85–111. See also Anthony Grafton, *Defenders of the Text: The Traditions of Scholarship in an Age of Science, 1450–1800* (Cambridge, MA: Harvard University Press, 1991), 76–103; and Borchardt, *German Antiquity*, 89–91.

184 I use the 1511 Strasbourg edition: Annius of Viterbo, *Berosvs Babilonicvs De His Quæ præcesserunt inundationem terrarum. Item. Myrsilus de origine Turrhenorum. Cato in fragmentis. Archilochus in Epitheto de temporibus. Metasthenes de iudicio temporum. Philo in breuiario temporum. Xenophon de equiuocis temporum. Sempronius de diuisione Italiæ. Q. Fab. Pictor de aureo sæculo & origine vrbis Rhomæ. Fragmentum Itinerarij Antonini Pij. Altercatio Adriani Augusti & Epictici. Cornelij Taciti de origine & situ Germanorum opusculum. C.C. de situ & moribus Germanorum* ([Strasbourg]: [Grüninger], 1511). VD16 B 1649 [VD16 C 1902].

collection as a forgery,[185] but many Germans refused to dismiss it completely. The Annian forgeries seemed to provide new information about German origins, for example, Annius traced the ancestry of the Germans back to a fourth son of Noah, Tuisco, who is not named in Genesis.[186] As with Tacitus's *Germania*, German humanists quickly incorporated information from Annius into their works on German Antiquity.[187] In his *Chronicle*, Nauclerus was especially interested in the Annian collection because it traced the early, and otherwise fragmentary, history of the Four Monarchies, and it offered complete regnal lists.[188] As a result, his emphasis on the Monarchies was driven mostly by Annius's use of the Four Monarchies as an organizing framework in his forgeries, and by the new ability to provide a comprehensive list of ancient rulers.

Nauclerus was in some sense a "scholastic-humanist," and his *Chronicle* reflects both his expertise in canon law and his interest in humanist studies.[189] He approached the *Donation of Constantine* and the *translatio imperii* from both perspectives, which was typical of many important early sixteenth century humanists, such as Wimpfeling.[190] In his treatment of Constantine, Nauclerus offered a lengthy description of the background to the *Donation*.[191] He focused on the standard canon law references, such as *Venerabilem*, but he also noted general inconsistencies concerning Constantine's grant to the popes.[192] Furthermore, from a historical perspective, he drew attention to the lack of extant contemporaneous sources regarding the *Donation*.[193] He did not mention Cusa or Valla, but he commented on the diversity of opinion

---

185   See Christopher Ligota, "Annius of Viterbo and Historical Method," *Journal of the Warburg and Courtauld Institutes* 50 (1987): 44 n. 2.

186   On Tuisco generally, see Borchardt, *German Antiquity*; and Peter Hutter, *Germanische Stammväter und römisch-deutsches Kaisertum* (Hildesheim: Georg Olms Verlag, 2000), esp. 36–44.

187   See, for example, Borchardt, *German Antiquity*, 109–114, 144–148.

188   See his discussion at the opening of the *Chronicle* – Nauclerus, *Chronica* (1516), vol. 1, fol. I r; and specifically on the Assyrian kings – Nauclerus, *Chronica* (1516), vol. 1, Generatio XVIII, fol. XII v.

189   Joachimsen in his *Geschichtsauffassung* commented, "Im ganzen bleibt Schedels Buch eine scholastische Arbeit im humanistischen Gewande. Von der Chronik des Nauklers darf man das Umgekehrte sagen" (91), and he also refers to the *Chronicle* as "das erste kritische Geschichtswerk Deutschlands" (92).

190   Goez, *Translation imperii*, 252.

191   Nauclerus, *Chronica* (1516), vol. 2, Generatio XI, fol. XXXIX r–XL r.

192   "Qualia autem & quae Constantinus ecclesiae donauerit Romanae uariant in hoc scribentes...." Nauclerus, *Chronica* (1516), vol. 2, Generatio XI, fol. XXXIX r.

193   "[D]e dono eius aut concessione, apud nullos extat autores, praeterquam in libro decretorum idque in antiquis uoluminibus minime contineri, autor est Antoninus praesul Floretinus in chronicis." Nauclerus, *Chronica* (1516), vol. 2, Generatio XI, fol. XXXIX v.

THE FOURTH MONARCHY AND THE TRANSLATIO IMPERII 79

concerning the *Donation* and remarked "may the truth win out."[194] Later, however, in his discussion of Charlemagne, he rehearsed the standard account of the *Donation* without qualification.[195] The inconsistency may have been present in Nauclerus's manuscript of the *Chronicle*, but it is possible that Basellius or Melanchthon inserted the sceptical comments during the editing process. Nevertheless, the *Chronicle* demonstrates that, despite the critiques of Cusa and Valla, the canon law perspective on the *Donation of Constantine* was still accepted on the eve of the Reformation, even among some German humanists.

Regarding the *translatio imperii*, Nauclerus exemplifies the perspective of early sixteenth century German humanists who were deeply concerned about French claims to Imperial territory, especially Alsace, as well as the Imperial title itself.[196] The French had long cast greedy eyes on the Empire, and in the late fifteenth century, they circulated arguments about Charlemagne and the *translatio imperii* to lay the groundwork for seizing the Imperial title from the Germans. These efforts culminated in the Imperial Election of 1519, when Francis I was considered as a viable candidate for the Imperial throne. Although he ultimately lost to the Hapsburg candidate, Charles of Spain, the threat was not quickly forgotten by the Germans.

In essence, the French advanced two basic arguments to (re)claim the Imperial title.[197] First, they argued that Charlemagne had been French, rather than German, so his true successors were the French kings. Second, they argued that the pope had transferred the Empire from the Greeks to the Franks, and only later to the Germans. Thus, the French, as the true descendants of the Franks, had a claim to the Imperial title that was prior to the Germans. In response, German humanists vehemently argued that the evidence showing Charlemagne had been German was irrefutable, and they held that the Carolingian *translatio* had transferred the Empire specifically to the Germans.[198]

In his *Chronicle*, Nauclerus explicitly addressed the French-German debate, and he based his arguments on historical fact as well as the authority of canon

---

194 "[P]ro hac parte facit quod quae hodie dicuntur de patrimonio ecclesiae, fere omnia inueniuntur a sequentibus principibus donata, alii aliter sentiunt, uincat ueritas." Nauclerus, *Chronica* (1516), vol. 2, Generatio XI, fol. XXXIX v.
195 Nauclerus, *Chronica* (1516), vol. 2, Generatio XXVII, fol. CXXI v.
196 On these French-German debates, see especially Laubach, "Wahlpropaganda," 207–248; as well as Goez, *Translatio imperii*, 251; and Bernd Moeller, "Karl der Große im 16. Jahrhundert," in *Die Präsenz der Antike im Übergang vom Mittelalter zur Frühen Neuzeit: Bericht über Kolloquien der Kommission zur Erforschung der Kultur des Spätmittelalters 1999 bis 2002*, ed. Ludger Grenzmann et al. (Göttingen: Vandenhoeck & Ruprecht, 2004), 109–124.
197 See Goez, *Translatio imperii*, 251–252.
198 See Laubach, "Wahlpropaganda," 220; Goez, *Translatio imperii*, 251–252; Borchardt, *German Antiquity*, 123.

law. He declared Charlemagne German by birth, since he had been born at Ingelheim, he had reigned from Germany, and he was also buried there.[199] Furthermore, he had used German as has native tongue, and he named both the winds and the months in German.[200] Nauclerus also asserted that Charlemagne's successors had been German, and he refuted claims that Charles the Bald had transferred the Empire to the French by demonstrating that Charles was, in fact, German, since he had been born in Germany to German parents.[201]

Beyond this, however, Nauclerus argued that the French-German debate over Charlemagne was ultimately irrelevant because Charlemagne himself had only been the conduit through whom the Empire had been transferred to the Germans. On this point, he cited *Venerabilem* as proof of the transfer specifically to the Germans, since the decretal described the *translatio* as "*in Germanos.*"[202] Furthermore, he addressed the apparent inconsistency between canon law (transfer to the Germans) and the historical record (transfer to the Franks) by arguing that at the time of his coronation, Charlemagne, as king of the "Franks," had actually been king of both Gaul and Germany. No specific mention was made of "Germany" because it was included in Charlemagne's rule over the Franks.[203] Nauclerus also resolved the issue of the two translations that seemed to be found in his sources – one at the time of the young Charlemagne's anointment and the second at his Imperial coronation in Rome – by differentiating between Pope Stephen II (r. 752–757), who had presented

---

199 "Nam clare constat ex chronicis Carolum fuisse germanum in germania natum sedem habuisse & sepultum, natus enim inuenitur in Ingelhem haud longe a Moguntia, quod satis colligitur ex historia Francorum & Eusebii." Nauclerus, *Chronica* (1516), vol. 2, Generatio XXVII, fol. CXIX r.

200 "Legitur etiam in Spe. histo. quod Carolus xii. uentis imposuit nomina, & xii. mensibus iuxta propriam id est teutonicam linguam." Nauclerus, *Chronica* (1516), vol. 2, Generatio XXVII, fol. CXIX r.

201 "Sed eo mortuo successit in imperio Carolus secundus qui natus fuit in germania ex Ludouico pio & Iuditha Guelfi teutonici filia...." Nauclerus, *Chronica* (1516), vol. 2, Generatio XXVII, fol. CXIX r.

202 "Magna admodum et uenerdana dignitas Germanorum, apud quos residet monarchia mundi Romanum imperium, de quo Innocentius tertius extra de elec. in c. uenerabilem, scribens asserit Romanum imperium a graecis in persona magnifici Caroli in Germanos esse translatum...." Nauclerus, *Chronica* (1516), vol. 2, Generatio XXVII, fol. CXVIII v–CXIX r. See Laubach, "Wahlpropaganda," 220; Goez, *Translatio imperii*, 251.

203 "Nec sine mysterio hoc factum uidetur & ad tollendam omnem ambiguitatem ita fuit exprimendum quod ita clarum fiet. Carolus enim magnus tempore translationis rex fuit non solum Galliae sed & germaniae & id est indubitatum, & licet utriusque regni rex fuerit a neutro tamen regno appellabatur, sed Carolus rex Francorum dicebatur, quod idem erat ac si nominatus fuisset rex germaniae & galliae...." Nauclerus, *Chronica* (1516), vol. 2, Generatio XXVII, fol. CXIX r.

THE FOURTH MONARCHY AND THE TRANSLATIO IMPERII   81

the argument for the *translatio imperii*, and Pope Leo III (795–816), who had carried it out.[204] In this way, Nauclerus harmonized canon law with the historical record to defend against French claims to Charlemagne and the Empire.

The chapter on Charlemagne (Generatio XXVII) also included lengthy sections on "Praise of Germany," as well as an "Admonition to the Princes," which discussed the geography and history of Germany and the Germans down to Charlemagne. This overt German patriotism was less pronounced in the *Nuremberg Chronicle*, and Schedel had reserved his extended digressions on the Germans and the Empire for the Ottonian period. Indeed, although Schedel presented Charlemagne as "German born," he held that prior to Otto I the "Gauls" and the "Lombards" had held the Empire.[205] By the time Nauclerus wrote, Schedel's perspective had become politically unacceptable among German humanists.

Despite his German patriotism, Nauclerus rejected the idea that Charlemagne had established the Electoral College to preserve the Empire among the Germans.[206] Instead, he seemed to favour Martin of Troppau's view that the foundation could be traced to Otto III and Gregory V with the creation of the seven Imperial Electors dated to 1002.[207] Even though he actively refuted French claims, Nauclerus was still deeply concerned that the Germans might lose the Empire. Schedel had written at the beginning of Emperor Maximilian's

---

204   "Itaque quod Stephanus argumentum transferendi imperii ostendit Leo pontifex consummauit." Nauclerus, *Chronica* (1516), vol. 2, Generatio XXVI, fol. CXII r.

205   "Von disem kaiser Karolo bis auff kaiser Ludwigen den sun Arnulphi hat das kaiserthumb in hundert vnd zehen iarn bey den galliern nit klaine zunemung gehabt. vnd darnach auff gie Lombardier gelangt. vnnd ist zu letst an die teütschen. an hertzog Otten könig Heinrich sun gewenndt worden." Schedel, *Chronicle of the World* (London, 2001), fol. CLXXVIII r.

206   "[N]ec etiam, reor, probari potest, Carolum, mandante Leone papa, constitutionem aliquam fecisse, quod Moguntinens. Treuerens. Coloniens. archiepiscopi, cum comite Palatino Rheni debeant imperatorem eligere. concedamus autem quod ita sit, imperium tamen Romanum non in illos translatum est, sed sine omni distinctione in Germanos: quod & euentus docet, & omne ius, & ratio simul, & consuetudo." Nauclerus, *Chronica* (1516), vol. 2, Generatio XXVII, fol. CXXII r.

207   "Hoc in tempore electores imperii primum instituti leguntur, de quo aliqui scribunt quod Otho III cum haeredes ex se descendentes mares non haberet, constituit ex consilio principum Germaniae ut imperatore mortuo in oppido Francofurt perpetuo fieret electio, electoresque constituit tres archiepiscopus, Moguntinensem Germaniae, Coloniensem Italiae, Treuerensem Galliae nomine, & cum his alios quatuor seculares principes, Palatinum comitem Rheni, ut ex officio etiam esset dapifer, ducem Saxoniae qui esset Mariscalcus, Marchionem Brandenburgensem qui esset Camerarius, & regem Bohemiae qui archipincerna imperii esset, hi septem principes eligendi imperatoris ius & potestatem sic acceperunt." Nauclerus, *Chronica* (1516), vol. 2, Generatio XXXIIII, fol. CXLIIII v.

reign, and in closing he stressed the threats Maximilian faced from the French, who had robbed him of his bride, Anne of Brittany, and from the Turks, who by then had conquered large portions of the eastern Mediterranean.[208] For Nauclerus, the adversaries remained the same. The French invasions of Italy that began in 1494 had already brought foreign armies into regions the Germans still considered Imperial territory, and the Turks remained a threat to Hungary and the eastern frontier.[209] Nauclerus expressed a very real fear that just as the Germans had "earned" the Empire through virtue, they might now lose it through sloth and vice.[210]

In the end, Nauclerus set his hopes for the future of Europe on the papacy rather than the Emperor. For him, the glory days of the medieval German Emperors had faded into the past, and the papacy remained as the institution that could bring stability to Europe.[211] Nevertheless, the sound historical sense of Nauclerus, and the sheer volume of information he offered, ensured that his *Chronicle* remained a ready source for German historians, Catholic and Protestant, throughout the sixteenth century.

13 Conclusion

In Late Antiquity, Christian scholars developed frameworks of historical periodization that contributed to a broader debate about the past, present and future of the Roman Empire. Although they drew on earlier interpretive patterns, they revised these schemes to address the specific concerns of an empire in decline. In this context, the Six Ages reflected St. Augustine's ambivalence about the permanence of the Roman Empire, whereas the Four Monarchies became a patriotic assertion of Rome's place in the divine plan for the world.

After the collapse of Roman rule in the West, the historiographical paradigms of Antiquity lost much of their political significance. Indeed, the Four Monarchies fell out of use among historians for five hundred years. The scheme reappeared, however, during the papal-Imperial strife of the Investiture Controversy, and by the twelfth century, it had again become a fixture of European intellectual culture. Nevertheless, in the Middle Ages, the specific sequence of world-empires held less importance than the idea of transfer itself (*translatio*

---

208 Schedel, *Chronicle of the World* (London, 2001), fol. CCLVIII v.
209 See Nauclerus, *Chronica* (1516), vol. 2, Generatio L, fol. CCC r–CCC v.
210 "Sicut Germani uirtutibus meruerunt imperium, ita ignauia & uitiis amittere possunt." Nauclerus, *Chronica* (1516), vol. 2, Generatio L, fol. CCC v.
211 Haering, "Johannes Vergenhans," 8.

imperii). As popes asserted stronger claims to supremacy, they developed a language of typology that marked the political debates of the medieval world. For historians, the pronouncements found in canon law eventually became historical authority, rather than a mere source, and this perspective lasted into the sixteenth century.

The Imperial controversialists of the Middle Ages never drafted an effective response to the narrative of pro-papal historiography, and in form and argument, history on the eve of the Reformation remained in the possession of the papacy. The foundation for change had, however, been laid in the Middle Ages, and by reforming the historiographical legacy he inherited, Melanchthon ultimately succeeded in overturning the pro-papal narrative that had dominated historical thought for centuries.

CHAPTER 3

Johann Carion of Bietigheim: The Berlin Court Astronomer

1   Introduction

When Melanchthon arrived at Wittenberg in 1518, he was only twenty-one years old, but by then he had already spent nearly a decade at universities, first at Heidelberg and then at Tübingen.[1] This initial experience in South Germany had immersed him in the world of early German humanism, and he brought many of its concerns with him to Wittenberg, not only in the sense of a general interest in eloquence and learned culture, but more specifically in questions and frameworks of interpretation that had been developed there since the late fifteenth century. From the time he arrived in Wittenberg to his death, Melanchthon remained deeply attached to two institutions, the University of Wittenberg and the court of Electoral Saxony. As a result, he brought a different lived experience to historical studies than many of his predecessors and contemporaries, who lived in Imperial free cities or served the Hapsburgs. Melanchthon's defining model was not Florence, Rome or Vienna, but the distinctly German humanism of the Rhine region.

In the early sixteenth century, history had slowly begun to enter the course offerings at German universities, but it was taught infrequently and mainly through the study of classical historians. Conrad Celtis, for example, lectured on the *Germania* of Tacitus at Vienna in 1500;[2] and at Wittenberg, the early

---

1   On Melanchthon generally, see Heinz Scheible, *Melanchthon: Eine Biographie* (München: Verlag C.H. Beck, 1997); Wilhelm Maurer, *Der junge Melanchthon*, 2 vols. (Göttingen: Vandenhoeck & Ruprecht, 1967–1969); Karl Hartfelder, *Philipp Melanchthon als Praeceptor Germaniae* (Berlin: A. Hofmann & comp., 1889); and Clyde Manschreck, *Melanchthon: The Quiet Reformer* (New York: Abingdon Press, 1958).

2   Emil Clemens Scherer, *Geschichte und Kirchengeschichte an den deutschen Universitäten: Ihre Anfänge im Zeitalter des Humanismus und ihre Ausbildung zu selbständigen Disziplinen* (Freiburg i. B.: Herder, 1927), 14–20; the first chair of history in Germany was founded at the University of Mainz in 1504 (21). For Wittenberg, see especially Eugen Rambeau, "Über die Geschichtswissenschaft an der Universität Wittenberg," in *450 Jahre Martin-Luther-Universität Halle-Wittenberg* (Halle: [s.n.], 1953), vol. 1, 255–270; as well as the references in Walter Friedensburg, *Geschichte der Universität Wittenberg* (Halle a.S.: Niemeyer, 1917). See also Arnaldo Momigliano, "The Introduction of the Teaching of History as an Academic Subject and its Implications," *Minerva* 21, no. 1 (March 1983): 1–15.

German humanist Christoph Scheurl (1481–1542) lectured on Suetonius in 1507.[3] Through Melanchthon's influence, history eventually became an integral part of the German university curriculum and an independent discipline separate from rhetoric or other subjects. In his inaugural address at Wittenberg on 28 August 1518, Melanchthon outlined a program for reforming education, and he emphasized history as central to learning.[4] Already in 1520, he advocated setting up a chair of history at Wittenberg as part of the proposed reforms of the university,[5] and later, several of his students took up newly established history professorships at the Protestant universities he had helped to found or reform. This institutionalization of historical studies was hardly inevitable, and it had no parallel in Italy, where Renaissance humanism had first taken root.[6]

Like his contemporaries, Melanchthon taught from classical historians, both Greek and Latin. At Tübingen, he delivered his first lectures on Livy,[7] an author to whom he returned several times in his career,[8] and after moving to

---

[3] Heinz Kathe, *Die Wittenberger Philosophische Fakultät 1502–1817* (Köln: Böhlau, 2002), 21.

[4] CR XI, 5–14. Even before he arrived at Wittenberg, Melanchthon had spoken in similar terms about the importance of humanist studies, and at Tübingen he had composed an oration entitled *On the Liberal Arts*, and dedicated to Stöffler, in which he extolled the traditional subjects of the trivium and quadrivium and aligned each of the arts with a corresponding muse. After finishing his discussion of the seven arts and muses, he pointed out that two were missing from their ranks – Clio and Calliope, history and poetry. CR XI, 12. See Heinz Scheible, "Reuchlins Einfluß auf Melanchthon," in *Reuchlin und die Juden*, ed. Arno Herzig (Sigmaringen: Thorbecke, 1993), 145–146; Heinz Scheible, "Melanchthons Bildungsprogramm," in *Lebenslehren und Weltentwürfe im Übergang vom Mittelalter zur Neuzeit: Politik, Bildung, Naturkunde, Theologie*, ed. Hartmut Boockmann (Göttingen: Vandenhoeck & Ruprecht, 1989), 233–248; Heinz Scheible, "Melanchthon und die oberrheinischen Humanisten," *Zeitschrift für die Geschichte des Oberrheins* 149 (2001): 125; Heinz Scheible, "Melanchthons Werdegang," in *Humanismus im deutschen Südwesten: Biographische Profile*, ed. Paul Gerhard Schmidt (Sigmaringen: Thorbecke, 1993), 236–237.

[5] Scherer, *Geschichte und Kirchengeschichte*, 27, 30–31. Scherer points out that Melanchthon's efforts seem to have been unsuccessful, and the need for Wittenberg to have a chair specifically devoted to history became less pressing because of Melanchthon's own lectures.

[6] There is no separate discussion of history at the Italian universities in the two major works on these subjects: Eric Cochrane, *Historians and Historiography in the Italian Renaissance* (Chicago: University of Chicago Press, 1981); and Paul Grendler, *The Universities of the Italian Renaissance* (Baltimore: Johns Hopkins University Press, 2002). See also Momigliano, "The Introduction of the Teaching of History," 1–15.

[7] CR X, 297. See the list of Melanchthon's lectures in Hartfelder, *Philipp Melanchthon*, 555–566.

[8] At Tübingen, Melanchthon had lectured on six books of Livy, and he seems to have lectured on Book 21 of *Ab Vrbe Condita* at Wittenberg in 1535 (CR X, 547 Nr. 129). In addition to this, a student notebook includes material from lectures by Melanchthon on Livy's preface and Book 1, beginning in 23 January 1555. Some remarks on Greek and Roman historians are also included in this section. For a full description, see Marianne Pade, "A Melanchthonian

Wittenberg, he also worked with Greek historians, particularly Thucydides.[9] Wittenberg was a young university, it had only been founded in 1502,[10] but through the generosity of the Elector of Saxony, the faculty had access to a substantial research library.[11] For teaching, however, Melanchthon needed inexpensive, but accurate, editions of the texts used by students for their courses. The early Wittenberg printers were notoriously bad,[12] so in 1519 Luther and Melanchthon convinced Melchior Lotter the Elder, a Leipzig printer, to establish a satellite shop in Wittenberg that would supply the Latin, and especially the Greek, editions Melanchthon needed.[13] The vast majority of these have

Commentary to the First Three Books of Thucydides? Cod. Philol. 166, Staats- und Universitätsbiliothek Hamburg," in *Reformation and Latin Literature in Northern Europe*, ed. Inger Ekrem et al. (Oslo: Scandinavian University Press, 1996), 193–206.

9   Melanchthon also translated selections from Thucydides into Latin for his students (VD16 T 1131). This is reproduced in CR XVII, 1074–1080. In 1562, Caspar Peucer published a posthumous collection of Melanchthon's Latin translations of orations from Thucydides. A small part of this material had appeared in print before, but most of it is found for the first time in this edition (VD16 P 2017). See Pade, "A Melanchthonian Commentary," 195–196. Besides the various individual printings, Melanchthon's work was incorporated into the Latin translation of Thucydides prepared by Vitus Winsemius (Veit Oertel, 1501–1570) one of Melanchthon's students, and then colleagues, at Wittenberg. The translation was published in 1569 (VD16 T 1122). In addition to Pade, "A Melanchthonian Commentary," see Marianne Pade, "Thucydides," in *Catalogus Translationum et Commentariorum*, ed. Virginia Brown (Washington, D.C.: The Catholic University of America Press, 2003), 130–136, 164–166; and generally, Udo Klee, *Beiträge zur Thukydides-Rezeption während des 15. und 16. Jahrhunderts in Italien und Deutschland* (Frankfurt a.M.: Lang, 1990).

10 For the history of the university, see Friedensburg, *Geschichte der Universität Wittenberg*; Maria Grossmann, *Humanism in Wittenberg, 1485–1517* (Nieuwkoop: De Graaf, 1975); Ernest Schwiebert, *The Reformation*, Vol. 2, *The Reformation as a University Movement* (Minneapolis: Fortress Press, 1996); and Kathe, *Die Wittenberger Philosophische Fakultät*.

11 See especially Grossmann, *Humanism in Wittenberg*, 100–112; and Sachiko Kusukawa, *A Wittenberg University library catalogue of 1536* (Binghamton, N.Y.: Medieval & Renaissance Texts & Studies, 1995), xi–xix, with additional references given there. After the Schmalkaldic War, the University of Wittenberg library was claimed by the Ernestine branch of the house of Wettin, and it was transferred to Jena, where it became the foundation for the library of the new university there.

12 On this point, see Richard Cole, "Reformation Printers: Unsung Heroes," *Sixteenth Century Journal* 15, no. 3 (Autumn 1984): 328. See generally Maria Grossmann, "Wittenberg Printing, Early Sixteenth Century," *Sixteenth Century Essays and Studies* 1 (January 1970): 53–74; and the relevant entries in Christoph Reske, *Die Buchdrucker des 16. und 17. Jahrhunderts im deutschen Sprachgebiet: Auf der Grundlage des gleichnamigen Werkes von Josef Benzing* (Wiesbaden: Harrassowitz, 2007).

13 Cole, "Reformation Printers," 333–334. One of Melanchthon's early Lotter editions was a short collection of biographies drawn from Eusebius and the continuation of Rufinus, along with Cassiodorus's *Tripartite History* (VD16 E 4705). This pamphlet for the classroom lacks any introduction or notes, and the text is entirely in Greek with capsule

been lost, but among the few survivors is a collection of excerpts from Lucian and Thucydides with a brief introduction in Greek by Melanchthon.[14]

During the 1510s and 1520s, Melanchthon also drafted commentaries and textbooks on several important subjects: grammar, rhetoric, dialectic, as well as his *Loci Communes*, an introduction to Protestant theology. In subsequent years, he contributed to other fields, such as ethics and natural philosophy, and he frequently revised and reissued his earlier works.[15] Textbooks were an integral part of Melanchthon's broader efforts to reform German education, and the extent of his influence is truly remarkable. By discarding or reforming the structure and content of the medieval education system, he effectively transformed an entire mental world.

Despite his interest in historical studies, Melanchthon did not prepare a history textbook during the 1520s. Then in 1531, Johann Carion (1499–1537), an old classmate from Tübingen, sent the manuscript of a history book he wanted to have printed in Wittenberg. Melanchthon reworked Carion's text into an engaging compendium of universal history, and it was published in 1532.[16] Unlike Melanchthon's textbooks, *Carion's Chronicle* did not arise from specific needs at Wittenberg, and initially it lacked a recognized place in the curriculum. In subsequent decades, however, history instruction gradually shifted from reading classical authors to learning from textbooks.[17] The vast popularity of *Carion's Chronicle* was a product, but also a catalyst, of that change.

Although his enduring fame rests on the *Chronicle*, during his lifetime, Carion was known mostly for his astrological writings, and he earned his living as a court astronomer to the Elector of Brandenburg.[18] He also served as a princely

---

biographies. Many of Melanchthon's shorter editions would have been similar to this one, with a text for student use and little or no commentary. Another example is his small edition of Aristophanes's *Clouds* (VD16 A 3274), see MBW 89. On Melanchthon's editions of Aristophanes, see CR XVIII, 1131–1136. See also Reske, *Die Buchdrucker*, 994–995.

14   VD16 L 2989. For Melanchthon's introduction, see MBW 79.
15   See the chronological listing in Hartfelder, *Philipp Melanchthon*, 577–620.
16   Johann Carion, *Chronica durch Magistru[m] Johan Carion / vleissig zusamen gezogen / meniglich nützlich zu lesen* (Wittenberg: Rhau, [1532]). VD16 C 998.
17   See generally Scherer, *Geschichte und Kirchengeschichte*.
18   On Carion see Georg Theodor Strobel, "Von Carions Leben und Schriften," *Miscellaneen literarischen Innhalts, Sechste Sammlung* (Nürnberg, 1782): [139]-206; Johann Christoph Adelung, *Geschichte der menschlichen Narrheit, oder Lebensbeschreibungen berühmter Schwarzkünstler, Goldmacher, Teufelsbanner, Zeichen- und Liniendeuter, Schwärmer, Wahrsager, und anderer philosophischer Unholden* (Leipzig: Weygandsche Buchhandlung, 1787), vol. 3, 110–147; Hildegard Ziegler, *Chronicon Carionis: ein Beitrag zur Geschichtschreibung des 16. Jahrhunderts* (Halle a.S.: Niemeyer, 1898), 1–10; Otto Tschirch, "Johannes Carion, Kurbrandenburgischer Hofastrolog," *Jahresbericht des Historischen Vereins zu Brandenburg* 36/37 (1906): 54–62; Gottfried Münch, "Das Chronicon Carionis

tutor at the Hohenzollern court, and he designed the *Chronicle* as a *Fürstenspiegel*, or "mirror of princes," text to influence the moral development of the Elector's son.[19] The *Chronicle* derived from the training Melanchthon and Carion received in South Germany, but it was also grounded in their experience at the courts of Brandenburg and Saxony. An introduction to Carion's career and his other publications is essential for understanding this context, especially because he was such an unlikely candidate for scholarly distinction. Indeed, in 1532 neither Carion nor Melanchthon could have imagined that the brief *Chronicle* they wrote for the Electoral Prince of Brandenburg would decisively influence the development of European historiography.

2 Carion's Early Career

According to his horoscope, Carion was born on 22 March 1499 at 1:46pm in Bietigheim, near Stuttgart (Württemberg).[20] The circumstances of his family and early life remain unknown, but Bietigheim had a Latin school in those

---

Philippicum: ein Beitrag zur Würdigung Melanchthons als Historiker," *Sachsen und Anhalt* 1 (1925): 201–212; Hermann Kuhlow, "Johannes Carion (1499–1537): Ein Wittenberger am Hofe Joachim I," *Jahrbuch für Berlin-Brandenburgische Kirchengeschichte* 54 (1983): 53–66; Dietmar Fürst and Jürgen Hamel, eds., *Johann Carion (1499–1537): Der erste Berliner Astronom mit einem Reprint der Schrift Carions "Bedeutnuss und Offenbarung" (1527)* (Berlin-Treptow: Archenhold-Sternwarte, 1988), 3–24; Almut Fricke-Hilgers, "'…das der historiographus auch sei ein erfarner der gschicht des himels.' Die Sintflutprognose des Johannes Carion für 1524 mit einer Vorhersage für das Jahr 1789," *Pirckheimer Jahrbuch* 5 (1989/1990): 33–68; Reiner Reisinger, *Historische Horoskopie: Das iudicium magnum des Johannes Carion für Albrecht Dürers Patenkind* (Wiesbaden: Harrassowitz, 1997), 245–263; Karl-Reinhart Trauner, "Carion, Johann(es)," in *Biographisch-Bibliographischen Kirchenlexikons* (Hamm: Traugott Bautz, 2007), vol. 28, 287–300. See also the articles collected in Elke Osterloh, ed., *Himmelszeichen und Erdenwege: Johannes Carion (1499–1537) und Sebastian Hornmold (1500–1581) in ihrer Zeit* (Ubstadt-Weiher: Verlag Regionalkultur, 1999). A collection of transcribed documents related to Carion is currently available on-line at: http://www.pascua.de/carion/carion-start.htm.

19 See Georg Schuster and Friedrich Wagner, *Die Jugend und Erziehung der Kürfursten von Brandenburg und Könige von Preußen*, Erster Band, *Die Kürfursten Friedrich I. und II., Albrecht, Johann, Joachim I. und II.* (Berlin: A. Hofmann & Comp., 1906), 356–357, 371–372.

20 An image of this nativity is reprinted with description in Andrea Liebers, "Johannes Carions Arbeiten zur Horoskopie im Vergleich zum heutigen Stand der Astrologie," in *Himmelszeichen und Erdenwege*, 322–325. See also Almut Fricke-Hilgers, "Die Sintflutprognose des Johannes Carion für 1524 mit einer Vorhersage für das Jahr 1789," in *Himmelszeichen und Erdenwege*, 294 n. 3.

years, and Carion may have received his initial education there.[21] The matriculation book at the University of Tübingen shows that on 21 April 1514, at the age of fifteen, he enrolled under the name, "Johannes Negelin de Büticken."[22] There Carion studied with Johannes Stöffler (1452–1531), a famous astronomer, and he met Melanchthon, who was two years older and a fellow student of Stöffler.[23] In later years, Melanchthon and Carion both remembered Stöffler fondly, and they attributed much of their own intellectual formation to his teaching in Tübingen.[24]

Already by 1518, Carion found employment as court astronomer to the Margrave of Brandenburg, Elector Joachim I (r. 1499–1535).[25] Therefore, he moved to Berlin around the same time that Melanchthon also left South Germany for Wittenberg. Until recently, however, Carion's activities in the late 1510s and down to 1521 had remained uncertain. In his *Vitae Germanorum Philosophorum* (1615), the standard collection of early modern German biographies, Melchior Adam mentioned that Carion had studied in Wittenberg and that he taught mathematics at Frankfurt an der Oder, but both are unlikely.[26] The reference to Frankfurt is possibly due to confusion with another Johannes Naegelin, who came from Gunzenhausen,[27] and the comment about studying in Wittenberg may stem from Carion's signature in the Wittenberg matriculation book during

---

21   Fricke-Hilgers, "Die Sintflutprognose" (1999), 277; Stefan Benning, "Johannes Carion aus Bietigheim: Eine biographische Skizze," in *Himmelszeichen und Erdenwege*, 193.

22   Tschirch, "Johannes Carion," 57; Heinrich Hermelink, ed., *Die Matrikeln der Universität Tübingen, Bd. 1: Die Matrikeln von 1477–1600* (Stuttgart: Kohlhammer, 1906), 200, Nr. 109.

23   For a brief biographical sketch, see Günther Oestmann, *Schicksalsdeutung und Astronomie: der Himmelsglobus des Johannes Stoeffler von 1493* (Stuttgart: Württembergisches Landesmuseum, 1993), 5–21. On his relationship with Melanchthon, see Günther Oestmann, "Johannes Stoeffler, Melanchthons Lehrer in Tübingen," in *Philipp Melanchthon in Südwestdeutschland: Bildungsstationen eines Reformators*, ed. Stefan Rhein (Karlsruhe: Badische Landesbibliothek, 1997), 75–86; Maurer, *Der junge Melanchthon*, vol. 1, 129–170.

24   CR XI, 382. See also the collection of articles in Günther Frank, ed., *Melanchthon und die Naturwissenschaften seiner Zeit* (Sigmaringen: Thorbecke, 1998). For Carion, see Johann Carion, *Ivdicivm Magistri Iohannis Carionis de Anno M.D.XXXIII. Cum purgatione in qua respondet Perlachio*. ([Wittenberg]: [Hans Weiß], 1532), sig. aiij v. VD16 C 1021. See also Fricke-Hilgers, "Die Sintflutprognose" (1999), 277 n. 6.

25   On Elector Joachim I, see ADB 14:71–78.

26   "Ioannes Cario nascitur A.C. 1499. A teneris optimarum literarum & artium studiosus fuit, inque pluribus Germaniae Academiis, praesertim in Witebergensi, tum facile omnium principe, cum laude versatus. Dedit autem operam cognitioni tum omnium disciplinarum, tum inprimis Matheseos; cuius & professioni in Academia Francofurtana praefuit." Melchior Adam, *Vitae Germanorum philosophorum* (Heidelberg: Jonas Rosa, 1615), 104.

27   See Tschirch, "Johannes Carion," 57.

FIGURE 4
Johann Carion, *Practica* ([Augsburg], 1518)
STAATS- UND STADTBIBLIOTHEK
AUGSBURG: 4 KULT 186–109,
URN:NBN:DE:BVB:12-BSB11216306-6

his visit in 1532. Some of the older biographical dictionaries also described Carion as a monk in Berlin.[28]

The first clear indication of Carion's post-Tübingen activities comes only in 1518, when he published a four leaf *practica* at Augsburg with predictions for the year 1519 (Figure 4).[29] Professional astrologers used the term *practica* to refer to the "art," or *Kunst*, of proceeding by fixed rules, thereby giving their predictions greater authority through methodological proof.[30] Thus, the art of

---

28   Adelung summarized many of these inaccuracies in his *Geschichte* (112–115).
29   Johann Carion, *Practica M. Joa[n]nis Nägelin von Bütighaim auff das 15.19. iar. Des durchleüchtigsten Fürsten vn[d] herren herr Joachim Margraue[n] zů Brandenburg &c. Astronomus.* ([Augsburg]: [Johann Miller], [1518]). VD16 ZV 24181. This pamphlet was first discussed in Heike Talkenberger, *Sintflut: Prophetie und Zeitgeschehen in Texten und Holzschnitten astrologischer Flugschriften 1488–1528* (Tübingen: Niemeyer, 1990), 211.
30   Helga Robinson Hammerstein, "The Battle of the Booklets: Prognostic Tradition and Proclamation of the Word in early sixteenth-century Germany," in *"Astrologi hallucinati": Stars and the End of the World in Luther's Time*, ed. Paola Zambelli (Berlin: de Gruyter, 1986), 130. On the *practica* literature generally, see Robin B. Barnes, "Hope and Despair in Sixteenth-Century German Almanacs," in *Die Reformation in Deutschland und Europa: Interpretationen und Debatten*, ed. Hans R. Guggisberg and Gottfried G. Krodel (Gütersloh: Gütersloher Verlagshaus Mohn, 1993), 440–461; and Robin B. Barnes, "Astrology and

producing a *practica* distinguished its predictions from prophecies based on inspiration (*uaticinia*). Carion probably issued an annual *practica* for each year after he became court astronomer in Berlin, but only a limited number of these have survived.

In this case, Carion's *Practica* provides two important pieces of historical information. At this point, he used the title *magister*; and since his name has not been found in other university matriculation books during this period, it is likely that he completed the degree at Tübingen. More important still, the title page indicates that Carion had already become an *astronomus* to Elector Joachim I. Until the discovery of this pamphlet at Augsburg in the 1990s, the earliest evidence for Carion's activities came from his *Prognosticatio* of 1521, which had left doubts about his role in the education and upbringing of the Electoral Prince, the future Elector Joachim II (1505–1571), who by 1521 was already in his late teens.[31] This earlier dating for Carion's arrival in Berlin argues for more extensive contact than previously thought, and only reinforces that he had opportunity to develop a close relationship with the Electoral Prince over the years. The pamphlet also helps to place Carion in Brandenburg during the initial years of the Reformation.

3   *Sintflut* of 1524

By his next known publication, the *Prognosticatio* from 1521,[32] Carion had adopted the hellenised version of his name, Carion, from the original *Nägelein*, which then meant either "small nail" or also "clove" (*Nelke*, i.e. *Gewürznelke*). The corresponding Greek term is *cariophyllon*.[33] The *Prognosticatio* itself deals

---

the Confessions in the Empire, c. 1550–1620," in *Confessionalization in Europe, 1555–1570: Essays in Honor and Memory of Bodo Nischan*, ed. John Headley et al. (Burlington, VT: Ashgate, 2004), 131–153.

31   See Schuster, *Die Jugend und Erziehung der Kürfursten*, 356. On Elector Joachim II generally, see ABD 14:78–86.

32   Johann Carion, *Prognosticatio vnd erklerung der grossen wesserung / Auch anderer erschrockenlichenn würckungen. So sich begeben nach Christi vnsers lieben hern geburt / Funfftzehen hundert vn[d] xxiiij. Jar. Durch mich Magistru[m] Joha[n]nem Carion vo[n] Buetikaym Churfürstlicher gnaden tzu Brandenburg Astronomu[m] mit fleyssiger arbeit tzusame[n] gebracht. Gantz erbermlich tzulesen / in nutz vn[d] warnung aller Christglaubigen menschen &c.* ([Leipzig]: [Martin Landsberg], [1521]). VD16 C 1030. Frequently, 1522 is given as the year of the *editio princeps*.

33   See Max Friedeberg, "Das Bildnis des Philosophen Johannes Carion von Crispin Herranth. Hofmaler des Herzogs Albrecht von Preußen," *Zeitschrift für Bildende Kunst, Neue Folge* XXX, 54 (1919): 309–316; and Benning, "Johannes Carion," 195.

especially with one of the most important astrological predictions of the sixteenth century, that a massive flood would inundate Europe in 1524.[34] As Aby Warburg pointed out, the title page of the *editio princeps* contains three images: the first shows the deluge of 1524, the second presents the comet that appeared in 1521, and below these are five figures that represent the planetary configurations at the time of the comet.[35] The pope kneeling and facing execution is Jupiter. The knight with drawn sword is Mars. The peasant, also bearing a sword, is Saturn. The cardinal with arms raised in despair is perhaps Mercury. The final figure, the Emperor, stands for the Sun and covers his face to avert the horrific scene before him (Figure 7).

Carion's reckonings in his *Prognosticatio* demonstrate a clear debt to Stöffler, whose *Almanach nova* contained exact positions of the stars down to 1531.[36] At the start of his entry on 1524, Stöffler had included additional comments about the appearance of many comets, and the dangers they foretold. Carion inserted a German version of these remarks into the *Prognosticatio*, virtually word for word, though without direct reference to Stöffler.[37] Regarding the flood itself, the astrologers based their expectations of a great deluge on Stöffler's prediction for 1524 of twenty planetary conjunctions, with sixteen in the watery sign of Pisces (the fish), including a great conjunction of Saturn and Jupiter.

---

34   For a description and explanation of this pamphlet, see Almut Fricke-Hilgers, "Die Sintflutprognose" (1999), 277–302; see also Talkenberger, *Sintflut*, 210–219.

35   Aby Warburg, "Pagan-Antique Prophecy in Words and Images in the Age of Luther (1920)," in *The Renewal of Pagan Antiquity: Contributions to the Cultural History of the European Renaissance*, trans. David Britt (Los Angeles: Getty Research Institute for the History of Art and the Humanities, 1999), 618.

36   I use the later edition – Johannes Stöffler, *Almanach nova plurimis annis venturis inservientia* (Venice: Liechtensteyn, 1504). Wolfenbüttel: A: 30.4 Astron. (2). The book was actually an updated version of Regiomantanus's *Ephemeriden*, which Stöffler had revised together with Jacob Pflaum, an astronomer from Ulm, and extended down to 1531. Oestmann, *Schicksalsdeutung und Astronomie*, 9.

37   "Als dann so man wirt tzelen Tausent funffhundert vnd xxiiij iar &c. Jn dißem Jar wirt weder Son noch Mon befinstert Aber ym anfang des Hornungs werden vil Cometen gesehen von aller planeten geburt / vnd werden bescheen geschichten der irrenden stern (welche billich tzu verwundern sein) dann in obgenantem monat werden tzweintzig tzusamenfügungen (fur war nicht gering) von welchen coniunctionibus ir xvi werden das wesserig tzeychen der visch besitzen / welche gar nahe der gantzen vmbkreysung der welt / Climaten / Köngreychen / Prouincien / Stenden / würden / vnuernünfftigen thiern / merwundern / vnd allen wachsenden dingen hie auff ertrich ein verkerung / verwandlung / vnd enderung bedeuten / Welchs wir von vilen so da haben geschriben alte historien vnd geschichten nicht oder kaum vernummen haben vnd von alten leuten schwerlich erfarn vnd in wissen gebracht mag werden." Carion, *Prognosticatio* (Leipzig, 1521), sig. [Aiiij]v – B r. This parallel is discussed by Fricke-Hilgers, "Die Sintflutprognose" (1999), 280–281.

FIGURE 5
Leonhard Reynmann, *Practica*
(Nuremberg, 1523)
HERZOG AUGUST BIBLIOTHEK
WOLFENBÜTTEL: A: 171.21 QUOD.
(51)

The title page of Leonhard Reynmann's 1523 *Practica*, for example, shows the planetary conjunctions within Pisces and the ensuing deluge (Figure 5).[38]

Despite its ominous predictions, Carion meant his *Prognosticatio* to calm the fears raised by other astrologers regarding the flood of 1524, especially Alexander Seitz († ca. 1545), an itinerant South German physician.[39] During 1520–1521, Seitz had been on a campaign to raise alarm over the impending deluge, and he meant to bring collective repentance as had happened in Old Testament Nineveh after Jonah's preaching. Apparently, Seitz first composed a tract on the coming flood for one of the Bavarian dukes.[40] Then in 1520, he wrote a shorter pamphlet for mass circulation; it was published anonymously late that year or early 1521 and reprinted in several cities. At the Diet of Worms

---

38   Leonhard Reynmann, *Practica vber die grossen vnd manigfeltigen Coniunction der Planeten / die im jar M.D.XXiiij. erscheinen / vn[d] vngezweiffelt vil wunderparlicher ding geperen werden* (Nuremberg: Hieronymus Höltzel, 1523). VD16 R 1620.
39   On Seitz, see Talkenberger, *Sintflut*, 184–192; and Robin B. Barnes, "Alexander Seitz and the Medical Calling: Physic, Faith and Reform," in *Ideas and Cultural Margins in Early Modern Germany: Essays in Honor of H.C. Erik Midelfort*, ed. Majorie Elizabeth Plummer and Robin B. Barnes (Burlington, VT: Ashgate, 2009), esp. 195–196.
40   Talkenberger, *Sintflut*, 185.

FIGURE 6
Alexander Seitz, *Ain Warnung*
([Augsburg], [1520])
STAATS- UND STADTBIBLIOTHEK
AUGSBURG: 4 KULT 186-114,
URN:NBN:DE:BVB:12-BSB11216311-4

(1521), which Carion, from his description, may have attended, Seitz also circulated his dire warnings in broadsheets (*in grossen gemalten brieffen*).[41] As a result, once the attendees of the Diet left Worms, the fear of a deluge spread with them. By late 1521, Seitz had succeeded in causing alarm in Germany over the anticipated flood, and Carion decided it was time to respond.

Of Seitz's writings on the flood, only his short pamphlet has survived.[42] With this pamphlet, Seitz addressed his warnings specifically to the common people; and he predicted not just a great flood but a universal deluge (*Sintflut*)

---

41 "Bedeutend mit sampt aller coniunction der irrenden stern / erhebung vnnd anfangs des wassers in greulicher ungestimmigkeyt / auff den ersten tag des Hornungs mit getzeugnus der Venus welche dann den ersten punckten der visch eintrit wie wol es angeuer xxx. tag sich vor neygt tzu wesserlicher vnd regenlicher gestalt / wirt es doch langsam sich begeben / vnnd nicht als sagt Alexander Seytz von Marpach der löblichen Fürsten von Beyrn Phisicus in grossen gemalten brieffen / welche er tzuuorkauffen auff dem reychstag gen Worms verordnet / mit vil thiern vnd mülredleyn aber ich acht es seyen wintmuln." Carion, *Prognosticatio* (Leipzig, 1521), sig. B r. See Fricke-Hilgers, "Die Sintflutprognose" (1989/90), 56–57.

42 Alexander Seitz, *Ain Warnung des Sündtfluss oder erschrockenlichen wassers Des XXIIII. jars auß natürlicher art des hymels zu besorgen mit sambt außlegung der grossen Wunderzaichen zu Wien in Osterreych erschinen, des XX iars.* ([Augsburg]: [Erhard Oeglin (Heirs)], [1520]). VD16 S 5396. See also the critical edition: Alexander Seitz, *Sämtliche Schriften*,

that would be the worst since Noah's time, perhaps also bringing the end of the world. To lend greater weight to his predictions, Seitz presented his dire warnings as grounded in the art of astronomy and recent celestial portents. In the first half of the pamphlet, Seitz argued that even the rainbow, which attested to the divine promise never to destroy the earth again by a flood, was itself no guarantee that divine punishment would not be visited with water.[43] He then appealed both to Scripture and to Ptolemy, among other authorities, to argue that astronomers can indeed recognize future events. As an example, he cited a *practica* by Johann Virdung of Hassfurt that had correctly predicted the death of Emperor Maximilian.

In the second half of the pamphlet, Seitz pointed to recent portents, especially at Vienna, that were indications of the worse disaster to come. Importantly, Seitz interpreted the portents through historical correlations. At the time of Emperor Henry IV and the Investiture controversy, for instance, similar portents were reported, and the strife between pope and Emperor led Henry to replace Gregory VII.[44] The pamphlet's title page woodcut also added to the sense of impending disaster (Figure 6).[45] The upper half shows the recent portents at Vienna – multiple suns, rainbows, and the moon in a cross – as well as the seven-headed dragon from Revelation 12:3. The lower half shows the ark upon the waters with the world destroyed. The difference from Noah's time is that fire and brimstone fall from the sky; a comet is also visible, as well as a dragon's head. The aim of the pamphlet was to cause panic, and Seitz was apparently successful.[46]

Carion directed his response at the first half of Seitz's pamphlet, which dealt with the 1524 flood. As for the portents at Vienna, Carion noted at the end of the *Prognosticatio* that these events were naturally occurring, and he promised to address them in a separate tract, which has not survived or was never written.[47] Carion divided the *Prognosticatio* material into a series of distinct, but still interlocking, sections:

---

    vol. 2, ed. Peter Ukena (Berlin: Walter de Gruyter, 1975), 56–69, with description of the editions at 424–456.

43 Talkenberger, *Sintflut*, 188.

44 "Zů der zeit Kayser Hainrichs des iiij. schwebet ob der Sonnen ain grosser Throm / do erstůnd groß durchechtu[n]g / durch vnainigkeit Kaysers vn[d] Bapsts. Der kayser satzt wider den bapst Gregoriu[m] ain andern bapst." Seitz, *Ain Warnung* (Augsburg, 1520), sig. [v] v.

45 One printer eventually combined Carion's *Prognosticatio* with Seitz's image – VD16 C 1032.

46 See Talkenberger, *Sintflut*, 190–192.

47 "Es seyen ettliche gesicht gesehen worden als iij. Sonnen / regenbogen / prinnent balcken / circkel vnd des dinges vill die hierinn keyn bedeutnuß haben. Wie nun die naturlich geborn werden wil ich kürtzlich ein tractat euch geben / tzutzeyten seyen sie etzlicher würckligkeyt vnd bedeutnuß / tzutzeyten auch gar keyner. Nach dem vnd dann würcken

FIGURE 7
Johann Carion, *Prognosticatio* (Leipzig, 1521)
HERZOG AUGUST BIBLIOTHEK
WOLFENBÜTTEL: 57 QUOD 4°

Prognosticatio vnd er=||klerung der grossen wesserung / Auch anderer erschrockenlichenn || würckungen. So sich begeben nach Christi vnsers lieben hern || geburt / Funfftzehen hundert vn[d] xxiiij. Jar. Durch mich || Magistru[m] Joha[n]nem Carion vo[n] Buetikaym Chur||fürstlicher gnaden tzu Brandenburg Astrono||mu[m] mit fleyssiger arbeit tzusame[n] gebracht. || Gantz erbermlich tzulesen / in nutz vn[d] || warnung aller Christglaubi=||gen menschen &c.

1. Rhymed Allegorical Verses   [Ai]v – Aij v
2. Explication (*Erklerung*)   Aiij r – Aiij v
3. Prophecy (*Weyssagung*)
    Introduction on Astronomy   Aiij v – [Aiiij]r
    From the Comet of 1521 down to 1524   [Aiiij]r – [Aiiij]v
    1524 Deluge   [Aiiij]v – Bij r
        Celestial events in 1524
        The Deluge

---

die wolken vnd andre corperliche ding des hymels / von wegen ires entzwischensatz Son vnd erdrichs &c." Carion, *Prognosticatio* (Leipzig, 1521), sig. [B iiij] r.

	Response to Alexander Seitz	
	Historical examples	
	Aftermath of the 1524 Deluge	
	Influence and meaning of the 1524	Bij r – Bij v
	planetary conjunction for religion and politics	
4.	Birth of the "Antichrist" (*Geburt des Endchrist*)	Bij v – [Biiij]r
	Birth of the Antichrist in 1693	
	Upheavals of 1789	
	Prophecy of the Last Emperor	
5.	Divine Invocation (*Gotlich anruffung*)	[Biiij]r
6.	Note on Portents at Vienna	[Biiij]r

Carion did not deny that the coming flood would be a great deluge, but he rejected Seitz's predictive methodology and the dire warning he had announced. The *Prognosticatio* opens with rhymed allegorical verses in which the characters stand for the planets. The verses tell a story that explains the sequence of celestial events from 1521 to 1524, and an explication (*Erklerung*) of their celestial correlation follows. Image, poetry and allegory then give way to explicit prose explanation. Carion briefly defended the arts of astrology and astronomy, and he lamented their improper use. He then outlined again the celestial events from 1521 to 1524, culminating in the flood, which would take place between 1 February and 3 March. Carion described the deluge as equivalent to nothing that had previously been seen.[48] The repercussions would continue long after the rain had stopped, and the winter of that year would be so harsh that even the birds would try to come indoors.[49]

Carion countered Seitz's claim that the flood would be the worst since Noah by turning to historical astronomy. Seitz had used history when discussing the

---

48 "Aber ich wil glauben das von sölcher obgemelter wesserung biß hieher / keyn grössere wesserung sich begeben hab / dann sich ietzunt in dem xxiiij. iar begeben wirt. Welche dann nimbt iren volkummen anfang auff den ersten tag des Hornungs weret biß auff den dritten tag des Martzens / vertzeucht sich tzu tzeyten ein wenig / als ein tag oder halben vnd facht bald wider an." Carion, *Prognosticatio* (Leipzig, 1521), sig. Bij r.

49 "Vnnd von sölcher vberflüssigkeyt des wassers / werden verschleyfft ecker / wisen / und ligende güter / vnd in nachuolgenden iarn nicht frucht bringen. Darauß groß hunger vnd not armen leuten entsteen wirt / vnd von solcher vberflüssigkeyt der grossen wesserung / wirt das erdrich also mit bösen dunsten vmbgeben / das durch die Summerlichen würckligkeyt der Sonnen / auff den Herbst des selben Jars. Ein eylender tzufelliger / vnd süchtiger sterben kummen wirt / vnd der winter gar hefftig kalt. Das yr etlich sagenn das die vogel des lufffts / werden suchen die wonung der menschen / von grosser kelten wegen." Carion, *Prognosticatio* (Leipzig, 1521), sig. Bij r.

meaning of portents to kindle greater apprehension. In contrast, Carion used history in a consoling way by pointing to the occurrence of even greater floods at earlier conjunctions. Carion focused on the conjunction in 618 and the ensuing floods in Italy, but he actually conflated events in 589–590 with 618, including the election of Pope Gregory the Great (590), so the chronology is confused.[50] Chronological problems aside, Carion used the earlier astronomical moment and the subsequent events to refute the claim that the 1524 flood would be the greatest disaster since Noah. The *Prognosticatio* indicates that Carion valued the role history could play in contemporary interpretation, and even if he had not yet decided to write the *Chronicle*, already by this time, he might have been assembling historical materials.

In the *Prognosticatio*, Carion also spoke of the 1524 conjunctions in relation to religion and politics. He foresaw great changes and reformation in the Christian Church during 1524. Both that year and the next would also see a great outpouring of Christian blood.[51] After addressing immediate concerns, Carion turned to more distant events by melding astronomy with the medieval prophecies of Pierre d'Ailly, Hildegard of Bingen, Joachim of Fiore and pseudo-Methodius. Using these sources, he wove together a description of the period from the birth of the Antichrist (*Endchrist*) in 1693 to the great upheavals that would take place in 1789.[52] Drawing especially on pseudo-Methodius, a seventh century Syrian writer, Carion continued with the prophecy of the Last Emperor who would journey to Jerusalem and lay down his crown at Calvary,

---

50   Carion, *Prognosticatio* (Leipzig, 1521), sig. B v – Bij r. See Fricke-Hilgers, "Die Sintflutprognose" (1989/90), 56–57.

51   "Auch ist leyder solcher tzusamenfügung wurckung vnd bedeutnuß nicht allein in wasser / als gesagt ist. Sonder auch wie oben angetzeygt / tzwitracht vnd vneinigkeyt der geystlichen vnd weltlichen / Auch dartzu ein gantze veranderung vnd reformation der Christlichen kirchen. Jn dem selben vnd nachuolgenden Jar / vnd grosses blutuorgiessens Christenliches volckes...." Carion, *Prognosticatio* (Leipzig, 1521), sig. Bij r – Bij v.

52   "Vnd von der geburt Christi vnsers seligmachers .i.M.vi.C. vnd drey vnd neuntzig Jar. Wo sich dann wirt begeben eyne von den grösten coniunctionibus vnd wirt ein gantze erfullung tzehen Saturnischer vm weltzung. Welches nach Christi vnsers liben hern geburt Tausent siben hundert vnd lxxxix. Jar gar geendet wirt.... O dann werden grosse wunderbarliche geschichten geschehen von enderungen / wanderungen vnd tzerstörungen / beforder in den gesatzen vnd seckten Christenlicher ordnung." Carion, *Prognosticatio* (Leipzig, 1521), sig. Biij r. See also Fricke-Hilgers, "Die Sintflutprognose" (1999), 280 n. 28. Carion does mention that Pierre d'Ailly had made a similar prediction regarding 1789, see Fricke-Hilgers, "Die Sintflutprognose" (1999), 292; and Fricke-Hilgers, "Die Sintflutprognose" (1989/90), 40.

an event that was to usher in the last days and the return of Christ.[53] The pamphlet ends with a plea for divine mercy.

Not surprisingly, some sixteenth century interpreters, with the benefit of hindsight, saw the literature on the conjunctions of 1524 as foretelling the Peasants' War.[54] The deluge then became the destruction from the war, which began in 1524, peaked in 1525, and continued to some extent into 1526. Likewise, Carion's prediction for 1789 was never entirely forgotten. Notably, Johann Christoph Adelung (1732–1806), an Enlightenment linguist and biographer, included Carion in his *Geschichte der menschlichen Narrheit* (1787), designating him as a "Sterndeuter."[55] In his biographical entry, Adelung presented Carion as an astrologer and charlatan, dismissing and ridiculing his prophecies and predictions. Writing from Saxony in 1787, Adelung noted how Carion would soon be proven a liar once again, since 1789 was fast approaching, and for that year, the "fool" had predicted the upheaval of the entire world.[56] Adelung also dismissed another ridiculous prediction Carion had made in his *Bedeutnus und Offenbarung* (1526), the rise of the Hohenzollerns to the Imperial throne.[57]

4 A Second Flood Prediction

The next record of Carion occurs in 1525, and it is unclear, but the event might have been a colophon to the flood predictions for 1524. The incident is known

---

53   For this prophecy generally, see Paul J. Alexander, "The Medieval Legend of the Last Roman Emperor and Its Messianic Origin," *Journal of the Warburg and Courtauld Institutes* 41 (1978): 1–15.
54   See Fürst, *Johann Carion*, 12.
55   Adelung, *Geschichte*, 110–147.
56   "Noch unbarmherziger sollte es in dem Jahre 1789 ergehen; das sollte das schrecklichste unter allen seyn, indem in demselben große und wunderbare Geschichte, Veränderungen und Zerstörungen vorfallen würden. Allein, so sehr sich der Narr in Ansehung des 1693sten Jahres betrogen hat, so sehr wird er vermuthlich auch 1789 zum Lügner werden." Adelung, *Geschichte*, 118.
57   On this prophecy, see Franz Kampers, *Die deutsche Kaiseridee in Prophetie und Sage* (München: Lüneburg, 1896), 145; Adelung, *Geschichte*, 116; Fricke-Hilgers, "Die Sintflutprognose" (1989/90), 34 n. 4. The contemporary interpretation was given as: "Der rote Adler wirt steigen in Eeren / vnnd wirdt mit hilff zwayer guldenen Löwen Eere erlangen / vnd ain schartzer Püffels kopff / vnd ain roter Greiff in ainem weissen felde / werden jm anhangen. Das ist / ain Marggraff zů Brandenburg / der wirt zů grossen Eeren kommen / mit hülff der Herren zů Braunschweig / Pomern / vnd Mechelnburg." Johann Carion, *Außlegung der verborgenen Weissagung / Doctor Johannis Carionis / von verenderung vnd zůfelligem glück / der höchsten Potentaten des Römischen Reichs* ([Augsburg]: [Otmar], 1546), sig. C iij r. VD16 C 952.

only from Peter Hafftiz († 1601), a Brandenburg chronicler, who included an account in his unpublished *Microchronologicum* of 1595.[58] The report first appeared in print as an excerpt in *Historical Description of Electoral and Mark Brandenburg* (1751), in a section on famous thunderstorms.[59] In his chronicle, Hafftiz related that for 15 July 1525 an astronomer, presumably Carion, had secretly warned the Elector of Brandenburg about horrible weather and a huge flood, which might even destroy the two cities of Berlin and Kölln. As a precaution, the Elector, his wife and part of their retinue took refuge on top of the Tempelhofer Berg; but eventually, the pious Electress encouraged her husband to return to his people and suffer with them whatever the will of God might be. In the evening, they rode back to the Schloß in Kölln. On the way, however, harsh weather did indeed come up, and as they drove through the castle gate, lightning struck their horses and the coachman.[60] Although Hafftiz does not mention Carion by name, he is likely the *astronomus* who gave this advice to the Elector, and the account is sometimes cited as an example of Carion's influence as a Renaissance court astrologer.[61]

---

58 See Fricke-Hilgers, "Die Sintflutprognose" (1999), 279 n. 24; Benning, "Johannes Carion," 196; and Fürst, *Johann Carion (1499–1537)*, 9.

59 Johann Christoph Becmann and Bernhard Ludwig Beckmann, *Historische Beschreibung der Chur und Mark Brandenburg* (Berlin: Christian Friedrich Voß, 1751), vol. 1, Part 3, Chapter 1, section xv: *Naturgeschichte der Mark Brandenburg – Von dem zustand der Luft, unterschieden Luftzeichen und würkungen derselben – Große Donnerwetter: merckwürdige exempel vom Blitz.*

60 "Vor andern ist merkwürdig was sich besage Haftitii erzehlung Anno 1525. den 15 Jul. zu Berlin mit Churfürst Joachimo I. begeben. Diesem hatte ein Astronomus heimlich gewarnet, daß an demselben tag ein groß Wetter würde kommen, und wäre zubesorgen, beide Stäte Berlin und Kölln möchten untergehen. Ist also mit seiner Gemahlin, der jungen Herrschafft und vornemsten Bedienten auf den Tempelhofischen berg gezogen, um die begebenheit der beiden Stäte abzuwarten. Als er aber sich lange da aufgehalten, und nichts daraus worden, hat ihn seine Gemahlin, wie sie dann eine sehr Gottesfürchtige und Christliche Fürstin gewesen, gebeten, daß er möchte wieder hineinziehen, und bei seinen armen Unterthanen auswarten, was GOtt thun wollte, weil sie es vielleicht nicht allein verschuldet, darüber er bewogen, und um 4 Uhr gegen abend wieder gen Kölln gefahren. Ehe er aber an das Schloß gelanget, hat sich ein Wetter bewiesen, und wie er unter das Schloßthor gekommen, dem Churfürsten 4 Pferde vor dem wagen samt dem Kutscher erschlagen, iedoch sonst keinen schaden mehr gethan." Becmann, *Historische Beschreibung der Chur und Mark Brandenburg* (1751), vol. 1, col. 509–510.

61 See Lynn Thorndike, *A History of Magic and Experimental Science*, vol. 5, *The Sixteenth Century* (New York: Columbia University Press, 1941), 202; and drawing on Thorndike, Robin Barnes, *Prophecy and Gnosis: Apocalypticism in the Wake of the Lutheran Reformation* (Stanford: Stanford University Press, 1988), 143.

5   Natural Art of Astrology

In 1526, what proved to be Carion's most popular pamphlet, *Bedeutnus und Offenbarung wahrer himmlischer Influxion*, was published at Augsburg, Nuremberg, and perhaps Frankfurt an der Oder;[62] but the printers may have issued it without Carion's consent and against his wishes. In a cover letter to Christoph Rigler, a priest in Mainz, Carion wrote that he had prepared the text for Rigler's personal use, and he cautioned that the material should not be printed, since common people would not understand it.[63] Throughout his career, Carion repeatedly stressed the professional, mathematical nature of his work, and in his letter to Rigler, he lamented the prophecies in circulation that were based on nothing more than inner musings. He recognized that printers, not just the prophets, were to blame, and he expressed disgust with those printers who published useless prognostications but made the title pages so intriguing that readers felt compelled to buy them.[64] Whether Carion genuinely intended *Bedeutnus und Offenbarung* to remain unprinted is questionable. Nevertheless,

---

62 Johann Carion, *Bedeütnusz vnnd Offenbarung / warer Hymlischer Jnfluxion / des Hocherfarnen Magistri Johannis Carionis Buetikaimensis / Churfürstlicher gnaden vo[n] Brandenburg &c. Mathematici / von Jarn zů Jaren werende / biß man schreybt. M.D.vn[d] xxxx. jar. Alle Landtschafft / Stende vnd einflüß clarlich betreffend.* ([Augsburg]: [Philipp Ulhart d.Ä.], 1526). VD16 C 962. A 1527 edition of the pamphlet is reprinted with an introduction in Dietmar Fürst and Jürgen Hamel, eds., *Johann Carion (1499–1537): Der erste Berliner Astronom mit einem Reprint der Schrift Carions "Bedeutnuss und Offenbarung" (1527)* (Berlin-Treptow: Archenhold-Sternwarte, 1988).

63 "Darumb Wirdiger vnd Andechtiger Herr / hab ich euch nit weniger als meynen vater / der jr euch an mir vnd den meinen väterlich erzaigt / diß prognostication zů sonderlichen willen / für euch gemacht. Deßhalben nit von nöten ist / solchs in druck zůbringen / dann sachen / so da auß ainem grund geen / soll man nit mit der menge vnter die vnuerstendigen werffen / sondern zů nutz vnd warnung für sich behalten. Wie vnd auch Orpheus seine Ceremonien verbarg...." Carion, *Bedeütnusz vnnd Offenbarung* (Augsburg, 1526), sig. Aij r.

64 "Es geen hin vnd wider / ja allenthalben in disen vnsern Jaren / Propheceyen vnnd Weyssagung auß / yetz von disem / dann von ihenem / Ettlich auß aygnem gůtduncken / derselbigen schreyber oder Propheten / Auch etlich auß ainem grund / der doch bißher wenig gesehen sein / Deßhalben ich es dafür hab / das sy die Bůchdrucker selbs etwann erdichten / also vnter das volck für Newe mär außgiessen / vnd blasen solche Propheceyen hoch auff / vnd geben jnen ain solchen waydelichen vnd dapffern Tittel / das der leser so er die anfichtig wirdt nit wol vnderlassen kan / můß aine kauffen / Vnd so er dann in die materi kompt / ist es mit ainem quarck versigelt / vnd etwann die vorred lenger / dann das gantz werck dauon der Tittel lautend ist." Carion, *Bedeütnusz vnnd Offenbarung* (Augsburg, 1526), sig. [Aj] r.

FIGURE 8
Johann Carion, *Bedeütnusz vnnd Offenbarung* (Augsburg, 1526)
HERZOG AUGUST BIBLIOTHEK
WOLFENBÜTTEL: A: 44.10
ASTRON. (15)

he repeatedly denied authorizing its release, and all the editions from 1526 omit both the publisher and place of publication.[65]

The *editio princeps* of the pamphlet has a title page image (Figure 8), in the form of a horoscope, of the heavens at the beginning of the world. Instead of a name and birth date, at the centre is a battle scene (*Figura celi tempore principij mundi*). Before his annual predictions, Carion inserted an "Admonition to all Christian Rulers" in which he explicitly placed himself in the tradition of Old Testament prophecy. He quoted at length from Habakkuk, and argued that the prophet's words were just as fitting then as they had been in Old Testament times, since the Turkish Sultan and king of Babylon were so similar in their oppression of the true believers.[66] Carion then launched, humbly but forcefully,

---

65   The cover letter is dated 1 December 1526: "Datum Berlin / Sonnabent nach Katharine / Anno &c. M.D.XXVI." Carion, *Bedeütnusz vnnd Offenbarung* (Augsburg, 1526), sig. Aij v.
66   "Darumb auch die Prophecey Abacuc / nit allain den Babilonischen künig / sonder soll vnd mag auch auff dise vnser zeyt / dem Türckischen Kayser wol vergleichet werden / Dann ye der Prophet anfechtung der rechtglaubigen verkündet / welche in dem alten Testament die Juden waren / vnd yetzundt wir Christen. / dann der recht glaub vnd das Euangelion / ye vnd ye von anfang vorfolgung leyden müß / Darumb hab ich die wort

into an admonition for peace among Christian rulers.[67] He used a story to illustrate the situation then facing Europe: a frog and mouse sat on the banks of a river and each one tried to force the other to come into his dwelling, the one into the water the other onto the land, though the place would be contrary to his natural habitation. As they argued and fought over what to do, a stork snatched them both up and devoured them.[68] From Carion's perspective, the same fate might befall Europe if the Christian princes remain divided in the face of the Turkish threat.

In the pamphlet, the yearly entries from 1527 to 1540 follow a set pattern: astronomical information, predictions in general, predictions for different geographical regions, and specific predictions for different social groups.[69] Of these annual entries, Carion's remarks for 1529 were perhaps the most ominous and certainly the most controversial. After the Ottoman Turks defeated the Hungarian army at Mohács in 1526, Europeans feared, rightly, that the Turks would seek to expand their control over the Balkans. In these circumstances, predicting conflict with the Turks was almost inevitable, but Carion's approach was unique. Instead of foretelling constant wars with the Ottomans, or continual border skirmishes, he singled out 1529 as the year when Austria would

---

Abacuc des propheten / wie sy in seinem aygen bůch beschriben lautend / vnd von ainem rechuerstendigen verteutscht...." Carion, *Bedeütnusz vnnd Offenbarung* (Augsburg, 1526), sig. Aij v – Aiij r.

67 "...Nit das ich mein mainung / über ewer so hochuerstendige vernünfften vnd weyßhaiten preyse / denselben ewern hohen verstanden zů ratten / der ich doch dem wenigsten vnter euch zů kainem fůßtůch wirdig / můß geschweygen ain radgeber.... Darumb jr Chrstenliche Künig / vnd jr edlen Fürsten / nempt an euch in disem jamer / ain milten vnd eintrechtigklichen fryden / vnd lassend Creütz vnnd Creütz gegen ainander nit fechten / Ain Christ dem andern entgegen / Lernet dieweyl vns die zeyt so grewlich ansicht / milt / gütig / vnd barmhertzig zůsein / Nempt behaltet vnd schützet was ewer ist / vnd was nitt ewer / so handthabend / helffend vnnd beschirment / dem / dem es zů erretten vnd behalten gehört / dann der ärmest vnter euch ye seins leybs narung etwann hatt / dann der gayst weniger weltlicher gůtter / aber der leyb das gegentayl allweg begerend ist." Carion, *Bedeütnusz vnnd Offenbarung* (Augsburg, 1526), sig. [Aiiij] r.

68 "Deß zů ainem beyspyl will ich euch ain gleychnuß sagen / Es begab sich auf ain zeyt / bey ainem bach oder fluß / das ain Frosch vnd ain Mauß mit ainander kriegten vnd zancketen / ye aines das ander zwingende / das es mit jm in sein wonung solt / Die mauß in das wasser / vnd der Frosch auff das land / das doch jrer bayder natur entgegen was / wurden der sach ains / vnd bunden sich mitt ainem faden zůsamen / vnd solt yetlichs ziehen / welches das ander in sein wonung zug vnd schlept / da solt es bleyben. Jn dem als sy kriegten / Ersach das ain Storck / vnd nam sy bayde hinweg / můßten also dise bayde krieger / yetlichs sein wonung verlassen / vnd darzů gefressen werden." Carion, *Bedeütnusz vnnd Offenbarung* (Augsburg, 1526), sig. [Aiiij] v.

69 See the description in Fürst, *Johann Carion*, 12–13.

"weep and grieve over Hungary."[70] Carion did not offer a more specific explanation, but the obvious implication was that in 1529 the Turks would overrun Hungary and threaten Austria.

6   The Dispute with Andreas Perlach

Because of the alarm Carion's predications were creating in Austria, Andreas Perlach (1490–1551), an astronomer and physician from Slovenia, attempted to reassure the Viennese by challenging Carion's reliability.[71] In the late 1520s, Perlach was working to enhance his reputation at the University of Vienna, and through a series of attacks on Carion, he sought to ingratiate himself at the court of the Hapsburg Archduke Ferdinand. In response to Carion's *Bedeutnus und Offenbarung*, Perlach published his *Ephemerides for the year 1529* and dedicated the text to the Archduke.[72]

In the *Ephemerides*, Perlach predicted illnesses, lootings and killings, as well as conflicts for the Viennese during 1529. Even so, his forecast was not as frightful as Carion's "grieving over Hungary."[73] In the *Ephemerides*, Perlach specifically attacked Carion's *Bedeutnus und Offenbarung* by arguing that the analysis of the celestial configurations for 1529 was erroneous. Perlach dissected Carion's interpretation of the lunar eclipse predicted for 1529, and he tried, not necessarily with success, to reconstruct Carion's interpretive methods and show that his predictions contradicted both Ptolemaic authority and recent experience.[74] Perlach argued that because Carion's predictions were based on slipshod methodology, they were wrong with regard to the effects caused, the locations affected, and the timing of those effects.[75]

In late 1529, Carion responded to Perlach's rebuke by revising his *Bedeutnus und Offenbarung*. He extended the text down to 1550 and dedicated this new, authorized edition to Electoral Prince Joachim.[76] In his preface, Carion

---

70   "Vnnd Ostereych wirdt waynen / vnd sich bekümmern mit Vngern." Carion, *Bedeütnusz vnnd Offenbarung* (Augsburg, 1526), sig. [Biiij] r.
71   For the discussion of Perlach, I have relied especially on Darin Hayton, "Astrology as Political Propaganda: Humanist Responses to the Turkish Threat in Early Sixteenth-Century Vienna," *Austrian History Yearbook* 38 (2007): 61–91.
72   The text is VD16 P 1445. I rely on the description in Hayton, "Astrology as Political Propaganda."
73   Hayton, "Astrology as Political Propaganda," 85.
74   Hayton, "Astrology as Political Propaganda," 86–87.
75   Hayton, "Astrology as Political Propaganda," 87.
76   The dedication is dated 28 December 1529, so the revised editions started to circulate in 1530. The new material is included in the Wittenberg edition of 1530 (VD16 ZV 17958). After

described the circumstances that compelled him to reissue the work, and he stressed that the original text was published without his consent.[77] To counter his critics, Carion pointed to his success in predicting the events of the later 1520s, especially the Sack of Rome in 1527 and the Siege of Vienna in 1529.[78] He also prided himself on the way the princes took his "Admonition" from 1526 to heart and drove back the Turks.[79] Against the accusations of Perlach,[80]

    1531, the title of the pamphlet consistently changes to *Bedeutnus und Offenbarung wahrer himmlischer Influentz*, and the material prior to 1530 is omitted: Johann Carion, *Bedeutnus vnd Offenbarung warer hymlischer jnfluentz des hocherfarnen Magistri Johannis Carionis Bütickheymensis C.F.G. von Brandenburg Mathematici / von jaren zů jarn werende / Biß man schreibt. 1550. Jar / alle Landschafft Stände vnnd einfluß / klerlich betreffendt. Gebessert vnnd verlengt mit anhang einer verborgnen Prophecey / auch Johannis Carionis.* ([Augsburg]: [Heinrich Steiner], 1531). VD16 C 972.

77   "Der wegen gnediger Herr / würd ich auff das newe bewegt zů ehern E.F.G. vnd nutz sunst aller menschen mein Prognostication / so ich vngefar vor vier jarenn gemacht / die dannocht on meinenwillen in den truck kam / vnd yetz auff das new hinder meinem ruck getruckt / mit anhang etlicher loser fratzen / Lolharts / Brigite / Methodij &c. denen ich all meyn leben lang gram gewesen / Vnd darzů gehen sie auß kainem grund / hette derhalben wol mügen leydenn / so sie ye mein Practick trucken hetten wöllen / das sie es bey meinen worten bleiben hetten lassen dörfftenn mir weder München / Nolbrüder oder Nonnen treüm hinein schreiben. Diß alles zů confutierenn würd ich geraitzt die zůuerbessern vnd verlengen / biß man screiben würde nach der Gepurt Christi Fünfftzehenhundert / vnd fünfftzig jar / wer als dann leben wirdt / mag die weyter erstrecken." Carion, *Bedeutnus vnd Offenbarung* (Augsburg, 1531), sig. Aij r – Aij v.

78   "Vnd wiewol ich doch in diser Prognostication vast vberall die maynung inn warhait getroffen / befoder inn dem / was schaden vnd erschrecken Jtalia vnd Rom im 1527. Jar haben werden / wie jhm 1528. Jar der falschen vnd erdichten pündtnus halben yhn Hessen / gar nahe ein mörderische aufrůr worden war / who man ym nicht durch fromer leut rath fürkommen were. Auch in vergangnen 1529. Jar / mit des Türcken zůkunfft / vnd mit der greülichen weheklagung Wien / Ofen / vnd anderen vmbligenden Vngerischen vnd Osterreichischen Stetten / Schlössern vnd Flecken / Auch das Mayland in dem selben Jar erst wyderumb dem Römischen Reych gegeben würde / vnd in sein rechte hand komen / vnd zwischen Kay. May. vnd dem Künig in Franckreich fryden gemacht / vnd das Kay. May. in Italia ehr vnnd würdin erzaigt werden / vnnd Florentz mit sampt andern stetten beschwerung haben &c." Carion, *Bedeutnus vnd Offenbarung* (Augsburg, 1531), sig. [Aiiij] r.

79   "Aber eins wolt ich dannoch / vnnd gebe mein rock darumb / das die Fürsten Teutscher nation mein meinung zu oren genummen vnd zu hertzen gezogen hetten / inn dem das ich die so trewlich vnnd hertzlich vor vier Jaren zu jnen allen schrib / vnnd sie so trewlich ermanet dem Türcken bey zeyt durch jr aller lieb vnnd einigkeyt fürzůkommen...." Carion, *Bedeutnus vnd Offenbarung* (Augsburg, 1531), sig. [Aiiij] v.

80   "Noch dannocht hab ich unangefochten nicht bleyben künden / sonder einer der sich nennet Andreas Perlachius von Wien hat wider mich schriben / vnnd mich nicht mit geryngen scheltworten gegenn Künigklicher May. vonn Vngern vnnd Behem geschmehet / wellicher mir entgegen / vnnd den von Wyen / frewd / fryd vnd glückliche zeyt verkündet / Eben da sie layder Gott erparm es mit allen engsten vnd nötten vmbfangen waren. Doch wie dem allen / welchem vnder vns bayden die warhait haimfellet / laß ich E.F.G.

Carion defended his predications by emphasizing the orderly, professional nature of his work, and he offered to supply more detailed information about his methodology:

> Indeed, anyone who is halfway competent in astronomy sees that this little book is not written without a sound basis, and that my interpretation and explication hold to an orderly process drawn from valid principles. If, however, anyone wants to ask me, then I will provide complete information and gladly share my reasoning.[81]

The issue was important. While Carion provided a discussion of the anticipated celestial events for each year, in *Bedeutnus und Offenbarung* he did not clearly explain the steps he used to reach specific, as opposed to general, predictions. Despite the criticism from Vienna, Carion did not avoid Hapsburg issues, and for 1548, he foretold the possibility of the Emperor's death.[82] He also predicted that a false prophet would arise in 1547. Margrave Johann of Brandenburg-Küstrin (r. 1535–1571), another son of Elector Joachim I, later applied this prediction to the Augsburg Interim, the religious settlement imposed by Emperor Charles V on the Protestants after their defeat in the Schmalkaldic War.[83]

---

vnnd alle Ständ erkennenn / wolt aber dannoch das ich gelogen vnd er war gesagt hette / were Kü. Maye. von Vngern &c. vnd der selben armen vnderthon vil leidlicher / Achte aber derhalben getachter Perlach / habe sich mehr geschendet / vnd verachtet dann ich jme ymmer aufflegen möchte / will das also jm zu lon vnd newen Jar geschenckt / vnnd hiemit verantwort haben / gegen E.F.G. vnd sunst aller menigklich &c." Carion, *Bedeutnus vnd Offenbarung* (Augsburg, 1531), sig. [Aiiij] r – [Aiiij] v.

81 "Es sicht doch ein yeder halb erfarner inn Astronomia / das diß büchlin one ein sonderlich grundt nicht geschryben ist / vnnd das mein außlegen vnnd bedeutnus eynen ordenlichen proces auß rechten fundamenten halten / Will aber einen yedenn der mich fragen wirt / allen beschayd vnnd ursach gern mitthailen vnd sagen." Carion, *Bedeutnus vnd Offenbarung* (Augsburg, 1531), sig. [Aiiij] r.

82 "Der Römisch Keyser wirdt in disem jar vnderligen / vnnd seines leybs grosse schwachheyt bekommen / vnd als zů besorgen den tod. Andere Fürsten vnd herren werden auch nicht inn sunderlichem glück erhalten." Carion, *Bedeutnus vnd Offenbarung* (Augsburg, 1531), sig. [Fiiij] v – G r.

83 "Vnd die Sonn wirdt yres scheines auf zehenthalb punct vonn oben herab beraubt / auff Sonabend nach Martini nach mittag vmb 1. vnd 58. minut / im 30. grad des Scorpions / vnd gehet die Sonn inn den erstenn puncten des Wydders auff den 11. tag Martij vor mittag vmb 8. vnd 29. minut ist der 12. grad des Zwillings in dem Ascendenten / welche Constellationes vns samptlich bedeuten / das da werde komen ein grosser feynd der Christen / welchen man kein vntrew vertrauwen werde. Aber er wirt der vil brauchen vnd vben vnder dem scheyn des gůten / wie vns dann die collocation Saturni scheyn barlich antzaygt." Carion, *Bedeutnus vnd Offenbarung* (Augsburg, 1531), sig. Fiij v. See Benning, "Johannes Carion," 198–199; Münch, "Das Chronicon," 203–204.

In 1531, the dispute between the astronomers of Berlin and Vienna intensified when Perlach published a direct attack on Carion.[84] In 1530, Perlach had issued a new *Ephemerides for the year 1531*, which again sought to undermine Carion for his supposed failure to understand the effects of lunar eclipses.[85] The following year brought an unexpected celestial event, as Halley's Comet returned to the sky that August. In November, Perlach wrote a pamphlet on the meaning of the comet, and he used the opportunity to lodge even more serious accusations against Carion.[86] In his two *Ephemerides*, Perlach had called into question Carion's competence as an astrologer; in *The Comet of 1531*, he shifted tactics by accusing Carion of using black magic.

In the new pamphlet, Perlach set up a contrast between his own predictions, based on the natural art of astrology, and Carion's, which must derive from "unnatural arts," since they did not agree with standard astrological practice. As before, Perlach demonstrated point by point how the revised *Bedeutnus und Offenbarung* made basic errors in astrology. Furthermore, not only was Carion's method faulty, his failure to provide clear astrological explanations indicated that he had something to hide: his reliance on unnatural arts and occult, rather than astrological, sources.[87] In fact, Perlach traced Carion's predictions to his use of books by the late fifteenth century hermit Pelagius of Majorca:

> Indeed, I am entirely convinced that he has taken his predictions from the books of Master Pelagius, the hermit of Majorca, concerning the conjuring of spirits. For one such book was transcribed in Berlin and then brought to Austria with all the accessories [for divination]; indeed, I have seen it with my own eyes. As Ptolemy indicates, in earlier times there were certain people associated with arts like these, and they

---

84   Hayton, "Astrology as Political Propaganda," 84–85.
85   Hayton, "Astrology as Political Propaganda," 88.
86   Andreas Perlach, *Des Cometen vn[d] ander erscheinung in den lüfften / Jm XXXI. Jar gesehenn bedütung Durch Andreen Perlach von Witschein / der sibenn freyen / vnd natürlichen kunst maister / Diser zeyt auff der löbliche[n] hohen schůl zů Wien / in der Astronomey / was die himlische[n] leüff würckung vnd jre einflüß betreffen ist / verordenter Läser. Darbey auch ein anzaigung / das Charion seine Judicia nicht auß der natürliche[n] kunst Astrologia gemacht hat*. ([Nuremberg]: [Johann Stuchs], [1531]). VD16 P 1448.
87   "So hab ich alzeyt in meinen Juditijs / disen prauch gehabt / das ich an natrülich vrsach / nichts hab wöllen schreiben vnd an tag geben / da mit ein yetlicher ab nem / das ich mich allain des grundts der natürlichen kunst Astrologia genant behilff / vnd kainer andern / darumb kainer mein Juditia / vergleichen sol / gegen des Charion/ welcher nit auß dem grundt / der natürlichen kunst Astrologia / sonder auß ainer andern / die er villeicht nit melden darff / genomen hat...." Perlach, *Des Cometen... bedütung* (1531), sig. [Aij] r.

claimed that they derived their predictions from astrology, even though – as with Carion – they had no proper grounding in it.[88]

The charge against Carion was not without basis. Well before Carion's arrival, Elector Joachim I had developed interests not just in mathematical astrology but also in the occult. The potential connection between Pelagius and Berlin comes through Johannes Trithemius (1463–1516), who claimed to be a student of Pelagius's disciple Libanius Gallus.[89] Pelagius and Libanius are obscure figures at best, and at worst inventions of Trithemius.[90] Trithemius was for many years the abbot of Sponheim, near Bad Kreuznach, and in later life he became abbot of St. James's Abbey in Würzburg. He was a prolific scholar, a forger of histories and a student of the occult. Elector Joachim I had been one of abbot's most important patrons; and during 1505–1506, Trithemius spent several months at the Hohenzollern court. Thus, it is entirely plausible that books by Pelagius, whether real or forgeries, had made their way into the Electoral library in Berlin.

---

[88] "Die weyl aber sein Juditia / bey solcher vnwissenhait nichts dester weniger zůtreten / vnd sich also begeben / vnd er den rechten grundt der Astrologey nit kan / welcher wil also vnnuerstendig sein / vnd sprechen / er habs auß der natürlichen kunst Astrologia / muß auch von nöten folgen das er seine Juditia / auß einer andern kunst nympt / vnd vermaint es sein auff allen vniuersitetn̅ lauter narren / man wür sein vnwissenhait vnd vnuerstandt in der kunst Astrologia nit spürn / oder auß nemen / Mich dunckt auch gentzlich er hab sein Juditia genommen / auß den püchern magistri Pelagi heremite in regno maioricarum von der beschwerung der geyst / dann ein solchs zů Perlin abgeschriben ist worden / vnnd mit aller zů gehörung gen Osterreich pracht / das ich mit meinen augen gesehen hab. Es sein vorzeyten auch solch lewt gewesen / wie Ptholomeus anzaigt / die mit solchen künsten vmb sein gangen vnd gesagt / sy nemen yr Juditia auß der Astrologey / so sy doch keinen rechten grundt (wie diser Charion) darjnn hetten." Perlach, *Des Cometen... bedütung* (1531), sig. [Aiij] v – [Aiiij] r.

[89] On Trithemius, see Klaus Arnold, *Johannes Trithemius (1462–1516)* (Würzburg: Kommissionsverlag F. Schöningh, 1991), and Noel Brann, *The Abbot Trithemius (1462–1516): The Renaissance of Monastic Humanism* (Leiden: Brill, 1981).

[90] Trithemius sometimes identified Pelagius as Fernando of Cordova († 1486), but this is questionable at best. See especially the sceptical discussion in Paola Zambelli, *White Magic, Black Magic in the European Renaissance: From Ficino, Pico, Della Porta to Trithemius, Agrippa, Bruno* (Leiden: Brill, 2007), 77–78. On the historical Fernando, see John Monfasani, *Fernando of Cordova: A Biographical and Intellectual Profile* (Philadelphia: American Philosophical Society, 1992). On Pelagius, see Jean Dupèbe, "L'écriture chez l'ermite Pelagius: Un cas de théurgie chrétienne au xve siècle," in *Le Texte et son inscription*, ed. R. Laufer (Paris: Editions du C.N.R.S., 1989), 113–153.

Perlach's pamphlet reached Carion in April 1532, possibly while he was in Wittenberg to finish revising his *Chronicle*.[91] In response, Carion composed his only extant publication in Latin, an *Apology* (*purgatio*) combined with a *Iudicium for 1533*. The choice of language was a strategic move. Carion clearly intended to end the dispute or at least restrict it to a learned audience. From Carion's perspective, throughout the controversy, Perlach had done nothing more than make malicious accusations.[92] Even so, in his *Apology*, Carion responded point by point to each of Perlach's six allegations from *The Comet of 1531*.

With regard to the accusations of "unnatural" arts and the use of occult literature, Carion categorically denied all of Perlach's charges:

> This ought to be a sufficient response for now to the arguments of Perlach, from which he falsely concludes that I have made predictions by arts prohibited and shameful to an upright man, and inflicts a notorious and unbearable injury upon me. Furthermore, I do not understand what he says about the book of the Hermit Pelagius. I have never seen it, and I absolutely abhor that entire class of forbidden arts.[93]

In his conclusion, Carion appealed to professional courtesy and the standing of the discipline to stop, or at least temper, Perlach's harsh attacks.[94] Carion

---

91 "Editus est libellus de Cometa ab Andrea Perlachio, in quo de me fere plura atque atrociora quam de ipso Cameta scripsit. Detrahit mihi in totum philosophiae atque Astronomiae scientiam, quod facile pateret nisi per eam calumniam conaretur alteri cuidam iniustissimae ac falsissimae criminationi fidem facere, quam dissimulare non est boni uiri. Accessit autem ad id incommodum hoc quoque, quod libellus Perlachij sero admodum ad me peruenit. Reperio Anno superiore Mense Nouembri scriptum esse, Cum ego nunc primum hoc Anno Mense Aprili acceperim, quare nolim mihi fraudi esse quod serius respondeo." Johann Carion, *Ivdicivm Magistri Iohannis Carionis de Anno M.D.XXXIII. Cum purgatione in qua respondet Perlachio*. ([Wittenberg]: [Hans Weiß], 1532), sig. aij r. VD16 C 1021. See Fricke-Hilgers, "Die Sintflutprognose" (1999), 294 n. 6, 294–295 n. 7, and 299 n. 49.

92 "Sed uenio ad causam ubi candor eius magis estimari poterit, Facillimum est enim uel me tacente, iudicare, nihil afferri contra me, nisi meras calumnias." Carion, *Ivdicivm* (Wittenberg, 1532), sig. aij v.

93 "Haec satis sit hoc tempore respondisse ad argumenta Perlachij ex quibus falso raciocinatur me ex artibus indignis bono uiro ac prohibitis diuinare, meque insigni & non ferenda iniuria afficit. Neque intelligo quid dicat de Pelagi heremitae libro, ego enim nunquam uidi & a toto illo genere artium interdictarum prorsus abhorreo." Carion, *Ivdicivm* (Wittenberg, 1532), sig. [a v] v.

94 "Spero me candidis Lectoribus satis purgatum esse, Et quia sine conuiciis & maledictis respondi, a Perlachio etiam peto, ut siquid rescripturus est ciuiliter agat, quod si fecisset in hoc libello, ego plane nihil respondissem. Non enim libenter rixor cum homine meae professionis, Et uterque hoc tempus collocare melius potest, quam in huiusmodi odiosas concertationes." Carion, *Ivdicivm* (Wittenberg, 1532), sig. [a v] v.

may have embarrassed Perlach into silence; but irrespective of the reason, the dispute ended.

After the exchanges with Perlach, Carion continued to write an annual *Practica*, but he did not publish any astrological works on the scale of his 1521 *Prognosticatio* or his *Bedeutnus und Offenbarung*. Ultimately, Perlach may have been more right than wrong in his accusations. Given that Carion held his position as Joachim's astronomer for so long, he likely engaged in occultism at the Berlin court. Throughout his career, Carion consistently referred to himself as an *astronomus*, rather than an *astrologus*. Nevertheless, in a 1540 letter addressed to multiple recipients, including Melanchthon, Luther called Carion a *magus*, a term with occult overtones;[95] and Erasmus Reinhold (1511–1553), a Wittenberg professor of mathematics, went so far as to label Carion a "notorious necromancer" (*insignis necromanticus*).[96]

Without question, Carion was engaged in copying obscure manuscripts at Berlin, such as Zebel the Arab's book on portents, of which Joachim I also had a display copy made.[97] Indeed, the library assembled by Joachim long served as a repository of occult texts. For example, a manuscript of Trithemius's *Antipalus maleficiorum* with a bibliography for necromancers indicates that it was copied by Heinrich Khunrath († 1605) from the original in the Electoral collection (*ex libro manuscripto Serenissimi Electoris Joachimi*).[98] More telling, however, is a letter Carion addressed to Albrecht Duke of Prussia in August 1527. In the letter, Carion included detailed instructions for conjuring spirits through a ritual requiring a twelve year old child and a series of Latin incantations.[99] Since the letter was essentially an advertisement of potential services to Duke Albrecht, it is doubtful that Carion sent something he had not already tried himself.

7   Carion and Königsberg

Although Carion was most closely connected to the Electors of Brandenburg, his service was not limited to the Hohenzollern court in Berlin.[100] In 1527,

---

95   "Venit aliquando in mentem Charionis Magi signum, quod scidit in eo loco brachii per diploidem et indusium." WA Br 9:64 [Luther to Jonas, Bugenhagen and Melanchthon, 26 February 1540].
96   Warburg, "Pagan-Antique Prophecy," 648.
97   Warburg, "Pagan-Antique Prophecy," 647–648.
98   Zambelli, *White Magic*, 82, 101.
99   Johannes Voigt, *Briefwechsel der berühmtesten Gelehrten des Zeitalters der Reformation mit Herzog Albrecht von Preußen* (Königsberg: Bornträger, 1844), 142–143. Voigt includes the text of the ritual from Carion's letter.
100   For Carion's relationship to the court in Königsberg, see Voigt, *Briefwechsel*, 139–160.

Albrecht Duke of Prussia (1490–1568) requested horoscopes from Carion for himself and for the newly constituted Duchy of Prussia, which Albrecht had created, on Luther's advice, from the lands of the Teutonic Knights.[101] Albrecht was born in Franconia and he was descended from the Brandenburg-Ansbach line of Hohenzollerns; his mother was a Polish royal princess. In 1511, Albrecht had been chosen Grand Master of the Teutonic Knights, with the task of addressing the strife between the Order and the King of Poland over lands in Prussia. During the Diet of Nuremberg (1522), Albrecht met Andreas Osiander (1498–1552), a Lutheran preacher, who was instrumental in his conversion to Protestantism. (Decades later, Albrecht would provide Osiander with a place of refuge when he was forced to flee Nuremberg.) In 1525, Albrecht converted Prussia into a Hohenzollern duchy, which became a fief of the King of Poland; the following year, he joined the Torgau League, a Protestant defensive alliance dominated by Hesse and Electoral Saxony.[102]

At some point in 1527, Albrecht entered into contact with Carion. The circumstances are unclear, but apparently he requested horoscopes. In his response to Albrecht that August, Carion apologized for the delay in sending the duke's material.[103] He explained that he lacked the resources he needed, since he only had access to his natal charts, but he promised to write again as soon as he consulted his charts of revolutions. At this point, Carion offered his expertise not only as an astronomer, but also as a diplomatic agent.[104] Albrecht, however, was not pleased. By October, Carion continued to delay in sending the material, claiming that similar projects for the Electoral court were monopolizing his time.[105] Worse still, by November, the duke wrote to Carion and rebuked him for failing to keep the whole matter secret.[106] For years, Carion sent profuse apologies to Königsberg, along with promises to keep quiet in the future, but the duke simply ignored him.[107]

In 1531, Carion finally had an opportunity to restore his relationship with Albrecht.[108] After Albrecht converted to Protestantism and seized Prussia, Walter von Cronberg († 1545) had claimed the office of Grand Master and

---

101   Voigt, *Briefwechsel*, 141. On Albrecht, see ADB 1: 293–310.
102   Reiner Groß, "Ernestinisches Kurfürstentum und albertinisches Herzogtum Sachsen zur Reformationszeit: Grundzüge außen- und innenpolitscher Entwicklung," in *Glaube & Macht: Sachsen im Europa der Reformationszeit*, ed. Harald Marx and Eckhard Kluth (Dresden: Sandstein, 2004), vol. 2, 55.
103   Voigt, *Briefwechsel*, 141.
104   Voigt, *Briefwechsel*, 141; Fricke-Hilgers, "Die Sintflutprognose" (1989/90), 36.
105   Voigt, *Briefwechsel*, 144.
106   Voigt, *Briefwechsel*, 144.
107   Voigt, *Briefwechsel*, 146.
108   Voigt, *Briefwechsel*, 146–147.

began agitating for the return of the Order's lands. By 1531, Albrecht had suspicions that Elector Joachim I was planning to release embarrassing material about the disputes with Cronberg. To help mend ties with Königsberg, Carion wrote to Albrecht and explained that Joachim did not intend to publicize the material in question. Furthermore, the Elector had quietly, but strenuously, worked against Walter von Cronberg on the duke's behalf.[109] Carion's mediation proved successful, and he began sending regular dispatches to Königsberg. By 1534, he was considered valuable enough to the Prussian court that he was given a new contract and paid fifty gulden for services rendered.[110] From that time on, Carion became an important diplomatic agent for Duke Albrecht, and he travelled widely in the service of both Berlin and Königsberg.

8 Carion and Melanchthon

Unless new evidence comes to light, Carion's relationship to Wittenberg in the 1520s will remain largely uncertain.[111] Despite his employment for the strongly Catholic Elector of Brandenburg,[112] Carion had started to embrace the Reformation's teachings already before the Diet of Augsburg (1530). His extant correspondence from the 1520s is silent about religious matters, but his published works are nevertheless revealing. In his *Bedeutnus und Offenbarung* (1526), for instance, he quoted from Luther's German edition of Habakkuk, and he referred to "the translator" as one with proper understanding of the Bible.[113] In 1529, Elector Joachim invited Lucas Cranach the Elder to Berlin, and it seems that Carion sat for a portrait (Figure 9).[114] Nevertheless, the interaction with

---

109 Voigt, *Briefwechsel*, 146–148.
110 Voigt, *Briefwechsel*, 151.
111 On Carion and Wittenberg, see Kuhlow, "Johannes Carion," 60–65.
112 See Bodo Nischan, *Prince, People, and Confession: The Second Reformation in Brandenburg* (Philadelphia: University of Pennsylvania Press, 1994), 5–11.
113 "Darumb hab ich die wort Abacuc des propheten / wie sy in seinem aygen bůch beschriben lautend / vnd von ainem rechuerstendigen verteutscht...." Carion, *Bedeütnusz vnnd Offenbarung* (Augsburg, 1526), sig. Aij v – Aiij r. See Kuhlow, "Johannes Carion," 61–62.
114 The portrait, now displayed in the Berlin Gemäldegalerie, is dated "ca. 1530." On the likely connection with Cranach's 1529 visit to Berlin, see Dieter Koepplin and Tilman Falk, *Lukas Cranach: Gemälde, Zeichungen, Druckgraphik* (Basel: Birkhäuser Verlag, 1976), vol. 1, 268. The inscription reads: "SI QVIB[VS] EST LECTIS MEA COGNITA FAMA LIBELLIS, || QVOS MEA SOLERTI CVRA LABORE DEDIT. || ILLE EGO SV[M] CARION, COELI QVI SYDERA TRACTO || CLARVS ET ASTORV[M] NOMEN AB ARTE FERO". It has been translated as: "If any of you know of my renown by reading the books that my zeal has produced with ingenious labor, I am the Carion who treats of the constellations of heaven and made his

FIGURE 9   Lucas Cranach the Elder, *Johann Carion* (ca. 1530)
STAATSBIBLIOTHEK ZU BERLIN (ON LOAN TO STAATLICHE MUSEEN ZU BERLIN, GEMÄLDEGALERIE)
PHOTO CREDIT: THE WARBURG INSTITUTE, UNIVERSITY OF LONDON, PHOTOGRAPHIC COLLECTION

Cranach does not indicate religious sympathies, since he painted both Catholics and Protestants. The Diet of Augsburg, however, marked a clear change in Carion's relationship with Wittenberg. From that time on, he was in regular contact with Melanchthon, and he also befriended Luther.

The Diet was the most important in a decade. For the first time since Worms (1521), Emperor Charles V attended, and he came intent on resolving the religious issues in Germany to facilitate his wars against the Turks.[115] As had been the case at the late medieval councils, the various princely entourages arriving in the city included many humanists, who used the opportunity provided by the gathering to meet and discuss their work. Beatus Rhenanus, for example, claimed that his *Three Books on German History* (1531) arose from questions posed at the Diet,[116] and *Carion's Chronicle* may also owe a debt to discussions at Augsburg.[117] Melanchthon and Carion were reacquainted in Augsburg, and during these months Carion also became friends with Melanchthon's future son-in-law, Georg Sabinus (1508–1560). These closer ties to Wittenberg are evident not only from Carion's visit there in 1532, but also his use of Wittenberg printers for his works published after 1530.

The first mention of Carion in Melanchthon's correspondence appears at the start of the next year. On 1 January 1531, Melanchthon sent letters to two friends in Nuremberg that describe how he was engaged in revising the *Apology* to the *Augsburg Confession*. He was also investigating Luther's birth horoscope, and he included material from Carion,[118] whose reckoning he was inclined to

---

name in the art of the stars." – Harry Vredeveld, "'Lend a Voice': The Humanistic Portrait Epigraph in the Age of Erasmus and Dürer," *Renaissance Quarterly* 66, no. 2 (Summer 2013), 555.

115 See Stephen A. Fischer-Galati, *Ottoman Imperialism and German Protestantism, 1521–1555* (Cambridge, M.A.: Harvard University Press, 1959), 40–47.

116 At the Diet of Augsburg in 1530, Beatus had been asked various questions about the Roman provinces in Germany, and his *Three Books on German History* was meant to clarify this and a wide range of issues relating to ancient Germany. See John D'Amico, *Theory and Practice in Renaissance Textual Criticism: Beatus Rhenanus between Conjecture and History* (Berkeley: University of California Press, 1988), 185.

117 "Nach dem mich zum offtermal etliche / besonder gute freunde gebeten / ein kurtze Chronica zu stellen / Daraus ein iglicher die furnemisten Historien / ordenlich fassen vnd lernen kont / welche zum teil nicht allein nützlich / sondern auch not ist zu wissen / Habe ich solche Chronica zu machen furgenomen / vnd nach meinem vermögen auff das aller ordenlichest die Monarchien / darein Gott die welt fur vnd fur wünderlich gefasset hat / vnd die grösten hendel vnd venderung / so darin furgefallen / kürtzlich zusamen gezogen vnd erzelet." Carion, *Chronica* (Wittenberg, 1532), sig. Aij r.

118 "Verum et valetudine dolorosa conflictor et totus sum in Apologia, quam scribere talem conor, ut ex ea posteritas non modo de nostris controversiis iudicare possit, sed omnino cognoscere totius doctrinae christianae summam. Hic labor me pene conficit, sed sustento me animi viribus. Mitto tibi geneses mihi a Carione missas [...] Episcopi Moguntini et

follow.[119] Although Luther generally believed that he had been born on 10 November 1483, in the early 1530s, various Italian astrologers were trying to move his birthday to 22 October 1484.[120] By doing so, they sought to associate him with the great conjunction of planets in 1484, which was supposed to mark a new era in religion. The problem for Melanchthon was that depending on the time of birth that day, Luther could be interpreted as a malignant force. If so, then the horoscope would facilitate doubt and accusations of heresy. Melanchthon collected various horoscopes to address the question, and the one provided by Carion offered a solution to the problem. By shifting the time of birth from 1:10 a.m. to 9:00 a.m., Carion was able to reconfigure the horoscope to avert the darker findings but preserve the astrologically significant date, 22 October 1484. Doubts remained, and Melanchthon frequently revisited the issue, but at the time, he gravitated toward Carion's conjecture.

The first indication that *Carion's Chronicle* was being prepared for publication comes a few months later in a letter of 15 June 1531 from Melanchthon to his friend, Joachim Camerarius (1500–1574), then in Nuremberg. Melanchthon wrote in response to receiving a disputation by Camerarius on Carion's predictions, but neither the letter from Camerarius nor the disputation seem to be extant. The exchange with Camerarius precedes Perlach's harshest attacks by at least five months, so well before the accusations of using "unnatural arts," Carion was under considerable pressure, even from his friends, to account for his remarkable predictions.

At the outset, Melanchthon addressed the suspicions that Carion had used more than the stars in making his predictions; he himself remained sceptical – despite Carion's vehement denials – because the specificity of the predictions

---

aliorum dignas cognicione. Et est in his Lutheri genesis, quam inquisivit Philo. Opinor te nosse hominem ac vidisse Lipsiae: den Pfeyl. Annus et dies conveniunt, hora est incerta. Mater dicit Lutherum natum esse ante dimidium noctis. Sed puto eam falli. Ego a Philone poetam, ut mihi significet, ubi tempus exploraverit. Ceterum quacumque hora natus est, haec mira coniunctio in scorpio non potuit non efficere virum acerrimum...." MBW 1112.3-4.

119 "Philippus ad Schonerum. Genesim Lutheri, quam Philo inquisivit, transtulit Carion in horam 9. Mater enim dicit Lutherum natum esse ante dimidium noctis (sed puto eam falli). Ego alteram figuram praefero, et praefert ipse Carion, etsi quoque haec est mirifica propter locum Martis et coniunctionem in domo quinta, quae habet coniunctionem magnam cum ascendente. Caeterum quacumque hora natus est: haec mira coniunctio in Scorpione non potuit non efficere virum acerrimum." MBW 1113 [Text complete here]. For a reproduction of this letter, including the horoscope, see Warburg, "Pagan-Antique Prophecy," 609. For a discussion of Carion's horoscopes, see Reisinger, *Historische Horoskopie*, 1–98; and Liebers, "Johannes Carions Arbeiten zur Horoskopie," 303–332.

120 The problem of Luther's horoscope is addressed in Warburg, "Pagan-Antique Prophecy," 603–613; see also Anthony Grafton, *Cardano's Cosmos: The Worlds and Works of a Renaissance Astrologer* (Cambridge, MA: Harvard University Press, 1999), 75–77.

was far more exact than he was prepared to allow for the usual art of astrology. Even his appeal to Carion's character was guarded and cautious: "But the man is, at least so far as I have known, upright and he very much calls to mind Swabian simplicity."[121] Immediately following, Melanchthon remarked:

> He has sent a chronicle to us to be published, on the condition that I should make corrections. You have seen nothing written so carelessly. Therefore, I am reworking the entire piece, but in German, and I have decided to describe the principal changes of the great empires.[122]

The questions Melanchthon posed at that time dealt primarily with the history of Hercules, especially whether there had been more than one figure by that name in Antiquity.[123] A week later, 23 June 1531, Melanchthon sent another letter to Camerarius concerning Hercules,[124] and the next month, 26 July 1531, he wrote again with comments about the *Chronicle*.[125] In the July letter, Melanchthon mentioned one of the most perplexing historical problems of early modern ethnography, the origins of the Franks. He did not believe that they had originated from the Baltic region. Rather, based on Strabo and Livy, he placed them in upper Germany, near the present French border, and he had decided to insert this discussion at his treatment of Charlemagne.[126]

---

121 "S.D. Accepi tuam disputacionem de praedictionibus Carionis. Quanquam autem iste vehementer affirmat se nihil praeter siderum positum in consilium adhibere, tamen mihi non satis persuadet hoc. Nam ars meo iudicio non potest tam diserte de particularis eventibus pronunciare. Sed vir est, quantum ego quidem cognovi, candidus et Suevicae simplicitatis plurimum referens." MBW 1159.1.

122 "Misit huc χρονικά excudenda, sed ea lege, ut ego emendarem. Nihil vidisti scriptum negligentius. Itaque ego totum opus retexo, et quidem Germanice, et constitui complecti praecipuas mutationes maximorum imperiorum." MBW 1159.2.

123 By this time, Melanchthon had decided to follow the view that there had been only one Hercules: "De Hercule valde laboro. Ego enim in ea opinione sum unum tantum Herculem fuisse. Nec multo aliter sentit Herodotus. Rogo igitur te, ut diligenter perscribas mihi, et cuias fuerit Hercules et quomodo existimes ab illo Alexandrum Macedonem ortum esse, cuius genus valde cupio nosse. Materno genere Aeacides est, sed paterno Isocrates facit Heracliden." MBW 1159.2.

124 "De Hercule deque toto genere Alexandri, quantum potes, inquire mihi seriem gratiam mihi feceris." CR II, 508 (MBW 1162 dates the letter as 27 June 1531).

125 "De Hercule plane mihi satisfactum est. Ego unum aliquem, et quidem illum Thebanum Amphitryonis extitisse arbitror, qui fama rerum gestarum occasionem fingendi aliis dedit, qui plures Hercules commenti sunt. Neque haec Graecis tantum licentia concessa est. Fingunt similia nunc quoque nostri homines." MBW 1167.11.

126 "De Francis tuis haud dubie falsum est eos a Baltico exortos esse. Fuerunt enim vicini Alpibus sicut Boii Strabonis tempore. Et Livius in Hannibalis transitu mencionem Branci facit, qui bellum gessit cum Allobrogibus. Habeo multa argumenta, quae fidem minime

Afterwards, he explained the difficulties he had had with arranging the material in the *Chronicle*, and how one idea lead to another, which complicated the process of composition.[127]

9 Melanchthon and Annius of Viterbo

The letters to Camerarius are symptomatic of Melanchthon's general approach to historical sources.[128] For *Carion's Chronicle*, Melanchthon did not work in archives or rely heavily on manuscripts; instead, he synthesized printed sources into a concise narrative. Melanchthon was adamant about clarity and accuracy, and already in 1521, he had cautioned Andreas Althamer († 1538/39), another former Tübingen student, against incorporating mythical or fabulous material into historical narratives. Indeed, he criticized two other Tübingen scholars, Franciscus Irenicus (1494–1553) and Heinrich Bebel (1472–1518),[129] for including "fabulous" material in their works.[130] A decade later, Melanchthon put his advice into practice, and with a few exceptions, *Carion's Chronicle* is virtually devoid of legendary accounts. In the letters to Camerarius, for example, Melanchthon did not even mention the Trojan origin of the Franks, a myth that had circulated since the early Middle Ages and remained popular in the

---

dubiam faciunt primas sedes Francorum in hac superiore Germania fuisse fere iisdem locis, quae nunc sunt Francorum. Strabo βρέγκους scribit Vindelicis vicinos et nescio quibus aliis. Non enim vacat inspicere librum. Itaque te non insertum alienae genti, sed vere Francum dici et haberi volo. Idque disputabo in χρονικοῖς in Carolo, quem ornabo, quantum potero." MBW 1167.12.

127 "Nescio an omnia scripserim, quae volui, cum quidem aliud ex alio sine ordine in mentem venerit inter scribendum. Teque oro, ut veniam des huic meae negligentiae. Sed nosti meas miserias, quibus condonare te haec quoque existimo." MBW 1167.13.

128 See the extensive source analysis in Münch, "Das Chronicon Carionis Philippicum," 238–253.

129 On the "fables" in Bebel and Irenicus, see Frank Borchardt, *German Antiquity in Renaissance Myth* (Baltimore: The Johns Hopkins Press, 1971), 109–114, 144–148.

130 "Quare non est, cur praecipites edicionem. Opto equidem, ut in lucem prodeat, sed candoris mei est consulere, ut quam emendatissime exeat. Vides, qualia sint Germanorum hominum hodie iudicia quibus te committis. Ipse meo malo didici, quam sit infoelix praecipitancia. Relegi bonam libelli tui partem; atque utinam audias me! Nam et Franciscum Irenicum sepe penituit non audisse meo consilio. Iam hoc quoque displicet, quod novicios et ignobiles scriptores crebrius citas, per quos operi tum auctoritas tum gracia derogabitur. Non erant mihi ad manum literae tuae: quare de omnibus respondere non possum. De Tudro est quod habemus. De Ascipurgo non placent illa vulgi commenta; et praeter alios insigniter ibi deliravit Bebelius. Vale et boni consule meam sentenciam; scribo enim amico et candido pectore." Addressed to Andreas Althamer, ca. June 1521. MBW 148.2–3.

sixteenth century. Nor did he include the fanciful legend about the Macedonian origins of the Saxons, or the myth that the Germans had left Babel before the confusion of the languages.[131] Instead, he explicitly set the time of Augustus as the point beyond which nothing about Germany was known.[132]

Not all decisions were so easy. In 1498, a papal official, Annius of Viterbo (1432–1502),[133] had published a collection of writings by "ancient authors" that addressed various gaps in classical and biblical sources.[134] Some scholars quickly, and correctly, recognized the texts as forgeries,[135] but others, especially in Germany, refused to dismiss them completely. Nauclerus drew extensively from the Annian collection for his *Chronicle*,[136] and prior to *Carion's Chronicle*, Melanchthon had also collaborated on a new edition of Justin's *Epitome* (1526)[137] that included supplementary chronological information drawn from Annius's pseudo-Berosus and pseudo-Metasthenes.[138] Melanchthon's qualified

---

131   See Borchardt, *German Antiquity*, 17–18, 31.
132   In addition to the letters, see the discission in the *Chronicle* itself: "Woher aber die francken erstlich her komen / dauon schreiben etliche seltzam Fabulas / Die Francken sind on zweiuel Hochdeudschen von der zeit Augusti an gewesen / Denn ferner zurürck kan man nicht eigentlichs von Deudschland wissen / Das aber die Francken so alt jnn hoch Deudschland sind / kan man klerlich beweisen aus Strabo / der zur zeit Augusti geschrieben hat / vnd mit den Römern den kriegen nachgezogen ist / Dieser Strabo setzt die Francken klar neben die Vindelicos / das ist / neben Baiern / daran sie noch zum teil rüren." Carion, *Chronica* (Wittenberg, 1532), fol. 114r.
133   See, with reference to earlier literature, Wilhelm Schmidt-Biggemann, "Heilsgeschichtliche Inventionen. Annius von Viterbos 'Berosus' und die Geschichte der Sintflut," in *Sintflut und Gedächtnis: Erinnern und Vergessen des Ursprungs*, ed. Martin Mulsow and Jan Assmann (München: Fink, 2006), 85–111. See also Anthony Grafton, *Defenders of the Text: The Traditions of Scholarship in an Age of Science, 1450–1800* (Cambridge, MA: Harvard University Press, 1991), 76–103; and Borchardt, *German Antiquity*, 89–91.
134   I use the 1511 Strasbourg edition: Annius of Viterbo, *Berosvs Babilonicvs De His Quæ præcesserunt inundationem terrarum. Item. Myrsilus de origine Turrhenorum. Cato in fragmentis. Archilochus in Epitheto de temporibus. Metasthenes de iudicio temporum. Philo in breuiario temporum. Xenophon de equiuocis temporum. Sempronius de diuisione Italiæ. Q. Fab. Pictor de aureo sæculo & origine vrbis Rhomæ. Fragmentum Itinerarij Antonini Pij. Altercatio Adriani Augusti & Epictici. Cornelij Taciti de origine & situ Germanorum opusculum. C.C. de situ & moribus Germanorum* ([Strasbourg]: [Grüninger], 1511). VD16 B 1649 [VD16 C 1902].
135   See Christopher Ligota, "Annius of Viterbo and Historical Method," *Journal of the Warburg and Courtauld Institutes* 50 (1987): 44 n. 2.
136   See, for example, his discussion at the opening of the *Chronicle* – Nauclerus, *Chronica* (1516), vol. 1, fol. I r.
137   Justin, *Ivstini Ex Trogo Pompeio Historia* (Hagenau: Johann Setzer, 1526). VD16 T 2051. The edition was reprinted and later revised, see MBW 435; see also VD16 T 2051, 2053–2055, 2058–2062, ZV 15048–15049.
138   "Quanqvam in monarchiis et annorvm ratione constiuenda, uehementer uarient autores, tamen ut historiae series atque ordo facilius a pueris posset percipi, adnotauimus, partim

endorsement of the Annian collection in *Carion's Chronicle* contributed to its continuing relevance among European historians, and Luther likewise used it in his *Reckoning of the Years of the World*.[139] The last early modern editions were published in 1659 at Leipzig and Wittenberg.[140]

Although Melanchthon used the Annian forgeries, he remained a critical reader of their content, and he weighed the information in the collection by comparing it with other sources. Some of the material in Annius was "fabulous" or did not conform to biblical narratives, so Melanchthon rejected it. Pseudo-Berosus, for example, named a fourth son of Noah, Tuisco, and presented him as the father of the Germans.[141] In *Carion's Chronicle*, Melanchthon tacitly denied this, and using the biblical genealogy in Genesis 10, he presented the Germans as descendants of Japheth.[142] He also incorporated this perspective into the *Chronicle's* map that shows the dispersion of Noah's descendants (Figure 10). Later, in the Wittenberg edition of Tacitus's *Germania* (1538), he explicitly rejected the "fables" in pseudo-Berosus about Tuisco and the origins of the Germans.[143] The multiple Hercules problem also derived from the genealogies found in the Annian collection,[144] and after comparison with classical sources, Melanchthon again rejected the forged information.[145]

---

ex Eusebio, partim ex Beroso & Metasthene, ea tamen quae ad planiorem paulo & explicatiorem Iustini lectionem conducere uidebantur." Justin, *Ivstini Ex Trogo Pompeio Historia* (Hagenau, 1526), sig. x iii r. The tables are found at sig. x iii r – [x iiii] r.

139 The text is edited in WA 53:1–184.
140 Leipzig (VD17 7:704503Q), and Wittenberg (Wittenberg, Lutherhalle Museum: CGH 194).
141 On Tuisco generally, see Borchardt, *German Antiquity*; and Peter Hutter, *Germanische Stammväter und römisch-deutsches Kaisertum* (Hildesheim: Georg Olms Verlag, 2000), esp. 36–44. See also Arno Borst, *Der Turmbau von Babel: Geschichte der Meinungen über Ursprung und Vielfalt der Sprachen und Völker* (Stuttgart: Anton Hiersemann, 1960), vol. III, part 1, 975–977, 1069–1074.
142 "Japhet hat auch andere söne gehabt / den Gomer / Magog / Tyras vnd Mesech / Von Gomer komen Cimmerij oder Cimbri / wie Eusebius anzeiget / Vnd von Ascanes dem son Gomer / komen Tuiscones / das ist / die Deudschen / Von Magog komen Scithe / daher die Türcken ihren vrsprung haben / Von Tyras Thraces. Das sey hie gnug zu einer kurtzen anleitung / wilchen teil der welt jder son Noe besetzt habe / welchs dienet / viel Historien klarer zu vernemen." Carion, *Chronica* (Wittenberg, 1532), sig. Ciij v.
143 "*Tuisco*. Omitto fabulas, quae sunt apud Berosum de ortu Tuisconis et aliorum." CR XVII, 622.
144 See Annius, *Berosvs Babilonicvs....* (Strasbourg, 1511), fol. IX v, X r, XVIII v, XXIIII r. See Melanchthon's comment in his 1521 letter to Althamer: "Alioqui quae est gloria patriae, si figmentis celebratur? Et quid dissimilius veri quam quod fingunt de Hercule Germanico, de filiis Herculis apud nos et multa hoc genus?" MBW 148.1 – see also the note there with reference to pseudo-Berosus.
145 See MBW 1159.2 and MBW 1167.11 (text quoted above).

FIGURE 10   Carion, *Chronica* (Wittenberg, 1532), sig. Cij v
HERZOG AUGUST BIBLIOTHEK WOLFENBÜTTEL: GB 56

After discarding the clearly erroneous material, Melanchthon and Carion used the Annian texts to supplement classical and biblical narratives. In those cases, they had limited, or even no sources, against which to judge the validity of the information from the Annian collection. Instead, they viewed the texts as filling important gaps in ancient history. Even in these instances, however, they still recognized that the Annian texts could be problematic, and they did not use them indiscriminately. Nauclerus had adopted the "complete" list of Assyrian kings from pseudo-Metasthenes,[146] but *Carion's Chronicle* pointedly omitted the "mere names" of the otherwise little known Assyrian rulers.[147] For the Persian Empire, Melanchthon and Carion used the regnal lists and chronological information in pseudo-Metasthenes and pseudo-Philo, but they

---

146   Nauclerus, *Chronica* (1516), vol. 1, Generatio XVIII, fol. XII v.
147   "Dieweil aber nicht viel von der folgenden König thaten vnd Historien geschrieben ist / wil ich die blossen namen auch nicht erzelen / denn der deudsch leser kan sie schwerlich gedencken / vnd wer sie haben wil / findet sie bey vielen Scribenten." Carion, *Chronica* (Wittenberg, 1532), sig. D v.

acknowledged that some rejected the Annian texts completely. Furthermore, they conceded that it was necessary to reconcile certain aspects of pseudo-Metasthenes with Greek historians, and they offered various explanations to resolve the inconsistencies.[148] The approach to the Annian collection demonstrates a critical mindset, but it also betrays a willingness to harmonize rather than discard questionable, though still plausible, information. Melanchthon never completely rejected the Annian forgeries, and he still included pseudo-Metasthenes when he revised *Carion's Chronicle* in the 1550s.[149]

10 Carion's 1532 Visit to Wittenberg

Only one letter from Melanchthon to Carion is extant, and none from Carion to Melanchthon are known to have survived. Aby Warburg discovered this single letter among the remnants of Carion's correspondence, then kept in Königsberg, and he published it for the first time. The text is dated 17 August 1531 from Wittenberg and was addressed to Carion in Berlin.[150] Because of trimming to the upper edge of the first leaf, the text is incomplete. The result is that part of Melanchthon's discussion of the *Chronicle* has been lost. The letter begins with the remaining comments on the *Chronicle*, and they indicate that Melanchthon himself had made the decision to order the work according to the Talmudic "Prophecy of Elias." To that point, he had been delayed by his revisions of the *Apology* to the *Augsburg Confession*, but he hoped to have the *Chronicle* finished in the winter, a statement implying that Carion was concerned about the delay in publication.[151]

---

148 "Jnn Daniele vnd Esdra / wird der Persen König gedacht / vnd werden etliche anders genent denn bey den Greken / Darümb wil ich zu vnterricht mein meinung dauon kürtzlich anzeigen / Etliche verwerffen Metasthenem / der etliche Persen König anders nennet / denn die Greken / Dieweil aber Esdra vnd Philo so gantz zusamen stimmen / wil ich sie nicht verwerffen...." Carion, *Chronica* (Wittenberg, 1532), fol. 31v [= sig. Hiiij v].
149 See, for example, CR XII, 779.
150 MBW 1177. For an English translation of the letter, see Warburg, "Pagan-Antique Prophecy," 600–601.
151 "[...] ornare honstissimis laudibus conatus sum. Quid assecutus sim, aliorum sit iudicium. Dictum Heliae extat non in Bibliis, sed apud Rabinos, et est celeberrimum. Burgensis allegat et disputat ex eo contra Iudeos, quod Messias apparuerit. Receptissima apud Ebreos sentencia est et a me posita in principio tuae historiae, ut omnibus fieret notissima et afferret commendationem tuo operi. Tales locos multos deinceps admiscebo. Vides autem prorsus esse propheticam vocem, tam concinna temporum distributio est. Historiam, ut spero, hac hyeme absolvemus. Nam hactenus fui impeditus recognitione meae Apologiae, quam in certis locis feci meliorem. Sed vix credas, quam tenui valetudine utar, consumor enim curis et laboribus." MBW 1177.1. See Warburg, "Pagan-Antique Prophecy," 600–603;

Afterwards, Melanchthon announced the birth of a daughter and sent her horoscope to Carion for his advice, commenting that she would become a nun.[152] (This daughter, Magdalena, eventually married Caspar Peucer.) Melanchthon noted the appearance of a comet – it was Halley's – and asked Carion what it could mean for worldly affairs, probably the death of princes.[153] He then shifted to the political situation at that time, and the prophecies that were circulating about current events. In closing, he added that he would forward his preface in praise of astrology and astronomy through Georg Sabinus and would wait for Carion's opinion of the piece.[154] Melanchthon mentioned Carion only once more in his correspondence for 1531, in another letter to Camerarius from 29 September, where he wrote that he was including one of Carion's annual prognostications.[155] No further reference is made in this letter or elsewhere to the *Chronicle* before its publication.[156]

Eventually, Carion seems to have become frustrated with the delays, because he decided to visit Wittenberg during the 1532 winter term. During his stay, he inscribed his name in the university matriculation book as "Johannes Carion Astronomus," which is perhaps the source for the tradition that he had studied there in earlier years.[157] Carion's presence in Wittenberg during April

---

and specifically on the Elias prophecy, Julius Köstlin, "Ein Beitrag zur Eschatologie der Reformatoren." *Theologische Studien und Kritiken* 51 (1878): 125–135. See also Münch, "Das Chronicon Carionis Philippicum," 240–241; Volker Leppin, *Antichrist und Jüngster Tag: Das Profil apokalyptischer Flugschriftenpublizistik im deutschen Luthertum 1548–1618* (Gütersloh: Gütersloher Verlagshaus Mohn, 1999), 63–65, 130–139.

152 "Mea uxor dei beneficio filiam enixa est, cuius thema tibi mitto, non ut faciam tibi negocium, video enim monacham fore." MBW 1177.2.

153 "Cometen vidimus diebus plus octo. Tu quid iudicas? Videtur supra cancrum constitisse, occidit enim statim post solem et paulo ante solem exoritur. Quod si ruberet, magis me terreret. Haud dubie principum mortem significat. Sed videtur caudam vertere versus Poloniam. Sed expecto tuum iudicium." MBW 1177.3. See Fricke-Hilgers, "Die Sintflutprognose" (1999), 298 n. 36.

154 "Sabinus mittit tibi prefacionem meam de laudibus astronomiae et astrologiae, de qua expecto quid sencias." MBW 1177.5.

155 "Mitto tibi huius anni προγνοστικὸν scriptum a Carione, teque rogo, mihi ut vicissim huius generis mittas, quaecunque digna lectione putabis." MBW 1190.5., esp. n. 41.

156 Melanchthon made disparaging remarks about medieval historians, presumably as part of revising *Carion's Chronicle*, in a letter of 2 November 1531 to Camerarius, but he did not mention the *Chronicle*: "Fama huc affertur de pugna ad Turegum facta, in qua dicitur et Cinglius periisse, si quid habes comperti, totam historiam velim te mihi perscribere, non ut Germanorum scriptores solent, qui nullas causas, nullas occasiones, nulla consilia, nullas περιστάσεις exponunt." CR II, 551 (MBW 1201 dates the letter as 6 November 1531).

157 Karl Eduard Förstemann, ed., *Album academiae Viterbergensis ab a. Ch. 1502 usque ad a. 1560* (Leipzig: Tauchnitz, 1841), 144b, Nr. 19. Carion's signature is not dated, but it appears several signatures after an entry marked as "30 Martij."

1532 helps to explain the lack of correspondence regarding the *Chronicle's* final revisions and publication. Carion's dedicatory epistle to Electoral Prince Joachim is dated "Berlin, 1531" so it cannot be said with certainty when he completed the manuscript, except that Melanchthon had received it by mid-June 1531. The last event mentioned in the *editio princeps* is the arrival of the princes at the Imperial Diet that opened on 17 April 1532.[158] Therefore, the editing process must have continued after Carion arrived in Wittenberg, but other than internal evidence, no record survives to indicate the state of the revisions at the time of Carion's visit.

In addition to the *Chronicle*, an important mission from Electoral Prince Joachim had brought Carion to Wittenberg. Before his departure from Berlin, Joachim had instructed Carion to convey a message to Luther and Melanchthon, asking whether he should continue to take the sacrament in only one form. (In contrast to his father, who was an ardent Catholic, the prince had Protestant inclinations.)[159] In his response of 23 April 1532, Melanchthon wrote to acknowledge that he had received the prince's inquiry through Carion.[160] Luther also composed a reply that same day, with a similar reference to Carion.[161] The dating of the letters indicates that Carion left Wittenberg sometime in late April or early May, and it is likely that he took copies of the *Chronicle* back with him to Berlin.

In May or early June 1532, Melanchthon sent a copy of the *Chronicle* to Antonius Corvinus in Witzenhausen, and his accompanying letter offers the only contemporary description of the *Chronicle's* composition:

> I am sending you a *Chronicle*, in which although certain passages belong to me, nevertheless the raw material of the work is not mine. For Carion sent to me a kind of hodgepodge rather carelessly heaped together. That has been put in order by me, arranged to the extent possible, that is, in a most summary account. At the end, I have added a useful and accurate table with the years of the world, which I hope will please you and other

---

158   See Fischer-Galati, *Ottoman Imperialism*, 51–52.
159   See Nischan, *Prince, People, and Confession*, 11–13; Kuhlow, "Johannes Carion," 59–65.
160   "Haec scripsi ad ea mandata, quae celsitudo vestra dedit Carioni nobis exponenda." MBW 1234.3.
161   Luther recommended that the prince abstain, rather than receive only the bread: "Denn es eben so wohl wider Gott ist, wissentlich eine Gestalt wider seine Ordnung zu nehmen, als es wider ihn ist, wissentlich rauben, morden oder andere Sünde begehen, wie E.F.G. solchs selb wohl bedenken mögen. So ist es nun besser, gar vom Sacrament sich enthalten, und (wo es nicht anders sein kann) sich ungeschickt, krank oder sonst gebrechlich stellen, denn wider das Gewissen tun." WA Br 6:304, 12–17.

scholars. And if our graphic artists reprint the work, I will add evidence from Ptolemy.[162]

In *Corpus Reformatorum*, Melanchthon's cover letter to Corvinus was mistakenly dated six months earlier, to January 1532. As a result, scholars puzzled over whether Melanchthon had sent Corvinus a manuscript copy of the *Chronicle* or an early edition that had not survived.[163] In fact, Melanchthon must have sent a copy of the *editio princeps* soon after it was published.

Decades later, when Melanchthon's son-in-law, Caspar Peucer (1525–1602), rededicated the new edition of the *Chronicle* (1572) to Elector August of Saxony, he attributed the original 1532 *Chronicle* almost exclusively to Melanchthon.[164] According to Peucer, Melanchthon completely rewrote Carion's manuscript, so much so that he really composed a new chronicle; nevertheless, he affixed Carion's name to the final text. Peucer explained that even after Melanchthon began to revise the *Chronicle* in the 1550s, he continued to use the title "*Carion's Chronicle*" as a memorial to his deceased friend rather than an indication of authorship. By the 1570s, Peucer was actively promoting *Carion's Chronicle* as a distinctly Wittenberg text, so he had good reason to downplay Carion's role in writing the original edition. Likewise, there is no indication that Peucer knew of Carion's visit to Wittenberg in 1532. For Peucer, contemporary politics were also a consideration. Elector Joachim II, the original dedicatee, had died in 1571, and by that time, Peucer clearly sought to associate the *Chronicle* with Saxony rather than Brandenburg.

The best explanation for the authorship question is probably the description Melanchthon sent to Corvinus. The raw material came from Carion, but Melanchthon improved the organization, and at several points he inserted new

---

162 "Mitto tibi χρονικὸν, in quo etsi sunt mei quidam loci, tamen ipsa operis sylva non est mea. Misit enim Carion ad me farraginem quandam negligentius coacervatam, quae a me disposita est, quantum quidem in compendio fieri potuit. In fine adieci tabellam annorum mundi utilem et veram, quam spero tibi et aliis doctis placituram esse. Et si recudent opus nostri χαλκογράφοι, addam ex Ptolemaeo testimonia." MBW 1250.2.

163 See Münch, "Das Chronicon," 214–215.

164 "Nomen Chronici Carionis retinui, quod mutare illud autor primus sanctae beataeque memoriae Philippus Melanthon socer meus noluit. Occasio nominis huius inde extitit, quod cum Iohannes Carion Mathematicus ante annos quadraginta coepisset contexere Chronicon, & recognoscendum illud atque emendandum, priusquam prelo subijceretur, misisset ad Philippum Melanthonem, hic, quod parum probaretur totum aboleuit vna litura, alio conscripto, cui tamen Carionis nomen praefixit, Sed & hoc cum retexuisset, amici nomen & memoriam, a cuius primordijs ἀφορμὴ prima Chronici contexendi nata atque profecta esset, titulo posteritati commendare voluit. Quae desunt peculiari volumine descripta, &, quantum omnino fieri potest, optima fide integre explicata, DEO adiuuante edemus seorsum, de quibus vera explorataque nos edituros profiteri ac polliceri possumus." Caspar Peucer, *Chronicon Carionis* (1580), sig. [a7] v. VD16 P 1960.

sections or refined the narrative. In his correspondence, Melanchthon claimed responsibility for the account of the early Franks, as well as the brief "Tabula annorum" that he derived from the Bible and Annius's pseudo-Philo. Other sections, such as the descriptions of Cyrus the Great and Charlemagne, are so well written that it is difficult to doubt Melanchthon's intervention. The *Chronicle* frequently slips into first person narrative, and it sometimes has an almost conversational tone, as if Carion were speaking directly to Electoral Prince Joachim. Nevertheless, in some instances, the "*ich*" probably includes both Carion and Melanchthon. The introductory section on the Prophecy of Elias, for example, uses first person, and the 17 August 1531 letter to Carion clearly indicates that Melanchthon had contributed that material. The original manuscript of the *Chronicle* has never been located and is presumably lost; therefore, most questions about revision and authorship will remain unanswerable.

Even though Melanchthon's name did not appear on the title page of the early editions, in the sixteenth century, the *Chronicle* was widely considered to be his work; and over the years, he exhibited more concern for Carion's little compendium than for other texts he helped to edit for publication. Whether Melanchthon wanted to claim the *Chronicle* as his own or not, after Carion's death, the contemporary understanding of his involvement eventually forced him to engage with the text, and its transmission, as if he had originally been the primary author. Questions of authorship often concentrate on the generation of a text, but here the more appropriate focus is on reception, and from this perspective, *Carion's Chronicle* belonged to Melanchthon.

Five editions of the *Chronicle* appeared in 1532. Georg Rhau published the *editio princeps* at Wittenberg in the spring (Figure 11), and he soon issued the text again, with some variants, mostly typographical.[165] Heinrich Steiner published an edition at Augsburg with more illustrations, dated 16 July 1532;[166] and Francis Rhode published another at Marburg.[167] Then sometime after September, Rhau published a revised edition at Wittenberg in octavo format.[168]

---

165 On Georg Rhau, see Christoph Reske, *Die Buchdrucker des 16. und 17. Jahrhunderts im deutschen Sprachgebiet: Auf der Grundlage des gleichnamigen Werkes von Josef Benzing* (Wiesbaden: Harrassowitz, 2007), 997–998. The initial editions are VD16 C 998 and VD16 C 995.

166 VD16 C 996. On Steiner, see Reske, *Die Buchdrucker*, 34–35.

167 VD16 ZV 20310. Rhode had matriculated at the University of Wittenberg on 10 June 1525, and was active as a printer in Marburg, Hamburg and finally Danzig, see Reske, *Die Buchdrucker*, 146, 334, 602. He also published Carion's *Almanach* from 1537, see Lajos Borda, "Ein unbekannter Hamburger Druck. Der Almanach von Johannes Carion (1537)," *Gutenberg Jahrbuch* 79 (2004): 183–186.

168 VD16 C 997.

FIGURE 11
Carion, *Chronica* (Wittenberg, 1532)
HERZOG AUGUST BIBLIOTHEK
WOLFENBÜTTEL: GB 56

This last edition became the standard text, and it served as the basis for the Latin translation of 1537.

Melanchthon and Carion seem to have collaborated on the revised Rhau edition, but as with the *editio princeps* itself, no record survives of the division of labour between the two.[169] Sixteenth century sources are also silent about the reasons for making revisions so quickly, literally within months of the *editio princeps*. After Carion left Wittenberg, Melanchthon's surviving

---

169 A likely indication of Melanchthon's involvement is the improved description of Ulrich Zwingli's death. In late 1531, Melanchthon had been keenly interested in the circumstances of Zwingli's demise, and the improved account of the revised *Chronicle* probably derives from the reports reaching Wittenberg that year. See Carion, *Chronica* (Wittenberg, 1538), fol. 229r. Carion's involvement is not specifically attested in internal or external sources, but it is apparent from the content, form and extent of the revisions. The most obvious indications of his involvement are the extensive use of first person and the description of Electoral Prince Joachim's departure for the 1532 Turkish campaign: "Den tag / als Marggraue Joachim ausgezogen ist / habe junge Henichen die erst vor zweien tagen ausgebrütet sind / den gangen tag / vnd hernach die nacht vnd tag / stettigs laut gedreet / das doch ein vngewönlich ding ist / derhalben es fur ein zeichen gehalten ...." Carion, *Chronica* (Wittenberg, 1538), fol. 230v–231r.

correspondence mentions him only once more that year in a letter (29 June 1532) to Camerarius, but in connection with the horoscopes of Emperor Charles V and his brother Ferdinand, rather than the *Chronicle*.[170]

The revisions themselves, however, offer an explanation for the decision to rework the text so soon after it was published. Carion probably visited Wittenberg during the 1532 winter term specifically to finish editing the *Chronicle*. Nevertheless, the resulting product shows signs of haste. Carion likely wanted to have copies in hand when he returned to Berlin, which may have forced him to send the manuscript to the printer before thorough editing. It is possible that Carion was simply slipshod, or that he was flustered after learning of Perlach's latest attack, but time pressure seems the best explanation for the failings of the *editio princeps*. The specific problems in the text and the extent of the revisions tend to bear this out.

11 Seventy Weeks of Daniel

Melanchthon and Carion soon realized, or early readers pointed out to them, that the *Chronicle* was riddled with chronological errors and contradictions. The problem was pervasive, and it was surely embarrassing for both of them. Melanchthon had used the Prophecy of Elias and the Four Monarchies as the principal organizing frameworks for the *Chronicle*, but for ancient history important chronological questions were bound to Daniel's prophecy of the "Seventy Weeks" (Daniel 9:20–27).[171] Melanchthon's prophetic scheme did not require precise chronological reckoning, since even the two thousand year intervals in the Prophecy of Elias were somewhat flexible. In fact, Melanchthon and Carion openly admitted that they lacked the necessary astronomical information to chart ancient chronology with absolute certainty.[172] In contrast,

---

170 "Mitto tibi geneses Caroli et Fernandi. Ac Fernandi quidem et altera circumfertur. Sed Gauricus affirmabat hanc veram esse. Si recte memini, Mars erat in fovea in eo catalogo, quem Cornelius Scepperus habebat. Neque hic multo aliter se habet. Carion habet τήν Caroli, quae paululum ab hac differt, in qua Saturnus et Mars sunt in quinta. Sed exemplum non habeo, misissem enim alioqui." MBW 1261.3.

171 On the Seventy Weeks, see CR XII, 784–787; also the lengthy discussion in CR XIII, 874–902. Carion had referred to the prophecy in his *Bedeutnuss und Offenbarung* (Augsburg, 1526), sig. Aiij v, but he did not offer an extended discussion. Luther's own *Reckoning of the Years of the World* contains a discussion of the Seventy Weeks, and it is the only chronological problem that he addressed in depth – WA 53:173–182.

172 "Wer aber die zeit gantz gewis rechnen wolt / der müste zu rück such die Eclipses jnn Ptolemeo / vnd daraus alle iar nach einander eigentlich rechnen / Dieses ist aber nicht eines einigen mans arbeit. Vnd solten die Bischoue auff solche sach etwas wenden...." Carion, *Chronica* (Wittenberg, 1532), fol. 48r.

the Seventy Weeks required greater precision, because aligning the chronology with the prophecy allowed little margin of error. Ultimately, to "correct" the section on Daniel's prophecy, Melanchthon and Carion had to rework the entire chronology, which even required shifting the year of Creation.

The prophecy of the Seventy Weeks was thought to foretell the exact time of Christ's ministry on earth, so it offered a striking example of how history and chronology could be used to demonstrate the fulfilment of biblical prophecy.[173] According to the interpretation in *Carion's Chronicle*, the interval from the rebuilding of the Temple in Jerusalem to the rule of Christ was to encompass sixty-nine weeks, each week being seven years, so 483 years altogether. Christ was baptized at sixty-nine weeks, actually 482 years after the rebuilding of the Temple, but the prophecy was called the "Seventy Weeks" because he was put to death four years later, i.e. within the seventieth week. Explicating the prophecy required an exact year for the rebuilding of the Temple. The date itself hinged on the complicated series of events related to the Temple's reconstruction, and the need to compare biblical events with ancient chronology. Because the date of Christ's death was taken as certain, it was possible to use that as a fixed marker in the chronology and work backwards through Greek and Persian history (with help from pseudo-Metasthenes) to the edict of Artaxerxes Longimanus, which authorized the rebuilding of the Temple.

In the *editio princeps* the reckoning for the Seventy Weeks included 320 years from the start of Alexander the Great's reign to the birth of Christ, with an additional 30 years until his baptism and beginning of the public ministry, giving 350 years; to this was added the 132 years counting backwards from Darius, the last king of Persia, to the second year of Artaxerxes Longimanus, which the *Chronicle* took as the date of the edict. According to this method, the reckoning came to 482 years.[174]

---

173 "Diese rechnung ist am richtigisten. Jch hab auch wol andere rechnung / Aber man rechne diese zeit / wie man wöll / wenn man bey den historien bleibet / so findet man nicht grosse vngleicheit / vnd ist hie zusehen / wie nützlich vnd not den Christen ist / historien zu wissen / die Propheten zuuerstehen / vnd zu sterckung jhres glaubens." Carion, *Chronica* (Wittenberg, 1532), fol. 48r.

174 "Nu sind vom anfang Alexandri bis auff die gepurt Christi 320. iar. Also hab ichs jnn diesem buch allenthalb gerechnet / vnd volge hierin Philoni. Von der geburt Christi bis auff seine Tauff sind 30. iar. Macht zusamen vom anfang Alexandri auff die tauff Christi 350. iar. Dazu thue die zeit vom letzten Dario an bis auff das ander iar Longimani / das sind nach der Grecken rechnung 132. jar. Vnd mit dieser rechnung trifft Metasthenes auch zu / so mans recht ansihet / denn das buch ist corrumpirt / Vnd die iar so Artaxerxes Mnemon hat in Metasthene / gehoren dem Longimano. Auch hat er Xerxen vnd Longimanum zusamen gefasset / wie ich droben gesagt habe. Vnd dieweil die Grecken Xerxen vnd Longimanum vnterscheiden / ist recht / das man hie der Grecken rechnung volget. Summir dieses zusamen / so macht es alles vom andern iar Longimani bis auff die tauff Christi 482. iar.

In the revised edition, this chapter on the Seventy Weeks was completely reworked. The calculations were made with new numbers: 310 years from Christ's birth to the beginning of Alexander's reign, as marked by the death of Darius, together with 30 years until Christ's baptism, which came to 340 years. The time from Artaxerxes Longimanus to the death of Darius was given as 145 years; altogether the interval then became 485 years, instead of 482.[175] The *Chronicle* also included the reckoning based on the Greek historians, which gave 280 years from Alexander to Augustus, so 322 from Alexander to Christ, with 30 years to the baptism, adding the Greek count of 132 years from the second year of Artaxerxes Longimanus gave 484, instead of 482, years.[176] Because the interval from Alexander to Christ was changed to 310 years rather than 320, the time from Creation to Christ was also recalculated by ten years. Therefore, all *anno mundi* dates became ten years less than in the *editio princeps*, and Christ was now born *anno mundi* 3944 instead of 3954.[177]

The chronological questions related to the Seventy Weeks hinged on source questions and the need to harmonize multiple ancient chronologies with the requirements of Old Testament prophecy. Other chronological and numerical problems in the *editio princeps* were more mundane, and most, though not all, were corrected in the revised edition. The Roman Emperors Alexander Severus

---

Dis sind eben 69. iarwochen / vnd jnn der volgenden halben wochen predigt Christus / vnd wird getödtet / Denn Christus ist im vierden iar nach seiner Tauff getödtet worden. So man nu diese volgende woch zu den 69. wochen thut / macht alles 70. wochen." Carion, *Chronica* (Wittenberg, 1532), fol. 47v–48r.

175 "Nu findet sich aus dem Buch Machabeorum / vnd Josepho / das vom anfang Alexandri / nach Darij des letzten tod / bis auff die Geburt Christi / sind 310. jar. Von der Geburt Christi / bis auff seine Tauff / sind 30. jar. Summa / Vom anfang Alexandri / auff die Tauff Christi 340. jar. Dazu thu die zeit / vom andern jar Longimani / bis nach dem letzten Dario / auff Alexandrum / das sind nach Metasthene 145. jar. Summa / vom andern jar Longimani / bis auff die Tauff Christi 485. jar." Carion, *Chronica* (Wittenberg, 1538), fol. 64v.

176 "Ich habe diese rechnung der 70. wochen Danielis / mit vleis nachgesuch / vnd finde nicht grosse vngleicheit / so man bey den Historien bleiben wil / Denn ob man gleich nicht Metastheni volgen wil / trifft doch der Greken zal auch fein zu / Denn zwischen dem tod Alexandri vnd anfang Augusti / sind nach der Greken zal 280. jar / das kan ich starck beweisen / So man nu der Persen jar nimmet / nach dem andern jar Longimani / bey den Greken / so findet man abermal. Nach Alexander / auff die Geburt Chrsti 322. Nach der Geburt Christi / auff die Tauff Christi 30. Adde Persen zal / vom andern jar Longimani 132. bey Greken. Summa 484. Also genaw concordirn der Greken Historien / mit der zeit / so man findet in Josepho vnd Philone / daraus allenthalben abzunemen ist / das Daniel die zeit der zukunfft Christi/ eigentlich bestimmet hat." Carion, *Chronica* (Wittenberg, 1538), fol. 65r–65v.

177 "Denn Christus vnser Heiland / Herr vnd Gott / ist geborn von Maria der Jungfrawen. Im 42. jar / der regirung Augusti. Im 3944. jar / nach der welt anfang." Carion, *Chronica* (Wittenberg, 1538), fol. 107; "Denn Christus vnser Heiland / Herr vnd Gott / ist geporn von Maria der Jungfrawen. Jm .42. jar der regirung Augusti. Jm .3954. jar nach der welt anfang." Carion, *Chronica* (Wittenberg, 1532), fol. 80r.

and Maximinus had both been designated as the twenty-second Emperor, so all the subsequent Emperors had been numbered incorrectly.[178] The *editio princeps* made an even worse chronological mistake after Emperor Marcus Aurelius. The dating for Emperor Hadrian's reign was given as Anno Mundi 4074, Anno Romae 873, Anno Christi 120.[179] Antoninus Pius was listed only as Anno Christi 140; but Marcus Aurelius was designated as Anno Mundi 4207, Anno Romae 916, Anno Christi 163 – a mistake of ninety years.[180]

The problem probably stems from a simple mathematical mistake. In adding the years 4074 + 20 + 23 = 4117, the 11 might have been read as a 2, giving 4207. Otherwise, it could be a common counting error, here related to the reign of Philip the Arabian. From the last "correct" date of *anno mundi* 4074, Emperor Philip should be 128 years later, but instead he was listed as 218 years later, *anno mundi* 4292, so the numbers have been inverted.[181] The mistake could have been read back into the previous *anno mundi* date for Marcus Aurelius. Regardless of how the error was introduced, from that point on the reckoning in the revised edition was one hundred years different from the *editio princeps*. The confusion only increased, since at Charlemagne the *editio princeps* made another *anno mundi* mistake, this time of two years, so it listed Charlemagne at Anno Christi 801, Anno Mundi 4843, and Anno Romae 1551, while the revised edition gave Anno Christi 801, Anno Mundi 4745, and Anno Romae 1551.[182] As a result, the difference between the two editions shifted to 98 years:

	Editio Princeps		Revised Edition		
	Text	Tabula Annorum	Text	LXX Weeks	Tabula Annorum
Incarnation	3954	3942	3944	3948	3944
A.D. 248	4292		4192		
A.D. 801 [800]	4843		4745		
A.D. 1532	5574	5474	5476	5480	5476

---

178 Carion, *Chronica* (Wittenberg, 1532), fol. 88r–88v.
179 Carion, *Chronica* (Wittenberg, 1532), fol. 86r.
180 Carion, *Chronica* (Wittenberg, 1532), fol. 86v–87r.
181 Carion, *Chronica* (Wittenberg, 1532), fol. 89r.
182 In medieval and early modern Europe, some regions began the New Year at Christmas, rather than 1 January, so 25 December 800 was considered to be 25 December 801. On this issue, see John J. Bond, *Handy-Book of Rules and Tables for Verifying Dates with the Christian Era* (New York: Russell & Russell, 1966 [Reprint]), 94.

In his letter to Corvinus, Melanchthon seems to have been genuinely unaware of the inaccuracies in the text of the *editio princeps*.[183] No contemporary criticism is known to survive, but the situation after the discovery of the muddled chronology must have been awkward, especially because Melanchthon consistently stressed the importance of chronological accuracy.[184] Indeed, he felt compelled to expand the explanation of his reckonings in the "Tabula annorum" that he had appended to the *editio princeps*.[185] For Carion, the mistakes must also have been embarrassing. Just as he was working to defend his professional reputation, and specifically his methodological competency, he was faced with serious flaws in his *Chronicle*. In view of this, it is hardly surprising that the revised edition appeared so quickly.

12 Celestial Signs and Portents

Besides the reworked chronology, the revised *Chronicle* also contained a newly drafted section with prophecies about the 1532 Turkish campaign.[186] Carion is the more likely source of these additions, but it is possible that Melanchthon also contributed.[187] Although Carion often used history in his astrological works, he did not reciprocate by including extensive astrological material in the *Chronicle*. At various points he discussed important figures in the history of astronomy and astrology,[188] but celestial signs and portents were rarely noted. In fact, Melanchthon and Carion referred to them no more, and perhaps less,

---

183   MBW 1250.2.
184   See Scheible, "Reuchlins Einfluß," 146; and Heinz Scheible, *Die Anfänge der reformatorischen Geschichtsschreibung: Melanchthon, Sleidan, Flacius und die Magdeburger Zenturien* (Gütersloh: Mohn, [1966]), 27 n. 43.
185   Carion, *Chronica* (Wittenberg, 1538), fol. 236r–238r.
186   Carion, *Chronica* (Wittenberg, 1538), fol. 226r–231v. For the situation in 1532, see Fischer-Galati, *Ottoman Imperialism*, 49–56.
187   The prophetic material is found in the same section as the description of Electoral Prince Joachim's departure for the 1532 Turkish campaign, and first person narrative is used in several places. Carion, *Chronica* (Wittenberg, 1538), fol. 230v–231r.
188   The *Chronicle* traced the study of the heavens back to Adam, and it validated astronomy and astrology through an intellectual chain of succession from the ancient Near East, to the Greeks and Romans, and finally to Germany: Adam and Seth (sig. [Biiij]v); Egypt and Thales (fol. 36v); Eudoxus, specifically astrology (fol. 54r); Egypt and Julius Caesar (fol. 77r); Hadrian (fol. 86v); Ptolemy, extended discussion (fol. 87r–87v); Charlemagne (fol. 116v); Emperor Frederick II (fol. 146r); and Alfonso of Aragon (fol. 149r).

than Schedel or Nauclerus. The *Chronicle* does not even include the historical portents that Carion had used in 1521 to refute Alexander Seitz.[189]

Melanchthon and Carion recognized the importance of eclipses for fixing dates in ancient chronology,[190] but they mentioned them only twice, at Xerxes I and Emperor Gordian III.[191] Comets were noted more frequently, perhaps because of the interest generated by the 1531 appearance of Halley's Comet.[192] The common interpretation in the sixteenth century was that these unpredictable wanderers foretold changes, especially among those of "high estate,"[193] and in *Carion's Chronicle* they invariably corresponded to upheavals in political or religious affairs.[194] At Xerxes's invasion of Greece, besides the eclipse, a comet appeared and a misbirth was discovered, all indicating his coming

---

189 For Melanchthon and astrology, see Barnes, "Astrology and the Confessions," 137–146; Charlotte Methuen, "The Role of the Heavens in the Thought of Philip Melanchthon," *Journal of the History of Ideas* 57 (July 1996): 385–403; Sachiko Kusukawa, "*Aspectio divinorum operum:* Melanchthon and astrology for Lutheran medics," in *Medicine and the Reformation*, ed. Ole Peter Grell and Andrew Cunningham (London: Routledge, 1993), 33–56; and Stefano Caroti, "Melanchthon's Astrology," in *"Astrologi hallucinati": Stars and the End of the World in Luther's Time*, ed. Paola Zambelli (Berlin: de Gruyter, 1986), 109–121.

190 "Wer aber die zeit gantz gewis rechnen wolt / der müste zu rück such die Eclipses jnn Ptolemeo / vnd daraus alle iar nach einander eigentlich rechnen / Dieses ist aber nicht eines einigen mans arbeit. Vnd solten die Bischoue auff solche sach etwas wenden...." Carion, *Chronica* (Wittenberg, 1532), fol. 48r.

191 In addition to the eclipse, the sole mention of an earthquake comes at the time of Gordian: "Da Gordianus Keisar ist worden / ist ein solche grosse Eclipsis der Sonnen gewesen / das man dieweil hat liechter brauchen müssen / Es sind auch Terremotus gewesen / vnd etliche Stedte versuncken." Carion, *Chronica* (Wittenberg, 1532), fol. 89r.

192 See Methuen, "The Role of the Heavens," 395–396. One of the earliest recorded observations of a comet's secondary tail is attributed to Carion, see Jürgen Hamel, "Johann Carion – Entdecker der Kometen Gegenschweife?" in *Beiträge zur Astronomiegeschichte*, Bd. 3, ed. Wolfgang R. Dick and Jürgen Hamel (Frankfurt a.M.: H. Deutsch, 2000), 201–202.

193 Carion, for instance, remarked: "Das gibt die erfarung / das man in gemein weis / das Cometen ein schrecklich zeichen sind / vnd bedeuten furnemlich verenderung der hohen Stend vnd personen..." Johann Carion, *Vom Cometen den man newlich jm M.D.XXXII. jar gesehen hat / iudicium gestellet durch Magistrum Johan. Carion.* (Wittenberg: Rhau, 1533), fol. [1 v]. VD16 C 1036. See also Methuen, "The Role of the Heavens," 395–396.

194 In Carion, *Chronica* (Wittenberg, 1532), the comets are mentioned at: Xerxes (fol. 43r); Emperor Claudius (fol. 83r); Constantine (fol. 94r); Justinian (fol. 107r); grandsons of Charlemagne (fol. 118v); Halley's Comet and Zwingli (fol. 168v). Under Emperor Claudius, a comet appeared and three suns were seen, which foretold the struggle for the Empire after Nero's death. In Nero's own time, a comet was visible for six months; it was connected with the turmoil after his reign, and especially the coming destruction of Jerusalem. Near the end of Constantine's life, a huge comet was seen for several months, which indicated the unrest that was to follow his death, due in part to Arianism. The *Chronicle* also mentioned the appearance of a burning sword above Jerusalem before the destruction of the Temple in A.D. 70 (fol. 84r–84v).

misfortunes. Many comets were seen when Charlemagne's grandsons fought over their inheritance and then divided the realm. Perhaps most striking of all, during Justinian's reign, there were horrible signs in the heavens combined with multiple comets, foretelling the collapse of the Roman Empire and the Church, since Muhammad came soon afterwards.[195] As for Halley's Comet, the authors implied that it had presaged Zwingli's death in battle. On the whole, however, Carion did not emphasize the correlation of historical and astrological events, and the celestial portents were comparatively few.

In contrast to the limited references in the *editio princeps*, the new material on prophecies and portents in the revised edition demonstrates Carion's continued interest in shaping expectations about the future and in seeing history through an astrological lens. Originally, the *Chronicle* had ended with the Emperor's journey to the Diet of Regensburg during Lent of 1532. In the revised edition, Carion continued with the departure of Electoral Prince Joachim for the Turkish campaign on 10 August 1532 and the gathering of Imperial forces in Austria. He portrayed the coming engagement with the Turks as the greatest battle since the collapse of the Roman Empire, even since Constantine;[196] and he introduced a series of prophecies for consideration.

Shortly before the fall of Constantinople, a monk near the city had prophesied that the Turks would destroy the Greek Empire, but they would lose Constantinople again eighty years later.[197] The astrologer in Naples, Lorenzo Bonincontri (fl. 1460), had written verses about a ruler who would eventually dominate the world, and they are included here and applied to Charles V.[198]

---

195   "Zu diesen zeiten hat man viel greulicher zeichen am himel jn Jtalia gesehen / feurige schlachten / Cometen / Auch hat die Tiber Rom schier erseufft / Diese zeichen haben den fall des Römischen Reichs vnd der Kirchen bedeut / der geuolget ist / Denn es wird Mahomet bald nu komen." Carion, *Chronica* (Wittenberg, 1532), fol. 107r.

196   "Item / der Keiser hat ein gros volck auffs Meer verordnet / jnn die 50. tausent / an des Türcken lender zu schiffen / vnd anzugreiffen / Also rüstet sich widdereinander mit der höhisten macht / beide Orient vnd Occident / dergleichen keine macht widdernander gezogen ist / nach dem fall des Römischen Reichs / nach Constantino Magno / vnd schicket sich die sach zu einer ewigen verenderung der welt / Gott gebe der Christenheit vnd vnserm fromen Keiser / gnad vnd sieg." Carion, *Chronica* (Wittenber, 1538), fol. 231v.

197   "Ich habe gelesen / das kurtz zuuor / ehe die Türcken haben Constantinopolin gewonnen / sey ein Mönch nicht fern von Constantinopoli gewesen / der habe geweissaget / das die Türcken würden Constantinopolin eröbern / vnd das Grekisch Reich zerstören / Aber die Türcken würden Constantinopolin bald nach 80. jarn widderumb verlieren / vnd jnn Europa vertilget werden / Nu nahet sich die zeit / denn im nechst künfftigen jar / sinds 80. jar / das die Türcken Constantinopolin gewonnen haben." Carion, *Chronica* (Wittenberg, 1538), fol. 231v–232r.

198   "Auch hat ein rechter gelarter Astrologus zu Neapoli / genant Laurentius Miniatensis / des Pontani preceptor vor 60. jarn jnn sein dritten buch zu letzt diese volgende verse gesatzt /

A prophecy recently found in a chronicle at Magdeburg foretold the coming of an Emperor named Charles, a descendant of Charlemagne and also the Kings of France, who would rule all of Europe and reform both the Church and the Empire; this was now combined with part of the Cedar of Lebanon prophecy to the effect that there should be great changes of regimes, from which the monks would utterly perish.[199] Joachim of Fiore was mentioned briefly as well. Another prophecy stated that an Emperor would be awakened, as if from sleep, who would march against the Turks, defeat them, and seize all their lands.[200] Likewise, the story was told that an astrologer once explained to Ferdinand of Aragon, an ancestor of Charles V, that one day a king from Spain would destroy the Turkish empire.[201]

Carion also noted the appearance of a comet that September, but he did not mention that it was still visible the next month, so he presumably finished his

---

von der Coniunctio Saturni vnd Jouis / jnn Cancro / dauon er redet als künfftig / vnd ist gewesen / Anno 1504...." Carion, *Chronica* (Wittenberg, 1538), fol. 232r.

199 "Zu Magdeburg ist ein Chronica vor hundert jarn geschrieben darin diese wort Latinisch am ende stehen / Vom stam des Keisars Caroli / vnd der Könige aus Franckreich wird ein Keiser komen / mit namen Carolus / der wird herr werden jnn gantzem Europa / vnd wird reformirn die Christliche Kirch vnd das Reich / Denn es wird ein volck komen / das heisst das volck on ein heubt / vnd denn wehe den Priestern / Das schifflin Petri wird grosse not leiden / Aber es wird entlich widder zu rugen komen / vnd sieg behalten. Es werden schreckliche verenderung aller Reich / von die Mönch werden vntergehen / Die bestia von Occident / vnd der Leo von Orient / werden herschen jnn aller welt / vnd werden die Christen frey ziehen 15. jar lang jnn Asien. Darnach wird man grewliche mehr vom Antichristo hören." Carion, *Chronica* (Wittenberg, 1538), fol. 232v. See the chapter dealing with Carion in Robert Lerner, *The Powers of Prophecy: The Cedar of Lebanon vision from the Mongol onslaught to the dawn of the Enlightenment* (Berkeley: University of California Press, 1983), [157]–182; the "Magdeburg Chronicle" manuscript (now lost) was actually a copy of the thirteenth century *Memoriale* by Alexander of Roes.

200 "Jtem / ich finde ein weissagung / die mit etlichen deutlichen worten gestalt ist / Ein Keiser wird erweckt werden / gleich als ein mensch der sussiglich schleffet / von dem schlaff den werden die menschen achten vnd schetzen gleich als tod / der wird auffsitzen auff dem grossen Meer / vnd widder die Türcken ziehen / vnd wird sie vberwinden / vnd jhre weiber vnd kinder fahen / Grosse forcht vnd grosser schrecken wird vber die Türcken komen / vnd jhre weiber vnd kinder werden weinen vnd klagen / vnd alles land der Türcken wird vbergeben / jnn die hende eins Römischen Keisers." Carion, *Chronica* (Wittenberg, 1538), fol. 233r.

201 "Jch habe auch gehört von eim Portugaleser / der sagt / Ein Astrologus hette König Ferdinando / vnsers Keisers anherrn gesagt / ein König von Hispania würde das Türckisch Reich demütigen vnd zerstören / Vnd hette solche weissagung auff gedachten König Ferdinandum / des Keisers anherrn / deuten wöllen / darauff hat König Ferdinandus geantwort / Er würde solchs nicht thun / sondern er hielte / seine erben würden das ausrichten." Carion, *Chronica* (Wittenberg, 1538), fol. 233r.

revisions sometime in late September or early October.²⁰² He described the appearance of two comets in such rapid succession as truly terrifying (*schrecklich*), and he associated them with the wars in Hungary and Denmark.²⁰³ A sense of triumph and foreboding also permeates the revised concluding chapter entitled, "Ende der Chronica." In the *editio princeps*, this chapter had been written in an anticlimactic fashion, with a basic review of the Prophecy of Elias. While the revised edition also included aspects of this summary, the chapter is longer, and it presents a more cogent view of the world in 1532, with a sense of resignation in the face of all the problems facing Europe, both political and religious.²⁰⁴ As a colophon, either Melanchthon or Carion appended the "Homeric Oracle" that prophesied concerning the Roman Empire.²⁰⁵

Carion's revisions changed the tenor of the *Chronicle's* concluding sections, and the prophecies concentrated attention on expectations and apprehensions about the Turkish wars. In many ways, the new material seems fitting for a history written by a court astronomer, and it makes the absence of prophetic material from the *editio princeps* all the more striking. By mid-September of 1532, the Ottoman army had already started to withdraw, and the world-changing clash of East and West did not take place.²⁰⁶ News of those events apparently reached Berlin and Wittenberg too late to be incorporated into the *Chronicle*, and Carion never updated the text to account for them. After months of delays, a trip to Wittenberg to supervise publication, and then what must have been a frenzied few weeks of revisions, he seems, at last, to have been content

---

202   Carion, *Chronica* (Wittenberg, 1538), fol. 233v.
203   "Es ist aber schrecklich / das zwen Cometen so bald auff einander komen sind...." Carion, *Chronica* (Wittenberg, 1538), fol. 233v.
204   "Denn warlich / verenderung vnd zerrüttung / der Regiment vnd Religion / sind nicht geringe sachen / hohe vnd nider Stend müssens jnnen werden / an leib vnd seel. Die welt ist wie ein gros alt gebew / das da reisset / vnd fallen wil / vnd felt itzund da ein wand / denn dort eine / Also schickt sich nu die welt auch zum fall / vnd gewint jtzund da ein riss / denn dort ein / da felt ein Königreich dahin / denn aber eins / vnd sol niemand gedencken / das solch gebew sanfft nidder sitzen werde / Gott gebe gnad / das vns die schrecklichen drawungen / so im Euangelio stehen / zu hertzen gehen / das wir auch bey Christo trost vnd hülff suchen / vnd die grossen herrn / mit Gottes furcht vnd weisheit vnd gedult handeln / zu linderung alles arges vnd jammers / denn sie sind ja von Gott dazu gesatzt / das sie das elend / schwach / menschlich geschlecht / durch ihren vleis / regirn vnd erhalten sollen / Vnd so sie jhr ampt in Gottes furcht füren / wil Gott dabey sein / vnd jnen helffen." Carion, *Chronica* (Wittenberg, 1538), 235r–235v.
205   "ORACVLVM HOMERI- || cum, quod vaticinatur de || imperio Romano. || Nunc genus inuisum Priami Saturniuus odit || Sed pius Aeneas Troas dominabitur inter || Et nati natorum & qui nascentur ab illis. || Finis." Carion, *Chronica* (Wittenberg, 1538), fol. 238v. See Homer, *Iliad* 20.306–308; see also Strabo, *Geographia* 13.1.53.39–41.
206   See Fischer-Galati, *Ottoman Imperialism*, 55.

with his *Chronicle*. At his death in 1537 he was working with Hermann Bonnus (1504–1548) on the Latin translation, but no record survives of his involvement or his plans, if any, to revise the text.[207]

13 Carion's Career after 1532

1532 had been a busy year. Besides his response to Perlach and the two editions of the *Chronicle*, Carion also published a *Practica* at Wittenberg for 1533, dedicated to Elector Joachim.[208] In January of 1533 he finished writing a short interpretation of the 1532 comet, but at that point his scholarly production seems to have peaked. He continued to issue an annual *practica*, but he did not publish anything on the scale of his *Bedeutnus und Offenbarung* or the *Chronicle*.[209]

In subsequent years, Carion travelled among the Hohenzollern courts, and on diplomatic missions within and beyond the Empire. During Easter of 1533 he accompanied Elector Joachim I on a trip to Halle to visit his brother, Archbishop Albrecht of Mainz; and in a letter of 23 April 1533, he informed Duke Albrecht of the splendour at the Archbishop's court.[210] At some point during 1533–1534, Carion also travelled to East Prussia to visit Duke Albrecht in Königsberg.[211] Besides his skill in astronomy, Carion was also considered an expert on heraldry, and his assistance was sought by Albrecht, among others, to explicate coats of arms.[212] Melanchthon and Carion remained in contact during this time, and in 1534, Melanchthon asked his advice about restructuring the University of Tübingen.[213]

---

207 The title page refers to Carion's involvement, but there is otherwise no indication of his work with Bonnus: Johann Carion, *Chronica Ioannis Carionis conuersa ex Germanico in Latinum à doctissimo uiro Herma[n]no Bono, & ab autore diligenter recognita. Halæ Sueuorum ex officina Petri Brubachij, Anno M.D.XXXVII.* (Schwäbish Hall: Peter Brubach, 1537). VD16 ZV 2943.

208 VD16 C 1024. See Fricke-Hilgers, "Die Sintflutprognose" (1999), 295 n. 11.

209 Carion's *practica* pamphlets for some of these years have survived: 1533 (VD16 C 1024); 1534 (VD16 C 1025); and 1536 (VD16 ZV 17959). See also Lajos Borda, "Ein unbekannter Hamburger Druck. Der Almanach von Johannes Carion (1537)," *Gutenberg Jahrbuch* 79 (2004): 183–186.

210 Michael Wiemers, "1533 in Halle: Johannes Carion zu Gast bei Albrecht von Brandenburg," in *Ein "höchst stattliches Bauwerk:" Die Moritzburg in der hallischen Stadtgeschichte 1503–2003*, ed. Michael Rockmann (Halle a. S: Mitteldeutscher Verlag, 2004): 95–106. See also Münch, "Das Chronicon," 204 n. 27.

211 Münch, "Das Chronicon," 204 n. 27.

212 Münch, "Das Chronicon," 205; Voigt, *Briefwechsel*, 159.

213 Voigt, *Briefwechsel*, 152.

The year 1535 brought a series of changes to Carion's life. Through Georg Sabinus, he was granted the title doctor of medicine. In recognition of his abilities as a poet, Sabinus had been made a papal count palatine in Italy on 1 September 1534, and as such, he had the right to bestow doctorates (*doctor bullatus*).[214] Already in 1533, Sabinus, who had been born in Brandenburg an der Havel, had published a poem on the Electoral Prince's return from the Turkish wars, with introductory verses addressed to Carion, and granting the new title seems to have been a further attempt to ingratiate himself at the court in Berlin.[215]

On 13 April 1535, Luther sent Carion a letter to congratulate him on his new rank, while at the same time interweaving jokes about his immense weight. He played on Carion's name by referring to him as *Charon*, who ferried the dead to the underworld, an allusion perhaps to Carion's work as a physician; and he comments that if Charon himself catches sight of Carion, he will be fearful that a doctor so great (in size) might even sink the boat.[216] On the title pages of his subsequent works, Carion now designated himself as *doctor* instead of

---

214 See Max Töppen, *Die Gründung der Universität zu Königsberg und das Leben ihres ersten Rectors Georg Sabinus: Nach gedruckten und ungedruckten Quellen dargestellt und bei Gelegenheit der dritten Säcularfeier der Universität mitgetheilt* (Königsberg: Verlag der Universitäts-Buchhandlung, 1844), 39–40.

215 Georg Sabinus, *Descriptio reditus illustris Principis ac Domini D. Ioachimi II. Marchionis Brandenburgensis etc. depulsis Turcis anno MDXXXII* (Wittenberg: Rhau, 1533), sig. [Aj] v. VD16 S 104. See Münch, "Das Chronicon," 205–206.

216 "Egregio et ornatissimo viro, Domino Iohanni Carioni, astronomiae et medicinae Doctori, amico suo sincere amato. G. et p. in Christo! Gratae fuerunt literae tuae, optime Charon; et cum aliud non possem ostendere viro bono, de quo scripsisti, quam ut ostenderem ei favorem meum et salutantem salutarem, affuit simul ille comes Palatinus Georgius Sabinus, qui forte et ipse ad te scribet. Gratulor certe non tantum tibi, quod dignitate doctorali amplificatus es, sed etiam illi ipsi Palatino, quod tam magnum et grandem et sublimem Doctorem promoverit. Crede mihi, paucos creabit deinceps Doctores tanta magnitudine et sublimitate. Mirabitur ipse (si olim te viderit ad littus suum venientem) Charon, et metuet, ne magnitudine tanti Doctoris cymba eius tam fragilis et umbratilis vel frangatur vel mergatur. Vel certe cogeris pro magnitudine tanti Doctoris magnum etiam dare naulum. Quare tu videris, ut, qui te fecit tam magnum Doctorem, impetret etiam tibi tam magnum stipendium. Et utinam tam magnum (sed totum aureum), quia tu es magnus Doctor. Tum eris certe tutissimus a Charonte illo, caetera avarissimo, ut qui habeas, quo illum largiter remuneres etiam, nedum naulum solvas. Haec iocari libuit tecum, quia et tu mihi visus es in literis tuis iocari. Commenda me illustrissimo tuo Principi iuniori. Nam quid aurae mihi sit apud patrem, nescio. Vale in Domino, mi Charon, et ora pro me. 1535, fer. 3. post D. Misericord. *Martinus Luther D.* Salsamenta missa per tuas literas accepit meus Ketha Dominus, et miratur multitudinem et magnitudinem, dicens: D. Speratus, magnus episcopus, misit satis magnum vas piscium. Cui ego dixi: etiam per magnum virum Charontem. Omnia, inquit, igitur magna sunt hodie?" WA Br 7:173–174, Nr. 2188 a [Text complete here]. On the Carion-Charon association, see Kuhlow, "Johannes Carion," 62–63.

magister, though his earlier publications continued to circulate under the old title.[217] A year later, Carion was still complaining about the costs of the degree to Duke Albrecht.[218]

In 1535, Carion also made two longer journeys away from Berlin. In the first part of the year, he visited the Danish court on behalf of Elector Joachim I and Duke Albrecht.[219] More significant events, however, came to pass that summer. The Brandenburg court was preparing for the wedding of the Electoral Prince to Hedwig, the daughter of the King of Poland, when on 11 July, Elector Joachim died. The Electoral Prince succeeded his father as Elector Joachim II (r. 1535–1571), and the change in rulers eventually meant sweeping changes in Brandenburg's religious policy, despite the attempts of Joachim I to guarantee that his lands would remain Catholic.[220] In September, Elector Joachim II travelled with his entourage to Krakow, and Carion accompanied him.[221] For the trip, Melanchthon supplied a letter of recommendation addressed to Johannes Laski in Krakow (31 July 1535), on behalf of both Carion and Sabinus, and he referred to Carion as a mathematician and doctor of medicine.[222] Early the next year, Carion conveyed greetings to Duke Albrecht from Luther and Melanchthon, and he asked Albrecht how he might receive more money from the King of Poland for his services in connection with the Elector's wedding.[223] Not only did Carion have the costs of his new degree to consider, but at some point before or during 1535, he had also married Margaretha Rehm, though the circumstances are unknown.[224]

At Easter of 1536, Carion and Elector Joachim II visited the court of Archbishop Albrecht of Mainz in Halle; and at the end of the month, Carion

217 The first extant example of this seems to be VD16 ZV 17959.
218 Voigt, *Briefwechsel*, 154.
219 Voigt, *Briefwechsel*, 153.
220 See Nischan, *Prince, People, and Confession*, 11.
221 Voigt, *Briefwechsel*, 152–154.
222 "Comitantur autem Marchionem viri tres eximia doctrina et virtute praediti: dominus Iohannes Carion, mathematicus et medicinae doctor, Franciscus iurisconsultus et Georgius Sabinus poeta. Hi cum incensi essent studio tui videndi ac salutandi, propter admirationem tuae excellentis virtutis, me rogarunt, ut sibi litteras ad te darem." MBW 1592.
223 Voigt, *Briefwechsel*, 155.
224 Prince Georg of Anhalt also briefly mentions Carion in a letter to Melanchthon of 22 February 1536: "Clarrissimo viro domino magistro Philippo Melanchthoni, sibi unice charo. Georgius princeps Anhaltinus, praepositus Magdeburgensis etc. S.D. Vix hesterno vesperi ex Marchia domum redieram, attulit ad me noster magister Georgius literas tuas exoptatissimas una cum enarratione magistri Milichii in secundum librum Plinii. Quae sane hilari animo 'obviisque,' ut aiunt, 'manibus' accepi: primum, quod intellexi te cum scholae maiore parte Witenbergam revertisse, id quod mihi etiam obiter ex Marchia remeanti dominus Carion antea nunciaverat." MBW 1704.1.

reported that Joachim had taken the sacrament according to the old way, so he asked Duke Albrecht to bring the matter up, but without mentioning him.[225] In late spring or early summer, Carion travelled home to Bietigheim, and Melanchthon commended him to Camerarius, who was then in Tübingen.[226] By November of that year, Carion had returned north and he was in Wittenberg for Sabinus's wedding to Melanchthon's daughter Anna.[227] By January of 1537, he was again in Brandenburg, and on 17 January, he apparently sent what would be his last letter from Berlin to Duke Albrecht.[228] To the surprise of all, he died suddenly on 2 February 1537 in Magdeburg, apparently from alcohol poisoning.[229]

From Schmalkalden, Melanchthon mentioned the news to Jakob Milichius, then at Wittenberg, in a letter of 2 March 1537.[230] Duke Albrecht wrote to Carion on 21 March 1537 regarding a visit to Denmark that he had planned to make on behalf of the Elector, so by then the report had not yet reached Königsberg. A month later, the duke sent a letter of condolence to Carion's widow.[231] Georg Sabinus wrote an epitaph for Carion;[232] but the most famous comment on his death comes from Luther's *Tischreden*: "Carion, long ago my adversary, once dared to predict in his *Practica* the day and year in which Luther was to be burned. But the day on which he so drowned himself in drink that he died, this he never predicted."[233]

---

225 Voigt, *Briefwechsel*, 158.
226 "Carionem tibi commendo, qui me properantem Lipsiam cum coniuge et familia non potuit alloqui, sed Sabinus eum expectabat. Etiam Eobanum, ut spero, Lipsiae videbo, qui erit nostri itineris comes." MBW 1732.2. See also Voigt, *Briefwechsel*, 159.
227 Kuhlow, "Johannes Carion," 61.
228 Carion's letter of 17 January 1537, addressed to Duke Albrecht, seems to be lost. Duke Albrecht noted the date and place of Carion's letter in a return letter he sent from Königsberg on 3 February 1537. Voigt refers to Duke Albrecht's letter (Voigt, *Briefwechsel*, 159) but does not include a transcription. Therefore, I have relied on the transcription at: http://www.pascua.de/carion/carion-briefe/ha.carion-1537-02-03.htm.
229 Melchior Adam gave the death year as 1538, which has led to confusion for centuries: "Mortuus Cario in flore aetatis Berlini anno 1538. aetat. suae 39." Melchior Adam, *Vitae Germanorum Philosophorum* (Heidelberg, 1615), 105.
230 "Saluta dominum doctorem Augustinum et dominum Crucigerum. De Carionis morte cito huc allata est fama." MBW 1860.
231 Voigt, *Briefwechsel*, 160.
232 Fricke-Hilgers, "Die Sintflutprognose" (1999), 278–279; Benning, "Johannes Carion," 193.
233 "Carion, olim adversarius meus, semel ausus est in sua practica diem et annum praedicere, in quo Lutherus esset cremandus. – Sed diem, in quo tantum se potu obruit, ut moreretur, nunquam praedixit." WA TR, Nr. 2394. The reference to Carion's *Practica* has never been located.

14 Conclusion

In the 1510s, Tübingen trained many of the scholars who would lead the next generation of German humanists. As they dispersed across Germany, the centre of intellectual activity gradually shifted north to Wittenberg, which became an increasingly important transit point for ideas. There, Melanchthon fostered the humanist studies that had marked his training in South Germany, and within this, he advocated a greater role for history in university life. From the late 1510s onward, Melanchthon wrote textbooks that adapted his ideas to classroom use, and they became a vehicle for his own Reformation of intellectual culture.

Nevertheless, the impetus for composing a new history textbook came not from Wittenberg, but rather from the Hohenzollern court in Berlin. Melanchthon was actively involved in the process, but the plan originated with another former Tübingen student, Johann Carion. Carion was, like Melanchthon, a teacher, but he taught at a princely court, rather than a university. His needs and his aims were similar, but yet distinct. Unlike Melanchthon, Carion and other princely tutors were not bound by the structures of the university curriculum, and *Carion's Chronicle*, the history textbook he composed, reflects these differences. Carion wrote in German, rather than Latin, the language of university instruction. Likewise, the tone is often conversational, as if a tutor were speaking to his young charge, and in the *Fürstenspiegel* tradition, the focus is on princely morals. Despite Peucer's claims to the contrary, *Carion's Chronicle* reflects Carion's own circumstances and his perspective as a Protestant courtier in the service of a German Electoral dynasty.

Despite its later fame, the origins of the *Chronicle* in 1531–1532 were not auspicious. If Melanchthon is to be believed, Carion's manuscript arrived in Wittenberg as a disordered assemblage of material. The editing process continued for months, and delays held back publication. After Georg Rhau printed the *editio princeps* in the spring of 1532, lingering problems quickly became apparent. The chronology and numbering systems were both inaccurate, so much so that Melanchthon and Carion felt compelled to issue a revised edition within a matter of months. At the time, Carion's professional reputation as an astrologer was under attack; there was rampant speculation about his sources and persistent doubts about his methodological competency. The *Chronicle* could easily have added to his scholarly woes. Indeed, if accuracy were a true indication of future popularity and influence, then *Carion's Chronicle* should have become just one more forgotten book from the sixteenth century.

But it did not. Instead, the text became the foundation for historical studies in Germany, both at princely courts, as Carion had intended, and at universities.

The reasons for the *Chronicle's* success were its timing, its content and its associations with Wittenberg. Individually, none of these factors explains the *Chronicle's* vast diffusion and influence, but together they made Carion's little compendium a basis of Western historical thought. Its circumstances were fortuitous, and its message resonated with a German, and indeed a European audience. Books have their own fate, and despite its inauspicious beginnings, *Carion's Chronicle* would ultimately assume extraordinary significance.

CHAPTER 4

Carion's Chronicle: A Wittenberg View of the Past

1   Introduction

On the eve of the Reformation, Germans increasingly turned to the legacy of Antiquity and the Middle Ages to address contemporary concerns. The *Germania Illustrata* movement sought to provide a comprehensive description of German history and geography, but in the early sixteenth century, the humanists tended to concentrate more narrowly on the question of origins and the right of the Germans to hold the Imperial dignity. These emphases reflected the anti-Italian and anti-French bias of many Germans. In general, they resented Italian scholars, such as Aeneas Sylvius (Pope Pius II), who justified the transfer of German wealth to Rome as the payment of an incalculable debt owed for early papal missions. At the same time, they feared French designs on Alsace and the left bank of the Rhine, as well as French claims to the Imperial dignity.[1]

In the initial years of the Reformation, Luther built on aspects of this earlier humanist discourse, but the parallels were fortuitous rather than part of a conscious plan to use history to support theology. In the mid-1510s, German scholars had limited access to medieval historical sources, and what they did have mostly presented a pro-papal view of the past. Even if Luther had decided to write a new anti-papal history of the Middle Ages, he would have had limited

---

1   See generally, Paul Joachimsen, *Geschichtsauffassung und Geschichtsschreibung in Deutschland unter dem Einfluß des Humanismus* (Leipzig and Berlin: Teubner, 1910); Gerald Strauss, *Sixteenth Century Germany: Its Topography and Topographers* (Madison: University of Wisconsin Press, 1959); Ernst Laubach, "Wahlpropaganda im Wahlkampf um die deutsche Königswürde 1519," *Archiv für Kulturgeschichte* 53 (1971): 207–248; Donald Kelley, "Tacitus Noster: The *Germania* in the Renaissance and Reformation," in *Tacitus and the Tacitean Tradition*, ed. T.J. Luce and A.J. Woodman (Princeton: Princeton University Press, 1993), 152–167; Larry Silver, "Germanic Patriotism in the Age of Dürer," in *Dürer and His Culture*, ed. Dagmar Eichberger and Charles Zika (New York: Cambridge University Press, 1998), 38–68; Gernot Müller, *Die "Germania generalis" des Conrad Celtis: Studien mit Edition, Übersetzung und Kommentar* (Tübingen: Niemeyer, 2001); Dieter Mertens, "Die Instrumentalisierung der 'Germania' des Tacitus durch die deutschen Humanisten," in *Zur Geschichte der Gleichung "germanisch – deutsch": Sprache und Namen, Geschichte und Institutionen*, ed. Heinrich Beck (Berlin: De Gruyter, 2004), 37–101.

resources available to support a comprehensive revision of the prevailing historical narrative.[2]

By the late 1520s, the situation had changed dramatically. In contrast to their Italian counterparts, German humanists were keenly interested in medieval history, the period of German Imperial glory, and the anti-papalism of the Reformation encouraged the search for medieval sources that had begun already in the late fifteenth century. By combing through libraries, German humanists, such as Ulrich von Hutten (1488–1532), discovered exactly what they hoped to find, a body of medieval sources that countered the received narrative of papal-Imperial history and the claims of canon law. Hutten reissued Lorenzo Valla's *On the Donation of Constantine*, which brought greater attention to the oration in Germany, but more importantly, the humanists discovered, and then published, a series of pro-Imperial sources related to the Investiture Controversy and the struggles of Emperor Ludwig the Bavarian against the Avignon popes. These newly available texts facilitated a fundamental reinterpretation of European history that overturned centuries of pro-papal historiography.[3]

Nevertheless, during the 1520s, neither the Wittenbergers nor the German humanists composed a new history of the Middle Ages. Indeed, Luther himself later observed that he had used theology rather than history to attack the papacy, and a historical dimension was only added later and mostly by others.[4] Earlier papal-Imperial conflicts had, like the Reformation, resulted in a flood of controversial literature, but as during the Middle Ages, early German

---

2 On this point, see John D'Amico, "Ulrich von Hutten and Beatus Rhenanus as Medieval Historians and Religious Propagandists in the Early Reformation," in *Roman and German Humanism, 1450–1550*, ed. Paul F. Grendler (Brookfield, VT: Variorum, 1993), XII:1–33.

3 See D'Amico, "Ulrich von Hutten and Beatus Rhenanus;" and on historiography in the Reformation, see generally Reinhard Schwarz, "Die Wahrheit der Geschichte im Verständnis der Wittenberger Reformation," *Zeitschrift für Theologie und Kirche* 76 (1979): 159–190; and Matthias Pohlig, *Zwischen Gelehrsamkeit und konfessioneller Identitätsstiftung Lutherische Kirchen- und Universalgeschichtsschreibung 1546–1617* (Tübingen: Mohr Siebeck, 2007).

4 "Ego sane in principio non valde gnarus nec peritus historiarum a priori (ut dicitur) invasi papatum, hoc est ex scripturis sanctis, Nunc mirifice gaudeo alios idem facere a posteriori, hoc est ex historiis. Et plane mihi triumphare videor, cum luce apparente historias cum scripturis consentire intelligo. Nam quod ego S. Paulo et Daniele Magistris didici et docui, Papam esse illum Adversarium Dei et omnium, hoc mihi historiae clamantes re ipsa velut digito monstrant et non genus neque speciem, sed ipsum individuum, non vagum (ut vocant) ostendunt." Luther, *Vorrede zu R. Barns, Vitae Romanorum pontificum* (1536), WA 50:5. Luther had, however, already cited to history in the *Ninety-Five Theses* (1517) and the *Explanations of the Ninety-Five Theses* (1518). WA 1:233–238; and WA 1:525–628. See especially Thesis 12 and explanation.

humanists failed to offer a comprehensive revision of the historical past.[5] When Carion dispatched the manuscript of his *Chronicle* in 1531, Melanchthon was, in some sense, forced to draft a coherent narrative of German history, and the final product reflected a Wittenberg perspective on the most pressing issues of contemporary Europe.

The 1520s had been a decade of change, upheaval and disorder. Emperor Maximilian I died at the beginning of 1519, and his grandson, Charles V, was elected as successor later that year. The Reformation gained momentum, and outbursts of radicalism and fanaticism became ever more disturbing. In 1522–1523, Germany witnessed the Knights' Revolt, which the territorial princes crushed, and then in 1524–1526 the even more tumultuous Peasants' War devastated large parts of Germany. German soldiers, many of them Lutheran, sacked Rome in 1527, and under Suleyman the Magnificent (r. 1520–1566), the Turks marched through the Balkans, overran Hungary and besieged Vienna in 1529. As Melanchthon remarked, somewhat prophetically, in an oration at the death of the Emperor, "When was Germany ever more at peace than as we saw it under Maximilian?"[6]

In response to all this, Melanchthon presented a patriotic narrative that sought to restore order to the contemporary world. He exposed the continual plotting of the papacy and the French, but he also addressed the more recent problems of civil unrest, religious reform and the rise of the Turks. By developing these themes, Melanchthon effectively overturned the dominant pro-papal narrative of late medieval historiography, and he replaced it with a Wittenberg view of the past. *Carion's Chronicle* may now seem conventional, but at the time, it marked a revolution in historical thought. Melanchthon accomplished this transformation of received narratives through a fundamental rethinking of the papacy's role in Imperial politics. Only a decade earlier, the library collections at Berlin and Wittenberg would have been inadequate to support a wholescale transformation of universal history. Through newly printed materials, however, by the late 1520s, Melanchthon and Carion had access to a larger collection of historical texts than even the best medieval library could have offered. They not only saw the past differently from their medieval forebears, but

---

5   See Hanns Gross, *Empire and Sovereignty: A History of the Public Law Literature in the Holy Roman Empire, 1599–1804* (Chicago: University of Chicago Press, 1973), 8–73; and Werner Goez, *Translatio imperii: Ein Beitrag zur Geschichte des Geschichtsdenkens und der politischen Theorien im Mittelalter und in der frühen Neuzeit* (Tübingen: Mohr, 1958).

6   "Quando enim unquam fuit Germania pacatior, quam sub Maximiliano fuisse vidimus?" CR XI, 31.

newly printed texts also facilitated, and even compelled, their reinterpretation of German history.[7]

In the 1550s, Melanchthon decided to revise *Carion's Chronicle*, and in some sense, he worked to complete the task he had undertaken in 1532. By then, Carion had been dead for almost twenty years, and the contemporary situation had changed dramatically. The 1540s had been a tumultuous decade marked by Luther's death (1546) and the upheavals of the Schmalkaldic War (1546–1547). At some points, it even seemed that Emperor Charles V might finally reimpose Catholicism on all of Germany. By the mid-1550s, however, the political situation had improved immensely for the Wittenbergers. The Princes' War (1552) and the Peace of Augsburg (1555) had given the Protestants permanent legitimacy within the Empire; and King Ferdinand was more willing to compromise with the Protestant princes, because he needed their support to secure his elevation to the Imperial throne after Charles abdicated in 1556. However, even as political stability returned to Germany, the situation within German Protestantism became increasingly divisive. After the Schmalkaldic War, the relative unity among the Wittenbergers was shattered by internal theological turmoil, and Melanchthon's later years were embittered by these controversies with his former students.[8]

In his new edition, Melanchthon adapted the *Chronicle* to the changed circumstances of his later years, and he clearly articulated the ideas that he had developed implicitly in 1532. In some instances, Melanchthon rejected aspects of the earlier *Chronicle*'s narrative, but more often he clarified and refined his perspective. Melanchthon died before he completed the new edition, and Caspar Peucer (1525–1602), his son-in-law, finished the later sections, from Charlemagne to the sixteenth century. Peucer struck at the papacy and the Turks in uncompromising terms, and his account of the Middle Ages became an attack not just on papal politics but on the entire medieval religious world. In 1532, Melanchthon had worked a subtle reformation of medieval historiography to wrest history from papal control. Thirty years later, Peucer dispensed with delicate persuasion, and he presented a past that was unambiguously Protestant and Imperial.

---

7 On this point, see generally Elizabeth L. Eisenstein, "Clio and Chronos an Essay on the Making and Breaking of History-Book Time," *History and Theory* 6, no. 6 (1966): 36–64.
8 See generally Bodo Nischan, "Germany after 1550," in *The Reformation World*, ed. Andrew Pettegree (London: Routledge, 2000), 393–396.

2   The Reformation of Form and Structure

In *Carion's Chronicle*, Melanchthon reformed patterns of narration to facilitate a broader historical reconceptualization.[9] Important early printed histories, such as Rolevinck's *Fasciculus Temporum* and Hartmann Schedel's *Nuremberg Chronicle*, had used the Six Ages as their primary frame of reference.[10] The Four Monarchies were present, but from the perspective of periodization, their incorporation was mostly perfunctory. The Six Ages was, by design, a theologically grounded framework, and it stressed biblical, and later papal, lineages. Accordingly, late medieval historians, such as Rolevinck, used the lineage of the popes as the guiding thread for their narrative of Roman Antiquity and the Middle Ages. The focus on papal history and lineages made an argument, sometimes explicit, sometimes tacit, for papal supremacy. Even Martin of Troppau's *Papal-Imperial Chronicle*, which did not use the Six Ages, emphasized the supremacy of the papacy by setting the popes before the Emperors in the page layout.[11]

Melanchthon rejected these late medieval approaches to periodization. Indeed, he dismissed the Six Ages as nothing but "disorder" (*vnordnung*). In its place, he substituted a Christianized version of the so-called "Prophecy of Elias,"[12] which he found in the writings of Paul of Burgos († 1435), a Jewish

---

9   For background, see Roderich Schmidt, "Aetates mundi: Die Weltalter als Gliederungsprinzip der Geschichte," *Zeitschrift für Kirchengeschichte* LXVII (Vierte Folge V) (1955/56): 288–317.

10 I have used the facsimile editions: Werner Rolevinck, *Fasciculus Temporum: Compendio Cronológico* (León: Universidad de León, 1993); and Hartmann Schedel, *Chronicle of the World: The Complete and Annotated Nuremberg Chronicle of 1493*, ed. Stephan Füssel (London: Taschen, 2001). See also Laviece C. Ward, "A Carthusian View of the Holy Roman Empire: Werner Rolevinck's *Fasciculus Temporum*," in *Die Kartäuser und das Heilige Römische Reich* (Salzburg: Institut für Anglistik und Amerikanistik, 1999), 23–44.

11 Anna-Dorothee von den Brincken, "Martin von Troppau," in *Geschichtsschreibung und Geschichtsbewusstsein im Späten Mittelalter*, ed. Hans Patze (Sigmaringen: Jan Thorbecke Verlag, 1987), 168–169.

12 "Wer Historien nützlich lesen wil / sol alle zeit vom anfang der welt / jnn ein richtige ordnung fassen / darümb haben etlich die welt geteilet / jnn sieben Etates / vnd rechen die selbigen mancherley / machen damit mehr ein vnordnung denn ein ordnung / Ich wil fur mich nemen / den köstlichen spruch des trefflichen Propheten Elia / der hat die welt fein geteilet jnn drey alter / vnd damit angezeiget die höchsten verenderung jnn der welt / auch / wenn Christus hat kommen sollen / wie lang auch diese welt weren sol / vnd lautet also. Der spruch des hauses Elia. Sechs tausent jar ist die welt / vnd darnach wird sie zubrechen. Zwei tausent oed. Zwey tausent / das gesetz. Zwey tausent / die zeit Christi. Vnd so die zeit nicht gantz erfüllet wird / wird es feilen vmb vnser sunde willen / wilche gros sind." Carion, *Chronica* (Wittenberg, 1532), sig. B v.

convert to Christianity.[13] The prophecy divided past, present and future into three intervals of approximately two thousand years. Each interval corresponded to a different period in salvation history: before the law, under the law, and under Christ. Melanchthon did not fix a definite date for the end of the world, but with the Prophecy of Elias, he set an outer limit. This was exactly the perspective Augustine had sought to counteract through the Six Ages, which assigned an unknown duration to the period from Christ to the Last Days.

The first two thousand years, from Creation to Abraham, form Book I of the *Chronicle*, and it presents the fundamental principles that govern all human affairs until the end of time.[14] Book II covers the two thousand years from Abraham to Christ, and it traces the succession of the Four Monarchies from Assyria to Persia then to Greece and finally to Rome.[15] Book III, the last age, focuses on the Roman Empire, and it concentrates on three major themes: first, the changes in the Empire, and how it came to be held by the Germans; second, how the Muslim empire came into existence; and last, how the papacy entered into secular affairs.[16]

---

13 See especially Schwarz, "Die Wahrheit der Geschichte," 168–174; and Aby Warburg, "Pagan-Antique Prophecy in Words and Images in the Age of Luther (1920)," in *The Renewal of Pagan Antiquity: Contributions to the Cultural History of the European Renaissance*, trans. David Britt (Los Angeles: Getty Research Institute for the History of Art and the Humanities, 1999), 693–696. See also Julius Köstlin, "Ein Beitrag zur Eschatologie der Reformatoren," *Theologische Studien und Kritiken* 51 (1878): 125–135; Münch, "Das Chronicon Carionis Philippicum," 240–241; Volker Leppin, *Antichrist und Jüngster Tag: Das Profil apokalyptischer Flugschriftenpublizistik im deutschen Luthertum 1548–1618* (Gütersloh: Gütersloher Verlagshaus Mohn, 1999), 63–65, 130–139. See also WA 53:9:15; CR XI, 416 Nr. 6431 (Statement on Prophecy of Elias from 1557); CR XXIV, 17–32.

14 "Diese ordnung wollen wir halten / vnd dieses buch in drey stück teilen / Das erst meret von Adam auff Abraham / denn diese sind die ersten zwey tausent jar / dauon wenig / aber grosse sachen beschrieben / vnd man findet von dieser zeit nichts gründlichs / denn allein jn der Bibel." Carion, *Chronica* (Wittenberg, 1532), sig. Bij r.

15 "Die andern zwey tausent jar / sollen gerechnet werden / von Abraham bis auff die geburt vnsers HERRN Jhesu Christi / wie wol es nicht gantz zwey tausent jar machet / denn (wie gesagt) Gott eilet zum end / Vnd diese zeit ist der welt rechtes vermöglichs alter / darinnen die grossen reich vnd Monarchien nach einander komen / vnd die welt all ihr macht erzeiget hat / Darümb müssen wir diese zeit teilen jnn die vier Monarchien / denn Gott hat die welt jnn ein Regiment fassen wöllen / zucht zu erhalten / vnd den bösen zu weren." Carion, *Chronica* (Wittenberg, 1532), sig. Bij r.

16 "Die letzte zeit / sind zwey tausent iar von Christus geburt an zu ende der welt / wiewol dabey angezeiget / das nicht gantz zwey tausent iar sein sollen / Vnd warlich dieser spruch begreifft viel nützlicher lere / vnd ist sonderlich wol zu mercken / das er von der zeit Christi / auch wenn der welt ende komen sol / weissaget / Derhalben / ich yhn gern hie forn angezogen habe / damit er meniglich bekant werde / Wie aber die Römisch Monarchi nach Christus geburt sich verendert / vnd auff die Deudschen komen / wie auch das Mahometisch reich entstanden / vnd wie das Bapstumb ynn weltlichem gewalt

The Four Monarchies and the Prophecy of Elias together give *Carion's Chronicle* a framework of on-going prophetic fulfilment and a teleology that advances toward Judgment Day. In this regard, it is important to stress that Melanchthon did not present the Reformation as the culmination of history or Luther as the figure who would usher in the last days. The Reformer is mentioned once and only in passing.[17] In contrast, Melanchthon focused on the fulfilment of Old Testament prophecy as the key to understanding the course of history and its advance to the end of time. Indeed, as he observed the decline of the Holy Roman Empire, Melanchthon emphasized that "Holy Scripture comforts us and clearly teaches that the Last Day shall come soon after the collapse of the German Empire."[18] As a result, the third, and final, age of the Prophecy of Elias essentially becomes coterminous with the Fourth Monarchy:

Book I	1	–	Creation
	1656	–	Flood
Book II	2000	–	1st Monarchy = Assyria || Abraham
	3443	–	2nd Monarchy = Persia
	3634	–	3rd Monarchy = Greece
	3907	–	4th Monarchy = Rome
Book III	3954		Incarnation
	4843		Translatio Imperii || A.D. 801
	5044		Electoral College || A.D. 1002
	5474		Present Year || A.D. 1532
			End of Time

By focusing on chronology, rather than biblical and papal lineages, Melanchthon was able to remove the papacy from its central place in historical thought. This initial step allowed him to reorient the narrative away from ecclesiastical history to political, and especially Imperial, history. Melanchthon then turned to the Four Monarchies to provide the structure for the Second and Third Ages of the Prophet Elias. He followed the sequence of Monarchies from

---

        gestigen / wil ich jnn diesem dritten teil anzeigen." Carion, *Chronica* (Wittenberg, 1532), sig. Bij v – Biij r.

17   "Nach Julio secundo / warde Bapst Leo x. ein son Laurentii Medici / Zur zeit Leonis anno 1517 hat Martinus Luther erstlich widder den Ablas geschrieben / vnd sind hernach viel disputationes erreget / Daraus nu eine grosse spaltung jnn Deudschland worden ist." Carion, *Chronica* (Wittenberg, 1532), fol. 167r.

18   "Denn die heilig schrifft tröstet / vnd leret vns klerlich / das der Jungste tag bald komen sol / nach zurstörung dieses Deudschen Reichs." Carion, *Chronica* (Wittenberg, 1532), sig. Bij v.

the Eusebius-Jerome *Chronicle*, so Assyria, Persia, Greece and Rome; and in some ways, the narrative reads, especially in Book II, like a series of columns converted into prose.

With the Four Monarchies, Melanchthon developed several themes that were to varying degrees interconnected. As in the late Middle Ages, Melanchthon did not limit "*translationes imperii*" specifically to the Four Monarchies. However, instead of treating these transfers as a typological justification for ecclesiastical power, he converted them into moral examples for princes. In this way, he preserved the general theme of "*translatio*," but he removed its pro-papal interpretation.[19] Regarding the Fourth Monarchy, Melanchthon traced its history from Antiquity to the sixteenth century, and he imbued his narrative with a sense that the German Empire had a unique role in the divine plan for human history. From Melanchthon's perspective, Daniel's Monarchies were hegemonic, rather than universal, and they were distinguished by their importance in upholding order. This interpretation allowed him to distinguish the Holy Roman Empire from the Turks, who upset, rather than upheld, peace and order. Like Jerome and Orosius in Late Antiquity, Melanchthon used the Four Monarchies to provide reassurance in the face of external threats, political turmoil and accusations of disloyalty to the Empire.

3   *Translationes Imperii*

In the *Chronicle*, Melanchthon presented political history as a system of divine reward and punishment.[20] From this perspective, history contained a trove of examples that demonstrated the importance of princely virtue (*Tugend*) for maintaining stable political rule. Kingdoms were won through virtue, but they could easily be lost through tyranny, blasphemy or immorality. Furthermore, the lessons of the past had present significance because people came and went, but the world ultimately remained the same (*Welt bleibt welt*).[21] Melanchthon

---

19   See Goez, *Translatio Imperii*, 262–264.
20   See Goez, *Translatio Imperii*, 263.
21   "Welt bleibt welt / darumb bleiben auch gleiche hendel jn der welt / ob schon die personen absterben / Derhalben sagt Thucidides / der ein erfarner krigsman gewesen ist / vnd ein grossen langen krieg vnd seltzam hendel / die sich vntern Grecken zugetragen / beschriben hat / das Historia ein schatz sein sol / den man bey der hand haben sol / damit man sich ynn gleiche felle schicken könne / Dieweil immer gleiche sachen widder furfallen / vnd ist warlich Historia ein rechter Fürstlicher schatz dadurch sich ein regent mancherley erinnern kan." Carion, *Chronica* (Wittenberg, 1532), sig. Aiij v.

accordingly treated the *translationes imperii* of history as a *Fürstenspiegel*, a mirror of princes, that offered a cautionary narrative for young German princes.

From this perspective, ancient history abounded with bad rulers, who received fitting punishments for their wicked deeds. The blasphemous Belshazzar (Babylon)[22] and the morally depraved Cambyses (Persia)[23] caused their own demise. Troy fell as a result of Paris's affair with Helen,[24] and the Roman Republic coalesced after the rape of Lucretia and the expulsion of the tyrannical kings.[25] Later, as punishment for Emperor Decius's persecution of Christians, the Goths and other tribes tore apart the Roman Empire.[26]

Melanchthon balanced these negative examples with the lessons of princes who were rewarded for their virtuous deeds. Cyrus the Great, for instance, possessed princely virtue, extensive victories, and through Daniel, he had come to a knowledge of the true God, the ultimate source of his success.[27] Similarly, Melanchthon presented Charlemagne, the first German Emperor, as an ideal ruler,[28] not only for his great victories but also for his interests in religion, law and learned culture.[29]

---

22 Carion, *Chronica* (Wittenberg, 1532), fol. 23r–23v.
23 Carion, *Chronica* (Wittenberg, 1532), fol. 38r–38v.
24 Carion, *Chronica* (Wittenberg, 1532), fol. 24v.
25 Carion, *Chronica* (Wittenberg, 1532), fol. 29v.
26 Carion, *Chronica* (Wittenberg, 1532), fol. 89r.
27 "Cyrus der erst Monarcha aus Persia / ist der aller berümbtisten helten vnd König einer auff erden gewesen / Denn Gott hat ihm allerley hohe vnd Fürstliche tugent / vnd sonderlich glück vnd wolfart im regiment / vnd viel herrlicher sieg geben / ja hat ihn auch zu rechtem Gottes dienst gebracht durch den hohen Propheten Daniel / wie die heilig schrifft bezeuget / Solche Fürsten / die Gott also hoch begabet hat / sol man ansehen nicht wie sie etliche vnuerstendige halten / sondern fur hohe Gottes gaben / dadurch Gott der welt hat helffen wollen / zucht / friden vnd recht auff erden angericht / vnter diese Gottes diener vnd Heroes sol man den Cyrum auch zelen." Carion, *Chronica* (Wittenberg, 1532), fol. 32r.
28 "Aus diesem allem ist zu mercken / wie Gott diesen Keisar mit allen hohen tügenden vnd mit grossem glück begabet vnd gezieret hat / darumb er billich Magnus genant wird." Carion, *Chronica* (Wittenberg, 1532), fol. 117r.
29 "Es gehöret aber grossen Helden / das sie nicht allein kriegen / sondern auch die Regiment fassen mit recht vnd Religion / das hat Carolus auch gethan / Concilia etlich mal gehalten zu Rom / zu Franckfort / vnd etliche jnn Gallia / Auch hat er drey Schulen fundirt / Christliche lahr zu pflantzen vnd zu erhalten / Nemlich / die Schulen zu Bononia / zu Paris vnd zu Paui / Jnn Deudschland hat er viel Clöster gestifft / welche dazumal auch Schulen gewesen sind / Er hat auch das Frenckisch recht zusamen getragen / vnd Recht bücher machen lassen / Denn das alte Römisch Recht war lang durch die Longobarden vnd Francken vnterdruckt. Item / der alten Deudschen Historias vnd lieder hat er zusamen bringen lassen / welche er auch selber hat aussen gelernt." Carion, *Chronica* (Wittenberg, 1532), fol. 116v.

In contrast to his narrative of ancient history, Melanchthon did not attribute the changes in German Imperial dynasties to specific moral failings. Indeed, he did not present any of the German Emperors as tyrannical or corrupt, which implicitly explained why the Empire had remained among the Germans since the time of Charlemagne. By making the Imperial succession central to his narrative, Melanchthon subordinated the lineage of the popes to the German Emperors, and he made an important, though tacit, argument about the Imperial constitution. Earlier historians, such as Rolevinck, had refused to include some of the German kings among the Emperors, because they had not been crowned by the pope. In contrast, Melanchthon designated all the German kings as Emperors, including the founder of the Ottonian dynasty, Henry the Fowler, who had adamantly refused anointing by ecclesiastical officials.[30]

By providing a continuous enumeration of the Emperors from Charlemagne to the sixteenth century, Melanchthon rejected papal claims to political supremacy, as well as French claims to the Imperial dignity. Indeed, Melanchthon referred to Charles the Bald (823–877) as "Carolus Caluus Keisar aus Gallia" rather than his usual designation (such as the later "Carolus Crassus / der fünfft Deudsch Keisar"), and he was pointedly omitted in the numbered series of the distinctly German Emperors. Rather than claim Charles the Bald as a German, as Nauclerus had in his *Chronicle*,[31] Melanchthon presented his coronation as an illegitimate, and failed, attempt by the French and the papacy to permanently transfer the Imperial dignity to the French.[32]

---

30   "Anno Christi 920. ist Keisar worden Henricus primus genant Auceps / ein Hertzog jnn Saxen / vnd hat regirt 17 jar / Er ist nicht vom Bapst gekrönet / ist auch nicht jnn Italien gezogen / wiewol sich zween darinne fur Keisar auffworffen / vnd viel auffrhur anrichten / vnd etlich mal einander schlugen / Denn Henricus hatt jnn Deudschland genug zu thun / das hat er als ein weiser fürst widerümb zu frieden bracht / vnd hoch erhaben." Carion, *Chronica* (Wittenberg, 1532), fol. 123r.

31   "Sed eo mortuo successit in imperio Carolus secundus qui natus fuit in germania ex Ludouico pio & Iuditha Guelfi teutonici filia...." Nauclerus, *Chronica* (1516), vol. 2, Generatio XXVII, fol. CXIX r.

32   "Anno Christi 876 kam Carolus Caluus gen Rom vnd practicirt mit Bapst Johanne nono / das er ihn zu Keisar machet / vnd regirt 2 jar / Nu war Caluus Lotharij bruder / des Pij son / vnd warde jhm jnn der teilung Gallia / Vnd hett der Bapst das Keisarthumb gern jnn Gallien von den Deudschen transferirt / Aber Ludouici Germanici söne woltens nicht leiden / Da drawet er ihn / er wolte ein solch gros volck widder sie vber Rhein bringen / das die pferd den Rhein aussauffen / vnd das volck drucken hindurch ziehen solt / Das hiessen Gallicae minae / Vnd zoge gegen ihn 50 tausent starck / bis gen Cöllen / da ward er geschlagen bey Andernach von den zweien sönen Ludouici Germanici. Im anderen jar zoge Caluus jnn Italiam / da zogen ihm nach die zween sön Ludouici Germanici / Da fiel Caluus aus forcht in kranckheit vnd starb / Noch liesse Bapst Johannes nicht abe / sondern wolte Calui son zu Keisar machen / Darumb warde er zu Rom von den Deudschen legaten

Early modern scholars, such as Hermann Conring (1606–1681), recognized that the way Melanchthon numbered the German Emperors made an important political statement about the source of the Emperor's authority.[33] While Melanchthon made the argument silently, Cyriakus Spangenberg (1528–1604), one of his students, adopted the same approach for enumerating the Emperors in his *Saxon Chronicle*, and he explained:

> Against the custom of some chroniclers, I designate all the Roman kings as Roman Emperors as soon as they were properly elected and crowned after the death of an Emperor. I do so notwithstanding that they were only slowly thereafter crowned and anointed by the pope, in fact a good number were not even crowned at all. Many historians do not do this, rather they designate such elected monarchs and potentates as kings (*reges*), until such time as they are crowned by the pope, at that point these historians give them the Imperial title. This is particularly the custom of papal and Italian writers. Even so, it is not the assent and confirmation of the pope, but rather the election by the proper estates of the Empire that makes an Emperor. Indeed, it is also apparent from histories that many who were the best and most effective Emperors and princes of the Empire were never anointed, consecrated or crowned by the Roman pope.[34]

---

vnd ihrem anhang gefangen / Aber er entranne widder vnd flohe jnn Gallien / Da krönet er Ludouicum Balbum Calui son zu Keisar / Dieser Balbus lebet nach seines vaters des Calui tod nicht lenger denn 2 jar. Also hat das Keisarthumb jnn Gallia ein ende / vnd feileten dem Bapst seine anschlege vnd practiken." Carion, *Chronica* (Wittenberg, 1532), fol. 119r – 119v.

33   "Neque enim verum est, quod nonnulli evincere pertendunt, Henricum Aucupem fuisse caesarem." Hermann Conring, *New Discourse on the Roman-German Emperor*, ed. Constantin Fasolt (Tempe: Arizona Center for Medieval and Renaissance Studies, 2005), 46.

34   "Wider den gebrauch etlicher Chronikenschreiber / nenne ich die Römischen Könige / als balt sie nach absterben eines Keysers ordentlichen erwelet vnd erkoren worden / Römische Keyser / vngeachtet daß sie langsam hernach / oder auch wol eins theils gar nicht / vom Bapst gekrönet noch gesalbet worden / welches viel Historici nicht thun / sondern sölche erwelete Monarchen vnnd Potentaten / nur Reges / Könige nennen / biß so lange sie vom Bapst gekrönet worden / den geben sie ihnen erst Keyserlichen Tittel / vnd ist sölches sonderlichen der Bäpstischen vnnd Welschen Schribenten gar gemeiner brauch / so doch nicht deß Bapsts Jawort vnd Confirmation / sondern die wahl ordentlicher Stände deß Reichs einen Keyser machet. So ist auch auß den Historien kund / daß jr viele die besten vnd nützlichsten Keyser vnd fürsteher deß Reichs gewesen / die vom Römischen Bapst weder Geölet / Gesalbet noch Gekrönet worden." Cyriacus Spangenberg, *Sächssische Chronica* (Frankfurt a.M.: Feyerabend, 1585), sig.)(5 r. VD16 S 7636. On Spangenberg, see Siegfried Bräuer, "Cyriakus Spangenberg als mansfeldisch-sächsischer Reformationshistoriker," in *Reformatoren im Mansfelder Land: Erasmus Sarcerius und Cyriakus Spangenberg*, ed. Stefan Rhein (Leipzig: Evangelische Verlagsanstalt, 2006), 171–189.

Carion's Chronicle was still a papal-Imperial *Chronicle* in the sense that Melanchthon listed both the Emperors and popes, but he confined the papal lineage to brief notes given at the conclusion of each Emperor's reign. Thus, Melanchthon used a medieval scheme, but he inverted its usual argument about political supremacy and turned it into an Imperial framework.

4 The Holy Roman Empire

In Book III of the *Chronicle*, Melanchthon developed a historical foundation for his view of the Imperial constitution.[35] First, he showed that through Charlemagne the Germans were the rightful holders of the Imperial dignity.[36] Second, he demonstrated that papal involvement in German political affairs was illegitimate and destabilizing. Third, he explained how the Electoral College had been formed to prevent civil war and to hinder French and papal efforts to transfer the Imperial title. Fourth, he offered historical proof that Roman Law had been reintroduced to Germany during the Middle Ages and it remained in force as the law of the Empire. Fifth, he admonished the German princes that through compromise within the framework of the Imperial constitution they could achieve peace at home and mount a strong defence against the Turks.

---

35 On Melanchthon's political thought generally, see Speros Thomas Thomaidis, "The Political Theory of Philip Melanchthon" (Ph.D. diss., Columbia University, 1965).

36 Melanchthon used the first half of Book III to tacitly set the stage for the transfer of the Empire to the Germans. Already in the first chapter, for example, he dealt with the Germans at the time of Augustus, and the triumph of Arminius ("Hermann the German") over the Roman legions in the Teutobergerwald: "Augustus hat inn seim Regiment kein Regiment kein sonderlichen grossen vnfal gehabt / denn inn Deudschen landen / Denn zu seiner zeit haben die Römer erstlich sich vmb Deudsch land angenomen / vnd den Reinstrom vnten von Cöllen herauff bis gen Mentz eröbert / Denn die Römer sind inn Deutsch land aus Gallia gefallen / vnd sind von Cöllen gegen Westwalen vnd Saxen / welche zum teil dazumal haben geheissen Longobardi / gezogen. Da war ein Fürst mit namen Herman / die Römer nennen ihn Harminium / Der vberfiel die Römer an der Weser / vnd schulg ihn ab .21. tausent man / dazu ein grossen hauffen ihrer bundgenossen / so bey den Römern lagen. Der Römer haubtman Quintilius Varus / erstach sich selb / vnd war ein schrecken zu Rom / nicht geringer / denn da die Cimbri in Italiam fielen / Denn man besorget / dieser Hertzog Herman / würde mit macht gegen Italien ziehen / Augustus war auch inn solcher angst / das er mit grossem klagen schrey / Quintili redde legiones. Doch practicirt er / das diesen Harminium seine eigene freund verrieten vnd vmbrachten. Das sey gnug von Augusto." Carion, *Chronica* (Wittenberg, 1532), f. 80r–80v. The revised octavo edition converts this description of Arminius into a separate chapter entitled "Von Deudschen" and it becomes the first chapter after the introduction to Book III. See Carion, *Chronica* (Wittenberg, 1538), f. 107r–108r.

Melanchthon and Carion were conscious of the change that they were making to earlier narratives of German history, and they offered *Carion's Chronicle* as the realization of the pro-Imperial history that earlier generations had desired, but ultimately failed to produce:

> Our German historians were such foolish people that any reasonable person who reads them becomes annoyed. Emperor Maximilian's Mathematician, Johann Stabius, often told me how the Emperor complained about German historians and the way they corrupted and described so incompetently the deeds and affairs of noble, wise, and divinely favoured princes. Indeed, the Emperor commanded that all histories should diligently be collected, and from all of these a satisfactory chronicle was to be made; this would undoubtedly have happened had he lived longer or had he not been hindered by other more important matters.[37]

After five hundred years of papal-Imperial conflicts, *Carion's Chronicle* would finally tell the German side of the story.

To begin, Melanchthon gave the German Empire a foundation that was not based on the will of the papacy.[38] At this point, he did not address the

---

[37] "Vnsere Deudschen Historici sind so vnuerstendige leut gewesen / das ein billich verdreusset / der sie lieset / Johannes Stabius des Hochlöblichen Keisars Maximiliani Mathematicus hat mir offt gesaget / wie Keisar Maximilian vber die Deudschen Historicos geklaget hat / das sie der hohen / weisen vnd von Gott begnadeten Fürsten / hendel vnd thaten / so vngeschicklich beschrieben vnd corrumpirt haben / Vnd hat beuohlen vleissig alle Historicos zusamen zu bringen / vnd aus allen ein leideliche Chronica zu machen / Wie on zweiuel geschehen were / so er lenger gelebet / odder durch andere grösser gescheftt nicht verhindert were." Carion, *Chronica* (Wittenberg, 1532), fol. 129r. See Uwe Neddermeyer, *Das Mittelalter in der deutschen Historiographie vom 15. bis zum 18. Jahrhundert: Geschichtsgliederung und Epochenverständnis in der frühen Neuzeit* (Köln: Böhlau, 1988), 27.

[38] "Anno Christi 801 Anno Mundi 4843 Anno Romae 1551 Jst Carolus Magnus zu Rom am Christag zu Keisar gekrönet worden vom Bapst Leone tertio / Vnd ist dieses der anfang des Keisarthumbs jnn Deudsch land / vnd hat Italia vnd Occident durch diese translatio widderumb ein gewaltig haubt / vnd ein mechtigen schutz vberkomen / Denn wiewol die Deudschen Keisar nicht alle gleich mechtig gewesen sind / wie jnn keinem Reich die Könige gleiche macht vnd glück gehabt haben / so sind doch fur vnd fur etliche Keisar seer mechtig gewesen vnd haben Italia geredtet / vnd viel grosser löblicher thaten gethan / vnd sachen gehandelt / dadurch sie friede / Regiment vnd Religion jnn Occident erhalten haben / Vnd so man unser Deudschen Keisar hendel erweget / findet man / das warlich hohe weise Fürsten / vnd nicht barbari gewesen sind / vnd sind wol zu vergleichen den löblichsten Römern / als Augusto / Traiano / Adriano / Constantino. Dazu spüret man / ja mehr erbarkeit jnn den vnsern / denn jn den selbigen / Auch findet man das die vnsern furnemisten Keisar / nicht aus eigenem ehrgeitz odder eigenem nutz krieg angefangen

Carolingian *translatio imperii* in depth, and in fact, most striking is what Melanchthon left out. Earlier German humanists, such as Wimpfeling, had followed late medieval practice and treated canon law as a historical authority. In contrast, Melanchthon says nothing about *Venerabilem* or the curial *translatio imperii* theory in the *Chronicle*. His approach marked an important shift in historical thought, because he focused on sources and evidence, rather than authorities, both for facts themselves and for interpretive issues. In this respect, his approach was closer to Nicolas of Cusa, who had used historical evidence to discredit the *Donation of Constantine*, than to Lorenzo Valla, who had attacked the *Donation* with rhetoric and logic. Thus, in the *Chronicle*, Melanchthon dismissed the *Donation of Constantine* simply by noting that the transfer was not recorded in any reliable histories.[39]

In addition, Melanchthon implicitly refuted the curial *translatio imperii* theory through his description of historical events. He presented the collapse (*Zerstörung*) of the Western Roman Empire as a process that accelerated after the time of Theodosius I,[40] and after Valentinian III, the Eastern Emperors provide the chronological outline down to Constantine VI and Irene.[41] Melanchthon then emphasized that the Carolingians had taken control of Italy and the lands belonging to the old Roman Emperors,[42] and he credits Charlemagne with the formation of the Papal States, rather than Pippin or Constantine. By concentrating on Charlemagne's control of Italy, the old Imperial heartland, Melanchthon implicitly presented *de facto* rule as the real basis for his assumption of the Imperial title. Indeed, although Melanchthon noted that Constantinople recognized Charlemagne's use of the Imperial title, he

---

haben / sondern allein aus hoher not / zu rettung der Religion / landen vnd leuten." Carion, *Chronica* (Wittenberg, 1532), fol. 112v–113r.

39 "Aber das Constantinus dem Bapst sol Rom vnd das halb Keisarthumb geschenckt haben / wie etliche fabuliren / findet man jnn keinen glaubwirdigen Historien." Carion, *Chronica* (Wittenberg, 1532), fol. 93r.

40 Carion, *Chronica* (Wittenberg, 1532), fol. 97v.

41 "Nach Valentiniano ist das Römisch Reich wüst zerrissen worden / haben sich viel Keisar genennet jnn Italia / Doch ist der Keisarliche name / vnd dennoch ein grosse macht zu Constantinopoli blieben / vnd hat hernach Justinianus auch das Reich jnn Occident widder zum teil zusamen gebracht / durch Bellisarium vnd Narsen. Aber nach Valentiniano worffen sich viel aufffur Keisar jnn Italia / vnd hatt Italia neher den jnn 20 jarn 9 Regenten nacheinander / vnd warde fur vnd fur einer vom andern erstochen. Der letzt nennet sich Augustulum / welcher name ein zeichen gewesen ist / das das Reich Augustorum jnn Italia fallen solt / Diesen Augustulum veriaget Othaker / Widder Othakern ward Dierich von Bern jnn Italien gesand zur zeit Zenonis / Also kam Italia auff die Gotthen / Hernach worden die Gotthen wider / gedempfft / vnter Justiniano / wie droben gesagt ist." Carion, *Chronica* (Wittenberg, 1532), fol. 105r–105v.

42 Carion, *Chronica* (Wittenberg, 1532), fol. 115r.

presents the recognition as perfunctory, since the Eastern Emperors no longer held the lands in the West.[43]

Carolingian history addressed the formation of the German Empire. Ottonian history then accounted for the Empire's constitutional structure. Melanchthon and Carion were both tied to Electoral courts, and the Electoral College itself is, in some sense, the hero of their *Chronicle*.[44] To this day, the origins of the Electoral College remain uncertain, and Melanchthon's argument – ultimately derived from Martin of Troppau – that Emperor Otto III simply chose the first Electors in 1002 is not unreasonable, but without contemporary witness.[45]

43 "Anno 32 zoge Carolus gen Rom / vnd setzt den Bapst Leo widder ein / widder welchen die Römer ein gros auffrhur erreget hatten / das der Bapst fliehen muste / Da nu Carolus befande / das kein friede jnn Italia sein kont / dieweil die Stedte frey waren / vnd allen mutwillen trieben / muste er sich des Regiments annemen / Also ward er herr vber gantz Italien / vnd gabe dem Bapst etlich land vnd stedte / zu vnterhaltung des kirchen regiments / Vnd an der Christnacht ruffet der Bapst in der kirchen / Carolus solte Römischer Keisar and Augustus sein / Hie schreibet man / Carolus habe gesagt / er wolde nicht jnn die kirchen komen sein / wo er sich dieses versehen hette / Auch wolt er sich nicht Keisar schreiben / bis er sich mit den zu Constantinopoli vertrug / Da willigeten Irene Constantini mutter / vnd Nicephorus das Carolus solt Keisar jnn Occident genant werden / vnd solchs war ihnen leicht zu willigen / denn die Keisar zu Constantinopoli hatten doch die land nicht mehr." Carion, *Chronica* (Wittenberg, 1532), fol. 115v -116r.

44 "Vnd solten die Deudschen Fürsten / vnd sonderlich die Chürfursten / solche jhr ehre billich hoch vnd tewer achten / das yhnen Gott die hoheit jnn der welt beuohlen / Religion / recht vnd friede zu erhalten / Denn ist warlich viel an dieser Monarchi / wiewol sie gering scheinet / gelegen / vnd sollen billich die Fürsten vneinigkeit vnd zwitracht / zwischen ihnen selbst verhüten / Damit sie nicht vrsach geben / das dieses Reich zerrissen / vnd das rechte heubt der gantzen weltordnung zerstöret werde / dadurch hernach vnordnung folgen müste jnn gantzer Christenheit / als ich leider besorge / das geschehen werde / Gott gebe nur gnad / das als denn der Jünste tag bald kome / dem vnrat zu stewren / Denn die heilige schrifft tröstet / vnd leret vns klerlich / das der Jungste tag bald komen sol / nach zustörung dieses Deudschen Reichs." Carion, *Chronica* (Wittenberg, 1532), sig. Bij v.

45 It is likely that Melanchthon used *Nauclerus's Chronicle* as his immediate source. The founding in 1002 is found in Nauclerus, *Chronica* (1516), vol. 2, Generatio XXXIIII, fol. CX-LIIII v. The section in *Carion's Chronicle* reads: "Nu war Otho bey 28 jar alt / vnd hatt solchen verstand / das er von wegen seiner klugheit genennet ist / Mirabilia mundi / Dazu hatten die Saxen als geschwinde leute / nu die Wellischen practiken gelernet / Darumb dieweil sie sahen / das die Bäpst zu Rom souiel auffrhuren widder die Keisar / vnd sonst / erregten / machet Otho ein Deudschen / seinen vetter Bruno zu Bapst / der wird genennet Gregorius .v. Von diesem ist Otho tertius gekrönet / Dieweil auch Otho befunden hat / wie sich Galli vnd Itali fur vnd fur vnterstunden / das Keisarthumb von Deudschen auff sich zu wenden / Item / das auch in Deudschland viel auffrhuren gewesen waren / widder alle seine voreltern / der wahl halben / vnd doch der Christenheit ein solcher potentat not ist / der Rom vnd den Bapst schützet / einigkeit der Religion in Europa zu erhalten / vnd aber nicht bestendig sein möchte / wo nicht solcher potentat gewislich auff ein sonderliche vnd mechtige natio gestifft vnd geordnet würde / hat er sampt dem Bapst Gregorio / der

Indeed, Melanchthon acknowledged the gaps in his sources about the Electoral College,[46] and he complained:

> I have not found further information on how this matter played out, for our German historians were unable to describe affairs thoroughly with reasons and circumstances, because they were monks, and they were not accustomed to political dealings. As a result, they lacked adequate understanding of many things that they should have inquired about, or paid attention to, [characteristics] that belong to a proper historian.[47]

Based on the broader context, Melanchthon believed that the Electoral College represented a compromise between Otto III and Gregory V, a German pope, to bring stability to the Imperial succession and an end to the recurring civil wars in Germany. By drawing the Electors from among the German princes, Otto decided to exclude the French and the papacy from German affairs, and Melanchthon saw this principle as fundamental for German political stability.[48] The Electoral College recognized internal ecclesiastical interests through

---

ihm als ein Deudscher dazu gern geholffen hat / die ordnung der Chürfürsten eingesetzt vnd instituirt / Also das die furnemisten geistlichen vnd weltlichen Fürsten dazu solten gezogen werden / einigkeit der wahl zwischen geistlichen vnd weltlichen zu erhalten / der Religion zu gut." Carion, *Chronica* (Wittenberg, 1532), fol. 128v.

46 "Vnd sind nemlich diese drey Ertzbischoff zu Chürfursten gemacht / Mentz / Cöllen / Trier / Daneben diese vier weltlichen Fürsten / Der Fürst von Behem / Denn dazumal hat Behem noch nicht König gehabt / Der Pfaltzgraue am Rhein / Der Hertzog zu Saxen / Der Marggraue zu Brandenburg. Mich wundert aber / das nicht andere Fürsten / so dazumal mechtiger gewesen sind / zu solcher hohen ehr gezogen sind / Als Hertzogen in Bairn / Schwaben / Francken / Sonderlich dieweil der Hertzog zu Baiern dazumal Othonis naher vetter vnd ein seer mechtiger Fürst gewesen ist / Denn er hat gehabt Baiern vnd Ostrich bis gen Aquileia / welches Henricus Othonis primi bruder gewonnen hat / Auch ware der Hertzog von Schwaben Othonis naher vetter / denn Hertzog Herman von Schwaben vnter Othone primo / hatt kein manlichen erben / darumb gabe er seine tochter dem Ludolff Othonis primi son / mit welchem der vater gekrieget hat / Von diesem Ludolff sind die Hertzogen jnn Schwaben hernach komen / Derhalben mag es wol ein wundern / wie sichs mit der Churfürsten Jnstitutio zugetragen hat." Carion, *Chronica* (Wittenberg, 1532), fol. 128r–129v.

47 "Wie sich aber die sachen weiter zugetragen haben / finde ich auch nicht Denn vnsere Deudschen Historici haben kein handel gruntlich beschreiben können / mit vrsachen vnd vmbstenden / denn es sind Mönche gewesen / vnd sind nicht zun hendeln gezogen worden / So haben sie so viel verstands nicht gehabt / das sie darnach gefraget hetten / odder bedacht / was zu eim Historico gehöret." Carion, *Chronica* (Wittenberg, 1532), fol. 125r.

48 "Wie hoch aber diese ordnung vnd einsetzung der Churfürsten zu loben sey / kan ich nach notturfft hie nicht gnugsam erzelen / Die sach beweiset selb / das diese ordnung

the three Archbishop Electors, and its structure insulated the Electoral regime, to some degree, from French and papal machinations. With his description of the Electoral College, Melanchthon implicitly argued that the German Electors chose the Emperor, and subsequent papal confirmation or coronation was unnecessary and meaningless.

Once the German Empire had been formed and its political structure set in place, Melanchthon demonstrated how it had withstood continuing French and papal efforts to destroy it. The struggle for the stability of the Empire against papal interference reached its high point during the Investiture Controversy and the associated German civil war (1075–1122). For these events, Melanchthon preferred material from the strongly Imperial *Chronicle* by Sigebert of Gembloux († 1112) to the pro-papal narrative in Nauclerus. Indeed, Melanchthon explicitly referred to Sigebert, which he did less often for his medieval sources than his ancient ones.[49]

In contrast to late medieval historians, Melanchthon presented Hildebrand (Pope Gregory VII) as destabilizing European order,[50] and he blamed the pope and his attempts to change the practice of papal and episcopal elections[51] for

---

viel guts bracht hat / Denn dadurch ist nu das Reich lenger denn 500 jar jnn dieser natio erhalten / Nu ist auff erden kein menschlich ding nützlicher / besser vnd seliger / denn verhüten / weren vnd vorkomen verenderung der Regiment / welchs durch diese ordnung mit Gottes gnaden also geschehen / Vnd sind der Bäpst vnd Frantzosen praktiken gehindert / die sich seer offt vnterstanden haben / das Reich jnn Gallien zu transferirn / Vnd hat ein Keisar mehr anhangs von fürsten / dieweil er von ihnen gewelet wird / Es kan auch weniger auffrhur der wahl halben werden / so die furnemisten Fürsten jnn einen gewilliget haben." Carion, *Chronica* (Wittenberg, 1532), fol. 129v.

49 "Sigebertus Historicus lobet Hilbrand nicht seer / sondern strafft seine handlungen hart / das er on billiche vrsach solche zerruttung der Kirchen vnd des Reichs angericht habe / Schreibt auch / Hiltebrand habe solchs vor seinem tod selb beklaget / vnd Henricum bitten lassen / das er ihm verzeihen wolt / Hiltebrand hat auch den priestern jnn Deudschland die Ehe verboten / vnd viel Ehe widder zerrissen." Carion, *Chronica* (Wittenberg, 1532), fol. 135v.

50 "Anno 1057 hat angefangen zu regieren nach seines vaters tod Henricus der vierde / noch seer jung / vnd regirt 50 jar / Nu ist das aureum seculum dieses geschlechts auch aus / Ja das gantz Deudsche Reich fahet hie an zu fallen / vnd ist nie widder recht jnn alten stand vnd vorige macht komen / Vnd das spiel hat Bapst Hellbrand angericht / der seer grosse schreckliche krieg vnter den Deudschen erreget hat." Carion, *Chronica* (Wittenberg, 1532), fol. 134 r.

51 "Ich kan seine hendel nicht alle erzelen / Die furnemiste sache wil ich kürtzlich anzeigen / Der vater Henricus Niger / hat guter meinung die ordnung der Bepstlichen wahl halben gemacht / das keiner Bapst sein solt / one des Keisars bewilligung / Da nu Bapst Helbrand gewelet ward / facht er diese ordnung an / vnd ordnet dagegen / das man des Keisars confirmatio nicht suchen solt / Nu wolt der Keisar ob seines vaters ordnung halten / Item / vor dieser zeit hatte der Keisar gewalt die Bistumb im Reich zu leihen / das wolt Bapst

the civil wars that permanently damaged the Empire and initiated its long decline.[52] Melanchthon omits Emperor Henry IV's humiliating penance at Canossa, and instead he emphasizes Henry's triumph, as rightful Emperor, over the uprising of his rival, Rudolf of Rheinfelden.[53] After Henry's victory, Melanchthon recounts the wretched end of Hildebrand. The Emperor marched on Rome and received the Imperial crown from the rival pope he had set up. Hildebrand died shortly thereafter in misery. Thus, the Empire, though weakened, once again survived papal attempts to undermine the Germans, and the pope who had sought to overturn the order of Church and Empire met a fitting end.[54]

After the formation of the Electoral College, the next important constitutional development in the Empire was the reintroduction of Roman Law in the early twelfth century. To explain this medieval renewal, Melanchthon inserted the "Lotharingian Legend" that in the early twelfth century Emperor Lothar III (r. 1125–1137) reintroduced Roman Law to the West:

Helbrand auch nicht leiden / Vnd begab sich / so ein Bischoff starb / das der Keisar einen setzet / vnd der Bapst auch einen / vnd excommunicirt den andern / Entlich aus diesen vrsachen excommunicirt der Bapst den Keisar / vnd triebe die gewaltigen Fürsten / das sie vom Keisar fallen / vnd ein andern Keisar welen solten." Carion, *Chronica* (Wittenberg, 1532), fol. 134v.

52 "Wie schedlich das Ciuile bellum jnn Deudschland / durch des Bapsts practiken erreget / gewesen ist / kan man daraus abnemen / das so viel Fürsten vnd hoher leut erschlagen / vnd die Fürstenthumb verendert sind. Henricus quartus hat Baiern den Welffen gegeben / die waren schwaben / Das Hertzogthumb Schwaben nach dem tod Rudolffi / gabe Henricus seinem tochterman Friderico von Stauffen / das jnn Schwaben ligt bey Gemund / Der Francken geschlecht ist auch bald gefallen / Eckbert der Marggraue von Meissen ist erschlagen / Gebhart ist erschlagen / der vater Lotharii / der hernach Keisar worden ist / Jnn summa / Deudschland ist gantz geschwecht vnd verendert worden." Carion, *Chronica* (Wittenberg, 1532), fol. 136v.

53 "Also starb Rudolff im 4 jar nach seiner wahl. Es müst freilich ein eifern hertz sein / den dieses schrecklich exempel nicht schrecket / vnd zu gehorsam vermanet / Aber die Bischoue sind gleich wol furt gefaren / vnd haben nach diesem vnfal den son widder den vater erreget. Bapst Helbrand rhümet er hett ein visio gehabt / dis jar solt der vnrecht Keisar vmbkomen / Das war ein Caiphas Prophecey / denn sie traff des Bapsts anhang / vnd nicht Henricum." Carion, *Chronica* (Wittenberg, 1532), fol. 135r.

54 "Nach dieser victoria zoge Henricus gen Rom / vnd nam Rom ein mit gewalt / fienge vnd entsetzet Bapst Helbrand / vnd machet zu Bapst ein Bischoff von Rauenna / der heist Clemens / Dieser hat Henricum quartum zu Keisar gekrönet / vnd ist Hiltebrand jnn kürtz jm elend gestorben. Sigebertus Historicus lobet Hilbrand nicht seer / sondern strafft seine handlungen hart / das er on billiche vrsach solche zerruttung der Kirchen vnd des Reichs angericht habe / Schreibt auch / Hiltebrand habe solchs vor seinem tod selb beklaget / vnd Henricum bitten lassen / das er ihm verzeihen wolt / Hiltebrand hat auch den priestern jnn Deudschland die Ehe verboten / vnd viel Ehe widder zerrissen." Carion, *Chronica* (Wittenberg, 1532), fol. 135v.

Lothar is highly praised, not only on account of his victories, through which he brought peace to Germany and Italy, but also that he treasured law and religion. At his time, there was in the Empire a learned man named Werner in the circles of Countess Matilda in Italy, whom Accursius often calls Irnerius. He found the books of Roman Law in [Italian] libraries, and brought them back to light. Lothar ordered that they be read in the schools, and that Imperial judgments once again be pronounced according to them. In this way, this noble treasure was again brought forth, and much good has followed from it, namely that there is once again a rational law in all of Europe.[55]

Melanchthon's source for the Lotharingian Legend is unknown. For the rediscovery of Roman Law in Italy, Melanchthon probably relied on the *Ursberger Chronicle*,[56] but the crucial idea that Emperor Lothar reintroduced Roman Law as binding in the Empire is not found there, or anywhere else in surviving sources. Therefore, Melanchthon probably relied on bad information from Carion or confused some of his sources.[57] It is also possible that he fabricated his assertion that Lothar reintroduced Roman Law to the West, but no sources have ever emerged to condemn or exonerate him.

By 1532, Melanchthon stressed the importance of Roman Law for three reasons. First, he had turned to Roman Law in the face of the Peasants' War, because he had become convinced that biblical and customary laws were incapable of preventing disorder and violence. In contrast, Roman law, as a written law, provided a firm basis for an orderly society. Second, by the 1530s, he had come to believe that Roman Law was a law of peace, and its impartiality could serve as a restraint on a hostile Emperor. Accordingly, Melanchthon

---

55 "Lotharius wird seer gelobet / nicht allein von wegen seiner sieg / dadurch er Deudsch land vnd Jtalien zu frieden bracht hat / sondern auch das er Religion vnd recht / seer lieb gehabt hat / Zu seiner zeit ist ein gelart man genant Wernherus / den Accursius offt nennet Jrnerium / jm Reich jnn Jtalia gewesen / bey der Fürstin Mechtildis / der hat die Römische recht bücher jnn Bibliotheken gefunden / vnd widder an das liecht bracht / Die hat Lotharius befolen jnn Schulen zu lesen / vnd widderumb darnach zu sprechen jnn Keisarlichen gerichten / Also ist dieser edel schatz widder herfur komen daraus viel guts geuolget nemlich / das man widderumb ein vernünfftig recht jnn gantzem Europa hat / Denn es richten sich doch alle land vnd recht / nach diesem Römischen recht / dieweil man befindet / das es der erbarkeit so gantz genies ist / So ist auch sonst viel guts daraus komen / Denn man findet keine besser lahr von guten sitten / denn diese." Carion, *Chronica* (Wittenberg, 1532), fol. 138v–139r.
56 Burchard of Ursberg, *Chronicvm Abbatis Vrspergensis* (Strasbourg: Mylius, 1537), CCXCI. VD16 B 9801.
57 See Gross, *Empire and Sovereignty*, 84–87.

embraced Roman Law as it had been used and interpreted in the Middle Ages (*mos Italicus*), rather than the purified Roman Law of French humanists (*mos Gallicus*).[58] Third, Melanchthon associated Roman Law with the Fourth Monarchy and the successors to the ancient Roman Empire. On this basis, he argued that the Fourth Monarchy could not be transferred to the Turks, because rather than upholding justice and peace, their laws spread the teachings of Islam. This understanding of "Monarchy" was a crucial aspect of his intellectual defence against the Ottoman threat.

5 The Four Monarchies and the Turks

During Emperor Maximilian's reign, his propagandists had used the Turkish threat to solicit support, and funding, for Hapsburg aims in the Balkans.[59] Nevertheless, many humanists, including Erasmus and Ulrich von Hutten, remained unpersuaded by Hapsburg and papal pleas for money to combat the Ottomans, and they criticized the attempts to wage a new crusade.[60] The Wittenbergers joined this chorus in the 1520s, but they did so just as the situation in the East started to change dramatically; and by 1529, Suleyman the Magnificent's policy of military expansion had brought the Turks to the gates of Vienna. As a result, the Wittenbergers were forced to counter accusations of Turkish sympathies,[61] and in doing so, they addressed the historical and prophetic foundations of both the Holy Roman Empire and the Ottoman Empire. In particular, they enlisted the Book of Daniel to make the confrontation between the Germans and

---

58 For these two points, I rely on James Q. Whitman, *The Legacy of Roman Law in the German Romantic Era: Historical Vision and Legal Change* (Princeton: Princeton University Press, 1990), 1–40. See also Gross, *Empire and Sovereignty*, 73–91; Guido Kisch, *Melanchthons Rechts- und Soziallehre* (Berlin: de Gruyter, 1967), 189–209; and generally Isabelle Deflers, *Lex und Ordo: Eine rechtshistorische Untersuchung der Rechtsauffassung Melanchthons* (Berlin: Duncker & Humblot, 2005).

59 See Darin Hayton, "Astrology as Political Propaganda: Humanist Responses to the Turkish Threat in Early Sixteenth-Century Vienna," *Austrian History Yearbook* 38 (2007): 61–66; and Gregory J. Miller, "Holy War and Holy Terror: Views of Islam in German Pamphlet Literature, 1520–1545" (Ph.D. diss., Boston University, 1994), 49–55.

60 See WA 30^II:90–91; Martin Brecht, "Luther und die Türken," in *Europa und die Türken in der Renaissance*, ed. Bodo Guthmüller and Wilhelm Kühlmann (Tübingen: Niemeyer, 2000), 10.

61 Johannes Cochlaeus (1479–1552) was especially harsh on the Protestants in his 1529 pamphlets on the "Seven-Headed Luther," see VD16 C 4386, 4389–4391.

the Turks the fulfilment of divine prophecy. The turn to Daniel was, however, a process of gradual interpretive development.[62]

Aside from isolated examples, Daniel did not appear prominently in the early Wittenberg Reformation. In *To the Christian Nobility of the German Nation* (1520), Luther presented the creation of the Holy Roman Empire as a papal trick to steal the title of "Roman Empire" from the Eastern Emperors. Because the pope claimed responsibility for this *translatio imperii*, the Germans supposedly owed him an incalculable debt, which they had been repaying for centuries. For Luther, the old Roman Empire, the one prophesied by Daniel, was long dead, and he argued that the Germans should take charge of the defence against the Turks rather than send money to Rome for crusades that were never launched.[63]

The next year, Luther published a pamphlet on Daniel 7, but he focused on the papacy as the Antichrist rather than the Holy Roman Empire or the Turks.[64] In 1524, Thomas Müntzer (ca. 1489–1525), one of the leaders of the peasant uprising in Thuringia, based a famous sermon, his *Fürstenpredigt*, on Daniel 2. He presented the Holy Roman Empire as the Fifth Empire, and he offered a vivid image of its decay through the mingling of secular and ecclesiastical spheres. The priests and the religious were snakes, the princes and rulers were eels, and they were all heaped together in one slithering, immoral mass.[65] Nevertheless, the Wittenbergers did not respond to Müntzer's interpretation, and he was executed the next year after his defeat in the Peasants' War. Even

---

62 See generally Arno Seifert, *Der Rückzug der biblischen Prophetie von der neueren Geschichte: Studien zur Geschichte der Reichstheologie des frühneuzeitlichen deutschen Protestantismus* (Cologne: Böhlau Verlag, 1990); and Hans Volz's introduction to the *Lutherbibel* translation of Daniel, WA DB 11^{II}:XXIV–LVII.

63 Luther, *An den christlichen Adel deutscher Nation von des christlichen Standes Besserung* (1520), WA 6:462–465.

64 Luther, *Ad Librvm Eximii Magistrinostri Magistri Ambrosii Catharini, Defensoris Silvestri Prieratis Acerrimi, Responsio Martini Lutheri. Cum exposita Visione Danielis vii. De Antichristo*, WA 7:722–723. See Seifert, *Der Rückzug*, 9–10.

65 The sermon is found in Thomas Müntzer, *Schriften und Briefe: Kritische Gesamtausgabe*, ed. Günther Franz (Gütersloh: Verlaghaus Gerd Mohn, 1968), 241–263; and Thomas Müntzer, *The Collected Works of Thomas Müntzer*, trans. Peter Matheson (Edinburgh: T & T Clark, 1988), 230–252. See Tom Scott, *Thomas Müntzer: Theology and Revolution in the German Reformation* (London: Macmillan, 1989), 69–76; Hans Jürgen Goertz, *Thomas Müntzer: Mystiker, Apokalyptiker, Revolutionär* (Munich: Verlag C.H. Beck, 1989), 105–115; and Eike Wolgast, "Thomas Müntzer's 'Fürstenpredigt' 1524," in *Recht, Kultur, Finanzen: Festschrift für Reinhard Mußgnug zum 70. Geburtstag am 26. Oktober 2005*, ed. Klaus Grupp (Heidelberg: Müller, 2005), 543–554.

as late as 1526, Melanchthon could write a preface to Justin's *Epitome* without mentioning Daniel or presenting the Roman Empire as the Fourth Monarchy.[66] As the Turks continued their march toward Vienna, the Wittenbergers started to distance themselves from the perspectives of the early 1520s.[67] In 1527, Melanchthon began to associate the Ottomans with Daniel's prophecies,[68] and he declared that through their cruelty the Turks had shown they were the fulfilment of Daniel's vision of Four Beasts in which a people would arise long after Roman times to oppress Christians (Daniel 7:21).[69] Then in 1529–1530, in the wake of the Ottoman Siege of Vienna, the Wittenbergers offered a concerted response to the Turkish threat that asserted their Imperial patriotism and countered Catholic accusations of disloyalty.[70] Melanchthon was chiefly responsible for moulding a new interpretation of Daniel to address these

---

66   Justin, *Ivstini Ex Trogo Pompeio Historia* (Hagenau: Johann Setzer, 1526). VD16 T 2051. See Hans Volz, "Neue Beiträge zu Luthers Bibelübersetzung: Luthers Arbeiten am Propheten Daniel," *Beiträge zur Geschichte der deutschen Sprache und Literatur* 77 (1955): 405–408; and also his comments in WA DB 11^II:XLVI–XLVIII. The editions are also listed at MBW 435.

67   See WA 30^II:81–106; John Bohnstedt, "The Infidel Scourge of God: The Turkish Menace as Seen by German Pamphleteers of the Reformation Era," *Transactions of the American Philosophical Society* New Ser. 58, no. 9 (1968): 12; Kenneth M. Setton, "Lutheranism and the Turkish Peril," *Balkan Studies* 3 (1962): 133–168. See also Brecht, "Luther und die Türken," 9–28; Rudolf Mau, "Luthers Stellung zu den Türken," in *Leben und Werk Martin Luthers von 1526–1546*, ed. Helmar Junghans (Berlin: Evangelische Verlaganstalt, 1983), vol. 1, 647–662; Harvey Buchanan, "Luther and the Turks 1519–1529," *Archiv für Reformationsgeschichte* 47 (1956): 145–160.

68   See MBW 546. The text is a letter preface to Jacques Fontaine, *De Bello Rhodio, Libri Tres* (Hagenau: Johann Setzer, 1527). VD16 F 1843. See also Arthur Freeman, "Editions of Fontanus, *De bello Rhodio*," *The Library* 5th series, 24 (1969): 336–339.

69   "Praedixerunt de Turcico regno etiam sacrae literae monueruntque fore aliquam nationem quae longe post Romana tempora summa crudelitate christianos delere et religionem ac doctrinam coelo traditam abolere conetur. Si nulla exempla extarent in quibus Turcicae gentis furor cerni posset, tamen haec una prophetia Danielis commonere nos debebat non leve periculum gentibus omnibus quae christianam religionem profitentur a Turcis impendere." MBW 546.2.

70   See Seifert, *Der Rückzug*, 7–20; Mark U. Edwards, *Luther's Last Battles: Politics and Polemics, 1531–46* (Ithaca: Cornell University Press, 1983), 97–114; Edgar Marsch, *Biblische Prophetie und chronographische Dichtung: Stoff- und Wirkungsgeschichte der Vision des Propheten Daniel nach Dan. VII* (Berlin: Erich Schmidt Verlag, 1972), 110–147; Volz, "Neue Beiträge zu Luthers Bibelübersetzung," 393–423; Hans Volz, "Beiträge zu Melanchthons and Calvins Auslegungen des Propheten Daniel," *Zeitschrift für Kirchengeschichte* 67 (1955/56): 93–118; and especially Volz's introduction to the *Lutherbibel* translation, WA DB 11^II:XXIV–LVII.

needs,[71] and the Wittenbergers quickly issued a series of texts that incorporated his perspective.[72]

Because the Wittenbergers believed that a force as powerful as the Turks must have been foretold in Scripture, they were faced with the problem of how to fit the Ottomans into the historical fulfilment of biblical prophecy in general and Daniel's prophecies in particular. By 1529, Melanchthon had decided to follow St. Jerome's interpretation that Nebuchadnezzar's dream (Daniel 2) and Daniel's vision of Four Beasts (Daniel 7) referred to the same sequence of Four Monarchies, with successors to Rome added to account for subsequent centuries:

	Daniel 2 Nebuchadnezzar's Dream Statue		Daniel 7 Daniel's Vision Four Beasts
1st Monarchy	Head of Gold	Assyria	Lion
2nd Monarchy	Chest of Silver	Persia	Bear
3rd Monarchy	Midsection of Bronze	Greece	Leopard
4th Monarchy	Legs of Iron	Rome	Terrifying Beast
4th Monarchy (After Rome)	Feet of Iron and Clay	Successors to Rome	Ten Horns

---

71   On Melanchthon and the Turks, see especially Manfred Köhler, *Melanchthon und der Islam: ein Beitrag zur Klärung des Verhältnisses zwischen Christentum und Fremdreligion in der Reformationszeit* (Leipzig: Klotz, 1938); and Heinz Scheible, "Melanchthons Verständnis des Danielbuchs," in *Die Geschichte der Daniel-Auslegung in Judentum, Christentum und Islam: Studien zur Kommentierung des Danielbuches in Literatur und Kunst*, ed. Katharina Bracht and David S. du Toit (Berlin: Walter de Gruyter, 2007), 293–321. Melanchthon's projects included: MBW 769 (dedicatory epistle to a commentary on Daniel that he did not finish writing). Justus Jonas, *Das siebend Capitel Danielis / von des Türcken Gottes lesterung vnd schrecklicher morderey / mit vnterricht Justi Jonae* (Wittenberg: Lufft, [1529]). VD16 J 897. On the collaboration between Jonas and Melanchthon, see Wilhelm Bonacker and Hans Volz, "Eine Wittenberger Weltkarte aus dem Jahr 1529," *Die Erde* 8, no. 2 (1956): 154–156. See also Köhler, *Melanchthon und der Islam*, 20–21; and WA DB 11[II]:XXX n. 93–94. Johann Brenz, *Wie sich Prediger vnd Leyen halten sollen / so der Turck das deutsche land vberfallen würde / Christliche vnd notturfftige vnterricht / Johannis Brentij Predigers zu Hall in Swaben* (Wittenberg: Rhau, 1531). VD16 B 7985. See WA DB 11[II]:XXXI n. 95; Bohnstedt, "The Infidel Scourge of God" 13, with translation of the Wittenberg edition of 1537 (46–50); Köhler, *Melanchthon und der Islam*, 21. See also Hans Volz, "Melanchthons Anteil an der Lutherbibel," *Archiv für Reformationsgeschichte* 45 (1954): 196–233. Melanchthon did not publish a Daniel commentary under his own name until 1543. CR XIII, 823–980.

72   Luther's texts included: *Vom Kriege wider die Türken*, WA 30[II]:81–148; *Heerpredigt wider den Türken*, WA 30[II]:149–197; *Vorwort zu dem Libellus de ritu et moribus Turcorum*, WA

Nebuchadnezzar's dream in Daniel 2 allowed for only Four Monarchies (not five), so the difficulty for the Wittenbergers lay in how to interpret the statue's feet of iron mixed with clay. As a first possibility, they looked for fulfilment in the successors to the title of Roman Emperor. Some of the German Emperors had been as strong as iron, like Charlemagne or Henry the Fowler, while others had been weak like clay. Therefore, the Empire preserved something of Rome's former might, but the Holy Roman Empire itself had known periods of strength and weakness, and it no longer equalled the power of ancient Rome.[73]

The second possibility was that some of the successor states to the Roman Empire would be strong and others weak; this seemed to align better with the geographical focus in Daniel 7. Thus the Turks, who ruled parts of the old Empire, were like iron and the Eastern successor kingdoms they had conquered like clay.[74] Regardless of how the prophecy was interpreted, the finality of the Monarchical succession provided consolation, because the passing of all Four Monarchies indicated that the end of the world was drawing near.[75]

In contrast to Daniel 2, Daniel's vision of the Four Beasts (Daniel 7) allowed the Wittenbergers to include the Turks with less concern about violating the finality of Rome. Daniel's dreadful fourth beast with ten horns signified that the terrifying final Empire would contain within itself ten kingdoms – which the Wittenbergers interpreted as the ten major provinces of the ancient Roman Empire[76] – and a later king would arise who would take control of three of these provinces. The Wittenbergers saw the fulfilment of this prophecy in the

---

30ᴵᴵ:198–208; *Das XXXVIII. und XXXIX Capitel Hesechiel vom Gog*, WA 30ᴵᴵ, 220–236; see also WA DB 11ᴵᴵ:LVI; *Der Prophet Daniel 1530. Luthers Vorrede über den Propheten Daniel*, WA DB 11ᴵᴵ:1–48, for the dating and sequence, see WA DB 11ᴵᴵ:XXVI.

73 See Köhler, *Melanchthon und der Islam*, 77. Luther adopted this interpretation in his preface to Daniel (1530), WA 11ᴵᴵ:4–6. See also CR XII, 719.

74 Köhler, *Melanchthon und der Islam*, 77. See also CR XXV, 854; CR X, 635–636.

75 "Es sind alle Monarchien fur vber / gefallen vnd vergangen / dauon die schrifft vermeldet / Vnd das Türkisch Reich hat auch schon lang gestanden / vnd ist zu hoffen / das die zeit / da Daniel von gesagt / auch nu fast zum ende lauffe / da er sagt / die heiligen werden ynn sein hende geben ein zeit lang / vnd aber ein zeit lang / vnd noch ein kleine weile." Jonas, *Das Siebend Capital Danielis* (Wittenberg, 1529), sig. Hiij r.

76 "Das aber Daniel sagt / die bestia habe zehen horner / zeiget er an / da das Römisch Reich verstöret vnd gefallen ist / das zehn ander Königreich aus dem selbigen sind auffkomen / welche hernach die vornemesten ynn der welt gewesen / dar von die Historien melden. Das königreich Franckreich / der Longobarden ynn Welschland / der Gotthen ynn Hispanien / der Wenden ynn Affrica / vnd sonst das Deudsche / Engelland / Hungerisch / der Griechen / das Asiatisch / das Aegyptisch." Jonas, *Das Siebend Capital Danielis* (1529), sig. Ciij v – [Ciiij] r. Luther substituted Syria for Hungary in his list of the provinces: "Er malet aber das selbige Romische Königriech also, das zum ersten sol zertrennet werden ynn

successor kingdoms to the Roman Empire and then in the Ottoman conquests of three of these kingdoms, specifically Asia, Egypt and Greece.[77] Thus, here too the interpretation of Daniel's vision provided reassurance to contemporary Germans, because the Ottomans had reached the extent of their expansion foretold by Daniel.[78]

6 The Wittenberg World Map

In 1529, the Wittenbergers also produced a world map that presented Melanchthon's interpretation of Daniel 7 and his synthesis of prophecies about the Turks (Figure 12).[79] The map contains the traditional three continents – Europe,

---

zehen Königreich, das sind die zehen horner, Als Syria, Aegypten, Asia, Grecia, Affrica, Hispania, Gallia, Italia, Germania, Anglia, etc." WA 11ᴵᴵ:12, see also n. 3.

[77] "Es folget ym text / das der bestien ein klein horn sey da forn am hewbt auffgangen / welchees andern drey horner vmb gestossen hat / Das klein horn bedeut das Türkisch Reich / welch drey königreich ynn morgen lendern hat eingenomen / das Aegyptisch / das Asiatisch vnd das Grekisch / Vnd das solch Türckisch Reich dadurch bedeut sey / findet sich daraus / dann es ist kein ander königreich gewaltiger odder mechtiger gewesen nach der Römischen Monarchey. Der text aber sagt / das dis königreich sol mechtiger sein denn die andern." Jonas, *Das Siebend Capital Danielis* (Wittenberg, 1529), sig. [Ciiij] r. The interpretation offered by Melanchthon and Jonas is paralleled in Luther's contemporaneous *Heerpredigt wider den Türken*, WA 30ᴵᴵ:166–167. The "little horn" presented a particular problem for the Wittenbergers because Luther had first interpreted it as the papacy. The shift to the Turks meant that they had to retract the earlier interpretation or modify it enough to make the Turkish fulfillment plausible. In the end, they frequently saw a "double fulfillment" of the Antichrist in both the papacy and the Turks. See Arno Seifert, *Der Rückzug*, 7–37.

[78] "Zum dritten / ist auch dem Türcken ein ziel ynn der schrifft gesteckt / wie weit er reichen sol vnd herschen / das ist bey Gott beschlossen / Das ist abermal ein trost das er weiter nicht wird komen konnen / von dem aber wollen wir hernach etwas sagen." Jonas, *Das Siebend Capital Danielis* (Wittenberg, 1529), sig. [Biiij] r. See also WA 30ᴵᴵ:171–172.

[79] See WA DB 11ᴵᴵ:XXX–XXXI n. 95, XLIX–L, and Tafeln 3a-3b for reproductions of the images. See Wilhelm Bonacker and Hans Volz, "Eine Wittenberger Weltkarte aus dem Jahr 1529," *Die Erde* 8, no. 2 (1956): 154–170; Hans Volz, "Zu der Wittenberger Landkarte aus dem Jahr 1529," *Die Erde* 89, no. 2 (1958): 136–139; Edgar Marsch, *Biblische Prophetie und chronographische Dichtung: Stoff- und Wirkungsgeschichte der Vision des Propheten Daniel nach Dan. VII.* (Berlin: Erich Schmidt Verlag, 1972), 119–120, also with reproductions. There are at least fourteen known variants. These images are cataloged and reproduced by Ernst Gallner at http://www.daniels-dream-map.com/index.htm. Gallner also

FIGURE 12   Justus Jonas, *Das Siebend Capital Danielis* (Wittenberg, 1529), sig. [Aj] v
HERZOG AUGUST BIBLIOTHEK WOLFENBÜTTEL: H: T 454.4° HELMST. (4)

Africa and Asia. Although it shows some of the Spanish and Portuguese discoveries, no reference is made to the Americas, and both Scandinavia and the British Isles are missing as well. After starting with this traditional cartographic base, the anonymous artist then imposes the vision from Daniel 7 onto the map.[80] At the compass points, the four winds stir up the sea. The Four Beasts have already emerged from the water and are standing on dry land facing inward to the centre of the map. The first two beasts are set in Asia, with the

---

    discusses the history of the map and its variants. See also Ernst Gallner, "Daniel's Dream Map: The Wittenberg World Map 1529–1661," *International Map Collector's Society Journal* 114, no. 3 (Autumn 2008): 49–53.
80 Around 1522–1523, Lucas Cranach had created an important early map of the Holy Land. See Armin Kunz, "Cranach as Cartographer: The Rediscovered *Map of the Holy Land*," *Print Quarterly* 12, no. 2 (June 1995): 123–144. For the 1529 Wittenberg World Map, however, the original graphic artist is likely the anonymous Monogrammist AW. See Bonacker, "Eine Wittenberger Weltkarte," 157.

FIGURE 13   Martin Luther, *Eine Heerpredigt* (Wittenberg, 1542), sig. B r
HERZOG AUGUST BIBLIOTHEK WOLFENBÜTTEL: M: LI 5530 SLG. HARDT (58, 1172)

winged lion (Assyria-Babylon) standing farthest to the East and the bear (Persia) immediately below it. The third beast, the four-headed leopard (Greece), is set in Europe, but it is missing the four wings described in Daniel. Later versions of the map would correct this error (Figure 13). The fourth terrifying beast (Rome) stands in Africa below the Atlas Mountains, and the head of a man speaking arrogantly has already appeared among its horns. The map then reflects the particular Wittenberg interpretation of Daniel by portraying the Turks at the centre, walled up behind the Caspian Mountains waiting to be released.[81]

---

81 Bonacker, "Eine Wittenberger Weltkarte," 154–156. The map first appeared in Jonas, *Das Siebend Capital Danielis* (Wittenberg, 1529).

The 1529 Wittenberg World Map (also referred to as Daniel's Dream Map) has no known direct antecedent, and it seems to be a composite of some of the maps then in circulation. The upper half of the image possibly derives from a world map by Martin Waldseemüller (ca. 1470–1518) and the lower part from a world map by Peter Apian (1495–1552), who was a friend of Melanchthon.[82] The prophetic elements of the map, however, are a distinctly Wittenberg contribution. Although the map aligned with the interpretation of Daniel subsequently developed in *Carion's Chronicle*, the image itself was never incorporated into any of the many editions. Nevertheless, the 1529 world map frequently reappeared in other Wittenberg texts, and it was included in successive editions of the Luther Bible. Through these subsequent reprints, Melanchthon's interpretation of Daniel and the Four Monarchies – bound, literally, into the Bible – retained canonical status among the Wittenbergers into the seventeenth century.[83]

7 The Turks in *Carion's Chronicle*

Melanchthon incorporated the Wittenberg perspective on the Turks into *Carion's Chronicle*. Although he had named the Four Monarchies in 1529, and denied that the Turks could be a Fifth, Melanchthon had not offered a precise definition of "Monarchy." In 1532, when he edited *Carion's Chronicle*, he refined his analysis and offered an explanation of what was meant by "Monarchy":

> And this [second] age [from Abraham to Christ] is the truly powerful age of the world, in which the great empires and the Monarchies followed one after another, and the world displayed all its might. Therefore, we must divide this age into the Four Monarchies, for God wanted to constrain the world by a governing authority in order to uphold moral decency and restrain the wicked. Therefore, he set up the Monarchies – that is, those empires in which a single person holds the greatest and highest power – to preserve peace and justice. The power of the Monarchy was such that other kings, although they were not subject to it, could nevertheless not set themselves against it. And there were Four Monarchies that followed one after another. First the Assyrians ruled, then the Persians, then the

---

82   Bonacker, "Eine Wittenberger Weltkarte," 159–161.
83   See Bonacker, "Eine Wittenberger Weltkarte," 162–170; Volz, "Zu der Wittenberger Landkarte," 136–139; and Ernst Gallner at http://www.daniels-dream-map.com/index.htm.

Greeks, then the Romans, and lastly God has brought the Germans above other nations to this honour and highest position in the world.[84]

For Melanchthon, designation of "Monarchy" did not hinge on specific territorial control; rather, during its period of rule, each Monarchy had a special role in preserving civil order. Indeed, Melanchthon saw continuity with Rome in the use of Roman Law among the successor kingdoms.[85] This emphasis on Roman culture as a civilizing force allowed Melanchthon to distinguish between the Germans and the Turks. In a 1529 pamphlet, for example, he had argued that the Turkish Empire was different from other kingdoms because it was directed toward spreading Islam, rather than upholding justice and peace.[86]

In *Carion's Chronicle*, Melanchthon concentrated on Islam and the Turks in two lengthy chapters, the first on Muhammad and the second on the Ottomans. Although he gave some attention to religious issues, the primary focus was on Islam as a political force. Melanchthon presented Muhammad as both a prophet and a king whose rise to power was occasioned by specific political events. During his wars against the Persians, Emperor Heraclius (r. 610–641) had paid the Arabs for their support, but when his officials stopped the payments, an uprising against the Romans broke out. During this uprising, Muhammad seized the opportunity to become the leader of the mob (*pöfel*). Muhammad understood the problems that religion could cause in secular affairs, and he

---

[84] "Vnd diese zeit ist der welt rechtes vermöglichs alter / darinnen die grossen reich vnd Monarchien nach einander komen / vnd die welt all ihr macht erzeiget hat / Darümb müssen wir diese zeit teilen jnn die vier Monarchien / denn Gott hat die welt jnn ein regiment fassen wollen / zucht zu erhalten / vnd den bösen zu weren. Darumb hat er Monarchien angericht / das ist / solche reich / da ein potestat den grösten vnd besten teil jnnen gehabt / fride vnd recht zu erhalten / der solchs vermögens gewesen / das dennoch andere König / ob sie schon nicht vnterthan gewesen / sich widder solchen potestat nicht haben setzen können / vnd sind nach einander vier Monarchien gewesen. Erstlich haben regirt die Assyrier / darnach die Persen / darnach die Greken / darnach die Römer / Vnd hat Got die Deudschen fur andere Nation / zu dieser ehre vnd hoheit der welt auffs letzt gezogen." Carion, *Chronica* (Wittenberg, 1532), sig. Bij r.

[85] "Dis seind die furnemesten Königreich / ynn welche die Römische Monarchey zu trennet vnd zu teilet ist / vnd welche aus der Römischen Monarchey sind auff komen / Diese sind auch die furnemesten Prouincien / so die Römer vnter sich gehabt / daraus darnach eigen Königreich worden. Vnd die andern königreiche alle haben Römische recht vnd gesetz behalten / ane die / so er nach den Majomet vnd sein lare angenomen." Jonas, *Das Siebend Capital Danielis* (Wittenberg, 1529), sig. [Ciiij] r.

[86] "Aber des Türcken Reich ist diesen nicht gleich / dan es ist nicht vornemlich darumb auffgericht / gemeinen fried / gericht vnd recht zuerhalten / sondern den Alcoran ynn die welt zu bringen / vnd zu erhalten die Mahometische lare." Jonas, *Das Siebend Capital Danielis* (Wittenberg, 1529), sig. Eij r.

was particularly aware of the struggles involving Arianism. Therefore, he decided to found a new religion to strengthen his position; and by doing away with christological doctrines, he removed the cause of the religious controversies that had splintered the Eastern Church.[87] Melanchthon did not discuss the specific teachings of Islam, and even polygamy, a favourite subject of other chroniclers, goes unmentioned. Instead, he emphasized the political impact of Muhammad and the Arab armies.[88]

Melanchthon identified the Muslim empire, rather than the papacy, with the "Antichrist," and he showed how it fulfilled Daniel's prophecy of the Four Beasts (Daniel 7:8). Muhammad was the horn that formed on the last, terrifying beast (the Roman Empire), and its eyes and speech were equated with the Koran and Muhammad's teachings.[89] Melanchthon closed the section on

---

87   "Mahomet hat sich jnn Arabia bey den Agarener vnd Sarracener auffgeworffen / fur ein Propheten vnd König / vnd ist also zugangen. Die Agareni forn jnn Arabia / sind allezeit reubische leut vnd krieger gewesen / Nu waren sie durch die Persen krieg erreget / vnd hatten sold gehabt von Heraclio / Da ihn aber des Keisars haubtleut den sold nicht lenger geben wolten / machet dieses kriegsuolck ein auffrhur widder die Römischen haubtleut / Durch diese auffrhur ist Mahomet gewaltig worden / denn der pöfel must ein haubt haben / derhalben hengten sie sich an Mahomet / denn er war reich / vnd hatt ein gros ansehen von wegen seiner geschickligkeit / Damit aber das volck jnn ein eintrechtig Regiment gefasset würde / bedacht Mahomet nicht allein ein weltlich recht zu stellen / sondern auch ein newe Religion / Denn er sahe / das viel auffrhuren noch jm land waren / von wegen der Religion / Denn die Kirchen waren zerrissen durch viel Ketzereien / vnd sonderlich durch die Ketzerey Arij." Carion, *Chronica* (Wittenberg, 1532), fol. 108r–108v.

88   "Wo nu die gewissen jrre sind vnd jnn zweiuel stehen / werden sie der lahr Christi feind / vnd fallen leichtlich gantz dauon. Also fand Mahomet die hertzen bereit zum abfal / darumb stellet er ein newen glauben / darinne hube er auff alle hohe Artikel von Christo / das der glaube nicht viel Disputationes machen solt / sondern were ein vernunfftige weltliche lahr von eusserlichen sitten / Das gefalt der vernunfft zum höhisten / da fielen zu Heiden / Jüden / Arianer / böse Christen / Denn dieser glaub war allen eben das der hauffe gros vnd eintrechtig ward / vnd den Römern gewaltigen widderstand thun mocht / Namen erstlich ein Arabien / vnd ein teil Syrie / Denn zu Damasco ist Mahomets Regia gewesen / Hernach haben sie auch Egyptum eröbert. Dis ist der anfang kurtz erzelet / des schrecklichen Reichs Mahometi / darinne erstlich die Araben vnd Egypcier regirt haben / vnd sich genent Sultan / das heist ein fürst / Hernach ist das reich auff die Türcken komen." Carion, *Chronica* (Wittenberg, 1532), fol. 108v–109r.

89   "Vnd dieses Reich ist furnemlich der Antichrist / Vnd hat vns Gott durch die Propheten ernstlich dauor gewarnet / Daniel malets also. Auff der Bestia die das Römisch Reich bedeut / wachsse ein horn / das stosse drey hörner weg / das hat augen / vnd redet grausam lesterung widder Gott / Dieses horn ist Mahomet / die augen vnd grausame lesterung widder Gott / ist der Alcoran vnd lahr Mahomets / die viel weiter gelauffen ist denn das Reich / Denn schier gantz Orient hat diese Teufflische lahr angenomen. Die drey hörner sind drey Königreich / die Mahomet eingenomen hat / Arabia / Egyptus vnd Syria. Solchs alles hat Gott vns zuuor angezeiget / das wir vns hüten sollen vor diesem ergernis / Jtem / das wir wissen / das es das letzte Reich ist / vnd der Jüngste tag denn nicht fern sein würde /

Muhammad with a discussion of the name "Saracen empire." Muhammad himself was a descendant of Hagar, but he knew the divine promises belonged to the children of Abraham and Sarah. Therefore, since he interpreted the promise as an expression of eventual world domination, rather than salvation, he changed the name of the Hagarenes to Saracens, and thus made them children of Sarah.[90]

In the chapter on the Turks, Melanchthon explained the origins and rise of the Ottoman Empire. In 870, when the Saracens attacked the Persians, the Persians sought help from the Turks, or Tartars. The Turks, first invited as guests, remained in Asia, and eventually took over the Muslim empire, and the Ottomans in particular came to prominence around 1300 under Osman.[91] Regarding Turkish origins, Melanchthon repeated the discussion from an earlier Wittenberg pamphlet on Daniel 7:

> Ezekiel and St. John call the Turks "Gog and Magog." Gog means a tent. Magog means the people out of the tents. Indeed, the Tartars dwell in tents, and Ezekiel clearly says that God will have allowed Gog to become powerful on account of our sins. Muhammad means wrath. Turk means a warrior or destroyer. Methodius [i.e. pseudo-Methodius] called this people the "Red Jews" because they took over certain ceremonies from the Jews. They are not, however, actual Jews, but rather "Red Jews," either

---

Aber Mahomets nachkomen haben weiter gegriffen / vnd sich lang mit den Keisarn von Constantinopoli vmb Asia geschlagen." Carion, *Chronica* (Wittenberg, 1532), fol. 109r.

[90] "Vnd ist erstlich das Reich genennet worden / das Sarracener Reich / Denn wiewol Mahomet ein Agarener war / hat er doch diesen namen aus der vrsach verwandelt / Die Göttliche verheissung gehöret den kindern Abrahe / von der Sara geporn nicht von Agar / Nu waren die Agarener von Agar / Dieweil aber Mahomet furgabe / sein volck solt Gottes volck sein / vnd die verheissung haben / das sie solten jnn aller welt herrn werden / Denn also deutet Mahomet die verheissung auffs weltlich Reich / darumb nennet er sie Sarracener / als kinder Sarae / vnd nicht Agarener." Carion, *Chronica* (Wittenberg, 1532), fol. 109r.

[91] "Hernach sind die Türcken aus der Tartarei jnn Asia komen / aus dieser vrsach / Die Sarraceni krigten mit den Persen / Da suchten die Persen hülff bey den Türcken / das waren Tartarn am gebirg Caucaso / Dis geschahe kurtz vor Carolo Caluo / vmb das jar Christi 870 / Nach diesem auszug / sind die Türcken fur vnd fur blieben jnn Asia / wie es pflegt zu gehen / wenn man ein frembde volck zu gast ladet / Vnd dieweil sie krieger waren / ist das Reich entlich auff sie komen / Vnd ist sonderlich der Türck Othoman mechtig worden / vmb die zeit des Keisars Alberti Austriaci des ersten / der keisar Rudolphs son war / das ist vmb das jar Christi 1300 / Von diesem an / wird nu Mahomets Reich / das Türkisch Reich genennet / Vnd ist zu mercken / das das jetzig Türkisch geschlecht hat angefangen zu regirn / zur zeit des ersten Osterreichischen Keisars / zu hoffen / ein Osterreichischer Keisar werde sie widder demütigen." Carion, *Chronica* (Wittenberg, 1532), fol. 109v.

because they are blood thirsty or because Muhammad came from Edom in Arabia, for Edom means "red." Methodius says, however, that Gog and Magog were locked up beyond the Caspian Mountains, that is the Caucasus, and a fox would make an opening for them. This fox is Muhammad, for through the law of Muhammad, they have been enticed out and have thus grown powerful.[92]

In his description, Melanchthon conflated a series of prophecies: the vision in Daniel 7, the biblical prophecies of Gog and Magog in Ezekiel 38–39 and Revelation 20, the legend of Alexander's Gates, and the later prophecies of the Red Jews found in the *Apocalypse* of pseudo-Methodius, a seventh century Syrian writer.[93] From Melanchthon's perspective, the Turks fulfilled this prophetic amalgam that a people from Asia would break out of the region near the Caspian Sea, where Alexander had walled them up centuries ago, to plague the Christian West near the end of time. The chapter concludes with a list of the areas that had already fallen to the Muslims, including Egypt, Syria, Asia, Africa, and now Greece.[94]

---

92 "Ezechiel vnd Johannes nennen die Türcken Gog vnd Magog. Gog heisset ein hütte / Magog heist das volck aus den hütten / Denn die Tartarn wonen jnn hütten / Vnd sagt Ezechiel klar / das Gott den Gog habe lassen mechtig werden / vmb vnser sunde willen. Mahomet heisset grim. Turck heisset ein krieger odder verderber / Methodius hat dis volck genennet rote Jüden / darumb das sie etliche Ceremonien von Juden nemen würden / Es sind aber nicht rechte Jüden / sondern rote Jüden / darumb das es bluthund sind / odder darumb / das Mahomet von Edom aus Arabia komen ist / Denn Edom heisset Rod / Methodius spricht aber / Gog vnd Magog sey hinter dem Caspien gebirg / das ist Caucasus / verschlossen gewesen / vnd ein fuchs werde jhn ein loch machen / Dieser fuchs ist Mahomet / denn durch das gesetz Mahomets / sind sie heraus gelocket / vnd also mechtig worden." Carion, *Chronica* (Wittenberg, 1532), fol. 110r. See the parallel in Jonas, *Das Siebend Capital Danielis* (Wittenberg, 1529), sig. [Diiij] r – [Diiij] v. The Red Jews appear inconsistently in Luther's writings. They are found not in the *Military Sermon* (1529) or his introduction to Daniel (1530), but they appear in the later introduction to Ezekial (1530), WA 30^(II):224, and the introduction to Revelation (1530), WA DB 7:417.

93 See especially Köhler, *Melanchthon und der Islam*, 61–82; and Margaret Meserve, *Empires of Islam in Renaissance Historical Thought* (Cambridge, MA: Harvard University Press, 2008), 18–21. See also Timothy Wengert, "Philip Melanchthon and the Jews: A reappraisal," in *Jews, Judaism and the Reformation in sixteenth-century Germany*, ed. Dean Phillip Bell (Leiden: Brill, 2006), 130; Andrew Runni Anderson, *Alexander's Gate, Gog and Magog, and the Inclosed Nations* (Cambridge, MA: The Mediaeval Academy of America, 1932), 44–51, 72–74; Bohnstedt, "The Infidel Scourge of God," 50; and generally Andrew Gow, *The Red Jews: Antisemitism in an Apocalyptic Age 1200–1600* (Leiden: Brill, 1995).

94 "Droben habe ich gesagt / wie jnn Occident die Römische Mönarchi zerfallen ist / Nu haben die Mahometischen den Keisarn / Egypten / Syrien / Asien vnd Aphricam genomen /

The Turks did not correspond to one of Daniel's Monarchies, but Melanchthon could nevertheless present the Ottoman rise to power as having been foretold in biblical and extra-biblical prophecy. In the *Chronicle*, Melanchthon did not explicitly engage with the old anti-Roman prophecies about the return of the Empire to the East. Nevertheless, those prophecies were well-known in Germany, and Johann Hilten, a fifteenth century monk, had similarly predicted that Gog and Magog would rule Germany by 1600.[95] Melanchthon often returned to Hilten during his career, but in *Carion's Chronicle*, he was more concerned with asserting a patriotic view of Germany's destiny. Accordingly, he avoided using prophecy to add to the collective panic, and as in Late Antiquity, he turned to the Four Monarchies to argue that the Holy Roman Empire would endure until the Last Days.[96]

8 Ecclesiastical History

In the *Chronicle*, Melanchthon's presentation of religious matters is less a concentrated discussion than an aggregate picture woven with threads reaching from Adam to the sixteenth century. Melanchthon did not directly attack Catholicism; rather he developed a Protestant perspective on ecclesiastical history that implicitly demonstrated the legitimacy of the Wittenberg Reformation. With this, one of the unstated purposes of the *Chronicle* was to persuade princes, and especially Electoral Prince Joachim, to choose wisely among the competing religious voices of the early sixteenth century. Melanchthon saw heresy as invariably leading to political uprisings, which allowed him to distinguish the Wittenberg Reformation from religious movements of past and present. He also tacitly contrasted the efforts of the medieval popes to undermine the German Empire with the patriotism of the Wittenbergers.

Melanchthon assigned the beginnings of the Church to the word of God given to Adam and Eve in the Garden of Eden:

> The Church also began with the Word of God, as the command was given that Adam and Eve should practice their obedience toward God.

---

bis nu die Türcken Greciam vnd das vbrig gewonnen vnd verwüstet haben." Carion, *Chronica* (Wittenberg, 1532), fol. 110r.

95 See Robin Barnes, *Prophecy and Gnosis: Apocalypticism in the Wake of the Lutheran Reformation* (Stanford: Stanford University Press, 1988), 1, 79.

96 "Denn die heilig schrifft tröstet / vnd leret vns klerlich / das der Jungste tag bald komen sol / nach zurstörung dieses Deudschen Reichs." Carion, *Chronica* (Wittenberg, 1532), sig. Bij v.

However, after they sinned, God revealed the power of the Devil, and against this, He promised the holy Gospel of Christ, that Christ should come to destroy the kingdom of the Devil and make us free again from sin and death. And this was the first preaching of the holy Gospel, with which began the Church and the kingdom of Christ. For in the Church and the kingdom of Christ, the command of good works must not be preached alone, rather also the forgiveness of sins through Christ. For in this way, we are reconciled to God and comforted in death and all anguish, that by faith we receive forgiveness.[97]

In this way, Melanchthon couched the foundation of the Church in mild, but nevertheless Protestant, language, and he set the tone for subsequent discussions of ecclesiastical affairs.

Under the reigns of Augustus and Tiberius, Melanchthon inserted broad introductory remarks about the history of the early Christian Church,[98] and he emphasized especially the destructive effects of heresy, which was even more devastating than the persecutions were.[99] In the chapters that follow,

---

[97] "Die Kirch ist auch angefangen mit dem Gottes wort / als das gebot geben / darinn Adam vnd Eua solten yhren gehorsam gegen Gott vben / Aber nach dem sie gesundiget haben / hat Gott des Teuffels gewalt geoffenbart / vnd dagegen das heilig Euangelium von Christo verheissen / das Christus komen solt / des Teuffels reich zustören vnd vns widder von sund vnd tod los zu machen / Vnd ist dis die erste predige des heiligen Euangelij gewesen / damit die Kirch vnd das Reich Christi angefangen hat / Denn ynn der Kirchen vnd dem reich Christi / müssen nicht allein die gebot guter werck geprediget werden / sondern auch vergebung der sund durch Christum / Denn also werden wir mit Gott versönet / vnd getrost ym tod vnd aller angst / so wir solche vergebung mit dem glauben entpfahen." Carion, *Chronica* (Wittenberg, 1532), sig. Biij v.

[98] "Jm .18. jar Tiberii ist vnser Heiland Christus gecreutziget / gestorben / vnd widderumb am dritten tag vom tod aufferstanden / Vnd hat nach seiner aufferstehung den Aposteln befehl geben / das Euangelium jnn alle welt zu predigen / Diesem jhrem befehl haben die Apostel angefangen volg zuthun / am Pfingstag als sie den heiligen Geist empfangen hatten / nach dem Christus zuuor gen himel sichtiglich gefaren ist. Vnd ist nu Gottes wort vnd das geistlich Reich vnd die heilige Kirch vnd Christenheit / nicht allein jm Jüdischen volck zu suchen / sondern jnn aller welt / wo der Apostel predig erschollen / vnd jhre schrifft gefunden wird / Denn Gott hat zugesagt / durch die selbige predigt vnd Euangelium zu wircken / Darumb wo es ist / da sind etliche die jnn das Reich Christi gehören / jnn welchen Christus herschet vnd wircket / wie er spricht / Jch wil bey euch sein bis zu ende der welt / Diesem Herrn Christo / vnserm Heiland vnd Gott sey lob preis / vnd danck ewiglich / Amen." Carion, *Chronica* (Wittenberg, 1532), fol. 78r [=81r] –78v [=81v].

[99] "Nu wil ich fürter anzeigen / wie die Christenheit grossen harten widderstand gehabt hat / durch leibliche verfolgung / vnd durch Ketzer / die allezeit die Kirch so jemmerlich zerrissen haben / das sie dadurch viel grössern schaden empfangen hat / vnd veracht worden ist / denn durch leipliche verfolgung." Carion, *Chronica* (Wittenberg, 1532), fol. 78v [=81v].

ecclesiastical history is treated primarily in connection with the succession of popes, whose reigns are described briefly after each Emperor. A standard set of topoi are included: the arrival of the Christian Church in Rome,[100] the execution of Peter and Paul under Nero,[101] and Trajan's tolerance of Christians.[102] More than any of the other apostles, including St. Paul, the *Chronicle* focuses on St. John, because of his struggle against heretics, and in particular against Cerinthus, who blasphemed Christ.[103] The destruction of Jerusalem in A.D. 70 receives a separate chapter, both as an example of God's wrath and as testimony that faithful Gentile Christians have now become the people of God.[104]

Regarding the Church fathers, occasional reference is made to Augustine, and briefly to Ambrose.[105] Gregory the Great receives a short, positive treatment, especially for writing against the title of "universal bishop" in his disputes with the Patriarch of Constantinople.[106] While Gregory is also recalled as having introduced new ceremonies, his pontificate does not specifically mark the beginning of medieval Christianity or decline within the Church, nor does it serve as a break between Antiquity and the Middle Ages. Melanchthon deals with the papacy's entrance into secular affairs more in connection with the struggles against the German Emperors than with the way the popes filled the power vacuum in Italy at the end of the Western Empire.

Of the ancient Christian heresies, Melanchthon focuses especially on Arianism and Manichaeism, devoting separate chapters to each; in contrast to this,

---

100 Carion, *Chronica* (Wittenberg, 1532), fol. 82r.
101 Carion, *Chronica* (Wittenberg, 1532), fol. 82v.
102 Carion, *Chronica* (Wittenberg, 1532), fol. 86r.
103 "Man screibet / er sey auff ein zeit jnn ein bad komen / da fand er Cherinthum den Ketzer / das er da sein hauffen vmb sich hatt / vnd disputirt vnter jhn hefftig / vnd lestert Christum / das er nicht Gott sein solt / Also stunde Johannes auff / vnd saget seinen freunden / die bey ihm sassen / sie solten weg gehen / Gott würde ein ende mit diesem lesterer machen / Als bald Johannes vor das bad hinaus kömpt / fellet das haus ein / vnd schlehet Cherinthum vnd seine rott zu tod. Jnn diesem Exempel ist zu sehen / wie sich Gott erzeiget / widder die jhenigen / so seinen namen lestern vnd schenden." Carion, *Chronica* (Wittenberg, 1532), fol. 85v–86r.
104 Carion, *Chronica* (Wittenberg, 1532), fol. 84r.
105 Carion, *Chronica* (Wittenberg, 1532), fol. 97v.
106 "Nach Pelagio Secundo warde der 67 Bapst Gregorius Primus / Der hat viel Ceremonias geordenet / Denn durch kriege vnd Ketzereien / war ein wüst wesen allenthalben worden / Darumb fieng er an die Kirchen mit Ceremonien widder zusamen zu bringen / zu dieser zeit hat sich auch der zanck zugetragen / De primatu / Vnd wolt der Keisar Mauricius / das der Patriarch zu Constantinopoli solt Oecumenicus / odder vniuersalis Episcopus / das ist / der öberst Bischoff jnn der Christenheit sein / Aber Gregorius wolt nicht darein willigen / vnd hielt sich Christlich / vnd schreibet / Es solt sich kein Bischoff jnn der Christenheit / vniuersalem rhümen." Carion, *Chronica* (Wittenberg, 1532), fol. 107v.

he addresses Pelagianism[107] and Novatianism[108] only briefly. Regarding Origen, Melanchthon links the intermingling of Platonic philosophy and Christian doctrine with the rise of heresy; in contrast, he argues for the utility of Aristotle.[109] Above all, Melanchthon blamed Arianism for enduring troubles in both East and West. Especially in the East, these problems led to sects and apostasy, and eventually Arianism opened the door through which Muhammad stepped.[110] In this respect, Melanchthon presents heresy not just as a religious issue, but also a political one, since it leads to uprisings and revolts. In the section on Manichaeism, he states outright:

> [O]ne sees what a horrible thing false teaching is, and how all heretics are insurrectionaries, and they think to protect and spread their error through uprisings, for the Devil is their master, and he is at the same time a liar and a murderer. Both of these aspects present themselves in all heretics – that they teach lies, and that they cause murder through insurrection and shattering of political order.[111]

---

107 "Nach Anastasio warde der 43 Bapst Innocentius / der erst dieses namens / Zu dieses Bapsts zeiten / ist gewesen Pelagius jnn Britannia / der leret / das der mensch für Gott gerecht vnd selig würde / aus eigen natürlichen wercken / vnd nicht durch glauben an Christum / Diesen jrrthumb hat dazumal Augustinus angefochten / vnd ist Pelagius jn Concilien verworffen." Carion, *Chronica* (Wittenberg, 1532), fol. 97v.

108 "Nach Fabiano ward der .20. Bapst Cornelius / der hat die Ketzerey Nouati verworffen / der vnrecht von der Bus leret / Das / so ein Christ nach der Tauff gefallen were / möcht jhm nicht widder geholffen werden / Vnd hat durch diese vnrechte lahr seer viel leute betrübet / vnd viel Kirchen zerrut." Carion, *Chronica* (Wittenberg, 1532), fol. 89v.

109 "Nach Eleutherio ward der .14. Bapst Victor / Nach Victore ward der .15. Bapst Zephyrinus / Zu diesen zeiten ist gewesen Origenes / der hat die heilige schrifft zu Alexandria gelert / vnd sind seine bücher hernach verpoten worden / derhalben das er viel vnnützer disputationes vnd allegorien eingeführet hat / Nach jhm ists gemein worden / das man die Philosophi Platonis / jnn die Theologi gemenget hat / daraus viel böses gefolget ist / Denn Platonis Philosophi gantz ein vnrichtige lahr / Dagegen ist Aristotelis Philosophi fein richtig / vnd so man sie recht braucht vnd verstehet / ist sie den gelerten Christen nützlich zu wissen." Carion, *Chronica* (Wittenberg, 1532), fol. 87v–88r.

110 "Jnn diese spaltung ist entlich Mahomet komen / dem hat Arius das loch gemacht vnd ist des greulichen Antichristi vorgenger gewesen / Denn da die leut also jrre waren / kam Mahomet / vnd macht das dritte / das fein vernünfftig war / vnd hube die disputaciones auff / das gefiel der welt / dauon wil ich hernach sagen." Carion, *Chronica* (Wittenberg, 1532), fol. 94v. On the Turk as Antichrist, see Seifert, *Der Rückzug*, 13–14.

111 "[M]an sehe / wilch schedlich ding ist vnrechte lahr / Vnd wie alle Ketzer affrürisch sind / vnd jhre jrthumb mit auffruren gedencken zu schützen vnd aus zubreiten / Denn jhr meister der Teuffel / ist zugleich ein lügner vnd ein mörder / Diese beide stück erzeigen sich jnn allen Ketzern / das sie lügen leren / vnd mord durch auffrhur vnd zerruttung der Regiment anrichten." Carion, *Chronica* (Wittenberg, 1532), fol. 91r. Later, Melanchthon wrote: "Dieses sey gnug hie von Ario vnd andern der gleichen ketzereien / welche ich

This understanding of heresy underpins the discussion of early Christian heretics and the rise of Islam. It was also a commentary on the religious movements of the 1520s.

The discussion of ecclesiastical affairs in Book III is directed primarily at the involvement of the papacy in secular affairs, and papal efforts to transfer or destroy the Empire underpin much of the political history of these centuries. The history of the papacy itself is treated only in a cursory fashion, with small and specific elements occasionally included in the sections on the popes: Boniface III had Emperor Phocas declare that the pope was the highest bishop in Christendom,[112] the first pope to change his name at the beginning of his pontificate was Sergius II,[113] Sylvester II supposedly was a magus,[114] the college of cardinals was formed under Nicolas II,[115] etc. Melanchthon draws attention to the brutality and tyranny of the ninth century popes,[116] and he includes the legend of Pope Joan, though it is not entirely clear whether he believed it to be true.[117]

For Melanchthon, Hildebrand and the Investiture controversy demonstrated the destructive potential of the papacy when it meddled in German affairs. However, as the case of Gregory V, the German pope appointed by Otto III,

gemeldet hab / das man dabey bedenck / wilche schaden / mord / auffrhur / zerruttung geistlichs vnd weltlichs Regiments / aus ketzereien volge." Carion, *Chronica* (Wittenberg, 1532), fol. 94v.

112 "Nach Sabiniano warde der 69 Bapst Bonifacius Tertius / Dieser hat vom Keisar Foca durch grossen zanck erhalten / das der Bapst zu Rom solt Oecumenicus vnd der höhist Bischoff jnn der Christenheit sein / Also haben nu fürter die Bepst auch nach erhöhung jhrer macht vnd ehren getracht." Carion, *Chronica* (Wittenberg, 1532), fol. 107v.

113 "Nach Gregorio quarto warde der 105 Bapst Sergius secundus / Dieser ist der erst / der sein namen verendert hat / denn man sagt er habe zuuor Os porci geheissen / Dieser hat Ludouicum secundum den son Lotharij gekrönet." Carion, *Chronica* (Wittenberg, 1532), fol. 118v.

114 "Nach Gregorio v. warde der 145 Bapst Syluester secundus / sol ein Magus gewesen sein." Carion, *Chronica* (Wittenberg, 1532), fol. 130v.

115 "Nach Benedicto nono warde der 158 Bapst Nicolaus secundus / Der hat Benedictum abgesatzt / Vnd sol erstlich geordnet haben / das die Cardinel allein solten die wahl eins Bapsts haben / Hat auch Berengarium widderumb damnirt / vnd zu der reuocatio gedrungen." Carion, *Chronica* (Wittenberg, 1532), fol. 133v.

116 "Nach Christophoro warde der 123 Bapst Sergius tertius / Der ists / der den todten leib Formosi hat köpffen lassen / Es ist schrecklich zu lesen solche lermen vnd tyranney / so die Bepst gegen einander geübet haben / Bey solchem Heidnischen wesen / haben sie Christlicher lahr wenig achten können / das nicht wunder ist / ob etliche misbreuch eingerissen sind." Carion, *Chronica* (Wittenberg, 1532), fol. 121r.

117 "Nach Leone quarto / warde Johannes octauus Bapst / Von diesem sagt man / er sey ein weib / vnd von Meintz gewesen." Carion, *Chronica* (Wittenberg, 1532), fol. 118v.

demonstrated, the papacy could also be a force for peace in the Empire;[118] and overall, Melanchthon's criticism is aimed as much at individual popes as it is at the papacy as an institution. The years in Avignon are not converted into a commentary on the degenerate state of the papacy. Instead the *Chronicle* focuses more on the mutual treachery of the French and popes, for example, when the pope worked with the German Electors to have Henry VII made Emperor instead of the King of France.[119]

The Great Schism (1378–1417) is presented as the fault of the French and the Italians. In contrast, Melanchthon demonstrates how its resolution at the Council of Constance was brought about by Emperor Sigismund working in consensus, not only with other major European rulers, including the kings of France, Spain and England, but also with the papacy.[120] After Constance, the Renaissance popes continued to cause occasional troubles for the Emperors, but they are treated no differently, or in more detail, than their predecessors. By the early fifteenth century, Melanchthon's emphasis gradually shifts from the struggle between the popes and the Emperors to the rising threat posed by the Turks. Melanchthon praises Pope Nicolas V for his support of scholars in Italy and especially for helping the Greeks who escaped as Constantinople

---

118 "Nach Johanne xvii. warde der 144 Bapst Gregorius v. ein fürst zu Saxen / aus den vrsachen / wie droben angezeigt / das die Jtalianer jmer widder die Keisar practicirten / vnd sonst ein auffrhur vber die ander erregten / ist bedacht worden / das es zu frieden dienen solt / so ein Deudscher Bapst gemacht würde / Noch ward dieser Gregorius von den Jtalianern veriagt / vnd einer genant Johannes / zu Bapst gemacht / Aber Otho satzet sein vettern widder ein." Carion, *Chronica* (Wittenberg, 1532), fol. 130v.

119 "Anno Christi 1309 ist zu Keisar gewelet Henricus ein Fürst von Lucelburg / vnd regirt 6 jar / Denn dieweil der Bapst jnn Franckrich lag / vnterstund sich der König zu Franckrich Keisar zu werden / vnd das bey dem Bapst zu erhalten / Aber Bapst vnd Franckrich bey einander / konten auch nicht wol einig bleiben / Darumb practicirt der Bapst / das die Churfursten / die sich lang der wahl nicht hatten vereinigen können solten eilen / vnd den Fürsten von Ludelburg welen / der dazumal fur ein weisen / vnd ernsten Fürsten gepreiset ward / Vnd als bald er gewelet ward / confirmirt jhn der Bapst / Also feyleten dem König von Franckrich seine anschlege / dadurch er verhofft das Reich zu sich zubringen." Carion, *Chronica* (Wittenberg, 1532), fol. 152r.

120 "Jm anfang seines Keisarlichen Regiments / ist er jnn Jtalien gezogen / vnd hat mit dem Bapst Johanne geradschlaget von eim Concilio / das Schisma auff zu heben / Er ist auch jnn eigener person zum König von Franckrich gezogen / vnd hat mit jhm gehandelt jnn ein Concilium zu willigen / Also mit bewilligung des Bapsts Johannis / des Keisars / der König Franckrich / Hispania vnd England / ist das Concilium zu Constantz angefangen / anno 1414. dahin Bapst Johannes selb komen ist." Carion, *Chronica* (Wittenberg, 1532), fol. 158r.

collapsed. They in turn aided in the revival of learning.[121] He also briefly mentions two German inventions that changed Europe, printing and firearms.[122]

Melanchthon praises councils, and he uses the examples of Constantine, Charlemagne and Sigismund to demonstrate that an Emperor can summon a council. Even so, he did not develop the idea of councils as a tool against papal tyranny. The Council of Jerusalem (ca. 50) is not mentioned, and the Council of Pisa (1511), which was meant to rein in Pope Julius II, is presented as the destructive meddling of the French.[123] The lesson to be learned from earlier councils is that they can be a means to peace and stability, if they have the backing of both religious and secular leaders. The Council of Basel fell apart because the pope and the French worked to undermine it,[124] and then Emperor Sigismund died, leaving it without Imperial support. The Council of Ferrara-Florence is cited only as a papal countermeasure to Basel, and the reunification of East and West at Florence goes unmentioned, the Emperor was not present.[125]

Of the modern heresies, Melanchthon mentions the Hussites on several occasions, and he points out that Jan Hus († 1415) began by preaching against indulgences. Even so, Melanchthon concentrates less on Hus's theology than

---

121 "Nach Eugenio iiii. warde Bapst Nicolaus v. der hat Fridericum zu Keisar gekrönet / vnd hat die gelarten jnn Jtalia seer gnediglich gehalten / Vnd sonderlich die jhenigen / so von Constantinopoli jnn Jtalien geflohen waren / als Gasam / Trapezontium / Argyropylos / durch welche alle gute künsten vernewet vnd gebessert sind." Carion, *Chronica* (Wittenberg, 1532), fol. 163v–164r.

122 "Den anfang der Druckerey / setzt man vnter keisar Friderich den dritten / Vnd sol diese kunst Bücher zu drücken zu Mentz erfunden sein / anno 1440. Die kunst Büchssen schiessen ist viel / vnd sol auch jnn Deudsch land erfunden sein / anno 1380." Carion, *Chronica* (Wittenberg, 1532), fol. 164v.

123 "Nach Pio tertio / warde Bapst Julius secundus / Widder diesen ward ein Concilium ausgeschrieben durch Bernardinum den Cardinal / jm Venediger krieg / vnd war die sach schier zu eim schisma geraten / wo es der frome Keisar Maximilianus durch seine weisheit nicht sonderlich verhut hett." Carion, *Chronica* (Wittenberg, 1532), fol. 166v.

124 "Anno 1444 ist der Delphin mit den Armeniacis jnn das Elsas gezogen / bis zur Basel / vnd hat grossen greulichen schaden gethan / Man helt / Bapst Eugenius habe jhn jnn Deudsch land gesand / das Concilium zu Basel zu zerstören / Der Delphin hat 25 tausent man / Widder diese sendeten die Schweitzer zu rettung der Stad Basel / vier tausent man." Carion, *Chronica* (Wittenberg, 1532), fol. 162r.

125 "Anno 1434 bey leben Sigismundi / ist das Concilium zu Basel angefangen / wie denn zu Constantz beschlossen war / nach zwelff jarn widder ein Concilium zu halten / Aber dieweil Keisar Sigmund starb / verhindert der Bapst das Concilium / vnd macht ein gegen Concilium / erstlich zu Ferraria / darnach zu Florentz / damit ward das Concilium zu Basel zertrennet / denn es hielt kein potestat darob / nach Sigismundi tod." Carion, *Chronica* (Wittenberg, 1532), fol. 160r.

on the wars in Bohemia after his death.[126] He notes the burnings of Hus and Jerome of Prague († 1416) as part of the Council of Constance.[127] Afterwards, he refers to the Hussite leader Jan Zizka († 1424) and his armies as rebels, who plundered churches and monasteries.[128] The more militant Hussites are also mentioned for their role in trying to invite the king of Poland to take the Bohemian crown.[129] Although Melanchthon does not explicitly label Hus as a heretic, he tacitly distinguished between Wittenberg and Prague by presenting the Hussites as insurrectionaries.

While Melanchthon was somewhat guarded in his discussion of Hus, he repeatedly attacks the Anabaptists as heretics and argues that earlier heresies are now reflected once again in them. The Essenes had followed similar social teachings, including the way they disavowed marriage.[130] Likewise, at the time of the Avignon papacy, the Fraticelli appeared, who did not believe in private

---

126 "Anno 1378 hat nach Caroli tod angefangen zu regirn Wenceslaus sein son / vnd hat regirt nach seins vaters tod allein 22 jar / Zu dieses zeiten hat Johannes Hus zu Praga angefangen widder den Bapst zu predigen / durch ein ausschreiben von Jndulgentiis verursacht / Also ist der schedliche lermen jnn Behem widder die Priester vnd Mönche erreget." Carion, *Chronica* (Wittenberg, 1532), fol. 156v.

127 "Keisar Sigmund ist dahin komen jnn der nacht Natalis Christi / vnd hat das Euangelium jnn der Mess als ein Diacon gesungen / Exiit edictum a Caesare Augusto / Darnach hat man jm Concilio von Hussen vnd seim anhang gehandelt / Johannem Hus vnd Hieronymum verbrant / Darnach ist gehandelt worden vom Schismate / vnd sind die drey Bepst Johannes xxiii. Gregorius vnd Benedictus entsetzt / vnd ist Otho de Columna Bapst worden / vnd genant Martinus v." Carion, *Chronica* (Wittenberg, 1532), fol. 158r.

128 "Nach dem Concilio / hat man viel züge jnn Behem furgenomen / widder die auffrhürer vnd wüsten leut / die nach dem tod Hussi / kirchen vnd Clöster zerrissen vnd plünderten / Welcher haubtman hies Zisca / Vnd ist viel schaden auff beiden seiten geschehen / den Behemen vnd den Deudschen / die widder sie zogen / Vnd ist doch die sach nicht zum ende bracht." Carion, *Chronica* (Wittenberg, 1532), fol. 159r.

129 "Etliche Behem henten sich an König zu Poln / vnd wolten das Königreich Behem auff Poln wenden / vnd furten die Poln ein gros volck jnn Behem / vnd henten an sich die auffrhürigen Thaboriten / Widder diese sendet der Keisar den Marggrauen von Brandenburg Albertum / der that viel kleiner schlagten mit jhn / bis die sach zwischen Keisar vnd Poln vertragen ward." Carion, *Chronica* (Wittenberg, 1532), fol. 160v.

130 "Essei / sind die dritten gewesen / die haben gesehen / das beide teil / Pharisei vnd Saducei / viel rhümeten von frömkeit / vnd nichts thaten / Darumb haben sie es mit ernst wollen angreiffen / vnd haben sich genant Essei / das ist / Operarij / vom wort Assa / das ist wircken. Wie jtzund die Anabaptisten schelten die andere zween teil / vnd wollen heiliger sein / Es haben auch die Essei eben ein solch Anaptisten leben geführt / nicht weiber gehabt / alle ding gemein wollen haben Vnd ist ein törichte / grobe Möncherey vnd heucheley gewesen / hat auch nicht lang geweret." Carion, *Chronica* (Wittenberg, 1532), fol. 68v–69r.

property or in civil government.[131] Melanchthon labels Thomas Müntzer as the founder of modern Anabaptism; and he argues that Müntzer's teachings bore many similarities to Manichaeism, since he believed in direct, personal revelation and attempted to do away with marriage and civil government.[132] In his discussion of the Peasants' War, Melanchthon presents Müntzer as both a liar and a rebel, since he claimed that he had been given the sword of Gideon to smite the godless and then roused the rabble to plunder the nobles. Melanchthon recognized, however, that Müntzer's defeat had not completely halted the unrest caused by Anabaptist teachings.[133]

In the *Chronicle*, Melanchthon also presents Zwingli, Oecolampadius and Karlstadt as religious errorists, and vehemently condemns them.[134] At the Marburg Colloquy, Luther and Zwingli had failed to reach agreement on the teaching of the Lord's Supper. Afterwards, Melanchthon showed no sympathy for Zwingli, and in the *Chronicle,* he presents Swiss teachings as the revival of heresy. In Book III, Melanchthon essentially ignores medieval heresy, but he does include Berengar of Tours († 1088), who had argued that the body and blood of Christ are not present in the sacrament.[135] Although Berengar was

---

131 "Zu dieser zeit sind gewesen Fratricelli / das ist gantz der Anabaptisten lahr gewesen / welche jtzund jrre lauffen / das man nicht sol eigens haben / das man nicht sol regirn / vnd der gleichen teufelische fantasien." Carion, *Chronica* (Wittenberg, 1532), fol. 152r.

132 "Dazu rhümeten sie besonder offenbarung / vnd sagten / sie geben den heiligen Geist / Vnd haben dazu viel Ceremonien angericht / speis vnd Ehe verpoten / dadurch den heiligen Geist zuerlangen / Haben auch weltlich Regiment verworffen / vnd geleret / das Ehe vnd weltlich Regiment / were vom bösen Gott geschaffen / nicht vom guten Gott. Zu unsern zeiten war Thomas Müntzer seer auff diese ban geraten." Carion, *Chronica* (Wittenberg, 1532), fol. 91v.

133 "Jnn Düringen zu Mülhausen / ist ein prediger gewesen / mit namen Thomas Müntzer / der gabe fur / er wolde die kirchen reformirn / vnd rhümet Got hett jm sonderlich offenbarung / vnd das schwerdt Gedeon gegeben / alle gotlosen zu erschlagen / Vnd füret den pöfel aus / lies sie der Edelleut heuser plündern / Aber die Fursten von Saxen vnd der Landgraue / schlugen den hauffen vnd fiengen den Müntzer vnd etliche seiner gesellen / vnd köpfften sie. Dieser Münzter hat erstlich die lahr vom Widdertauff angefangen / die noch inn viel landen vnruge macht." Carion, *Chronica* (Wittenberg, 1532), fol. 167r–167v.

134 "Anno 1525 haben Johannes Oecolampadius zu Basel / vnd Vlrich Zwingli / erstlich schrifften ausgehen lassen / darinn sie den verdampten jrrthumb Berengarij vernewet haben / das Christus leib vnd blut nicht jm Nachtmal Christi warhafftiglich gegenwertig sey / Wiewol der vnsinnig man Andreas Carolostad / jm jar zuuor den vnlust angefangen hat." Carion, *Chronica* (Wittenberg, 1532), fol. 167v.

135 "Nach Damaso secundo warde der 154 Bapst Leo ix. Er ist jm Synodo zu Mentz gewesen / vnd hernach lang bey Henrico Nigro blieben / Zu seiner zeit hat Berengarius ein Diaconus von Andegaui jnn Gallia gelart / das leib vnd blut Christi nicht warlich im brod vnd wein des Sacraments sey / Welcher jrthumb zu vnser zeit jnn Schweitz durch Zwingli erreget ist / Vnd hat Leo in Concilio Vercellensi diesen jrthumb verworffen / wiewol dennoch

condemned by both pope and council, his teaching could not be eradicated, and Melanchthon saw its revival among the Swiss. Besides these associations with earlier heresy, Melanchthon emphasizes the political unrest Zwingli caused, since under his leadership Zürich tried to impose an economic blockade on other Swiss cities. Like Müntzer, Zwingli's heresy led to his own demise, and he was killed on the battlefield in 1531.[136]

Melanchthon mentions Luther only once, under the description of Leo X's pontificate:

> After Julius II, Leo X, the son of Lorenzo de' Medici became pope. At the time of Leo, in the year 1517, Martin Luther first wrote against the indulgence, and since then many disputes have arisen; from this, a great rift has now come into being in Germany."[137]

Thus, the Reformer is treated in the same manner as most of the Renaissance popes, i.e. briefly, and without explicit commentary, good or bad. The sanitized approach may have seemed prudent given Carion's position at the Catholic court in Berlin, and it made the *Chronicle* less hostile to a Catholic audience, especially young Catholic princes. In a similar way, the description of the Diet of Augsburg (1530) does not name the Protestants. Instead, it tells how Charles V convoked the assembly in the hope of bringing peace and unity to religious matters. A large number of the princes attended, and as faithful subjects, they showed due reverence to their lord, the Emperor. Despite his good intentions, nothing was brought to conclusion, and in the end, Charles permitted an

---

das vndraut nicht gantz auff ein mal ausgerot ist / Man hat hernach mehr damit zuthun gehabt." Carion, *Chronica* (Wittenberg, 1532), fol. 133v.

[136] "Darnach jnn Octobri / ist geuolget ein krieg jnn Schweitz / Denn die Züricher hatten ihren nachbarn / den von Zug / Vri / Schweitz / Vnterwalden vnd Lucern die straffen verlegt / vnd liessen jhn nicht zufüren / Darumb zogen die von Zug / Vri / Schweitz / Vnterwalden vnd Lucern widder die von Zürich / vnd worden die von Zürich mit ihrem anhang dreymal geschlagen nacheinander / Jnn der ersten schlacht ist der Züricher Prediger Zwinglius mit erschlagen / Vnd ist die jarzal inn diesen Versen. Occubuit patrio bellator Cinglius ense. Et pressa est armis gens populosa suis. Mitler zeit ward vleissig durch die nachbarn gehandelt / die Eidgenossen widder zuuertragen / vnd ist nach ausgang 6 wochen der lerm gestillet / Vnd acht man / es sind auff der Züricher seiten vmbkomen bey funff tausent / Auff der andern seiten seer wenig." Carion, *Chronica* (Wittenberg, 1532), fol. 168v.

[137] "Nach Julio secundo / warde Bapst Leo X. ein son Laurentii Medici / Zur zeit Leonis anno 1517 hat Martinus Luther erstlich widder den Ablas geschrieben / vnd sind hernach viel disputationes erreget / Daraus nu eine grosse spaltung jnn Deudschland worden ist." Carion, *Chronica* (Wittenberg, 1532), fol. 167r.

edict to be issued that upheld the old ceremonies and teachings of the Roman Church.[138]

Despite the *Chronicle's* Protestant tone, there is no sense that the Church ever reached a point of total corruption from the perspective of doctrine or practice. Instead, religious questions are framed to accord with contemporary needs. By pointing out how St. Paul wrote to the "Germans" in Galatia, Melanchthon moves the emphasis away from St. Peter and the papal missions to the Germanic tribes under his successors.[139] Melanchthon does not mention the conversion of Clovis or Gregory the Great's mission to England, but he notes the seventh century journeys of St. Gall, the Irish missionary to Germany.[140] By drawing attention to St. Gall, Melanchthon implied that the Christianization of the Germans had preceded the later work of St. Boniface, who had official support from the papacy. In the *Chronicle*, St. Boniface, the "Apostle to the Germans," receives only a single sentence: "At the time of this [Pope] Zachary, St. Boniface preached in Germany."[141] Melanchthon neither emphasized nor celebrated the Christianization of Europe; and implicitly, he used historical silence concerning the early missions to the Germanic tribes to undermine papal claims to German gratitude.

Ultimately, Melanchthon offers no comprehensive lineage of dissent from the Roman Church, a perspective that would become characteristic of later Protestant historiography. The Church is present already in Eden, but its development is treated more incidentally than systematically. Instead, Melanchthon stresses the need for harmony between the religious and secular worlds. They are shown to interact constantly, and in times of harmony, they bring peace and religious concord. In this respect, the cooperation of Emperor Otto III and his German pope to form the Electoral College served as a model of how pope and Emperor together could bring stability to Europe.

---

138 "Darnach ist Keisar Carolus jnn Deudsch land gezogn / vnd den abend Corporis Christi zu Augspurg einkomen / dahin er ein Reichstag ausgeschrieben hat / Vnd waren des mehrer teil Fürsten da / vnd empfiengen jhren herrn vnd Keisar mit aller reuerentz / Vnd wiewol der Keisar viel handlung furname / die vneinigkeit jnn der Religion / mit güte zu frieden vnd einigkeit zu bringen / ists doch nicht vollendet / sondern entlich hat der Keisar lassen ein Edict ausgehen / die alten Ceremonien vnd lahr inn der Römischen Kirchen gewönlich zu halten." Carion, *Chronica* (Wittenberg, 1532), fol. 168r.

139 Carion, *Chronica* (Wittenberg, 1532), fol. 61v.

140 Carion, *Chronica* (Wittenberg, 1532), fol. 110 r.

141 "Zur zeit dieses Zachariae hat Sanct Bonifacius jnn Deudsch land gepredigt." Carion, *Chronica* (Wittenberg, 1532), fol. 112r.

9 The Melanchthon-Peucer *Chronicle* of 1572

In 1532, Melanchthon built on the traditions of Antiquity, the Middle Ages and the German Renaissance, but he offered an interpretation of the past aligned with the perspective of Reformation Wittenberg. Between 1558 and 1565, Melanchthon and his son-in-law, Caspar Peucer, revised and expanded the original 1532 *Chronicle*. Peucer then published a complete edition in 1572. Much had changed, and the revised *Chronicle* reflects these developments in politics and religion, as well as historical scholarship generally.

Amidst the troubles of his later years, Melanchthon often nostalgically recalled the early days of German humanism. In 1532, Melanchthon and Carion had presented the *Chronicle* as the fulfilment of Emperor Maximilian I's desire for an Imperial history of Germany. For the new edition, Melanchthon looked to an Electoral precedent rather than a Hapsburg one. In his dedicatory epistle, he recalled how Reuchlin used to tell stories about the Wittelsbach court of Philip, Elector Palatine (1476–1508), and Bishop Johann von Dalberg (1445–1503), an important early German humanist.[142] According to Melanchthon, Dalberg's humanist circle composed a chronicle dealing with the importance of historical examples and the succession of Empires. The chronicle is lost, or perhaps never existed, and it seems to be otherwise unknown. Regardless, Melanchthon used the story to set *Carion's Chronicle* in the tradition of South German humanism.[143] Melanchthon did not discuss the *Chronicle's* origins in 1531–1532 or Carion's role in preparing the original manuscript.

---

142 For Dalberg see the collection of articles: Gerold Bönnen and Burkard Keilmann, eds., *Der Wormser Bischof Johann von Dalberg (1482–1503) und seine Zeit* (Trier: Gesellschaft für Mittelrheinische Kirchengeschichte, 2005).

143 "Est omnino necessaria singulis hominibus historiae cognitio, sed maxime gubernatoribus, quae sine temporum serie, sine gentium distinctione, et non monstrato Imperiorum ordine, lucem non habet. Saepe audivi narrare Capnionem, cum apud Philippum Principem Palatinum Electorem essent Dalburgius Episcopus Vangionum, Rudolphus Agricola et ipse, et non solum in familiaribus colloquiis, sed etiam in deliberationibus de re publica saepe narrarent insignia exempla vel Persica, vel Graeca, vel Romana, mirifice accensum esse Principem studio cognoscendae historiae, sed dixisse, se animadvertere, distinctione temporum, gentium et imperiorum opus esse, eamque ob causam petivisse, ut sibi ex tota antiquitate, quantum nota esset, ex Ebraeis fontibus, et ex Graecis ac Latinis Scriptoribus ordine contexerent Monarchias, ut mente complecti tempora mundi, et seriem maximarum mutationum posset. Nulli tunc extabant scripti lingua Germanica libri de veteribus imperiis. Nec Latina praeter Iustini confusaneam Epitomen, quae tamen distinctione temporum caret, habeantur. Erat ocium tunc illis doctis viris, et hoc labore delectabantur. Ordine igitur ex Ebraeis, Graecis et Latinis monumentis Monarchias recensent, et maxime digna memoria suo loco adhibita temporum et gentium distinctione inserunt. Legit avidissime id Scriptum Princeps ingeniosus, seque laetari dicebat, divinitus conservatam

10 Melanchthon's Revisions

In the new edition, Melanchthon followed the original outline and structure of the Carion-Melanchthon *Chronicle*, but his revision involved both refinement and vast expansion of the narrative. As before, he focused on moral examples, good and bad, but he removed his salient "*Welt bleibt welt*" remark, and he added a cautionary category, "misguided imitation" (κακοζηλία). Melanchthon noted Cicero, who opposed Mark Anthony, as he had Catiline, and the Jews, who, in imitation of the Maccabees, revolted at various times against the Romans.[144] Thus, changed circumstances could invalidate formerly appropriate behaviour and examples.

The differences from the 1532 *Chronicle* are most noticeable for religious matters. Instead of focusing on individual, Christian virtue (*Tugend*), Melanchthon concentrated on ecclesiastical history itself. As such, he argued that history is particularly necessary in the Church:

> First, because God in his immense goodness has made himself manifest, and he has desired that his manifestations be recorded in writing...

---

esse temporum seriem, et rerum praecipuarum memoriam." CR IX, 532–533. Melanchthon gave a parallel to the remarks here in his oration on Reuchlin: "Exulabat igitur Capnio, sed in Aula Palatina tunc quidem florente, cum et Principis Philippi virtus egregia esset, et multi viri docti simul versarentur, quorum singuli magnas Academias ornare poterant. Talium amicorum consuetudo exilium ei leniebat. Ibi et Philippo Palatino Epitomen historiarum composuit, recitata serie monarchiarum ex Herodoto ex Xenophonte, et ex aliis bonis scriptoribus, qui postea res Macedonicas et Romanas descripserunt: ibi comoediam scripsit, Capitis caput, plenam nigri salis et acerbitatis adversus monachum, qui eius vitae insidiatus erat." *De Capnione Phorcensi*, CR XI, 1004; see also CR III, 216–217; CR III 675–676; CR IV, 929; CR VIII, 406; CR VIII, 811–812; CR XI, 444–445. See Emil Clemens Scherer, *Geschichte und Kirchengeschichte an den deutschen Universitäten: Ihre Anfänge im Zeitalter des Humanismus und ihre Ausbildung zu selbständigen Disziplinen* (Freiburg i. B.: Herder, 1927), 14; James Michael Weiss, "The Six Lives of Rudolph Agricola: Forms and Functions of the Humanist Biography," *Humanistica Lovaniensia* 30 (1981): 19–39; Quirinus Breen, "Melanchthon's Sources for a Life of Agricola: The Heidelberg Memories and the Writings," *Archiv für Reformationsgeschichte* 52 (1961): 49–74.

144 "Interdum moventur animi κακοζηλία. Ut, Demosthenes imaginatur suum consilium esse Themistocleum, defendendam esse Graeciae libertatem contra exteros reges. Cicero quia antea Catilinam oppresserat, sperat se simili foelicitate Antonium oppressurum esse. Hoc modo saepe in Ecclesia peccatur. Ut Zedechias scit, a prioribus regibus defensum esse templum, ac sperat suam defensionem fore foelicem, quam Ieremias contra superiorum Prophetarum exempla dissuadebat. Iudaei aliquoties adversus Romanos moverunt seditiones, tanquam imitaturi Iosuam aut Maccabaeos etc." CR XII, 713. On this point, see Asaph Ben-Tov, *Lutheran Humanists and Greek Antiquity: Melanchthonian Scholarship between Universal History and Pedagogy* (Leiden: Brill, 2009), 38.

Second, so that the prophetic books might be better understood, the history of all times is to be embraced as an intellectual whole...
Third, to have become familiar with histories is useful for discerning the differences in the gravest theological controversies....
Finally, it is also of considerable utility to reflect continually upon the collation of pagan histories with our own [ecclesiastical] histories.[145]

The framework is indicative of Melanchthon's shift in emphasis. In 1532, he had not concentrated on theological controversies; now he made them an integral part of historical understanding. Theology did not become all encompassing, but it is noticeably more prevalent.[146]

Melanchthon did not retreat from the Prophecy of Elias or from the Four Monarchies, but he refined his interpretation of each. Regarding the Prophecy of Elias, Melanchthon expanded his remarks from 1532 to give a different, or more nuanced, explanation of each age.[147] For example, in 1532, Melanchthon had written that the first age was "void" (*Zwey tausent oed*), because it lacked rule prescribed through God's Word.[148] In 1558, he rejected this earlier view and wrote instead that "void" (*Duo millia inane*) simply meant that before the founding of Babylon men had not yet occupied distant regions.[149] The refinement continued in the *Chronicle* itself, and Melanchthon now assigned a specific characterization to each two thousand year interval. The first age (ἡγεμονικὸν) was characterized by authority, reason and invention.[150]

---

145 "Praecipue historia opus est in ecclesia. Primum quia Deus immensa bonitate sua se patefecit et patefactiones suas scribi voluit.... Secundo, ut libri prophetici melius intelligantur, omnium temporum historia complectenda est.... Tertio ad diiudicationes gravissimarum controversiarum prodest nosse historias.... Postremo et haec ingens utilitas adsidue cogitanda est in collatione historiarum ethnicarum et nostrarum." CR XII, 713–716.

146 See generally Pierre Fraenkel, *Testimonia Patrum: The Function of the Patristic Argument in the Theology of Philip Melanchthon* (Geneva: Librairie E. Droz, 1961).

147 See Ben-Tov, *Lutheran Humanists*, 42–46; and Warburg, "Pagan-Antique Prophecy," 693–696, which includes an English translation of the 1532 and 1558 versions of the prophecy.

148 "Das ist / zwey tausent jar sol die welt stehen oed / das ist / one ein gefasset regiment durch Gottes wort." Carion, *Chronica* (Wittenberg, 1532), sig. B v.

149 "Duos primos millenarios nominat inane, quod simplicissime sic interpretor, nondum homines procul dissitas regiones occupasse, ante conditam Babylonem. Alii dicunt, nominari Inane, quia nondum certa politia Ecclesiae constituta fuit, et nondum segregata fuit Ecclesiae a caeteris gentibus. Nondum etiam erant imperia, qualia postea in monarchiis fuerunt." CR XII, 717.

150 "Ut in homine praecipuae vires sunt ἡγεμονικὸν, θυμικὸν et ἐπιθυμητικὸν, ita dicunt initio in genere humano praecipue regnasse ἡγεμονικὸν, id est, excelluisse sapientiam cum artes inventae sunt, et gubernatio adhuc paterna fuit, plena sapientiae, iusticiae et autoritatis." CR XII, 726.

The second age (θυμικὸν) was marked by strength and spirit, especially fortitude in war, and it included the foundation of the Four Monarchies. The third age (ἐπιθυμητικὸν) is both similar and different; its defining characteristics are lust and desire. Thus, wars are waged, but they do not have the same vigour, and the age is marked by a general decline.[151] Melanchthon also reworked the chronology according to the reckonings from Johann Funck's *Chronologia*, so the birth of Christ now appeared at Anno Mundi 3963, instead of 3954 as in the revised Carion-Melanchthon edition of 1532.[152]

Regarding the Monarchies, Melanchthon clarified the position he had adopted in 1532. Thus, he now referred to the First Monarchy as the "Chaldean," rather than the Assyrian, and he explained the distinction between Babylon and Nineveh.[153] So too, Melanchthon had by now settled on the interpretation of the feet of Daniel's statue, iron mixed with clay, as the Roman-German Emperors, and he explicitly rejected any interpretation that saw fulfilment in the Turks. He explained that the Turks could not be included among the Four Monarchies of Daniel 2 because they committed manifest blasphemy against the Word of God, and the Turkish kingdom was not constituted to uphold law and learning, but rather to destroy it.[154] The association with blasphemy and

---

151 "Secunda aetas fuit θυμικὴ, in qua excelluit fortitudo in bellis, et imperia constituta sunt. In hac aetate complector quatuor monarchias, sic, ut initium sit a Nimroth, usque ad Iulium Caesarem, post quem secuta est senectus hominum languida et dedita voluptatibus. In hac regnat ἐπιθυμητικὸν. Etsi enim et in postrema senecta multum est bellorum, tamen non geritur res simili vigore animorum et labore." CR XII, 726.

152 "In dicto Eliae etiam tempora Mundi sic distributa sunt, vt significetur, Messiam se ostensurum esse mundo post quatuor millenarios. Natus est Christus ex Virgine anno Mundi ter millesimo, nongentesimo, sexagesimo tertio. Ita apparet, fere completos esse quatuor millenarios. Estque hic annus a morte Alexandri, annus trecentesimus vicesimus quartus. Annus urbis Romae septingentesimus quinquagesimus primus." CR XII, 904. Compare to the reckoning in Funck – "[Anno Mundi 396]3 IESVS CHRISTVS AETERNVS ET COAEQVALIS DEI FILIVS HOMO NATVS." Funck, *Chronologia* (Königsberg: Lufft, 1552), sig. P2 v. VD16 F 3382.

153 "1. Prima est Chaldaeorum, qua et Assyrii vicini comprehenduntur. Nam alias statim initio potentiores fuerunt reges in Babylone, alias vicini reges in Ninive. Nec dubium est, Babylonem et Niniven diversas urbes esse." CR XII, 719.

154 "Quarta Romanorum, quam significat Daniel tandem dilacerandam esse, et pedes partim ferreos, partim luteos fore. Etsi alii ferreos pedes intelligunt regnum Turcicum, caeteros luteos pedes: tamen ego existimo, Turcicum regnum, quod manifestas blasphemias contra verbum Dei profitetur, et ex professo delere nomen Christi conatur, non annumerari monarchiis, quas Deus legum et disciplinae causa constituit. Sed ferreos pedes intelligo aliquot potentes imperatores Germanicos, ut Carolum primum, Ludovicum filium, Henricum Saxonem, quem usitate Aucupem nominant. Veteres Germanicae historiae nominant eum Humilem, ut sic dicam. Deinde Otthones, Henricum Bombergensem. Postea fuerunt multi imbecilliores, quos significant lutei pedes. Sed mixti fuerunt et fortes

destruction, however, allowed Melanchthon to maintain that the Turks were foretold in Daniel 7. As before, he interpreted the little horn that displaces three of the ten horns on the Fourth Beast as the Turks, and he still equated them with Gog and Magog. In contrast to 1532, however, he no longer referred to extra-biblical prophecies regarding Turkish origins, including the "Red Jews" of pseudo-Methodius.[155]

In his revised introduction, Melanchthon again presented the Investiture Controversy and the German Civil Wars as the episode that set the Empire on its long decline. Likewise, he clearly laid out his belief that the Electors were the foundation of order within Europe and the true defenders of Germany against the Turks.[156] Based on the introduction, Melanchthon probably would have developed the same three themes in his treatment of Imperial Germany: the transfer of the Empire to the Germans, the entrance of the papacy into secular affairs, and the rise of the Turks.

The revised narrative follows the basic framework of the original *Chronicle*, but expatiates broadly on religious matters.[157] Melanchthon added more detail to his treatment of the early Christian heresies, and especially the theological struggles after the death of Constantine the Great.[158] He reserved much of this material for new chapters entitled, "*De Ecclessia*," and his discussion of Paul of Samosata is an example of the changes between 1532 and 1560. In the original

---

Principes, qui res utiles gesserunt, ut Lotharius Saxo. Nam Turcicum imperium prorsus a monarchiis seiungo, quas Deus legum et disciplinae causa constituit." CR XII, 719.

155 "Sunt igitur peculiares descriptiones Turcicae tyrannidis. Ut apud Ezechielem prophetia de Gog and Magog proprie ad Turcas pertinet. Et cornu loquens blasphemias, et conterens Ecclesiam apud Danielem, de toto Mahometico regno concionatur. Singularis furor est ortus a diabolis in hac ultima senecta mundi, Deo permittente propter horribilia hominum peccata, tyrannis Mahometica, dissimilis omnium regnorum: quia ex professo conatur delere nomen Christi. Nec ornat genus humanum legis aut disciplina: Sed vasta orbem terrarum, ut et nomen Turca vastionem seu vastatorem significat." CR XII, 719.

156 "Post hunc cum iam Romanorum Pontificum potentia crevisset, furiae pontificiae accenderunt in Germania bella civilia, quibus potentia Germanici imperii praecipue languefacta est. Non enim procul abest dies triumphi, in quo se filius Dei palam ostendet generi ornabit, et omnes impios in aeternas poenas abiiciet. Interea tamen, ut minus sit confusionum, optandum est, ut Principes in Germania privatis discordiis Germaniam ipsi dilacerent. Hanc curam praecipuam esse oportebat summi in terris Senatus, videlicet collegii Electorum, ut Europa et caput et vires haberet contra Turcicam barbariem, et tryrannos, qui iniusta bella movent, perniciosa toti Europae. Nos autem in hac turbulenta senecta mundi et ruinis imperiorum servet aliqua Ecclesiae hospitia, et tribuat eis salutarem gubernationem." CR XII, 720.

157 "Ut semper in historiis quaerendum est, ubi et quae Ecclesia Dei in genere humano fuerit: ita et series imperiorum consideranda est, quae voluit Deus constitui et disciplinae causa, et propter defensionem communis societatis." CR XII, 739.

158 "Ecclesiae certamina post mortem Constantini Magni." CR XII, 983–991.

Chronicle, Paul of Samosata, a third century anti-trinitarian bishop, was never mentioned. There was no need, since the doctrine of the Trinity was not at issue in the early Reformation. Beginning in the 1530s, however, the Spanish physician Michael Servetus (1511–1553) published a series of books that denied the Trinity, arguing that the doctrine was not biblical but rather a development grounded in Greek philosophy. Both Catholics and Protestants were agreed in condemning Servetus, and after fleeing the French Inquisition, he was captured at Geneva and executed by the Calvinists.[159] In the revised *Chronicle*, Melanchthon disingenuously stated that he was adding a "few things" about Paul of Samosata. In fact, he inserted several pages on the heretic and his condemnation by the ancient Church.[160] Melanchthon did not make an explicit comparison to Servetus, but contemporary readers would have recognized his discussion as a timely defence of trinitarian doctrines.

The treatment of Muhammad likewise shifted from the political focus of the original *Chronicle* to a more specific engagement with the basic teachings of Islam. Polygamy is now briefly mentioned in the context of Islamic law[161] and again as a sign of impiety,[162] but unlike Nauclerus, Melanchthon still did not draw attention to the Islamic view of "heaven" as a pleasure paradise.[163]

---

159   On Servetus, see RE 18: 228–236.
160   CR XII, 959–961. At the beginning of the section, Melanchthon remarks: "Addiiciam pauca et de Paulo Samosateno, qui blasphemiam renovavit, quam non tantum ab Ebione et Cerintho post Apostolos sparsam esse iudico, sed existimo primum ad Diabolis impulsum esse Cain, ut doctrinam de Messia irrideret, et negaret tunc adesse Ecclesiae filium Dei" (959).
161   "Ut autem et illecebras addat, concedit πολυγαμίαν, et sinit fieri divortia privato arbitrio sine cognitione Iudicum, et sine manifesta causa. Deinde ut sit occassio beneficentiae, quae prodest ad concordiam, non solum iubet largiri pauperibus, sed etiam pro delictis ordinat mulctas dandas pauperibus. Ita remissionem peccatorum transfert in satisfactionem: et si quis fecit stuprum aut adulterium, aut iuravit falso, dives vestiat decem inopes, aut redimat precio captivum. Inops vestiat duos pauperes. Homicidia et furta punit sicut lex Mosi. Ita duo praecepta utilitatis causa utcunque retinet: Non occides, et: Non furtum." CR XII 1076.
162   "Semper confusiones libidinum sunt signa impietatis. Mahometus reipsa delet coniugium, concedens divortia pro cuiusque arbitrio, etiamsi nullae probabiles causae sint. Nam ducere et abiicere cum libet, reipsa est vulgaris scortatio. Dissentiunt etiam a doctrina divina prohibitio vini et suillae carnis." CR XII, 1078–1079.
163   "Deinde ut regno Arabum potiretur consilio Sergii legem suam composuit, hic uero monachus erat, ideo ordinauit ut eius legis sectatores cuculla uterentur, quod hodie Saraceni seruant, deinde multas genuflexiones fieri mandauit & ut meridiem uersus adorarent, lotiones etiam usque ad uerenda instituit, & ut orantes unum confiterentur deum, unde trinitatem negant, se non deum sed dei prophetam eximium haberi, quod omnes carnes praeter porcinas & morticinia ac sanguinem comedere possent, quod quatuor legitimas uxores cuique habere liceret, & de propria cognatione liceat eas accipere, docuit autem

Instead, Melanchthon concentrated especially on the question of whether the teachings of Muhammad belong to the true Church, and he rejected the idea that this might be possible.[164] While the 1532 *Chronicle* had moved from Muhammad directly to the origins of the Turks, Melanchthon omitted that section and its discussion of the Red Jews. Instead, he incorporated various observations about the Turks into the general chapter on Muhammad. Melanchthon's contribution ends with the state of the church at the time of Empress Irene, without any conclusion or transition to the Carolingians.

11 Caspar Peucer's Revisions

In the original *Chronicle*, Melanchthon had forcefully argued for excluding the papacy from German political affairs, but he nevertheless maintained a moderate tone in describing religious matters. By the time Peucer began revising the text in the 1560s, hope for reconciliation between the Protestants and Rome had faded. Accordingly, Peucer abandoned Melanchthon's approach, and he transformed the later sections of the *Chronicle* into an unmitigated attack on both papal politics and the papal church. Through these revisions, the *Chronicle* became a forceful statement of a distinctly Protestant view of history.

Peucer's revisions mark both change and continuity with the 1532 *Chronicle*. The revised *Chronicle* remained strongly Imperial, and Peucer lauded the wisdom, strength and piety of the German Emperors and princes, who defended Christendom both at home and abroad.[165] Nevertheless, Peucer divided his attention between East (*Imperatores Orientis*) and West (*Imperatores Occidentis*),

---

auditores suos quod qui occidit inimicum uel occiditur ab inimico, paradisium ingreditur, paradisium uero, carnalis cibi ac potus locum, & indulgendis mulieribus perhibebat, fluuium quoque uini & mellis ac lactis ibi esse & affluentem uoluptate, multaque alia stultitiae plena quae stultis uidebantur credibilia, uel eo quod delectabilia, his & aliis prophetam dei se affirmans illius regionis obtinuit principatum, omnesque Arabes suasione uel tandem gladii timore ad ipsum uenerandum & legem suam seruandam." Nauclerus, *Memorabilivm omnis aetatis et omnivm gentivm chronici commentarii* (Tübingen: Anshelm, 1516), vol. 2, Generatio XXII, fol. XCVII v.

164 "Manifestum est autem Mahometi doctrinam plus quingentis annis posteriorum esse apostolica, et ab apostolica dissentire. Non est igitur vera. Huic Argumento et hoc addatur: Impossibile est esse Ecclesiam Dei coetum ex professo reiicientem scripta prophetica et apostolica. Mahometistiae ex professo reiiciunt scripta prophetica et apostolica. Non igitur sunt Ecclesia Dei." CR XII, 1077. The entire section on Islam is found in CR XII, 1073–1080.

165 "Praeterea celebranda erat & illustranda sapientia, virtus, pietas, ac foelicitas nostrorum Principum, quorum multi excitati & adiuti diuinitus gesserunt res orbi Christiano salutares domi forisque, repressis exerternis gentibus, & orbe Christiano pacato. Aliqui enim

rather than focusing exclusively on the German Emperors, and he offered an uninterrupted succession of rule that included both the Byzantines and the Turks.

As Melanchthon's heir, Peucer had inherited much of his library and *Nachlass*, and during these years he was engaged in preparing a new edition of Melanchthon's collected works.[166] Therefore, he was able to build on the historical foundation Melanchthon had laid in his revisions, literally with building blocks carved by Melanchthon's own pen. The revised chapters on Charlemagne and the *translatio imperii* exemplify this approach. Here, Peucer drew on Melanchthon's earlier writings to continue arguments that Melanchthon had started to develop in the revisions. Indeed, Peucer inserted so much of this material that some sections are literally Melanchthon's own work.[167]

After the abdication of Charles V in 1556, Melanchthon wrote a series of consilia for the Saxon court that addressed the papacy's role in Imperial elections, since Pope Paul IV (r. 1555–1559), who hated the Hapsburgs, was refusing to recognize Ferdinand I as Emperor.[168] In his responses, Melanchthon made two arguments for Charlemagne's assumption of the Imperial title.[169] First, he argued that Charlemagne had gained control of Italy, the Western Imperial

---

Imperium Occidentis, velut de collectis ex naufragio tabulis instaurarunt, vt Carolus Magnus." Peucer, *Chronicon Carionis* (Wittenberg, 1580), 292.

[166] Before his death, Melanchthon had been preparing a collection of his doctrinal writings (*Corpus Doctrinae*), which was published at Leipzig in 1560. Peucer followed this with a four-volume edition of Melanchthon's works, published between 1562 and 1564. He supplemented this collection with a selection of Melanchthon's letters (1565), and he edited various other texts, such as Melanchthon's declamations. For these editions, see the bibliography in Hans-Peter Hasse and Günther Wartenberg, eds., *Caspar Peucer (1525–1602): Wissenschaft, Glaube und Politik im konfessionellen Zeitalter* (Leipzig: Evangelische Verlagsanstalt, 2004), 327–368.

[167] On this point, see especially Uwe Neddermeyer, "Kaspar Peucer (1525–1602). Melanchthons Universalgeschichtsschreibung," in *Melanchthon in Seinen Schülern*, ed. Heinz Scheible (Wiesbaden: Harrassowitz, 1997), 69–101.

[168] In his *Annales*, Melanchthon discussed how Paul IV refused to recognize the election of Ferdinand as Holy Roman Emperor because he had confirmed the rights of the Protestant princes – "Ueber das begehret auch der Kaiser an die Fürsten des Reichs, daß sie zurathen sollten, wie dem unbilligen Fürnehmen des Papsts Pauli IV., Caraphae, zu begegnen, so die Wahl Kaisers Ferdinandi nicht confirmiren wollt darum, daß er den Fürsten und Städten der Augsburgischen Confession Frieden zugesagt hätte." CR IX, 1012; [1559].

[169] "An Romanus Pontifex ius habeat transferendae dignitatis Romani Imperatoris, et Principum Electorum? Anno 1558." CR IX, 703–705; "Quo iure Carolus Magnus habuerit imperium Occidentis, et titulum Imperatoris? Anno 1559." CR IX, 800–802; and in July of 1559, "Fragstück von Kaiserlicher und Päpstlischer Gewalt, Herrn Philippo Melanthoni seligen fürgestellet zu beantworten." CR IX, 851–889. See generally Goez, *Translatio imperii*, 257–304. See also Thomaidis, "The Political Theory of Philip Melanchthon," esp. 195–223;

heartland, through a just war against the Lombards. Second, he stressed that Charlemagne had been unwilling to use the Imperial title before negotiations with Constantinople. These two bases – the law of war (*ius belli*) and the agreement (*transactio*) with Constantinople – gave Charlemagne the right to the Imperial title.[170] Melanchthon's analysis did not disagree with the corresponding section in the 1532 *Chronicle*, but it was much more refined.

In his revisions to the *Chronicle*, Melanchthon carefully constructed a historical foundation for the Carolingian *translatio imperii*. The strands of his argument wind through Late Antiquity and the early Middle Ages, and his line of reasoning hinged on demonstrating that the papacy first gained political control over Italy only in the ninth century. Melanchthon set the *translatio imperii* from Rome to Constantinople at the time of Constantine the Great.[171] While the 1532 *Chronicle* had simply dismissed the notion that Constantine ceded the Western Empire to the pope,[172] in his revisions, Melanchthon explicitly refuted papal claims concerning the *Donation of Constantine* through a series of historical arguments.[173]

In contrast to the 1532 *Chronicle*, Melanchthon did not mention every Western Emperor after Constantine, since by then Roman rule had been transferred to Constantinople. He also removed the numbering of the Imperial succession. The change is striking, since it is one of the few instances where the revised *Chronicle* provides less information than the original. After the fall of Romulus Augustulus, the last "Italian Emperor,"[174] however, Melanchthon carefully traced the succession of political rule in Italy to the Emperors at Constantinople, who retained control over Italy through their vicars, the Exarchs of Ravenna, and then to the Lombards.

---

and Deflers, *Lex und Ordo*. In 1530, Melanchthon had written an opinion, "Von der Wahl eines neuen römischen Königs, daß dieselbe zuvor auch gebräuchlich." CR II, 447–448.

170 See, for example, "Habuit igitur iuste Carolus et terras, et titulum Imperatoris Occidentalis, iure belli et transactione. Et magna admiratione et laude digna est sapientia et iustitia Caroli, quod titulo uti noluit ante transactionem." CR IX, 800.

171 "Verum est, urbis Romae, Italiae et imperii statum valde languefactum esse, translata et dignitate et translatis familiis et opibus ex Italia in Thraciam." CR XII, 971.

172 "Aber das Constantinus dem Bapst sol Rom vnd das halb Keisarthumb geschenckt haben / wie etliche fabuliren / findet man jnn keinen glaubwirdigen Historien." Carion, *Chronica* (Wittenberg, 1532), fol. 93r.

173 The chapter is entitled: "An Constantinus urbem Romam et Occidentis imperium Romano Episcopo donaverit?" CR XII, 971–974.

174 "Augustulus fugiens imperio se abdicat, quod circiter annum unum tenuerat, ac deinde in Campania privatus vixit tanquam exulans. Hic finis fuit imperatorum Italicorum anno Christi quadringentesimo septuagesimo quinto, cum adhuc Leo Constantinopoli viveret." CR XII, 1034.

The purpose of Melanchthon's revised narrative was to demonstrate that Charlemagne had, by the law of war, succeeded to the Exarchs and the Lombards, and that at the time of the Imperial coronation the pope had never held a political claim to the city of Rome or to the West.[175] Accordingly, Melanchthon stressed not only that Charlemagne had conquered the Lombards in a just war, but also that the creation of the papal states took place under Charlemagne's son, Louis the Pious, and thus after the Imperial coronation, rather than earlier, under Charlemagne's father, Pippin.[176] By stripping the pope of any claim to political authority at the time of Charlemagne's coronation, Melanchthon sought to remove political significance from the act of coronation itself.

Peucer adopted Melanchthon's analysis from the consilia, and he inserted a paraphrase of these arguments into the chapter on Charlemagne.[177] Nevertheless, Peucer tended to describe the Carolingian *translatio imperii* as the "separation" (*separatio*) or "split" (*diuulsio*) of the Eastern and Western Empires; those terms are not specifically used in Melanchthon's consilia.[178] Even so, Peucer argued that the Greeks lost control of the West for two reasons, both of which Melanchthon had sketched earlier in the *Chronicle*.[179] First, the Exarchs of Ravenna had become tyrannical, luxurious and lazy. Second, after the eighth century iconoclasm disputes in the Eastern Empire, the Seventh Ecumenical Council was convened at Nicaea and recognized the impious and idolatrous

175 "Deinde Exarchi imperatorum vicarii fuerunt circiter annos centum et sexaginta a Iustino Secundo usque ad Pipinum. Testis est igitur *historia*, Romanos Episcopos non tenuisse imperium urbis Romae aut Occidentis." CR XII, 973.
176 "His initiis pars illa Romae proprior cepit esse propria Pontificum, non Pipini aut Caroli donatione, sed Ludovici Pii." CR XII, 972.
177 "Ita CAROLVS MAGNVS factus est Imperator Occidentis: primum iure belli: occupata armis Italia & vrbe Roma, Longobardorum regno destructo, & pace restituta, atque legibus ac praesidijs communita: deinde transactione cum Imperatoribus Graecis, qui vt veri domini, omne ius, quod habuerunt in Imperium Occidentis, CAROLO electio fuit, neque traditio: sed declaratio saltem, quod CAROLVS esset verè Imperator iure belli & concessione Imperatorum Orientis, consensuque & subiectione populi Romani. Nec Pontifices in vrbem Romam iuris quidquam sibi vendicasse, aut vsurpasse tunc, sed ea tantum, quae ad res sacras pertineret, procurasse prodiderunt omnes." Peucer, *Chronicon Carionis* (Wittenberg, 1580), 330.
178 In describing the Latin sources for the Fourth Monarchy, Peucer divides them into two categories: "Vetustiores ante diuulsionem Imperij Orientalis & Occidentalis" and "Recentiores circa & post diuulsionem." Peucer, *Chronicon Carionis* (Wittenberg, 1580), *Tabella*.
179 Melanchthon had followed a similar perspective on the Exarchs of Ravenna – "Erant alioqui magno in odio Graeci imperatores, et Exarchi magnam crudelitatem in Italia exercebant." CR XII, 1088. See Ben-Tov, *Lutheran Humanists*, 87–88.

adoration of images.[180] Thus, the Eastern Emperors lost political control through tyranny and idolatry, like so many rulers before them.

12 The Electoral College

The way that Peucer adapted and redeployed material from Melanchthon to describe the *translatio imperii* is characteristic of his working methods in many sections of the revised *Chronicle*.[181] Nevertheless, he also engaged in independent research; and at times, his studies led him to doubt his father-in-law. Perhaps most notably, Peucer questioned Melanchthon's view that the sixteenth century form of the Electoral College had been established by Emperor Otto III in 1002. In the original *Chronicle*, Melanchthon had complained that he could not discover from his sources why the Emperor had chosen the seven Electors.[182] Nevertheless, he consistently maintained that Otto III had established the Electoral College, and that it had continued unchanged to the sixteenth century.[183]

In his chapter on Otto III, Peucer gives a lengthy account of the reasons for the Electoral College.[184] There, he discusses the lack of contemporary sources regarding its supposed Ottonian foundation and notes general uncertainty about the issue.[185] In a preface from earlier that year addressed to Georg Sigismund Seld (1516–1565), the Imperial Vice-Chancellor, Peucer mentioned his research on this topic, and his doubts about the date of the foundation.[186]

---

180 "Mutationi autem, quae in orbe Christiano hoc tempore facta est separatione Imperij Occidentis ab Orientiali, caussam praebuit praeter tyrranidem, ignauiam, luxuriam, & luxum Exarchorum Graecorum in Italia, certamen de adoratione statuarum & imaginum cultuque sanctorum: de quo crudelia certamina fuerunt in Ecclesijs Graecis, Episcopis vrgentibus & propugnantibus, Imperatoribus prohibentibus & abolentibus cultum statuarum." Peucer, *Chronicon Carionis* (Wittenberg, 1580), 332.

181 See Neddermeyer, "Kaspar Peucer (1525–1602)," 69–101.

182 Carion, *Chronica* (Wittenberg, 1532), fol. 128r–129v.

183 "Noster Saxo sapienter viros doctos et bellatores miscuit, tribus Episcopis, Moguntino, Treverensi et Coloniensi adiunxit ex bellicosissimis gentibus tres Duces, Bohemicum, Saxonicum et Marchicum, et adiunctus est Palatinus Rheni, vel quia e stirpe Caroli fuit, vel ut Rheni ripam continuam quasi limitem Electores quatuor custodirent, ut alibi limitem orientalem tenuerunt caeteri." Melanchthon, *De dignitate Principum Electorum* [1554], CR XII, 82.

184 Peucer, *Chronicon Carionis* (Wittenberg, 1580), 383–393.

185 "Huius constitutionis author an fuerit OTTO, vt multi dubitent, non leues sunt causae." Peucer, *Chronicon Carionis* (Wittenberg, 1580), 389.

186 "Non minorem admirationem commouet intelligentibus omnibus industria tua, qui enim inter illos ingentes labores tuos, quibus gubernationis in Romano Imperio maximae

In the *Chronicle*, Peucer presented the Electoral College and the Imperial constitution as the result of a long process of development. He still held that the Electoral College was created by Otto III, but the year and the exact composition could not be determined from the sources.[187] Peucer maintained that the number of Electors had been permanently established at seven only later, under the Hohenstaufen Emperors.[188] Even then, he placed the final designation of the individual Electors later still. Here too, he was uncertain about the exact date or circumstances.[189] In the end, Peucer set the definitive establishment of the Imperial constitution with Emperor Charles IV and the Golden Bull of 1356.[190] For Peucer, as for Melanchthon, the Electors were the foundation of German political order.[191] Nevertheless, he conceded that in its actual political form, the German Empire was really an *aristocracy* rather than a *monarchy*.[192]

---

negotia administras, uix ad respirandum tibi tempus concedi existimarunt, ii cognoscunt tibi in promptu esse, ad ea respondere, quae nos in scholastico ocio nostro uix reperimus. Exercuit me in Chronico nostro Regum Galliae familia et successio, de quibus quaerenti mihi seriem generis horum, misisti et diligentissime a te conquisitam et ordine pulcherrimo descriptam. Torsit me postea altera dubitatio de origine Septemuiratus Imperatori creando, in hoc etiam ipso quanta diligentia notasti atque consignasti ea, quae paucissimi attendunt." Caspar Peucer, ed., *Orationes ex historia Thucydidis et insigniores aliquot Demosthenis et aliorum oratorum Graecorum* (Wittenberg: Rhau, 1562), sig. † 3 v – † 4 r. VD16 P 2017. On Seld, see ADB 33: 673–679.

187 "Hoc decretum quo anno factum sit non traditur, sed non multo ante mortem OTTONIS factum esse narratur, qua in re flagitiosa scriptorum negligentia detestanda est, vt in plerisque alijs rebus maximis." Peucer, *Chronicon Carionis* (Wittenberg, 1580), 388.

188 "Post FRIDERICVM secundum & numerus septenarius exprimitur crebroque repetitur, & familiae indicantur suffragantium." Peucer, *Chronicon Carionis* (Wittenberg, 1580), 390, see also 496–498.

189 Peucer, *Chronicon Carionis* (Wittenberg, 1580), 391.

190 "Etsi ergo nec quibus authoribus institutus sit, nec quando esse coeperit Senatus septem Electorum, certis argumentis historiarum concludi potest, tamen nullam eorum fieri mentionem ante Sueuorum Imperium certum est. Secutus tandem CAROLVS Quartus ordines Imperij accuratius distinxit, & leges cum Electoribus, tum caeteris Principibus imposuit, etiam Imperibus ipsis, quae extant comprehensae in ea formula, quam vocant Bullam auream, sicut infra dicemus." Peucer, *Chronicon Carionis* (Wittenberg, 1580), 393.

191 "Ita septem Electorum Senatus non tantum Germaniam assiduis ciuilibus bellis grauiter quassatam ac fluctuantem, restituit in tranquillum, sed, quod vna cum Imperatore est, & fuit, religionis Christianae, legum, iudiciorum, disciplinae, custos vigilantissimus, & defensor acerrimus: inter sese ordines omnes sic copulauit, atque coagmentauit, vt interrumpi, aut dissolui haec tam concina Imperij harmonia hactenus, nullis domi seditiosis motibus, nullo foris violentiae impetu potuerit." Peucer, *Chronicon Carionis* (Wittenberg, 1580), 495.

192 "Ita Monarchia Occidentis temperata est & fuit honestissima Aristocratia, in qua vnus rerum potitur, qui statuit & sancit pleraque, de consilio & sententia Septemuirum, quorum inter se est aequalitas Arithmetica." Peucer, *Chronicon Carionis* (Wittenberg, 1580), 495.

13 The Medieval Papacy

For Peucer, the political history of the Middle Ages was ultimately the story of how the papacy wrecked the Empire:

> That the Western Empire was shattered and torn to pieces chiefly by the machinations and ambition of the Roman pontiffs, no one can be in doubt, unless he is ignorant of histories or influenced more by affection than judgment.[193]

Although Peucer retained the thread of Melanchthon's original argument for maintaining peace and stability within Europe by adhering to the compromise formula of the Imperial constitution, he abandoned the previous focus on the positive aspects of cooperation between pope and Emperor. Instead, Peucer's account of the seven hundred years from Charlemagne to the Reformation became an unbridled attack on papal tyranny and the superstitions of the "Roman religion."

Based on his revisions to the earlier sections, Melanchthon had clearly intended to be much harsher on the papal church in the Middle Ages. At the close of Book 3, for example, he had blamed Pope Gregory the Great for introducing two degenerate practices – the invocation of the dead and masses for the dead – and he promised to address the harm done to the Church later and in more detail.[194] In contrast, Melanchthon's 1518 inaugural oration had praised Gregory for his preservation of learning, and the original *Chronicle* had presented him in a positive way for his resistance to the idea of "universal bishop."[195] In 1532, Melanchthon had attacked papal interference in German

---

[193] "Imperium Occidentis Pontificum Romanorum artibus & ambitione potissimum conuulsum esse atque dilaceratum, nemini dubium esse potest, nisi aut historias ignoranti, aut affectioni, quam iudicio, plus tribuenti." Peucer, *Chronicon Carionis* (Wittenberg, 1580), 493.

[194] "Imperatorum Mauricii et Phocae tempore fuit Gregorius Romanus Episcopus, primus eius nominis, qui ut vir Romanus, politica negocia multa egit, sed duas res in Ecclesia perniciosas auxit: Invocationem hominum mortuorum, et sacrificia pro mortuis, quae duae res horribiliter nocuerunt Ecclesiae, ut alibi copiose exponitur." CR XII, 1092.

[195] In *Carion's Chronicle* of 1532, the section reads: "Nach Pelagio Secundo warde der 67 Bapst Gregorius Primus / Der hat viel Ceremonias geordenet / Denn durch kriege vnd Ketzereien / war ein wüst wesen allenthalben worden / Darumb fieng er an die Kirchen mit Ceremonien widder zusamen zu bringen / zu dieser zeit hat sich auch der zanck zugetragen / De primatu / Vnd wolt der Keisar Mauricius / das der Patriarch zu Constantinopoli solt Oecumenicus / odder vniuersalis Episcopus / das ist / der öberst Bischoff jnn der Christenheit sein / Aber Gregorius wolt nicht darein willigen / vnd hielt sich Christlich / vnd

political affairs; in the revisions, he clearly planned to add theological condemnations of the papacy.

While Melanchthon intended to be less reserved, Peucer was completely unrestrained. With his revisions, he transformed the *Chronicle* into an unrelenting polemic against the doctrine, practice, and politics of papal Catholicism.[196] His attack on monasticism, scholasticism and papal tyranny is essentially a Protestant indictment of the papal church and a justification for the Reformation. With this, Melanchthon's earlier perspective of unity through compromise was utterly lost.

In the 1532 *Chronicle*, Melanchthon had traced the succession of popes, usually through a brief description at the end of each Emperor's reign. His discussions of theology were few and carefully chosen. For the revised *Chronicle*, he abandoned this practice, and instead he generally confined ecclesiastical matters to specifically dedicated chapters (*De Ecclesia*). As a result, ecclesiastical history was divorced from papal lineages, and the focus expanded beyond papal involvement in political affairs to developments in doctrine and practice. To some extent, Peucer followed this narrative pattern, but he intertwined more descriptions of ecclesiastical matters into the chapters about the Emperors.[197] Peucer made limited mention of individual popes, and he concentrated instead on broader developments in the Church. The doctrinal topics that had been hinted at or mentioned only in passing are developed in detail, and the

---

schreibet / Es solt sich kein Bischoff jnn der Christenheit / vniuersalem rhümen." Carion, *Chronica* (Wittenberg, 1532), fol. 107v. See Fraenkel, *Testimonia Patrum*, 96–100. For Luther's perspective on Gregory, see John Headley, *Luther's View of Church History* (New Haven: Yale University Press, 1963), 189–192.

196 "Relicta est enim pars operis pene difficilma, in qua dicendum erat de mutationibus, quas perpessa est Ecclesia, de inuectis in eam ac cumulatis abusibus atque idolatrijs, de abolita memoria legis diuinae superstitiosa obseruatione traditionum humanarum, de obruta multipliciter puriore doctrina Euangelij, & extincta pene vera DEI inuocatione, de conditis nouis dogmatibus, & institutis contra mandatum DEI cultibus, & sancitis legibus impijs, de converso Ministerio verbi in Monarchiam politicam, & rapta atque occupata à Pontificibus Romanis tyrannide in Ecclesia & Imperio." Peucer, *Chronicon Carionis* (Wittenberg, 1580), 291.

197 In his introduction to the German translation of this fasicle, Eusebius Menius noted, and specifically addressed, this change in perpsective: "Weil aber in diesem teil der Chronica / durch der Bepste vnmessige ehrgeitz tyranney vnd vntrew / offtmals vrsachen geben wird / das dauon nach der lenge mus geredt werden / wil ich den Leser dohin verwisen haben / da den nach der lenge nütze erinnerung geschehen / wie die Bepste wider iren beruff die weltliche Herrschaft vnd Monarchi zu sich gerissen haben / was sie dadurch für schaden / jamers vnd elendes angerichtet / vnd darüber die Kirchen verseumet / ja dieselben gleichfalls auch gar in ein weltlich Reich verstellet haben." Carion, *Chronica* (Wittenberg, 1564), sig. c v – cij r.

interference of the papacy in Imperial affairs is treated at even greater length than in the 1532 *Chronicle*.

14 Ecclesiastical History and Periodization

As Peucer recounted the developments in ecclesiastical affairs, he was especially interested in tracing the rise of tyranny, superstition and idolatry in the post-Apostolic Church. Here too, Peucer was deeply indebted to Melanchthon, but at the same time he showed an independent perspective. In a 1548 oration on *Luther and the Ages of the Church*, Melanchthon had divided New Testament ecclesiastical history into five ages:[198]

1. *Apostolic and post-Apostolic Age* – doctrine was pure and had not yet been diluted by Platonic philosophy and superstitious rites.[199]
2. *Age of Origen* – doctrine became clouded, and the churches were widely dominated by Platonic philosophy and superstition.[200]
3. *Age of Augustine* – God cleansed the Church through the voice of Augustine, and there was a return to the sources.[201]
4. *Age of the Monks* – after the invasions of the Goths and the Vandals, darkness slowly crept into the Church. The age was marked by scholastic theology, the worship of idols, namely the abuse of the Lord's Supper, the invocation of the dead, celibacy and the superstitions of the monks.[202]
5. *Age of Luther* – God has again recalled the Church to the sources, and through Luther, the light of the Gospel has driven away the darkness of the fourth age.[203]

---

198   Melanchthon, *De Luthero et aetatibus Ecclesiae* [8 Novemenber 1548], CR XI, 783–788.
199   "Sed consideremus tempora post praedicationem Apostolorum, quae etiamsi alius aliter distribuere potest, tamen opinor perspicue hoc modo discerni, ut prima aetas ac pura, sit ipsa apostolica, et promixa discipulorum, qui doctrinam nondum dilatum Platonicis opinionibus ac superstitiosis ritibus tradebant." CR XI, 786.
200   "Secunda aetas est Origenica, in qua iam caligo effusa erat doctrinae de fide, et in Ecclesiis late dominabantur philosophia Platonica et superstitio." CR XI, 786.
201   "Etsi semper Deus semina purae doctrinae in aliqua parte servat, tamen saepe diu vagantur errores in magna parte Ecclesiae, quos tamen postea Deus emendat, ut post Origenicam aetatem Augustini voce Ecclesia repurgata est. Sit igitur Augustini aetas tertia, in qua ad fontes revocata sunt hominum studia." CR XI, 786.
202   "Sed mox propter bella Gothica et Vandalica dissipatis Ecclesiis, secuta est quarta aetas monachorum, in qua paulatim tenebrae creverunt. Quid est enim doctrina Thomae aut Scoti, nisi barbaries conflata ex confusione duarum malarum rerum, ineruditae et nimis garrulae Philosophiae, et cultus idolorum, videlicet abusus Coenae Domini, invocationis mortuorum, coelibatus, superstitionum monasticarum." CR XI, 786.
203   "Etsi igitur, ut antea dixi, tunc quoque Deus semina purae doctrinae in aliquibus servavit: tamen manifestum est, maiorem partem Ecclesiae tenebris obrutam fuisse. Has depellere

Melanchthon did not specifically outline this scheme in his revisions to *Carion's Chronicle*, but it nevertheless guided his approach as he expanded the ecclesiastical sections.

In his own revisions, Peucer adopted a different periodization for ecclesiastical history, and he used it to add greater nuance to the religious history in the final age of the prophecy of Elias. Like Melanchthon, Peucer believed that major changes in politics and religion often occur at two-hundred-fifty and five-hundred year intervals.[204] Accordingly, he divided Melanchthon's third age (*aetas* or *tempus*) into three periods (*periodus*) of roughly five hundred years, followed by a nascent fourth period:[205]

1. *First Period* – Apostles to Gregory the Great
2. *Second Period* – Gregory the Great to the Investiture Controversy
3. *Third Period* – Investiture Controversy to the Reformation
4. *Fourth Period* – Reformation Era initiated by Luther and Melanchthon

The first period had been purer in doctrine, but it contained within it the seeds of later errors and superstitions. The transition to the second period occurred as the Roman Empire collapsed in the West, and Peucer blames Pope Gregory the Great for much of the superstition that developed during these years, including the invocation of the saints and masses for the dead.[206] The third period

---

cepit Deus immensa misericordia, luce Evangelii per Lutherum rursus accensa. Et quanquam multae gentes voci Evangelii adversatae sunt, ut semper accidit: tamen in multis regionibus pia constitutio Ecclesiarum facta est, et integrae doctrinae summa sine corruptelis extat. Sit igitur haec quinta aetas, in qua Deus Ecclesiam iterum ad fontes revocavit." CR XI, 786.

204 "Ferè enim aut integra quingentorum, aut dimidia ducentorum quinquaginta annorum periodo circumacta, accidere solent mutationes quasi fatales non regnis solum & Rebuspublicis: sed etiam Ecclesiae, quae quales inciderint in haec tempora, eò diligentius cognosci debent, quod inuexerunt in Ecclesiam regnum nouum politijs simile, & ab illo Christi regno, quod promittunt & describunt literae sacrae, diuersissimum." Peucer, *Chronicon Carionis* (Wittenberg, 1580), 416

205 Peucer, *Chronicon Carionis* (Wittenberg, 1580), 417–422, see also the *Tabella*.

206 "Talia ergo cum iacta essent impiarum superstitionum fundamenta initio, & aetate confirmata, iam alte insedissent in hominum animis, accessit publica authoritas Gregorigij Magni Pontificis Romani, qui Pontificatum adijt anno Christi quingentesimo, nonagesimo tertio. Hic publicum ritum inuocationis diuorum instiuit, & ossibus ac puluerbius sanctorum templa dedicari iussit. Auxit plurimum falsam persuasionem de Monachatu, & de operibus sine mandato Dei excogitatis, de satisfactionibus Canonicis, de votis, de coelibatu, quo onerauit Diaconos Siculos, qui eo vsque iuxta consuetudinem Ecclesiae Graecae & Synodorum veterum decreta, retinuerant coniugia in omnibus gradibus Ecclesiasticis. Irrepsit tunc etiam opinio de oblatione corporis & sanguinis Christi facienda pro mortuis, quae horribilem peperit prophanationem Sacramenti, hanc GREGORIVS comprobauit motus spectris." Peucer, *Chronicon Carionis* (Wittenberg, 1580), 418.

began with Henry IV and the Investiture Controversy. Indeed, Henry's reign, which began in 1057 (actually 1056), was marked for great upheavals, since it came 250 years after Charlemagne and a thousand years after the beginnings of the New Testament Church. Earlier tyranny, superstition and idolatry were all confirmed in this third age, and the degeneration only increased with the introduction of the adoration of the host (*artolatria*).[207] From Henry IV onwards, Peucer is also especially harsh in condemning monasticism.[208] Indeed, rather than characterizing the monks as "ministers of the Christian Church," Peucer refers to them as "accomplices of the popes," "devourers of consciences," and "priests of barbarian superstitions."[209]

In describing the third age, Peucer presented a thorough discussion of papal errors in doctrine and practice, and the entrenchment of the Protestant position stands in marked contrast to the presentation of these issues in the original *Chronicle*. While Melanchthon and Carion had hinted at papal abuses and theological problems in 1532, Peucer addressed them now thirty years later in uncompromising terms. Indeed, Peucer argued that because of its doctrinal errors, the papal church could not even be called "Christian":

> But we strip from [the papists] the title of "The Christian Church," because they have forsaken the foundation of Christ and the Apostles. And in truth, we judge the Roman Religion to be the abomination of desolation, concerning which the Son of God prophesied, i.e. it is the idol that effects universal devastation in the Church.

---

207 "Secuta est deinceps tertia periodus Ecclesiae, quae coepit huius HENRICI Quarti aetate, in quam incidit dimidia Imperij, inde vsque à CAROLO. Haec insignem mutationem Ecclesiae atque Imperio attulit. Confirmata est enim Tyrannis & superstitionum atque Idolatriae in Ecclesia contra regnum, id est, doctrinam, cultum atque legitimam potestatem Imperatorum. Introductus est in Ecclesiam ad priores Idolatrias & abusus cultus Idoli Maozim, quod occupauit in Ecclesia locum & honorem adorationis soli DEO debitum, & ad se oculos hominum mentesque conuertit. Hoc sese in processionem & threatricae Missae spectaculis vndique ostentate, conticuit vox doctrinae, hoc ordinis Ecclesiastici dignitatem euexit, amplificauit potentiam, auxit opes, muniuit regum." Peucer, *Chronicon Carionis* (Wittenberg, 1580), 420.

208 See the lengthy discussion at the end of Book 4 – Peucer, *Chronicon Carionis* (Wittenberg, 1580), 482–484.

209 "Haec monere hoc in loco volui, vt consideretur, qualem hi noui doctores, qui fuerent non ministri Ecclesiae Christi, sed Pontificum satellites, conscientiarum carnifices, superstitionis barbaricae architecti & antistites, omnis doctrinae liberalioris iurati hostes, qualem ergo hi pepererint doctrinam, & quando tyrannis horum, quae intolerabilis fuit orbi Christiano, esse ceperit, & sit confirmata." Pecuer, *Chronicon Carionis* (Wittenberg, 1580), 484.

The abomination consists, furthermore, of four great errors:

[1] The first of these errors is that it abolishes the doctrine of law and justification by faith, and introduces doubt. From this source flows the utter chaos of papal errors and idolatry.

[2] The second error is that it transfers the merits of the Son of God and the worship properly owed him to the adoration, oblation and application of the consecrated bread, for the living and dead, *ex opere operato* in the theatre of the Mass (*Missa Theatrica*) and also outside the Mass. [This is error] since [in truth] each one applies the good works of the Son of God to himself only by his own faith.

[3] The third error is that it directs the invocation that must be kept for God alone to the human dead, according to the custom of the pagans.

[4] The fourth error is that under the supposition of benefit, reverence and necessity, it has substituted rituals instituted by human authority, such as monastic vows and innumerable similar examples, for the precepts and works required by divine law, as the divine saying expressly teaches: In vain is God worshiped by the commands of men [Matthew 15:9].[210]

Peucer consistently attacked the "Roman religion" as illegitimate, and in doing so, he set in contrast the Reformation church as the true Church. Within this, Peucer developed two interrelated themes that Melanchthon had generally resisted in *Carion's Chronicle*. First, he incorporated the idea of "forerunners" of the Reformation, those pious men who had earlier opposed papal abuses. Second, he presented Luther as a turning point in history and the beginning of a new period.

In the 1532 *Chronicle*, Melanchthon had mentioned Jan Hus († 1415), but he portrayed his followers as insurrectionaries, and he completely omitted

---

210 "Sed titulum eis Ecclesiae Christi detrahimus, eo quod discesserunt à fundamento Christi & Apostolorum, & vere iudicamus Religionem Romanam esse abominationem desolationis, de qua vaticinatus est filius Dei, id est, Idolum, quod effecit vastationem vniversalem in Ecclesia. Consistit autem in quatuor maximis erroribus, quorum Primus est, quia delet doctrinam de Lege & Iustitia Fidei, & praecipit dubitationem, ex quo fonte scaturijt totum Chaos errorum Pontificiorum, & Idolatriae. Secundus est, quia merita, & cultus Filij Dei proprios, transfert in adorationem, oblationem, & applicationem panis consecrati, pro viuis & mortuis, ex opere operato in Missa Theatrica, & extra Missam, cum beneficia Filij Dei applicet sibi vnusquisque non nisi fide propria. Tertio, quia inuocationem soli Deo praestandam, Ethnico more, dirigit ad homines mortuos. Quarto, quia ritus humana autoritate institutos, vt vota monastica, & similes innumeros, cum opinione meriti, cultus, ac necessitatis, anteponit praeceptis ac requisitis lege diuina operibus, voce diuina expresse docente: Frustra Deum coli mandatis hominum." Peucer, *Chronicon Carionis* (Wittenberg, 1580), 508. The corresponding section in the German edition is found at Peucer, *Chronica Carionis* (Wittenberg, 1573), 797.

the English reformer John Wyclif († 1384). Melanchthon was always cautious about drawing parallels between the Reformation and earlier condemnations of "heresy." Even when he noted similarities, he remained especially guarded about Hussitism;[211] and in the *Apology* to the *Augsburg Confession* (1531), he explicitly rejected Wyclif's teachings.[212] Peucer, however, was more interested in demonstrating that others had previously condemned papal errors and abuses, and that the true Church had always existed amidst the degeneration of the philosophers and the monks. Accordingly, he draws attention to earlier "reformers," such as Johannes Tauler († 1361), Wessel Gansfort (1419–1489), and Jerome of Prague († 1416).[213] Furthermore, in marked contrast to Melanchthon's earlier account of Constance, which portrayed the gathering as an example of compromise,[214] Peucer viewed councils through the lens of Trent, and he presents the late medieval councils as a weapon in the papal arsenal to stifle ecclesiastical reform.[215]

Of the late medieval dissidents, Peucer gives special consideration to Hus, and he writes that the angels themselves must have fought on the side of the Hussites in the Bohemian Wars.[216] Peucer portrays the Czech reformer as a

---

211 For example, Melanchthon had written in his oration at Luther's funeral: "Ac post Apostolos sequitur agmen, quod etsi fuit imbecillius, tamen Dei testimoniis ornatum est: Polycarpus, Irenaeus, Gregorius Neocaesariensis, Basilius, Augustinus, Prosper, Maximus, Hugo, Bernardus, Taulerus, et alibi alii. Etsi enim haec postrema senecta squalidior est: tamen Deus semper aliquas reliquias servavit. Et lucem Evangelii splendidiorem accensam esse voce Lutheri, manifestum est." Melanchthon, *In funere Lutheri* [1546], CR XI, 728.

212 *Die Bekenntnisschriften der evangelisch-lutherischen Kirche* (Göttingen: Vandenhoeck & Ruprecht, 1998), 241 (*Apologie der Konfession*, VII.29), 309 (*Apologie der Konfession*, XVI.12).

213 "Colligant pij & exempla illorum, qui errores & abusus Pontificos reprehenderunt & refutarunt, sicut Prophetae fecerunt in populo Dei, quales fuerunt TAVLERVS, WESSELVS Groningensis, IOHANNES Huss, HIERONYMVS Pragensis, Hiltenius Isennacensis & alij." Peucer, *Chronicon Carionis* (Wittenberg, 1580), 463.

214 "Jm anfang seines Keisarlichen Regiments / ist er jnn Jtalien gezogen / vnd hat mit dem Bapst Johanne geradschlaget von eim Concilio / das Schisma auff zu heben / Er ist auch jnn eigener person zum König von Franckrich gezogen / vnd hat mit jhm gehandelt jnn ein Concilium zu willigen / Also mit bewilligung des Bapsts Johannis / des Keisars / der König Franckrich / Hispania vnd England / ist das Concilium zu Constantz angefangen / anno 1414. dahin Bapst Johannes selb komen ist." Carion, *Chronica* (Wittenberg, 1532), fol. 158r.

215 "Sed, vt toties monui, non doctrinae, non morum & disciplinae emendatio, non legum Pontificarum laxatio quaesita est, quae nerui fuerunt abominandae impietatis, Sed Idolatriae, errorum, abusuum, superstitionis & Tyrannidis Pontificae confirmatio." Peucer, *Chronicon Carionis* (Wittenberg, 1580), 703.

216 "Quinquies tentatam tunc esse Boemiam, & toties eos, qui contra Hussitas arma tulerunt, exutos esse castris atque omnibus impedimentis citra praelium tradunt, vt dubium non sit, pro pio grege amplexo sinceram doctrinam Filij Dei pugnasse sanctos Angelos, qui

forerunner of Luther, both in his methods and in the unfolding of his career, and he draws attention to the methodological example set by Wyclif. In their disputes, both Wyclif and Hus searched the sources and consulted a purer antiquity against papal tyranny and monkish superstition.[217] At the Council of Basel (1414–1418), the teachings of Wyclif were condemned,[218] and Hus was pronounced a heretic,[219] but their example prefigured Luther's own struggle. To remove any doubts about the correlation, Peucer relates the famous story that before his execution, Hus prophesied that a hundred years later a swan would arise from his ashes who could not be burned.[220] It was, of course, exactly a century between Constance and the posting of the *Ninety-Five Theses*.

The clearest indication of Peucer's overall change in perspective comes at the end of the *Chronicle*. Peucer did not reject Melanchthon's original framework of prophetic fulfilment. Nevertheless, he transformed the teleological sense of the *Chronicle*. Melanchthon had concentrated primary attention on politics, so he looked to the eventual fall of the Fourth Monarchy as the sign that the last age (*aetas*) of the Prophet Elias was drawing to a close. In contrast, Peucer focuses on the transition from the third period (*periodus*) of ecclesiastical history into the fourth, the Age of the Reformation. Accordingly,

hostes conterritos palantesque ac trepidantes sola consternatione animorum tota exegerunt Boemia." Peucer, *Chronicon Carionis* (Wittenberg, 1580), 634.

[217] "Initium disputationum harum fecerat paulo ante Wicleffus in Anglia circiter millesimum, trecentesimum, septuagesimum secundum, cuius exemplo Hussus inuitatus, fontibus accuratius inquisitis, & consulta antiquitate sinceriore, ita se confirmauit aduersus Tyrannidem superstitiosam Pontificum, & superstitionem rabiosam Monachorum, vt quidquid ab his produceretur, id omne autoritate testimoniorum coelstium protinus configeret." Peucer, *Chroncion Carionis* (Wittenberg, 1580), 618.

[218] "Condemnauit haec Synodus dogmata Iohannis Wicleffi Angli, digesta in capita quadraginta quinque, Condemnauit ad rogum & duos Martyres Boëmos, viros sanctimonia vitae, & doctrina fidei Christiae analoga antecellentes, violata vide publica, qua ab Imperatore praemuniti accesserant." Peucer, *Chronicon Carionis* (Wittenberg, 1580), 634.

[219] "Vtrunque & Iohannem Hussum & Hieronymum Pragensem postquam Synodus pronunciasset Haereticum, Hussum vsitato ipsis ritu exutum dignitate sacerdotali tradidit exurendum Magistratui ciuili." Peucer, *Chronicon Carionis* (Wittenberg, 1580), 634.

[220] "Fertur ante mortem ceu praesagiens vatidico Spiritu sequuturam inclinationem regni Pontificij, dixisse, nasciturum esse ex suis cineribus olorem, quem non ita exusturi sint, sicut anserem torrerent. Significat autem Boëmica lingua Hussus anserem. Sunt & hae ex eo auditae voces: Post annos centum vos Deo & mihi respondebitis, quae verba Boëmi in ambitu monetae cuiusdam signatae imagine Hussi expresserunt. Vatcinij fidem comprobauit euentus. Intercesserunt enim inter finem Synodi Constantiensis & initia disputationum Martini Lutheri anni centum. Crematus est deinceps similiter Hieronymus Pragensis quinta Iduum Septembris." Peucer, *Chronicon Carionis* (Wittenberg, 1580), 634.

political history ends with Emperor Maximilian I – rather than Charles V and Ferdinand I as in the original *Chronicle* – and ecclesiastical history culminates with the restoration of "divine light" through Luther and his Wittenberg colleagues.[221] Unlike Melanchthon, Peucer made the Reformation the defining event of history.

In his revisions, Peucer abandoned any remaining hope for Christian unity, and he transformed *Carion's Chronicle* into a quintessentially Protestant text. The centuries after Charlemagne became the story of how the papacy wrecked the Empire, and the thousand years from Gregory the Great to Luther were reduced to a prelude to the Reformation. The shift itself is indicative of the change in generations and in circumstances over the thirty years that separated the two editions. Thus, with Peucer, *Carion's Chronicle* became exemplary of the move away from efforts at compromise to self-legitimating critiques of incompatible theological positions.

15   Conclusion

In the sixteenth century, Melanchthon and the Wittenbergers gave new life to the prophecy of Four Monarchies, and their interpretative framework set a standard with which all later commentators had to engage. Melanchthon drew on patterns of interpretation from Antiquity and the Middle Ages, but he deployed them in new ways to address the specific context of his day. On the eve of the Reformation, historians used the Four Monarchies as an interpretative pattern, but they generally treated it as subordinate to the Six Ages. With *Carion's Chronicle*, Melanchthon rejected this approach, and although he used the Three Ages, his concurrent, and indeed primary, focus was on the Monarchies. The shift in historiographical paradigms indicated more than a change in method. The Four Monarchies were integral to Melanchthon's assertion of a Wittenberg interpretation of history, prophecy and the Imperial constitution.

With *Carion's Chronicle* Melanchthon developed two positions that were of lasting importance for political discourse in Europe. First, he presented the Holy Roman Empire as Daniel's Fourth Monarchy, which was to endure until the end of time, and second, he refuted the curial *translatio imperii* theory to preclude papal involvement in Imperial elections and more generally in Imperial political affairs. Ultimately, the arguments that Melanchthon articulated in *Carion's Chronicle* established patterns of thought concerning the Four

---

221   Peucer, *Chronicon Carionis* (Wittenberg, 1580), 701–706.

Monarchies, the *translatio imperii* and the Imperial constitution that animated discussions among theologians, historians and jurists for centuries.[222]

Melanchthon's perspective on these issues, however, changed over time, so his written corpus, like Luther's, is marked by inconsistencies or developments that can only be explained by reference to immediate circumstances.[223] As Melanchthon revised texts, he silently adapted them to changes in his thought and to situational differences. In this respect, the two major editions of *Carion's Chronicle* from 1532 and 1572 reflect a process of interpretive development and a refinement in Melanchthon's thinking about the Imperial constitution.

In its initial form (1532), *Carion's Chronicle* was a response to the political problems that Germany had faced during the 1520s, especially the interference of the papacy and the French in German affairs and the rise of the Turks as a threat to the Eastern frontier of the Empire. The situation was similar to the one Jerome, Augustine and Orosius had faced a millennium before. The Empire was wavering under the stress of invasion and the turmoil of internal discord. In response, Melanchthon turned to the Four Monarchies to emphasize the permanence of the Empire, and he used Daniel's prophecy to explain the struggle between the Empire and Turks.

In its later form (1572), the *Chronicle* concentrated on the papacy and the Turks, the twin foes of Wittenberg and the Empire, as political, and now more specifically religious, threats. After Melanchthon's death, Caspar Peucer completed the most important sections of the *Chronicle*, the history of the medieval Empire. Peucer refined, and sometimes reworked, Melanchthon's earlier arguments about political supremacy, but just as important, he reoriented the politically focused narrative into an overt attack on the medieval papacy. In doing so, he presented Wittenberg historiography as a vision for Europe that rejected not just papal supremacy, but any role at all for the papacy, in politics or religion. For Peucer, the Wittenberg Reformation marked the beginning of a new period in history, and *Carion's Chronicle* became a foundational text for understanding the divide between Protestant and Catholic worlds.

---

222 See Gross, *Empire and Sovereignty*; and Seifert, *Der Rückzug*.
223 See Seifert, *Der Rückzug*, 7–37.

CHAPTER 5

The Transmission and Reception of Carion's Chronicle

1   Introduction

After 1532, *Carion's Chronicle* spread from Wittenberg to the far corners of Europe. As Melanchthon and Carion had intended, the *Chronicle's* thematic content and its manageable size meant it was well suited for use as a textbook. In Germany, court tutors relied on the *Chronicle* for instructing young princes, and from the 1550s, professors regularly used Melanchthon's expanded text as the basis for university lectures. As the first printed history textbook, the *Chronicle* set a standard for the discipline, and it conditioned expectations of what it meant to study history.

Carion did not live to enjoy the fame of his *Chronicle*. At his death in 1537, the Latin translation had not yet been published, so the *Chronicle's* circulation was still confined to a German-speaking audience. Initially, Melanchthon did not intervene in the *Chronicle's* transmission, and the text spread through the well-worn routes of the European book trade. The situation changed, however, from the mid-1540s onward, when the convergence of several forces pushed Melanchthon to reengage with the *Chronicle*.

The vast number of editions attests to the *Chronicle's* popularity as a history textbook. Print not only made this broad dissemination possible but also strained Melanchthon's ability to control his own text. Furthermore, he struggled against practices that had been accepted and common among scholars both in the Middle Ages and in the early days of printing. Down to the sixteenth century, annalists and historians could generally expect that subsequent writers would continue their narrative or adapt their material. Burchard of Ursberg († ca. 1231), for instance, continued the earlier Frutolf-Ekkehard *Chronicle*, and then in the 1530s, Caspar Hedio re-edited the text and added a new continuation down to the sixteenth century.[1] Martin of Troppau's *Chronicle* probably offers the most extreme example of these tendencies. Over the centuries, translators and continuators adapted his work to a wide range of

---

1   Burchard of Ursberg, *Chronicvm Abbatis Vrspergensis* (Strasbourg: Mylius, 1537). VD16 B 9801.

contexts, and by the fifteenth century, hundreds of manuscripts transmitted an array of variant editions and continuations.[2]

Print changed and accelerated this process. As a result, the adaptation of *Carion's Chronicle* unfolded in Melanchthon's own lifetime, a situation that would have been far more rare, and certainly less widespread, in the Middle Ages. Sixteenth century historians and printers treated the *Chronicle* much like a medieval text. They translated it, wrote continuations, and adapted the content. Eventually, Melanchthon, and later Caspar Peucer, tried to push back against this process. At the time, however, few effective tools were available to maintain control over a text once it had been released into the world of print.

In the sixteenth century, authors could not assert "copyright" over their works to prevent unauthorized uses, and other protections were limited.[3] In England, printing was centred in London, and the crown could, and to some degree did, impose measures to regulate the presses.[4] Germany, however, had multiple printing centres and a fragmented political landscape.[5] Authors, or more commonly printers, sometimes applied to their princes or to the Emperor for a printing "privilege," which usually granted exclusive rights to print a text for a fixed amount of time.[6] Nevertheless, German printers were keenly aware that there was no legal prohibition on "pirating" a text, unless it was protected by a privilege valid in the printer's jurisdiction.[7] As a result, jurisdictional lines prevented the establishment of publishing monopolies, and reprinting was rampant.

The Wittenbergers, and especially Luther, were at the forefront of attempts to strengthen printing protections in Germany. During the 1520s and 1530s, Wittenberg texts sold well, and printers outside of Electoral Saxony were sometimes unscrupulous in their efforts to capture a share of the market. Wittenberg sermons and lectures were published without permission, manuscripts

---

2 See Anna-Dorothee von den Brincken, "Studien zur Überlieferung der Chronik des Martin von Troppau," *Deutsches Archiv für Erforschung des Mittelalters* 41 (1985): 460–531; and Anna-Dorothee von den Brincken, "Studien zur Überlieferung der Chronik des Martin von Troppau: Zweiter Teil," *Deutsches Archiv für Erforschung des Mittelalters* 45 (1989): 551–591.

3 See generally Elizabeth Armstrong, *Before Copyright: The French Book-Privilege System 1498–1526* (Cambridge: Cambridge University Press, 1990).

4 For England, see generally Lyman Ray Patterson, *Copyright in Historical Perspective* (Nashville: Vanderbilt University Press, 1968); and Joseph Loewenstein, *The Author's Due: Printing and the Prehistory of Copyright* (Chicago: University of Chicago Press, 2002).

5 For Germany, see generally Ludwig Gieseke, *Vom Privileg zum Urheberrecht: Die Entwicklung des Urheberrechts in Deutschland bis 1845* (Baden-Baden: Nomos Verlagsgesellschaft, 1995).

6 See Gieseke, *Vom Privileg zum Urheberrecht*, 39–92.

7 See Karl Hubert Haug, "Luthers Bedeutung in der Geschichte des Urheberrechts," *Archiv für Urheber-, Film-, Funk- Und Theaterrecht* 135 (1997): 135.

were stolen before an approved edition was released, and reprints, often shoddy and inaccurate, were quickly issued to compete with official imprints. Printers even falsely indicated "Wittenberg" as the place of publication to enhance sales.[8]

In response, Luther and his colleagues tried various techniques to protect their works and the economic interests of the Wittenberg printers. They published "corrected" editions, or they added new prefaces to official imprints to undercut the marketability of earlier reprints.[9] Luther publicly admonished printers, and he condemned the practice of reprinting, which he eventually referred to as "robbery."[10] Sometimes, he appealed directly to the relevant authorities, whether city officials or princes, to halt deceptive printing practices, and he sought, but failed to obtain, Imperial printing privileges.[11] He had some success in Saxony, where an automatic one-year prohibition on reprints was instituted in 1526, but he never obtained protections that would be enforceable throughout the Empire.[12]

The transmission of *Carion's Chronicle* was marked by this tension between the fluidity of print and the desire to control. The *Chronicle* was a Wittenberg text, which made it desirable for reprinting, but it also fell into a category of texts for which there was generally less expectation of fixity and integrity. This combination of factors made the *Chronicle* particularly susceptible to the problems the Wittenbergers had experienced with their texts, and these were compounded by the issue of attribution for continuations and adaptations.

The focus here is on the diffusion and adaptation of *Carion's Chronicle* in different geographic, linguistic and religious contexts. Over the years, Melanchthon and Peucer tried to establish an official Wittenberg text of the *Chronicle*, but ultimately, "*Carion's Chronicle*" became a rubric for an array of texts that to varying degrees resembled the original 1532 *Chronicle*. The complexity of the *Chronicle's* transmission has long posed a barrier to understanding the extent of its influence on European historical thought. The account here resolves many lingering questions, and in doing so, addresses more than the generation and dissemination of texts. Reception, especially of a textbook, is difficult to chart, but extant copies of the *Chronicle* offer some indications of how it was received and read, and these books provide a sense of its broader European influence.

---

8   On these practices, see Haug, "Luthers Bedeutung," 156–232; Gieseke, *Vom Privileg zum Urheberrecht*, 21–28.
9   Haug, "Luthers Bedeutung," 220–232; Gieseke, *Vom Privileg zum Urheberrecht*, 22.
10 Haug, "Luthers Bedeutung," 194–197, 213–216; Gieseke, *Vom Privileg zum Urheberrecht*, 25.
11 Haug, "Luthers Bedeutung," 170–171, 207–213; Gieseke, *Vom Privileg zum Urheberrecht*, 25.
12 Haug, "Luthers Bedeutung," 170–179; Gieseke, *Vom Privileg zum Urheberrecht*, 25.

2 The Early Transmission of *Carion's Chronicle*

In the spring of 1532, Georg Rhau published the *editio princeps* of *Carion's Chronicle* in quarto format at Wittenberg,[13] which served as the basis for the editions published that year at Augsburg, with additional illustrations, and at Marburg.[14] Within a few weeks of the *editio princeps*, Rhau reprinted the text with some variants, mostly typographical.[15] Then in late 1532, he published a revised edition in octavo format.[16] The revision presented a reworked chronology, added some new material, and included a series of prophecies about the 1532 Turkish campaign. The revised text immediately became the standard, and it was reprinted the next year in Wittenberg and Augsburg.[17] In 1534, the first translation for an even wider audience was published at Magdeburg in Low German (*Plattdeutsch*).[18] The frequency of German reprintings then slowed dramatically, but this was not unusual.[19] Following an initial flood of editions, the market often could not sustain serial reprinting of Wittenberg texts. Furthermore, Carion had died in 1537, so there was no possibility of preparing a new edition under his joint direction.

As soon as *Carion's Chronicle* was published in 1532, German historians started to draw on it for their own works. Several sections, including Melanchthon's introduction on the Prophecy of Elias, were copied or adapted by Christoph Egenolff (1502–1555), a Frankfurt printer, and inserted into an illustrated chronicle he published in 1533. The borrowings from *Carion's Chronicle* are

---

13   Johann Carion, *Chronica durch Magistru[m] Johan Carion / vleissig zusamen gezogen / meniglich nützlich zu lesen* (Wittenberg: Rhau, [1532]). VD16 C 998. For a discussion of the *editio princeps*, see Frank Prietz, *Das Mittelalter im Dienst der Reformation: Die Chronica Carions und Melanchthons von 1532. Zur Vermittlung mittelalterlicher Geschichtskonzeptionen in die protestantische Historiographie* (Stuttgart: W. Kohlhammer Verlag, 2014), 43–64.

14   These editions are: Augsburg, Steiner [dated 16 July 1532] (VD16 C 996); and Marburg, Rhode (VD16 ZV 20310).

15   Carion, *Chronica* (Wittenberg: Rhau, 1532). VD16 C 995.

16   Johann Carion, *Chronica durch Magistrum Johan Carion / vleissig zusamen gezogen / meniglich nützlich zu lesen. Wittemberg. M.D.XXXII.* (Wittenberg: Rhau, 1532). VD16 C 997.

17   The 1533 editions are: Wittenberg, Rhau – VD16 ZV 2942; and Augsburg, Steiner – VD16 C 999. The 1532 Wittenberg octavo edition was also reissued with a new title page in 1533 (Tübingen, Universitätsbibliothek: Fn 81 t). See Prietz, *Das Mittelalter im Dienst der Reformation*, 56–58.

18   Johann Carion, *Chronica dorch M. Johan. Carion / vlitich tosamende getagen / mennichlick nütlick tho lesen. M.D.XXXIIII.* (Magdeburg: Michael Lotter, 1534). VD16 C 1011.

19   German editions were published at Wittenberg in 1538 (VD16 C 1001) and at Augsburg in 1534 (VD16 C 1000) and 1540 (VD16 C 1002). A second Low German (*Plattdeutsch*) edition was published at Magdeburg, probably in 1542 (VD16 C 1012).

most noticeable in the early chapters of *Egenolff's Chronicle*, and the opening sentence was even copied verbatim.[20] More so than *Carion's Chronicle*, however, Egenolff drew from the *Nuremberg Chronicle*. He reconfigured and abridged Schedel's complex layout and unwieldy narrative, and for the period after Christ he reduced the text to a chronicle of the Emperors. Despite his debt to Schedel, Egenolff did not use the Six Ages, the principal organizing framework for the *Nuremberg Chronicle*. It is plausible, though not entirely clear, that he made the decision in response to Melanchthon's negative view of Schedel's periodization scheme.[21]

Georg Major (1502–1574), a former Wittenberg student, also quickly incorporated material from *Carion's Chronicle* into one of his works.[22] In 1526, Major had published a new edition of Justin's *Epitome* with a preface by Melanchthon.[23] In 1537, he was again in Wittenberg, and that year he prepared a revision of his Justin edition, which was published at Magdeburg by Lotter. For this 1537 edition, Major inserted additional chronological information, and he added Melanchthon's "Tabula annorum," all of which he derived from *Carion's Chronicle*.[24] Major also added a brief introduction on reading history

---

[20] Christian Egenolff, *Chronic von an vn[d] abgang aller Weltwesenn. Auß den glawbwirdigsten Historien / On alle Gloß vnnd Zůsatz / Nach Historischer warheyt beschriben. Künig / Keyser / vnnd fürneme Personen / nach warer fürbildung Controfeit*. (Frankfurt a.M.: Egenolff, 1533), fol. II v. VD16 E 573.

[21] Interestingly, however, Egenolff removed Melanchthon's specific comment that the Six Ages created disorder (*vnordnung*). See Egenolff, *Chronic* (Frankfurt, 1533), fol. II v; and compare to Carion, *Chronica* (Wittenberg, 1532), sig. B v.

[22] On Major, see Timothy Wengert, "Georg Major (1502–1574): Defender of Wittenberg's faith an Melanchthonian exegete," in *Melanchthon in Seinen Schülern*, ed. Heinz Scheible (Wiesbaden: Harrassowitz, 1997), 129–156; and Robert Kolb, "Georg Major as Controversialist: Polemics in the Late Reformation," *Church History* 45, no. 4 (December 1976): 455–468.

[23] Justin, *Ivstini Ex Trogo Pompeio Historia* (Hagenau: Johann Setzer, 1526). VD16 T 2051. On Major's editions of Justin see Irene Dingel and Günther Wartenberg, eds., *Georg Major (1502–1574): Ein Theologe der Wittenberger Reformation* (Leipzig: Evangelische Verlagsanstalt, 2005), 273–274; H. Holstein, "Das altstädtische gymnasium zu Mageburg," *Neue Jahrbücher Für Philologie Und Pädagogik* 130 (1884): 23–24; and Hans Volz, "Neue Beiträge zu Luthers Bibelübersetzung: Luthers Arbeiten am Propheten Daniel," *Beiträge zur Geschichte der deutschen Sprache und Literatur* 77 (1955): 405–408; and also his comments in WA DB 11^II:XLVI–XLVIII. The editions are also listed at MBW 435; see also VD16 T 2051, 2053–2055, 2058–2062, ZV 15048–15049.

[24] "Haec, quae ex Carionis Chronico de Monarchiarum temporibus & mutatione addidimus, nouisse, non tam ad Iustini, quam aliorum historicorum lectionem plurimum proderit." Justin, *Ivstini Ex Trogo Pompeio Historia* (Magdeburg: Lotter, 1537), sig. B v; the table is found on sig. [A viii r], with the section from *Carion's Chronicle* at sig. [A viii r] – B v. VD16 T 2055.

("*Brevissima Legendae historiae ratio*"),[25] which made his revised edition of the *Epitome* even more similar to *Carion's Chronicle* in its presentation.

Another early example of engagement with *Carion's Chronicle* is the *German Chronicle* of the spiritualist historian Sebastian Franck (1499–1543?).[26] At the beginning of the *German Chronicle*, Franck provided a list of his sources, and he divided them into ancient and modern, among whom he included Wimpfeling, Nauclerus and *Carion's Chronicle*. Franck frequently noted his sources, but not always; and he sometimes copied or adapted material from *Carion's Chronicle*, such as the Lotharingian legend, without explicit reference.[27] In other instances, he implicitly rejected Melanchthon's position. For example, he began by addressing the origins of the Germans, but in contrast to Melanchthon, who held that the Germans descended from Japheth, Franck followed pseudo-Berosus, and he traced the lineage of the Germans back to the "fourth" son of Noah, Tuisco.[28]

In other sections Franck acknowledged his debt to Melanchthon and Carion; for example, he drew his discussion of the German tribes from *Carion's Chronicle*.[29] Furthermore, in one instance, Franck explicitly addressed the factual content in *Carion's Chronicle*. In the chapter on Emperor Charles IV, Melanchthon and Carion had written: "Charles besieged Ulm, but I have not been able to find the reason, because our foolish German historians did not pay attention to the circumstances of the affair."[30] In response, Franck explained that during his own archival research in Ulm he had discovered an old book that provided the answer to the question. According to the manuscript, which Franck had no reason to doubt, Charles had been allied at that time with Count Eberhard II of

---

25   Justin, *Ivstini Ex Trogo Pompeio Historia* (Magdeburg, 1537), sig. A iiij v – [A vii v].
26   Sebastian Franck, *Germaniae Chronicon* (Augsburg: Hans Westermair, 1538). VD16 F 2088. The *editio princeps* from Frankfurt am Main is VD16 F 2089. On Franck, see the essays in Jan-Dirk Müller, ed., *Sebastian Franck (1499–1542)* (Weisbaden: Harrasowitz Verlag, 1993); and Yvonne Dellsperger, *Lebendige Historien und Erfahrungen: Studien zu Sebastian Francks "Chronica Zeitbuoch vnnd Geschichtbibell" (1531/1536)* (Berlin: E. Schmidt, 2008).
27   Franck, *Germaniae Chronicon* (Augsburg, 1538), fol. CLIX r.
28   "Teutschen aber werden sie von Tuisco dem sun Noe genant / Der hat den teil Europe eingenomen / vnd durch sein nachkommen regiert / Sein sun hatt geheissen Mannus / von dem die Teutschen Alemanni seind gnant worden." Franck, *Germaniae Chronicon* (Augsburg, 1538), sig. [aa vj] v.
29   "Von Teutschland vnd anfang desz Fränckischen Reichs / auß Carione." Franck, *Germaniae Chronicon* (Augsburg, 1538), fol. LXXVIII v.
30   "Carolus hat Vlm belagert / Aber warumb / das finde ich nicht / Denn vnsere vnuerstendige Deudsche Historici haben vmbstende der hendel nicht geacht." Carion, *Chronica* (Wittenberg, 1532), fol. 156 r.

Württemberg (r. 1344–1392), who spent his reign trying to enlarge his territory at the expense of the Imperial Free Cities, such as Ulm.[31]

As Franck demonstrates, contemporary historians did more than copy the *Chronicle*, they engaged critically with its content and they reacted to specific historical problems that it posed. Furthermore, they viewed the *Chronicle* as a contribution to the *Germania Illustrata* tradition, rather than a specifically Protestant text. In his 1536 *Commentary on Tacitus's Germania*, for instance, Andreas Althamer († 1538/39), another former Tübingen student, set his work in the tradition of famous modern writers on German antiquity, including Beatus Rhenanus, Conrad Peutinger, Sebastian Münster, and most recently Johann Carion.[32]

3   The Latin Transmission of the Carion-Melanchthon *Chronicle*

The broad dissemination of *Carion's Chronicle* across Europe was due chiefly to the Latin translation of Hermann Bonnus (1504–1548).[33] Bonnus had studied in Wittenberg from 1523 to 1525, and he was heavily influenced by Melanchthon. He taught in Greifswald, later served as a princely tutor at the Danish Court, and eventually was appointed superintendent (essentially Protestant bishop) of Lübeck. In addition to his translation of *Carion's Chronicle*, Bonnus

---

31   "Anno M.CCC.lxxvij. war Carolus vnd Graff Eberhart von Wirtenberg so eins / das sie Vlm belägerten. Carion schreibt / er künde die vähde oder vrsach nit finden oder wissen / so vberhupfft sie Nauclerus / weiß nit aus willen oder onwissenheit / auch. Ich hab aber zů Vlm die vrsach inn einem alten geschriben bůch gefunden / die will ich inn jrem werd geleich bald hernach setzen oder zelen / doch sihets er warheyt nit onenlich." Sebastian Franck, *Germaniae Chronicon* (Augsburg: Westermair, 1538), fol. CCV r. VD16 F 2088. On this point see, Gotthard Münch, "Das Chronicon Carionis Philippicum: ein Beitrag zur Würdigung Melanchthons als Historiker," *Sachsen und Anhalt* 1 (1925): 253, esp. n. 111.

32   "Nauant enim eandem operam, ut historiis Germanicis & antiquitati lucem adferant, qui adhuc superstites sunt Beatus Rhenanus, Chonradus Peutinger, Iacobus Spiegel, Ioannes Huttichius, Sebastianus Munsterus, Ioachimus Vadianus, Gerhardus Nouiomagus, Petrus Appianus, Hieronymus Gebuylerus, Iohannes Schonerus, Iohannes Carion, & alij quorum nomina nondum teneo." Andreas Althamer, *Commentaria Germaniae In P. Cornelij Taciti Equitis Rom. libellum de situ, moribus, & populis Germanorvm.* (Nuremberg: Petreius, 1536), 340. VD16 ZV 14839.

33   On Bonnus, see Petra Savvidis, *Hermann Bonnus, Superintendent von Lübeck (1504–1548): sein kirchenpolitisch-organisatorisches Wirken und sein praktisch-theologisches Schrifttum* (Lübeck: Schmidt-Römhild, 1992).

was an historian in his own right, and like many of Melanchthon's students, he composed a local history, a *Chronicle of Lübeck* (1539).[34]

In 1537, Peter Brubach, one of Melanchthon's favoured printers in South Germany, published Bonnus's translation at Schwäbish Hall.[35] Brubach had succeeded his father-in-law, Johann Setzer, who in turn had succeeded his own father-in-law, Thomas Anshelm, for whom Melanchthon had worked as corrector in Tübingen.[36] The revised German edition was used as the basis for the translation, so it was this improved version that was disseminated in Latin, as in the vernacular translations. The title page indicates that Carion himself had been consulted for the project (*"ab autore diligenter recognita"*), so it is possible that he saw parts of Bonnus's work before his death in early 1537. Nevertheless, either Carion chose not to revise the *Chronicle*, or his unexpected death cut short any such effort. With the exception of an introductory "epigram to the reader," no new material was added.

As the *Chronicle* was republished across Europe, it generated into distinct textual families, and these followed well known patterns of European book distribution. After the Latin translation issued in Schwäbish Hall (1537), it promptly appeared in Antwerp (1537). From Schwäbish Hall, it soon spread also to Paris and from there to Lyon (both 1543). Once the *Chronicle* reached Paris, it was republished as often in France as in Germany. Additional Latin editions soon followed at Venice (1548) and then at Basel (1552).

The process of adaptation continued as soon as the *Chronicle* left Germany. The 1537 Antwerp edition includes an *Appendix* on events from 1533–1537, and it added a catalogue of the Emperors and popes.[37] From 1544, *De rebus in Belgica gestis* was added to various Latin editions at Paris and Lyon.[38] (The text is an epistolary report by the French historian Guillaume Paradin (1510–1590) on the Emperor's siege of Landrecies in Picardy during autumn of 1543). Then in 1548,

---

34 On Bonnus's chronicle, see Savvidis, *Hermann Bonnus*, 194–204. The 1539 edition is VD16 B 6619.

35 Johann Carion, *Chronica Ioannis Carionis conuersa ex Germanico in Latinum à doctissimo uiro Herma[n]no Bono, & ab autore diligenter recognita. Halæ Sueuorum ex officina Petri Brubachij, Anno M.D.XXXVII*. (Schwäbish Hall: Peter Brubach, 1537).

36 Heinz Scheible, "Melanchthons Verhältnis zu Johannes Setzer," in *Buchwesen in Spätmittelalter und Früher Neuzeit: Festschrift für Helmut Claus zum 75. Geburtstag*, ed. Ulman Weiß (Ependorf/Neckar: Bibliotheca Academica Verlag, 2008), 318–319.

37 Johann Carion, *Chronica Ioannis Caronis conuersa ex Germanico in Latinu[m] à doctissimo viro Hermanno Bono, & ab auctore diligenter recognita. Accessit Catalogus omnium Regum, Imperatorum, & Pontificum Romanorum, cum Appendice. Antuerpiae per Ioannem Steelsium in scuto Burgundiae, Anno M.D.XXXVII*. (Antwerp: Jan Steels [by Jan Grapheus], 1537).

38 Guillaume Paradin, *Gulielmvs Paradinus de rebus in Belgica gestis ad Philippum Gayanum*. ([Paris]: Vivant Gaultherot, 1544).

Guillaume Morel (1505–1564) added an *Appendix* in annalistic format that sketched the history of the years 1532–1547.[39] Morel's *Appendix* is distinct from the earlier Antwerp *Appendix*, and it was expanded in subsequent Latin editions to bring them up to date. These supplementary texts were addressed to a wider European audience, and they stand in marked contrast to the German focus of the *Chronicle's* main text, which these early editions reproduced in the original Bonnus translation.

In 1551, Jacques du Puys published the first reworked Latin edition of *Carion's Chronicle* at Paris. This edition kept Bonnus's text as its base, but it inserted additional information about events in France or other regions of Europe into the narrative; for example, it expanded the section on Merovingian history, which Melanchthon had largely glossed over in the German original.[40] In doing so, the du Puys edition gave the *Chronicle* a more European character and it diluted the original German orientation. The Morel *Appendix* likewise had a European perspective. Luther's death, for example, was noted only in passing, and the theological struggles in Germany after the Schmalkaldic War not at all.[41] At Venice in 1553, the French humanist Guillaume Postel (1510–1581) re-edited the du Puys text with the Morel *Appendix* and added several sections on Venetian history.[42]

---

39   Johann Carion, *Io. Carionis Mathematici Bvetickheinensis Chronicorum libri tres in Latinum sermonem conuersi, Hermanno Bonno interprete. Appendix De Rebvs Ab anno Christi 1532 gestis ad annum 1547, ex optimis quibusque Historicis & Chronographis excerpta. Catalogus Regum, Consulum, Cæsarum, & Pontificum Romanorum. Cum Priuilegio. Parisiis, Apud Iacobum Bogardum, & Gulielmum Moreliu[m], sub insigni D. Christophori, è regione gymnasii Cameracensium, 1548.* (Paris: Jacques Bogard & Guillaume Morel, 1548).

40   Johann Carion, *Ioannis Carionis Mathematici Buticheimensis Chronicorum libri tres, è Germanico in Latinum sermonem conuersi, Hermanno Bonno interprete. Huic postremæ editioni accessere permulta scitu dignissima, suis locis passim inserta, cum accurata calculi recognitione, & eorum appendice quæ à fine Carionis ad annum 1551. contigêre. Praeterea Catalogus Regum, Cæsarum, Pontificum Romanorum ad hoc regum Franc. Angl. & Sco. & Index alphabeticus amplissimus. Complectitur hic libellus apto ordine maximas quasque res gestas ab initio mundi ad nostra vsque tempora: vt annorum ratio, ac præcipuæ vicißitudines quæ in regna, in religionem, & in alias res magnas incidunt, quam rectißimè cognosci & obseruari queant* (Paris: Jacques du Puys, 1551), 338–349.

41   "Martinus Lutherus Islebiæ in patria sua moritur, vnde funus Vuittembergam perductum, & in templo arcis sepultum est, 18. Cal. Feb." Carion, *Chronicorum libri tres* (Paris: Jacques du Puys, 1551), 613.

42   On Postel's edition, see Johann Georg Schelhorn, *Amoenitates Historiæ Ecclesiasticæ Et Literariæ Quibus Variæ observationes, Scripta item quædam anecdota & rariora Opuscula, diversis utriusque historiæ capitibus elucidandis inservientia, exhibentur. Tomus Secvndvs.* (Frankfurt & Leipzig: Daniel Bartholomaeus & Sons, 1738), 642–647; Georg Theodor Strobel, "Von Carions Leben und Schriften," *Miscellaneen literarischen Innhalts, Sechste Sammlung* (Nürnberg, 1782): 176–184; François Secret, "Notes Sur Guillaume Postel XV. L'Appendice De Postel Aux *Chronicorum libri tres* De Carion," *Bibliothèque d'Humanisme*

The *Chronicle's* transmission took on a dynamic, or rather dynamics, beyond the concerns and sociology of knowledge at Wittenberg; and Carion's name became part of the title as much as an indication of actual authorship.[43] Initially, the Bonnus and du Puys texts circulated side by side, but by the mid-1550s, the du Puys text had become the standard. The final Latin edition of the Carion-Melanchthon *Chronicle* was published by Johannes Oporinus at Basel (1564),[44] and it derives from the Paris editions published by Jacques du Puys in the 1560s. These later editions offered a Europeanized *Chronicle*. They included the expanded du Puys text and an updated version of Morel's *Appendix*. Furthermore, the regnal catalogues were no longer limited to the popes and Emperors, but included the Kings of France, Spain, England, and Scotland, as well as the Venetian doges. They also appended a brief description of religious orders. Thus, by the time it reached its final Latin form, publishers had succeeded in adapting the original German oriented *Chronicle* to a broader European audience. The last Paris edition of 1563 shows the results of this process:

IO. CARIONIS || CHRONICORVM || AB ORBE CONDITO AD || hanc vsque nostram ætatem Libri III. || primùm ab ipso authore conscripti: || deinde multis accessionibus docto-||rum virorum aucti: postremò tandem || ad annum D. 1560 & veteribus & || recentibus historiis Pontificu[m] Rom[anorum] || atque Cæsaru[m] Regúmque insignium || Catalogis, & aliis nonnulis mirum in || modum locupletati. || Accessit præftereà huic editioni Index || alphabeticus amplissimus. || Ad Lectorem. || Continent hic prima gestas ab origine mundi || Historias nostrum tempus adusque

---

et *Renaissance Travaux et Documents* XXII, no. 3 (Septemter 1960): 552–555; François Secret, "L'Emithologie de Guillaume Postel," *Archivio di Filosofia* (1960) [*Umanesimo e Esoterismo*]: 399, 437; Guillaume Postel, *Apologies et Rétractions Manuscrits inédits publiés avec une introduction et des notes par François Secret* (Nieuwkoop: De Graaf, 1972), 18; Marion Leathers Kuntz, "The Myth of Venice in the thought of Guillaume Postel," in *Svpplementvm Festivvm Studies in Honor of Paul Oskar Kristeller*, ed. James Hankins et al. (Binghamton, NY: Medieval & Renaissance Texts & Studies, 1987), 509–510. See also Postel's comment, "cuius vita est a me in multis locis subindicata magis quam descripta, videlicet, in expositione tabulae de restitutione sive de quaternariis, et in principio evangelii aeterni, et in appendice ad Chronicum Charionis anno 1553 ad signum capitis Erasmi Venetiis excusa, et in historia de immutatione mea Parisiis scripta." London, British Library: MS Sloane 1411, fol. 2v; quoted in Secret, "Notes Sur Guillaume Postel XV," 552 n. 2.

43   In the American context, an analogous situation has occurred, for example, with respect to the title "*Webster's Dictionary*" which includes an array of texts – authorized and unauthorized – that derive to varying degrees from the original work of Noah Webster (1758–1843).

44   Johann Carion, *Io. Carionis Chronicorvm Ab Orbe Condito Ad hanc usq[ue] nostram œtatem Libri III*... (Basel: [Oporinus], 1564). VD16 ZV 2950.

liber. || Grande sub exiguo comprensum fasce volume[n], || Exiguo ære tibi candide lector eme. || PARISIIS, || Ex officina Puteana, || 1563. || CVM PRIVILEGIO.

1.	EXTRAICT DV PRIVILEGE	[†i]v
2.	EPISTOLA NVNCVPATORIA	†ij r – †iij v
3.	Errata sic repone.	[†iiij]r
4.	IOANNIS CARIONIS IN CHRONICA SVA PRAEFATIO	1–14
	VSVS LECTIONIS HISTORIARVM	1–8
	ORDO LEGENDI HISTORIAS	9–14
5.	CHRONICORVM liber primus: Qui primam ætatem, hoc est, annorum duo millia, ab Adam vsque ad Abrahæ tempora continet.	15–27
6.	CHRONICORVM LIBER SECVNDVS, de quatuor Monarchiis, qui similiter bis mille annos complecitur.	28–209
	PRIMA MONARCHIA Assyriorum	29–75
	DE SECVNDA Monarchia	76–146
	DE TERTIA MONARCHIA	147–202
	QVARTA ET VLTIMA Monarchia, quæ est Imperij Romani	202–209
7.	CHRONICORVM LIBER TERTIVS, qui continet tempus à nato Christo.	210–590
8.	SVPPLEMENTVM, seu appendix ad præcentia.	591–684
9.	CARION	[V vij]r – [V viij]v
10.	TABVLA ANNOrum mu[n]di ex Bibliis & Philone.	X r – X iij r
11.	ORACVLVM HOmericu[m], quod vaticinatur de Imperio Romano.	X iij r
12.	CATALOVS REGVM, CAESARVM, & Pontificum Romanorum, usque ad Carolum huius nominis quintum, & Pium quartum.	X iiij r – [X vj]v
13.	CATALOGVS PONTIFICVM ROMANORVM VSQUE AD PIVM huius nominis quartum.	[V vij]r – Y iij v
14.	SERIES ET ORdo Regum Fra[n]corum in Gallia.	Y iiij r – [Y vj]r
15.	SERIES ET ORDO REGVM HISPANIAE post Honorium Imperatorem, qui more Cæsarum prioru[m] unà cum Theodosio fatre suo Hispaniarum regnum administrauit.	[Y vj]r – [Y viij]v

16. ANGLORVM REGVM SERIES Post Christu[m] natum.   [Y viij]v –
                                                    Z v
17. SERIES ET ORDO SCOTORVM REGVM   Z ij r –
                                                    Z iiij v
18. CATALOGVS DVCVM VENETORVM omnium qui   Zv r –
    hactenus fuere, de libro Petri Marcelli Patritij [Z vij]r
    Veneti & aliis nonnullis excerptus.
19. DE ORDINIBVS RELIGIOnum ex Ioanne Lucido.   [Z vij]r –
                                                    [Z iij]v
20. INDEX RERVM memorabilium quæ hoc libro   Aa r –
    continentur.   [Ii iiij]v

4 Translations

In the sixteenth century, the Latin editions of *Carion's Chronicle* made the text widely accessible across geographic and linguistic barriers. The *Chronicle* also had a remarkable reception in vernacular translations. Indeed, few, if any, Wittenberg texts achieved such a broad vernacular circulation in the sixteenth and seventeenth century. Various forms of the *Chronicle* were eventually translated into Low German (1534), Latin (1537), Czech (1541/1584), Italian (1543), Dutch (1543/1586), French (1546/1579), Spanish (1549?/1553), English (1550), Danish (1554/1595), Swedish (1649), Turkish (1654), and Icelandic (1692). Through the Latin and vernacular translations, the *Chronicle* entered multiple historiographical traditions, and it became a standard point of reference across the learned communities of Europe.

Of these vernacular translations, the French translation of Jean le Blond (†1553) was republished the most often, with new editions into the seventeenth century.[45] From the start, these included an *Appendix* on events in France, beginning in 1514, with the reign of Francis I, and over the years, the material was updated or extended as appropriate. In France, much more so than in Germany, the Carion-Melanchthon *Chronicle* continued to circulate after the Melanchthon-Peucer edition began to appear in 1558. Le Blond's translation was published only in Paris and Lyons, never in Geneva or the Low Countries.

---

45 For his translation activities, see Björn-Olav Dozo, "Jean Le Blond, premier traducteur français de l'*Utopie*," *Lettres Romanes* 49 (2005): 187–210.

In contrast, Simon Goulart's French translation (1579) of the Melanchthon-Peucer edition was published only in Geneva and Leiden. Both, however, were widely circulated, and they are found in libraries across Europe. Many of these editions survive in single copies, so it is likely that many others have been lost over the centuries.

As in France, the *Chronicle's* reception in England involved issues of textual integrity, including both adaptation and continuation, but as in Germany, it also concerned questions of attribution. A Latin edition of the *Chronicle* was never published in England. The *Chronicle* was translated into English twice, but only one of these translations acknowledged *Carion's Chronicle* as its source. As a result, the text circulated widely in English, but it was not necessarily recognized as *Carion's Chronicle*. Both translations enhanced the otherwise limited English character of the original text by adding sections on recent British history.

Before his death, the English historian Thomas Lanquet († 1545) had begun a translation adapted to English readers, and Thomas Cooper († 1594), an Oxford scholar and later Elizabethan bishop, finished Lanquet's work.[46] The edition was published in 1549 as *An Epitome Of Chronicles*.[47] Cooper removed any attribution to Melanchthon or Carion, so this translation has generally been known as *Cooper's Chronicle*. At his death, Lanquet had completed the translation from Creation down to Tiberius,[48] and Cooper continued the narrative to 1548. One of the major changes Lanquet made was to insert references to the pre-Roman history of England throughout Book II of the *Chronicle*. He conceded that British history lacked any credible source base prior to Roman times, but he decided to follow "common opinion" and begin the lineage of English rulers with Brutus, the legendary first king of England and founder of London.[49] In the margins, Lanquet accordingly traced three timelines: "the yere of the worlde," "the yere before Christe," and "before Britayn knowen." Then

---

46   See "Lanquet, Thomas (1520/21–1545)" and "Cooper, Thomas (c.1517–1594)" in Oxford DNB.
47   Thomas Lanquet and Thomas Cooper, *An Epitome Of Chronicles Conteining the whole discourse of the histories as well of this realme of England, as all other countreis, with the succession of their kynges, the tyme of their reigne, & what notable actes thei did : much profitable to be redde namely of magistrates and suche as haue auctoritee in co[m]men weales : gathered out of most p[ro]bable auctors, fyrst, by Thomas Lanquet, from the beginnyng of the world to the incarnacion of Christ, and now finished and continued to the reigne of our soueraine lorde kynge Edwarde the sixt by Thomas Cooper. Anno. M.D.LXIX.* (London: Thomas Berthelet, 1549).
48   See the note at Lanquet, *An Epitome Of Chronicles* (London, 1549), fol. 84 r [= sig. Ziii r].
49   Lanquet, *An Epitome Of Chronicles* (London, 1549), fol. 32r–32v.

after Caesar's invasion of Britain, he shifted the last category to "Anni regum Britannie."[50] Cooper's intervention marked a change in approach. Indeed, he included so much material that *Carion's Chronicle* became one source among many rather than the foundation of the narrative, as it had been for Lanquet. Cooper also enhanced the Protestant tone. Under the year 1517, for instance, he inserted a longer section on Luther and the Wittenberg reformers.[51] Thus, in its final form, *Cooper's Chronicle* was to varying degrees a translation, adaptation and continuation of *Carion's Chronicle*.

In 1559, Robert Crowley († 1588), one of the Marian exiles, published a new edition of *Cooper's Chronicle*, but he changed the character of the later sections on English history by adding material that maligned several important Edwardian figures, including Northumberland and Cooper's original dedicatee, Somerset.[52] Cooper was furious, and he countered with new editions in 1560 and 1565 that removed much of the offensive material.[53] Besides the revisions, he added "An admonicion to the reader" that lamented Crowley's failings as an historian, though without mentioning him by name, and he explicitly repudiated the 1559 edition.[54] The 1560 edition also included an exclusive printing privilege in the colophon.[55]

---

50   Lanquet, *An Epitome Of Chronicles* (London, 1549), fol. 83r–83v.
51   Lanquet, *An Epitome Of Chronicles* (London, 1549), fol. 275r–275v.
52   See Barrett L. Beer, "Robert Crowley and Cooper's Chronicle: The Unauthorized Edition of 1559," *Notes and Queries* 55, no. 2 (June 2008): 148–152. See also "Crowley, Robert (1517x19–1588)" in Oxford DNB.
53   See Marcia Lee Metzger, "Controversy and 'Correctness': English Chronicles and the Chroniclers, 1553–1568," *Sixteenth Century Journal* 27, no. 2 (Summer 1996): 455–449.
54   "I had gathered longe sens (gentle reader) dyvers profytable things out of moste commendable hystories, thynkynge, when tyme serued, to adde them to this my chronicle : but vpon certayne occasions I deferred the matter vntill this last yere. At that tyme entendyng to goe forward with my purpose, I vnderstoode by reporte that certaine persons, for lukers sake contrare to honestie, had caused my chronicle to be prynted without my knowledge, alterynge in my dooynge what they lysted, and anneryng an other mans addicions vnto my woorke. Wherfore I, not purposynge to leaue of that I entended, ouerlooked theyr edicion. Wherein as I saw some thynges of myne lefte out, and many thynges of others annexed : so dyd I finde almost fiue hundred fautes and errours eyther of the prynter, or els of hym that vndertooke the correction : yea and many of them in those thynges, that are in this woorke chiefly to be regarded. I can not therfore doe other wyse but greatly blame their vnhonest dealynge, and openly protest that the Edicion of this chronicle set foorth by Marshe and Seres in the yere of Christe .1559. is none of myne, but the attempte of certayne persons vtterly vnlearned. This, gentle reader, I thought good to aduertise thee, leste the fautes, by other mens lewdnesse committed, should be fathered vpon me, to my reproch and sclaunder." Thomas Cooper, *Coopers Chronicle* (London: Thomas Berthelette (Heirs), 1560).
55   Cooper, *Coopers Chronicle* (London, 1560), sig. [Cij v].

The dispute between Cooper and Crowley concerned interpretations of sixteenth century English history, rather than the more distant past, and it turned on issues of adaptation, continuation and attribution. Even though Crowley indicated on the title page of his edition that Cooper's contribution had ended at the reign of King Edward, Cooper was obviously troubled by the association with Crowley's added content. Cooper's response – publish a new, corrected edition, publicly disavow the unauthorized one and make stronger claims to exclusive control – is strikingly similar to techniques Melanchthon and Caspar Peucer used to address problems in Germany with the transmission of *Carion's Chronicle*. After the authorized editions of 1560 and 1565, Crowley's 1559 edition was not republished as a competitor.

In 1550, Walter Lynne († in or before 1571) published the only complete English translation of *Carion's Chronicle*, which he dedicated to King Edward VI.[56] The text itself was printed by Steven Mierdman († 1559), a Netherlandish printer who had settled in London.[57] Lynne had likewise come to England from Antwerp, and he specialized in publishing English editions of works by Continental Protestants.[58] He based his translation on the Latin text of the *Chronicle*, and he worked independently of Lanquet and Cooper.[59] Indeed, although he made some modifications for English readers, Lynne was far more faithful to the original text than *Cooper's Chronicle*. Furthermore, unlike Cooper, Lynne did not compose his own narrative for the events of 1532–1546. Instead, he translated a continuation prepared by a former Wittenberg student, Johann Funck (1518–1566). The anti-Catholic tone of Funck's *Continuation* may have appealed to Lynne, but his exact source remains uncertain. The version of Funck's *Continuation* that he presented is otherwise unknown in German or Latin, and it is closest to a Low German (*Plattdeutsch*) edition from Magdeburg published in 1547. Lynne may have had access to this Low German edition, or perhaps he used a now lost Latin manuscript intermediary. He gave no

---

56 Johann Carion, *The thre bokes of Cronicles, whyche Iohn Carion (a man syngularly well sene in the Mathematycall sciences) Gathered wyth great diligence of the beste Authours that haue written in Hebrue, Greke or Latine : Whervnto is added an Appendix, conteynyng all such notable thynges as be mentyoned in Cronicles to haue chaunced in sundry partes of the worlde from the yeare of Christ. 1532. To thys present yeare of. 1550. Gathered by Iohn Funcke of Nurenborough. Whyche was neuer afore prynted in Englysh. Cum Priuilegio ad Imprimendum solum* (London: Gwalter Lynne [by Steven Mierdman], 1550).

57 See "Mierdman, Steven [Niclaes von Oldenborch] (c. 1510x12–1559)" in Oxford DNB.

58 See "Lynne, Walter (*d.* in or before 1571)" in Oxford DNB.

59 "But yet yf my knowledge would haue serued me to haue translated it as eloquently as it is written in latyne: I doubt not but the learned also myghte haue founde some swetnes in my laboures." Carion, *The thre bokes of Cronicles* (London, 1550), sig. *.ij. v.

explanation for why he combined the Latin text of the *Chronicle* with Funck's material, and the two did otherwise circulate together at that time.

By including Funck's voluminous *Continuation*, Lynne presented a version of the *Chronicle* to English readers that set greater emphasis on the sixteenth century, and Funck had actually included a substantial amount of English history. For the remaining years, Lynne added some "Brefe Annotations" from "dyuers historiographers" to bring the narrative down to 1550.[60] Despite its brevity, Lynne's annalistic sketch of 1547–1550 retains some source value for Tudor history, since it provides an early account of the 1549 rebellions.[61] In contrast to the 1549 edition of *Cooper's Chronicle*, Lynne's edition indicated a printing privilege on the title page, and his translation was never republished.

In its various Latin and vernacular forms, *Carion's Chronicle* circulated widely within the English intellectual community. Tudor historians, such as Richard Grafton († 1573) and John Stow († 1605), tended to concentrate on British history,[62] so in the absence of strong indigenous competition, the *Chronicle* became a default reference for pre-Christian Antiquity and it influenced interpretations of history more generally.[63] In Scotland, Sir David Lyndsay († 1555) structured his poetic history, *The Monarche* (1554), according to the Four Monarchies and the Prophecy of Elias, and his verses refer explicitly to *Carion's Chronicle*.[64] Earlier, an anonymous poem, *The Complaynt of Scotland* (ca. 1550), had also adopted the Prophecy of Elias, apparently from Melanchthon.[65] Sir Philip Sydney (1554–1586) used *Carion's Chronicle* as an important source for

---

60 "The ende of the Appendix or addition compyled by Maister John Funke. Brefe Annotations added unto the premisses gathered out of dyuers historiographers." Carion, *The thre bokes of Cronicles* (London, 1550), fol. cclxix v.

61 Barrett L. Beer, "John Stow and Tudor Rebellions, 1549–1569," *The Journal of British Studies* 27, no. 4 (October 1988): 355.

62 See F.J. Levy, *Tudor Historical Thought* (San Marino, CA: The Huntington Library, 1967), esp. 167–201; see also "Grafton, Richard (c.1511–1573)" and "Stow, John (1524/5–1605)" in Oxford DNB.

63 See Daniel R. Woolf, *Reading History in early modern England* (Cambridge: Cambridge University Press, 2000), 143.

64 Albrecht Lange, "Lyndesay's Monarche und die Chronica Carionis," *Anglia* 28, no. 1 (January 1905): 101–102; Alasdair M. Stewart, "Carion, Wedderburn, Lindsay," *Aberdeen University Review* XLIV, no. 147 (1972): 271–274; and Carol Edington, *Court and Culture in Renaissance Scotland: Sir David Lindsay of the Mount* (Amherst: University of Massachusetts Press, 1994), 197–199. See also "Lyndsay, Sir David (c.1486–1555)" in Oxford DNB.

65 See Lange, "Lyndesay's Monarche," 99–100; and Stewart, "Carion, Wedderburn, Lindsay," 271–274. Regarding the attribution of the *Complaynt* to Robert Wedderburn, see "Wedderburn, James (c.1495–1553)" in Oxford DNB.

the presentation of Cyrus in his *Defense of Poesy*,[66] and traces of the *Chronicle* can even be found in Milton's *Paradise Lost*.[67] Among sixteenth century English historians, William Harrison (1535–1593) was especially influenced by the *Chronicle*; and although he patriotically resisted the German-oriented interpretation of the Four Monarchies, important aspects of his unpublished "Chronology" show an intellectual debt to Wittenberg.[68] As on the Continent, the *Chronicle* had a long history in England. By the early seventeenth century, Sir Walter Ralegh (1554–1618) treated Melanchthon and Peucer as broadly recognized authorities on Antiquity in his *History of the World* (1614).[69] Even Sir Isaac Newton (1642–1727) owned a copy of the *Chronicle*, still listed among the holdings of Trinity College in Cambridge.[70]

5 *Carion's Chronicle* in the Catholic Context

In the years before the Counter-Reformation gained momentum, *Carion's Chronicle* circulated widely from centres sympathetic, or at least open, to Reformation ideas, such as Antwerp, Lyon and Venice. Since Carion himself was not directly associated with Wittenberg, the *Chronicle* was perhaps not as suspect as if Melanchthon had figured openly as the author. Within a few years this situation changed, and Carion, like many other Northern humanists, was listed as a heretic and all of his works forbidden by Pope Paul IV on the *Roman Index* of 1557, which after 1559 become known as the *Index of Prohibited Books* (*Index Librorum Prohibitorum*).[71] After Pope Paul IV's death, the new pope, Pius IV, decided to mitigate some of the *Pauline Index's* prohibitions, and in

---

66 On Melanchthon and Sydney, see generally Robert E. Stillman, *Philip Sydney and the Poetics of Renaissance Cosmopolitanism* (Burlington, VT: Ashgate, 2008), esp. xiv, 227 for *Carion's Chronicle*.
67 Don Cameron Allen, "Milton's Busiris," *Modern Language Notes* 65 (February 1950): 115–116; and John M. Steadman, "Busiris, the Exodus, and Renaissance Chronography," *Revue belge de Philologie et d'Histoire* 39–3 (1961): 799.
68 G.J.R. Parry, *A Protestant Vision: William Harrison and the Reformation of Elizabethan England* (Cambridge: Cambridge University Press, 1987), esp. 96–107.
69 Walter Ralegh, *The History of the World* (London: Walter Burre, 1614 [1617]), esp. 139–148.
70 Philip Melanchthon, *Chronicon Carionis* (Geneva: Crespin, 1625) – Cambridge, Trinity College Library: NQ.8.124.
71 Jesús Martínez de Bujanda, ed., *Index des livres interdits*, vol. VIII, *Index De Rome 1557, 1559, 1564* (Sherbrooke: Centre d'Études de la Renaissance, 1990), 521, with reproduction of the original *Index* (730).

1564, he promulgated the new *Tridentine Index*, so-called because the Council of Trent had authorized it.[72]

As Catholic monarchs regulated the press, they did not categorically follow the *Tridentine Index*, in part because blanket prohibitions on "heretical" authors hindered Catholic access to Protestant scientific works and damaged the book trade.[73] Accordingly, in 1571 the King of Spain and the Duke of Alva issued a new *Index Expurgatorius Librorum (Belgian Index)*, which allowed for some books by Protestant authors to be used, provided that they were corrected or expunged of offensive material.[74] In contrast to the absolute prohibition of the *Roman Index*, the *Belgian Index* listed the *Chronicle* as a book to be corrected and expurgated, not entirely forbidden. The editors of the 1571 *Index* collated Latin copies of the *Chronicle* from Paris, Basel, and Antwerp. They also mentioned the French translation of Jean le Blond, but not the German original. Subsequent versions of the *Belgian Index* were revised to include additional editions of the *Chronicle*, such as the 1556 Venetian edition of Valgrisi.[75]

Not surprisingly, the sections marked for revision by the editors dealt principally with Reformation theology or with anti-papal political sentiments. The *Index* indicated that the *Chronicle's* chapter on the ancient heretic Pelagius, with its anti-Catholic tone, should be completely expunged.[76] So too, the editors removed a section comparing inter-testamental Jewish sects to sixteenth

---

72   On Catholic press censorship, see Paul Grendler, "Printing and Censorship," in *The Cambridge History of Renaissance Philosophy*, ed. Charles B. Schmitt et al. (Cambridge: Cambridge University Press, 1991), 45–48.

73   Grendler, "Printing and Censorship," 45–48.

74   The *Belgian Index* of 1571 is reproduced in Jesús Martínez de Bujanda, ed., *Index des livres interdits*, vol. VII, *Index d'Anvers 1569, 1570, 1571* (Sherbrooke: Centre d'Études de la Renaissance, 1988), 788–791 for *Carion's Chronicle*.

75   "In Chronicon IOANNIS Carionis Mathematici excusum Parisiis apud Ioan. Roigny, anno 1550 in 16°. Et in aliud exemplar eiusdem Basil. impress. in eadem forma 16. anno 1564. Estque praeterea aliud exemplar Antuerpiae impressum, apud Stelsium, anno 1540. & 1547. Duplex aliquando foliorum ponitur numerus, quorum prior Paris. posterior Basil. est editionis: & vbi agitur de versuum numero, foliorum principio, medio, aut fine, de Paris. intellige editione." *Index Expvrgatorivs Librorvm Qvi Hoc Secvlo Prodiervnt, vel doctrinæ non sanæ erroribus inspersis, vel inutilis & offensiuæ maledicentiæ fellibus permixtis, iuxta sacri Concilij Tridentini decretum: Philippi II Regis Catholici iussu & auctoritate, atque Albani Ducis consilio ac ministerio in Belgia concinnatus; anno M D LXXI* (Lyon: Mareschallus, 1586), 172–173. The cross-references to the Venice edition (1556) are found in the margin, and the reference to an Antwerp edition of 1547 has not otherwise been located. I use this edition since it agrees with the annotated copy of *Carion's Chronicle* discussed below.

76   "*Pap. 271. al. pag. 287. de Pelagiano haeretico, illud deleatur*, Is docuit, &c. *Vsque ad*, Arcadium Imperatorem. *Item subiungitur illud linea 3. esse ibidem delendum.* Sine nostro merito ad. *Item illud infra*, Et gratia tutatus, &c. *vsque ad*, In conciliis aliquot." *Index Expvrgatorivs Librorvm* (Lyon, 1586), 175.

century religious divisions.[77] In the case of Pope Benedict VIII, the *Index* struck embarrassing references to selling the papacy for money.[78] Interestingly, the *Chronicle's* brief section on Luther was also slightly revised, but not entirely expunged.[79] From a political perspective, the general anti-French and anti-Papal tenor of the *Chronicle* is not specifically mentioned, but the *Index* removed offending remarks about the political dealings of the popes. In particular, the editors revised the *Chronicle's* treatment of Pope Gregory VII (Hildebrand) and the Investiture Controversy, which Melanchthon and Carion had presented from a strongly German Imperial perspective.[80] Indeed, the editors specifically removed the section on the Investiture Controversy where the *Chronicle* had shifted from Nauclerus to Sigebert of Gembloux as the principal source.[81]

The *Index's* instructions extended to problematic material in the *Chronicle's* index and its printed marginal notes. The deletions and corrections to the index were treated separately, and the editors again showed concern mostly for anti-papal remarks.[82] With regard to marginalia, the editors noted when these

---

77   "*Pag. 191. alias pag. 181. lin. 18. illud,* de Essaeis, fuit omnino haec stulta, &c. *vsque ad illud pagi. sequent.* Exortae hae sectae. *Et quod est in margine,* Ecclesiae status horum temporum." *Index Expvrgatorivs Librorvm* (Lyon, 1586), 174. For example, see the section on the Essenes: "Essei / sind die dritten gewesen / die haben gesehen / das beide teil / Pharisei vnd Saducei / viel rhümeten von frömkeit / vnd nichts thaten / Darumb haben sie es mit ernst wollen angreiffen / vnd haben sich genant Essei / das ist / Operarij / vom wort Assa / das ist wircken. Wie jtzund die Anabaptisten schelten die andere zween teil / vnd wollen heiliger sein / Es haben auch die Essei eben ein solch Anabaptisten leben gefüret / nicht weiber gehabt / alle ding gemein wollen haben Vnd ist ein törichte / grobe Möncherey vnd heucheley gewesen / hat auch nicht lang geweret." Carion, *Chronica* (Wittenberg, 1532), fol. 68v–69r.
78   "*Pag. 370. lin. 12. sic legatur,* Post Ioannem 20. factus est papa 151. Benedictus 8. quo fugato Siluester quidam papatum occupauit: Porro reuersus Benedictus contra Siluestrum tertio cuidam, qui Gregorius VI. dictus est, cessit ius suum in Pontificatu." *Index Expvrgatorivs Librorvm* (Lyon, 1586), 176.
79   "*Pag. 464. lin. 7.* de Luthero, *corrigatur sic, pro,* Non vulgarem vicissitudinem, *ponatur,* non vulgares tumultus. Sic enim habet Parisiensis editio, anni 1551. apud Iacobum de Puys, & 1557. apud Gul. Iulianum. *qui hac sequentia adiecit.*" *Index Expvrgatorivs Librorvm* (Lyon, 1586), 180.
80   "*Pag. 374 lin. 3. del.* Tragœdiæ huius auctor papa Hildebrandus, *vsque ad,* In pueritia." *Index Expvrgatorivs Librorvm* (Lyon, 1586), 177.
81   "*Pag. 377. lin. 2. del.* Quem quæso, &c. *vsque ad,* Post hanc victoriam. *Et annotatio marginalis,* Hildebrandus papa, alter Caiphas. *Item lin.* 22. Sibebertus historicus, &c. *vsque ad ilud pag. sequentis,* Anno. 1103. *cum annot. marginali.*" *Index Expvrgatorivs Librorvm* (Lyon, 1586), 177.
82   "*In litera A in Indice Alphabetico,* impress. Parisiensis, *illa delantur,* de Adriano Papa, Papae querela quin moreretur. *Lit. B.* de Bonifacio Papa, *illud dele,* vniuersalis & summus vt esset Episcopus, obtinet a Phoca. *Item illud,* Vulpes, leo, canis." *Index expuratorius librorum* (Lyon, 1586), 173.

comments should be deleted in relationship to the main text, for example in the section on Jewish sects, they indicated that the marginal note, "*Ecclesiae status horum temporum*," should also be cancelled out.[83] Likewise, the note, "*Hildebrandus papa, alter Caiphas*," was deleted from the Investiture Controversy.[84] Although the editors of the *Index* painstakingly corrected certain details, they ultimately deemed the *Chronicle* harmless enough, or useful enough, to remain in Catholic hands.

While the *Belgian Index* provides an official Catholic position on the *Chronicle*, an example of its treatment by an individual reader is found in a 1540 Augsburg German edition from the Benedictine Abbey of Einsiedeln (Switzerland). Inside the cover, a Catholic reader from the later sixteenth century wrote:

> Greetings to the Reader.
> This book is most useful for correctly reading and understanding histories: but it is to be read with discernment, especially in those places where the author examines the Roman, or chief, Pontiffs. As for what pertains to the rest, concerning these things, one should see the *Index expurgatorius Librorum*, produced in Belgium, pages 172, 173, and following.
>
> Johannes Besingerus, D.[85]

Besinger inherited the book from his father, who had died in 1563, and the references in his notation correspond to the *Belgian Index* of 1586, published at Lyon. As such, his comments are in the spirit of proper Catholic reading rather than precise correction, because the *Index* gave instructions only for the Latin text, not the German. Thus, Besinger's note was meant to demonstrate that the *Chronicle* was allowed if read with appropriate recognition of its anti-papal bias, precise line-by-line correction of the text might be helpful, but it was not strictly necessary. In this respect, Besinger appealed to the *Chronicle's* intrinsic

---

83 "*Pag.* 191. *alias pag.* 181. *lin.* 18. *illud*, de Essaeis, fuit omnino haec stulta, &c. *vsque ad illud pagi. sequent.* Exortae hae sectae. *Et quod est in margine*, Ecclesiae status horum temporum." *Index Expvrgatorivs Librorvm* (Lyon, 1586), 174.

84 "*Pag.* 377. *lin.* 2. *del.* Quem quæso, &c. *vsque ad*, Post hanc victoriam. *Et annotatio marginalis*, Hildebrandus papa, alter Caiphas." *Index Expvrgatorivs Librorvm* (Lyon, 1586), 177.

85 "Lectori, S.P.D. Hic Liber ad Historias recte legendas et intelligendas utilissimus est: sed cum judicio legendus, in ijs praesertim locis, ubi Romanos seu summos Pontifices taxat Auctor. Quod ad reliqua attinet, de illis videndus est Index expurgatorius Librorum, in Belgio concinnatus, pag. 172. 173. et seq. Joan. Besingerus, D." Johann Carion, *Chronica durch Magistrum Johann Carion / fleissig zůsamen gezogenn / menigklych nutzlich zů lesen. Gemert vnd gebessert.* M.D.XXXX. (Augsburg: Heinrich Steiner, 1540) – Einsiedeln, Stiftsbibliothek: He 2860.

utility for Catholic readers, which the editors of the *Belgian Index* had implicitly recognized.

Einsiedeln is only one example of the many Catholic monastic and cathedral libraries that hold at least one, and often multiple copies, of *Carion's Chronicle* in their inventories. (Einsiedeln has four editions in Latin and three in German.) Besinger's copy from 1540 is perhaps unique in the way that he made specific reference to the *Chronicle's* status on the *Belgian Index*. In some Catholic libraries, title pages were presumably torn out to avoid zealous censors, a simpler approach than Besinger's attempts at explanation. The Abbey Library of Sankt Gallen, also in Switzerland, holds a 1557 Paris edition that has lost its title page. Another example is the 1557 Paris edition found in the Bibliothèque Municipale of Valognes, and additional examples are found in many other libraries.[86] Other editions of the *Chronicle* may have been mutilated for their title page woodcuts or their Melanchthon portraits, and several copies presumably damaged for those reasons are found at the Herzog August Bibliothek in Wolfenbüttel.[87] In contrast to this, the examples from Sankt Gallen and Valognes lacked any title page iconography, so the most likely explanation for their lost title pages is the desire by some earlier owner to protect the copy from destruction.

Somewhere between the two extremes of the Einsiedeln and Sankt Gallen copies are those copies with notes or alterations to the title pages themselves. The Bayerische Staatsbibliothek in Munich, for example, has a 1546 German edition from Wittenberg with the warning "*Author damnatus*" inscribed on the title page.[88] Likewise, the Hessische Landesbibliothek in Wiesbaden has a 1557 Latin edition from Basel with a title page warning against the *Chronicle's* heretical author and content: "*NB Hic Liber est haeretici et c[on]tinet haereses.*"[89] The efforts to preserve *Carion's Chronicle* from the flames are even more apparent

---

86   Sankt Gallen, Stiftsbibliothek: SGST 8221; and Valognes, Bibliothèque municipale: C. 328; additional examples include Carcassonne, Bibliothèque municipale: 8 22–2.

87   Among other examples, see the editions from Magdeburg (1534) – Wolfenbüttel, Herzog August Bibliothek: H: T 293.8° Helmst. (3); Wittenberg (1566) – Wolfenbüttel, Herzog August Bibliothek: H: T 245.8° Helmst.; and Wittenberg (1573) – Wolfenbüttel, Herzog August Bibliothek: M: Gb 52 I.

88   Johann Carion, *Chronica Durch M. Johan Carion / vleissig zusamen gezogen / meniglich nützlich zulesen* (Wittenberg: Rhau, 1546) – München, Bayerische Staatsbibliothek: Chron. 200 z.

89   Johann Carion, *Io. Carionis Mathematici Bvetikheimensis Chronicorum libri tres, ut sunt in Latinum sermonem conuersi, Hermanno Bonno Interp.* (Basel: [Michael Isengrin], 1557) – Wiesbaden, Hessische Landesbibliothek: Wielb 404.

from a copy now at the Biblioteca Nazionale Centrale in Florence.[90] In this instance, someone avoided the censors by changing Carion's name from *CARIONIS* to the nonsense word *OABFONIS*. Here, however, the clever attempt at deception extended beyond the title page to the section headings in the *Chronicle* itself, where Carion's name was again changed to *Oabfonis*.[91]

As these examples demonstrate, Catholic readers across Europe recognized the value of *Carion's Chronicle* as a history textbook. The title pages are sometimes missing or they were mutilated to deceive censors, but the copies were preserved nonetheless. In the second half of the sixteenth century, when the Jesuits became active in education, they were faced, especially in Germany, with students who expected to use *Carion's Chronicle* in the classroom. In 1567, Peter Canisius (1521–1597), the most important Jesuit in Germany, wrote to the Catholic historian Onofrio Panvinio († 1568) to inquire about the chronicle he was preparing to counter *Carion's Chronicle*. The Jesuits hoped to use the book in Germany, but despite Canisius's high expectations, Panvinio's work remained only in manuscript.[92] As a result, it was not until the end of the sixteenth century that Orazio Torsellini's *Epitome Historiarum* (1598) gave the Jesuits a Catholic counterpart to *Carion's Chronicle*.[93]

6   Johann Funck and the 1542 Turkish Campaign

After 1532, Melanchthon demonstrated no particular interest in the *Chronicle* for over a decade. Then, in 1546, Cyriakus Jacob, a publisher at Frankfurt am Main, produced a new German edition of *Carion's Chronicle* with a

---

90   Johann Carion, *Io. Carionis Mathematici Chronicorvm Libri Tres. Appendix Eorvm, quæ à fine Carionis ad hæc vsque tempora contigêre. Catalogvs Pontificvm, Caesarvm, Regvm, & Ducum Venetorum, cum Indice copiosißimo*. (Venice: Vincenzo Valgrisi, 1553) – Firenze, Biblioteca Nazionale Centrale: MAGL.4.8.8.

91   Carion, *Chronicorvm Libri Tres* (Venice, 1553), sig. a2 r, A r. Firenze, Biblioteca Nazionale Centrale: MAGL.4.8.8.

92   The letter to Panvinio is dated 29 September 1567: "Prima vorria fra le altre sue opere volontieri Chronicum ecclesiasticum a Iulii Caesaris imperio etc. Item tres libros contra historiam Magdeburgicam. Jtem Chronicum universale instar Carionis. Et ancora xv libros rituales." Peter Canisius, *Beati Petri Canisii, Societatis Iesu, epistulae et acta collegit et adnotationibus illustravit Otto Braunsberger*, Vol. 6, *1567–1571* (Freiburg i.B.: Herder, 1913), 70 [Nr. 1504]. See also the editor's note (70 n. 5): "Chronologicum hoc opus, quod ab initio mundi usque ad a. 1562 perventurum erat, neque a Panvinio perfectum, neque unquam typis excusum est; exstat Panvinii manu scriptum in bibliotheca vaticana, Cod. Vat. lat. 6785 (*Perini* l.c. 104–106 196)."

93   See Uwe Neddermeyer, "Das katholische Geschichtslehrbuch des 17. Jahrhunderts: Orazio Torsellinis *Epitome Historiarum*," *Historisches Jahrbuch* 108 (1988): 469–483.

Continuation (Volstreckung) by Johann Funck (1518–1566),[94] the first since 1532.[95] The Cyriakus Jacob edition started a twenty-year struggle between Wittenberg and Frankfurt over the right to control and market *Carion's Chronicle*. The actors changed over time, but the central issue remained the content added to the *Chronicle* by the Frankfurt publishers. The dispute is unusually well documented, and it provides a unique window into sixteenth century views about the rights of authors and publishers.

Funck had received his *magister artium* from Wittenberg in 1539, and after completing his studies, he took up various ecclesiastical positions around Nuremberg.[96] Prior to his work on *Carion's Chronicle*, he had written a *Chronologia* (1545), which soon established his reputation as one of the finest chronologists in Europe.[97] Funck finished his *Continuation* to *Carion's Chronicle* in either January or early February of 1546,[98] but, news of Luther's death on 18 February 1546 held back publication. Within a month, Funck had translated Melanchthon's biographical oration from the funeral ceremonies in Wittenberg, and he reworked the *Continuation* by adding a detailed discussion

---

94 For Cyriakus Jacob (active 1539–1551), see Reske, *Die Buchdrucker des 16. und 17. Jahrhunderts im deutschen Sprachgebiet: auf der Grundlage des gleichnamigen Werkes von Josef Benzing* (Wiesbaden: Harrassowitz, 2007), 226–227; and Josef Benzing, "Der Drucker Cyriacus Jacob zu Frankfurt a. M. 1533 (1539)-1551," *Archiv für Geschichte des Buchwesens* 3 (1961): 1–18.

95 "Vnnd nach dem ich von meinem günstigen Herrn Ciriaco Jacob Burger vnd Druckerherrn zů Franckfurt in schrifften gebeten / jme die geschicht / so sindher Johannis Charionis Chronica ans liecht kommen ist / verlauffen sein zubeschreiben / denn er willens were solche Chronica dieses jars wider an tag zugeben / sintemal sie kůrtz / vnd ordnung halben nützlich ist zulesen." Carion, *Chronica Durch Magistrum Johan Carion / fleissig zusamen gezogen / meniglich nützlich zulesen. Sampt eynem Register / darinn alle fürnemisten geschichten vnnd trefflichsten Historien / von anfang der Welt biß yetzt kürtzlich angezeygt sindt. Volstreckung dieser Chronica / vom 32. Jar der mindern zal / biß in 46. Durch M. Johan Funcken zusamen getragen. Cum Gratia & Priuilegio Imperiali.* ([Frankfurt a.M]: [Cyriakus Jacob], 1546), sig. Aiii r.

96 On Funck, see Karl Alfred von Hase, *Herzog Albrecht von Preussen und sein Hofprediger: Eine Königsberger Tragödie aus dem Zeitalter der Reformation* (Leipzig: Breitkopf und Härtel, 1879), esp. 105 for his work on Carion (von Hase states that the Cyriakus Jacob edition of 1546 has 369 pages, this is a reference to 368, [1] fol.). For Funck's activities during the key months in 1546 see also Siegfried Bräuer, "Die Überlieferung von Melanchthons Leichenrede auf Luther," in *Humanismus und Wittenberger Reformation: Festgabe anläßlich des 500. Geburtstages des Praeceptor Germaniae Philipp Melanchthon am 16. Februar 1997*, ed. Michael Beyer (Leipzig: Evangelische Verlagsanstalt, 1996), 192–195.

97 The edition is VD16 F 3381.

98 His letter preface is dated Epiphany 1546, but the text itself ends with the colophon, "completed on the twelfth of February." – "Volendet am zwelfften Februarij 1546." Carion, *Chronica* (Frankfurt, 1546), fol. [369] v.

of Luther's significance.[99] With these additions, Funck abandoned the mildly Protestant tone of the original 1532 editions, and he transformed the *Chronicle* into an overtly Protestant work culminating in Luther.[100]

In his *Continuation*, Funck dispensed with the *Chronicle's* characteristic brevity, and he filled page after page with events from 1532 to 1546.[101] For each year, Funck followed a set narrative pattern. He began with events in the Holy Roman Empire then moved geographically outward, with special attention to England. Funck also increased the emphasis on signs and wonders, and at the conclusion of each year he recounted various portents, particularly those involving the weather, misbirths and celestial events. Amidst this mass of information, he dwelt especially on the Turkish wars, the Anabaptist kingdom in Münster, and the siege of Wolfenbüttel, all of which he described in graphic detail. While the *Chronicle* itself had not mentioned the voyages to Asia or the Americas, Funck commented briefly on them.[102]

Because Imperial troops were stationed near Frankfurt, and the prohibition on printing Protestant books was being enforced,[103] Cyriakus Jacob printed the *Chronicle* without designating a publisher or place of publication. He indicated on the title page that his edition was protected by an Imperial privilege, but the notation was presumably false (Figure 14). There is no surviving record

---

99 Carion, *Chronica* (Frankfurt, 1546), fol. 365r–368r.
100 Melanchthon was praised too, and Funck referred to him as a beloved teacher: "Dieweil sich solches im Niderlandt verlauffen / ist ein tag vnnd gesprech die Religion belangend auß Kayserliche Maiestat beuel zu Worms gehalten worden. Seyn zu beyden partheien Collocutores gewesen Herr Philippus Melanchthon / mein getrewer preceptor / welcher von wegen der Euangelischen Stend geredt / vnd Doctor Johan Eck von Ingelstadt / der des Bapst teil zuuertedigen fürgehabt." Carion, *Chronica* (Frankfurt, 1546), fol. 312v.
101 "Vnnd damit jr ja an den Historien keynen zweiffel hetten / hab ich dieselben dermassen beschrieben / entweder wie ichs zum theyl selber gegenwertig gesehen vnnd erfaren / oder ja von glaubwirdigen leutten gehört / die der warheyt ein gůt zeugnuß haben / oder wie ichs in den glaubwirdigsten schrifften dieser zeit gefunden hab / denn ich nicht eynem jeden von hören sagen hab glauben geben wollen / Vnd ist mir derhalben auch widerfaren (wie geschicht / wo man alle sach mit fleiß handelen wil) daß ich inn vielen stücken lenger bin gewesen / denn des Charionis Chronica art vnd gewonheyt ist / Aber inn diesem wird mich niemand leichtlich verdencken mögen / so er meine vrsach erwieget / welche ist / daß sonst soliche Historien von wenigen oder ja von keynem in eynem theyl zuhauff beschrieben publiciert sein / welche ich dem leser auff eynem büntel (wie man spricht) hab wöllen zuhauff vberantworten." Carion, *Chronica* (Frankfurt, 1546), sig. Aiii v.
102 "Hernach haben die Spanischen schiffleut durch anleitung Kei. Ma. etliche zuuor vnbekante Insulen im Meer gefunden / welche an silber vnd golt so vberschwencklich reich sein / daß nit dauon zusagen ist Diese haben sie mit gewalt eingenomen / vnd dem Keiser vnterthenig gemacht." Carion, *Chronica* (Frankfurt, 1546), fol. 270r–270v.
103 See Hase, *Herzog Albrecht*, 105.

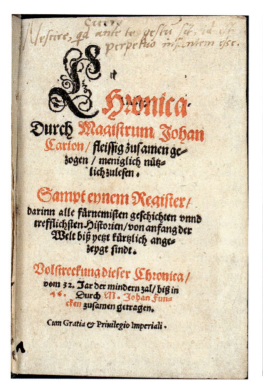
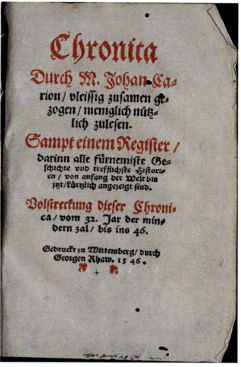

FIGURE 14 Carion, *Chronica* (Frankfurt a.M., 1546)
HERZOG AUGUST BIBLIOTHEK WOLFENBÜTTEL: H: T 226.8° HELMST

FIGURE 15 Carion, *Chronica* (Wittenberg, 1546)
HERZOG AUGUST BIBLIOTHEK WOLFENBÜTTEL: H: T 224.8° HELMST

of Jacob receiving it from Imperial officials, and adding it to the title page was probably a ploy to discourage reprinting. Indeed, the practice of using false privileges was so common in early modern Germany that Imperial statutes eventually banned such privileges altogether.[104]

From the start, Funck's edition met with dissatisfaction in Wittenberg. Not only did his *Continuation* fail to match the *Chronicle's* concise narrative style, the edition resurrected the problematic text of the initial 1532 German quarto editions, with all of their typographical and chronological errors. These were minor issues, however, compared to the added content. Melanchthon was furious when he learned of Funck's work. On 14 May 1546, he wrote to Hieronymus Baumgartner, a Nuremberg senator, to discuss various news, and at the end of

---

104 Gieseke, *Vom Privileg zum Urheberrecht*, 40–41.

the letter, he remarked that "your Funck" would do well to consider the fate of Timaeus, the historian and chronologist who was subjected to torture for his political agitation against the Sicilian tyrant Agathocles.[105]

On 26 May 1546, Hieronymus Besold also wrote to Nuremberg, and this second letter from Wittenberg clarifies Melanchthon's cryptic comments to Baumgartner. After Luther's death, his wife dismissed all of the guests from the house, and Besold, who had been staying there, was taken in by Melanchthon. In his letter to Veit Dietrich, Besold mentioned that Melanchthon had told him about writing to Baumgartner, and he informed Dietrich that Melanchthon was enraged at the Frankfurt edition because Funck had deeply insulted the Margrave of Brandenburg, Elector Joachim II, through references to his command of the Imperial army in Hungary.[106]

The 1542 campaign that Besold referred to is little known today, and it is generally treated, if at all, as a footnote to the decades of conflict along the Ottoman-Hungarian frontier.[107] The sixteenth century interpretation, however, was different, because the campaign was one of the few occasions when the Empire actually fielded a major army to fight the Turks in Hungary. In 1541, the Ottomans conquered Buda and Pest, and they took direct control of Hungarian territory to create a buffer zone against the Hapsburgs. In response, the German princes agreed the next year to support a major campaign against the Turks, and Elector Joachim II was chosen to lead the forces. The Imperial army marched for Hungary with high hopes, but the campaign was a complete disas-

---

[105] "Vestrum historicum Funkium doleo quaedam narrasse minus circumspecte, qui si cogitaret Timaeum ab Agathocle in crucem actum, stylum retraxisset." CR VI, 135; MBW 4259. On Melanchthon's letter to Baumgartner, see Bräuer, "Die Überlieferung von Melanchthons Leichenrede auf Luther," 194–195; and James Michael Weiss, "Erasmus at Luther's Funeral: Melanchthon's Commemorations of Luther in 1546," *Sixteenth Century Journal* 16 (Spring 1985): 108 n. 64.

[106] "Etiam ex Ungaria quaedam allata sunt de mulierculis defendentibus arcem quampiam, quid sit, nondum comperi, sed D. Philippus dicebat se scriptum ad Hieronymum. Funckium magnam injuriam fecisse Marchioni, quod tantis convitijs incessisset eum. Si enim dimicasset, omnes fuisse occissos, cum tantum animi et roboris sit in mulieribus prae nostris ducibus et militibus." Besold to Dietrich (26 May 1546) in O. Albrecht and P. Flemming, "Das sogenannte Manuscriptum Thomasianum. V. Aus Knaakes Abschrift veröffentlicht von O. Albrecht und P. Flemming. Dritter Teil. Nr. 94–126. Briefe Besolds an Dietrich aus den Jahren 1541–1546. Zweiter Abschnitt: Nr. 111–126," *Archiv für Reformationsgeschichte* 13 (1916): 184, see esp. n. 11, where the editors refer to *Carion's Chronicle*.

[107] On the 1542 campaign, see Hermann Traut, *Kurfürst Joachim II. von Brandenburg und der Türkenfeldzug vom Jahre 1542* (Gummersbach: Luyken, 1892); see also Stephan A. Fischer-Galati, *Ottoman Imperialism and German Protestantism, 1521–1555* (Cambridge, M.A.: Harvard University Press, 1959), 84–91.

ter. Unlike his success of 1532 as Electoral Prince, when he had returned from the Turkish front as "Hector," Joachim now met with total failure. The Imperial troops attacked Pest in late September, but after a few days discipline broke down, and the army began to retreat and finally disintegrated.[108] The Elector returned to Germany in disgrace.

The 1542 campaign was a turning point in the wars between the Hapsburgs and the Ottomans. Rather than raise another army, the Hapsburgs decided to conclude a peace with the Sultan that recognized the status quo, and the two sides reached an agreement in November of 1545. The ensuing calm on the Hungarian front allowed the Hapsburgs to prepare for the Schmalkaldic War, but it also gave the Turks time to strengthen their control over the Hungarian heartlands they had conquered in 1541.[109]

In his *Continuation* to the *Chronicle*, Funck wrote that the massive Imperial army gathered at Vienna too late to wage war, but Elector Joachim insisted on taking the troops into the field for his own glory. Furthermore, his leadership on the campaign was miserable. After a few days of besieging Pest, disease started to spread through the Imperial camp, and by the time the retreat was over, only a tenth of the army was left.[110]

---

108 Traut, *Kurfürst Joachim II. von Brandenburg*, 107–120.
109 See Fischer-Galati, *Ottoman Imperialism*, 94–96.
110 "Vnter des hat man sich im gantzem Reich gerüstet / vnnd ein gewaltigen zug in Vngern (wie denn zu Regenspurg beschlossen war) wider den Türcken fürgenummen / vnnd ist vonn allen enden Teutscher Nation volck zugeschickt worden / Welches sich vmb Wien versammelt. Da mann nū mit dem volck fort rucken solte (welches vber hundert tausent mann gewesen) wartet der Obriste Marckgraff Joachim von Brandenburck / seines Pancketirens / ließ die knecht on alle vbung / in sauffen / hurerey / vnnd müssiggang verderben (da doch kein grösser noch schedlicher gifft dem kriegvolk seyn mag / wie die alten Historien sampt dieser genugsam beweysen) biß das sie die zeyt mit gwalt triebe etwas zu schaffen. Denn da der Herbst mit gewalt herdrang / vnnd schier zeyt sein wolte / das man sich ins winterläger begebe / da zog der Obriste erst mit dem volck fort (da mit er nit gar vngeschafft abzüge) vnnd belegert Pest / welches der Türck des jars zuuor im winter vbereilt / vnnd erobret hette. Thet auch ein sturm mit grossem schaden daran / in welchem nit wenig der vnsern vmbkommen sein / vnnd als die in der Stadt offt herauß fielen zu scharmützelen / hat sich Hertzog Moritz von Sachsen (welcher auff sein eigen köstung / freiwillig zu solchem krieg sich begeben / etwas zu erfaren / vnd der Christenheit zu dienen) vielmals mit den seinen menlich vnd tapffer ertzeiget / biß er eins mals / als er zu hefftig den feynden nachiaget / vnnd zu ferr von den seynen kam / von den Türcken vmbringet vnnd gefangen wurde. Da sie jm aber im küres nichts vermochten antzugewinnen / sonder jhn lieber lebendig daruon gebracht hetten / hat sich einer seiner Edelleudt (welches namen mir itzt nicht kund ist) so dapffer vber dem Fursten gewehret / den von den feinden zu erledigen / biß die andern Reisigen ihres Herren gemangelt / vnd in gefangen erfaren / kommen sein / vnd jn nach erlegung der feind entlediget haben

In contrast to some of his aggressive contemporaries, Melanchthon was loath to antagonize the German princes. Indeed, he believed that silence about controversial or embarrassing historical events was preferable to a "complete" narrative that risked causing offense. In 1539, for example, Melanchthon denounced the *Chronicle* (*Geschichtbibel*) by the spiritualist historian Sebastian Franck as a "*schmachbuch*"[111] that slandered the authorities.[112] Later, Melanch-

---

/ Doch ist gemelter Edelman / in dem er ritterlich für seinen Herren gestritten / von den Türcken vmbracht worden.

Vnter diesem hat sich jmmer als gemach / ein schedliche / erschröckliche vnd gifftige seuch / vnter dem kriegsvolck erhaben / welche je mehr einreissend wurde. Derhalben man entlich auß dem feld abziehen muste / vnd den hauffen vrlauben / das also durch nachlessickeit des Obristen / oder vielleicht durch Gottes schickung (der vns lenger mit dem Turcken plagen wil / Wie wir denn gentzlich wol verdienen / mit vndanck vnd vervolgung seines worts vnd genaden) nichts anders ist außgericht worden / denn das wir beide volck vnd gelt / mit aller muhe vnd fleiß verloren haben / vnnd vns selbs dem Turcken zum gespöt gemacht.

Jm abziehen hat die vorgemelte seuch also grewlich vnter den knechten rumort / das nit der zehende / ja nit der zwentzigst widerumb heim kommen ist. Die kranckheit daran sie sturben / war so ein starcke gifft / das auch die von den siechen angeatmet / von solcher seuch begriffen wurden vnd starben. Dieweil sie aber darnider lagen / hetten sie seltzame fantasey / vnnd geberden / gleich als sie der sinn gentzlich beraubet weren. Vnnd als bald sich solches leget / gingen sie on sonderliche angst als schlieffen sie dahin / wenig sein von solcher kranckheit auffkommen / welche aber genesen / habens ein lange zeyt besichen mussen.

Dieweil der Marckgraff / wie gesaget ist / mit seinen hauffen in Vngern müssig lage / Dieweil namen die durchleuchtigesten Johan Friderich Hertzog zu Sachsen / Churfurst &c. vnd Philippus Landtgraff zu Hessen / sampt jren Bundtsgenossen / ein zimlichen hauffen volcks zu Roß vnnd fueß an / wider den Hertzog Heinrich den Jungern / des zuuor mehr gedacht ist." Carion, *Chronica* (Frankfurt, 1546), fol. 333v–335v.

111 "Man tregt sich jetzund mit Sebastian Francken chronicka, welche billicher möchte ein schmachbuch dann ein historia genant werden. Dann neben den geschichten hat er seine declamationes daran gehenget, lobliche weltliche potestaten schandtlich gelestert und sonst vil on warheit dabei geschriben, schmucket die anabaptisten, und ist wol zu mercken auß dem gesang, was er für ein vogel ist. Polibius spricht: Oculus historiae est veritas. Das achtet Sebastian Franck wenig, sondern macht ein blinde historien, darein er seine eigne affectus außgossen. Darzu irret er als ein ongelerter oft in der zeit und in den geschichten." Text from Heinz Scheible, ed., *Die Anfänge der reformatorischen Geschichtsschreibung: Melanchthon, Sleidan, Flacius und die Magdeburger Zenturien* (Gütersloh: Mohn, 1966), 25; see CR III, 877–884; MBW 2138.

112 For the infamous section denouncing the nobility for being as rapacious as the eagles on their coats of arms, see Sebastian Franck, *Chronica, Zeytbuch und geschycht bibel von anbegyn biß inn diß gegenwertig M.D. xxxj. jar...* (Strasbourg: Beck, 1531), fol. cxix r – cxxv r. VD16 F 2064. On this so-called *Adlervorrede*, see Klaus Deppermann, "Sebastian Francks Straßburger Aufenhalt," in *Sebastian Franck (1499–1542)*, ed. Jan Dirk Müller (Wiesbaden: Harrassowitz, 1993), 113–115; and Dellsperger, *Lebendige Historien und Erfahrungen*, 70–76. Franck made the clever comparison by drawing on material from Erasmus's *Adagia*, a

thon was annoyed that Johann Sleidanus (1506–1556), the official historian of the Schmalkaldic League,[113] included much that should have been buried in "eternal silence"[114] in his *Commentaries on Religion and Politics during the Reign of Charles V* (1555).[115]

The 1532 edition of *Carion's Chronicle* had avoided recent controversial events or presented them in a relatively neutral manner. Funck dispensed with that cautious approach, and in the process he endangered the relationship between the Wittenbergers and Elector Joachim. For the next twenty years,

---

collection of Greek and Roman adages, and in the offending passage, Franck explicitly acknowledged Erasmus as his source. In response, Erasmus immediately sought to have the book suppressed. See Desiderius Erasmus, *Opus epistolarum des Erasmi Roterdami*, ed. P.S. Allen (Oxford: Oxford University Press, 1992 [Reprint]), vol. 9, 153–156 Nr. 2441, and 445–457 Nr. 2615.

[113] On Sleidanus generally, see Alexandra Kess, *Johann Sleidan and the Protestant Vision of History* (Burlington, VT: Ashgate, 2008). See also Hermann Ehmer, "Reformatorische Geschichtsschreibung am Oberrhein: Franciscus Irenicus, Kaspar Hedio, Johannes Sleidanus," in *Historiographie am Oberrhein im Späten Mittelalter und in der Frühen Neuzeit*, ed. Kurt Andermann (Sigmaringen: Jan Thorbecke Verlag, 1988), 230–244, esp. 242; Donald Kelley, "Johann Sleidan and the Origins of History as a Profession," *The Jounal of Modern History* 52, no. 4 (December 1980): 591–596; and Richard Fester, "Sleidan, Sabinus, Melanchthon," *Historische Zeitschrift* 89 (1902), 1–16.

[114] "Cristophoro Libio, Pastori Ecclesiae Brandenburgensis. S.D. Reverende vir et cariss. frater. Edita est Sledani historia de germanicis motibus, qui his triginta annis extiterunt, ac praecipue de Ecclesiarum mutationibus. Liber dedicatus est Duci Saxoniae Augusto, qui misit scriptori ducentos Ioachimicos. Liberalitatem principis laudo, sed historiam non laudo, quia ἀπὸ ἔργων οὐ καλῶν οὐκ ἔστιν ἔκη καλά. Multa narrat, quae malim obruta esse aeterno silentio. Si voles videre librum, huc ad nos venias. Nam apud vos exemplum non haberi existimo. Tria vobis exempla mitto Enarrationum Salomonis, quorum unum retinebis, alterum dabis vicino tuo Simoni, tertium collegae Kittelio. Scio pueriles libellos esse, sed lectionem hanc utiliorem esse iunioribus censeo, quam lectionem tumultum, qui stultiam et ignaviam nostram ostendunt. Quaeso ut respondeas mihi ac significes, an istuc Sledani liber allatus sit. Bene vale. Die 18. Maii 1555. Philippus." CR VIII, 483; MBW 7492. [Text complete here.]

[115] Johann Sleidanus, *Ioan. Sleidani, De Statv Religionis Et Reipvblicae, Carolo Qvinto, Caesare, Commentarij. Cvm indice luculentißimo* (Strasbourg: Rihel, 1555). VD16 S 6668. Sleidanus had offended Margrave Albrecht Alcibiades of Brandenburg-Kulmbach (1522–1557) by describing his wars of plunder in Germany. See Karl Schottenloher, "Johann Sleidanus und Markgraf Albrecht Alcibiades,"*Archiv für Reformationsgeschichte* 35 (1938): 193–202; and Kess, *Johann Sleidan*, 79. Sleidanus was also criticized for his account of the 1542 Turkish campaign. See Kess, *Johann Sleidan*, 79. The Turkish campaign is described in Books 14–15 of the *Commentaries*. On 1 September 1556, Melanchthon's son-in-law, Georg Sabinus, who was then employed by Elector Joachim II, sent Sleidanus a letter, castigating him for the section on the 1542 campaign. See Georg Sabinus, *Poëmata* (Leipzig: Steinmann, 1589), 475–476. VD16 S 139.

the history of *Carion's Chronicle* in Germany turns on the Wittenberg efforts to suppress Funck's *Continuation*.

7   The 1546 Wittenberg Edition

Besides putting pressure on the authorities in Frankfurt, Melanchthon apparently responded to Funck's *Continuation* by having *Carion's Chronicle* republished at Wittenberg for the first time since 1538. Contemporary sources are silent about the circumstances of this new edition, but it was clearly meant to counteract the Frankfurt imprint. The title page is similar, the standard revised German text was used, and Rhau added an index as Cyriakus Jacob had done (Figure 15). The new *Chronicle* also included a *Continuation* (*Volstreckung*) covering the events from 1532 to May of 1546, so it must have appeared within a few months of the Frankfurt edition.

In contrast to Funck's *Continuation*, the Wittenberg version corresponds to the style of the original *Chronicle*, and no author is given, but Melanchthon likely wrote the *Continuation* himself or at least supervised its preparation.[116] The Wittenberg *Continuation* maintained the earlier, relatively neutral, perspective on recent events. It contained a brief account of Luther's death, but despite high praise for the Reformer, it did not treat him as the culmination of history.[117] The last event mentioned is the Diet at Regensburg in May of 1546, but the *Continuation* actually ends with Melanchthon's account of Juan and Alfonso Diaz,[118] which he had published separately as a pamphlet, dated 17

---

116   Melanchthon is mentioned in the Wittenberg continuation at the Diet of Worms (1540), "Dis ist auffgemelten Reichstage zu Wormbs / durch den Ehrwirdigen herrn Philippum Melanthon / vnd Doctor Eck angefangen worden / wie dann dis Colloquium Wormaciense / inn ein eigen Buch beschrieben / vnd an tag gegeben ist." Carion, *Chronica* (Wittenberg, 1546), fol. 236r.

117   "Anno 1546. am 18. Februarij / ist der Ehrwirdige herr Doctor Martinus Luther / seliglichen in Gott verschieden / zu Eisleben in seinem Vaterlande / dahin er erfordert worden / von wegen etlicher handlung / zwischen den Graffen von Mansfelt / seinen Landsherrn / Die Leich aber ist gen Wittenberg gebracht / vnd in die Schlos Kirchen begraben worden." Carion, *Chronica* (Wittenberg, 1546), fol. 238v.

118   Philipp Melanchthon, *Wie newlich zu Newburg jn Beiern einer genant Alphonsus Diasius seinen bruder Johanem, grausamlich ermort hatt, alleine aus has Wider die Einige Ewige Christliche lahr, wie Cain den Abel ermordet* ([Wittenberg]: [Klug], 1546). VD16 M 4415. The text is reproduced in CR VI, 112–114; and CR XX, 515–518. See Kathrin Stegbauer, "Perspektivierungen des Mordfalles Diaz (1546) im Streit der Konfessionen: Publizistische Möglichkeiten im Spannungsfeld zwischen reichspolitischer Argumentation und heilsgeschichtlicher Einordnung," in *Wahrnehmungsgeschichte und Wissensdiskurs im illustrierten Flugblatt der Frühen Neuzeit (1450–1700)*, ed. Wolfgang Harms (Basel: Schwabe, 2002), 371–414.

April 1546. The Diaz affair was a recent *cause célèbre* of fratricide, in which a lawyer for the papal court murdered his Protestant brother for refusing to return to Catholicism. By comparing the Diaz brothers to Cain and Abel, the Wittenberg edition used these martyrdom-fratricides to provide bookends to the *Chronicle* as a whole.[119] The episode also foreshadowed the impending war in Germany between the Protestants and the Emperor.

Regarding the Turkish campaign of 1542, the Wittenberg account mentions the leadership of Elector Joachim II, but the colourless description simply states that plague forced the army to withdraw from Pest:

> In the year 1542, the army of the entire Empire marched into Hungary, as had been decided at the Diet of Regensburg, and Margrave Joachim of Brandenburg, the field commander, accompanied in person. At first, there were a few skirmishes with the Turks; however, such horrible and foul plague and sickness soon broke out among the soldiers that the army had to be ordered to withdraw again.[120]

The new Wittenberg edition was reprinted in Wittenberg and Leipzig down to 1554. Although the title pages of the later editions claim to include additional material, the *Continuation* actually remained the same, with no information on the years after 1546.[121] At Frankfurt in 1550, Peter Brubach published a Latin

---

119 "Aber aus dieser that ist abzunemen / wie die feind Göttlicher warheit / gegen allen fromen glidmassen Christi / gesind sein / nemlich / wie Cain gegen Abel / Darumb ist nicht zweifel / das allein / durch gnedigen Gottes schutz / diese Fürsten / Kirchen / Predicanten / vnd zuhörer / die reine Göttliche lere lieben vnd ehren / widder so grimmigen hass / so lang erhalten sind / Vnd sollen alle Gottfürchtige hertzen bitten / das Gott vns forthin / schützen vnd regiren wölle / vmb seiner ehr willen / wie er gesprochen hat / Esaie 51. Meine wort habe ich in deinen Mund gelegt / vnd wil dich mit dem schatten meiner hand bewaren / das du mir den Himel / wie einen schönen garten pflantzest. Geschrieben Anno 1546. am 17. tag Aprilis / daran vor 3852 / jar Nohe in die Arca getretten ist / Durch welchs exempel Gott bewisen / vnd vns wil erinnert haben / das wir gleuben vnd wissen sollen / vnd darumb bitten / Das Gott selbs die Kirch wunderbarlich erhalten wöl / wenn gleich die Welt in hauffen felt." Carion, *Chronica* (Wittenberg, 1546), fol. 240v.

120 "Anno 1542. ist der Zug in vngern / so zu Regenspurg beschlossen / von dem gantzen Reich furgenomen / vnd Marggraff Joachim von Brandenburg / öberster Feldheuptman selbst inn eigner Person mit zogen / Vnd sein erstlich etlich scharmützeln mit dem Türcken geschehen / aber balt ist so ein grewliche schedliche seuche vnd kranckheit / vnter das Kriegsvolckkomen / das man das Volck widerumb hat abziehen lassen." Carion, *Chronica* (Wittenberg, 1546) fol. 237r.

121 Johann Carion, *Chronica Durch M. Johan Carion / vleissig zusamen gezogen / meniglich nützlich zu lesen. Sampt einem Register darin alle fürnemeste Geschichte vnd trefflichste Historien / von anfang der Welt bis jtzt / kürtzlich angezeigt sind. Volstreckung dieser Chronica / vom 32. Jar der mindern zal / bis ins 46. vnd etliche jar hernach. Gedruckt zu*

translation of the Wittenberg edition, but he did not expand the *Continuation*.[122] Ultimately, the Wittenberg editions remained fixed in their 1546 form, and they were not modified to address subsequent events, such as the Schmalkaldic War and the Interims.

8   The Schmalkaldic War

In 1546, after Luther's death, war finally broke out in Germany between the Protestants and the Emperor.[123] Although the Protestant forces of the Schmalkaldic League had a military advantage, the war was poorly run by the princes, and Moritz of Saxony, from the Albertine branch of the house of Wettin, agreed to turn against his cousin, Elector John Frederick, and his father-in-law, Philip of Hesse, in exchange for the lands of Electoral Saxony and the Electoral title. After initial victories for the Protestant side, the Emperor marched into Saxony and defeated the Elector at Mühlberg on 24 April 1547. Both Elector John Frederick and Philip of Hesse were imprisoned, and a month later on 19 May 1547, the city of Wittenberg, which had prepared for a siege, capitulated after threats by the Emperor to execute John Frederick. The Emperor transferred the Electoral title and Saxon lands to Moritz, and the Ernestine branch of the Wettins

---

Wittemberg / Durch Georgen Rhawen Erben. 1554. (Wittenberg: Rhau (Heirs), 1554). VD16 C 1008.

122   "ANNO 1542. Bellum contra Turcam, de quo in conuentu Ratisbonensi deliberatum erat, à toto Imperio susceptu[m] est. Estq[ue] summus gubernator & dux super omnes copias constitutus Ioachimus Marchio Brandenburgensis. Initio autem aliquot conflictus fuere Christianorum & Turcarum. Sed propter morbos contagiosos in exercitu grassantes, milites sunt dimißi." Johann Carion, *Io. Carionis Mathematici Bvetickheinensis Chronicorum libri tres in Latinum sermonem conuersi, Hermanno Bonno interprete. Continvatio Chronicorvm Ab Anno 1532. Ad Annvm 1547. Vnà cum Catalogo Regum, Cæsarum, & Pontificum Romanorum. Complectitur hic libellus apto ordine maximas quasque res gestas, ab initio Mundi, usq[ue] ad nostra tempora, ut annorum ratio, ac præcipuæ uicissitudines, quæ in Regna, in Religionem, & in alias res magnas incidunt, quàm rectissimè cognosci & obseruari queant. Francoforti, M.D.L.* (Frankfurt: Peter Brubach, 1550), fol. 223r–223v.

123   On the Schmalkaldic War and the Interims, see Clyde Manschreck, *Melanchthon: The Quiet Reformer* (New York: Abingdon Press, 1958), 277–292; and Christian Winter, "Die Außenpolitik des Kurfürsten Moritz von Sachsen," in *Glaube & Macht: Sachsen im Europa der Reformationszeit*, ed. Harald Marx and Eckhard Kluth (Dresden: Sandstein, 2004), vol. 2, 124–136; as well as Curt Christmann, *Melanchthons Haltung im schmalkaldischen Kriege* (Berlin: E. Ebering, 1902). For the Magdeburg perspective, see Nathan Rein, *The Chancery of God: Protestant Print, Polemic and Propaganda against the Empire, Magdeburg 1546–1551* (Burlington, VT: Ashgate, 2008); and Oliver Olson, *Matthias Flacius and the Survival of Luther's Reform* (Wiesbaden: Harrassowitz Verlag, 2002).

was reduced to ruling the territory around Jena and Weimar. Of the Northern cities, only Bremen and Magdeburg continued to resist the Emperor.

The University of Wittenberg had closed during the war, and Melanchthon along with many others had fled the city. When Moritz came to power, he offered Melanchthon the opportunity to return to Wittenberg and to resume his activities at the university. Melanchthon agreed, and many of his former students never forgave him for this. In order to try to achieve religious peace in the Empire, Charles V set up a transitional arrangement, the Augsburg Interim of 1548. Because of its uncompromising Catholicism, Moritz was hesitant to impose the Augsburg Interim on his newly won lands, so he commissioned Melanchthon to help draw up a milder version for Saxony, the so-called Leipzig Interim. Melanchthon's role in these events caused a fierce reaction and many branded him a traitor to Luther's cause. As a result, a bitter pamphlet war broke out, especially between Wittenberg and Magdeburg, which had defiantly resisted the Emperor. The intra-Protestant feuding clouded the rest of Melanchthon's life,[124] and historical scholarship eventually became part of this competition over the future of the Reformation.[125]

9 Unauthorized Editions of the *Chronicle*

In 1547, a new Low German edition of *Carion's Chronicle* was published at Magdeburg, which preserves a later version of Funck's *Continuation*, otherwise unknown in any German or Latin form.[126] This edition includes the first account of the Schmalkaldic War appended to *Carion's Chronicle*, but it concludes in November 1546, midway through the war, with Moritz of Saxony threatening both Torgau and Wittenberg.[127] Funck may have contributed new material, but the authorship remains uncertain.

---

124 See generally Robert Kolb, "Dynamics of Party Conflict in the Saxon Late Reformation: Gnesio-Lutherans vs. Philippists," *The Journal of Modern History* 49 (1977): On Demand Supplement, D1289-D1305.

125 See Ronald Diener, "The Magdeburg Centuries: A Bibliothecal and Historiographical Analysis" (Ph.D. diss., Harvard Divinity School, 1978).

126 Johann Carion, *Chronica dorch Magistrum Johan Carion / Vlytich thosammen getagen / einem yedermanne nütte tho lesen. Mit einem Register / darynne alle vörnemesten Geschichten vnde Dreplickste Historien / van anfanck der Werlt beth tho desser Chronica vam xxxij. Jar an beth tho desser tydt / körtlick angetöget sint. Vormeringe desser Chronica vam xxxij. Jar an / beth vp dyth xlvij Jar / Dorch M. Johann Funcken / thosamen gedregen* (Magdeburg : Lotther, [1547]). On Michael Lotter see Reske, *Die Buchdrucker*, 580.

127 "Am 16. Nouembris / Hefft Hertog Mauritz einen Trommeter mith twen Breuen / einen an de Beuelhebber / den anderen an de Gemene to Wittenborch twisschen dren vnd

After 1546, or perhaps 1547 if he was involved with the Low German edition, Funck did not revisit *Carion's Chronicle*. In early 1547, he deserted his parish as Imperial troops drew closer to Nuremberg, and he eventually travelled in 1548 to Königsberg, where Viet Dietrich helped arrange for him to become court preacher to Duke Albrecht. From Königsberg, Funck continued to agitate in both political and religious affairs, and he became a follower of Andreas Osiander († 1552), which made him a bitter enemy of Melanchthon.[128] After Osiander's death, Funck married his mentor's daughter, and he became the leading proponent of Osiander's views on justification, which many considered heretical. He also continued to work on historical chronology, and he published an extensive revision of his *Chronologia* in 1552.[129] In Königsberg, Funck created further problems for himself by meddling in political affairs, and eventually his enemies appealed to Duke Albrecht's overlord, the king of Poland. In those years, Duke Albrecht's government had become unpopular; and because of his ties to the court, Funck was blamed for many of its failings. After an investigation, Funck and several other officials were arrested and condemned to death. This time there was no escape, and Funck was beheaded in Königsberg on 28 October 1566.[130]

Although Funck had left the Empire by 1548, his edition of *Carion's Chronicle* continued to plague Melanchthon and the Wittenbergers. After Cyriakus Jacob's death in 1551, his son-in-law David Zöpfel took over the printing shop. By 1558, Zöpfel had published five new editions of *Carion's Chronicle* at Frankfurt, including a Latin edition in 1555. These all included Funck's *Continuation*, with its scandalous account of the 1542 Turkish campaign.[131] In contrast to the Wittenberg-Leipzig editions, which remained unchanged after 1546, the Zöpfel

---

veeren vp den auent / vor dat Eluedor geschicket / Eer auerst de Breue angenamen / ys de Vorstadt angesticket / Dar mit thouorstan thogeuen / Dat men dachte sick syner tho wehren. Den suluigen dach hefft he ock den Börgeren von Torgaw / so yn der Besettinge tho Wittenborch gelegen / anteken lathen / Wo se sick den volgenden dach nicht by Sunnenschyn heim geuen würden / Wolde he ene Wyff vnde Kindt na yagen / dartho se alle erer Güder berouen." Carion, *Chronica* (Magdeburg, 1547), fol. CCCLXXVI r – CCCLXXVI v.

128 On Osiander, see ADB 24: 473–483.
129 Johann Funck, *Chronologia hoc est omnium temporum et annorum ab initio mundi, usque ad hunc praesentem a nato Christo annum M.D.LII. computatio.* (Königsberg: Lufft, 1552). VD16 F 3382.
130 On the events leading up to Funck's death, see Hase, *Herzog Albrecht*, 331–371.
131 On David Zöpfel (Zöpflin, Zephelius, Schöffel, active 1552–1563), see Reske, *Die Buchdrucker*, 228–229; Benzing, "Der Drucker Cyriacus Jacob," 1–4; and Heinrich Pallmann, *Sigmund Feyerabend, sein Leben und seine geschäftlichen Verbindungen* (Frankfurt a. M.: Völcker, 1881), 1–7. See also Diener, "The Magdeburg Centuries," esp. 177–203. Zöpfel was married to Cyriakus Jacob's daugher Sara.

FIGURE 16 Carion, *Chronica* (Frankfurt a.M., 1564)
HERZOG AUGUST BIBLIOTHEK WOLFENBÜTTEL: H: T 232.8° HELMST

FIGURE 17 Carion, *Chronica* (Frankfurt a.M., 1564), fol. 166r
HERZOG AUGUST BIBLIOTHEK WOLFENBÜTTEL: H: T 232.8° HELMST

editions continued to be revised and updated, down to the last edition of 1558. The identity of the editor, however, remains unknown.

In 1564, the Zöpfel press published a completely reworked edition of the *Chronicle* edited by Michael Beuther (1522–1587), a former Melanchthon student and distinguished historian in his own right (Figure 16).[132] Rather than

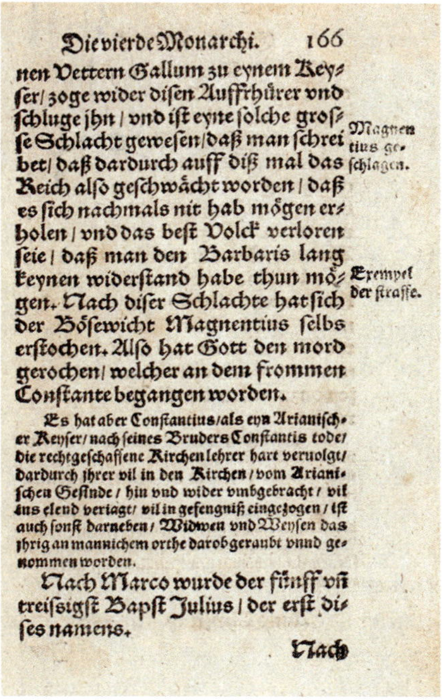

---

132 Johann Carion, *Chronica Johannis Carionis / Jetzt von newem vbersehen / vnd an vilen orten / da bißher durch mannicherley Truck / etwa mängel eingeschlichen / nach notturfft Corrigiert. Darzu auch Jm tritten Buch / souil die zeit nach Christi Geburt belangt / mit vilen namhafften Historien / so bei eyner kleynern Schriffte zuunterscheyden / erklärt vnd gemehrt. Deßgleichen Eyne Verzeychniß allerley gedenckwirdiger Sachen vnd Händel / so sich in etlichen vnd vierzig jaren bißher / vnder Keyser Carls des Füfften / vnd seines bruders Keyser Ferdinandes Regierungen / in vnd ausserhalb des heyligen Römischen Reichs Teutscher Nation zugetragen vnd verlauffen / jetz erstlich in Truck gegeben. Durch Michaelem Beuther von Carlstatt / der Rechten Doctorn. M.D.LXIIII.* (Frankfurt a.M.: David Zöpfel, 1564 [1563]).

leave the text itself intact, as every German edition since 1532 had done, Beuther added extensive interpolations, which were indicated with a smaller typeface (Figure 17).[133] Despite this reworking of the *Chronicle*, Beuther did not include Funck's *Continuation*, or any other appendix, to the main text of the *Chronicle*. This edition was never republished, at Frankfurt or anywhere else, so it probably met with little commercial success.

Zöpfel died in 1563, and his passing effectively ended the initial dispute between Frankfurt and Wittenberg over *Carion's Chronicle*. Zöpfel's ability to publish the *Chronicle* with impunity for over a decade demonstrates the lack of protections available to the Wittenbergers. In 1546, Melanchthon had pressed Hieronymus Baumgartner to deal with Funck, but in the wake of the Schmalkaldic War, the issue became irrelevant. It remains unknown whether he renewed his complaints in the 1550s when Zöpfel started to publish the *Chronicle*. Informal pressure had been ineffective and the channels available for official recourse were limited, so Melanchthon apparently tried to fight the Frankfurt edition in the marketplace. The 1546 Wittenberg edition was reprinted several times, so it may have enjoyed some commercial success, but it ultimately failed to discourage Zöpfel from publishing new editions at Frankfurt.

10 Melanchthon's Revised *Chronicle*

In the mid-1550s, Melanchthon finally decided to revise *Carion's Chronicle*, and in 1555, he started to lecture on the text in preparation for publishing a new edition. Several factors probably contributed to this decision. Funck's *Continuation* and the annoyance of Zöpfel's Frankfurt editions clearly played a role. The 1546 Wittenberg edition had proven ineffective as a response to the Frankfurt

---

The colophon is dated 1563, but the title page indicates 1564. On Beuther, see Otto Jung, *Dr. Michael Beuther aus Karlstadt: Ein Geschichtschreiber des XVI Jahrhunderts (1522–1587)* (Würzburg: Freunde mainfränkischer Kunst und Geschichte E.V., 1957), esp. 58–61; also Kelley, "Johann Sleidan," 583.

133 The text follows the revised octavo text of 1532, which had been used in the other Zöpfel editions. At the section on Constantius II, Beuther added these comments about Arianism: "Nach diser Schlachte hat sich der Bösewicht Magnentius selbs erstochen. Also had Gott den mord gerochen / welcher an dem frommen Constante begangen worden. *Es hat aber Constantius / als eyn Arianischer Keyser / nach seines Bruders Constantis tode / de rechtegeschaffene Kirchen lehrer hart veruolgt / dardurch ihrer vil in den Kirchen / vom Arianischen Gesinde / hin vnd wider vmbgebracht / vil ins elend veriagt / vil in gefengniß eingezogen / ist auch sonst darneben / Widwen vnd Weysen das jhrig an mannichem orthe darob geraubt vnnd genommen worden.* Nach Marco wurder der fünff vnd treissigst Bapst Julius / der erst dieses namens." Carion, *Chronica* (Frankfurt, 1564), fol. 166 r; italic added to mark the interpolation.

editions, and Melanchthon may have thought that a thorough revision would be more successful. That seems, in fact, to have been true, since Zöpfel did not reprint the original Melanchthon-Carion text after 1558, the same year that Melanchthon published the first fascicle of his new edition. Not surprisingly, Zöpfel started to reprint Melanchthon's new fascicles almost as soon as they were issued at Wittenberg.[134]

Developments at Magdeburg may have also influenced Melanchthon's decision. There, Matthias Flacius Illyricus,[135] one of Melanchthon's former students, had started to prepare a new ecclesiastical history, the *Magdeburg Centuries*.[136] The project as envisioned was too vast for a single scholar, so Basil Faber (1525–1576), Matthaeus Judex (1528–1564) and Johann Wigand (1523–1587) became involved. The team of historians became known as the Centuriators of Magdeburg, and Wigand, the superintendent (essentially a Protestant bishop) of Magdeburg, eventually became the overseer of the project. Because of their tremendous amount of source material, the Centuriators found funds to assemble a research team, which they divided into a hierarchy according to prescribed research, writing and editing tasks.[137] The organization was innovative and so was the methodological approach. Rather than produce a continuous narrative, the Centuriators divided their material according to strict hundred year intervals (*centuriae*),[138] which they arranged according to fifteen

---

134 Zöpfel published the first fascicle in 1559 (VD16 M 2700); and the second in 1560 (VD16 M 2702) and again in 1561 (VD16 ZV 16739).

135 On Flacius, see the entries in ADB 7: 88–101; TRE 11: 206–214; and RE 6: 82–92. See also Olson, *Matthias Flacius*.

136 See Diener, "The Magdeburg Centuries;" Heinz Scheible, *Die Entstehung der Magdeburger Zenturien: Ein Beitrag zur Geschichte der historiographischen Methode* ([Gütersloh]: Gerd Mohn, 1966); and Matthias Pohlig, *Zwischen Gelehrsamkeit und konfessioneller Identitätsstiftung Lutherische Kirchen- und Universalgeschichtsschreibung 1546–1617* (Tübingen: Mohr Siebeck, 2007), 370–389. See also Eckhart W. Peters and Günther Korbel, eds., *Die Magdeburger Centurien* (Dößel: Stekovics, 2007); Arno Mentzel-Reuters and Martina Hartmann, eds., *Catalogus und Centurien: Interdisziplinäre Studien zu Matthias Flacius und den Magdeburger Centurien* (Tübingen: Mohr Siebeck, 2008); Gregory Lyon, "Baudouin, Flacius, and the Plan for the Magdeburg Centuries," *Journal of the History of Ideas* 64 (April 2003): 253–272; Martina Hartmann, *Humanismus und Kirchenkritik: Matthias Flacius Illyricus als Erforscher des Mittelalters* (Stuttgart: Jan Thorbecke Verlag, 2001); and Harald Bollbuck, *Wahrheitszeugnis, Gottes Auftrag und Zeitkritik: Die Kirchengeschichte der Magdeburger Zenturien und ihre Arbeitstechniken* (Wiesbaden: Harrassowitz, 2014).

137 See Diener, "The Magdeburg Centuries," 183; also Anthony Grafton, "Where was Salomon's House? Ecclesiastical History and the Intellectual Origins of Bacon's *New Atlantis*," in *Die europäische Gelehrtenrepublik im Zeitalter des Konfessionalismus*, ed. Herbert Jaumann (Wiesbaden: Harrassowitz, 2001), 28–33; Lyon, "Baudouin, Flacius, and the Plan for the Magdeburg Centuries," 259.

138 The use of centuries for historical periodization was not strictly new. At Mainz, Hermann Piscator († 1526), a Benedictine monk, had used the division in his *Chronicle of the City*

topics (*loci*).¹³⁹ The periodic structure had medieval precedent, but its combination with the *loci* method was truly novel, and it reflected the Centuriators' Wittenberg training.¹⁴⁰ Over the course of fifteen years (1559–1574), the Oporinus publishing house issued thirteen volumes of the *Centuries* at Basel.¹⁴¹ The project eventually lost momentum due to several relocations and staff changes, but even in incomplete form, the output was genuinely impressive. Indeed, the *Centuries* were so compelling that they generated a direct Catholic response in the multi-volume *Ecclesiastical Annals* (1588–1607) of Cesare Baronio (1538–1607).¹⁴²

In the 1550s, Melanchthon was keenly aware of the massive project taking shape in Magdeburg, and it is clear that both the Magdeburgers and the Wittenbergers were keeping close watch on each other's work, sometimes even through spies.¹⁴³ Melanchthon and his colleagues genuinely feared that the

    and Church of Mainz. The Centuriators used Piscator's *Chronicle* for source material, and it seems that they may have adopted the centuries scheme based on his work. On this point, see Uta Goerlitz, "The Chronicle in the Age of Humanism: Chronological Structures and the Reckoning of Time between Tradition and Innovation," in *The Medieval Chronicle: Proceedings of the 1st International Conference on the Medieval Chronicle*, ed. Erik Kooper (Amsterdam and Atlanta: Rodopi, 1999), 133–143.

139 "De loco et propagatione ecclesiae, De persecutione et tranquillitate eius poenisque persecutorum, De doctrina eiusque inclinatione, De haeresibus, De ceremoniis diversis in locis, De gubernatione ecclesiae, De schismatibus, De conciliis, De personis illustribus in ecclesia, De haereticis, De martyribus, De miraculis, De rebus Iudaicis, De religionibus extra ecclesiam, De mutationibus politicis imperiorum." Scheible, *Die Anfänge der reformatorischen Geschichtsschreibung*, 68.

140 The *loci*, or commonplaces, method was a hallmark of Melanchthon's approach to structuring knowledge, and the Centuriators would have been exposed to it during their studies in Wittenberg. On this point, see Robert Kolb, "Philipp's Foes, but Followers Nonetheless: Late Humanism among the Gnesio-Lutherans," in *The Harvest of Humanism in Central Europe: Essays in Honor of Lewis W. Spitz*, ed. Manfred P. Fleischer (St Louis: Concordia Publishing House, 1992), 163–165.

141 Matthias Flacius, et al., *Ecclesiastica Historia*, 13 vols. (Basel: Oporinus, 1559–1574). VD16 E 218–238.

142 Cesare Baronio, *Annales ecclesiastici*, 37 vols. (Paris: Barri-Ducis, 1864–1883). See Hubert Jedin, *Kardinal Caesar Baronius: Der Anfang der katholischen Kirchengeschichtsschreibung im 16. Jahrhundert* (Münster: Aschendorff, 1978); Cyriac Pullapilly, *Caesar Baronius: Counter-Reformation Historian* (Notre Dame: University of Notre Dame Press, 1975).

143 On the question of spies in Wittenberg: "Wilhelm Radensis [Eccius] had matriculated in Wittenberg on 31 August 1555. On 1 September 1556 he wrote to Flacius (Cod. guelf. 20 Novi, fol. 24r, lines 34 to 40): Philippum iam texere historiam a principio ut et adiaphoricarum controversiarum ut etiam alijs innotescat quantis tui libri scateant mendacijs. Dicunt tibi iam multos non fauere qui antea optime de te senserint, putant te moueri quorundam clamoribus fabellis aut scriptis ut ita contendas, nihil de istis historijs compertum habres (for "habere"), tales his audiuntur querelae." Diener, "The Magdeburg Centuries," 190 n. 12.

Centuries would be as much an attack on them as it was on the papacy. Therefore, even before the *Centuries* were published, the Wittenbergers tried to discredit the project, in part by suggesting the Centuriators had misappropriated the research funds.[144] In one pamphlet from 1558, the Wittenbergers also mentioned the perceived competition between the *Centuries* and Melanchthon's new edition of *Carion's Chronicle*, and they argued that the *Chronicle* was no less laudable than the Magdeburg project.[145] In the end, the *Magdeburg Centuries* were widely read and referenced, but the classic texts of German humanism and the *Germania Illustrata* tradition competed with *Carion's Chronicle* in the marketplace more than the *Centuries*, despite the real and perceived rivalry between Melanchthon and his former students.[146]

---

144   Grafton, "Where was Salomon's House?" 30–32; Pohlig, *Zwischen Gelehrsamkeit und konfessioneller Identitätsstiftung*, 381.

145   "Quò nos etiam humana imbecillitas quædam abduxit, qui ex peruersitate hominum dolorem capientes, inuidemus uestro Præceptori Flacio, quod Deus nobis ignoscat, fortunam istam, cui tam liberaliter omnes contribuunt ad illam historiam, cum noster Præceptor, qui Chronicon scribit, non minus laudabile quam uestra historia esse potest, ne decimam quidem millesimam partem benignitatis similis sentiat." University of Wittenberg, *De Ecclesiastica Historia: Qvae Magdebvrgi Contexitvr, Narratio, Contra Menivm, Et Scholasticorvm Wittebergensivm Epistolas. A Gvbernatoribvs Et Operariis Eivs Historiae Edita Magdebvrgi. Cvm Responsione Scholasticorvm Witebergensivm Ad Eandem. Edita Witebergæ Anno M.D.LVIII*. (Wittenberg: [Rhau (Heirs)], 1558), sig. E r. VD16 E 242. See Emil Clemens Scherer, *Geschichte und Kirchengeschichte an den deutschen Universitäten: Ihre Anfänge im Zeitalter des Humanismus und ihre Ausbildung zu selbständigen Disziplinen* (Freiburg i. B.: Herder, 1927), 128–129.

146   In 1564, for example, Laurentius Surius (1523–1578), a Carthusian monk, published a new edition of *Nauclerus's Chronicle* as a competitor to *Carion's Chronicle*. (VD16 N 169). Surius's edition includes a Catholic continuation with the events of the sixteenth century, and Peucer viciously attacked the new edition (and its author) in his dedicatory epistle to Book V of *Carion's Chronicle* (1565). See Peucer's comments in Peucer, *Chronicon Carionis* (Wittenberg, 1580), 488–489, where he refers to Surius as *scurrilous*. Surius also attacked Peucer's *Commentary on Divination* for its comments on transubstantiation, see Roebel, "Humanistische Medizin," 232 n. 815. Similarly, in 1586, the publisher Jan Canin issued a new Dutch edition of *Carion's Chronicle* at Dordrecht, and he used his introduction to argue for the superiority of *Carion's Chronicle* to the spiritualist Sebastian Franck's *Chronicle* (1531) and *Weltbuch* (1534), which had appeared again at Leiden in 1583: "Melanchthon ende Peucerus ghedaen hebben / de welcke alle geleerde ende verstandighe des geruygenisse moeten geuen / daer ter contrarie alle vrome connen oordeelen / wat Fondament ofte sekerheyt wt het Werelt boeck ende de Chronijcke van Sebastiaen Franck te vinden is / twelck lichtelicken te beswijsen soude zijn / maer hier om de lanckheyts wille naer ghelaten wort: Doch int ouerlesen van dese herrlicke Chronijcke / sullen alle vrome ende verstandige Lesers selue connen oordeelen / wat een groot onderscheyt datter is tusschen dese voorsc. Chronijcke / ende de Chronijcken von Sebastiaen Franck / etc." Philipp Melanchthon, *Chronica Carionis* (Dordt: Jan Canin, 1586), sig. + ij v.

Besides his troubles from intra-Protestant feuding, Melanchthon was also under pressure from Catholic adversaries. By the mid-1550s, Catholicism had started to revive in Germany, and one of Melanchthon's former protégés, Friedrich Staphylus (1512–1564), was among those to return to the Catholic fold. At the Colloquy of Worms in 1557, he attacked the Wittenbergers and especially Melanchthon on fundamental points of doctrine, and Melanchthon remained bitter about the experience for the rest of his life.[147] The struggles of these later years meant that Melanchthon was constantly concerned with theological controversy, both in the present and in the past.

Against this background of religious tensions and publishing competition, Melanchthon began a series of history lectures at Wittenberg in 1555,[148] and he used these sessions to prepare a revised and expanded edition of *Carion's Chronicle*.[149] By 1558, the first fascicle was ready, and on 4 February,

---

147 On the events at Worms, see Benno von Bundschuh, *Das Wormser Religionsgespräch von 1557: unter besonderer Berücksichtigung der kaiserlichen Religionspolitik* (Münster: Aschendorff, 1988). Melanchthon attacked Staphylus in his preface to volume eight of the Wittenberg edition of Luther's German works: "So sind auch die päpstlichen Gotteslästerung und Irrthum also grob, daß sie leichtlich ein jeder Verständiger richten kann, und ist gewißlich wahr, daß die gelehrten Verfolger wider eigen Gewissen die erkannte Wahrheit verfolgen, als nämlich die neuen Scribenten, die itzund den großen Herrn zu gefallen sich herfür thun, und suchen neue Farben, die Irrthum zu schmücken, als in Anglia Polus, in Collen Gropperus, der den Cardinalhut verdient hat, in Oestreich der Cynicus Canisius, in Slesien Staphylus, zu Ingolstadt Georgius Theander, welche, so sie also fortfahren und erkannte Wahrheit mit boshaftiger Sophistery verfolgen, Irrthum und Abgötterey stärken, und das arme Volk an Erkenntniß der Wahrheit zu verhindern nicht uffhören, werden sie Judas Belohnung empfangen." [10 March 1556] CR VIII, 688–689; MBW 7739. On Staphylus, see Ute Mennecke-Haustein, *Conversio ad ecclesiam: der Weg des Friedrich Staphylus zurück zur vortridentinischen katholischen Kirche* (Gütersloh: Gütersloher Verlagshaus Mohn, 2003).

148 "[1555] Coepit dictare latinum Chronicon Carionis, exorsus 13 Julii: Editum postea anno 1558 & 1560." Martin Mylius, *Chronologia scriptorum Philippi Melanchthonis* (Görlitz: Fritschius, 1582), sig. [G6] v. VD16 M 7406. See Emil Clemens Scherer, "Die letzten Vorlesungen Melanchthons über Universalgeschichte," *Historisches Jahrbuch* 47 (1927): 359–366, Scherer includes a discussion of the frequency of the lectures; Samuel Berger, "Melanchthons Vorlesungen über Weltgeschichte," *Theologische Studien und Kritiken: Beiträge zur Theologie und Religionswissenschaft* 70 (1897): 781–790; Münch, "Das Chronicon Carionis Philippicum," 257–258; also Uwe Neddermeyer, "Kaspar Peucer (1525–1602). Melanchthons Universalgeschichtsschreibung," in *Melanchthon in Seinen Schülern*, ed. Heinz Scheible (Wiesbaden: Harrassowitz, 1997), 69–101. On Melanchthon's other history lectures in the 1550s, see Marianne Pade, "A Melanchthonian Commentary to the First Three Books of Thucydides? Cod. Philol. 166, Staats- und Universitätsbibliothek Hamburg," in *Reformation and Latin Literature in Northern Europe*, ed. Inger Ekrem et al. (Oslo: Scandinavian University Press, 1996), 193–206.

149 The *Chronicle* is printed in sections scattered through *Corpus Reformatorum* – Privilegium (12 February 1558) = CR XII, 711; Dedicatory Epistle to Archbishop Sigismund (April 1558) = CR IX, 531–538 [MBW 8600]; Prima Pars Chronici Carionis, Liber Primus & Liber Secundus

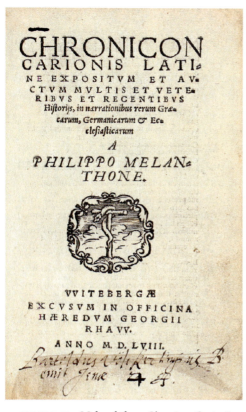 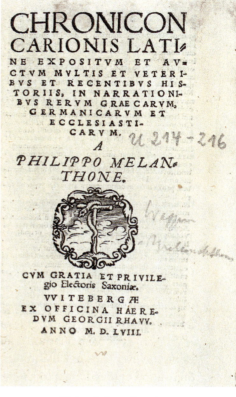

FIGURE 18 Melanchthon, *Chronicon Carionis* (Wittenberg, 1558)
HERZOG AUGUST BIBLIOTHEK WOLFENBÜTTEL: H: YT 39.8° HELMST

FIGURE 19 Melanchthon, *Chronicon Carionis* (Wittenberg, 1558)
HERZOG AUGUST BIBLIOTHEK WOLFENBÜTTEL: S: ALV.: U 214 (1)

Melanchthon wrote to Ulrich Mordeisen, a Saxon official, to request a printing privilege for his work. As Melanchthon explained, Georg Rhau had published the *editio princeps*, so he was requesting that Rhau's heirs receive exclusive rights to the new edition. Melanchthon did not mention his bitter experience with Funck's edition, even though this was undoubtedly a reason for seeking the privilege.[150] On 12 February, the Elector granted the request, and Melanchthon

= CR XII, 712–902; Dedicatory Epistle to Archbishop Sigismund (25 March 1560) = CR IX, 1073–1077 [MBW 9269]; Epigramma de Monarchiis = CR X, 635–636; Secunda Pars Chronici Carionis, Liber Tertius = CR XII, 901–1094.

150 "Ulrico Mordisin, Consiliario Duc. Sax. Elect. S.D. Clarissime vir, et Patrone colende. Quaeso, ut veniam mihi detis toties interpellanti vos. Sed hoc negocium, arbitror, non difficile fore. Libellum Chronicum propter adolescentes retexui, quia certe opus est,

had the Rhau press include the text of the privilege on the title page verso.[151] (This was unusual for a Wittenberg imprint.) The Elector gave the Rhau heirs the rights to the book not only in Latin but also in German for six years, and the printing, as well as the sale of copies printed elsewhere, was strictly forbidden within the lands covered by the Elector's privilege. The *editio princeps* did not advertise the privilege on the title page (Figure 18), but the Rhau press included it on the second edition from 1558 (Figure 19).

In addition to the printing privilege, Melanchthon also tried to protect the new edition by placing his personal seal on the title page. Already in the 1520s, the Wittenbergers had begun to use personal seals, especially Luther's, as an indication of authenticity.[152] In early disputes over reprintings of graphic art, Renaissance artists, most notably Albrecht Dürer, had been unable to win broad legal protection for their images.[153] Nevertheless, they had succeeded in preventing the unauthorized reproduction of personal seals or monograms. This allowed them to distinguish their works from reprints, and it offered a type of "trademark" protection. The Wittenbergers built on this tradition, and it proved effective, in the sense that printers might reprint a text without permission, but they would not reproduce the author's personal seal. As a result, only official Wittenberg editions of *Carion's Chronicle* bear Melanchthon's seal, and even Zöpfel did not infringe on his personal mark.

In April 1558, Melanchthon dedicated this first fascicle of the *Chronicle* covering the events from Creation to Augustus (Part I, Books 1–2) to Archbishop Sigismund of Magdeburg (1538–1566), a bitter enemy of the Flacians[154] and the son of Elector Joachim II, Carion's dedicatee of 1532.[155] (Although Sigismund

---

adolescentes nosse seriem temporum et Monarchiarum. Nec addam historias, quae laedere bonos possint. Editio autem inchoata est in familia Orphanorum Georgii Raw. Haec petit privilegium, ne alii in hac vicinia recudant. Hanc rem vobis commendo, quia scriptrum est: Esto orphano Pater, tunc Deus magis te diliget, quam diliget te Mater tua. Nuper reversus domum, in spexi Cuspiniani historiam de Lothario primo. Is ait, Pruliacum esse Monasterium in Lotharingia. Bene et feliciter valete. Die 4. Februarii. Philippus." CR IX, 443; MBW 8520. See also Diener, "The Magdeburg Centuries," 201–202.

151   Philipp Melanchthon, *Chronicon Carionis Latine Expositvm Et Auctvm Mvltis Et Veteribus Et Recentibus Historijs, in narrationibus rerum Graecarum, Germanicarum & Ecclesiasticarum. A Philippo Melanthone. Witebergæ Excvsvm In Officina Hæredvm Georgii Rhaw. Anno M.D.LVIII.* (Wittenberg: Rhau, 1558), sig. [‡ 1] v. VD16 M 2698.
152   See Haug, "Luthers Bedeutung," 223, 231–232; Gieseke, *Vom Privileg zum Urheberrecht*, 26.
153   See Christopher L.C.E. Witcombe, *Copyright in the Renaissance: Prints and the* Privilegio *in Sixteenth-Century Venice and Rome* (Leiden: Brill, 2004), 81–86.
154   The Flacians had prevented Sigismund from entering his see. See Diener, "The Magdeburg Centuries," 1–36, 192–193. On Sigismund's career, see also ADB 34: 294–297.
155   "Cum autem prima editio Illustrissimo Principi Electori patri tuo dedicata sit, ne transferre munus in aliam familiam videretur, filio dedicare hanc editionem volui, quia patrem ipsum, cui iam historia Ecclesiae et Imperiorum notissima est, scio velle talia iam a filiis

was openly Protestant, Pope Julius III had confirmed his appointment as Archbishop.) Melanchthon explained how the Latin translation of *Carion's Chronicle* had long since spread from a classroom text to a book that was read across Europe. While he praised Hermann Bonnus, Melanchthon nevertheless felt that a new edition was necessary because of the "Germanized Latin" Bonnus had used in his translation.[156] Melanchthon's simple, monocausal explanation for the new edition (to improve the Latin) glossed over the complex series of events that drove him to revisit the *Chronicle*, and it skirted the compelling reasons behind his desire to publish a new edition. Based on the quire signatures of the *editio princeps*, Melanchthon's dedicatory epistle was printed last, and by mid-May, he had started to distribute copies. Although Melanchthon did not rededicate the *Chronicle* to Joachim II, a signed copy addressed to the Elector has survived.[157]

---

legi, et se vivo vos in possessionem doctrinae venire. Cum igitur non dubitem, eum pro sua excellenti sapientia hanc notram inscriptionem probaturum esse, te oro, ut hunc librum accipias, ac non tam meum, quam paternum munus esse cogites, et propter patrem Principem sapientia et virtute exellentem, magis ames, et legas saepius." CR IX, 532. On 1 April 1558, Melanchthon had written another preface addressed to both Elector Joachim II and Archbishop Sigismund, as well as the other margraves of Brandenburg, for a brief verse history of the Hohenzollerns – Johannes Schosser, *Historia De Origine Et Incrementis Illvstrissimae Et Inclytae Familiae Marchionvm Brandeburgensium, Elegiaco carmine illustrata, à Iohanne Schossero Poëta Laureato. Cum praefatione Philippi Melanthonis* (Wittenberg: Rhau, 1558). VD16 S 3981. The preface summarizes many of the themes that Melanchthon would address in *Carion's Chronicle* and it also echoes some of his comments from his *Stadtgeschichte* of Wittenberg (CR IX, 582–587; MBW 8686), particularly the question of legitimate political order, "Sed veram esse agnoscamus Danielis concionem, Deus transfert regna et stabilit. Et Psalmus inquit: Nisi Dominus custodierit civitatem, frustra vigilat, qui custodit eam. Firmissime igitur statuamus, Deum vere custodem esse legitimae societatis hominum, et politicum ordinem propter voluntatem Dei amemus, veneremur, et grati celebremus hanc Dei praesentiam." CR IX, 512–513; MBW 8572.

156 "Excelluit ingenio, eruditione, consilio et virtute Hermannus Bonnus, qui in inclyta urbe Lubeca et doctrinae studia rexit, et Evangelium docuit. Is ante annos viginti Germanicum Libellum, cui titulus est Chronicon Carionis, ut adolescentia invitaretur ad historiarum lectionem, et illo compendio nonnihil adiuvaretur, in quo Monarchiarum seriem, et temporum collationem in praecipuis Ecclesiae, veteris Graeciae, et Romae negotiis probavit, latine interpretatus est. Eam interpretationem cum postea viderem non solum in manibus esse adolescentum, sed etiam vagari per exteras nationes, retexendam esse iudicavi, non tam ut augerem, (etsi enim quaedam addidi, tamen compendii modus servandus est), quam ut phrasin Germanicam, quam interpres suo quodam consilio studiosius retinuerat, cum quidem facundus et disertus esset, propter adolescentes et exteros mutarem. Nec alia causa fuit, cur hunc laborem susceperim. Ut enim lectio ametur intelligi orationem oportet." CR IX, 531–532; MBW 8600; Scheible, *Die Anfänge der reformatorischen Geschichtsschreibung*, 26–33.

157 The copy sent to Elector Joachim II is now Erlangen, Universitätsbibliothek: H62/CIM.F 7[1. For other recipients, Melanchthon handwrote his poem "De Monarchiis" on the flyleaf, for example – Atlanta, Emory University Pitts Theology Library: 1558 MELA A.

In the new edition, Melanchthon followed the original outline and structure of the Carion-Melanchthon *Chronicle*. As he explained in a letter to Konrad Heresbach (1496–1576), a princely tutor in Jülich-Cleves-Berg, he simply lacked the strength to write an entirely new work, so he expanded and revised the existing narrative.[158] In fact, Melanchthon seems to have been generally dissatisfied with the revised *Chronicle*. In a letter to Abdias Prätorius (1524–1573), a professor at Frankfurt an der Oder, Melanchthon commented that he had lacked the time to carry out proper revisions, and the final version was more ragged (*squallidior*) than he would have liked. Even so, he had determined to add the history of the subsequent periods, should he live that long.[159] Likewise, in a letter to David Chytraeus (1530–1600), a professor at Rostock, Melanchthon confessed that he had not been able to refine (*perpolire*) the text as thoroughly as he had intended.[160] Judging from the revised *Chronicle* itself, Melanchthon's modesty was not entirely false. As a whole, the printed text has a not-quite-finished character to it.

Once the *Chronicle* was published that spring, Melanchthon immediately began to send copies across Europe, and from its frequent appearance in his correspondence, it is clear that he was actively promoting the new edition, despite his own dissatisfaction with the final text.[161] At Wittenberg, he also began to lecture on the newly printed fascicle. This is the first time that a history professor is known to have taught his own printed textbook, and based

---

158　Melanchthon's letter is dated 18 November 1558: "De Chronico libello non libet scribere, quia non ratiocinor me ad illas recentiores historias perventurum esse. Donec vivo adolescentiae proponi curabo res utiles. Et haec ipsa χρονολογικά repeto, ut invitem plures ad legendas veteres historias. Nam novum et integrum opus condere, non est mearum virium. Scis sapientiae et eloquentiae non mediocris esse vel exiguam historiam scribere, quid de illa amplitudine integrae historiae, qualis est Polybii, non multorum annorum cogitare possumus? sed hoc omitto." CR IX, 976; MBW 8780.

159　"De chronicis quae scribis, ominari vos εὔφημα velim. Si vivam, addam seqentium temporum historias, et partem, quam edidi, probari tibi valde opto. Squallidior est quam velim, quia scis mihi tempus deesse ad emendationem. Sed institui, ut adolescentes invitentur ad veterum lectionem." CR IX, 560; MBW 8628.

160　"Te tamen velim placatorem nobis esse, apud inclytum Principem Ducem Iohannem Albertum, teque oro ut libellum χρονολογικὸν, quem nunc ad te mitto, ei exhibeas. Tibi etiam exemplum mitto, ac voluntatem meam vobis probari opto. Nam opus tenue esse scio et in his aerumnia et hac negociorum confusione, ne possum quidem perpolire ea quae instituo." CR IX, 564–565; MBW 8641.

161　MBW 8609 [Berlin, 8 May 1558]; MBW 8619 [Bremen, 16 May 1558]; MBW 8622 [Breslau, 18 May 1558]; MBW 8628 [Frankfurt an der Oder, 24 May 1558]; MBW 8631 [Breslau, 29 May 1558]; MBW 8637 [Frankfurt an der Oder, 1 June 1558]; MBW 8641 [Rostock (Chytraeus), 5 June 1558]; MBW 8643 [Frankfurt an der Oder, 7 June 1558]; MBW 8649 [Frankfurt an der Oder, 13 June 1558 – Melanchthon asks if the copies sent to Frankfurt have been received]; MBW 8780 [Lorward, 18 November 1558 – discussion of the *Chronicle's* contents]; MBW 9222 [Zossen, 5 February 1560].

on the student notes that survive from these lectures, it is possible to chart Melanchthon's progress through this fascicle and then into the new material for Book 3. The lectures also indicate that in the classroom Melanchthon drew on more than the printed sources available to him in Wittenberg, and he referred at times to monuments and Roman ruins in Germany, as well as coins and tomb inscriptions.[162] By mid-March of 1560, he had finished the material for the second fascicle, which covered the period from Augustus to Charlemagne (Part II, Book 3).

On 25 March 1560, Melanchthon wrote a second dedicatory epistle to Archbishop Sigismund, and he remarked that writing history is like a long journey, and he had become exhausted.[163] He freely admitted that he had preferred the material for the 1558 fascicle – based as it was on Scripture and his beloved classical authors, such as Xenophon – and he expressed the sentiment of many Italian humanists when he asked: "But after Caesar Augustus, except for the beginnings of the Christian Church, what is there amidst the rest that could possibly delight the reader?"[164] Based on the quire signatures, the dedicatory

---

162   See Scherer, "Die letzten Vorlesungen Melanchthons," 362–364. In 1534, Melanchthon had written the preface to a collection of inscriptions, CR II, 697–698; MBW 1396. While the opportunities to engage in antiquarian endeavours were limited in Wittenberg, Melanchton nevertheless published a short treatise on numismatics and measures already in 1529. According to the editors of CR this text was first published at Wittenberg in 1529 as a folio size chart. (A copy was still in existence at the University of Leipzig Library in the nineteenth century.) A specific title is lacking, but it has the inscription: *Nomina mensuarum. Vocabula rei numariae. Auctore Philipp Melanchthone Wittembergae per Nicol. Schirl. 1529* (CR XX, 413–414). It was converted to book format already that year (VD16 M 4366). For the complete text, see CR XX, 413–424. See also Hans Volz, "Melanchthons Anteil an der Lutherbibel," *Archiv für Reformationsgeschichte* 45 (1954): 208 n. 65. In the course of his lectures, Melanchthon mentioned coins in the possession of the Saxon princes as well as his own collection. See Scherer, "Die letzten Vorlesungen Melanchthons," 363–364. On collecting in Saxony more generally, see Hilda Lietzmann, "Der kaiserliche Antiquar Jacopo Strada und Kurfürst August von Sachsen," *Zeitschrift für Kunstgeschichte* 60 (1997): 377–399. Previous Electors has also been keenly interested in history, see for example the discussion between Elector Johann Frederick and Spalatin over his *Chronicle* – Irmgard Höss, *Georg Spalatin, 1484–1545: Ein Leben in der Zeit des Humanismus und der Reformation* (Weimar: Böhlau, 1989), 408–412.

163   "Ego quidem bono studio hoc Compendium institui, sed fateor, quod res est: Ut in longo itinere, ita in hoc opere quo longius progressus sum, eo magis defatigatus sum. Initia Mundi et Imperiorum habent et res splendidiores et scriptores meliores." CR IX, 1074; MBW 9269.

164   "Et quid dulcius est lectione scriptorum, ex quibus illorum Historiae excerpendae fuerunt, Prophetarum, deinde Herodoti, Thucydidis, Xenophontis, Diodori, Livii, Iulii. At post Augustum praeter initia Ecclesiae Christi, quid in caeteris est, quod delectare legentem possit?" CR IX, 1074.

epistle again appeared last, and by 27 March, Melanchthon could send the finished book off with a cover letter to Frankfurt an der Oder.

As he had done for the first fascicle, Melanchthon distributed Book 3 widely[165] to his eager followers.[166] At Wittenberg, Melanchthon lectured on the material for Book 4 of the *Chronicle* for about two weeks. By early April, however, he had fallen ill, and he never recovered. His son-in-law, Caspar Peucer, cared for him in those last days, but on 19 April 1560, after forty years at Wittenberg, Melanchthon died quietly in bed. His followers held large and well-attended funeral ceremonies, and they buried him in the Castle Church opposite Luther.[167] For almost thirty years, Melanchthon had worked intermittently on *Carion's Chronicle*. The project had begun with Carion's request for editorial assistance in 1531, and it continued to the last days of Melanchthon's life. By the end, Melanchthon treated the *Chronicle* as his own, and as one of the most important publications of his long career.

11   Caspar Peucer

After Melanchthon's death, the faculty at Wittenberg approached Elector August of Saxony to fund a new professor to continue Melanchthon's history lectures. Their first choice was Hubert Languet (1518–1581), who had been associated with Wittenberg since 1539. Languet was born in France, and the reading of Melanchthon's *Loci* was crucial to his conversion to Protestantism.[168] During the 1540s and 1550s, he travelled widely, sometimes combining the journeys with manuscript hunting for Melanchthon, and on occasion he spent the winter in Wittenberg.[169] Eventually, he became a diplomat, and spy, for the Saxon princes, and he later joined the court of Emperor Maximilian II. From the perspective of the faculty, Languet was a perfect candidate for the history post, but attempts to establish a new position were dropped when the Elector refused to provide funding.[170] After this initial failure, the faculty decided to

---

165   MBW 9272 [Frankfurt an der Oder, 27 March 1560]; MBW 9275 [Hamburg, 29 March 1560]; MBW 9285 [Nuremberg, 4 April 1560]; MBW 9290 [Olmütz, 7 April 1560]; MBW 9293 [Dessau, 12 April 1560].
166   See MBW 8947.4 [6 May 1559]; MBW 8995 [7 July 1559].
167   For the official description, see CR X, 250–251, and the German translation at CR X, 290–293; as well as the section "Scripta Quaedam Ad Vitam Et Obitum Melanthonis Spectantia," in CR X, 173–316.
168   On Languet, see ADB 17: 692–694. See also Diener, "The Magdeburg Centuries."
169   See CR VIII, 490–491, MBW 7510; CR VIII, 491–492; CR VIII, 765, MBW 7502.
170   Scherer, *Geschichte und Kirchengeschichte*, 53; Eugen Rambeau, "Über die Geschichtswissenschaft an der Universität Wittenberg," in *450 Jahre Martin-Luther-Universität Halle-Wittenberg* (Halle: [s.n.], 1953), vol. 1, 260.

turn the lectures over to Caspar Peucer (1525–1602), Melanchthon's son-in-law, physician, and companion in his final years. Since Peucer was already on the faculty, the lectures were continued without additional cost.

Peucer had been born in 1525 at Bautzen, a town to the east of Electoral Saxony in Upper Lusatia.[171] Bautzen was, and remains, populated by the Sorbs, a Slavic ethnic group with its own language. Peucer studied at Bautzen and then at Goldberg in Upper Silesia, where Valentin Friedland Trozendorf (1490–1566), one of Melanchthon's students, became his mentor and arranged for him to continue to Wittenberg in 1540. Peucer was fifteen years old when he arrived, and through Friedland's recommendation, he was able to lodge in Melanchthon's house. After studying in the preparatory school, he enrolled at the university in 1543, and received his master's degree in 1545. During the Schmalkaldic War, Peucer fled to Frankfurt an der Oder, where he studied medicine. Melanchthon returned to Wittenberg already in the summer of 1547, and the university officially re-opened the following year. Peucer also returned and joined the arts faculty.[172] In 1550, he married Melanchthon's youngest daughter, Magdalena (1531–1576). They first lived in Melanchthon's house and then in a house erected in the back garden.

During the 1550s, Peucer's career advanced rapidly. He published several important works on mathematics, astronomy and divination,[173] and in 1554, he succeeded Erasmus Reinhold (1511–1553) as professor of "higher mathematics." In these years, Peucer also accompanied Melanchthon on many of his

---

[171] For Peucer, I have relied on Ernst Ludwig Theodor Henke, *Caspar Peucer und Nicolaus Krell: Zur Geschichte des Lutherthums und der Union am Ende des 16. Jahrhunderts* (Marburg: Elwert, 1865); Robert Kolb, *Caspar Peucer's Library: Portrait of a Wittenberg Professor of the Mid-Sixteenth Century* (St. Louis: Center for Reformation Research, 1976); Uwe Koch et al., *Zwischen Katheder, Thron und Kerker: Leben und Werk des Humanisten Caspar Peucer, 1525–1602* (Bautzen: Domowina-Verlag [Stadtmuseum Bautzen], 2002); Hans-Peter Hasse and Günther Wartenberg, eds., *Caspar Peucer (1525–1602): Wissenschaft, Glaube und Politik im konfessionellen Zeitalter* (Leipzig: Evangelische Verlagsanstalt, 2004); Martin Roebel, "Humanistische Medizin und Kryptocalvinismus: Leben und medizinisches Werk des Wittenberger Medizinprofessors Caspar Peucer (1525–1602)" (Ph.D. diss., Ruprecht-Karls-Universität Heidelberg, 2004); and Claudia Brosseder, *Im Bann der Sterne: Caspar Peucer, Philipp Melanchthon und andere Wittenberger Astrologen* (Berlin: Akademie Verlag, 2004).

[172] For Peucer's early education, see especially Ulrike Ludwig, "Caspar Peucer als Professor an der Artistenfakultät der Universität Wittenberg," in *Caspar Peucer (1525–1602): Wissenschaft, Glaube und Politik im konfessionellen Zeitalter*, ed. Hans-Peter Hasse and Günther Wartenberg (Leipzig: Evangelische Verlagsanstalt, 2004), 34–38.

[173] *De dimensione terrae* (1550), *Elementa doctrinae de circulis coelestibus, et primo motu* (1551), *Commentarius de praecipuis divinationum generibus* ([1550?]/1553), *Logistice astronomica* (1556). See the bibliography in Hasse, *Caspar Peucer (1525–1602)*, 327–368.

journeys, including the ill-fated trip to the colloquy at Worms in 1557.[174] In 1560, the year Melanchthon died, Peucer received his doctorate in medicine, joined the medical faculty and become rector of the university.[175]

By the early 1560s, Peucer had become a dominant figure in Wittenberg, and he started to attract the attention of the Electoral Court.[176] In 1553, after the death of his brother Moritz, Duke August (r. 1553–1586) became Elector of Saxony; and by the mid-1560s, Peucer frequented the court as a trusted advisor. At the Diet of Augsburg in 1566, Emperor Maximilian II officially invested August with the Electoral dignity; and a few weeks later he also ennobled Peucer and his family.[177] In 1570, August made Peucer his personal physician, and the following year, he had Peucer stand as baptismal sponsor for his son Adolf. Peucer also became a favourite of the Elector's wife, Anna (1532–1585), a Danish royal princess, who was especially interested in medicine.[178]

After Melanchthon's death in 1560, the change in generations marked a change in perspective. The lingering resentment from the Interims plagued Melanchthon's later years, and other intra-Protestant doctrinal conflicts added to his struggles with Flacius and the "gnesio-Lutherans." With Melanchthon's passing, the terms of debate shifted, as his followers, the Philippists, renewed efforts to cultivate Protestant ecumenism and political solidarity, especially with the Calvinists in France and South Germany. They believed that doctrinal agreement, or at least lack of disagreement, between Wittenberg and Geneva would allow for a united political front, especially in France, against the rising tide of Catholicism. In response to these efforts, the gnesio-Lutherans branded the Philippists as crypto-Calvinists. During the 1560s, Saxon foreign policy was influenced by the Philippist perspective, but this increasingly led to tension between loyalty to the Hapsburg Emperor and a desire to cultivate closer religious and political ties with other Protestants. For the moment,

---

174   See Nicole Kuropka, "Caspar Peucer und Philipp Melanchthon: Biographische Einblicke in eine reformatorische Gelehrtenfreundschaft," in *Caspar Peucer (1525–1602): Wissenschaft, Glaube und Politik im konfessionellen Zeitalter*, ed. Hans-Peter Hasse and Günther Wartenberg (Leipzig: Evangelische Verlagsanstalt, 2004), 247–248.

175   On Peucer's rapid advance, see Ludwig, "Caspar Peucer als Professor," 37–38.

176   On Electoral Saxony during these decades, see generally Harald Marx and Eckhard Kluth, eds., *Glaube & Macht: Sachsen im Europa der Reformationszeit* (Dresden: Sandstein, 2004). For Peucer's role in Saxon politics, see the essays in Koch, *Zwischen Katheder, Thron und Kerker*, and Hasse, *Caspar Peucer (1525–1602)*.

177   Koch, *Zwischen Katheder, Thron und Kerker*, 122–123.

178   See Martin Roebel, "Caspar Peucer als Humanist und Mediziner," in *Caspar Peucer (1525–1602): Wissenschaft, Glaube und Politik im konfessionellen Zeitalter*, ed. Hans-Peter Hasse and Günther Wartenberg (Leipzig: Evangelische Verlagsanstalt, 2004), 51–73.

however, the Philippist party was clearly in ascendance both at court and at Wittenberg.[179]

12 Peucer and the *Chronicle*

As Peucer continued Melanchthon's history lectures, he also prepared the remaining portions of the *Chronicle* for publication.[180] He kept to the roughly two-year pace that Melanchthon had set with his instalments; and in 1562, he published the third fascicle on the events from Charlemagne to Frederick II (Part III, Book 4). Following Melanchthon, Peucer dedicated the new book to Archbishop Sigismund, with a letter dated 21 February 1562. There, he recounted the story of Apelles, the painter of Antiquity, who had such skill that when his creations were partially destroyed or left incomplete, no one could make them whole again. Peucer compared that situation to his own as he continued *Carion's Chronicle*, which Melanchthon had left unfinished at his death.[181]

In addition to revising the text, for this third fascicle Peucer prepared *A Table Showing in What Order the Series of Histories of the World are to be Read and Understood*.[182] The *Tabella* was a landmark in the systematization of historical thought, and its broad diffusion had a pervasive influence on discussions

---

179 See generally Kolb, "Dynamics of Party Conflict," D1289-D1305; and Jens Bruning, "Caspar Peucer und Kurfürst August: Grundlinien kursächsischer Reichs- und Konfessionspolitik nach dem Augsburger Religionsfrieden (1555–1586)," in *Caspar Peucer (1525–1602): Wissenschaft, Glaube und Politik im konfessionellen Zeitalter*, ed. Hans-Peter Hasse and Günther Wartenberg (Leipzig: Evangelische Verlagsanstalt, 2004), 157–174. The engagement with South German Calvinists included the marriage in 1570 of the Elector's daughter Elizabeth (1552–1590) to Palsgrave Johann Casimir (1543–1592), the son of the Elector Palatine, Frederick III (1515–1576). On Johann Casimir, see ADB 14: 307–314; and for Elizabeth, see ADB 6: 7–8. The Elector Palatine was openly Calvinist, rather than Lutheran, and had begun to follow an aggressive foreign policy. See generally, Claus Peter Clasen, *The Palatinate in European History 1555–1618* (Oxford: Blackwell, 1966).

180 On these lectures see Uwe Neddermeyer, "Kaspar Peucer (1525–1602). Melanchthons Universalgeschichtsschreibung," in *Melanchthon in Seinen Schülern*, ed. Heinz Scheible (Wiesbaden: Harrassowitz, 1997), 74–100; and Hildegard Ziegler, *Chronicon Carionis: ein Beitrag zur Geschichtschreibung des 16. Jahrhunderts* (Halle a.S: Niemeyer, 1898), 48. Student notes from these lectures are found in Wrocław – Wrocław, Biblioteka Uniwersytecka: Rehdigeriana 1330 – Caspar Peucer, annotationes in chronica Melanchthonis. (I have not consulted the manuscript in person.)

181 Peucer, *Chronicon Carionis* (Wittenberg, 1580), 291.

182 "TABELLA OSTENDENS QVO ORDINE LEGENDA ET COGNOSCENDA SIT SERIES HISTORIARVM MVNDI. DEDICATA SCHOLASTICIS ACADEMIAE WITEBERGENSIS." Peucer, *Chronicon Carionis* (Wittenberg, 1580), *Tabella* opposite sig. A r. First published in Peucer, *Tertia Pars Chronici Carionis* (Wittenberg: Seitz, 1562), *Tabella* opposite sig. [q 8] v.

of historical method.[183] Peucer divided histories into universal and particular, and then again into political and ecclesiastical. Nevertheless, the division between political and ecclesiastical was a practical matter rather than a firm demarcation, and Peucer emphasized interconnectedness:

> Ecclesiastical Histories deal especially with Church matters, and yet the affairs of the Monarchies and kingdoms are interwoven, which happens of necessity, since the Church is not able to exist without political institutions, and sometimes it is defended by empires, but indeed sometimes it is more closely pressed [by them].[184]

As Peucer subdivided histories from general to more specific categories, he also indicated the relevant sources for each section of the *Chronicle*. Furthermore, although he added the chart in 1562, Peucer already included the framework and source indications for the remaining material from Frederick II to the sixteenth century. Thus, it is clear that from early on Peucer had developed a comprehensive plan for revising the *Chronicle*. Peucer dedicated the *Tabella* to the "Scholars of the University of Wittenberg," in recognition of the collaborative nature of the project (Figure 20).

By 1565, Peucer was ready to publish the final sections of the *Chronicle*, and he continued the shift away from Brandenburg to Saxony by dedicating this fourth fascicle (Part III [IV], Book 5) to Elector August. The letter preface is dated 31 October, forty-eight years after Luther posted the *Ninety-Five Theses*. The dating is itself symptomatic of the ways that Peucer used his revisions to develop the historical background to the Reformation.[185]

183   On Peucer's *Tabella*, see Adalbert Klempt, *Die Säkularisierung der universalhistorischen Auffassung: zum Wandel des Geschichtsdenkens im 16. und 17. Jahrhundert* (Göttingen: Musterschmidt, 1960), 35–40. Bartholomaeus Keckermann, one of the most important philosophers of the early seventeenth century, included excerpts from Peucer's chart for analysis in his *ars historica*. See Bartholomaeus Keckermann, *Operum Omnium* (Geneva: Peter Aubert, 1614), vol. 2, col. 1345–1354.

184   "[Historiae sunt:] Aut vniuersales, quæ complectantur res Ecclesiæ & Monarchiaru[m], sunt ergo: Aut Ecclesiasticæ, quæ praecipuè tractant res Ecclesiasticas, etsi Monarchiarum & regnorum negocia miscent, quod fieri necesse est, cum Ecclesia non poßit esse sine politiis, & interdum ab imperiis defendatur, interdum & quidem crebrius prematur. Est autem historia Ecclesiæ prima & antiquißima, quæ facilius comprehenditur distinctis temporibus. Commodissima distinctio sumitur ex notissimo dicto domus Heliæ. Aut Politicae, quæ Imperiorum initia, constitutiones, gubernationes et mutationes exponunt. Sunt autem ex prædictionibus Danielis Monarchiæ quatuor:..." Peucer, *Chronicon Carionis* (Wittenberg, 1580), *Tabella* opposite sig. A r.

185   "Bene & foeliciter valeat Celsit: tua. Datae Witebergae pridie Calend: Nouemb: Anno 1565. Hoc die ante annos octo & quadraginta Lutherus Witebergae propositis thematibus ad

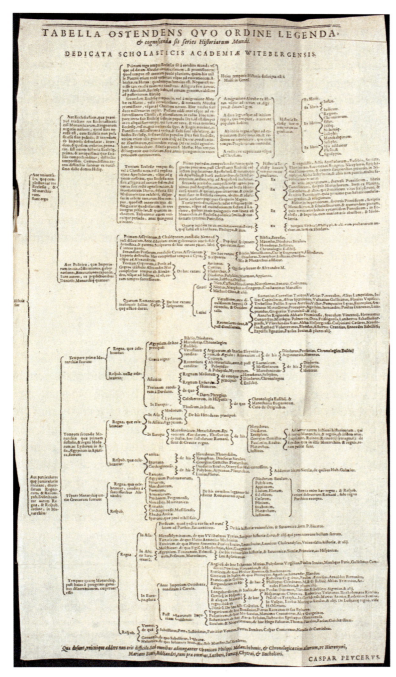

FIGURE 20 Peucer, *Chronicon Carionis* (Geneva, 1617), *Tabella*
HERZOG AUGUST BIBLIOTHEK WOLFENBÜTTEL: H: T 259.8° HELMST

In this fascicle, Peucer also acknowledged receiving extensive help from Hubert Languet and Georg Sigismund Seld (1516–1565), the Imperial Vice-Chancellor. Seld's involvement is particularly noteworthy, because it demonstrates the semi-official character of the *Chronicle* as an Imperial response to pro-papal historiography. In 1558, Seld had been responsible for drafting the legal opinion requested by the Hapsburgs when the pope refused to recognize the abdication of Charles V and the elevation of his brother Ferdinand to the Imperial throne. The extent of Seld's contribution is not entirely clear, but he presumably believed that Peucer's revised narrative would be a valuable tool in the papal-Imperial struggles that marked his own career.[186]

Melanchthon and Peucer had together taken a decade to rewrite *Carion's Chronicle*. If Melanchthon's aim was to drive the Zöpfel editions out of the marketplace, his strategy of producing a new edition was (initially) successful. The presses in Frankfurt and Basel stopped printing the old Carion-Melanchthon *Chronicle* and quickly switched to the new Wittenberg fascicles.

13 Wittenberg and Frankfurt

After David Zöpfel's death in 1563, his printing house was taken over by Sigmund Feyerabend (1528–1590), one of the most famous German publishers of the sixteenth century.[187] Feyerabend was based in Frankfurt am Main, and he published in a wide range of fields. After 1560, he had become especially well known for his Luther Bibles, which featured illustrations by Jost Amman and Vergil Solis, two of the leading graphic artists in Germany. Luther Bibles were among the most lucrative publications in the book trade, and the Wittenberg publishers were dismayed by Feyerabend's entry into the market.[188] In the early 1560s, Feyerabend also published Melanchthon's collection of theological works, the *Corpus Doctrinae*.

Before his death, Melanchthon had arranged for a new German translation of *Carion's Chronicle*, which was to be made after the publication of each Latin fascicle. Initially, he approached Justus Menius (1499–1558) to make the translations, since Menius was a close friend, and he had frequently translated

---

valuas templi, quod arci contiguum est, coepit oppugnare indulgentias Pontificum Romanorum, & restituere doctrinam puriorem, quam vt conseruet Deus & semper sibi inter nos colligat Ecclesiam celebraturam ipsum in tota aeternitate, ardentibus votis precor." Peucer, *Chronicon Carionis* (Wittenberg, 1580), 490.

186 For Seld, I rely on ADB 33: 673–679.
187 On Feyerabend, see Pallmann, *Sigmund Feyerabend*.
188 Pallmann, *Sigmund Feyerabend*, 10–11.

works by both Luther and Melanchthon.[189] Death intervened, however, and took Menius on 11 August 1558. Melanchthon then turned to Justus's son, Eusebius Menius (b. 1527), who had married Melanchthon's granddaughter, Anna Sabinus, on 27 June 1558.[190]

The Rhau press published the first German fascicle in August 1560. Eusebius again presented the German translation to Archbishop Sigismund, and Georg Major wrote a lengthy preface.[191] Eusebius ultimately translated the first three fascicles (Parts I–III, Books 1–4) of the new Latin edition into German, dedicating each to Archbishop Sigismund. The German fascicles were all published by the Rhau press at Wittenberg, and the title pages of 1560 and 1562 bear the Saxon privilege.[192] These both fell within the six years of original rights.

189   On Menius, see ADB 21: 354–356; and TRE 22: 439–442 for current bibliography.
190   Eusebius explains these circumstances in his letter to the Archbishop, and he remarks that he has now seen the death of both of his fathers: "Vnd demnach vor zweien Jaren mein lieber Vater Er Justus Menius mit vorwissen vnd bewilligung des Herrn Philippi (beide heiliger gedechtnis) Das erste teil dieser Chronica zu verdeudschen angefangen hatte / vnd aber vnser lieber Gott in nach seinem veterlichen willen / bald im anfang solcher arbeit / vnuersehens aus diesem Jamerthal zu sich in sein ewiges Reich abforderte / Als hat mein geliebter Vater vnd Praeceptor D. Philippvs nachmals solche arbeit mir bevohlen vnd aufferlegt / mit dem veterlichen erbieten / das er selber alles vbersehen / vnd seinem hohen verstand nach / wo er es von nöten achten würde / bessern vnd corrigieren wolte. Bin derwegen nicht aus gelt oder ehrgeitz / zu solchem vorhaben bewogen worden / sondern dieweil ich mich schüldig erkandt / meinem lieben Vater vnd Praeceptori / als dem ich nach Gott gleich meinem leiblichen Eltern alle reuerentz vnd gehorsam pflichtig war / auch in dem zu gehorsam." Melanchthon, *Chronica Carionis* (Wittenberg: Rhau, 1560), sig. [Biij] v – [Biiij] r.
191   Major focused on the utility of the *Chronicle*: "Derwegen ich für nötig vnd nützlich geachtet / hiervon den Christlichen Leser / vnd in sonderheit de liebe deudsche Kirchen / auffs aller kürtzest zu erinnern / welcher zu nutz vnd trost / solch Chronicken / so zuuor im Latein ausgangen ist / nu auch verdeudscht ausgehet / damit die Deudsche Kirche dieses schönen vnd herrlichen wercks / des Herrn Philippi / welchs dann seiner letzten / weisesten / nötigesten vnd nützlichsten Schrifft eine ist / nicht beraubt were / vnd obgemelte beide stück / nemlich von der Kirchen Gottes / vnd der Regiment pflantzung / affnemen / regierung / erhaltung vnd verendrung / mit so viel weisen vnd nötigen erinnerung selbs lesen vnd betrachten köndte / vnd es nicht allein den Gelehrten / sondern auch allen gemeinen leuten vnd Hausuetern in Deudschlandt gemein vnd bekandt würde." Melanchthon, *Chronica Carionis* (Wittenberg, 1560), sig. [Ciiij] v – D r.
192   The dedication to the second German fascicle (Secunda Pars, Liber Tertius) is dated as "Datum Wittemberg / Anno 1562. den 21 Aprilis / an welchem tag die Stadt Rom fur 2313. jaren zu bawen angefangen worden." Melanchthon, *Der Ander Teil der Chronica Carionis* (Wittenberg: Rhau, 1562), sig. [(.)iiii] v. VD16 M 2724. The dedication copy from Menius to Archbishop Sigismund of this second fascicle (1562) is still found in Berlin. Menius wrote, "Reuerrendissimo praesuli et illustrissimo Principi ac Domino, Domino Sigismundo Archiepiscopo Magdeburgensi, primati Germaniae, Administratori Halberstatensi, Marchioni Brandeburgensi, Duci Pomeraniae Stetini Cassubiorum, Vandalorum, et in

In 1564, the Rhau press published the third German fascicle (Part III, Book 4), but without the privilege, since by then it had expired.¹⁹³ In contrast to the Latin fascicles, which were quickly reprinted in other cities, the individual German fascicles were only published in Wittenberg.

In 1566, Feyerabend published a new edition of *Carion's Chronicle* at Frankfurt. In an introductory note, he claimed that "friends" had requested a German folio edition, since this would be preferable to the quarto fascicles published at Wittenberg.¹⁹⁴ By that time, Eusebius Menius had translated the first three

---

Silesia Crosnae, Burggrauio Noribergensi & Principi Rugiae & Domino suo suo ac principi elementissimo hunc librum humiliter offert seq[ue] ipsum submisse commendat. Humilis seruus, Eusebius Menius." Berlin, Staatsbibliothek zu Berlin Preußischer Kulturbesitz: 4" Libri impr. rari 44.

193   The dedication to the third German fascicle (Tertia Pars, Liber Quartus) is dated as "Geben zu Wittemberg den 25. tag des Hebstmonds / im Jar 1564." [= 25 September 1564] Melanchthon, *Der Dritte Teil der Chronica Carionis* (Wittenberg: Rhau, 1564), sig. cij r. VD16 P 1966. Both this printing (VD16 P 1966) and the printing of 1565 (VD16 P 1967) lack the privilege on the title page or in the colophon.

194   "An den guthertzigen wolmeynenden Leser. Nachdem das fürtreffliche herzliche werck der Chronick Carionis / wie es von Herrn Philippo Melanthone / vnd D. Casparo Peucero Latine beschrieben / von M. Eusebio Menio aber verdeutscht / stückweise nach einander getruckt / vnd in etliche Theil in der quarta gattirt worden / Also das deren Theil etliche nicht einem jeden angenem / vnnd so man die gleich alle hat / doch nicht in ein Buch zusammen einbinden kan / Bin ich von vielen wolmeynenden Herrn vnd Freunden jetzt vielmal ernstlich ersucht vnd auffs höchste gebeten / Das ich doch ihnen vnd andern günstigen Lesern zu sonderem dienst vnd wolgefallen / gemeldte Theil in ein Corpus / vnd in Folio zusammen trucken wolte / auff das allerfleissigst vnd Correct / Damit mans ordenlich bey einander finden vnd in einem Buch / wie sie der Jarzal nach eins auff das ander folgen / ohn alle zerrückung oder hinderniß ablesen vnd zur hand haben möchte. Dieweil aber auch gedachte Chronick von jren Authoren noch nicht gäntzlich vollendet / Vnd sich aber in den nechst verlauffenen Jaren viel mercklicher gedenckwiriger sachen allenthalben zugetragen / dauon mancher auch gern etwas gewisses erkündigen / vnd zum wenigsten ein kurtze anzeigung darauß verstünde / Haben obgedachte liebe Herrn vnd Freunde gleich so streng bey mir angehalten vnd getrieben / Ich wolte solchem auch rath suchen / vnd ernante Chronick vollends biß auff dieses gegenwertige Jar außstrecken lassen / welches ich auffs fleissigst (so es müglich) hab fürbracht.

Dieweil ich denn solcher lieben Herren vnd Freunde vielfeltiges ersuchen vnd bitte / gantz guthertzig vnd vielen Menschen vberauß nüntzlich vnd dienstlich / Habe ich (der ich ohne das weyß Gott viel mehr jedermeniglich zu seinem mercklichen guten zuwillfaren / denn meinen eigenen genieß oder nutzen in solchem oder anderem dergleichen zu suchen jeder zeit beflissen /) jnen gewillfaret / vnd die obbemelten Theil / wie sie vorhin besonders von einander getruckt / in diese Form / wie du es / Günstiger lieber Leser hie vor augen sihest / eincorporiren / vnd die Histori biß auff dieses Jar / auß glaubwirdigen gewissen Berichten vnd gründen erweitern / sampt einem ordentlichen Register (bey ein jedes Theil besonders hinzugethan) vollnziehen lassen. Welchen fleiß / ernst vnd vnkosten dir vnd vielgedachten meinen lieben Herren vnd Freunden zu dienst

fascicles of the revised *Chronicle*, and Feyerabend reset this material in folio format. The last Latin fascicle of 1565 had not yet been translated, so Feyerabend made a decision that would prove costly and almost ruinous. For the period after Frederick II, he reproduced the material in Zöpfel's 1558 *Chronicle* with an extension to 1565. Thus, the edition was a hybrid of the Carion-Melanchthon-Funck and Melanchthon-Peucer *Chronicles*. Through the Frankfurt printing lineage of Cyriakus Jacob, David Zöpfel and Sigmund Feyerabend, the form of *Carion's Chronicle* that the Wittenbergers had sought to suppress was again presented to the public.[195]

At the Leipzig book fair of 1568, Peucer discovered the new Frankfurt edition, which was being sold by Simon Hütter, one of Feyerabend's business partners. To Peucer's dismay, not only had Feyerabend resurrected the offensive remarks against Elector Joachim II, he had also changed the title page so Peucer himself, rather than Funck, was presented as the author of the *Continuation* (Figure 21). Peucer was furious at the misattribution, and he reacted swiftly. In 1566, he had obtained an Imperial privilege, in addition to the Saxon one, and he used both to attack Feyerabend and Hütter. Once he learned of the Frankfurt edition, Peucer lodged a complaint with the Elector of Saxony. On 7 January 1568, the Elector ordered the confiscation of all unauthorized copies of the *Chronicle* found at Leipzig.[196] Peucer, however, managed to have all of Hütter's bookstocks in Leipzig impounded, and he sought damages.[197] Based on the Imperial privilege, Peucer also tried to proceed against Feyerabend in Frankfurt, but the city fathers did not accede to his request as readily as the Elector of Saxony, since Feyerabend was such a prominent figure there.[198]

---

      angefangen / vnd zu sonderm ersprießlichem gehorsam vollendet / hoffe ich werde jedermenigklich getrewlich mit meinem vnterthenigen dienst / sampt andern dieses Werck zum besten gebrauchen. Hiemit sey dem Allmechtigen lieben Gott in sein gnad / schutz vnd schirm / gantz trewlich befohlen. Sigmund Feirabend Buchhändler in Franckfurt." Melanchthon, *Neuwe vollkommene Chronica* (Frankfurt a.M: Feyerabend, 1566), sig.)(ij r. VD16 M 2726.

195 See the discussion and collection of documents in Hansjörg Pohlmann, "Der Urheberrechtsstreit des Wittenberger Professors Dr. Med. Peuker mit dem Frankfurter Verleger Sigismund Feyerabend (1568 bis 1570): Ein Quellenbeitrag der Wirksamkeit des kaiserlichen und kursächsischen Autorenschutzes," *Archiv für Geschichte des Buchwesens* 6 (1965): 593–640. See also Ian Maclean, "Melanchthon at the book fairs, 1560–1601: Editors, markets and religious strife," in *Melanchthon und Europa*, ed. Günter Frank (Stuttgart: Thorbecke, 2002), vol. 2, 211–232; and Diener, "The Magdeburg Centuries," 190–205.

196 Pohlman, "Der Urheberrechtsstreit," 626.
197 Pohlman, "Der Urheberrechtsstreit," 602.
198 Pohlman, "Der Urheberrechtsstreit," 603.

FIGURE 21 Melanchthon, *Neuwe vollkommene Chronica* (Frankfurt a.M., 1566)
HERZOG AUGUST BIBLIOTHEK WOLFENBÜTTEL: H: T 365.2° HELMST

Peucer's case against Feyerabend has long provided a trove of information about sixteenth century publishing practices. Nevertheless, the reasons for Peucer's aggressive response are only hinted at in the records. In his complaint to the officials in Frankfurt, Peucer drew attention to the way Feyerabend's edition slandered "higher potentates," but he provided no further details.[199] The summary of the case drawn up by the Saxon officials is more specific and refers to embarrassing comments about the Elector of Brandenburg.[200] Both documents, however, fail to explain that the "slander" against Elector Joachim II was the discussion of the 1542 Turkish campaign in Funck's *Continuation*. Politics, rather than religion, had caused Melanchthon's troubles with Frankfurt, and Feyerabend's edition renewed and aggravated those earlier problems.

Initially, the case moved rapidly, with Electoral officials seizing the bookstocks in Leipzig already in January; and by February, the Saxons were in correspondence with Frankfurt officials about how to handle the case. On 16 March 1568, Feyerabend offered a lengthy response to the accusations, and in his own defence he gave a detailed account of sixteenth century publishing practices, including many of the marketing tactics that publishers used to enhance sales.[201] At the outset, Feyerabend disputed Peucer's right to a privilege for the *Chronicle* by arguing that the text had passed into a sort of "public domain" because it had been republished so often and in so many places. Furthermore, he claimed that no one, of high or low estate, had previously objected to any of those editions. He also attacked the indication of Peucer's privilege as confusingly vague. The title page stated only "with privilege" (*cum gratia et priuilegio*) and did not identify the privilege as Electoral or Imperial.[202] As a result, he reasonably assumed that it was a false privilege, which many publishers used as a matter of course. Cyriakus Jacob, for example, had used a false privilege for his 1546 edition.

Feyerabend also tried to prove that neither the Saxon nor the Imperial privileges prohibited his edition. First, he argued that he was not aware of the Saxon privilege granted to Peucer for all of Melanchthon's works, but this was in some sense irrelevant because a Saxon privilege was only valid within the Upper Saxon Circle (*Obersächsischer Reichskreis*), whereas his own publications fell under the jurisdiction of the Elector of the Palatinate and the Upper Rhenish Circle (*Oberrheinischer Reichskreis*).

---

199 Pohlman, "Der Urheberrechtsstreit," 622.
200 Pohlman, "Der Urheberrechtsstreit," 602, 621.
201 Feyerabend's "Rechtfertigung" is transcribed in Pohlman, "Der Urheberrechtsstreit," 622–629. The account here is based on that document and Pohlman's discussion.
202 Pohlman, "Der Urheberrechtsstreit," 600 n. 19.

With regard to the Imperial privilege, Feyerabend claimed that he had printed his edition in 1565, where the new continuation had ended, but he had used 1566 as the date of publication in anticipation of the book fairs.[203] From his perspective, this meant that the edition was not bound by Peucer's Imperial privilege, which had been issued on 18 April 1566. By 1565, the original six-year Electoral privilege had expired, so the Rhau press published the Latin fascicle of Book 5 without its protection. The heirs of Georg Rhau ended their printing operations in 1566, but Johann Schwertel republished Book 5 that same year, with an indication of the new Saxon and Imperial privileges. At the time, Saxony recognized Imperial privileges as valid, so Peucer was able to use both against Feyerabend for his activities in Leipzig. Only the Imperial privilege, however, was effective in Frankfurt.[204]

Feyerabend then moved to the publication history of *Carion's Chronicle* itself as a defence against Peucer's complaint, and especially as a counter to the accusations that the edition had slandered the Elector of Brandenburg.[205] Feyerabend's response presents the most detailed sixteenth century account of the continuations and supplements to the *Chronicle*, and his effort to distance himself from the text offers a candid, insider perspective on Renaissance printing practices. Feyerabend sought to separate the original *Chronicle* of 1532 from the later editions, and he argued that neither Melanchthon nor Peucer held rights to Funck's *Continuation*. Neither had written the material, and Cyriakus

---

203 The last copy of *Carion's Chronicle* printed by David Zöpfel had involved exactly this type of practice, since the colophon gives a date of 1563, while the title page indicates 1564. Zöpfel himself died in 1563.

204 Pohlmann, "Der Urheberrechtsstreit," 604.

205 "Es thut mich aber hiebeneben nit wenig befrembden, dass Herr Supplicant fürgibt, ob solte die erstreckung der Historien, Darinnen des Höchstgemelten Churfürsten zu Brandenburg gedacht wurdt, vnder seinen Namen ausgangen vnd Ihme vnd den seinen darauss schimpff auch große beschwerung an leib vnd ehern ervolgt sein, So doch solche appendices, Zusetz vnd erstreckung der Historien, Ihme gar nit zugeaignet worden, vnd er oder die seine derselben als frembden Werks, Dessen Author er nit ist, weder zu geniessen noch zu entgelten haben, wie dann die Vorrede, So in meinem namen dem durch mich getruckten Buch vorgesetzt, clarlich ausweiset, dass solches alles, was also hinzusetzt, nit der vorigen Authorn oder auch des vermeinten Supplicanten, sonder anderer gelärter Leuth seis, Kurtze halben vff dieselbe gezogen, Also dass mir zu viel vngutlich zugemessen wurdt, wie solte ich Ime dieselbe zugeschrieben, vnd er dardurch schaden erlitten, oder auch hinfürter zugewarten haben, So weiss auch one das Meniglich, dass die Latinische Cronica durch Herrn Philippum vnd Dr. Peucern weiter nit extendirt worden, als biss vff des Kaisers Otthonis des Vierten Zeit, so dann er solche anheng vnnd zusetz, darinnen etwas Hochstgedachten Churfürsten, meinem gnedigsten Herrn, zuwidder angezogen worden sein soll, nit gmacht, noch Ihme dieselbe durch mich vffgedrungen worden, Als hat er sich derhalben weder von mir zu beclagen, noch einiger beschwerung zu befaren, Dieweil er ein fremde Handlung zu verbussen nit schuldig, noch dahin getrungen werden khan vnd soll." Pohlmann, "Der Urheberrechtsstreit," 627.

Jacob had first published it under Funck's name with a (false) Imperial privilege. Feyerabend failed to mention, however, that even if the privilege had been genuine, Imperial grants usually lasted for only five to ten years.[206]

Peucer had demanded that Feyerabend identify everyone involved with the edition. In response, Feyerabend disavowed personal responsibility and named the scholars at fault. Dr. Justinus Göbler, an important jurist, had encouraged the new edition, and Johann Ulrich Strupp had helped him edit it. Nicolas Wolch of Düsseldorf had served as print corrector.[207] Feyerabend argued that these collaborators should bear the blame for the edition; but he pointed out that they were all already dead. In addition, Feyerabend stressed that he was not even responsible for printing the text, since Martin Lechler's print shop had prepared it. He and Hütter were simply the publishers, and Hütter in particular had no idea what was in the book he was selling.

Feyerabend also tried to counter Peucer's claims of false attribution. He passed over the title page, which had designated Melanchthon and Peucer as the editors, and instead drew attention to his introductory note. There, he had inserted a disclaimer about the *Chronicle's* fragmented authorship. Although he had not named the new contributors, he had indeed explained that the final sections of the edition did not come from Melanchthon, Peucer or Menius. Ultimately, he asserted that his publishing house had trusted Göbler and Strupp, and no one had checked the *Chronicle's* content before sale. As a result, he and Hütter were genuinely unaware of any offensive material.

In closing, Feyerabend offered to remove the final quires with the offensive material and sell only the remaining text. He asked that the charges against Hütter be dropped and his bookstocks returned.[208] The officials at Frankfurt forwarded Feyerabend's response to Dresden with cover letters addressed to Elector August and Peucer. By early 1569, Peucer seems to have given up his attempts to pursue the case in Frankfurt.[209] The process was potentially costly and time consuming, especially because he would have to appear in person. At Leipzig, however, Peucer probably succeeded in inflicting substantial financial harm before the confiscated bookstocks were released, and afterwards, Feyerabend and Hütter severed their partnership.[210]

Despite these problems, Feyerabend had the audacity to reissue *Carion's Chronicle* in 1569, just in time for the New Year's book fair at Leipzig.[211] Contrary to his promise, he failed to edit out the offensive material; instead, he had

---

206   Pohlmann, "Der Urheberrechtsstreit," 607 n. 45.
207   Pohlmann, "Der Urheberrechtsstreit," 610.
208   Pohlmann, "Der Urheberrechtsstreit," 628.
209   Pohlmann, "Der Urheberrechtsstreit," 611–612.
210   Pohlmann, "Der Urheberrechtsstreit," 612.
211   Pohlmann, "Der Urheberrechtsstreit," 612. The edition is VD16 ZV 10777.

simply redated the edition and removed Hütter from the colophon. Besides the *Chronicle*, Feyerabend's selling agent, Michael Stoll, also brought additional Frankfurt editions of Wittenberg texts to the Leipzig fair, and this time the Wittenbergers went after Feyerabend for these "pirate editions."[212]

Once again, the Saxon officials confiscated the bookstocks in Leipzig, an inventory was prepared and Feyerabend was faced with further proceedings initiated by Peucer and the Wittenberg publishers, who saw an opportunity to undermine Feyerabend's trade in Bibles.[213] This time the threat was more serious, and Feyerabend appealed directly to his own sovereign, the Elector of the Palatinate. Feyerabend presented his problems as Saxon interference in matters under the Elector's jurisdiction, and he begged for help lest he be ruined.[214] He pleaded ignorance of the bookstocks that his agent in Leipzig was selling; and if the hundreds of confiscated volumes were returned, he promised that he would never again print books from Wittenberg or Leipzig.[215]

In response, Elector Frederick interceded with Elector August on Feyerabend's behalf at the end of January 1570. Frederick asked that August convince Peucer and the Wittenberg printers to drop their case, seeing that Feyerabend had agreed to surrender the copies from his stock to which they objected, and he had promised to give up printing books from Leipzig and Wittenberg.[216] Feyerabend's plan apparently worked, since by mid-February August wrote to Peucer asking him to relent.[217] The actual outcome of the case is unknown, but after this second dispute, Feyerabend seems to have been frightened enough that he gave up publishing *Carion's Chronicle*.[218]

14   Wittenberg Chronicle

Against this background, Peucer issued the first complete Latin edition of the revised *Chronicle* in 1572. By dedicating the book to Elector August of Saxony, Peucer completed the transfer of the *Chronicle* from the Hohenzollerns to the Wettins; and in some sense, August came to view the *Chronicle* as the property

---

212   Pohlmann, "Der Urheberrechtsstreit," 612.
213   Pohlmann, "Der Urheberrechtsstreit," 612.
214   Pohlmann, "Der Urheberrechtsstreit," 613.
215   Pohlmann, "Der Urheberrechtsstreit," 635–636.
216   Pohlmann, "Der Urheberrechtsstreit," 614, 637–638.
217   Pohlmann, "Der Urheberrechtsstreit," 614, 638–639.
218   In 1594, Feyerabend's counsin, Johann Feyerabend, published a complete Latin edition at Frankfurt. The 1594 edition served as the basis for Gottfried Tambach's edition (1624), the last edition of *Carion's Chronicle* published in Germany. VD17 23:299941N.

of the Saxon court. The new edition was really a collection of Melanchthon's historical texts, and in 1601, it was reissued as volume five of Melanchthon's works.

After his dedicatory epistle to Elector August, Peucer inserted *An Oration on the Argument of Histories and the Profit to be Sought in Their Reading, Recited at the University of Wittenberg, in the Year 1568*, which had been delivered by Christoph Pezel (1539–1604). Peucer followed with his *Tabella* on the reading of history dedicated to the scholars of Wittenberg. He then arranged the texts chronologically: Melanchthon's *Description and History of Locations in Palestine*; the *Germania* of Tacitus with Melanchthon's *Vocabulary*; Carion's *Chronicle*, including all four previous dedicatory epistles; Melanchthon's *Exhortation of Emperor Maximilian on Waging War against the Turks*, and finally his *Description of the Election and Coronation of Charles V*. The collection served as the defining statement of Wittenberg historiography; and taken together, these texts presented a vision for church, state and society grounded in the experience of the recent and distant historical past:

> CHRONICON || CARIONIS || EXPOSITVM ET AVCTVM MVL=||TIS ET VETERIBVS ET RECENTIBVS HISTORIIS, || IN DESCRIPTIONIBVS REG-NORVM ET GENTIVM AN=||tiquarum, & narrationibus rerum Ecclesiasticarum, & Politicarum, Græ=||carum, Romanarum, Germanicarum & aliarum, ab exordio || Mundi vsq[ue] ad CAROLVM QVIN=||TVM Imperatorem. || A PHILIPPO MELANTHONE ET || CASPARO PEVCERO. || Adiecta est narratio historica de electione & coronatione || CAROLI V. Imperatoris. || Cum Gratia & Priuilegio. || WITEBERGÆ || EXCVDEBAT IOHANNES CRATO, || ANNO M.D.LXXX.

1. EPISTOLA DEDICATORIA [from Caspar Peucer to Elector August of Saxony (14 September 1572)]   a ij r – [a 8]r
2. ORATIO DE ARGVMENTO HISTORIARVM, ET FRVCTV PETENDO EX EARVM LECTIONE: RECITATA INACADEMIA WITEBERGENSI ANNO M.D.LXVIII.   b r – [b 6]v
3. ALIQVOT LOCORVM INSIGNIVM EXPLICATIO ET HISTORIÆPER PHILIPPVM MELANTHONEM.   c r – c iiij r
4. PVBLII CORNELLII TACITI HISTORICI, DE SITV ET MORIBVSET POPVLIS GERMANIÆ, LIBELLVS.   c iiij r – [d 5]r

5.	EPISTOLA NVNCVPATORIA	[d 5]v – [d 6]r
6.	VOCABVLA REGIONVM ET GENTIVM, QVÆ RECENSENTVR IN HOC LIBELLO TACITO	[d 6]v – [c iiij]v
7.	TABELLA OSTENDENS QVO ORDINE LEGENDA ET COGNOSCENDA SIT SERIES HISTORIARVM MVNDI. DEDICATA SCHOLASTICIS ACADEMIAE WITEBERGENSIS.	Fold-out Table
8.	[PRIMA PARS CHRONICI CARIONIS]	
	EPISTOLA DEDICATORIA [from Philipp Melanchthon to Archbishop Sigismund of Magdeburg (April 1558)]	1–5
	CHRONICON LIBER PRIMVS	6–27
	DE ORDINE LIBRI.	9–12
	ANNORVM SERIES EX PHILONE.	12–13
	LIBER PRIMVS, QVI COMPLECTITVR DVO MILLIA ANNORVM INDE vsq[ue] ab initio mundi.	13–27
	SECVNDVS LIBER CHRONICORVM	27–142
9.	SECVNDA PARS CHRONICI CARIONIS AB AVGVSTO CAESARE VSQVE AD CAROLVM MAGNVM	143–290
	EPISTOLA DEDICATORIA [from Philipp Melanchthon to Archbishop Sigismund of Magdeburg (25 March 1560)]	143–145
	EPIGRAMMA DE MONARCHIIS	145
	LIBER TERTIVS DE QVARTA MONARCHIA	146–290
10.	TERTIA PARS CHRONICI CARIONIS, A CAROLO MAGNO, VBI PHILIPPVS MELANTHON DESIIT, VSQVE AD FRIDERICVM SECVNDVM	291–484
	EPISTOLA DEDICATORIA [from Caspar Peucer to Archbishop Sigismund (23 February 1562)]	291–293
	LIBER QVARTVS CHRONICORVM	294–484
11.	LIBER QVINTVS CHRONICI CARIONIS A FRIDERICO SECVNDO VSQVE AD CAROLVM QVINTVM. EXPOSITVS ET AVCTVS A CASPARO PEVCERO. PERTINET HIC LIBER AD partem tertiam Chronici.	485–706
	EPISTOLA DEDICATORIA [from Caspar Peucer to Elector August of Saxony (31 October 1565)]	485–490

AD LECTOREM	491–492
VLTIMA PARS CHRONICI CARIONIS [LIBER QVINTVS]	493–706
12. EXHORTATIO MAXIMILIANI CÆSARIS AD BELLVM TVRCIS INFERENDVM SCRIPTA A PHILIPPO MELANTH.	707–720
13. DE ELECTIONE ET CORONATIONE CAROLI CÆSARIS HISTORIA. PHILIPP: MELANTH:	720–746
14. INDEX RERVM ET VERBORVM MEMORABILIVM OMNIVM CHRONICORVM PHILIPPI ET PEVCERI PARTIVM	Rrr ij r – [Xxx 5]r

In 1573, Peucer issued a new German edition of the *Chronicle* in collaboration with Christoph Pezel (Figure 22). He retained the connection to Saxony through a dedication to Electress Anna, but the edition was several hundred pages longer than its Latin counterpart from 1572. Peucer added extensive genealogical information,[219] he inserted the map of Noah's descendants from the original *Chronicle*,[220] and he revised the subject headings so the text would be easier to navigate. Peucer presented the new edition as final and definitive, and he warned printers against issuing revisions, continuations or supplements.[221] He also promised a new history of the sixteenth century, but it would

---

219 "DAmit nu ein jederman / der auch der Lateinischen Sprach vnerfaren / solch Chroniken mit nutz lesen köndte / hab ichs vffs newe von fornen an / fleissig vbersehen vnd bessern / vnd die andern theil / so bis an hero zum theil gantz vbel vertiret / zum theil gar daran gemangelt / von newem vffs beste vnd verstendtlichste / als es geschehen mügen / verdeudschen / vnd darüber hin vnd wider zu mehrer erklerung der Historien / viel Genealogias vnd Fürstlicher Stemme mit hinein setzen / auch das herrliche Büchlein des Herrn Philippi / so vnter dem Namen Georgij Sabini zuuorn ausgangen / von der erwehlung vnd krönung Keisers Caroli des Fünfften / hinten an drücken lassen." Peucer, *Chronica Carionis* (Wittenberg, 1573), sig. [av] r.
220 Peucer, *Chronica Carionis* (Wittenberg, 1573), 21.
221 "An den Leser. Es haben sich fur dieser zeit / etliche Drucker vnterstanden / dieses vnser Wittembergisch Chronicon nach zu drucken / vnd dasselbe jres gefallens zu endern vnd zu mehren / vnd also ein Corpus zusammen zu flicken jres gewins halben / darzu sie etliche Theil dieses Chronici / die do allbereit sind verdeudscht gewesen / genommen haben / die andern Theil die noch nicht verdeudscht gewesen / haben sie ausgelassen / vnd an derselben stat andere fremdbe Narrationes hinan geflickt / nicht one vnsern grossen nachtheil vnd beschwerung / Dieselben vnd alle andere wollen wir erinnert / vnd vmb jr selbst besten willen vermanet haben sie wollen sich forthin dieses vnser Chronicon nach zu drücken gentzlich enthalten / viel weniger wollen sie sich vnterstehen etwas hinein zuflicken oder darzu zusetzen / es sey was es wolle

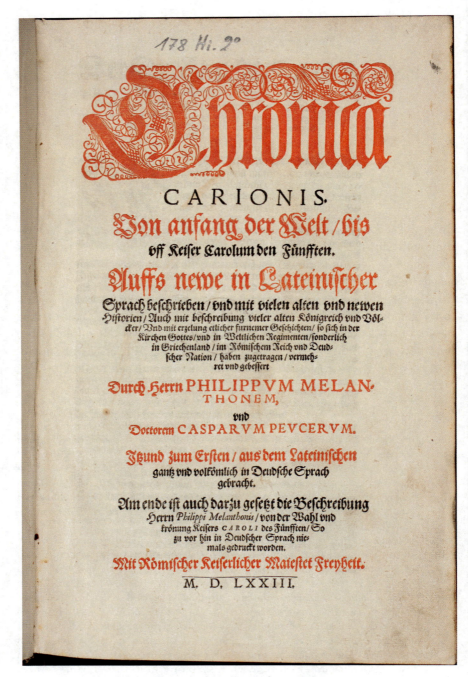

FIGURE 22   Melanchthon, *Chronica Carionis* (Wittenberg, 1573)
HERZOG AUGUST BIBLIOTHEK WOLFENBÜTTEL: A: 178 HIST. 2°

be published separately, not as part of *Carion's Chronicle*.[222] Peucer's 1573 edition marked the conclusion of the dispute between Wittenberg and Frankfurt over the *Chronicle*.

15   The Fall of the Philippists

By the early 1570s, Peucer had become one of the most powerful men in Saxony, but the situation was quickly changing.[223] The political agitation of the Calvinist Palatinate and the developments in France after the St. Bartholomew's Day Massacre (1572) had started to alarm the Electoral court.[224] Even as a group of Saxon theologians and courtiers were working to move the territory closer to Calvinism, Elector August was becoming more concerned about maintaining a "Lutheran" identity.[225] In 1574, the Saxon court undertook an extensive investigation of possible Calvinist agitation in the electorate. Suspicion fell especially on four courtiers: Christian Schütz (1526–1592), the court preacher; Georg Cracow (1525–1575), an electoral counsellor; Johann Stössel (1524–1576), the Elector's confessor; and Peucer, the Elector's physician. On 1 April 1574, Peucer was taken into custody at Wittenberg and then transferred to Dresden. His letters and papers were seized to reveal possible support for Calvinism. Eventually, the broader Saxon investigation uncovered incriminating correspondence

---

/ Sondern lassen vns dieses vnser Chronicon bleiben / wie wir es in Druck verfertigt haben / was ferner zu vollstreckung vnd ausfürung der Historien bis vff vnsere zeiten gehöret das sol vermittelst göttlicher hülff in ein eigenes abgesondertes Buch verfasset / vnd zu seiner zeit an tag gegeben werden." Peucer, *Chronica Carionis* (Wittenberg, 1573), sig. [avj] r.

222   "DAs vbrige / was sich bey zeiten der regierung Keiser Caroli des Fünfften / vnd folgends hernach bis zu vnsern zeiten zegetragen hat / das wil ich mit der hülffe Gottes in ein sonderlich Buch zusammen bringen / dieses Buch sol also ein theil fur sich sein vnd bleiben." Peucer, *Chronica Carionis* (Wittenberg, 1573), sig. [av] r – [av] v.

223   "Scholasticvm me natura fecerat, aulicum fortuna: sed fortuna, quæ vt in omnibus rebus humanis, sic maximè in aulis, stabilis aut diuturna minimè esse solet, citò mutata, ex schola me simul & aula eiecit: ex neutra tamen inuitum." Peucer, *Historia Carcerum et liberationis diuinae* (Zürich: [s.n.], 1605), 35. VD17 12:116322H.

224   Hans-Peter Hasse, "Peucers Prozeß und die 'Historia carcerum,'" in *Caspar Peucer (1525–1602): Wissenschaft, Glaube und Politik im konfessionellen Zeitalter*, ed. Hans-Peter Hasse and Günther Wartenberg (Leipzig: Evangelische Verlagsanstalt, 2004), 136–137.

225   For fall of the Philippists, I rely on Koch, *Zwischen Katheder, Thron und Kerker*, 132–136, and Hasse, "Peucers Prozeß," 136–147. See also Robert Calinich, *Kampf und Untergang des Melanchthonismus in Kursachsen in den Jahren 1570 bis 1574 und die Schicksale seiner vornehmsten Häupter: Aus den Quellen des königlichen Hauptstaatsarchivs zu Dresden* (Leipzig: Brockhaus, 1866), esp. 183–304.

among the other courtiers, including letters that ridiculed the Electoral court and referred to it as a regime of women (*gynaikokratie*).[226]

When the "plot" was discovered, the Elector believed his counsellors had deceived him, and he reacted as one betrayed.[227] Initially, Peucer was held under house arrest, but the Elector had him transferred to confinement in Rostlitz, then Zeitz, and finally to the Pleißenburg in Leipzig. August purged the university of Philippists; and Christoph Pezel, Eusebius Menius and others fled Saxony, never to return.[228] In response to these developments, August ordered a group of theologians to draft the *Formula of Concord* (1577), a document that attempted to impose religious uniformity on Saxony and other Protestant territories. August also sought to use it as a tool in asserting the primacy of Electoral Saxony within Protestant religious politics.[229]

As these events unfolded, the University of Wittenberg, the Saxon estates, and several German princes interceded with the Elector on Peucer's behalf, even Emperor Maximilian II asked August to release Peucer so that he could serve as an Imperial physician, but all to no avail.[230] The Elector personally controlled the minutiae of Peucer's imprisonment, and the Saxon court fully expected that he would die in confinement.[231] Peucer's wife died, probably from shock, while he was in prison,[232] and Georg Cracow, one of the other "conspirators," was tortured to death.[233]

---

226 Hasse, "Peucers Prozeß," 140.
227 Peucer was not the only historian to fall from favour with Elector August. See Otto Clemens, "Der Prozeß des Johannes Pollicarius," *Archiv für Reformationsgeschichte* 18 (1921): 63–74. Pollicarius, who had edited the collection of texts relating to Luther's death, became preacher and superindenent of Weißenfels, but was deposed by Elector August of Saxony in 1568. After his fall from favour, Pollicarius was imprisoned and forced to confess to dealings with a prostitute. He was set free only in 1578.
228 See Jürgen Moltmann, *Christoph Pezel (1539–1604) und der Calvinismus in Bremen* (Bremen: Verlag Einkehr, 1958).
229 See Bodo Nischan, "Germany after 1550," in *The Reformation World*, ed. Andrew Pettegree (London: Routledge, 2000), 393–396. The Lutheran confessional texts are edited in *Die Bekenntnisschriften der evangelisch-lutherischen Kirche* (Göttingen: Vandenhoeck & Ruprecht, 1998).
230 Peucer, *Historia Carcerum* (Zürich, 1605), 477–478. See also Roebel, "Humanistische Medizin," 87.
231 The Saxon court even drew up a *consilium* on whether Peucer, as an unrepentant heretic, deserved Christian burial. For a copy of the document, see Peucer, *Historia Carcerum* (Zürich, 1605), 755–758.
232 Calinich, *Kampf und Untergang des Melanchthonismus*, 247.
233 Roebel, "Humanistische Medizin," 88–90.

Despite his hatred for the conspirators, August approached Peucer twice about continuing *Carion's Chronicle*. The Elector had already been the dedicatee of Sleidanus's *Commentaries on Religion and Politics during the Reign of Charles V*. Any history of the Reformation by Peucer, however, would have even greater authority because of his ties to Wittenberg and his own prominence within the Protestant intellectual community. Furthermore, the Saxon court now had to be concerned that Peucer would write a history of contemporary events as a defence of his own views and an attack on those who had driven out the Philippists.

In 1575, while Peucer was being held at Zeitz, the Elector asked whether he would be willing to extend the *Chronicle* into the sixteenth century, as he had promised in the German edition of 1573.[234] Peucer responded that he could not work in confinement, without his books or research materials,[235] so if the Elector wanted the *Chronicle* finished, he should end the imprisonment.[236] August refused, and in 1576, he had Peucer transferred to the Pleißenburg in Leipzig, where the conditions were much more severe.

August was serious about asserting control over *Carion's Chronicle*, and that same year he had Gimel Bergen, one of the Saxon court printers, publish a new edition at Dresden (1576). Bergen's edition is massive, far larger than

---

[234] "Adiecta erat mandatis particula, *vt Præfectus & Quæstor, non Principis Electoris nomine, sed tanquam ex sese significarent mihi, posse ferre Principem Electorem vt Chronicon meum pertexam.*" Peucer, *Historia Carcerum* (Zürich, 1605), 302.

[235] Peucer had inherited Melanchthon's library, and his children removed much of it to Bautzen after Peucer was arrested. (The Elector seized the books that remained in Wittenberg.) An inventory survives from the collection at Bautzen, see Robert Kolb, *Caspar Peucer's Library*; and Roebel, "Humanistische Medizin," 89.

[236] "De Chronico respondi, hoc rerum mearu[m] statu & conditione mea nihil posse me aggredi aut præstare. Quid scriberem enim fractus ingenii viribus & corporis, animo mœsto & perturbato in solitudine, inter perpetuas & circumdatas ex omni parte insidias per subornatos Coryceos, praesertim si negata mihi sit facultas & coram & per literas consulendi explorandique præstantium virorum iudicia de maximis rebus? Multa enim deesse mihi ad tantum opus necessaria, atque haec quidem maxime, ingenii vigorem qui perierit, animi alacritatem, quam extinguant cruciatus perpetui metus, & carceris solitudo, vires corporis, quæ prorsus sint exhaustæ morbis & mœstitia, supellectilem librorum historicorum, quam transferre huc nequeam. Nec scripti futuram aliquam fidem vel auctoritatem, si palàm fiat in carcere à me esse confectum. Denique interdicto singulari ademptam mihi esse facultate[m] de Theologicis materiis tractandi; quas si attingere no[n] debeam, cum sine præcipua pars historiæ nostrorum temporu[m], opus futurum esse mutilum, mancum, & contemptum. Idcirco si me velint commentari aliquid de nostri seculi rebus gestis, vt me aresto & carcere solutum dimittant." Peucer, *Historia Carcerum* (Zürich, 1605), 303–304. See Ziegler, *Chronicon Carionis*, 42–43; Roebel, "Humanistische Medizin," 90.

the Wittenberg folio editions, and the surviving copies in Dresden and Berlin are both ornately bound.[237] August was willing to spend a small fortune on publishing these display copies, and the arms of Electoral Saxony, rather than Melanchthon's seal, are emblazoned on the title pages of each volume.

Likewise, in contrast to his earlier indifference, the Elector actively worked to fill the vacant history professorship at Wittenberg. When attempts to lure David Chytraeus and Reiner Reineccius failed, he hired Andreas Franckenberger (1536–1590) as professor of rhetoric.[238] Franckenberger continued the lectures on *Carion's Chronicle* and eventually published *Institutes of Antiquity and Histories* (1586), which is loosely based on the themes of *Carion's Chronicle* and its sources.[239] In 1589 he also published an oration in praise of Melanchthon and the *Chronicle*.[240]

In 1577, while Peucer was being held at the Pleißenburg, the Elector again approached him about continuing the *Chronicle*. In exchange, he offered milder prison conditions, but Peucer refused anything less than full release, as he had at Zeitz.[241] Around this time, Landgrave Wilhelm IV of Hesse-Kassel (1532–1592), who had earlier tried to intercede for Peucer, wrote to the Saxons with various astronomical and astrological questions for Peucer.[242] After receiving the Landgrave's request, the Elector decided to try giving Peucer some books and writing material to work on the Landgrave's projects and also on *Carion's Chronicle*.[243]

---

237 See the image in Margrit B. Krewson, ed., *Dresden: Treasures from the Saxon State Library* (Washington, D.C.: Library of Congress, 1996), Nr. 73. Only Book 5 has survived in Dresden. See also Peter Schmidt, *Unbekannter Jakob-Krause-Einband zum Chronicon Carionis in Freiberg* (Freiberg i.B.: Informationszentrum der Bergakademie, 1981). Schmidt's article discusses the binding of a 1572 Latin folio edition.

238 Detloff Klatt, "Chyträus als Geschichtslehrer und Geschichtschreiber," *Beiträge zur Geschichte der Stadt Rostock* 5 (1909): 147–149. On Franckenberger, see Scherer, *Geschichte und Kirchengeschichte*, 55.

239 Andreas Franckenberger, *Institvtionvm Antiqvitatis Et Historiarvm Pars Prima, In Libros Sex Distribvta* (Wittenberg: Crato, 1586). VD16 F 2198.

240 Andreas Franckenberger, *Oratio In Honorem Domini Philippi Melanthonis De Magnitvdine rerum diuinarum & politicarum, quae in Chronico eius continentur* (Wittenberg: Crato, 1589). VD16 ZV 6023.

241 Peucer, *Historia Carcerum* (Zürich, 1605), 358–359. See Henke, *Caspar Peucer*, 33–34; Ziegler, *Chronicon Carionis*, 42–43; Roebel, "Humanistische Medizin," 92.

242 On Peucer and Wilhelm IV, see Bruce Moran, "German Prince-Practitioners: Aspects in the Development of Courtly Science, Technology, and Procedures in the Renaissance," *Technology and Culture* 22, no. 2 (April 1981): 262–265; and Brosseder, *Im Bann der Sterne*, 100–103.

243 Peucer, *Historia Carcerum* (Zürich, 1605), 362; Henke, *Caspar Peucer*, 33–34; Roebel, "Humanistische Medizin," 92.

As soon as Peucer received ink and paper, he ignored the Elector's instructions and turned to writing the history of his imprisonment. Peucer's family managed to smuggle some of his work out of prison, but once the Saxon officials discovered what he was doing, they denied him access to writing materials and to most of his books.[244] Peucer was reduced to making ink from soot and ashes, and he used the margins of his few remaining books as writing paper.[245]

In 1586, after twelve years of confinement, circumstances changed in Peucer's favour. By that time, Electress Anna had died, and August had remarried to the daughter of Joachim Ernst of Anhalt, a territory situated between Saxony and Brandenburg. The Elector's new father-in-law supported the Philippists and had actively sought Peucer's release. (After the expulsion of the crypto-Calvinists in the 1570s, Anhalt had become a place of refuge for Philippists in exile.)[246] Peucer was finally set free on 8 February 1586, only a few days before the Elector's death.[247] Upon his release, Peucer immediately left Saxony and

---

244 See Koch, *Zwischen Katheder, Thron und Kerker*, 154, 176; Hasse, "Peucers Prozeß," 148–155.
245 "Animo tamen & ingenio nec languescebam, nec deficiebam. Qua propter ociosus numquam eram, sed omne quod a somno ac quiete liberum erat tempus, quamquam & hoc erat exiguum admodum, id precibus consumebam, aut lectionibus bibliorum, ac meditationibus, quas versibus concipiebam; cumque absumptis omnibus atramenti vestigiis, quae vspiam apparebant reliqua, deesset quo illas consignarem, monstrabat mihi Deus rationem & atramenti conficiendi ex cremata in cinerem crusta panis hyberno tempore, cum foculus strueretur conclaui calefaciendo fumoque de nigratis cineribus, qui per fornacis rimas atque ex luto denigrato delabebantur, & comparandi calamos cultro qui retusus prorsus acie, & apice carebat. Chartas suggerebant margines librorum, quos illatos mecum primo, postea ademptos restituerant. Saepe petebam his annis Testamentum Graecum, sed impetrare non poteram." Peucer, *Historia Carcerum* (Zürich, 1605), 363–364. This is the most famous paragraph Peucer wrote, however, it has circulated in two versions since the seventeenth century. The second, and more colorful, is found in Melchior Adam, *Vitae Germanorum medicorum* (Heidelberg: Rosa, 1620), 381–382. In this second version, Peucer also used beer to make his ink, and he wrote specifically in the margins and blank pages of a copy of the "*libri Concordiae*," the very book that had been composed against him.
246 See Koch, *Zwischen Katheder, Thron und Kerker*, 156–161.
247 In a letter of 1588, Tycho Brahe outlined the shortcomings of Ptolemaic astronomy for Caspar Peucer, an old teacher from his student days in Wittenberg. Tycho mentioned that he had once cast Peucer's horoscope, and he had seen that Peucer would suffer exile or imprisonment, but eventually regain his freedom. See J.L.E. Dreyer, *Tycho Brahe: A Picture of Scientific Life and Work in the Sixteenth Century* (Edinburgh: Adam and Charles Black, 1890), 21–23. For the letter, see Tycho Brahe, *Opera omnia*, VII, *Epistolae astronomicae*, ed. I.L.E. Dreyer (Copenhagen: Libraria Gyldendaliana, 1924), 127–141, esp. 137–138.

moved to Dessau. By then, he was already in his sixties, but he remarried and served as a physician to the princes of Anhalt.[248]

The Saxon court was aware that Peucer had continued writing in prison, and they knew of his plans to publish a defence of his position. Therefore, as a condition of release, the Elector forced Peucer to swear an oath that he would never speak or write about the events surrounding his imprisonment.[249] These terms effectively prevented Peucer from publishing his promised companion volume to *Carion's Chronicle*.

After August's death, the new Elector, Christian I (1560–1591), again purged the University of Wittenberg – this time of the strict Lutherans – and he worked to transform Electoral Saxony into a Calvinist stronghold.[250] In 1591, Christian travelled to Anhalt to rehabilitate Peucer, and he formally released him from the terms of his oath.[251] Peucer immediately published selections from his prison writings, which he quietly inserted into a new edition of his *Commentary on the Principal Forms of Divination*.[252] The caution was justified. The Elector died in 1591, and because Christian II (1583–1611) was underage, Duke Frederick Wilhelm I of Saxony-Weimar-Altenburg (1562–1602) became regent and ruled as "Administrator of Electoral Saxony."[253] The Duke returned Saxony to its position as leader among the Lutheran states, and he purged the

---

248 See Joachim Castan, "Caspar Peucers letzte Lebensperiode in Anhalt – eine Wiederentdeckung," in *Caspar Peucer (1525–1602): Wissenschaft, Glaube und Politik im konfessionellen Zeitalter*, ed. Hans-Peter Hasse and Günther Wartenberg (Leipzig: Evangelische Verlagsanstalt, 2004), 283–297.

249 "Und wen ich auch solcher meiner verhaftung in argkwohn / oder verdacht ziehen möchte / weder mündtlich / noch schriftlich / hiemlich oder offentlich in ungüten zugedencken / oder zu eifern / noch solches jemandts von meinet wegen zugestatten." Peucer, *Historia Carcerum* (Zürich, 1605), 776.

250 See Thomas Klein, *Der Kampf um die zweite Reformation in Kursachsen, 1586–1591* (Cologne: Böhlau, 1962).

251 Peucer, *Historia Carcerum* (Zürich, 1605), 782–786.

252 "Cum, post mirandam conseruationem & liberationem mei ex aresto & carcere annorum duodecim, iterum editurus essem commentarium meum de diuinationum generibus diuersis, (quem initio hoc consilio praesipue contexui, vt, quantum possem, ostenderem opera Dei propria, ordinata, ac perpetua, & extraordinaria ac miraculosa, in rerum natura, generisque humani societate, & in Ecclesia Filii Dei, quomodo a ludibriis Diaboli, imposturisque illorum aemulis, sint discernenda) Volui, ut debui, in prooemio, significatione aliqua publica, qualem ferret scripti ratio ac breuitas, Deo & Ecclesiae gratitudinem declarare meam...." Caspar Peucer, *Commentarivs De Præcipvis Divinationvm Generibvs* (Zerbst: Faber, 1591), sig. α2r; see also fol. 71r–132v, the new material begins at "Disserui hactenus de causis secundis & propinquis, obuiis & occultis, sed uerbo Dei tamen patefactis." VD16 P 1977.

253 On Frederick Wilhelm I, see ADB 7: 791–792.

territory of Calvinists. Because Peucer was living in Anhalt, he was able to avoid arrest, but the Duke threatened him with prison if he wrote against the *Formula of Concord* or the Wettins.[254] The danger was real. Almost immediately after assuming power, the Administrator imprisoned Christian I's chancellor, Nicolaus Krell. In 1601, he was publicly beheaded at Dresden.[255]

Peucer never revisited the *Chronicle*. The 1573 German edition was republished in 1576, 1578, and 1588, each time without alterations or continuations. The Latin editions subsequently published at Wittenberg and Frankfurt likewise followed Peucer's 1572 edition.[256] In contrast, some early seventeenth century Genevan editions added a *Supplement* for events after 1519, and the 1579 French translation of Simon Goulart (1543–1628) added an entire volume on sixteenth century history (Books 6–7). The Dutch editions of the 1620s and 1630s likewise contained additional material to supplement the main text. By the 1620s, however, the number of reprintings diminished, and the last early modern edition, a Swedish translation, was published at Nyköping in 1649.

In the end, Peucer never wrote his promised supplement to *Carion's Chronicle*. He composed a history, really a personal defence, of his beliefs and actions (*History of My Imprisonments and Divine Release*), but his oath to the Elector and the threats from Duke Frederick Wilhelm held back publication. After Peucer's death in 1602, Christoph Pezel edited this collection of texts, and it was published posthumously at Zürich in 1605.[257] It became the standard account of the Philippist movement in Saxony, but it was a disappointing substitute for a comprehensive history of the sixteenth century.

The *Chronicle's* immense popularity in the sixteenth century was due to several factors, but especially its timing, its content and its associations with Wittenberg. Peucer's efforts to define an official text of the *Chronicle* eventu-

---

254 Peucer, *Historia Carcerum* (Zürich, 1605), 784–785; see Roebel, "Humanistische Medizin," 97.
255 The execution sword was inscribed with the warning "CAVE CALVINIANE," see Koch, *Zwischen Katheder, Thron und Kerker*, 174; and a commemorative image was issued, see Carlos Eire, *Reformations: The Early Modern World, 1450–1650* (New Haven: Yale University Press, 2016), 587.
256 At Wittenberg, the individual fascicles of the revised *Chronicle* sold better than Peucer's complete edition (1572), probably because students preferred the smaller size for class. The revised *Chronicle* actually seems to have met with greater commercial success in Reformed Geneva, where compact-sized editions were published regularly between 1576 and 1625.
257 See Koch, *Zwischen Katheder, Thron und Kerker*, 154, 176; Hasse, "Peucers Prozeß," 148–155. The *Historia Carcerum* was published twice, in 1605 (VD17 12:116322H) and 1615 (VD17 1:049023V).

ally stifled the creative adaptation that had marked the early decades of the *Chronicle's* dissemination. In response, historians turned to other texts, especially Johann Sleidanus's *On the Four Chief Empires* (1556)[258] and Orazio Torsellini's *Epitome Historiarum* (1598),[259] which were not burdened by disputes over authorial rights and textual integrity. By 1601, the year before Peucer's death, enough copies of the 1580 Wittenberg Latin edition remained in inventory that they were redated and advertised as volume five of Melanchthon's collected works. Many of these editions arrived in England, presumably because they were not selling well in Germany.[260] The 1601 edition marked the last time that *Carion's Chronicle* was published at Wittenberg; and with that, a truly improbable chapter in the history of historical thought drew to a close.

16 Conclusion

In 1532, *Carion's Chronicle* was released into the world of print. From Wittenberg, the text spread across language and geography, and even sixteenth century observers commented on its remarkable dissemination. Reprints, adaptations and translations made the *Chronicle* widely available, and through this process of diffusion, the text reached a much broader audience than Melanchthon or Carion could ever have expected. The *Chronicle* was written to meet a specific need among princely tutors, and its circulation attests to the lack of a comparable compendium of European history. Indeed, its popularity in the Catholic world, and especially in France, is otherwise inexplicable. Melanchthon and Carion offered what earlier Renaissance humanists had never provided: a concise narrative history from Creation to the present that explained the foundations of the "modern" European world.

---

258 Johann Sleidanus, *Ioan. Sleidani, De Qvatvor Svmmis Imperiis, Libri Tres, In gratiam iuuentutis confecti. Cum gratia & priuilegio Cæsareo ad annos octo* (Strasbourg: Rihel, 1556). VD16 S 6657. On the editions of the text, see *Johann Sleidan (Johann Philippson): Bibliographie seiner gedruckten Werke und der von ihm übersetzten Schriften von Philippe de Comines, Jean Froissart und Claude de Seyssel, mit einem bibliographischen Anhang zur Sleidan Forschung* (Stuttgart: Hiersemann, 1996); and Scherer, *Geschichte und Kirchengeschichte*, 83.

259 See Neddermeyer, "Das katholische Geschichtslehrbuch," 469–483.

260 Ian Maclean, "Melanchthon at the book fairs, 1560–1601: Editors, markets and religious strife," in *Melanchthon und Europa*, ed. Günter Frank (Stuttgart: Thorbecke, 2002), vol. 2, 222–223.

During the Middle Ages, historians often built on the work of their predecessors by copying or continuing earlier narratives. The process was gradual and incremental, and it produced composite histories, such as Martin of Troppau's *Chronicle*, that extended long beyond the lifetime of the original author. The expectation of continuation persisted into the early years of printing. Indeed, rather than discourage the practice, some authors clearly endorsed it. Hartmann Schedel, for example, included blank pages in the *Nuremberg Chronicle* for later writers to fill in the events between 1493 and the Last Days.

In 1537, the year Carion died, the first continuation to the *Chronicle* appeared at Antwerp. Others soon followed at Paris, London and Frankfurt. Carion could not contest these uses from the grave, so adapting the *Chronicle* should have been no different than producing an updated version of a medieval text. In most contexts, this was, in fact, the case, but not in Germany. There, the *Chronicle* was associated more closely with Wittenberg, and particularly with Melanchthon. This association contributed to the *Chronicle's* popularity, but it also gave the Wittenbergers, and later the Electoral Saxon court, an interest in controlling the presentation of the text.

From the mid-1540s, Frankfurt printers compelled Melanchthon, and then Peucer, to assert greater control over the *Chronicle*. The reprinting of Wittenberg texts was common, and ultimately unpreventable, but Johann Funck's *Continuation* shifted concern from reprinting to textual integrity and attribution. The *Chronicle* was effectively a commentary on contemporary politics, which in a world ruled by princes was inherently dangerous. Melanchthon understood this, and he recognized that Funck's treatment of the 1542 Turkish campaign had the potential to damage the relationship between Wittenberg and the Elector of Brandenburg. His response was swift. He pressed the authorities in Frankfurt to address the situation, and within weeks, he issued a new official edition of the *Chronicle* at Wittenberg. He might have done more, but the Schmalkaldic War soon closed the university and made his family political refugees.

Two decades later, Caspar Peucer again confronted the problem of Funck's *Continuation*. By revising the *Chronicle*, Melanchthon and Peucer certainly had stronger claims over its text, and more importantly, Peucer had acquired broad legal rights over Melanchthon's printed works. A confluence of factors had probably encouraged Melanchthon to revisit the *Chronicle* in the 1550s. He clearly wanted an improved text for his university lectures, and revising the *Chronicle* also served as a preemptive response to Flacius and the *Magdeburg Centuries*. Peucer likewise used the *Chronicle* for his lectures, and he treated it as an important part of Melanchthon's legacy. Melanchthon obtained an Electoral printing privilege to enhance his ability to control the printing and distribution of the *Chronicle*. Peucer secured both Electoral and Imperial privileges for all of Melanchthon's works.

Because of his privileges, Peucer was better positioned than Melanchthon had been in 1546 to suppress the Frankfurt editions he discovered at Leipzig. Indeed, it seems that he successfully prevented further reprinting of Funck's *Continuation* after 1569. Peucer's response, however, went beyond the legal recourse he sought in Frankfurt and Saxony. Peucer knew that the means at his disposal were ultimately inadequate to prevent unauthorized reprintings. Therefore, he sought to fix the *Chronicle* in a definitive form by publishing official Latin and German editions that stressed the integrity and finality of the text. His perspective marked a fundamental change from centuries of historiographical practice that had treated adaptation and continuation as legitimate, and indeed important, aspects of historical scholarship. By asserting control over *Carion's Chronicle*, Peucer prevented further development and adaptation of the text, and he effectively divorced the history of sixteenth century Europe from the medieval past. In the end, he had transformed *Carion's Chronicle* into "our *Wittenberg Chronicle*" (*vnser Wittembergisch Chronicon*), and he presented it as the defining statement of Wittenberg historiography.

CHAPTER 6

The Legacy of Wittenberg Historiography

1   Introduction

By the mid-sixteenth century, *Carion's Chronicle* had spread from Wittenberg across Europe, and its diffusion through reprintings, adaptations and translations is truly remarkable, even for a text associated with the Reformation. Through the *Chronicle*, Melanchthon overturned the medieval papal view of history, and he finally provided the comprehensive pro-Imperial narrative that had been lacking in the Middle Ages. His intervention in the annals of Western historical thought was part of a broader engagement with the legacy of Antiquity and the Middle Ages that unfolded over the decades. During the Reformation, the texts that had governed medieval life and thought were replaced with a new canon, and *Carion's Chronicle* was an important contribution to this transformation of the European intellectual landscape.

By the later sixteenth century, Melanchthon's political vision had assumed a normative function at the courts and schools of the Empire.[1] Even after Melanchthon's works disappeared from the classroom, subsequent textbooks and teaching tools held to his perspective, to varying degrees, for centuries. Nevertheless, *Carion's Chronicle* did not remain unchallenged with regard to narrative content and argument. Initially, the most important opposition to Melanchthon's embedded political views emerged from France rather than

---

1   See, for example, an entry from 1573 regarding princely education: "Dazu dann insonderheit das klein Chronicon Philippi, so man Charionis nennt, dieweil es kurz, dienstlich und der gedechtnus behilfflich sein mag. Dann daraus ein kurze Memori von anfang der Wellt biß uff unnsere Zeit gefasst werden mag, besser dann in weitleufftigen büchern." Friedrich Schmidt, *Geschichte der Erziehung der Pfälzischen Wittelsbacher: Urkunden nebst geschichtlichem Überblick und Register* (Berlin: A. Hofmann & Comp., 1899), 44 n. 1 [Adam Schwartz wird zum Kammerdiener des Pfalzgrafen Otto Heinrich bestallt. Neuberg a. D., 1. Juli 1573.] See also an entry in a *Studienordnung* of 1623–1624: "Epitomen historicam Sleidani de quatuor Monarchiis subjungat ad pleniorem Ideae cognitionem. Addat Chronicon Melanchtonis et Peuceri, in quo omnis generis historiae, sacrae, profanae, magno judicio selectae et ad usum accommodatae sunt, in regendis moribus, augenda prudentia et accendo in animo Principis virtutum amore vitiorumque odio." Schmidt, *Geschichte der Erziehung der Pfälzischen Wittelsbacher*, 319 [Zwei Studienordnungen für Prinz Friedrich Heinrich. 1623 u. 1624]. See also, Emil Clemens Scherer, *Geschichte und Kirchengeschichte an den deutschen Universitäten: Ihre Anfänge im Zeitalter des Humanismus und ihre Ausbildung zu selbständigen Disziplinen* (Freiburg i. B.: Herder, 1927), 83.

from within the Empire. The early reception of *Carion's Chronicle* there had mostly been a process of adaptation and translation. The Latin text was expanded or continued to mitigate the German emphasis and make it more useful to a French audience. Likewise, the French translation by Jean le Blond included additional material about events in contemporary France. Indeed, in many respects, it is surprising how popular the *Chronicle* became in France during the sixteenth century, especially given the general anti-French tone of the original narrative.

In 1566, the French jurist Jean Bodin (1530–1596) finally launched an attack on the *Chronicle* in his *Method for the Easy Understanding of History*. From a political perspective, Bodin was mostly concerned with opposing Melanchthon's arguments for the importance of elected rule under the Imperial constitution. In contrast to the Imperial succession by election, Bodin argued for the superiority of hereditary royal rule, as in France; but in this context, he also attacked Melanchthon's interpretation of Daniel's Fourth Monarchy. A flurry of objections from German contempories followed, and Bodin's writings inspired responses from German intellectuals for decades. The Holy Roman Empire, despite all its shortcoming, provided a constitutional and legal framework of comprise that allowed the Germans to avoid the political and institutional crises that plagued France in the later sixteenth century. Moreover, the collective experience and the effects of the Reformation differed markedly in France and Germany. By 1555, the German princes and the Hapsburgs had come to terms over religious and political issues; and although tensions remained, especially over Calvinism, the Empire did not suffer the continued instability and violence of the French Wars of Religion. Therefore, the Germans could argue, with some justification, that the Holy Roman Empire offered a better example of peace and stability based on compromise and the rule of law than the situation of war torn France.

Although *Carion's Chronicle* was superseded by other texts in the seventeenth century, its underlying framework remained. During these decades, Melanchthon's interpretation of the Holy Roman Empire and the Four Monarchies continued as the standard view of both Daniel's prophecy and the Imperial constitution among German Protestants. Lutheran theologians long adhered to the Wittenberg perspective on Daniel as an article of faith, and their biblical commentaries held to the idea of the Holy Roman Empire as the Fourth Monarchy. Indeed, traces of Melanchthon's views persisted within the theological community even after the Empire itself dissolved. Imperial jurists similarly relied on Melanchthon's interpretation of Daniel well into the seventeenth century for their arguments about the relationship of the Holy Roman Empire to divine prophecy, though political pragmatists gradually began to question the relevance of Melanchthon's vision of Rome's legal and constitutional legacy among the Germans. The Wittenberg world of the 1520s had united law and theology in a compelling response to the problems of that day. Eventually, however, as the years wore on, that unity broke down in the face of changing European political realities, and the disciplines accordingly went their separate ways.

Through it all, German historians, particularly at Wittenberg, continued to rely on the Four Monarchies as a historiographical paradigm. After *Carion's Chronicle* fell out of use in the classroom, Wittenberg historians turned to *On the Four Chief Empires* (1556) by Johann Sleidanus (1506–1556), which similarly used the Four Monarchies to emphasize the continuity from Imperial Rome to Germany. As late as the 1720s, one Wittenberg professor still argued against all critics that the Holy Roman Empire would endure until the end of the world; and in the mid-eighteenth century, Wittenberg students were still required to listen to readings from *Carion's Chronicle* or Sleidanus at the evening meal. During these years, however, Wittenberg gradually receded from its position as a leading centre of historical scholarship, and other universities, such as Helmstedt, Halle and Göttingen took its place. Ultimately, Wittenberg historians would also abandon the Four Monarchies; but long after Daniel's prophecies had fallen out of favour, the arguments underlying Melanchthon's historical thought, and especially his interpretation of the medieval past, would remain an integral part of European intellectual culture.

2 Jean Bodin's Attack on German Political Thought

With *Carion's Chronicle*, Melanchthon contributed to a broader conversation about the constitution of the Holy Roman Empire, and through his influence, the Four Monarchies became the point of departure for theologians, historians and jurists to debate the past, present and future of the Holy Roman Empire.[2]

---

2 See generally Edgar Marsch, *Biblische Prophetie und chronographische Dichtung: Stoff- und Wirkungsgeschichte der Vision des Propheten Daniel nach Dan. VII* (Berlin: Erich Schmidt Verlag, 1972); Hanns Gross, *Empire and Sovereignty: A History of the Public Law Literature in the Holy Roman Empire, 1599–1804* (Chicago: University of Chicago Press, 1973); Arno Seifert, *Der Rückzug der biblischen Prophetie von der neueren Geschichte: Studien zur Geschichte der Reichstheologie des frühneuzeitlichen deutschen Protestantismus* (Cologne: Böhlau Verlag, 1990); Klaus Koch, *Europa, Rom und der Kaiser vor dem Hintergrund von zwei Jahrtausenden Rezeption des Buches Daniel* (Göttingen: Vandenhoeck & Ruprecht, 1997); and Mariano Delgado et al., eds., *Europa, Tausendjähriges Reich und Neue Welt: Zwei Jahrtausende Geschichte und Utopie in der Rezeption des Danielbuches* (Stuttgart: Kohlhammer, 2003).

In sixteenth century Europe, the ideas of "empire" and "universal monarchy" were changing in response to the rise of Spain and the world empire of Charles v.[3] Melanchthon himself remained in dialogue with medieval currents, yet in thinking about "monarchy," he focused on the struggle between the Germans and the Turks rather than the voyages of discovery and the formation of overseas empires.

In the later sixteenth century, Melanchthon's interpretive framework finally collided with the broader European reframing of the ideas of "monarchy" and "universal empire." In 1576, while Peucer languished in prison, Johann Wolf, a Protestant jurist, published his *Storehouse of the Historical Art*, which quickly caused a stir among German historians.[4] Despite the interest of early Renaissance humanists in historical scholarship, they had devoted limited attention to theoretical discussions of historical method.[5] Indeed, they inherited very little guidance on the subject from classical or medieval authors. Occasionally, a Renaissance scholar might insert a short discussion of historical writing into a text on the liberal arts or on education, but independent works on historical method started to appear only in the sixteenth century. In fact, the most widely circulated early modern discussion of historical thought was actually Melanchthon's brief introduction to *Carion's Chronicle*.

As the *ars historica* genre gradually developed, it became increasingly sophisticated, with contributions from across the European intellectual community. The texts in Wolf's *Storehouse of the Historical Art* reflect this increasing sophistication. Through an eclectic collection of orations and tracts on historical methodology, Wolf introduced German historians to trends in French and Italian historiography. A revised, enlarged edition was published in 1579, and the collection became a standard into the seventeenth century.[6] Wolf

---

3   See generally Franz Bosbach, "The European Debate on Universal Monarchy," in *Theories of Empire, 1450–1800*, ed. David Armitage (Brookfield, VT: Ashgate, 1998), 81–98.

4   Johann Wolf, ed., *Io. Bodoni Methodvs Historica, Dvodecim eiusdem argumenti Scriptorum, tam veterum quàm recentiorum, Commentariis adaucta: quorum elenchum Præfationi subiecimus.* (Basel: Perna, 1576). VD16 B 6274. For the complete contents, see John Brown, *The Methodus ad facilem historiarum cognitionem of Jean Bodin: A Critical Study* (Washington, D.C.: Catholic University of America Press, 1939), 47–49.

5   See Robert Black, "The New Laws of History," *Renaissance Studes* 1 (1987): 126–156; Anthony Grafton, "The Identities of History in Early Modern Europe: Prelude to a Study of the *Artes Historicae*," in *Historia: Empiricism and Erudition in Early Modern Europe*, ed. Gianna Pomata and Nancy Siraisi (Cambridge, MA: MIT Press, 2005), 41–74; and Anthony Grafton, *What was History? The Art of History in Early Modern Europe* (Cambridge: Cambridge University Press, 2007).

6   Johann Wolf, ed., *Artis Historicae Penvs Octodecim Scriptorum tam veterum quàm recentiorum monumentis & inter eos Io. præcipuè Bodini libri Methodi historicæ sex instructa.* (Basel: Perna, 1579). VD16 W 4208.

also included selections from German Protestants, and Melanchthon featured prominently, though indirectly, through the contributions by Christoph Pezel (1539–1604)[7] and David Chytraeus (1530–1600), who lectured on *Carion's Chronicle* at the University of Rostock.[8]

In particular, Wolf confronted Germans with Jean Bodin's *Method for the Easy Comprehension of History* (1566), which directly challenged Melanchthon's view of "monarchy" and the Imperial constitution.[9] Bodin considered *Carion's Chronicle* an accurate narrative,[10] but he rejected Melanchthon's underlying arguments about the Holy Roman Empire. Indeed, Bodin dismissed all those who clung to the belief that the Empire constituted the Fourth Monarchy of Daniel, and he devoted a chapter to the "Refutation of those who Postulate Four Monarchies and the Golden Age":[11]

> A long established, but mistaken, idea about four empires, made famous by the prestige of great men, has sent its roots down so far that it seems difficult to eradicate. It has won over countless interpreters of the Bible; it includes among modern writers Martin Luther, Melanchthon, Sleidan, Lucidus, Funck, and Panvinio – men well read in ancient history and things divine.[12]

---

7   Wolf printed a shortened version of the *Oratio de Argumento Historiarum* in the *Storehouse of the Historical Art*, omitting the introduction (*exordium*) – Wolf, *Artis Historicae Penvs* (Basel, 1579), vol. 2, 603–617.

8   David Chytraeus, *De Lectione Historiarum Recte Instituenda* (Wittenberg: Crato, 1563) VD16 C 2644; Wolf, *Artis Historicae Penvs* (Basel, 1579), vol. 2, 452–565.

9   Wolf, *Artis Historicae Penvs* (Basel, 1579), vol. 1, 1–396. The *editio princeps* is Jean Bodin, *Methodus, Ad Facilem Historiarum Cognitionem* (Paris: Martin le Jeune, 1566). An English translation is also available as Jean Bodin, *Method for the Easy Comprehension of History*, trans. Beatrice Reynolds (New York: Columbia University Press, 1945). See generally Brown, *The Methodus*; and Julian Franklin, *Jean Bodin and the Sixteenth-Century Revolution in the Methodology of Law and History* (New York: Columbia University Press, 1963).

10 "Ab eo scriptore aliquantùm informati de statu rerum omnium publicarum, Carionis aut veriùs Melancthonis historiam consimili diligentia percurremus. Est enim aliquanto copiosior in disputationibus de religione, vt erat religioni ac pietati deditus, quae si odiosa videntur, praeteriri facilè possunt: caetera quę in vniuersum de Rebuspublicis clarioribus dici potuerunt, breuiter & accuratè complexus mihi videtur. ac si quis est alius scriptor (sunt autem nonnulli) qui vniuersam mundi historiam Melancthone copiosiùs scripsit, hunc ego legendum censeo." Bodin, *Methodus* (Paris, 1566), 17.

11 Bodin *Methodus* (Paris, 1566), 346–361 (Chapter VII); Bodin, *Method* (New York, 1945), 291–302.

12 Bodin, *Method* (New York, 1945), 291. "Inveteratus error de quattuor imperiis, ac magnorum virorum opinione peruulgatus tam altè radices egit, vt vix euelli posse videatur, habet enim propè infinitos bibliorum interpretes: habet è inuioribus Martinum, Melanchthonem, Sleidanum, Lucidum, Funccium, Onuphrium; rerum diuinarum & antiquitatis homines valdè peritos." Bodin, *Methodus* (Paris, 1566), 346.

The French never came to terms with the idea that the Holy Roman Empire fulfilled Daniel's prophecy and that France was somehow excluded from divine favour, nor were they ever reconciled to the political supremacy of the Emperor. Since Melanchthon was the leading proponent of the Four Monarchies, Bodin's chapter was directed largely, though not entirely, against him.

Bodin attacked the idea that Germany was the Fourth Monarchy on two different grounds. First, he held that it was impossible to relate Daniel's prophecies of Four Monarchies to the flourishing "empires" of the sixteenth century.[13] Second, he argued that the German interpretation of Daniel was flawed, in part, because Germany itself failed to satisfy the definition of a "monarchy,"[14] both as a formal matter and in terms of practical reality.[15] Bodin considered Melanchthon's view on the German "monarchy" to be absurd – Germany was hardly the most powerful polity – and even more absurd was the idea that Germany held the Roman Imperium.[16] With regard to land or population, Germany did not compare to other kingdoms in Europe, such as Spain, and with its overseas holdings, even the king of Portugal controlled more territory.[17] In particular, Bodin pointed out the disparity between the power and vigour of the Turks and the Germans. The Turks ruled on three continents and they held Byzantium and Babylon, whereas the Empire was limited to a few border territories of the old Roman Empire.[18] In fact, none of the Four

---

13 "[I]ta non video quemadmodum beluas & statuam Danielis ad ea, quae nunc vbique florent, quaeque tot seculis floruerunt imperia traducamus." Bodin, *Methodus* (Paris, 1566), 346.

14 "[A]c primùm illud quod ait Philippus Melanchtho monarchiam sibi videre summam unius Reipublicae potentiam, quae aliarum opes & copias superare poßit." Bodin, *Methodus* (Paris, 1566), 347.

15 "Principiò monarchia nobis est imperij ac regionis quibusdam finibus constituenda, vel principis aut populi origine clara, vt intelligatur quid sit illud quod monarchiam vocant: quod cùm huius disputationis caput esset, non satis aptè definierunt interpretes oraculorum. posuerunt enim ex illa visione quattuor belluarum ac statuae, totidem imperia significari: puta Aßyriorum, Persarum, Gręcorum ac Romanorum, imperio praeesse. quod cùm à Germanis scriberetur, ad sui nominis & imperij gloriam scriptum esse iudicaui: est enim ab interpretatione Danielis omnino alienum. placet igitur suis ipsos rationibus confutare." Bodin, *Methodus* (Paris, 1566), 346–347.

16 "Absurdum est igitur quod Germani monarchiam, id est vt Philippus interpretatur, Rerum potentißimam: absurdius etiam quod imperium Romanorum se tenere putant: quod omnibus valde ridiculum videatur, qui orbis descriptionem animo penitus comprehensam habent." Bodin, *Methodus* (Paris, 1566), 348.

17 "[A]t ne regi quidem Lusitaniae pares sunt, si regionum logitudine imperium definiamus. nam is vniuersam pene oram Africae armis occupauit, ac fortißimis propugnaculis barbarorum impetus saepe repreßit." Bodin, *Methodus* (Paris, 1566), 347.

18 Bodin, *Methodus* (Paris, 1566), 348–349.

Monarchies exercised any sort of universal domination, and many kingdoms enjoyed greater power and prestige. If anything, Bodin argued that Daniel had meant the "Four Monarchies" to refer to the empires that would control Babylon, so the Medes, Persians, Greeks, and Parthians.[19] Bodin also revived the old French claims about Charlemagne to argue that he had not transferred the Empire from the Byzantines to the Germans.[20] Indeed, based on the historical record, Bodin suggested that the Fourth Monarchy should properly be called the French Monarchy rather than the German.[21]

More generally, in the *Method*, Bodin sought to present "royal power" (*regia potestas*), i.e. France's succession of dynastic rulers, as a superior political form to the elected "monarchy" of Germany.[22] Therefore, he portrays the elective principle as the cause of Germany's earlier political instability, rather than its enduring source of strength. Indeed, according to Bodin, Germany only attained a modicum of political calm once the German Emperors began to secure the election of hereditary successors. Accordingly, he presents the orderly succession of Frederick III to Maximilian I to Charles V as a striking contrast to the history of earlier Emperors, many of whom, he claims, were treacherously murdered.[23]

In an oration from 1554, Melanchthon had argued that the Electors constituted the Senate of the Empire, and they could both elect and, under some circumstances, depose the Emperor. Furthermore, the Emperor could not

---

19   "[A]c mihi diutiùs cogitanti quid propheta innuere vellet, nihil commodius occurrit, quàm interpretari de Babylone, quae in potestatem Medorum, Persarum, Graecorum, & Parthorum peruenit, quaeque saepiùs vastata est, ac tandem aliquando deleta." Bodin, *Methodus* (Paris, 1566), 352.

20   "Illud verò ineptius visum est, quòd Carolum magnum (qui quam monarchiam vocant primus occupauit) natione Gallum, in Gallia natum, lingua quoque, moribus & institutis Gallorum vnà cum suis maioribus educatum, modò Alemanum vocant." Bodin, *Methodus* (Paris, 1566), 351.

21   "[M]ultò veriùs igitur ac iustiùs Gallica monarchia dici debet, quae priùs virtute Gallorum parta est, quàm Germani monarchiae verbum audissent." Bodin, *Methodus* (Paris, 1566), 351.

22   For a more detailed discussion of Bodin's views, which can be inconsistent at times, see J.H.M. Salmon, "The Legacy of Jean Bodin: Absolutism, Populism or Constitutionalism," *History of Political Thought* 17, no. 4 (Winter 1996): 500–522.

23   "[N]ec priùs inter Germanorum principes bella pro imperio geri desierunt, quàm pater filium Caesarem designaret: vt Henricus III. filium adhuc puerum curauit eligendum, à quo nepos est adoptatus. & Carolus IIII. filium habuit successorem: hic fratrem Sigismundum, qui sibi generum adoptauit: Fridericus Maximilianum, hic nepotem. caeteri magna ex parte coniuratione aut veneno interierunt; Rudolphus, Albertus, Henricus VII. Fridericus III. Ludouicus Bauarus, Carolus Henrici nepos, Gutherus." Bodin, *Methodus* (Paris, 1566), 338.

promulgate legislation without a majority of the Electors. In view of this, Melanchthon maintained that the Empire was really an "aristocracy."[24] Peucer repeated this idea in *Carion's Chronicle*, but it seems to have attracted little attention at the time.[25] In a chapter on "Type of Government of the Germans," Bodin similarly claimed that the Empire was really an aristocracy, and this, together with his attack on the Fourth Monarchy, provided for decades of debate on whether the Empire was a "monarchy" or an "aristocracy."[26]

These discussions about the political structure of the Empire perpetuated the sixteenth century tension between "monarchy" as a political form and "monarchy" as the prophetic fulfilment of Daniel. Furthermore, they reflect the reality that the Emperors after Charles V were Austrian Hapsburgs, rather than the rulers of a vast empire that reached around the globe. Beyond this, Bodin developed ideas about sovereignty that forced the Germans to address questions about political supremacy between the Emperor and the territorial princes more precisely. Subsequent German political thought became consumed with these questions.

3   The Initial German Response to Bodin

Despite its incoherence and inconsistency, Bodin's assault on Melanchthon and the Four Monarchies sent shock waves through Germany. The Germans recognized that by attacking Melanchthon and his interpretation of Daniel's prophecy, Bodin might undercut both the certainty of their interpretation of the biblical text and the legal foundations for the Holy Roman Empire – two pillars of German Protestantism. For these later German humanists, the *translatio imperii* and the Four Monarchies were inextricably bound together.

In some sense, Bodin misrepresented Melanchthon's idea of "monarchy." He was correct that in *Carion's Chronicle* Melanchthon associated the Four Monarchies with territorial extent and authority over other rulers, even if not universal dominion.[27] Nevertheless, Bodin ignored the second, and more important, aspect of Melanchthon's perspective, his belief that God had established the Monarchies to uphold law and learning, and in the case of the

---

24   CR XII, 82–83.
25   "Ita Monarchia Occidentis temperata est & fuit honestissima Aristocratia, in qua vnus rerum potitur, qui statuit & sancit pleraque, de consilio & sententia Septemuirum, quorum inter se est aequalitas Arithmetica." Peucer, *Chronicon Carionis* (Wittenberg, 1580), 495.
26   Bodin *Methodus* (Paris, 1566), 242–243; Bodin, *Method* (New York, 1945), 206–208.
27   "Intelligas autem *monarchiam* non quidem complexam omnes regiones et gentes, sed tantam habuit potentiam, ut caeteros reges compescere posset." CR XII, 718.

Germans, religion.[28] On this basis, Melanchthon excluded the Turks from the Monarchies, not because they lacked political power, but rather because they were blasphemers who destroyed law and learning.[29] When the Germans set out to refute Bodin, they addressed his arguments about territorial control, but they concentrated much more on the issues that mattered – law, learning and religion.

The most important replies to Bodin's *Method* came from Leipzig and Wittenberg, the universities of Electoral Saxony. The Wittenberg response came from Andreas Franckenberger (1536–1590). Although Franckenberger has attracted little modern attention, in his own day, he ranked among the most influential German historians.[30] Franckenberger was born in Memmingen, and he had studied at Wittenberg. After Peucer's downfall, and the failed efforts to attract Reiner Reineccius, Franckenberger was called from Rostock back to Wittenberg. Although he was appointed as professor of rhetoric, he continued the lectures on *Carion's Chronicle*. In 1580, he was rewarded with additional compensation from Elector August for *lectio historiarum*.[31] Franckenberger's historical perspective was solidly Melanchthonian, and perhaps more than any other Late Reformation historian, he expressed the implicit notions behind the Protestant approach to history.[32] For this reason, he was highly regarded and frequently cited by his contemporaries. Indeed, almost a third of

---

28   "Ideo enim voluit Deus monarchias constitui, ut homines legibus, iudiciis et disciplina regerentur. Hoc ut fieret Deus dedit monarchas, instructos potentia, qui et leges honestas conderent, et iudicia ac disciplinam armis defenderent." CR XII, 718.

29   "Quarta Romanorum, quam significat Daniel tandem dilacerandam esse, et pedes partim ferreos, partim luteos fore. Etsi alii ferreos pedes intelligunt regnum Turcicum, caeteros luteos pedes: tamen ego existimo, Turcicum regnum, quod manifestas blasphemias contra verbum Dei profitetur, et ex professo delere nomen Christi conatur, non annumerari monarchiis, quas Deus legum et disciplinae causa constituit." CR XII, 719.

30   On Franckenberger, see Scherer, *Geschichte und Kirchengeschichte*, 55; and Heinz Kathe, *Die Wittenberger Philosophische Fakultät 1502–1817* (Köln: Böhlau, 2002), 151–154.

31   Scherer, *Geschichte und Kirchengeschichte*, 55; and Kathe, *Die Wittenberger Philosophische Fakultät*, 153.

32   Franckenberger focused especially on the pastoral interpretation of history that Melanchthon had outlined in the revision to *Carion's Chronicle* (CR XII, 900–902); e.g., "In distractionibus Theologorum nostra aetate, consolatur nos ex Histostoria [sic] recordatio dissidiorum inter ipsos Apostolos, & quidem ne labi possent, a Spiritu Sancto confirmatos: ac postea inter Patres praecipuos veteris ac purioris Ecclesiae, quorum imaginem in nostris dissensionibus uidere licet. Namque Diuus Paulus ad Galatas, secundo capite, Petrum Apostolum acriter reprehendit, eique in faciem resistit, quod, dum metuit alienationem Iudaeorum, ex gentibus conuersos offendit." Andreas Franckenberger, *Institvtionvm Antiqvitatis Et Historiarvm Pars Prima, In Libros Sex Distribvta* (Wittenberg: Crato, 1586), 447. VD16 F 2198. Cf. Wrocław, Biblioteka Uniwersytecka (Rehdigeriana) 429 – Andr. Franckenberger, observationes in chronicon Melanchthonis (1586).

Bartholomaus Keckermann's *ars historica*, which is generally considered one of the last major contributions to the genre, is actually a direct quotation from Franckenberger, who is rarely, if ever, mentioned in discussions of the *ars historica* tradition.[33]

To refute Bodin and vindicate prophetic history, Franckenberger wrote *On the Dignity of Prophetic History* (1580), a comprehensive defence of Protestant historiography.[34] From a theological standpoint, Franckenberger saw two major threats from the *Method*: first, it undermined the certainty of Daniel's prophecy about Christ's return, and second, it tore away the consolation found in the approaching Last Judgment and the resurrection of the dead.[35] Franckenberger also saw Bodin as declaring war on the Holy Roman Empire, based on such trivial questions as its size and population relative to other empires.[36]

33   Bartholomaus Keckermann remarked about Franckenberger's work, "Inter Effecta historiarum etiam est, quod ex iis liceat consolationes haurire in necessitatibus publicis ac priuatis. Sed & hunc effectum fusius quam alius quisquam deduxit Franckenbergerus, ideo ut omnia habeant studiosi quasi sub unum intuitum, in hac de effectis historiarum doctrina posita, non pudebit integrum locum huc transferre...." Bartholomaus Keckermann, *Operum omnium quae extant* (Geneva: Aubert, 1614), vol. 2, col. 1332. The parallel sections in Keckermann's *ars historica* are – Keckermann, *De natura ... historiae*, 54–90. Pages 54–65 (*Operum omnium*, col. 1327–1331) correspond to Franckenberger, *Institutionum antiquitatis*, 290–309; pages 65–68 (*Operum omnium*, col. 1331–1332) to Franckenberger, *Institutionum antiquitatis*, 309–314; and pages 68–90 (*Operum omnium*, col. 1332–1340) to Franckenberger, *Institutionum antiquitatis*, 428–468. The quotations are exact, except for occasional omissions of Greek translations and classical citations.

34   The Four Monarchies are treated specifically in Andreas Franckenberger, *De Amplitvdine Et Excellenti Historiæ Propheticae Dignitate: De Cavsis Ad Lectionem illius nos impellentibus: & adminiculis in meditatione: in quibus pleraq[ue] in hoc genere accuratè excutiuntur, quæ studiosis sacræ antiquitatis & historiarum scitu necessaria sunt: Authore M. Andrea Franckenbergero, Profeß. publico in Acad: VVitebergensi. Inserta est pagina 172, quòd res ita postularet, refutatio sententiæ Iohannis Bodini, Galli Andegaui, qui celebritate nominis multorum regnorum aures & animos compleuit, de monarchijs quatuor, pro Daniele Propheta: pro Imperio Romanorum Germanico: Doctore Luthero & Domino Philippo Melanthone, quibus iniuria facta est. Index ordinis & rerum memorabilium sequitur dedicationem.* (Wittenberg: Simon Gronenberg, [1580]), 160–222. VD16 F 2196.

35   "Primum eripitur nobis certitudo in isto Propheta excellentissimo de tempore aduentus Messiae.... Eripitur piis ualde aerumnosis in hac uita consolatio de appropinquante iudicio postremo: resuscitatione mortuorum, & de regni Seruatoris nostri aeterna maiestate...." Franckenberger, *De Amplitvdine* (Wittenberg, 1580), 185.

36   "Verum in eodem tractatu de monarchiis Bodinus, Vir Clarissimus, suscipit bellum contra Germanicum romanorum Imperium, non quidem armis, sed stylo, quem stringit contra ipsum, ut illa dignitas, quam adhuc Dei beneficio per neruum Collegii septem Electorum tenet patria nostra, communis omnium parens, in uniuersum auferatur. Negat enim Germanos habere monarchiam, id quod Doctor Lutherus, D. Philippus Melanthon, & doctissimi quique in orbe Christiano senserunt & sentiunt: atque illud probare eo modo instituit: Hispaniarum princeps imperium habet Germanico maius, tum populorum

To reassert the German interpretation of Daniel's prophecy, Franckenberger turned to Luther and Melanchthon and argued that Scripture should be allowed to interpret Scripture; wild theories should not intrude on prophecy.[37] To defend the Holy Roman Empire, Franckenberger outlined the distinguishing characteristics of the Four Monarchies. In this respect, their greatness did not lie in territorial possessions, but rather in their laws and relationship to true religion. Franckenberger repeated the standard claim that Christ would return during the Fourth Monarchy,[38] and he expressed the sentiment of every German Protestant: the Holy Roman Empire held a special place in the divine plan because the light that drove away the darkness of the papacy had come from Saxony. God had chosen Luther, and Luther was German.[39] No Protestant could deny Luther's decisive, positive intervention in the course of history, and Franckenberger used this to reinforce the special role of Germany in the divine plan for the Church. Aside from the intersection of true religion and the Empire, Franckenberger focused on the importance of law, and specifically Roman Law, for the greatness of Germany.[40]

The Leipzig reply came from Matthias Dresser (1536–1607), a professor at the university there. In contrast to Franckenberger, Dresser is generally recognized

---

multitudine, tum amplitudine regionum: ut omittam regiones Americas (quibus ex magna parte dominatur) Europa triplo maiores." Franckenberger, *De Amplitvdine* (Wittenberg, 1580), 191.

[37] "Danielis mentem ac sensum retinuerunt atque conseruarunt duo lumina Ecclesiae, Lutherus & Melanthon, qui nostra aetate diuinitus effloruerunt. Namque is tandem iudicatur uerus Scripturae sacrae interpres, qui intelligentiam ex scriptura, atque ex textuum collatione aufert, asportatque, non suis theoriis indulget, aut sensum alienum ex antro Trophonio, more haereticorum Vatibus diuinis et Apostolis affingit." Franckenberger, *De Amplitvdine* (Wittenberg, 1580), 183.

[38] "Praedicit [Daniel] enim Filium Dei in quarta monarchia uenturum esse, & sacrificium oblaturum, ad quod mittendus erat: ac deinde finem fore generationis hominum, & secuturam esse mortuorum resuscitationem." Franckenberger, *De Amplitvdine* (Wittenberg, 1580), 179.

[39] "Emicuit autem in Imperio Germanico lux Verbi diuini, ac fulgore claritatis omnia regna uicina praestrinxit, quae secundum Deum Ecclesiis nostris magnam gratiam habere debent. Nam ex hoc ipso Electoratu Saxoniae, & oppido Witeberga, doctrina de sordibus, & coeno Papistico perpurgata, longe lateque diffusa est in Angliam, Galliam, Daniam, Suecium, Poloniam, Vngariam, Bohemiam, quae res cunctis thesauris Turcicis anteferenda est. Quod itaque de magnitudine regionum detractum esse uidetur, id repuratione & instauratione Verbi coelestis per Lutherum facta, compensatum." Franckenberger, *De Amplitvdine* (Wittenberg, 1580), 194.

[40] "Neque uero humaniores leges & pulchriores in toto mundo inueniuntur, quam in iure ciuli romano, quemadmodum omnes sapientes una mente unoque ore iudicant & testantur." Franckenberger, *De Amplitvdine* (Wittenberg, 1580), 197.

as one of the last great German humanists of the sixteenth century.[41] He studied briefly at Wittenberg, and after teaching for a time at Erfurt, in 1574 he was called to replace Justus Lipsius at Jena. Already in 1575, however, Elector August of Saxony had lured Dresser away from Jena by offering him positions at the school in Meissen or the University of Leipzig. Dresser chose Meissen, but within a few years, Wittenberg and Leipzig were both trying to add him to their faculty. In the end, Leipzig won out, and Dresser stayed there until his death in 1607.

When Johann Wolf introduced Bodin's *Method* to Germany, Dresser quickly answered the challenge with an *Oration on the Four Monarchies* (1581).[42] The certainty of biblical prophecy stands at the centre of Dresser's arguments, and his oration focuses on the theological implications of the *Method* more than the political. Therefore, he treats Bodin as a heretic rather than a revolutionary. To start, Dresser counters Bodin's claim that Melanchthon had misused the term "monarchy," and by collating events against the prophecy itself, he dispels any misunderstandings about the monarchies. Dresser then argues that Bodin had failed to muster any patristic support for his ideas, as opposed to Melanchthon who relied on the consensus of the early Church.[43] In fact, by denying Rome fulfilled the prophecy of the Four Monarchies, Bodin had done nothing more than resurrect the "Jewish heresy" from Antiquity that Theodoret of Cyrus († ca. 457) had rejected in his writings on Daniel.[44] Dresser then

---

41 On Dresser, see especially Matthias Pohlig, *Zwischen Gelehrsamkeit und konfessioneller Identitätsstiftung Lutherische Kirchen- und Universalgeschichtsschreibung 1546–1617* (Tübingen: Mohr Siebeck, 2007), 189–198.

42 Matthaeus Dresser, *Oratio De Qvatvor Monarchiis, Sive Svmmis Imperiis, A Daniele Propheta Expressis. Contra Veterem Ivdaeorum errorem, hoc tempore à Ioanne Bodino Gallo, in methodo historica renouatum* (Leipzig: Beyer, 1581). VD16 D 2737. I cite to the later edition of the oration in Matthaeus Dresser, *Isagoges Historicae Pars prima* (Leipzig: Lantzenberger, 1598). VD16 D 2721. Dresser's *Isagoges* were an introduction to universal history divided by millennia.

43 "Possem quidem autoribus ad hoc confirmandum uti grauissimis, Hieronymo, Augustino, Theodoreto, Lyra, atque adeo totius antiquitatis consensu, sed plus ualeat apud nos Prophetae, non ambiguum neque obscurum, sed expressum, & experientia ipsa stabilitum testimonium. Quod si secutus esset in sua methodo historica Ioannes Bodinus, minus in dubitationem atque errorem raptus esset. Sed dum, relictis, uel certe non satis consideratis scripturae uerbis caecorum Magistrorum Iudaeorum interpretationi assentiri mauult, fieri non potest, quin in easdem erroris tenebras cum illis indicat." Dresser, *Oratio de Quatuor Monarchiis* (Leipzig, 1598), 597.

44 "Intelligo enim non nunc primum hanc a Ioanne Bodino in contentione poni, sed iam olim quoque a Iudaeis ipsis in controuersiam disceptationemque uocatam esse. Sic enim scribit Theodoretus oratione septima in Danielem: Ego in praesenti omissa Iudaeorum accusatione, uehementer admiror, quosdam pietatis magistros quartam bestiam vocasse regnum Macedonicum." Dresser, *Oratio de Quatuor Monarchiis* (Leipzig, 1598), 575.

explained how the Holy Roman Empire fit perfectly with Daniel's description of iron mixed with clay, sometimes strong and sometimes weak.[45] More importantly, the Roman Empire had seen Christ's nativity, and this stood as proof that the Holy Roman Empire would witness his return in glory.[46] While Franckenberger had countered the essence of Bodin's attack, Dresser unpacked the arguments point by point.

After the initial volleys, the dispute between Bodin and the Germans continued intermittently for several years. In 1576, Bodin had published his most famous work, *Six Books on the Republic*.[47] Although *On the Republic* developed many of the themes from the *Method*, the intervening years led Bodin to revise aspects of his political vision. In particular, he had come to favour absolutism: a strong French monarchy unconstrained by other political institutions. The change in Bodin's thinking was a reaction to Huguenot political thought and to the religious violence that had erupted in France during the 1570s. By the publication of *On the Republic*, Bodin viewed a strong monarchy as the only force capable of bringing peace and order back to France.

By the time Franckenberger wrote *On the Dignity of Prophetic History*, it had been almost fifteen years since the initial publication of Bodin's *Method*. Nevertheless, within a year, Bodin wrote an *Apology* (1581) to *On the Republic*, under the pseudonym René Herpin, that addressed the complaints from Wittenberg.[48] In the *Apology*, Bodin responded to several of his critics, but the

---

45 "Ex hac Prophetae ipsius interpretatione elucet inprimis illud, quod gemina sit forma seu facies Imperii Romani, ferrea & lutea, siue potens, & contrita, seu infirma. Id cum res euentusque clarissime demonstret, nemo de ueritate & conuenientia Imperii Romani & praedictionis Danielis dubitare potest." Dresser, *Oratio de Quatuor Monarchiis* (Leipzig, 1598), 582.

46 "Ita error est Iohannis Bodini uetus & quidem detestabilis, si serio; refellendus uero, si, ut ego suspicor, Iudaeorum causa simulate contra Monarchias disputauit. Verum mala & impia consuetudo est contra Deum, aut diuinum ipsius uerbum disputandi, siue ex animo id fit, siue simulate. Et decet sane nos Christianos nos incerta spe duci, aut pendere animis, cum de diuino uerbo agimus: Sed persuasum hoc penitus nobis habeamus, Christi nostri natiuitatem apte cum Danielis Propheta congruere, & in quartam Monarchiam incidisse. Cumque haec pars uaticinii Danielis certo euenerit: certi sumus, euenturum etiam alterum, ut in nubibus uenientem filium Dei uideamus, ad liberandum nos ab omni luto, & coeno, in quo misere haeremus atque luctamur: stante adhuc eo ipso ordine imperiorum, quem praedixit Daniel, nempe in Monarchia quarta & ultima. Idque ut quam primum fiat, uotis, suspiriis, & gemitibus assiduis te oramus, fili DEI Iesu Christe, quo in regnum illud tuum aeternum & perbeatum, laeticia & luce abundans, traducamur, & re factoque summa uaticinii atque promissi tui compleatur. [Finis]." Dresser, *Oratio de Quatuor Monarchiis* (Leipzig, 1598), 600–601.

47 See Quentin Skinner, *The Foundations of Modern Political Thought*, vol. 2, *The Age of Reformation* (Cambridge: Cambridge University Press, 1978), 284–301.

48 "Caeteri mitiores fuêre, & eorum reprehensio laudabilis ipsa per sese: qui aliud scribentes, locos è republica qui corrigi debere sibi videbantur, cum praefatione laudis, & sine

section devoted to Franckenberger appears at the beginning and is especially lengthy. Once again, Bodin stressed the uncertainty in deciding on the correct historical interpretation of the Four Monarchies, and he inserted extensive sections from the *Method* to reiterate his position.[49] Since Dresser's *Oration* was published only in 1581, the *Apology* does not mention it.

By 1586, however, Dresser's *Oration* had also come to Bodin's attention. In that year, Bodin prepared a new Latin edition of *On the Republic*. The edition does not include the *Apology*, but Bodin inserted new material into the text itself to answer his critics. In the chapter entitled, "whether it is possible to foresee changes in polities" (*An Rerumpublicarum conversiones prospici possit*), he added dismissive comments about Franckenberger, "the pontiff of the Leipzigers," and Dresser, "a schoolman lacking in reason."[50] Nevertheless, he did not explicitly engage with the criticism from Wittenberg, as he had in the *Apology*.

In 1587, Dresser again wrote against Bodin,[51] and he responded specifically to the arguments in *On the Republic*.[52] This time, Dresser focused more on the

---

contumelia notarunt. Inter quos est Ostatus Vasco, & Andreas Frankebergerus Saxo, qui non ita pridem Augusto Saxoniae duci librum de amplitudine, et excellenti historiae propheticae dignitate nuncupauit, quibus libenter responderem, si quid à negotiis et literis forensibus otij impetrare possem." Jean Bodin, *Apologie de Rene Herpin Pour la Republique de I. Bodin* (Paris: Jacques du Puys, 1581), fol. 2v; see esp. fol. 6r–10r.

49 Bodin, *Apologie de Rene Herpin* (Paris, 1581), esp. fol. 6r–10r.

50 "Quae verò de imperiis Daniel scripsit, apertè ille quidem Medos, Persas, & Graecos ad Babylonis imperium vocauit, praeter eos certè neminem. Quartum imperium ad Romanos non pertinere docuimus, cùm illic de Babylone quaeratur, quam Romani nunquam subegerunt: quod cùm tentauissent Euphrate transmisso, saepe illi & quidem ingentes ab inuictissimis Parthis clades acceperunt. Ineptiùs tamen, qui quartum illud imperium tribuunt Germanis, qui ne per somnium quidem vllam imperij Babylonici particulam viderunt. Quae quòd à nobis alibi disputata [In methodo historiarum] sunt, omitto: ea temen [i.e. tamen] Frankebergerus Saxo Lipsiorum Pontifex Lutheri autoritate: Dresserus verò homo de schola nulla subiecta ratione, maledictis refellit: hunc ego disertum putabo si quàm malè didicit tam bene dicere condiscat. Sed quoniam homo iracundus, commune ingeniosorum hominum malum, mihi subirascitur quòd de oraculis diuinis temere affirmare non ausim. ne quid in rebus tam arduis & ab omnium sensu retrusis offendam: docere debuerat, cur quinquaginta imperia, quae denotaui, decies Germanico maiora, quaeque imperij Babylonici magna partem complexa sunt Danielem omisisse putet?" Jean Bodin, *De Republica Libri Sex* (Paris: Jacques du Puys, 1586), 422. The section is found in Book 4, Chapter 11.

51 Matthaeus Dresser, *Oratio De Monarchia Qvarta Romano Germanica, quam Ioannes Bodinus, cum Iudaeis, conuellere nondum desistit. Separatim, & cum millenario isagoges historicae quinto coniuncte edita* (Leipzig: Defner, 1587). VD16 D 2713. I cite to the later edition of the oration in Matthaeus Dresser, *Isagoges Historicae Millenarius Quintus* (Leipzig: Lantzenberger, 1599). VD16 ZV 4777.

52 "Quid ergo? quoniam sua ille in uolumine de Repub. repetit, meque ad respondendum prouocat: faciendum mihi putaui, ut ne quid desiderare in me studii posset, quod

political implications of Bodin's ideas, and he warned the Elector of Saxony (to whom he dedicated the *Oration*) about the danger of dismissing the conventional interpretation of Daniel's prophecy.[53] If the Holy Roman Empire does not embody the Fourth Monarchy, then neither the Emperor nor the Electors would survive.[54] In the *Oration*, Dresser focuses especially on refuting Bodin's reordering of the succession of Monarchies. Since Bodin tried to bind Daniel's Monarchies to territorial possession of Babylon itself – thereby excluding Rome – Dresser separates the rule of the Monarchies from control of specific lands.[55] He also links the transfer of Empire from East to West with the spread of the Gospel, another sign of divine favour.[56]

Among German Protestants, Franckenberger and Dresser quickly became heroes for defending the Holy Roman Empire against the attacks of the French.[57] After his release from prison in 1586, Caspar Peucer's opinion was

---

ad causae disceptationem pertineret." Dresser, *Oratio de monarchia quarta Romano-germanica* (Leipzig, 1599), sig. Mm5v.

[53] "Mallem certe tacere, ac in communi, ab omnibusque Christianis hactenus accepta atque probata sententia acquiescere: idque affirmare omni asseueratione possum. Sed profecto res est maior grauiorque multo, quam ut deseri ab officio eius qui se Christianum, qui imperii Romani membrum aut subditum se profitetur, possit aut debeat. Nisi enim monarchiam quartam Romanorum & Germanorum a Daniele definitam esse statuamus: Deus bone, quantas tenebras, & quam horribilem confusionem in Ecclesiam & Rempublicam inuehemus?" Dresser, *Oratio de monarchia quarta Romano-germanica* (Leipzig, 1599), sig. Mm7v.

[54] "Et uero duces Electores imperii de gradu & dignitate omni deiicientur. Quibus concessis, quota pars imperii salua erit? Monarchia enim sublata, aut negata, nec rex, nec imperator, nec princeps elector imperii reliquus esse potest." Dresser, *Oratio de monarchia quarta Romano-germanica* (Leipzig, 1599), sig. Mm7v.

[55] "Hoc ergo inter Bodinum & me interest, quod is unum tantum statuit imperium Babylonicum, tanquam principale, quod alio tempore Chaldaei, alio Persae, alio Graeci tenuerit. Quod reipsa aliud nihil est, quam confundere monarchias, & ex quatuor unam efficere, quae uno eodemque loco consistens, diuersis dominis aliis atque aliis temporibus paruerit." Dresser, *Oratio de monarchia quarta Romano-germanica* (Leipzig, 1599), sig. Nn6v.

[56] "Vt enim ecclesiam peragrare totum orbem oportuit, ut omnib. gentibus atque populis Dei patefactiones innotescerent: sic monarchias etiam necesse fuit, ab Oriente in Occidentem, Meridiem, adeoque in Septentrionem penetrare: ut uterque Christi aduentus in carnem, & ad iudicium manifestus omnibus fieret, & series temporum rerumque maximarum momenta in mundo usque ad finem eius notari atque possent." Dresser, *Oratio de monarchia quarta Romano-germanica* (Leipzig, 1599), sig. Nn5v–Nn6r.

[57] Brown, *The Methodus*, 71–72. See "Nam praeter Andream Francobergerum Oratione erudita, collectisque argumentis firmissimis, istam istam σοφιστικὴν καὶ χρησολογίαν refellit MATTHAEVS DRESSERVS, & Bodinianum commentum antiquum Iudaeorum delirium esse demonstrat." Reiner Reineccius, *Methodus Legendi Cognoscendique Historiam tam sacram quàm profanam* (Helmstedt: Lucius, 1583), fol. 18v. VD16 R 890.

eagerly sought about the dispute, but he never published on the topic.[58] By then, the initial interlocutors were fading from the scene. Franckenberger died in 1590, Bodin in 1596, and Dresser in 1607. Unlike many intellectual disputes, however, this controversy did not die with the original antagonists. Instead, the tension between Melanchthon and Bodin over the Four Monarchies continued to influence the German intellectual community for decades. Indeed, the dispute continued to resurface among theologians, jurists and historians in ways both independent and interconnected.

4 The Fourth Monarchy and the Theologians

From the perspective of theology, the later sixteenth century and seventeenth century were the great age of Lutheran confessional orthodoxy.[59] After Peucer's fall in 1574, Elector August purged the University of Wittenberg of Philippists and replaced them with conservative Lutherans. After a brief interlude under his son, Elector Christian I (1586–1591), who was more inclined toward Calvinism, Wittenberg regained and then retained its status as a bastion of conservative Lutheranism throughout the seventeenth century. During these years, Lutheran theologians produced massive works of biblical interpretation and systematic theology, sometimes referred to as a new Protestant scholasticism. Within this world, Melanchthon's interpretation of the Holy Roman Empire and the Four Monarchies remained the standard view of both Daniel's prophecy and the Imperial constitution.

Luther's thought on the *translatio imperii* and the Fourth Monarchy had shifted over the course of his career. In his early treatise *To the Christian Nobility* (1520), Luther had devoted an entire chapter to an attack on the papal theory of the *translatio imperii*, and he rejected the Holy Roman Empire as the fulfilment of Daniel's prophecies.[60] By 1530, he had changed his position on Daniel, and in his introduction to the German translation of the book he adopted Melanchthon's view.[61] In one of his last major works, *Against the Roman Papacy, An Institution of the Devil* (1545), Luther again devoted an extended section

---

58 For Peucer's views on history after his release, see his letter preface of 1588 in Reiner Reineccius, *Historia Iulia* (Helmstedt: Lucius, 1594), fol. c2v–c3r. VD16 R 886.

59 See generally, Timothy Schmeling, ed., *Lives & Writings of the Great Fathers of the Lutheran Church* (St. Louis: Concordia Publishing House, 2016); and Robert D. Preus, *The Theology of Post-Reformation Lutheranism*, 2 vols. (St. Louis: Concordia Publishing House, 1970–1972).

60 WA 6:462–465.

61 WA 11ⁿ:4–6

to the *translatio imperii*, but without reference to Daniel.[62] Subsequent interpreters of Luther were thus left to ponder which of his shifting explanations reflected his actual view. Decades later, Matthias Flacius Illyricus, Melanchthon's great rival within Lutheranism, also joined the debate by publishing a treatise entitled *On the Translation of the Roman Empire to the Germans* (1566).[63] Flacius attacked the papal theory of the *translatio imperii*, and he asserted that God had transferred the Empire to the Germans through Charlemagne's sword rather than a papal blessing.[64] Although Flacius's treatise did elicit a direct reply from the Catholic controversialist Robert Bellarmine (1542–1621),[65] within Lutheran confessional circles, its impact remained limited.

By contrast, Melanchthon's view of the *translatio imperii* became fixed as an article of faith within Lutheranism. The official Lutheran confessional texts gathered in the *Book of Concord* (1580) included not only the *Augsburg Confession* (1530) and its *Apology* (1531), both authored by Melanchthon, but also his *Treatise on the Power and Primacy of the Pope* (1537).[66] In the *Treatise*, Melanchthon directly addressed, and rejected, papal involvement in secular affairs, including the curial theory of the *translatio imperii*:

> Christ gave to his apostles only spiritual authority.... He did not give them the power of the sword or the right to establish, take possessions, or dispose of the kingdoms of the world. ... For this reason [the *Unam Sanctam* of Pope Boniface VIII] and other similar statements, which contend that the pope is lord of the kingdoms of the world by divine right, are false and impious. This conviction brought horrible darkness upon the church and afterward precipitated great tumult in Europe. For the ministry of the gospel was neglected. Knowledge of faith and of the spiritual realm was destroyed. Christian righteousness was equated with that external government which the pope had created. Then the popes began grabbing

---

62   WA 54:206–299. The discussion of the *translatio imperii* is found in Part III.
63   Matthias Flacius, *De Translatione Imperii Romani Ad Germanos* (Basel: Perna, 1566). VD16 F 1502.
64   Werner Goez, *Translatio imperii: Ein Beitrag zur Geschichte des Geschichtsdenkens und der politischen Theorien im Mittelalter und in der frühen Neuzeit* (Tübingen: Mohr, 1958), 291–304.
65   Robert Bellarmine, *De Translatione Imperii Romani A Graecis Ad Francos, Adversvs Matthiam Flaccivm Illyricvm, Libri Tres* (Antwerp: Plantin, 1589).
66   *The Book of Concord: The Confessions of the Evangelical Lutheran Church*, ed. Robert Kolb and Timothy J. Wengert (Minneapolis: Fortress Press, 2000), 327–344 (*Treatise on the Power and Primacy of the Pope*); *Die Bekenntnisschriften der evangelisch-lutherischen Kirche* (Göttingen: Vandenhoeck & Ruprecht, 1998), 469–498 (*De potestate et primatu papae tractatus*).

an empire for themselves. They transferred kingships. They harassed the rulers of almost all the nations of Europe, but especially the emperors of Germany, with unjust excommunications and wars: sometimes to occupy Italian cities and other times to bring the German bishops into subjection and to deprive the emperors of the right to appoint bishops. Indeed, it is even written in the Clementines: "When the imperial office falls vacant, the pope is the legitimate successor." Thus, the pope, contrary to the command of Christ, has not only violated sovereignty [*dominatio*] but even exalted himself tyrannically over all rulers.[67]

Through the *Treatise*, Melanchthon's anti-papal narrative of medieval history was transmitted to subsequent generations as an authoritative confessional statement. The Lutheran confessions, however, do not specifically identify the Holy Roman Empire as the Fourth Monarchy, nor do they discuss Charlemagne's assumption of the Imperial title. Nevertheless, Melanchthon's interpretation of the Four Monarchies still found an audience whenever Luther's introduction to Daniel was included with the German Bible. Furthermore, some publishers continued to include the 1529 Wittenberg World Map (with its cartographic presentation of Daniel's prophecies) in German Bibles into the seventeenth and eighteenth centuries.[68] Initially, the distinction between history and prophecy made little difference. Eventually, however, later generations could retain Melanchthon's narrative of medieval history but abandon his interpretation of the Fourth Monarchy, because the Lutheran confessions themselves did not address the Holy Roman Empire as the fulfilment of Daniel's prophecies.

Within Protestantism more generally, Calvin and many Reformed theologians did not accept the Holy Roman Empire as the continuation of the ancient Roman Empire or as Daniel's Fourth Monarchy.[69] Instead, they believed that Daniel's prophecies were already fulfilled by the first century. Calvin himself still treated ancient Rome (though not the Holy Roman Empire) as the Fourth Monarchy, but some Reformed theologians adopted the view that the Four Monarchies referred to Babylon, Media, Persia and Greece, thereby omitting Rome entirely. Among these was Hugo Grotius (1583–1645) – most famous as the father of international law – who adopted this view in his influential

---

67   *The Book of Concord* (Minneapolis, 2000), 335–336.
68   These images are cataloged and reproduced by Ernst Gallner at http://www.daniels-dream-map.com/index.htm. See also Ernst Gallner, "Daniel's Dream Map: The Wittenberg World Map 1529–1661," *International Map Collector's Society Journal* 114, no. 3 (Autumn 2008): 49–53.
69   See generally, Seifert, *Der Rückzug*, 49–64; and Goez, *Translatio Imperii*, 370–377.

commentary on the Old Testament.[70] In general, Reformed thinkers showed much less investment in the Imperial constitution than the Lutherans. Calvin himself was French and his focus was primarily directed to Switzerland and France. Furthermore, Calvinism had been left out of the settlement established by the Peace of Augsburg in 1555. Thus, the Reformed were more inclined to challenge Melanchthon's view of the Four Monarchies because they lacked the same attachments to the established political order.

On the other end of the spectrum, Catholic thought tended to defend the *translatio imperii* theory to uphold the established Imperial order. The great controversialist Robert Bellarmine wrote a refutation of Flacius, but more generally, even he did not subscribe to the extreme positions of medieval political thought.[71] By contrast, although Cesare Baronio (1538–1607) cited Bellarmine in his *Ecclesiastical Annals* (1588–1607) – the monumental refutation of the *Magdeburg Centuries* – he still defended the medieval view of the *translatio imperii* that the pope had the right to transfer rule, including the Imperial title.[72] However, the 1556 abdication of Charles V in the presence of Imperial, rather than papal, officials had been a watershed moment. The exclusion of the papacy from the Peace of Westphalia also demonstrated unequivocally that papal claims to universal secular authority were a relic of the past.[73] As a result, later Catholic thought in the Empire actually tended to align more with the Lutherans in emphasizing the importance of the Imperial constitution against the destabilizing influence of the Calvinists.

Against this background, conservative Lutheran theologians of the seventeenth century had both theological and political pressure to maintain the Holy Roman Empire as Daniel's Fourth Monarchy. The standard Lutheran biblical commentaries of this era by the Wittenberg theologian Abraham Calov (1612–1686), for instance, held to Melanchthon's interpretation. Calov was a prolific scholar, but he was especially well-regarded in Lutheran confessional circles for his biblical commentaries.[74] In his *Biblia Illustrata* (1672–1676),

---

70 Seifert, *Der Rückzug*, 115–122.
71 Stefania Tutino, *Empire of Souls: Robert Bellarmine and the Christian Commonwealth* (Oxford: Oxford University Press, 2010), 33–39; Goez, *Translatio Imperii*, 305–328; and Seifert, *Der Rückzug*, 41–44.
72 Goez, *Translatio Imperii*, 324–325.
73 See Constantin Fasolt, "Sovereignty and Heresy," in *Infinite Boundaries: Order, Disorder, and Reorder in Early Modern German Culture*, ed. Max Reinhart (Kirksville: Sixteenth Century Journal Publishers, 1998), 385–386.
74 On Calov, see Timothy Schmeling, "Abraham Calov (1612–86): The Prussian on the *Cathedra Lutheri*," in *Lives & Writings of the Great Fathers of the Lutheran Church*, ed. Timothy Schmeling (St. Louis: Concordia Publishing House, 2016), 243–262.

he provided an extensive Latin commentary for a scholarly audience, and he wrote specifically to counter the Reformed biblical commentaries of Hugo Grotius.[75] For popular consumption, Calov produced the Luther-Calov German Bible, which included annotations for pious readers.[76] In both works, Calov presented the Holy Roman Empire as Daniel's Fourth Monarchy, which would endure until the end of the world.[77] Thus as German Protestants – such as Johann Sebastian Bach (1685–1750) – read their Luther-Calov Bibles, they saw Daniel through the lens of sixteenth century Wittenberg.

Within systematic theology, leading Lutheran dogmaticians likewise held to Melanchthon's interpretation of Daniel. In his *Loci Theologici* (1610–1625), for example, the University of Jena professor Johann Gerhard (1582–1637) specifically stated:

> Furthermore, from the prophecy of Daniel concerning the Four Monarchies it is correctly inferred that the Roman Monarchy, under which we are living, shall endure until the end of the world, for the end of this Monarchy and the coming of Christ in judgment shall be linked directly.[78]

Gerhard is generally considered the preeminent Lutheran theologian of the seventeenth century, and his works have remained influential in confessional circles to the present.[79] Although he did not specifically mention Bodin in this section of the *Loci Theologici*, other theologians continued to write against the attacks launched by the adversary of their intellectual forefathers. In 1654, for example, Gerhard's nephew, the Wittenberg dogmatician Johann Andreas Quenstedt (1617–1688), published a series of theological biographies in which he famously remarked that Bodin "vomits forth all sorts of slanders against the

---

75 Abraham Calov, *Biblia Testam. Veteris Illustrata*, vol. 2 (Frankfurt a.M.: Wustius, 1672). See Henk Nellen, "Bible Commentaries as a Platform for Polemical Debate: Abraham Calovius versus Hugo Grotius," in *Neo-Latin Commentaries and the Management of Knowledge in the Late Middle Ages and the Early Modern Period (1400–1700)*, ed. Karl Enenkel and Henk Nellen (Leuven: Leuven University Press, 2013), 445–472.
76 On the book of Daniel – Abraham Calov, *Das Andere VOLUMEN Der Göttlichen Schrifften Alten Testaments* (Wittenberg: Schrödter, 1682).
77 Calov, *Biblia Illustrata* (Frankfurt a.M., 1672), vol. 2, 592–599, 612–622; Calov, *Das Andere VOLUMEN Der Göttlichen Schrifften Alten Testaments* (Wittenberg, 1682), col. 933–939.
78 "Porrò ex Danielis de quatuor Monarchiis vaticinio rectè colligitur, *Romanam Monarchiam, sub qua vivimus, usque ad finem mundi duraturam*, cùm finis huius Monarchiae & Christi ad judicium adventus immediatè conjungantur." Johann Gerhard, *Loci Theologici* (1619), vol. VI, 779. See Seifert, *Der Rückzug*, 85.
79 See Preus, *The Theology of Post-Reformation Lutheranism*, vol. 1, 52–53.

Germans. He is always boasting about himself and his people, but too ready to tread others into the earth."[80]

Thus, among German Lutheran theologians, Melanchthon's interpretation of the Four Monarchies remained an enshrined article of faith. Challenges emerged as some Lutheran theologians adopted the critical methods of biblical interpretation pioneered during the Enlightenment. Nevertheless, the leading Lutheran biblical commentary of the eighteenth century, the *Biblical Synopsis* (1747) of Johann Georg Starke (1712–1762), still followed the standard sequence for the Four Monarchies – Assyria-Babylon, Persia, Greece and Rome – with the Holy Roman Empire becoming the successor to ancient Rome through Charlemagne.[81]

After the dissolution of the Empire in 1806, theologians, unlike jurists and historians, could not simply ignore Daniel's prophecies. Instead, they had to accommodate their exegesis of Daniel to changed political circumstances. As late as the early twentieth century, Lutheran theologians were still trying to preserve the idea of the Holy Roman Empire as the fulfilment of the Fourth Monarchy. Indeed, one widely circulated commentary, Paul Kretzmann's *Popular Commentary of the Bible* (1922–1924), actually reverted to a variation of the medieval views that had seen both Charlemagne and the papacy as the successors to the Roman Empire:

> The fourth beast is the Roman Empire with its insatiable fierceness and love of conquest, whose spiritual descendant and successor is the kingdom of Antichrist, of the Pope at Rome, just as delineated in the Book of Revelation. The ancient empire indeed came to an end, but it was revived in the empire of Charles the Great, and the political power of the Pope is felt in practically every nation of the earth today. [...] The kingdom of the Pope is unlike every other kingdom, since he exerts political

---

80   Quoted in Brown, *The Methodus*, 71–72; see Johann Andreas Quenstedt, *Dialogus De Patriis Illustrium Doctrina et Scriptis Virorum* (Wittenberg: Wendt, 1654), 46 – "Passim in Germanos tota mendaciorum plaustra evomit. Quod se & sua nimium praedicare, alios verò insolenter conculcare praeter meritum soleat ac rei veritatem, dictus est Anagrammatismo: ANDIUS SINE BONO."

81   "Etliche sagen von des eisens stärke etc. Er wil aber sagen, daß das Römische reich zur zeit, wenn es zertrennet seyn wird, versetzt, und gleichwie eine pflanze oder wurzel anders wohin komt, und sol doch dessen eisens oder reichspflanze, und nicht ein neu ander reich seyn. Dis ist alles geschehen, da das Römische reich von den Griechen auf die Teutschen gekommen ist, durch den pabst und Carolum magnum." Johann Georg Starke, *Synopsis Bibliothecae Exegeticae in Vetus Testamentum.... Fünfter Theil* (Leipzig: Breitkopf, 1747), col. 2435. Christoph Starke (1684–1744) was the primary author of the *Synopsis*, but his son completed the portions unfinished at his death. See ADB 35:493.

power under the guise of spreading the kingdom of God. [...] In spite of the reverses which the kingdom of Antichrist has suffered in the past, as when Emperor Otto I deposed Pope John XII, when the councils of the fifteenth century tried to effect at least an outward reformation, and, above all, when Martin Luther carried the fight into the enemy's ranks, the kingdom of Antichrist will remain till the end of time. Cp. 2 Thess. 2; Rev. 17. The prophecy of Daniel was fulfilled and is being fulfilled in a most remarkable manner, a fact which tends to strengthen our faith in every word of the Bible.[82]

Among twentieth century English-speaking Lutherans, Kretzmann's *Commentary* achieved a popularity similar to the status the Luther-Calov Bible had previously enjoyed in Germany. Although Kretzmann subverted the medieval perspective by making the papacy the antichrist, his *Commentary* nevertheless demonstrates the persistence of the *translatio imperii* to the Germans within Lutheran thought long after the Empire itself had vanished into history.

5   The Fourth Monarchy and the Imperial Publicists

In the struggles of the 1520s, Melanchthon had seen constitutional law as a defence against a hostile Emperor, and by the early seventeenth century, his intellectual heirs were systematizing that perspective. During those decades, German Protestants became increasingly concerned about the precariousness of their legal and constitutional standing after the Peace of Augsburg. In response, a new intellectual discipline developed that was devoted specifically to Imperial public law.[83] For the Imperial publicists (*Reichspublizisten*),

---

[82]   Paul Kretzmann, *Popular Commentary of the Bible: Old Testament* (St. Louis: Concordia Publishing House, 1924), vol. 2, s.v. Dan. 7:28.

[83]   See generally Seifert, *Der Rückzug*; Gross, *Empire and Sovereignty*; Heinz Duchhardt, *Protestantisches Kaisertum und Altes Reich: Die Diskussion über die Konfession des Kaisers in Politik, Publizistik und Staatsrecht* (Wiesbaden: Franz Steiner Verlag, 1977); Michael Stolleis, *Geschichte des öffentlichen Rechts in Deutschland: Erster Band 1600–1800*, 2d ed. (München: C.H. Beck Verlag, 2012); Robert von Friedeburg, *Luther's Legacy: The Thirty Years War and the Modern Notion of 'State' in the Empire, 1530s to 1790s* (Cambridge: Cambridge University Press, 2016); Michael Stolleis, *Public Law in Germany: A Historical Introduction from the 16th to the 21st Century*, trans. Thomas Dunlap (Oxford: Oxford University Press, 2017); Gertrude Lübbe-Wolff, "Die Bedeutung der Lehre von den Vier Weltreichen für das Staatsrecht des Römisch-Deutschen Reichs," *Der Staat* 23:3 (1984): 369–389; Notker Hammerstein, "Das Römische am Heiligen Römischen Reich Deutscher Nation in der Lehre der Reichs-Publicisten," *Zeitschrift der Savigny-Stiftung für Rechtsgeschichte*.

the principal issue was the division and exercise of authority (sovereignty) within the Empire. The Emperor, the Electors and the German princes all exercised degrees of authority both in their territories and within Imperial governance, but neither the extent nor the limits of their respective powers were precisely defined under the Imperial constitution. Thus, the Imperial publicists debated whether the Empire was an aristocracy, a monarchy or some mixture of both. In doing so, however, some eventually rejected the idea of the Holy Roman Empire as the fulfilment of Daniel and the continuation of ancient Rome.

The Thirty Years War (1618–1648) and the Peace of Westphalia (1648) permanently changed the Imperial constitution and the relationship of the territorial princes to the Emperor. Indeed, the resolution of the war assured that the Empire would remain decentralized and the Emperor would never become an absolute monarch. Nevertheless, traditionalists still vociferously defended the view of the Holy Roman Empire as the successor to ancient Rome. Among the Imperial publicists, Theodor von Reinkingk (1590–1664) is usually considered the great defender of the Four Monarchies.[84] Reinkingk was born along the Baltic in Courland (part of modern Latvia), but his family came from Germany and he was sent there for his education. After legal studies in Catholic Cologne, Calvinist Marburg and Lutheran Giessen, he was appointed professor at Giessen in 1617. Already the next year, however, he left academe and launched into a career of diplomacy and politics. He served the court of Hesse-Darmstadt, then Mecklenburg, and eventually the archbishopric of Bremen (then under the administration of a Danish prince). During the Thirty Years War, Reinkingk's views on the Imperial constitution earned him the animosity of the Swedes, and they imprisoned him twice. In 1648, after his second release, he became a high-ranking official in the service of his former prince from Bremen, who had now ascended to the Danish throne as King Friedrich III (1609–1670). The Emperor ennobled Reinkingk in 1656, and he continued serving the Danish court until his death in 1664.

Although Reinkingk made his career as a princely courtier, his fame rested on his political writings, particularly his early work, *A Tract Regarding Secular*

Germanistische Abtheilung 100:1 (1983): 119–144; Notker Hammerstein, "'Imperium Romanum cum omnibus suis qualitatibus ad Germanos est translatum': Das vierte Weltreich in der Lehre der Reichsjuristen," *Zeitschrift für Historische Forschung* Beiheft 3 (1987): 187–202.

84 On Reinkingk, see Christoph Link, "Dietrich Reinkingk," in *Staatsdenker in der Frühen Neuzeit*, 3d ed., ed. Michael Stolleis (München: C.H. Beck, 1995), 78–99; Gross, *Empire and Sovereignty*, esp. 192–204; ADB 28: 90–93; NDB 21: 375–376.

and Ecclesiastical Rule (1619), which he revised and expanded in later years.[85] The *Tract* sought to defend the constitutional order established under the 1555 Peace of Augsburg; and to accomplish this, Reinkingk strongly advocated for the sacred character of the Empire. In a series of chapters, he explicitly defended Melanchthon's view that the Roman Empire was the Fourth Monarchy of Daniel 2 and Daniel 7, and that through the *translatio imperii* to the Germans it would endure until the end of time.[86] In this context, he included a lengthy refutation of Bodin's position that the Empire was really an aristocracy, and argued instead that the Empire was a true monarchy, with ultimate authority vested in the Emperor.[87] Reinkingk also revisited medieval controversies regarding papal power. He rejected the notion that the Empire was a papal fief, that the pope had transferred the Empire to the Germans, or that the papacy held "two swords" – temporal power and ecclesiastical authority.[88] Despite contemporary political realities, Reinkingk defended traditional views of the Empire so effectively that his *Tract* continued to be republished into the eighteenth century.

On the other side of the debate stood Herman Conring (1606–1681), a professor at the Lutheran University of Helmstedt.[89] Conring was born in East Frisia, and he studied in Helmstedt and Leiden. He eventually returned to Helmstedt where over the course of his long career he held professorships in natural philosophy and rhetoric, medicine, and politics. He was also active as an advisor to princely courts including Braunschweig-Wolfenbüttel, East Frisia, Sweden, Denmark and France.

At Helmstedt, Conring developed a keen interest in German history, and later generations have often called him the father of Imperial legal history. In contrast to Reinkingk the traditionalist, Conring was pragmatic and modern. He saw the Empire of his day as German, not Roman, and he believed that the Empire should not be bound by misinterpretations of its past. He

---

85 Cited here according to Theodor von Reinkingk, *Tractatus De Regimine Seculari Et Ecclesiastico* (Marburg: Hampel, 1632).
86 Reinkingk, *Tractatus* (Marburg, 1632), class. II, chap. 1, p. 24–27. Reinkingk specifically cites *Carion's Chronicle* in his arguments, e.g., p. 25–26.
87 Reinkingk, *Tractatus* (Marburg, 1632), class. II, chap. 2, p. 27–46.
88 Reinkingk, *Tractatus* (Marburg, 1632), class. II, chap. 4–6, p. 50–62.
89 On Conring, see Gross, *Empire and Sovereignty*, esp. 255–292; Michael Stolleis, ed., *Hermann Conring (1606–1681): Beiträge zu Leben und Werk* (Berlin: Duncker & Humblot, 1983); Constantin Fasolt, *The Limits of History* (Chicago: University of Chicago Press, 2004); and Hermann Conring, *New Discourse on the Roman-German Emperor*, ed. Constantin Fasolt (Tempe: Arizona Center for Medieval and Renaissance Studies, 2005).

unequivocally rejected Melanchthon's view that the Holy Roman Empire was the continuing fulfilment of the Fourth Monarchy from Daniel's prophecies:

> For the whole idea that there will be only four great monarchies or world empires is more of a rumor than a fact. Even before the arrival of Alexander the Great, four very large empires – and not only two, as is commonly believed – had already flourished in Asia: the Assyrian, Babylonian, Median, and Persian. And after the destruction of the Roman empire, Asia again gave rise to vast realms under Saracens, Turks, Tartars, Persians, and Chinese, as it still does to some extent today. In Europe, moreover, the realm of the Franks was huge before Charles became emperor, and nowadays Spain and France are enjoying enormous power. Moreover, nothing in Sacred Scripture really establishes that the Roman empire will last forever, for neither the dream of Nebuchadnezzar nor that of Daniel, chapter seven, have much to do with Roman imperial times, as the learned recognize very well.[90]

Conring likewise rejected the idea of a *translatio imperii* from ancient Rome to the Germans, and he attacked the historical foundation that Melanchthon had used to establish the continuity of Roman Law in the Empire. Earlier scholars, including Melanchthon, had refuted the *Donation of Constantine* by arguing that it lacked any support in contemporary sources.[91] In his *Historical Commentary on the Origin of German Law* (1643), Conring similarly demonstrated that the Lotharingian Legend – the view that Emperor Lothar III had reintroduced Roman Law to the West – lacked contemporary historical witnesses.[92] In doing so, Conring sought to liberate German legal thought from the shackles of a false past.

Melanchthon had seen Roman Law and the Imperial constitution as a solution to the political instability of the 1520s. In the early seventeenth century, Reinkingk and other traditionalists still believed that retaining Melanchthon's solution remained the key to stability within the Empire. By contrast, Conring agreed with Melanchthon that the papacy had no role in German politics,

---

[90] Hermann Conring, *New Discourse on the Roman-German Emperor*, ed. Constantin Fasolt (Tempe: Arizona Center for Medieval and Renaissance Studies, 2005), 77.

[91] "Aber das Constantinus dem Bapst sol Rom vnd das halb Keisarthumb geschenckt haben / wie etliche fabuliren / findet man jnn keinen glaubwirdigen Historien." Carion, *Chronica* (Wittenberg, 1532), fol. 93r.

[92] See Constantin Fasolt, "Hermann Conring and the European History of Law," in *Politics and Reformations: Histories and Reformations. Essays in Honor of Thomas A. Brady, Jr.*, ed. Christopher Ocker et al. (Leiden: Brill, 2007), 128–129.

but he was among the vanguard of those who saw Melanchthon's arguments for continuity with ancient Rome, especially through Roman Law, as a constitutional problem, not a solution. In the wake of the Thirty Years War and the Peace of Westphalia, Conring believed that a revised constitutional order was necessary, but it took time to develop what that meant.

Throughout the later part of the seventeen century, the Imperial publicists continued to produce a vast literature on the Imperial constitution. During these decades, the most important work to emerge was Samuel von Pufendorf's study of the Imperial constitution, *The Present State of Germany* (1667).[93] Pufendorf (1632–1694) was from Saxony, and he studied at Leipzig and Jena.[94] After stays in Copenhagen and Leiden, he became a professor at Heidelberg, but he eventually left for Sweden where he taught at the University of Lund before becoming the royal historiographer in Stockholm. In the last years of his life, he was called to the court in Berlin as historian and advisor, and he died there in 1694.

In the *The Present State of Germany*, Pufendorf analysed the political condition of the Empire as if he were a foreign traveller. He used the fictive authorship of an Italian to describe the Empire as it actually existed in his day, rather than presenting an image distorted to reflect the theories of the Imperial publicists. Pufendorf discussed the origins of the Empire and its component territories, the position and authority of the Emperor and the Electors, as well as the overall political form of the Empire. In this context, he unequivocally rejected the view that the Holy Roman Empire was a continuation of ancient Rome:

> By all that has been said, it will appear how {childishly} they are mistaken, who think the Kingdom of *Germany* has succeeded in the Place of the old Roman Empire, and that it is continued in this Kingdom; when in truth, that Empire which was seated at *Rome*, was destroyed many Ages before *Germany* became one Kingdom.... The *Germans* also at this day do commonly call {their State}, *The Roman Empire of the Teutonick Nation*; which form of Speech seems to contain in it a contradiction, seeing it is very certain the present State of *Germany* [*modernam*

---

[93] Samuel Pufendorf, *The Present State of Germany*, ed. Michael J. Seidler (Indianapolis: Liberty Fund, 2007).

[94] On Pufendorf, see Gross, *Empire and Sovereignty*, 311–328; Notker Hammerstein, "Samuel Pufendorf," in *Staatsdenker in der Frühen Neuzeit*, 3d ed., ed. Michael Stolleis (München: C.H. Beck, 1995), 172–196; ADB 26:701–707; NDB 21:3–5.

Germanorum rempublicam] is not one and the same with the ancient Roman Empire.[95]

As Pufendorf's comment shows, the *translatio imperii* remained important enough within existing schools of thought that he still needed to explicitly reject it.

After Conring and Pufendorf, the fortunes of Roman Law and the *translatio imperii* waxed and waned among the Imperial jurists and publicists. Their writings had created a stir, but not an immediate legal or political revolution. The unresolved tension between the authority of the princes and the Emperor continued to frame discussions of the Imperial constitution and legal structure. Against this background, the tradition of Roman Law in the Empire continued to be reinvented into the nineteenth century, by scholars such as Friedrich Carl von Savigny (1779–1861), in response to changing constitutional and legal circumstances.[96] The prophetic elements of Melanchthon's interpretation of Daniel and the Four Monarchies faded away, but turning to Rome for contemporary solutions continued.

6   The Fourth Monarchy and the Historians

Over the centuries, historians occupied a middle ground between theologians and Imperial publicists. The demarcation among the disciplines was never absolute, and Protestant historians had good reasons for both retaining and rejecting the Four Monarchies. Indeed, despite changing currents, the Four Monarchies remained, at a minimum, a familiar and useful way to organize ancient history for student instruction. Johann Sleidanus (1506–1556), for example, emphasized Germany's exclusive right to Imperial title in his *On the Four Chief Empires* (1556), and he included a lengthy discussion of Daniel's prophecies.[97] The titlepage of *Gottfried's Chronicle* – the popular seventeenth century

---

95   Pufendorf, *The Present State of Germany*, 45–46 (Chap. 1.14).
96   See James Q. Whitman, *The Legacy of Roman Law in the German Romantic Era: Historical Vision and Legal Change* (Princeton: Princeton University Press, 1990).
97   "Germania quidem sola titulum ac posseßionem habet imperii...." Johann Sleidanus, *Ioan. Sleidani, De Qvatvor Svmmis Imperiis, Libri Tres* (Strasbourg: Rihel, 1556), 178 v. VD16 S 6657. On Sleidanus generally, see Alexandra Kess, *Johann Sleidan and the Protestant Vision of History* (Burlington, VT: Ashgate, 2008); and Emile Van der Vekene, *Johann Sleidan (Johann Philippson): Bibliographie seiner gedruckten Werke und der von ihm übersetzten Schriften von Philippe de Comines, Jean Froissart und Claude de Seyssel, mit einem bibliographischen Anhang zur Sleidan Forschung* (Stuttgart: Hiersemann, 1996).

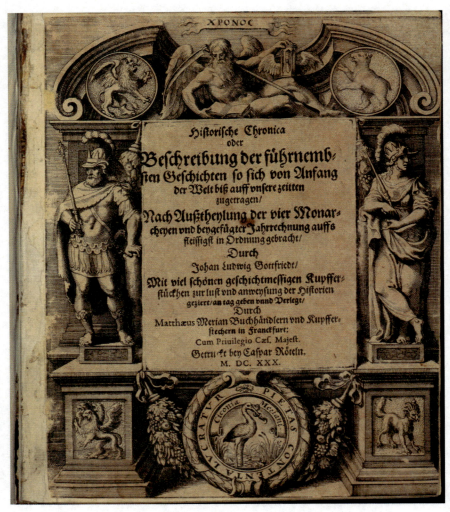

FIGURE 23   Johann Ludwig Gottfried, *Historische Chronica* (Frankfurt a.M., 1630)
BASEL UNIVERSITY LIBRARY: FALK 1079:1

universal history by Johann Ludwig Gottfried (1584–1633) and the publisher Matthäus Merian (1593–1650) – likewise advertised its adherence to the Four Monarchies (Figure 23).[98] Even Pufendorf, who rejected Melanchthon's view

---

98   VD17 23:236575H. For more than a century, *Gottfried's Chronicle* became a standard "popular" reference work for universal history in Germany, with reprintings and continuations into the 1750s. Johann Wolfgang von Goethe (1749–1832) still recommended it as an introduction to universal history. See Lucas Heinrich Wüthrich, *Matthaeus Merian d.Ä.: Eine*

of the *translatio imperii* to the Germans, still used the Four Monarchies (without reference to Daniel) to structure the chapter on the ancient empires in his compendium, *An Introduction to the History of the Principal Kingdoms and States of Europe* (1682).[99] Eventually, the realities of Imperial politics forced historians to abandon the interpretation of the Holy Roman Empire as Daniel's Fourth Monarchy. The process, however, took centuries and Wittenberg held out as one of the last places to assert the continuing vitality of the interpretation of Daniel forged in the 1520s.

After the purge of the Philippists in 1574, the University of Wittenberg remained an important destination for generations of Protestant students, but it never entirely regained its position as a preeminent centre of historical scholarship in Europe.[100] By the late sixteenth century, leadership in Protestant historiography shifted from Wittenberg to its newly created rival in Helmstedt. Duke Julius of Braunschweig founded the University of Helmstedt in 1576, and he soon hired two historians for the new faculty. In fact, he succeeded where Elector August had failed. In 1582, he was able to attract the most sought after historian in Germany, Reiner Reineccius (1541–1595). The next year he also appointed Heinrich Meibom (1555–1625).[101]

Reineccius had studied with Peucer in Wittenberg, and he fled Saxony in 1575 after the fall of the Philippists. Meibom, in contrast, was not a Wittenberg student. He had enrolled at Helmstedt soon after its foundation and completed his studies there. Of the two, Reineccius was the more famous, particularly for his publications on genealogy, yet as a teacher, Meibom had greater impact. At Helmstedt, Meibom taught from Sleidanus rather than *Carion's Chronicle*, and in 1586 he published a new expanded edition of *On the Four Chief Empires*.[102]

Biographie (Hamburg: Hoffmann und Campe Verlag, 2007), 137–143; and Lucas Heinrich Wüthrich, "Der Chronist Johann Ludwig Gottfried (ca. 1584–1633)." *Archiv für Kulturgeschichte* 43 (1961): 188–216.

99 Samuel Pufendorf, *An Introduction to the History of the Principal Kingdoms and States of Europe*, ed. Michael J. Seidler (Indianapolis: Liberty Fund, 2013), 13–39 (Chap. 1).

100 See Scherer, *Geschichte und Kirchengeschichte*; and Kathe, *Die Wittenberger Philosophische Fakultät*. See also Eugen Rambeau, "Über die Geschichtswissenschaft an der Universität Wittenberg," in *450 Jahre Martin-Luther-Universität Halle-Wittenberg* (Halle: [s.n.], 1953), vol. 1, 260–261; and Walter Zöllner, "Geschichte und Geschichtswissenschaft an der Universität Wittenberg," in *Recht – Idee – Geschichte: Beiträge zur Rechts- und Ideengeschichte für Rolf Lieberwirth anläßlich seines 80. Geburtstages*, ed. Heiner Lück and Bernd Schildt (Köln: Böhlau, 2000), 373–401.

101 For Reineccius and Meibom, I rely on Otto Herding, "Heinrich Meibom (1555–1625) und Reiner Reineccius (1541–1595) Eine Studie zur Historiographie in Westfalen und Niedersachsen," *Westfälische Forschungen* 18 (1965): 5–22.

102 The 1586 edition is VD16 S 6662.

Meibom's contribution consisted of extensive source annotations to the text, and his edition quickly became the standard at Helmstedt and eventually at Wittenberg.

Upon Andreas Franckenberger's death in 1590, the history lectures at Wittenberg passed from one scholar to another in rapid succession until Andreas's son, Reinhold Franckenberger (1585–1664), took up the professorship in 1616.[103] Reinhold taught at Wittenberg for almost half a century, and this long tenure by a cipher undoubtedly contributed to the decline of the university as a centre of historical thinking and research. The younger Franckenberger returned to *Carion's Chronicle* for his lectures. This was a surprising choice, since Melanchthon's textbooks had fallen out of favour with the anti-Philippist faculty;[104] but Reinhold probably embraced the *Chronicle* because his father had used the text decades earlier. Later, in 1660, Reinhold even revisited the debate between Bodin, Dresser, and his father. Eighty years after the initial controversy, he still felt obligated to vindicate Melanchthon's position on the Four Monarchies and defend his father and Dresser from Bodin's attacks in *On the Republic*.[105] In some sense, Reinhold offered the response to Bodin that

---

103 On Reinhold Franckenberger see Scherer, *Geschichte und Kirchengeschichte*, 55–57; Rambeau, "Über die Geschichtswissenschaft an der Universität Wittenberg," 260–261; Zöllner, "Geschichte und Geschichtswissenschaft," 381; Kathe, *Die Wittenberger Philosophische Fakultät*, 172–176.

104 See Clyde Manschreck, *Melanchthon: The Quiet Reformer* (New York: Abingdon Press, 1958), 15–16.

105 "Et licet hunc Bodini de 4 Monarchiis errorem & Parens meus p.m. Andreas Franckenberger in hac ipsa Academia ante 80 circiter annos Histor. Professor Publ. in erudito de Historiae Propheticae dignitate Libello, nec non Clarissimus Vir Matthaeus Dresserus itidem Historiarum Professor Publicus Lipsiensis sufficienter refutauerint: tamen Bodini de hac controuersia posteriores cogitationes in libr. 4. de Repub. in sequentibus uerbis prolatae minime sunt sapientiores: Ea tamen, inquit Bodinus ibidem, Andreas Franckenbergerus Saxo Lipsiorum Pontifex Lutheri autoritate, Dresserus uero homo de Schola, nulla subiecta ratione maledictis refellit. Hunc ego hominem disertum putabo, si, quam male didicit, tam bene dicere discat. Hactenus Bodinus. Cuius circumstantiarum ignorantia, per quam toties in uerbis errat, uel hinc manifesta est. Nam Parentum meum Saxonem uocat, cum fuerit Francus, Lipsiorum Pontificem indigitat, cum hic primo Eloquentiae & deinde Historiarum Professorem egerit, & denique Lutheri saltem autoritate pro argumento usum esse affirmat, cum tamen idem Parens meus ad Lutheri & Philippi beatorum ductum solum Danielis textum clarissimum ad historiam & experientiam accommodauerit. Similem errorem Bodinus in Dresseri, quem per iniuriam hominem de schola uocat, mentione committit, eoque ipso uel Parentis mei uel Dresseri Tractatus de hac re editos se nec uidisse nec legisse innuit. Etsi uero, 4 Monarchiis hac ratione a Bodino negatis, simul Germanis quarta denegata erat: tamen idem Bodinus non tantum in Historiarum Methodo: uerum etiam lib. 4. de Republica & alibi e peculiari erga Germanos odio contra Germanicum Romanorum Imperium bellum non armis sed stylo suscipit, tantum ut

his father had never written, and he demonstrated how deeply rooted Melanchthon's interpretation of Daniel and the Holy Roman Empire remained at Wittenberg.

The last surviving record of Wittenberg lectures on *Carion's Chronicle* is found in the university course catalogue for 1634,[106] and by the 1640s, Franckenberger had also abandoned the *Chronicle* for Sleidanus's *On the Four Chief Empires*.[107] From that time on, Sleidanus became synonymous with historical instruction at Wittenberg. Indeed, in 1658, Franckenberger's successor, Aegidius Strauch (1632–1682),[108] published a new edition of Sleidanus which included a frontispiece showing the Four Beasts from Daniel combined with a city-view of Wittenberg (Figure 24).[109] Interestingly, despite hundreds of editions, representations of the Four Monarchies or Wittenberg had never appeared on the titlepages of *Carion's Chronicle*.

Strauch's contemporaries had considered him something of a prodigy, and he had taken over the history lectures as Franckenberger's health declined in old age. Strauch's edition also included a continuation to Sleidanus, adding new material from Charles V down to the mid-seventeenth century. During the 1660s, Strauch published several works on history and chronology, including a study of the Four Monarchies – *Imago Tetrametallos Danielitica* (1662) – in which he affirmed the Wittenberg interpretation of Daniel as the recognized view of "nearly all historians and political theorists."[110] Eventually, Strauch extended his continuation of Sleidanus down to 1668, but by then he had

---

dignitas illa, quam Germania Patria nostra dulcissima per Collegii Electoralis neruum Dei beneficio hactenus tenuit, in uniuersum sublata uideatur." Reinhold Franckenberger, *Chronologiae Scaligero-Petavianae Breve Compendium* (Wittenberg: Henckel, 1661), sig. b3 v – [b4] r. VD17 23:299944L.

106 "M. Reinholdus Franckenberger Histor. P. & p. t. Academiae Rector, si officij ratione licebat, ea quae in Chronico Carionis Philippico & Peuceriano eiusque Libro IV restant paucissima, absolvet, & deinde ad Librum V. Deo volente, accedet Hora II." University of Wittenberg, *Rector Et Consilium Academiae Wittebergensis Publ.* (Wittenberg: Rothe, 1634). VD17 547:637629Z. See also VD17 547:637632C (1628); VD17 547:637631V (1629); VD17 547:637630N (1634).

107 See VD17 547:637647X (1645); VD17 547:637648E (1646); VD17 547:637658M (1647); VD17 547:637747C (1647).

108 On Strauch see Scherer, *Geschichte und Kirchengeschichte*, 160; Rambeau, "Über die Geschichtswissenschaft an der Universität Wittenberg," 261; Zöllner, "Geschichte und Geschichtswissenschaft," 398–399; Kathe, *Die Wittenberger Philosophische Fakultät*, 173–176; ADB 36:525–527.

109 VD17 3:006322C.

110 "Atq[ue] ità si consideremus Theologicè Monarchias, non nisi quatuor extitisse, ultimamq[ue] & quartam in Romano Imperio apud Germanos etiamnum durare secundùm vaticinium Danielis Dictum Cap. II. & VII. convenient Theologici & Politici ferè onmnes."

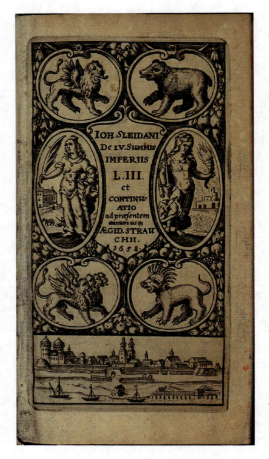

FIGURE 24
Johann Sleidanus, *De Quatuor Summis Imperiis* (Wittenberg, 1658)
BASEL UNIVERSITY LIBRARY: EA VI 8B

turned increasingly to theology and in 1669 left Wittenberg for Danzig. After Strauch's departure, Georg Green (1636–1691) took over the history lectures from 1670–1678, but published little of consequence. In 1678 he also left to become court preacher in Dresden.

After Green's departure, the history lectures fell to one of the most respected Wittenberg professors during these years, Konrad Samuel Schurzfleisch (1641–1708).[111] In his own day, Schurzfleisch enjoyed an international reputation.

Aegidius Strauch, *Imago Tetrametallos Danielitica: Exercitatione Historica Illustrata* (Wittenberg: Wendt, 1662), sig. A3 v. VD17 3:613041V. See Seifert, *Der Rückzug*, 128.

111 On Schurzfleisch see Scherer, *Geschichte und Kirchengeschichte*, 160–161; Rambeau, "Über die Geschichtswissenschaft an der Universität Wittenberg," 261–264; Zöllner, "Geschichte und Geschichtswissenschaft," 395–396; Kathe, *Die Wittenberger Philosophische Fakultät*, 283–289; ADB 33:97–99; NDB: 23:764–766; and Anthony Grafton, "The World of the Polyhistors: Humanism and Encyclopedism," *Central European History* 18:1 (March 1985): 43–47.

He had studied at Giessen, Helmstedt and Wittenberg, and his earliest works, published under a pseudonym, criticized Pufendorf's view of the Imperial constitution.[112] During his lifetime, he produced a wide array of publications, often in the form of orations and disputations, as well as letters, but much of his work on German history appeared only posthumously based on lecture notes or his working papers.[113] Indeed, his contemporary fame rested as much, or even more, on his personality and teaching than on his written works. Schurzfleisch did, however, publish a detailed study of Charlemagne and the Carolingians, entitled *On the Division of the Carolingian Empire* (1682), which was reprinted into the eighteenth century.[114] Furthermore, in 1678 he published a continuation to Strauch's edition of Sleidanus, which extended the text down to 1676. The last edition of Sleidanus published in Germany was actually a Schurzfleisch version that appeared at Dresden in 1713.[115]

Under Strauch, and especially Schurzfleisch, Wittenberg regained some of its lost lustre, but new competitors within the Protestant world quickly eclipsed its revival. The disruptions of the Thirty Years War had taken their toll on the German universities, but by the end of the century they had started to recover.[116] The Elector of Brandenburg founded the University of Halle in 1694, and it quickly became a leading intellectual centre of the Protestant world. Indeed, Christoph Cellarius (1638–1707), who popularized the tripartite division of universal history into ancient, medieval and modern, was a professor at Halle.[117] Then in 1734, the Elector of Hanover founded the University of

---

112   Christian A. Teuteburg, *Solida Ac Necessaria Disquisitio, De Forma Imperii Romano-Germananici, Ad Severini De Monzambano Caput VI. Diss. De Statu Imp. Germ.* ([Leipzig]: [s.n.], 1668). VD17 1:019283L. See NDB: 23:764–766. In his *Disquisitio*, Schurzfleisch offers a section by section response to the arguments that Pufendorf made in Chapter 6 ("Of the Form of the German Empire") of *The Present State of Germany*.

113   Rambeau, "Über die Geschichtswissenschaft an der Universität Wittenberg," 262; NDB: 23:764–766. In a letter of 1679, Schurzfleisch discussed the study of history. See Kathe, *Die Wittenberger Philosophische Fakultät*, 286 n. 115.

114   Konrad Schurzfleisch, *Divisionem Imperii Karolini* (Wittenberg: Fincelius, 1682). VD17 32:680963G.

115   The 1713 Dresden edition is the last surviving edition of *On the Four Chief Empires* published in Germany, though subsequent editions were actually published England in 1774 (Cambridge) and 1786 (Wolverhampton). See Emile Van der Vekene, *Johann Sleidan (Johann Philippson): Bibliographie seiner gedruckten Werke und der von ihm übersetzten Schriften von Philippe de Comines, Jean Froissart und Claude de Seyssel, mit einem bibliographischen Anhang zur Sleidan Forschung* (Stuttgart: Hiersemann, 1996), 101–104.

116   See generally Hans Erich Bödeker et al., eds., *Aufklärung und Geschichte: Studien zur deutschen Geschichtswissenschaft im 18. Jahrhundert* (Göttingen: Vandenhoeck & Ruprecht, 1992).

117   See generally Wallace K. Ferguson, *The Renaissance in Historical Thought: Five Centuries of Interpretation* (Boston: Houghton Mifflin, 1948), 73–77 for Cellarius; and Peter Schaeffer,

Göttingen, which became the most renowned centre for historical scholarship in Germany until the early nineteenth century.[118]

During all of these years, the Four Monarchies remained enshrined as the official teaching position at Wittenberg. Indeed, despite the increasing intellectual pressure from other German scholars, such as Conring, the Wittenberg university statutes of 1666 still provided that history should be taught according to the Four Monarchies, using a textbook such as Sleidanus.[119] As late as the early eighteenth century, the Wittenberg professor Johann Wilhelm Jahn (1681–1725), a student of Schurzfleisch, was still defending the traditional Wittenberg interpretation of the Four Monarchies against the most recent set of critics.[120]

Jahn is generally considered one of the last to publicly assert that the Holy Roman Empire would endure until the end of time.[121] In 1712, he published a dissertation on the Four Monarchies, and he later expanded this into a longer study, which appeared posthumously in 1728.[122] In comparison to Strauch's work from 1662, Jahn's study is comparatively lengthy, running to over a hundred pages. Indeed, Jahn offers an entire history of the disputes about the Four Monarchies from Antiquity to his own day, with specific chapters devoted to different stages in the development of the debate. Furthermore, he discusses the question from the perspective of theologians, Imperial publicists and

---

"The Emergence of the Concept '*Medieval*' in Central European Humanism," *Sixteenth Century Journal* 7, no. 2 (October 1976): 21–30.

118 Ernst Breisach, *Historiography: Ancient, Medieval, and Modern*, 2d ed. (Chicago: University of Chicago Press, 1994), 217–221.

119 "Historicus res in ecclesia et republica gestas seu utramque historiam, sacram et profanam, cum accurato temporum computo recenseat et subinde Sleidani de quatuor summis imperiis aut alterius compendium necnon Curtium, Justinum et similes explicet." Walter Friedensburg, ed., *Urkundenbuch der Universität Wittenberg* (Magdeburg: Selbstverlag der Historischen Kommission, 1927), vol. 2, 249. See also Kathe, *Die Wittenberger Philosophische Fakultät*, 175; and Seifert, *Der Rückzug*, 132 n. 29.

120 On Jahn see Scherer, *Geschichte und Kirchengeschichte*, 161–162; Zöllner, "Geschichte und Geschichtswissenschaft," 384–385; Kathe, *Die Wittenberger Philosophische Fakultät*, 289; Seifert, *Der Rückzug*, 142.

121 "Libris diuinis contineri, quod regno Babylonico, Nebucadnezaris auspicio ad summum potentiae gradum euecto, et omnium, quae tunc orbis terrarium habuit, facile principi, tria alia eiusmodi summa Imperia, nominatim Persicum, Graecum, et Romanum, ad finem usque mundi duraturum, suo quodque loco et ordine, succedere debuerint, primis et antiquissimis Christianis pridem creditum, constantique multorum seculorum consensus approbatum est." Johann Wilhelm Jahn, *Antiqvae Et Pervulgatae De Qvatvor Monarchiis Sententiae Contra Recentiorvm Qvorvndam Obiectiones Plenior Et Vberior Assertio* (Frankfurt a.M. and Leipzig: Knoch, 1728), [1].

122 Johann Wilhelm Jahn, *Dissertatio Historico-Politica De Qvatvor Monarchiis: Qva Recentiorvm Qvorvndam, Nominatim I.C. Becmanni, H. Hardtii, Et Observ. Halensis Sententiae Modeste Excvtivntvr* (Wittenberg: Kreusig, 1712); and Jahn, *De Qvatvor Monarchiis* (1728).

historians. Thus, among the more recent authors he notes Luther, Melanchthon and Bodin, but also Franckenberger and Dresser. He mentions Conring, as well as Grotius and Calov. Not surprisingly, he gives particular emphasis to Wittenberg historians, including Strauch and Schurzfleisch, and draws attention to the Wittenberg statute of 1666. Furthermore, as Jahn surveyed two centuries of controversy since the Reformation, he explicitly recognized the early importance of *Carion's Chronicle* in transmitting the Wittenberg interpretation of Daniel, and he considered the use of Sleidanus's textbook as a successor in the same tradition.[123]

After reviewing the history of the debate, Jahn specifically addressed three of the most recent writers: Johann Christoph Becmann (1641–1717), a professor at Frankfurt an der Oder; Hermann von der Hardt (1660–1746), a theologian at Helmstedt and an early proponent of historical-critical Biblical exegesis; and an anonymous work from Halle. Von der Hardt, for example, argued that Daniel's Four Beasts actually referred to four rulers of Babylon – Nebuchadnezzar, Evilmerdoch, Belshazzar, and Cyrus – and he asserted that charting prophetic fulfilment was the task of neither history nor political science.[124] Against these critics, Jahn maintained that the Four Monarchies referred to Babylon, Persia, Greece and Rome, with Roman rule transferred to the Germans through Charlemagne.[125] Jahn's tract *On the Four Monarchies* remained the classic defence

---

[123] "Praeterea, ut aliorum Theologorum, ac praecipue commentatorum Euangelicorum, consensum, in apricot positum, hic taceam, PHILIPPVS MELANCHTHON, communis ille Germaniae praeceptor, secundum ordinem quatuor monarchiarum, uniuersam fere historiam distribuit, ut patet ex *Chronico* eius, sub nomine IOANNIS CARIONIS a. 1528 primum edito, deinceps uero cum ipsius Philippi, tum generi eius, CASP. PEVCERI opera aucto, saepiusque recuso. Eandem methodum in tradenda historia, praetor ceteros secutus est IOANNES SLEIDANVS, in libello *de quatuor summis Imperiis*, a. 1556, qui autori emortualis fuit, primum edito, qui deinceps, GVLIELMI XYLANDRI, THEOPHILI MADERI, HENRICI MEIBOMII, aliorumque doctorum uirorum, annotationibus illustrates, et ab AEGIDIO STRAVCHIO et CONRADO SAMVELE SCHVRZFLEISCHIO continuatus, communis fere compendia historici uicem in Germania sustinuit, quod statute ordinis philosophici, in Academia nostra, anno MDCLXVI, ad Diuo Electore IOHANNE GEORGIO II. Confirmata, Professori historiae nominatim explicandum praescribunt." Jahn, *De Qvatvor Monarchiis* (1728), 70–71.

[124] "Quartam igitur & ultimam dicere *Monarchiam*, Imperium Romanum & orbis finem, non est *historici*, qui future nescit, nec *politici*, qui future non determinat, inprimis remota." Hermann von der Hardt, *Danielis Quatuor Animalia, non Quatuor Monarchiarum fabula, sed Quatuor Regvm Babylonis Nebucadnezaris, Evilmerodachi, Belsazaris & Cyri, historia, demonstrata* (Helmstedt: Hamm, 1715), 9.

[125] "Ex hactenus disputatis patere, existimo, Imperium Rom. non modo a Carolo M. in occidente instauratum, sed etiam ad posteros et successores eius transmissum esse. Restare nunc uidetur, ut hanc successionem inter omnes gentes, quae Carolo M. subiectae fuerunt, Germanorum propriam esse, demonstremus." Jahn, *De Qvatvor Monarchiis* (1728), 137.

of the Wittenberg interpretation of Daniel, and it was republished at Jena as late as 1805, the year before the Empire was dissolved.[126]

7 The Four Monarchies in the Graphic Arts

After Jahn, the Four Monarchies continued to decline among the historians. *Carion's Chronicle* had not been reprinted in Germany since 1624. Sleidanus's *On the Four Chief Empires* lasted almost a century longer, but after 1713, it too ceased. *Gottfried's Chronicle* survived both, with the last edition in 1759, though it had never been a teaching text.[127] Nevertheless, even after *Carion's Chronicle* and its successors declined in popularity, Melanchthon's basic interpretation of the past remained important as a framework for understanding universal history through the remainder of the eighteenth century. Indeed, when the University of Wittenberg issued revised regulations for the "common table" in 1748, they still prescribed that *Carion's Chronicle* or Sleidanus should be read at the evening meal.[128] Furthermore, the legacy of Melanchthon's historical thought is especially apparent from its transmission in graphic arts, which continued long after the *Chronicle* itself had fallen out of use.[129]

The Wittenberg World Map of 1529 had offered a cartographic interpretation of Daniel 7 (Figures 12–13). An image representing Melanchthon's interpretation of the statue from King Nebuchadnezzar's dream in Daniel 2 came only

---

126 Johann Wilhelm Jahn, "Antiquae et pervulgatae De Quatvor Monarchiis sententiae Contra Recentiorum Quorundam Objectiones Plenior et Uberior Assertio," in *Historisches Magazin*, ed. C.W.F. Breyer (Jena: Cröcker, 1805), vol. 1, 114–220.

127 Wüthrich, *Matthaeus Merian d.Ä.*, 137.

128 "80. Er soll sich bei Carenz der Mahlzeit vor Anfang derselben einfinden, damit er mit der ersten Viertelstunde, vor Auftragung der Suppe, das lateinische Tischgebet laut recitiren könne; sodann lieset er solange, nach der Ordnung, in der lateinischen Bibel des Mittags und im Sleidano oder Philippi chronico des Abends, bis die Mahlzeit vollendet, welches der famulus hebdomadarius mit einem Schlag an die Catheder bemerket, damit er kurz vor oder mit der dritten Viertelstunde das Gebet pro rege und darauf das Nachtischgebet ablesen könne. Sodann, und nicht eher, ist ihm erlaubt von der Catheder zu gehen, bei Strafe einer wöchentlichen Carenz." Friedensburg, *Urkundenbuch der Universität Wittenberg* (1927), vol. 2, 402.

129 Many examples of the Four Monarchies, in a variety of mediums, are associated with the Saxon court in Dresden. See generally Ernst Kramer, "Die Vier Monarchien: Der Traum Nebucadnezars als Thema keramischer Werke," *Keramos* 28 (1965): 3–27; Ingeborg Krueger, "Ein Prunkbecken des Barock: Zur Ikonographie der Vier Weltreiche nach Daniels Visionen," *Kunst & Antiquitäten* (1984): Heft 2, 36–45, Heft 3, 37–45; and Thomas Rahn, "Geschichtsgedächtnis am Körper – Fürstliche Merk- und Meditationsbilder nach der Weltreiche-Prophetie des 2. Buches Daniel," in *Seelenmaschinen – Gattungstraditionen, Funktionenund Leistungsgrenzen der Mnemotechniken bis zum Beginn der Moderne*, ed. Jörg-Jochen Berns and Wolfgang Neuber (Vienna: Böhlau Verlag, 2000), 521–561.

later, but it proved even more enduring. In 1562, Peucer had drawn up a *Tabella* that outlined the periodization structure of *Carion's Chronicle*, and it long remained an important tool for understanding universal history (Figure 20).[130] Nevertheless, neither he nor Melanchthon ever developed a graphic representation of the Four Monarchies as described in Daniel 2. Indeed, an illustrative form of Melanchthon's interpretation of Daniel never appeared in any copies of *Carion's Chronicle*. In the mid-1580s, however, Lorenz Faust (1532–1594) finally published a detailed image that combined the statue of Daniel 2 with the Four Beasts of Daniel 7 (Figure 25).[131]

Faust was from Saxony and had studied theology at Leipzig.[132] After ordination at Wittenberg, he returned to his hometown of Schirmentz as a Lutheran pastor. Although he was not a university professor, he had a life-long interest in historical studies, and in addition to his study of Daniel, he published a history of Saxon rulers and the Saxon city of Meissen. The image of Daniel 2 was included in Faust's first major historical work, entitled *Anatomy of Daniel's Statue*, which appeared at Leipzig in 1585/1586. Faust divided the book into four parts: the genealogy of Christ, the anatomy of Daniel's statue, the rulers of the Four Monarchies, and a genealogy of Saxon rulers. He followed Melanchthon's interpretation of the Four Monarchies, and the approval of the Saxon book censor specifically noted that the *Anatomy* conformed to the chronology in *Carion's Chronicle*.[133] Faust also included images to accompany each of the

---

130 See Adalbert Klempt, *Die Säkularisierung der universalhistorischen Auffassung: zum Wandel des Geschichtsdenkens im 16. und 17. Jahrhundert* (Göttingen: Musterschmidt, 1960), 35–40.

131 Lorenz Faust, *Anatomia Statuae Danielis. Kurtze und eigentliche erklerung der grossen Bildnis des Propheten Danielis* (Leipzig: Steinman, 1586 [1585]). VD16 F 660. On this image, see Daniel Rosenberg and Anthony Grafton, *Cartographies of Time: A History of the Timeline* (New York: Princeton Architectural Press, 2010), 54–57; Günter Irmscher, "Metalle als Symbole der Historiographie – zu den Statuae Danielis resp. Nabuchodonosoris von Lorenz Faust und Giovanni Maria Nosseni," *Anzeiger des Germanischen Nationalmuseums Nürnberg* (1995): 93–106; Rahn, "Geschichtsgedächtnis am Körper," esp. 523–531; Barbara Uppenkamp, "Representation of History: The Four Empires snd the Statua Danielis in the Castle of Güstrow," in *Beyond Scylla and Charybdis. European Courts and Court Residences outside Habsburg and Valois/Bourbon Territories 1500–1700*, ed. Birgitte Bøggild Jahannsen and Konrad Ottenheym (Copenhagen: University Press of Southern Denmark, 2016), 253–264.

132 On Faust, see Fritz Horbank, "Laurentius Faustus – Pfarrer und Geschichtsschreiber," *Mitteilungen des Vereins für Geschichte der Stadt Meißen* 1:2 (2010): 134–145.

133 "Gnedigster Herr / auff E. Churf. G. Cammerraht befehlich / habe ich diese Chronologiam durchlesen / vnd befinde / was die Historien anlanget / das dieselbe alle aus bewerten Authoribus genommen / stim[m]en auch die jarzal vberein mit dem Chronico Philippi, Chronologia Funcij vnd anderer / [et]c. Die ordnung betreffende / ists auff die statuam Danielis gerichtet / darinnen das güldene heupt bedeutet die Assyrische Monarchien / die silberne brust die Persische / der ehrne bauch die Griechische / die eiserne schenckel die Römische. Vnd sind in jeder Monarchien / alle Regenten ordentlich nacheinander

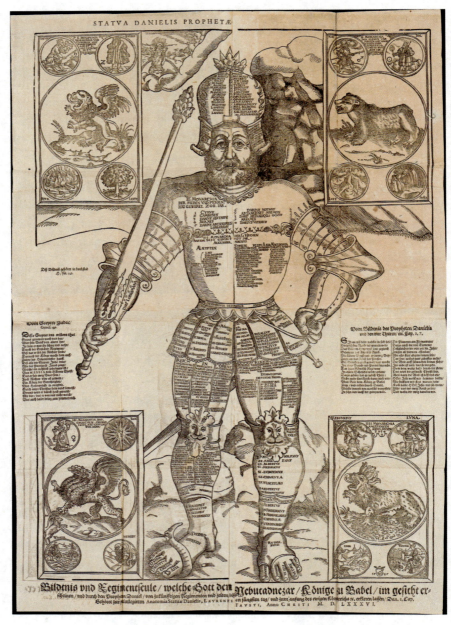

FIGURE 25   Lorenz Faust, *Anatomia Statuae Danielis* (Leipzig, 1585 [1586]), chart opposite sig. Hiij r
HERZOG AUGUST BIBLIOTHEK WOLFENBÜTTEL: A: 91.1 QUOD. (1)

three content elements in the *Anatomy*. For the genealogy of Christ, he used a family tree, literally in the form of a tree; and for the Saxon rulers, he used both a family tree and a hand, with the fingers showing different branches of the family.[134] The most striking image, however, is Faust's representation of the statue from Daniel 2 and the Four Monarchies.

At the centre of the image stands the statue from King Nebuchadnezzar's dream in Daniel 2. The Colossus, pictured in full armour, has a face resembling Elector August of Saxony, to whom Faust had dedicated the book. Inscribed on the helmet are the rulers of Assyria-Babylon, with the Persians following on the chest and the Greeks on the statue's midsection. The Fourth Monarchy extends down the legs to the feet, where the toes divide into the ten major provinces of the ancient Roman Empire. The image thus follows the pattern set in *Carion's Chronicle* of dividing Roman rule into East and West, with the Exarchate of Ravenna, for example, specifically noted in the Western succession. In the Eastern succession, the Turkish sultans also follow the Byzantine Emperors, as in *Carion's Chronicle*. The horn from Daniel 7, with the head of a man speaking arrogantly, rises from beneath the left foot of the statue (the Eastern Empire) and through its placement is associated with the Turks. Faust also explicitly links the statue's sceptre to the sceptre of Judah described in Genesis 49. Above the statue, Faust included an image of Christ at the Last Judgment and to the right the mountain from which a stone (the Kingdom of Christ) will descend and destroy the statue.

The beasts from Daniel 7 are shown in roundels at the four corners of the image. Each beast appears at the centre of a quincunx scheme, with the planetary gods, the elements and the seasons at the corners.[135] The winged lion (Assyria-Babylon), for example, is associated with Saturn and Jupiter, fire and spring. Although the image could be studied in isolation, it was best read in combination with Faust's text, which provided more detail about the "anatomy" of the statue through a process of "dissection." Gout, for instance, was associated with the way the papacy had harmed the Empire through meddling in Imperial religious and secular affairs.[136]

---

gesetzt / auch wie lang ein jeder regieret / vnd was sich bey seiner regierung sonderlichs zugetragen / ist alles mit der jahrzal auffgezeichnet." Faust, *Anatomia Statuae Danielis* (Leipzig, 1586), sig. Ciii r-v.

134 The images are reproduced in Rosenberg, *Cartographies of Time*, 50–51.
135 See Rahn, "Geschichtsgedächtnis am Körper," 526; and Uppenkamp, "Representation of History," 262.
136 "Podagra, Zipperlin / ist der Primat des Papsthumbs / da keyser Phocas den Bonifacium tertium zu Rom / Anno Christi 607. damit er mit jm dispensieret / vnd seinen bösen sachen vberhülff vnd beypflichtet / zum öbersten Heupt vber alle andere Bischoffe bestettiget /

Faust's image of the Colossus had a long afterlife, and it transmitted Melanchthon's interpretation of Daniel and the Four Monarchies for the next two centuries. In 1623, the Augsburg engraver Wolfgang Kilian (1581–1662) produced a new version of the Daniel statue, adapted from the original Faust image of 1586. Kilian's representation was issued as a broadsheet, rather than a book illustration, and sometimes survives with a brief explanatory text appended below the image (Figure 26). At the top, Kilian omits Christ and the Last Judgment, but adds a title in a mixture of Hebrew, Greek and Latin: "The Great Babylonian Image (or more specifically) An Image Representing the Four World Monarchies of Daniel." Despite various changes, such as repositioning the Four Beasts, the overall image retains the core aspects of Faust's representation, and thus Melanchthon's perspective on Daniel.[137] In 1667, an unknown artist at Altdorf or Nuremberg produced a less detailed variant of Faust's Colossus, though without the beasts from Daniel 7 (Figure 27).[138] To accompany the image, the Altdorf Professor Johann Paul Felwinger (1606–1681) prepared five additional sheets with succinct descriptions of each ruler of the Four Monarchies.[139]

Dardurch im Reich / beydes in geistlichen vnd weltlichen sachen / viel schedliche vnd schmertzliche plagen erfolget." Faust, *Anatomia Statuae Danielis* (Leipzig, 1586), 72.

137   As in Faust's representation, Kilian inscribes the rulers of the Four Monarchies on the statue, but he reverses the legs (so the left leg is now the Western Empire) and reorders the Roman provinces on the toes. He also adds an association of the statue's eyes with the Prophets Daniel and Ezekiel. More noticeable changes occur with respect to the beasts from Daniel 7. Kilian places them on islands in the lower half of the image, rather than in the four corners, and the bear and the four-headed leopard trade places. The descriptions of the beasts also lack Faust's quincunx scheme – Kilian did not carry over the associations with the elements or the seasons, and he mentions the planetary gods only with respect to Assyria-Babylon and Persia. Wolfgang Kilian, *Imago... Danielis 2.v.31* (Augsburg, 1623) (National Library of Sweden: KoB Tr. B. 2014_B. 17).

138   For a reproduction of the image with commentary, see Wolfgang Harms, *Deutsche Illustrierte Flugblätter des 16. Und 17. Jahrhunderts*, Band II, Wolfenbüttel Band 2: Historica (München: Kraus International Publications, 1980), 2–3. The artist replaced the lists of rulers with references to *translatio imperii* for each Monarchy. Within the Fourth Monarchy, for instance, he describes the division of Roman rule into East and West, and for the Western Empire, he notes the translation from the Exarchs of Ravenna to Charlemagne and the Germans. The artist omitted the Roman provinces from the statue's toes and the Colossus holds an orb and sceptre, rather than a sword and sceptre. Within the stone that will eventually destroy the statue, the artist incorporated an image of Christ's navitity, thereby clearly associating it with Christ's Kingdom.

139   Johann Paul Felwinger, *Declaratio Colossi, In Qua Recitatur Ordine, Ex Sacris Et Profanis Scriptoribus Desumta Monarcharum Series, Ad Nostra Usque Tempora, Et Historiae Quaedam Obiter Annotatae Sunt* (Altdorf: Schönnerstaedt, 1667). VD17 23:675074R. For the Fourth Monarchy, Felwinger used parallel columns for East and West after the division of Roman rule, continuing to his own day with the Emperors and the Turkish sultans. At the start of each Monarchy, he also incorporated brief associations with Daniel 2 and Daniel 7, following the traditional Wittenberg perspective on Daniel. Therefore,

FIGURE 26   Wolfgang Kilian, *Imago … Danielis 2.v.31* (Augsburg, 1623)
NATIONAL LIBRARY OF SWEDEN: KOB TR. B. 2014_B. 17
PHOTO CREDIT: ANN-SOFIE PERSSON, NATIONAL LIBRARY OF SWEDEN

FIGURE 27   Anonymous, *Colossus* (Altdorf, 1667)
HERZOG AUGUST BIBLIOTHEK WOLFENBÜTTEL: IH 2

Even as German intellectuals were abandoning Melanchthon's interpretation of Daniel, Faust's image of the Colossus continued to reappear down to the last years of the Holy Roman Empire. At Augsburg, Matthias Seutter (1678–1757), and later his son-in-law Tobias Lotter (1717–1777), produced the

---

although references to Daniel 7 did not appear in the image, they were still presented in the accompanying text.

best known versions of the Colossus image, based on Kilian's model from a century before. Seutter was trained as an engraver, and he worked especially as a mapmaker.[140] During this period, mapmakers would use their inventory to produce both standardized and customized atlases for clients, so the selection of individual maps often varied from copy to copy of the same work. As a result, the Colossus is sometimes found in Seutter atlases, but also sometimes in atlases by the Homann firm, another Augsburg publisher, or simply as an individual print.[141] Seutter also developed three other Colossi to create a historical set: the Four Monarchies, the Roman Pontiffs, the Rulers of Europe, and the Imperial Electors (Figures 28–31).

Although Seutter used Kilian's model, he nevertheless made his own contributions. In particular, he added a system of symbols to provide the reader with descriptions of each ruler. A key in the upper left of the image explains the system. The symbols indicate the ruler's temperament – charitable, warlike, learned, cruel, effeminate, etc. They also note how the ruler died (naturally, in battle or violently) and whether the ruler was deposed, abdicated or re-crowned. Constantine the Great and Charlemagne, for example, have the following symbols: ☉ (virtuous) ⁊ (charitable) ♂ (warlike) m (died naturally). Their ♂ (warlike) symbols also have rays emanating to indicate that they were victorious in battle. (The other Colossi contain similar symbolic systems.) For the beasts from Daniel 7, Seutter standardized the captions that had varied in Kilian's image. He omits the Greek descriptions and removes the remaining references to the planetary gods. The later versions by Lotter vary slightly and are aesthetically less pleasing (Figure 32), but they nevertheless continued to be produced down to the end of the eighteenth century.[142] A manuscript variant in Hebrew even survives (Figure 33).[143]

---

140 See Christian Sandler, *Johann Baptista Homann, Matthäus Seutter und ihre Landkarten: Ein Beitrag zur Geschichte der Kartographie* (Amsterdam: Meridian, 1963); Michael Ritter, "Seutter, Probst und Lotter: An Eighteenth-Century Map Publishing House in Germany," *Imago Mundi* 53 (2001): 130–135; Michael Diefenbacher et al., *"Auserlesene und allerneueste Landkarten": der Verlag Homann in Nürnberg 1702–1848* (Nürnberg: Tümmels, 2002); and Michael Ritter et al., *Die Welt aus Augsburg: Landkarten von Tobias Conrad Lotter (1717–1777) und seinen Nachfolgern* (Berlin: Deutscher Kunstverlag, 2014).
141 See, e.g., Basel University Library: Ew 397:2 Grossfolio – a Seutter atlas of 1734; and R.W. Shirley, *Maps in the Atlases of The British Library: A Descriptive Catalogue* (London: British Library, 2004), vol. 1, 549, Nr. 32 – a Homann heirs atlas.
142 See, with reproductions of the Lotter Colossi images, Ritter, *Die Welt aus Augsburg*, 74–78.
143 See Carol A. Newsom, with Brennan W. Breed, *Daniel: A Commentary* (Louisville: Westminster John Knox Press, 2014), 96; Kestenbaum & Company, *Fine Judaica: Printed Books, Manuscripts, Autograph Letters & Graphic Arts* (New York: Auction held on December 8, 2011), Nr. 322.

FIGURE 28 Matthias Seutter, *Colossus Monarchicus* (Augsburg, ca. 1734)
BASEL UNIVERSITY LIBRARY: EW 397:2 GROSSFOLIO

Overall, the Colossus images transmit a wealth of information to their readers, and they were a useful teaching tool in European schools.[144] By the time of Seutter's version, the direct association with *Carion's Chronicle* had long been lost, but the essence of Melanchthon's arguments was nevertheless still present. Indeed, the images demonstrate the continuing vitality of Melanchthon's interpretation of the Four Monarchies as a historical paradigm throughout the eighteenth century.

---

144   See Rosenberg, *Cartographies of Time*, 54–57; and Marsh, *Biblische Prophetie*, images 20–21.

FIGURE 29 Matthias Seutter, *Pontificum Romanorum Series Chronologica* (Augsburg, ca. 1734)
BASEL UNIVERSITY LIBRARY: EW 397:2 GROSSFOLIO

8 The Last Days of the Fourth Monarchy

After Jahn, the history lectures at Wittenberg again passed to a series of once famous, but now long forgotten, scholars until they finally descended upon Johann Matthias Schroeckh (1733–1808), the last great historian at Wittenberg.[145] Schroeckh had studied in Göttingen with two of the leading scholars

---

145 On Schroeckh see Scherer, *Geschichte und Kirchengeschichte*, 409–413; Rambeau, "Über die Geschichtswissenschaft an der Universität Wittenberg," 266–267; Zöllner, "Geschichte und Geschichtswissenschaft," 389–395; Kathe, *Die Wittenberger Philosophische Fakultät*,

FIGURE 30   Matthias Seutter, *Statua Regum Europæorum* (Augsburg, ca. 1734)
BASEL UNIVERSITY LIBRARY: EW 397:2 GROSSFOLIO

of the time, the historian Johann Lorenz von Mosheim (1693–1755) and the Orientalist Johann David Michaelis (1717–1791), but he completed his studies at Leipzig. He arrived at Wittenberg in 1767, and he took over the history lectures in 1775. Schroeckh published two works on world history, both introductory,

esp. 372–377; ADB 32:498–501; and Herbert Gutschera, *Reformation und Gegenreformation innerhalb der Kirchengeschichtsschreibung von Johann Matthias Schröckh* (Göppingen: Kümmerle, 1973).

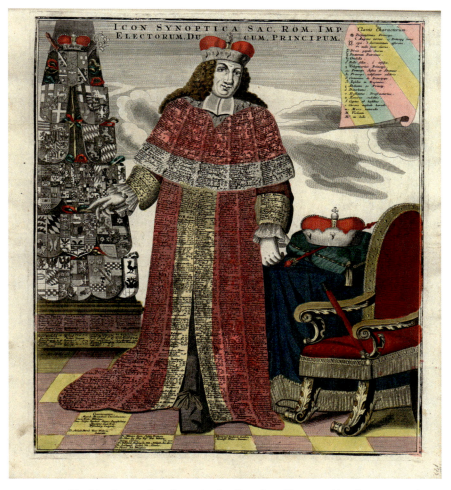

FIGURE 31   Matthias Seutter, *Icon Synoptica Sac. Rom. Imp. Electorum* (Augsburg, ca. 1734)
BASEL UNIVERSITY LIBRARY: EW 397:2 GROSSFOLIO

though comparatively detailed, texts for student instruction.[146] By then, the Four Monarchies had largely fallen out of use, and Schroeckh instead divided history into ancient (before Christ) and modern (after Christ), with each half subdivided into six eras. The history before Christ thus encompassed: [1] Adam

---

146   Matthias Schroeckh, *Allgemeine Weltgeschichte für Kinder*, 4 vols. (Leipzig: Weidmann und Reich, 1779–1784); and Matthias Schroeckh, *Lehrbuch der allgemeinen Weltgeschichte zum Gebrauche bey dem ersten Unterrichte der Jugend* (Berlin: Nicolai, 1774).

FIGURE 32   Tobias Lotter, *Colossus Monarchicus* (Augsburg, ca. 1775)
BERN UNIVERSITY LIBRARY: MUE RYH 8303: 31

to Noah, [2] Noah to Moses, [3] Moses to Romulus, [4] Romulus to Cyrus, [5] Cyrus to Alexander, and [6] Alexander to Christ. The history after the birth of Christ then followed as: [1] Christ to Theodosius and the Great Migrations, [2] Theodosius to Muhammad, [3] Muhammad to Charlemagne, [4] Charlemagne to Gregory VII and Godfrey of Bouillon, [5] Gregory VII and Godfrey of Bouillon to Columbus and Luther, and [6] Columbus and Luther to Joseph II and Frederick the Great. Although the periodization differed, like Melanchthon

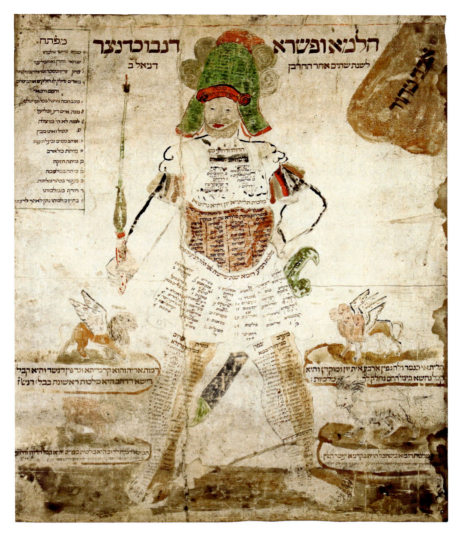

FIGURE 33   Anonymous, *Colossus Monarchicus* ([s.n.], ca. 1735)
PHOTO CREDIT: KESTENBAUM & COMPANY, NEW YORK

in *Carion's Chronicle*, Schroeckh still included a brief introduction on the study of history in which he pointed out the religious, moral and practical value of studying the past.[147] Despite the popularity of his world history texts,

---

147   Schroeckh, *Lehrbuch der allgemeinen Weltgeschichte* (Berlin, 1774), [3]–19; Rambeau, "Über die Geschichtswissenschaft an der Universität Wittenberg," 266.

Schroeckh remains most famous for his work in ecclesiastical history, which was also well-received in Catholic circles.[148] His forty-three volume ecclesiastical history (1768–1808) remains one of most comprehensive ever written.[149]

During Schroeckh's long career at Wittenberg, the European order that had endured since the Peace of Westphalia collapsed in the wake of the French Revolution (1789) and the Napoleonic Wars. For centuries, the Germans had seen the French and the papacy, and eventually the Turks, as the existential foes of the Empire. In the end, Hapsburg fears that Napoleon would finally achieve the centuries-old French goal of seizing the Imperial title lead to what had previously been unthinkable. On 6 August 1806, the Fourth Monarchy finally came to an end when the last Emperor, Francis II (r. 1792–1806), officially dissolved the Holy Roman Empire.[150] As with the fall of the old Roman Empire, questions that had animated scholarly discourse for centuries suddenly passed into irrelevance; and with that, Melanchthon's grand vision of the Imperial constitution and a peaceful Europe also lapsed from history.

After Schroeckh's death in 1808, the last historian at Wittenberg, Karl Heinrich Ludwig Pölitz (1772–1838), published a retrospective analysis of historical studies at Wittenberg from the sixteenth century to his own day.[151] Pölitz praised Melanchthon and *Carion's Chronicle* as path-breaking for their time;[152] but he lamented the failure of subsequent Wittenberg historians to adapt to developments in historical method. Furthermore, he specifically criticized the Wittenberg statue of 1666 – that had enshrined the Four Monarchies in the university curriculum – as perpetuating an outmoded and simplistic approach to history.[153] As for himself, although Pölitz wrote only in 1811, he had already

---

148   Rambeau, "Über die Geschichtswissenschaft an der Universität Wittenberg," 266; Kathe, *Die Wittenberger Philosophische Fakultät*, 376.
149   Matthias Schroeckh, *Christliche Kirchengeschichte*, 43 vols. (Leipzig: Schwickert, 1768–1808).
150   Joachim Whaley, *Germany and the Holy Roman Empire* (Oxford: Oxford University Press, 2012), vol. 2, 644.
151   Karl Heinrich Ludwig Pölitz, *Symbolae ad historiam Academiae Vitebergensis illustrandam* (Wittenberg: C.H. Grässlerus, 1811), 4–11.
152   "Ipse Melanchthon, vir immortalis memoriae, ad Carionis († 1537) chronicon enarravit historiam catholicam, et sua auctoritate, suo exemplo, stadium historicum mirifice promovit. Nemo ex eius coaevis magis, quam Melanchthon, Historiam quavis occasione commendavit, eamque *magistram vitae*, et *pragmatice* et vitae communis cognitionem sibi comparaverit, rite scribe et recitari posse, recte vidit." Pölitz, *Symbolae* (Wittenberg, 1811), 5–6.
153   "Quae tum temporis fuerit conditio disciplinarum historicarum, ex hoc decreto facile apparet. Distinguebatur tantum historia sacra et profana; profana enarrabatur ad Ordinem quatuor imperiorum, et ut sciret Historicus, quo modo lectiones ceteras expleret, commendabatur explicatio Curtii et Iustini! Ea aetate munus Historici levius fuisse, quam hoc

adopted the perspective that universal history should be divided into ancient, medieval (476–1492), early modern (1492–1789) and modern (after 1789).[154] With Pölitz's departure for Leipzig in 1815, the line of Wittenberg historians, which had started in the earliest days of the university, finally came to an end:[155]

(1507	Christoph Scheurl)
(1543–1551	Paul Eber)
(1555–1560	Philipp Melanchthon)
(1560–1574	Caspar Peucer)
(1579–1580	Andreas Franckenberger)
1580–1587	Andreas Franckenberger
1587–1588	Petrus Albinus
1588–1590	Andreas Franckenberger
1590–1592	Janus Gruterus
1592–1593	Nikolaus Todaeus
1593–1595	Johann Georg Volkmar
1595–1598	Friedrich Tilemann
1598–1601	Wolfgang Franz
1601–1606	Laurentius Rhodoman
1606–1616	Johannes Wanckel
1616–1664	Reinhold Franckenberger
(1656–1664	Aegidius Strauch)
1664–1669	Georg Green
1678–1702	Konrad Samuel Schurzfleisch
(1701–1702	Heinrich Leonhard Schurzfleisch)
1702–1713	Heinrich Leonhard Schurzfleisch
(1702–1708	Konrad Samuel Schurzfleisch)
1713–1719	Johann Wilhelm Jahn
1719–1730	Jakob Karl Spener
(1727–1732	Johann Gottlieb Krause)
1732–1736	Johann Gottlieb Krause

---

nostro tempore, quisque, spero intelligent." Pölitz, *Symbolae* (Wittenberg, 1811), 8; Kathe, *Die Wittenberger Philosophische Fakultät*, 175.

154 "[H]*istoria uniuersalis*, quae dividitur in antiquam, mediam (ab anno 476 usque ad a. 1492), recentiorem (ab a. 1492–1789), et recentissimam (inde ab anno 1789)...." Pölitz, *Symbolae* (Wittenberg, 1811), 10.

155 Kathe, *Die Wittenberger Philosophische Fakultät*, 458–459. The parenthetical notations indicate faculty who taught history but did not hold a specific appointment as history professor at that time. Melanchthon also seems to have lectured on classical historians at various times. See, e.g., CR X, 547 Nr. 129 (Livy – 1535?).

1737–1739   Johann Wilhelm Hoffmann
1742–1775   Johann Daniel Ritter
1775–1808   Johann Matthias Schroeckh
1808–1815   Karl Heinrich Ludwig Pölitz

By the time of Pölitz's departure, the Wittenberg world was collapsing. During the Napoleonic Wars, the Saxons sided with the French, and at the Congress of Vienna they lost the territory around Wittenberg to the Prussians. The University of Wittenberg was closed in 1813 during the last stages of the wars and permanently ceased to exist after 1817, when the Prussians merged it into the University of Halle.[156] For centuries, the Wittenberg intellectual community, following Melanchthon, had seen its fortunes as tied to the Fourth Monarchy. In the end, they were correct. Wittenberg did not survive the death of the Holy Roman Empire.

---

156   Kathe, *Die Wittenberger Philosophische Fakultät*, 440.

CHAPTER 7

Conclusion

The sixteenth century was an era of intellectual, religious and political upheaval not seen since the waning days of the old Roman Empire. Just as the Christian historians of Late Antiquity, such as Orosius, had sought to reframe "universal history" to conform to a new set of expectations, so also the Wittenbergers picked up where Orosius and Augustine had left off, and they rewrote the history of Late Antiquity and the Middle Ages to reflect a new perspective on the past. During the Reformation, for the first time in a thousand years, all of history was open for reinterpretation as it never has been again. The enduring legacy of the Wittenbergers was to craft a coherent, and still unfolding, story that reached from Creation to the present.

By transforming received narratives, Melanchthon used *Carion's Chronicle* to develop a distinctly Wittenberg perspective on the historical foundations of the "modern" European world. The *Chronicle* also offered an urgent response to political, religious and social upheaval in Germany during the early years of the Reformation, as well as to threats posed by the French, the papacy and the Turks. In this context, Melanchthon made forceful arguments about the Imperial constitution to restore peace and to promote a united resistance against the foes of the Empire. In doing so, Melanchthon effectively overturned the pro-papal narrative of the Middle Ages, and he presented a persuasive, though often tacit, argument for the legitimacy of the Wittenberg Reformation. At the same time, Melanchthon also reinterpreted Daniel's Four Monarchies to address the needs of Reformation Wittenberg. His intervention ended centuries of inconsistency about the sequence of the Four Monarchies, and from that point, Protestants in Germany consistently argued that the Fourth Monarchy meant Rome and its continuation among the Germans through Charlemagne.

Melanchthon's interpretation of Daniel provided a cohesive set of interlocking arguments about the Holy Roman Empire that cut across law, history and theology. The intellectual culture of Protestant Germany equipped generations of scholars with the tools needed to challenge received orthodoxies; but conformity within that same culture made it difficult to argue against the synthesis of prophecy, historical method and political theory that Melanchthon had developed in response to the struggles of his day. The initial attacks on Melanchthon and the Four Monarchies accordingly came from France; but during the seventeenth century, German Protestants themselves became more critical of the Wittenberg interpretation of Daniel. Defenders of Melanchthon's historical thought nevertheless persisted; and scholars, both pious and patriotic, continued to write new chapters in the struggle against Bodin and other critics. For the Imperial publicists, however, the pressing realities of seventeenth century German political culture eventually undermined the idea of the Empire as a sacred continuation of ancient Rome and turned it into a relic of the past. Theologians clung to the prophetic perspective longer, but they too slowly abandoned Melanchthon's interpretative framework. Among historians, many of the later Wittenbergers enjoyed fame across Europe in their own day, but few are now remembered as more than footnotes. From a modern perspective, the most dynamic centres of historical thought lay elsewhere. Even so, after students stopped using *Carion's Chronicle* at school, the Four Monarchies continued – with or without reference to Daniel – as a point of departure for studying the past. Ultimately, no clear demarcation defines when the Four Monarchies and the *translatio imperii* ceased to inform European intellectuals.[1] Eventually, however, the heirs of the Wittenberg Reformation mostly returned to Luther's early interpretation of Daniel, which saw the fulfilment of the Fourth Monarch in the old Roman Empire.[2] In the end, Melanchthon's patriotic defence of the Holy Roman Empire, after enduring for centuries as an article of faith, gradually ebbed away, until it was quietly forgotten.[3]

Wittenberg historiography, however, encompassed a broader perspective than simply the Empire as the Fourth Monarchy. As a result, even though the University of Wittenberg died with the Holy Roman Empire, its legacy permeated historical thought long after the university itself dissolved. The intellectual world that Melanchthon and his Wittenberg colleagues had created exercised a normative influence over the cultural and educational milieu of Northern Germany and Scandinavia well into the twentieth century. The

---

1 A copy of *Gottfried's Chronicle*, for example, was kept in the library of Adolf Hitler's retreat, the Eagle's Nest, built by the Nazis near Berchtesgaden. See Lucas Heinrich Wüthrich, *Matthaeus Merian d.Ä.: Eine Biographie* (Hamburg: Hoffmann und Campe Verlag, 2007), 143.
2 See, for example, Andrew Steinmann, *Daniel* (St. Louis: Concordia Publishing House, 2008), 144–157; and *Concordia Self-Study Bible* (St. Louis: Concordia Publishing House, 1986), s.v. Dan. 2:32–43: "The gold head represents the Neo-Babylonian empire (v. 38; Jer 51:7); the silver chest and arms, the Medo-Persian empire established by Cyrus in 539 B.C. (the date of the fall of Babylon); the bronze belly and thighs, the Greek empire established by Alexander the Great c. 330; the iron legs and feet, the Roman empire. The toes (v. 41) are understood by some to represent a later confederation of states occupying the territory formerly controlled by the Roman empire."
3 See, for example, *The Lutheran Study Bible* (St. Louis: Concordia Publishing House, 2008), s.v. Dan. 2:39–41: "Second, third and fourth kingdoms are not named. Suggested identifications are Media, Persia and Greece (cf. 7.17; 8:20–21). The chief message is that whichever kingdoms are meant, all have disappeared."

leading German historians of that era – including the father of modern historical studies, Leopold von Ranke (1795–1886) – were largely products of this Protestant tradition and intellectual heirs of Melanchthon.[4] Indeed, Ranke descended from a family of Lutheran theologians and jurists, he was educated in Saxony at schools established or reformed by Melanchthon, and his personal copy of *Carion's Chronicle* (a 1578 Wittenberg edition) still survives.[5]

Each generation develops its own understanding of the past to suit an ever-changing present. During the tumult of the Reformation, the labours of Melanchthon, the *Praeceptor Germaniae*, assumed extraordinary significance for the development of historical studies across early modern Europe and across the divides of language, geography and confession. With *Carion's Chronicle*, Melanchthon deftly transformed the historical "master narrative" of the Middle Ages. The *Chronicle's* immense popularity and formative influence ensured that Melanchthon established a basic narrative that historians and their students have followed, or reacted to, ever since. As scholars before and after can attest, overturning a dominant historical paradigm does not come easy. With his intervention, Melanchthon essentially defined what it meant to study history in the post-medieval world; and the script he set in place is still recognizable even now. Through *Carion's Chronicle*, the Wittenberg reformation of historical thought became an integral aspect of European intellectual culture for the centuries that followed. In the annals of the West, few such wholescale reinterpretations have proven so successful, resilient and enduring.

---

4   See ADB 27: 242–269; NDB 21: 140–142. Ranke's background and experience paralleled that of many young Protestants since the sixteenth century. As Protestant immigrants from Lutheran regions of Europe migrated to North America, they also brought this intellectual culture with them and re-established the same types of educational forms that they knew from Europe. As a result, a world that has largely vanished from Europe has in some ways been preserved in North America. See, e.g., Carl P.E. Springer, *Cicero in Heaven: The Roman Rhetor and Luther's Reformation* (Leiden: Brill, 2018), VIII–IX, 178–186; and Thomas I. Ziebell, "Establishing an Educational Subculture: The 19th Century German Gymnasium Arrangement of Northwestern College in Watertown, Wisconsin to 1915" (Ph.D. diss., University of Wisconsin (Madison), 1994).

5   Melanchthon, *Chronica Carionis* (Wittenberg, 1578) – Syracuse, Syracuse University Library: Ranke 909 C27 f.

APPENDIX A

Carion's Chronicle – Textual Transmission

1 Introduction

Curiosity about the origins and diffusion of *Carion's Chronicle* arose already in the sixteenth century. Indeed, the initial attempts to inventory the editions of the *Chronicle* began in Melanchthon's own lifetime, both as an inquiry in its own right and as part of the growing interest in compiling bibliographical volumes. Among the earliest of these reference works were Conrad Gesner's *Bibliotheca Vniuersalis* (1545),[1] which already then misunderstood the dating of the 1532 *editio princeps*, and Melchior Adam's *Vitae* (1609), which inscribed various mistakes about Carion.[2] Martin Mylius (1542–1611), an early Melanchthon scholar, likewise included *Carion's Chronicle* in his inventory of Melanchthon's works (1582), but he too misunderstood the dating of the *editio princeps*.[3]

Over the decades and centuries that followed, researchers were faced with an aggregate of information, good and bad, and repeated efforts were made to sift through library catalogues and bibliographical compilations to determine the *Chronicle's* textual transmission. Bayle's *Dictionaire*, for example, included a discussion of the editions and an analysis of the possible dates for the *editio princeps*,[4] as did Johann Georg Meusel's *Bibliotheca Historica* (1785),[5] but even the advent of computer resources, such as *Verzeichnis der im deutschen Sprachbereich erschienenen Drucke des 16. Jahrhunderts* (VD16), has not solved the problems associated with understanding the *Chronicle's* text and transmission.[6]

---

1 Conrad Gesner, *Bibliotheca Vniuersalis* (Zürich: Froschauer, 1545), fol. 399r–399v [VD16 G 1698]; Conrad Gesner, *Appendix Bibliothecae Conradi Gesneri* (Zürich: Froschauer, 1555), fol. 93v [VD16 G 1702]; Josias Simler, *Epitome Bibliothecæ Conradi Gesneri* (Zürich: Froschauer, 1555), fol. 93v [VD16 G 1703].
2 For example, Melchior Adam gave Carion's death year as 1538, rather than 1537, which has led to confusion for centuries: "Mortuus Cario in flore aetatis Berlini anno 1538. aetat. suae 39." Melchior Adam, *Vitae Germanorum philosophorum* Melchior Adam, *Vitae Germanorum philosophorum* (Heidelberg: Jonas Rosa, 1615), 105.
3 Martin Mylius, *Chronologia scriptorum Philippi Melanchthonis* (Görlitz: Fritschius, 1582), sig. C3 r. VD16 M 7406.
4 Pierre Bayle, *Dictionaire historique et critique* (Amsterdam: Brunel, 1740), vol. 2, 56–58.
5 Johann Georg Meusel, *Bibliotheca Historica* (Leipzig: Weidmannus & Reichius, 1784), vol. 1, part 1, 175–180.
6 Some later inventories include Carl Schmit von Tavera, *Bibliographie zur Geschichte des Österreichischen Kaiserstaats* (Vienna: L.W. Seidel, 1858), vol. 2., 2–6, Nr. 1038–1083; Uwe

The tradition of independent studies on *Carion's Chronicle* also began in the sixteenth century. The explanatory notes of Victorin Strigel (1524–1569), who taught history at Heidelberg, were published already in 1586.[7] At Wittenberg in the 1580s, Andreas Franckenberger (1536–1590) also published notes related to *Carion's Chronicle*,[8] and he even composed an oration in praise of Melanchthon and the *Chronicle*.[9] A century later, Daniel Wilhelm Moller (1642–1712), a polymath from Altdorf, wrote the first academic "dissertation" (*disputatio*) dedicated entirely to *Carion's Chronicle* (1697).[10] Through his analysis of the *Chronicle's* text and context, Moller set the standard for subsequent scholarship. Despite various problematic sections in his *Disputatio*, Moller's solutions to various textual issues have in fact often proven correct, such as his attribution of the 1564 Basel edition to Oporinus. Subsequent to Moller, three shorter analyses of the *Chronicle's* text were published in the early to mid-eighteenth century. Of these, the most interesting is Johann Christoph Dommerich's *Epistola* (1750), because it deals specifically with the editions at the Herzog August Bibliothek in Wolfenbüttel

    Neddermeyer, *Das Mittelalter in der deutschen Historiographie vom 15. bis zum 18. Jahrhundert: Geschichtsgliederung und Epochenverständnis in der frühen Neuzeit* (Köln: Böhlau, 1988), 363–364; and Karl-Reinhart Trauner, "Carion, Johann(es)," in *Biographisch-Bibliographischen Kirchenlexikons* (Hamm: Traugott Bautz, 2007), vol. 28, 287–300.

7   Victor Strigel, *Reverendae Et Clarissimae memoriae D. Victorini Strigelii. Scholae Historicae Quibus in Academia Heidelbergensi Chronicon viri incomparabilis D. Philippi Melanchthonis illustravit : proposita continua serie historiarum à condito mundo vsque ad Christum natum. Nunc primùm in lucem editae. Opera et studio Christophori Pezelii D.* (Neustadt an der Haardt: Harnisch, 1586). VD16 S 9645. On Strigel, see Viljo Adolf Nordman, *Victorinus Strigelius als Geschichtslehrer* (Abo Turku: Aura, 1930).

8   Andreas Franckenberger, *Institvtionvm Antiqvitatis Et Historiarvm Pars Prima, In Libros Sex Distribvta, Qvorvm Priores Tres Agunt de iudicio ac delectu Authorum, in Chronico Carionis Philippico, & in omni Antiquitate adhibendo : Posteriores idem Chronicon cum fontibus sacris, atq[ue] ethnicis græcis & latinis, ad vsum vitę humanæ transferunt, in cultu numinis diuini, consilijs, praedictionibus, morum emendatione, & consolationibus : Scripta Et Pvblice Proposita in Academia Witebergensi A M. Andrea Franckenbergero ibidem Professore. Ἀξίωμα : Nobilissima & difficilima pars est Historici Operis iudicare, non tantùm de Authorum elocutione & charactere, sed multò magis de rebus ipsis, & qua quisque fide dignus sit.* (Wittenberg: Crato, 1586). VD16 F 2198.

9   Andreas Franckenberger, *Oratio In Honorem Domini Philippi Melanthonis De Magnitvdine rerum diuinarum & politicarum, quae in Chronico eius continentur, Scripta et publicè habita VVitebergae A M. Andrea Franckenbergero, Antiquitatis & Historiarum Professore* (Wittenberg: Crato, 1589). VD16 ZV 6023.

10   Daniel Wilhelm Moller, *Disputationem Circularem De Joh. Carione, Sub Praesidio Dan. Guil. Molleri, Com. Palat. Caesar. & Prof. Publ. Facult. Philosoph. h.t. Decani, Iuventuti Karinophilus P.P. Joh. Leonhardus Kulmichius, Norimb. Altdorf. d. 13. Febr. A. MDCXCVII. H.L.Q.C.* ([Altdorf]: Meyerus, 1697). VD17 12:136858G. This was later reprinted in a collection of dissertations: Daniel Wilhelm Moller, *Dissertationes academicae : De vitis quinquaginta historicorum.* (Nuremberg & Altdorf: Tauber, 1726).

(probably the largest single surviving collection today).[11] The other studies were published at Leipzig (1731)[12] and again at Wolfenbüttel (1755),[13] but none of these offered an improvement on the research conducted by Moller, which had been republished in 1726.

In 1782, Georg Theodor Strobel (1736–1794), a minister living near Altdorf and Nuremberg, published an article on Carion that finally superseded Moller, and it has remained a standard point of departure.[14] Strobel was among the most distinguished Reformation historians of the eighteenth century, and his study of the German Peasant's War (1525) became an important source for nineteenth century interpretations.[15] Because he approached Carion from the perspective of Reformation historiography, Strobel focused especially on the interaction between Carion and Melanchthon, meaning that he provided an understanding of Carion's position within the Reformation world that is often lacking in Moller. Strobel's survey of the *Chronicle's* textual transmission addressed many of the problems raised by earlier scholarship, and as a whole, his research is a testament to the scholarly resources of his day.

A few decades after Strobel, Karl Gottlieb Bretschneider (1776–1848), a former Wittenberg student, began to edit Melanchthon's works, and he included selected portions of *Carion's Chronicle* in volume XII of *Corpus Reformatorum* (1844). Bretschneider relied on Strobel for much of his information about Carion, and he used the libraries in Gotha and Wolfenbüttel for his research on the *Chronicle's* textual transmission. Because Bretschneider's analysis was bound, literally, to the text reproduced in *Corpus Reformatorum*, his remarks on the text and transmission have had an important influence on subsequent scholarship. Although Bretschneider was an outstanding scholar,

---

11 Johann Christoph Dommerich, *De M. Ioannis Carionis Chronico Epistola Ad Virvm Svmme Venerabilem Eberhardvm Davidem Havbervm S. S. Theol. Doctor. Et Ad D. Petri Aedem Qvae Hafniae Est Pastorem Scripta A Joan. Christoph. Dommerich* (Wolfenbüttel: Bartschivs, 1750).

12 Christoph G. Grundig, *De optima historiae providentiam divinam feliciter pervestigandi ac eruendi methodo, itemque de Chronico Melanchthonis, quod Carionis vulgo audit, ob eandem maxime commedando, nonnulla disserit, qui viro nobilissimo atque doctissimo Johanni Henrico Blumbacho Lipsiensi, singulari s. theol. ejusdemque hist. cultori ac phil. baccal. summos in philosophia honores amice congratulatur Christophorus Gottlob Grundigius Dorffhaeyna Misnicus s. theol. cult. et philosoph. baccal* (Leipzig: Saalbach, 1731).

13 Erhard Ernst Hoch, *Disquisitio de chronici, quod extat sub nomine Ioannis Carionis, vera et genuina origine* (Wolfenbüttel: Meisner, 1755).

14 Georg Theodor Strobel, "Von Carions Leben und Schriften," *Miscellaneen literarischen Innhalts, Sechste Sammlung* (Nürnberg, 1782): 163.

15 Georg Theodor Strobel, *Leben, Schriften und Lehren Thomas Müntzers, des Urhebers des Bauernaufruhrs in Thüringen* (Nürnberg & Altdorf: Monath & Kussler, 1795). See generally, Abraham Friesen, "Philipp Melanchthon (1497–1560), Wilhelm Zimmermann (1807–1878) and the Dilemma of Muntzer Historiography," *Church History* 43, no. 2 (June 1974): 164–182.

he occasionally misinterpreted some of the information he found in Wolfenbüttel. As a result, *Corpus Reformatorum* both refined and complicated the understanding of the *Chronicle's* transmission.

After the publication of *Corpus Reformatorum*, a succession of studies on *Carion's Chronicle* appeared from the late nineteenth century to the 1920s. Some of these are sound, but conventional, contributions,[16] while others were truly innovative. Aby Warburg, for instance, discovered some of Carion's correspondence and used it as background to a path-breaking article on astrology in the Reformation.[17] This flurry of pre-War German scholarship culminated in Emil Clemens Scherer's monumental analysis of the foundations of history as an academic discipline: *Geschichte und Kirchengeschichte an den deutschen Universitäten* (1927).[18] In his early chapters, Scherer detailed the efforts of Melanchthon and his students to establish history lectures at the Protestant universities of Germany, and he emphasized the importance of Melanchthon and *Carion's Chronicle* for the development of professional historical studies. He also provided a detailed, and still invaluable, inventory of the books used for historical instruction over the centuries. Scherer cast his net more widely than any other researcher before the War, so he looked not only to German libraries but also to London and Paris, among others, to trace the dissemination of *Carion's Chronicle*. In particular, though, he was able to rely on the vast resources of the Berlin Staatsbibliothek, and his research is all the more valuable because the collection of *Carion's Chronicles* that he used there is now mostly lost (*kriegsverlust*). Since its publication, his study has remained a constant point of reference.

2 Text and Transmission

Georg Rhau (1488–1548) published the *editio princeps* of *Carion's Chronicle* at Wittenberg in the spring of 1532 [1]. A second printing was issued within the next few

---

16 Hildegard Ziegler, *Chronicon Carionis: ein Beitrag zur Geschichtschreibung des 16. Jahrhunderts* (Halle a.S.: Niemeyer, 1898); Emil Menke-Glückert, *Die Geschichtsschreibung der Reformation und Gegenreformation: Bodin und die Begründung der Geschichtsmethodologie durch Bartholomäus Keckermann*. Leipzig: J.C. Hinrichs, 1912; and Gotthard Münch, "Das Chronicon Carionis Philippicum: ein Beitrag zur Würdigung Melanchthons als Historiker," *Sachsen und Anhalt* 1 (1925): 199–283.

17 Aby Warburg, "Pagan-Antique Prophecy in Words and Images in the Age of Luther (1920)," in *The Renewal of Pagan Antiquity: Contributions to the Cultural History of the European Renaissance*, trans. David Britt (Los Angeles: Getty Research Institute for the History of Art and the Humanities, 1999).

18 Emil Clemens Scherer, *Geschichte und Kirchengeschichte an den deutschen Universitäten: Ihre Anfänge im Zeitalter des Humanismus und ihre Ausbildung zu selbständigen Disziplinen* (Freiburg i. B.: Herder, 1927).

weeks [2]. These Rhau editions are unillustrated except for a map with the dispersion of Noah's descendants, but the Augsburg publisher, Heinrich Steiner added a few illustrations to his own edition that appeared later the same year [3]. Later in 1532, Rhau also published a revised text of the *Chronicle* [5], which was used for all editions after 1532, with one exception [28]. The revision reworked the chronology and added a few new sections to the narrative, such as an extended discussion of the early heretic Pelagius. The superintendent of Lübeck, and former Wittenberg student, Hermann Bonnus (1504–1548), used this revised text as the basis for his Latin translation of 1537 [10]. Carion seems to have consulted with Bonnus on the Latin translation, but any efforts to expand the *Chronicle* were cut short by Carion's sudden death in early 1537.

Eventually, various forms of the *Chronicle* were translated into Low German (1534), Latin (1537), Czech (1541/1584), Italian (1543), Dutch (1543/1586), French (1546/1579), Spanish (1549?/1553), English (1550), Danish (1554/1595), Swedish (1649), Turkish (1654), and Icelandic (1692). Initially, the *Chronicle* was republished widely, with editions appearing in Germany, the Low Countries, France, Italy, England and Switzerland; but as Europe divided along religious lines, the *Chronicle's* transmission was increasingly confined to Protestant regions. Thus, by the later sixteenth century, republication occurred mostly in Germany, Switzerland, the Low Countries and Scandinavia. Even so, by then such a vast number of editions were in circulation that the *Chronicle* remained widely available across Europe. Indeed, even now, copies of the *Chronicle* are relatively easy to acquire and fairly inexpensive compared to other texts from the sixteenth century.

In 1546, Johann Funck (1518–1566), a former Wittenberg student, wrote a *Continuation* (*Volstreckung*) to the *Chronicle* on events from 1532 down to 1546 [28]. Funck's *Continuation* quickly came to Melanchthon's attention because it included a section blaming the disastrous 1542 campaign against the Turks on the leadership of Elector Joachim II, Margrave of Brandenburg.[19] Melanchthon was furious, because the *Chronicle* was widely known as his work, and a new Wittenberg edition was quickly published to counter Funck's *Continuation* [29]. Despite Melanchthon's efforts, Funck's scandalous remarks continued to resurface in editions of *Carion's Chronicle* published at Frankfurt by David Zöpfel and later by Sigmund Feyerabend [141].

By the mid-1550s, Melanchthon decided to revise and expand the *Chronicle*, and he also sought a printing privilege to protect the book from the Frankfurt publishers. The revised text was published in a series of four fascicles, but Melanchthon completed only two of these before his death in 1560. At the request of the Wittenberg faculty, the

---

19   See O. Albrecht and P. Flemming, "Das sogenannte Manuscriptum Thomasianum. V. Aus Knaakes Abschrift veröffentlicht von O. Albrecht und P. Flemming. Dritter Teil. Nr. 94–126. Briefe Besolds an Dietrich aus den Jahren 1541–1546. Zweiter Abschnitt: Nr. 111–126," *Archiv für Reformationsgeschichte* 13 (1916): 184, esp. n. 11, where the editors refer to Carion's Chronicle.

remaining two fascicles, on events from Charlemagne down to the sixteenth century, were prepared by Caspar Peucer (1525–1602), Melanchthon's son-in-law. Thus, *Carion's Chronicle* was issued in two different official Wittenberg versions: Carion-Melanchthon (1532) and Melanchthon-Peucer (1558–1565). Various continuations and supplements were appended to the *Chronicle* in the late sixteenth and early seventeenth century, and it continued to be used for history lectures at Wittenberg until the 1630s.[20]

3 The *Editio Princeps* of 1532

In the winter of 1532, Carion traveled to Wittenberg, where he inscribed at the university and consulted with Luther and Melanchthon on behalf of the Electoral Prince of Brandenburg. Georg Rhau (1488–1548) likely published the *editio princeps* of the *Chronicle* shortly before Carion's return to Berlin that spring, and copies were soon circulating around Germany. Nevertheless, at various times, the date of the *editio princeps* has been incorrectly given as 1528 or 1531. These dates can be dismissed from contextual and even internal evidence – the *Chronicle* itself includes material from early 1532 – but the false dates merit further attention because of their frequent recurrence over the centuries.

4 Ghost Edition (1528)

Although the 1532 Marburg edition of *Carion's Chronicle* has a title page image by Hans Brosamer dated "1528" [4], this does not seem to have been the source of the 1528 ghost edition. Rather, the edition was created by a typographical error in Conrad Gesner's *Appendix Bibliothecae* (1555) [21] and Josias Simler's *Epitome Bibliothecæ* (1555).[22] Earlier, in his *Bibliotheca Vniuersalis* (1545), Gesner had given the date of the *editio princeps*

---

20 "M. Reinholdus Franckenberger Histor. P. & p. t. Academiae Rector, si officij ratione licebat, ea quae in Chronico Carionis Philippico & Peuceriano eiusque Libro IV restant paucissima, absolvet, & deinde ad Librum V. Deo volente, accedet Hora II." University of Wittenberg, *Rector Et Consilium Academiae Wittebergensis Publ.* (Wittenberg: Rothe, 1634). Forschungsbibliothek Gotha: Phil 2° 268/11 (74). VD17 547:637629Z.

21 "Ioannes Carion mathematicus, natione Germanus, scripsit libros Chronicorum secundum quatuor monarchias mundi, lingua Germanica: qui Vuittenbergæ impressi sunt 1528. Idem opus Latine redditum ab Hermanno Bonno, excusum Halæ Sueuroum per Petrum Brubachium, 1539. & Lugduni apud Frellæos, 1543. Floruit anno 1534." Conrad Gesner, *Appendix Bibliothecae Conradi Gesneri* (Zürich: Froschauer, 1555), fol. 93v. VD16 G 1702.

22 "Ioannes Carion mathematicus, natione Germanus, scripsit libros Chronicorum secundum quatuor monarchias mundi, lingua Germanica: qui Vuittenbergæ impressi sunt 1528. Idem opus Latine redditum ab Hermanno Bonno, excusum Halæ Sueuroum per Petrum

as 1538, but the *Appendix* and the *Epitome* reproduced 1538 as 1528.[23] These mistaken entries caused confusion for centuries. In his study of *Carion's Chronicle* (1697), Daniel Moller discussed the 1528 ghost edition at two points, noting that he had never seen it, and he cites Simler's *Epitome* as his ultimate source.[24] (Moller was not aware that the correct date for the *editio princeps* is 1532.) The problem created by Gesner and Simler was widely transmitted, and the *Dictionaire* of Pierre Bayle, for example, provided an analysis dismissing the 1528 date in favor of 1531.[25] Although Emil Clemens Scherer noted Moller's references to a 1528 edition, he did not follow the trail back to the sixteenth century sources;[26] and since then, the issue has faded into learned

Brubachium, 1539. & Lugduni apud Frellæos, 1543. Floruit anno 1534." Josias Simler, *Epitome Bibliothecæ Conradi Gesneri* (Zürich: Froschauer, 1555), fol. 93v. VD16 G 1703.

23 "Ioannes Carion mathematicus, Buetickheimensis, natione Germanus, scripsit libros Chronicorum secundum quatuor monarchias mundi, lingua Germanica: qui Vuittembergæ impressus est, 1538 in 8. Obijt author ante paucos annos. Idem opus Latine redditum ab Hermanno Bonno, excusum Halæ Sueuoru[m] per Petru[m], 1539. in 8 chartis 35. & Lugduni apud Frellæos, 1543. hac inscriptione: Chronicorum libellus, maximas quasq[ue] res gestas ab initio mundi, apto ordine complectens, ita ut annorum ratio, ac præcipue uissitudines, quæ in regna, in religionem, & in alias res magnas incidunt, quàm rectissime cognosci queant. Ex præfactione authoris scripta anno 1531. ad Ioachimum Marchionem Brandenburgensem. 'Hæc Chronica conscribenda mihi sumpsi, in quibus pro uirili, ordine quàm potuit fieri accuratissimo, monarchias, & alias insignes res gestas mutationesq[ue], quæ subinde in imperijs acciderunt, breuiter comprehendere & commemorare sum conatus.'" Conrad Gesner, *Bibliotheca Vniuersalis* (Zürich: Froschauer, 1545), fol. 399r–399v. VD16 G 1698.

24 "*Scripta & Opuscula* ex ingenio Carionis prognata partim sunt *Historica*, partim *Mathematica*. Et quidem *historica* quod attinet, *unicus libellus Chronicorum*, germanico idiomate contextus, & *in quatuor Monarchias* distributus, ab Orbe condito usque ad A.C. 1521. sub Carionis nomine prodiit *Wittebergæ A. 1528 in 12*. quæ quidem Editio nunquam adhuc mihi visa est...." Daniel Wilhelm Moller, *Disputationem Circularem De Joh. Carione, Sub Praesidio Dan. Guil. Molleri, Com. Palat. Caesar. & Prof. Publ. Facult. Philosoph. h.t. Decani, Iuventuti Karinophilus P.P. Joh. Leonhardus Kulmichius, Norimb. Altdorf. d. 13. Febr. A. MDCXCVII. H.L.Q.C.* ([Altdorf]: Meyerus, 1697), 7. VD17 12:136858G. Moller continues with a further explanation (p. 7–8); and in a subsequent section, he adds, "(1) *Joh. Carionis Chronica / nach dem 4. Monarchien der Welt eingetheilt / Witteberg. 1528. in 12.* de quo libro *Josias Simler* in Epitom. Biblioth. Gesner. voc. Carion. *Scripsit Carion libros Chronicorum secundum quatuor Monarchias Mundi, lingua germanica, qui Wittenbergæ impressi sunt 1528.*" Moller, *Disputationem*, 17.

25 "Les Abbréviateurs de Gesner marquent une Edition de l'an 1528 : c'est une faute. La prémiere Edition n'a pu précéder l'an 1531." Bayle, *Dictionaire historique et critique* (Amsterdam, 1740), vol. 2, 56 n. (D).

26 "Moller a. a. O. 7 und 17 erwähnt eine Überlieferung, wonach schon 1528 zu Wittenberg eine deutsche Ausgabe der Chronik erschienen sei, die bis 1521 gereicht habe. Er habe jedoch diese nie zu Gesicht bekommen. Leider gibt er nicht an, aus welcher Quelle er die Nachricht geschöpft hat, so daß eine Nachprüfung nicht möglich war." Scherer, *Geschichte und Kirchengeschichte*, 468 n. 2.

obscurity. Based on the evidence, the 1528 edition was clearly a ghost, but it attests to the normative and enduring force of early reference literature in molding subsequent scholarship.

5   Ghost Edition (1531)

While the 1528 ghost edition can be traced to a typographical error, the reference to a 1531 edition generally derives from Carion's dedicatory epistle to the Electoral Prince of Brandenburg, which is dated: "Datum zu Berlin / Anno D[om]ni. xxxj." Neither Carion nor Rhau redated the letter from 1531 to 1532, despite the publication delays caused by Melanchthon. The 1532 Rhau editions do not include the date of publication on the title page or in the colophon, so scholars from the sixteenth century to the present have often treated the dedicatory epistle as a guide to the year of publication.

In his *Chronologia* (1582) of Melanchthon's works, Martin Mylius (1542–1611), the most important early Melanchthon bibliographer, listed the *editio princeps* among the entries under 1531.[27] For his dating, Mylius relied on Melanchthon's published correspondence with his friend Joachim Camerarius (1500–1575), in which he mentioned various revisions to Carion's manuscript during 1531. In his *Disputatio*, Moller discussed the contents of Carion's dedicatory epistle, but because he believed that the *editio princeps* must have been from 1528, he did not address the question of the 1531 dating.[28] The *Dictionaire* of Pierre Bayle, a good indication of eighteenth century tradition, dismissed the 1528 dating in favor of 1531.[29]

In contrast to this, Strobel clearly and unequivocally refuted the 1531 dating; and based on internal evidence, he correctly set the date for the *editio princeps* as 1532.[30] Bretschneider relied on Strobel's article for much of his information about Carion,

---

27 "[Anno Christi 1531, Aetat. Phil. xxxv] Chronicon Carionis scripsit, de quo Philip. in epistolis ad Camer. p. 163. sic. Cario misit huc χρονικά excudenda, sed ea lege ut ego emendarem, Sunt multa scripta negligentius. Itaque ego totum opus retexo & quidem germanicè, & constitui complecti praecipuas mutationes maximorum Imperiorum. De occasione nominis Carionis vide Peuceri praefationem in Chron. Philip. in fol. editum. De Carione Georgius Frabricius: Hos alius fecit, tu Cario nomine signas // Ingenio scriptos à meliore libros." Mylius, *Chronologia* (Görlitz 1582), sig. C2 r.
28 Moller, *Disputationem*, 7–10, 17.
29 "Les Abbréviateurs de Gesner marquent une Edition de l'an 1528 : c'est une faute. La prémiere Edition n'a pu précéder l'an 1531." Bayle, *Dictionaire historique et critique* (Amsterdam, 1740), vol. 2, 56 n. (D).
30 Strobel, "Von Carions Leben und Schriften," 163.

and he accordingly noted the 1532 dating in *Corpus Reformatorum*. Nevertheless, Bretschneider mistakenly listed the 1532 Rhau octavo edition [5], rather than the earlier quarto edition [1], as the *editio princeps*.[31] Although he mentioned the 1528 ghost edition, Scherer had little doubt that the *editio princeps* was published in 1532, but he was unaware that Rhau published multiple versions of the text in 1532. The on-line edition of VD16 has occasionally revised the date of initial Rhau quarto editions from 1532 to 1531, but the printed version correctly set the date for VD16 C 998 and VD16 C 995 as 1532. At present, Worldcat includes a false record for a 1531 edition, so the tradition of learned error has continued unabated.

6   Ghost edition (1532) – Nicolaus Schirlentz

A third ghost edition, a Nicolaus Schirlentz edition from 1532, deserves attention because it was created by Bretschneider in *Corpus Reformatorum* and subsequently taken up in the secondary literature on Carion. The bibliographical and descriptive information on *Carion's Chronicle* is frequently problematic in *Corpus Reformatorum*. Among other things, Bretschneider thought that Carion had dedicated the *editio princeps* to Margrave Joachim I, Elector of Brandenburg, rather than to his son Electoral Prince Joachim, the future Elector Joachim II. The mistake continues to be repeated, even in the most recent literature on Carion.[32]

Bretschneider discussed the Nicolaus Schirlentz ghost edition in the introduction to the text of *Carion's Chronicle* in *Corpus Reformatorum*,[33] and the reference can probably be traced to a *Sammelband* containing a copy of Rhau's second printing from 1532 [2] (Wolfenbüttel, Herzog August Bibliothek: H: T 252.4° Helmst.). The volume includes *Carion's Chronicle* as the first book within the binding, but the fifth book, *Von der winckelmesse vnd Pfaffen Weihe. D. Mart Luther* (VD16 L 7242), has the colophon "Gedrückt zu Wittemberg durch Nickel Schirlentz MDXXXIII" (sig. [Oiij] r). Because the Rhau edition has no publication information on the title page, turning to the colophon apparently lead Bretschneider to Schirlentz. Indeed, the binding opens naturally to that leaf, Schirlentz's typeface is similar to Rhau's, and Bretschneider must have simply misread the Roman numerals. Arguments based on the Schirlentz ghost edition

---

31   CR XII, [706].
32   "Dicavit libellum Carion Domino ac patrono suo Ioachimo I., Marchioni Elect., et data est epistola Berolini a. 1531" (CR XII, 708).
33   The publication information is given in a standarized format: "Gedruckt zu Wittenb. durch Nikel Schirlenz im J. 1532" (CR XII, 708).

are occasionally found in the secondary literature, and they all derive ultimately from *Corpus Reformatorum*.

7   Misattributed Augsburg *Chronica*

In addition to the ghost editions, at various times *Carion's Chronicle* has been confused with another *Chronica*,[34] first published at Augsburg in 1515.[35] The 1515 Augsburg *Chronica* consists of a brief annalistic sketch, with little extended narrative. It begins at A.D. 903 with the election of Saint Ulrich († 973) as Bishop of Augsburg – the date is actually a mistake for A.D. 923 – and it ends with events from 1515. In general, the little *Chronica* focuses especially on South Germany and on Augsburg. The entries are succinct, and the 1515 edition is quite short, less than thirty pages. In subsequent years, the *Chronica* was revised and expanded, and the title also varies in later editions.[36]

In 1531, Philip Ulhart published a vastly expanded edition,[37] and this new version of the Augsburg *Chronica* has sometimes been confused with *Carion's Chronicle* in the secondary literature. Instead of beginning with A.D. 903, the 1531 Ulhart edition begins at Anno Mundi 4071, with the foundation of Augsburg, but the annalistic account itself starts with Julius Caesar and the beginning of the Roman Empire in 47 B.C. (Anno Mundi 5153). Thus, Ulhart extended the chronological coverage to encompass the entire Roman Empire. In 1532, the same year as the *editio princeps* of *Carion's Chronicle*, Georg Rhau published an edition of this Augsburg *Chronica* at Wittenberg, making confusion with *Carion's Chronicle* all the more likely. In fact, the Augsburg *Chronica* is sometimes bound with the octavo edition of *Carion's Chronicle* (Figures 34–35).[38]

---

34   The Augsburg *Chronica* editions fall into three textual families: VD16 C 2478–2485, ZV 3285–3286; VD16 C 2470–2473; VD16 C 2457–2465, ZV 3287.

35   Anonymous, *Chronica Von vil Namhafftigen geschichten die geschehen seynd seid man zalt nach Christ geburt neün hundert vnd dreü iar in Ungern Behem Osterreich Steürmackt Bayern Schwab[e]n Francken Wälsch vnnd Teütsch landen biß auf das M.CCCCC.XV.* ([Augsburg]: [Erhard Oeglin], 1515). VD16 C 2478. See the editions: VD16 C 2478–2485, ZV 3285–3286.

36   Anonymous, *Chronica New: Manicherlay Historien / vnnd besondere geschichten / Kürtzlich begreyffend / Von dem Jar der geburt vnsers seligmachers Jesu Christi / biß in das M.D.vnd. xxviij. Erlengeret* (Augsburg: Ulhart, 1528). VD16 C 2471. See the editions: VD16 C 2470–2473.

37   Anonymous, *Chronica Darinn auff das kurtzest werden begriffen / die Namhafftigsten geschichten / so sich vnder allen Kaysern / von der geburt Christi / biß auff das M.D.vñ.xxxj. Jar / verlaffen haben.* (Augsburg: Ulhart, 1531). VD16 C 2457. See the editions: VD16 C 2457–2465, ZV 3287.

38   Anonymous, *Chronica Darynn auffs kürtzest werden begriffen / die namhafftigsten geschichten / so sich vnter allen Keisern / von der gepurt Christi / biß auff das Tausent Fünffhundert ein vnd dreyssigst Jar verlauffen haben. Auch findestu hinden jnn diesem Büchlein die Meissnische Chronica* (Wittenberg: Rhau, 1532). VD16 C 2461. See, e.g., Wolfenbüttel, Herzog August Bibliothek: H: T 223.8° Helmst. (1).

CARION'S CHRONICLE – TEXTUAL TRANSMISSION   347

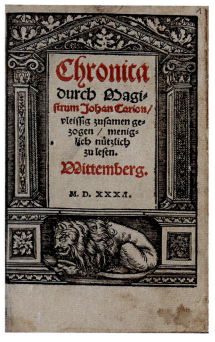

FIGURE 34 Carion, *Chronica* (Wittenberg, 1532).
HERZOG AUGUST BIBLIOTHEK WOLFENBÜTTEL: H: T 223.8° HELMST. (1)

FIGURE 35 Anonymous, *Chronica* (Wittenberg, 1532).
HERZOG AUGUST BIBLIOTHEK WOLFENBÜTTEL: H: T 223.8° HELMST. (2)

The last edition of the Augsburg *Chronica* was published by Peter Seitz at Wittenberg in 1553.[39]

8 Supplements to the *Chronicle*

Over the years, publishers added appendices and supplementary material to their editions of the *Chronicle* including various regnal lists, *De Rebus in Belgica gestis ad Philippum Gayanum* by the French historian Guillaume Paradin (1510–1590) [26, 27], and a *Supplementum seu Appendix ad praecentia* by Guillaume Morel (1505–1564) [36]. After 1551, a new expanded "du Puys Edition" of the *Chronicle* [51] circulated alongside

---

39 Anonymous, *Chronica Darin auffs kürtzest werden begriffen / die namhafftigsten Geschichten / so sich vnter allen Keisern / von der geburt Christi / bis auff das Tausent Fünffhundert ein vnd dreissigst jar verlauffen haben. Auch findestu hinden in diesem Büchlein die Meissnische Chronica* (Wittenberg: Seitz, 1553). VD16 C 2463.

Bonnus's original translation, and it added considerable material on events outside of Germany. In 1564, Johannes Oporinus published the last Latin edition of the Carion-Melanchthon *Chronicle* at Basel [123].

9   *Chronicon Carionis* (1558–1565)

In contrast to the 1532 Carion-Melanchthon version, the Melanchthon-Peucer version of the *Chronicle* was published in a series of fascicles: *Prima Pars, Liber Primus et Liber Secundus* (1558); *Secunda Pars, Liber Tertius* (1560); *Tertia Pars, Liber Quartus* (1562); *Tertia Pars, Liber Quintus* (1565). The final fascicle was also sometimes styled as *Quarta Pars*.[40] As a precaution, Melanchthon obtained a printing privilege for the new *Chronicle*, and all the fascicles were first published at Wittenberg. With the exception of *Liber Quartus*, published by Peter Seitz, the heirs of Georg Rhau were responsible for each fascicle. For *Liber Quartus*, Peucer also prepared his important tabella on reading history: *Tabella ostendens qvo ordine legenda et cognoscenda sit series historiarvm mvndi. Dedicata scholasticis Academiæ Witebergensis.*

Peucer did not issue a complete folio edition of all five books until 1572, published by Johannes Crato at Wittenberg [154]. The folio edition is really a collection of historical works including: Caspar Peucer's *Oratio de Argumento Historiarum*, Melanchthon's *Explicatio Locorum Palastinae*, Tacitus's *Germania*, Melanchthon's *Vocabula Regionum et Gentium*, the complete Wittenberg text of the *Chronicon Carionis*, the *Exhoratio Maximiliani Caesaris Ad Bellum Turcis Inferendum*, and the *De Electione et Coronatione Caroli V Caesaris Historia*.

Various reprintings of the complete Melanchthon-Peucer version followed in Wittenberg, Frankfurt am Main, Geneva and Bern. The editions at Wittenberg and Frankfurt reproduced the text of Peucer's 1572 edition. In contrast, the Swiss editions seem to have been based on the individual fascicles. The Swiss editions after 1610 include a continuation down to the seventeenth century, but none of these include the supplementary texts from the 1572 Wittenberg edition. The last Latin edition published in Germany appeared at Frankfurt am Main in 1624 [200]; and after the 1625 Geneva edition [201], the printing of *Carion's Chronicle* in Latin lapsed for over two hundred

---

40   Both Strobel and *Corpus Reformatorum* made mistakes concerning the *editio princeps* of the *Liber Quintus* fascicle. Strobel listed a *Quarta Pars* published in 1565, rather than a *Tertia Pars, Liber Quintus*. See Strobel, "Von Carions Leben und Schriften," 194. (The title *Quarta Pars* was, however, used somewhat confusedly by Matthias Welack in 1580 and 1591: "Qvarta Pars Chronici Carionis A Friderico Secvndo vsq[ue] ad Carolum Quintum. Expositvs Et Avctvs A Casparo Pevcero. Pertinet hic liber ad partem tertiam Chronici.") Bretschneider attempted to correct this mistake, but he erroneously asserted that *Liber Quintus* was first published by Schwertel in 1566, instead of Rhau in 1565. See CR XII, 709.

years until *Corpus Reformatorum*. The last early modern edition of *Carion's Chronicle* was the 1649 Swedish translation [204].

10 *Chronica Carionis* – German (1560–1564)

The first three Latin fascicles of the Melanchthon-Peucer version were translated into German by Eusebius Menius (b. 1527): *Chronica Carionis gantz new Latine geschrieben* (1560); *Der Ander Teil der Chronica Carionis* (1562); and *Der Dritte Teil der Chronica Carionis* (1564). Despite claims of being "newly translated," all subsequent German editions actually incorporate Menius's translation. Christoph Pezel translated the remaining sections of the *Chronicle* for the German folio edition published at Wittenberg in 1573 [157].

Scherer thought that three German translations had been made of the Melanchthon-Peucer *Chronicle*: Eusebius Menius (1560–1566); Anonymous (1573); and Christoph Pezel (1576).[41] Scherer was not aware of the 1564 German fascicle of *Liber Quartus*, and he assumed that the material had appeared for the first time in the Frankfurt hybrid edition of 1566. Because of their title pages, he also thought that the German text of the Wittenberg folio edition of 1573 had been made by an anonymous translator and that Christoph Pezel was responsible for the translation used in the Dresden edition of 1576. These are, in fact, all editions of the Menius-Pezel translation.

11 Frankfurt Hybrid Edition 1566/1569

In 1566, Sigmund Feyerabend published a hybrid edition of *Carion's Chronicle* [141]. Feyerabend used Menius's German translation of Libri 1–4, but then he turned to the original Carion-Melanchthon German text for the events that were included in Liber 5 of the Melanchthon-Peucer version. Furthermore, Feyerabend included Funck's *Continuation*, so the very text that Melanchthon had worked so hard to suppress was again republished in Frankfurt. Peucer was furious, because Feyerabend's title page made it appear as though Peucer himself had written Funck's *Continuation*, including the scandalous remarks about the Elector of Brandenburg. Despite Peucer's vehement protests, Feyerabend reissued the hybrid edition in 1569 [148]. These Frankfurt editions lead Peucer to assert greater control over the *Chronicle*, and his last official edition of 1573 included a request that the text be left unchanged in subsequent reprints.[42]

---

41 Scherer, *Geschichte und Kirchengeschichte*, 473.
42 "An den Leser. Es haben sich fur dieser zeit / etliche Drucker vnterstanden / dieses vnser Wittembergisch Chronicon nach zu drucken / vnd dasselbe jres gefallens zu endern vnd

12 Census of Editions

The census includes all the editions of *Carion's Chronicle* currently known to survive.[43] Earlier scholars have generally tried to account for all of the editions of the Carion-Melanchthon *Chronicle*, but even Scherer gave up in despair when confronted by the Melanchthon-Peucer editions. As a result, the sheer number of Carion imprints has never been fully appreciated; and in some sense even the census below is an incomplete inventory, because so many editions have undoubtedly been lost.

With the exception of the verse adaptation of the *Chronicle* (1596) [188] by Halvard Gunnarssøn (Halvardus Gunarius),[44] the bibliography is limited to editions of *Carion's Chronicle* proper. Accordingly, it excludes works that incorporate material from *Carion's Chronicle* but are textually distinct, such as Christoph Egenolff's *Chronic* (1533),[45] the Hungarian verse adaptation of András Batizi (1554),[46] the *Chronica* of István Székely

---

zu mehren / vnd also ein Corpus zusammen zu flicken jres gewins halben / darzu sie etliche Theil dieses Chronici / die do allbereit sind verdeudscht gewesen / genommen haben / die andern Theil die noch nicht verdeudscht gewesen / haben sie ausgelassen / vnd an derselben stat andere fremdbe Narrationes hinan geflickt / nicht one vnsern grossen nachtheil vnd beschwerung / Dieselben vnd alle andere wollen wir erinnert / vnd vmb jr selbst besten willen vermanet haben sie wollen sich forthin dieses vnser Chronicon nach zu drücken gentzlich enthalten / viel weniger wollen sie sich vnterstehen etwas hinein zuflicken oder darzu zusetzen / es sey was es wolle / Sondern lassen vns dieses vnser Chronicon bleiben / wie wir es in Druck verfertigt haben / was ferner zu vollstreckung vnd ausfürung der Historien bis vff vnsere zeiten gehöret das sol vermittelst göttlicher hülff in ein eigenes abgesondertes Buch verfasset / vnd zu seiner zeit an tag gegeben werden." Peucer, *Chronica Carionis* (Wittenberg, 1573), sig. [avj] r.

43   For Carion's other works, the best bibliography is Dietmar Fürst and Jürgen Hamel, eds., *Johann Carion (1499–1537): Der erste Berliner Astronom mit einem Reprint der Schrift Carions "Bedeutnuss und Offenbarung" (1527)* (Berlin-Treptow: Archenhold-Sternwarte, 1988), 18–24; see also Karl-Reinhart Trauner, "Carion, Johann(es)," in *Biographisch-Bibliographischen Kirchenlexikons* (Hamm: Traugott Bautz, 2007), vol. 28, 287–300.

44   See Inger Ekrem, *Historieskrivning og -undervisning på latin i Oslo omkring år 1600: Halvard Gunnarssøns Philippiske Carionkrønike, Rostock 1596. Med innledning, oversettelse og kommentar* (Oslo: Scandinavian University Press, 1998).

45   Christian Egenolff, *Chronic von an vn[d] abgang aller Weltwesenn. Auß den glawbwirdigsten Historien / On alle Gloß vnnd Zůsatz / Nach Historischer warheyt beschriben. Künig / Keyser / vnnd fürneme Personen / nach warer fürbildung Controfeit.* (Frankfurt a.M.: Egenolff, 1533). VD16 E 573.

46   András Batizi, "Meglött és megleendő dolgoknak teremtéstül fogva mind az ítéletig való história," in *xvi. századbeli magyar költők művei*, vol. 1 (1527–1546), ed. Áron Szilády (Budapest: Magyar Tudományos Akadémia, 1880), 95–113. The *editio princeps* is incomplete, see the facsimile with commentary: Márton Tarnóc and Varjas Béla, eds., *Hoffgreff-énekeskönyv. Kolozsvár, 1554–1555. A kísérő tanulmányt írta Tarnóc Márton. A fakszimile svővegét gondozta Varjas Béla*, Bibliotheca Hungarica Antiqua VII. (Budapest: Akadémiai

(1559),[47] and *Cooper's Chronicle* (1549), which is really an adaptation and expansion of *Carion's Chronicle* for an English audience.[48] So too, the bibliography excludes the copies of Melanchthon's "Tabula Annorum" that are found in other historical works, such as Georg Major's edition of Justin's *Epitome*[49] or Sleidanus's *Commentaries*.[50] It also excludes excerpts from the *Chronicle* found in periodicals. The history of the most important ghost editions receives attention above, others are addressed in the census of editions and in the footnotes. For the most part, the bibliography excludes references to ghost editions from earlier catalogs and bibliographies that are easily attributable to typographical mistakes.[51]

13 Census Numbers

The editions are numbered here for the first time, and I have included cross-references to standard bibliographies such as VD16 and French Vernacular Books. Different printing states – an edition that has been corrected by the printer while the book was in press, e.g., correcting page numbers – are subnumbered. Likewise, where the text and title page are identical except for the publisher subnumbers are also used; this occurs most frequently with editions printed at Paris and Lyon. In contrast to this, title page variants and textual variants receive individual numbers. In the sixteenth century, publishers commonly printed new title pages for unsold bookstocks to make them appear as if new for the bookfairs, and I have included colophons where appropriate to note this. Although I have generally excluded ghost editions, in some instances, I have used brackets to indicate editions that I have not seen but whose existence is plausible based on secondary references.

Kiadó, 1966). See also Magyar Tudományos Akadémia Országos Széchényi Könyvtár, *Régi Magyarországi Nyomtatványok (1473–1600)* (Budapest: Akadémiai Kiadó, 1971), Nr. 108.

47 István Székely, *Chronica Ez Vilagnac Yeles Dolgairol. Szekel Estvan. Craccoba Niomtatot. Striykouiai Lazar Altal, Christvs ßweletesenec M.D.L.LIX. eßtendeibe.* (Kraków: Lazar, 1559). See Magyar Tudományos Akadémia Országos Széchényi Könyvtár, *Régi Magyarországi Nyomtatványok (1473–1600)* (Budapest: Akadémiai Kiadó, 1971), Nr. 156.

48 Thomas Lanquet and Thomas Cooper, *An Epitome Of Chronicles* (London: Thomas Berthelet, 1549).

49 Justin, *Ivstini Ex Trogo Pompeio Historia* (Hagenau: Johann Setzer, 1526). VD16 T 2051.

50 Johannes Sleidanus, *De Statv Religionis Et Reipvblicae, Carolo Qvinto Caesare, Commentarii* (Frankfurt a.M.: Peter Schmidt, 1568), 739. VD16 S 6686.

51 See, for example Theophil Georgi's bibliography, which includes the 1528 ghost edition as well as an edition from 1684: Theophil Georgi, *Allgemeines Europäisches Bücher-Lexicon* (Leipzig: Theophil Georgi, 1742), vol. 1, 254.

APPENDIX B

Carion's Chronicle – Manuscript Notes

I note the following manuscripts because *Iter Italicum* or other bibliographical references indicate they are related to *Carion's Chronicle*. I have seen only those in Bonn, London and Wolfenbüttel.

Bonn, Universitäts- und Landesbibliothek

Ms. S1959 Melanchthon, Philipp. *Vorlesungsmitschrift – Chronicon Carionis*

Konya, Izzet Koyunoglu Library

Nr. 14031 – Târîh-i Firengî Tercümesi. [Turkish translation of *Carion's Chronicle* by Kātib Čelebi]

London, British Library

Add 11153 – Thesaurus multarum historiarum, annalium et narrationum, a Magno Jonæo, Vigrensi, compositus circa annum 1550. Islandice. [Includes "Vr Chronicu Johannis Carjonis" – Icelandic translation of *Carion's Chronicle*].

Rostock, Universitätsbibliothek

Hist. 5. – David Chytreaus, Index monstrans fontes ex quibus historiae in Chronico Carionis Philippeo depromptae sunt.

Wolfenbüttel, Herzog August Bibliothek

Extrav. 11. – Caspar Peucer, tabella ostendens quo ordine legenda et cognoscenda sit series historiarum mundi.

Wrocław, Biblioteka Uniwersytecka

Rehdigeriana 429 – Andr. Franckenberger, observationes in chronicon Melanchthonis (1586).
Rehdigeriana 447-449 – Melanchthon, observationes in Carionis Chronicon.
Rehdigeriana 1330 – Caspar Peucer, annotationes in chronica Melanchthonis.

Zürich, Zentralbibliothek

Z V 302. – In Philippi Melanthonis Chronicorum librum primum annotata ex ore D. Victorini Strigelii praeceptoris sui charissimi per Samuelem Hochholtzerum Tigurinum excepta quem salvis auspiciis 10. Maii anni salutis nostrae 1568 auspicatus est.

APPENDIX C

Carion's Chronicle – Stemma of Editions

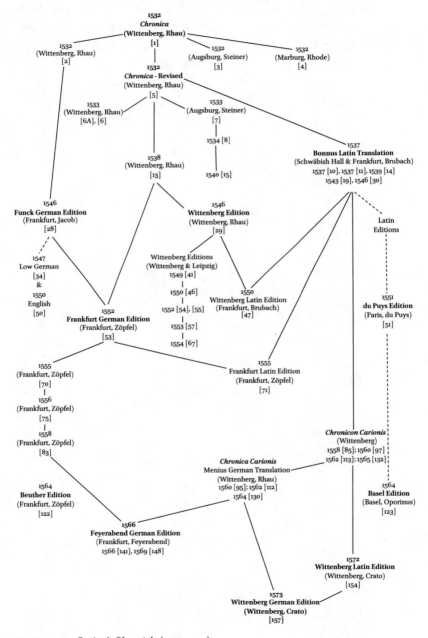

STEMMA 1   *Carion's Chronicle* (1532–1573)

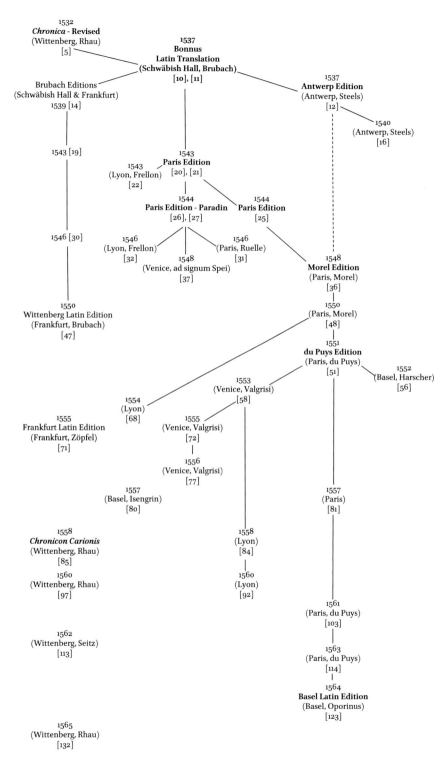

STEMMA 2   *Carion's Chronicle* Latin Editions (1537–1565)

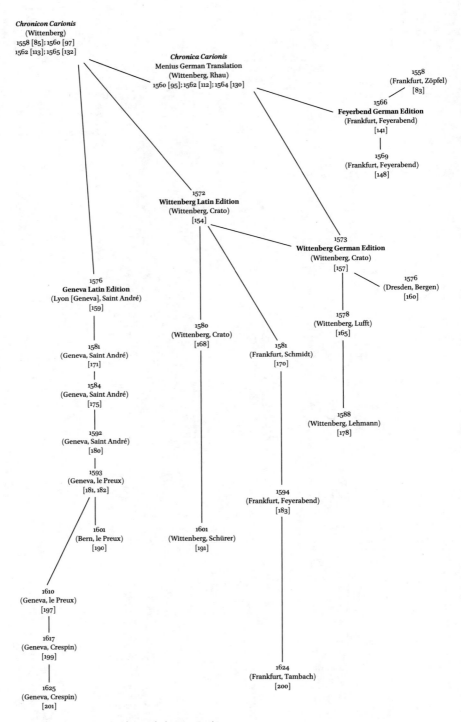

STEMMA 3   *Carion's Chronicle* (1558–1625)

CARION'S CHRONICLE — STEMMA OF EDITIONS 357

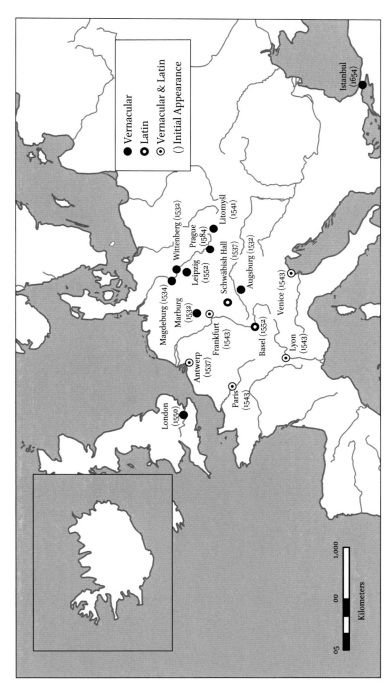

MAP 1   Carion-Melanchthon *Chronica* (1532) Textual Transmission

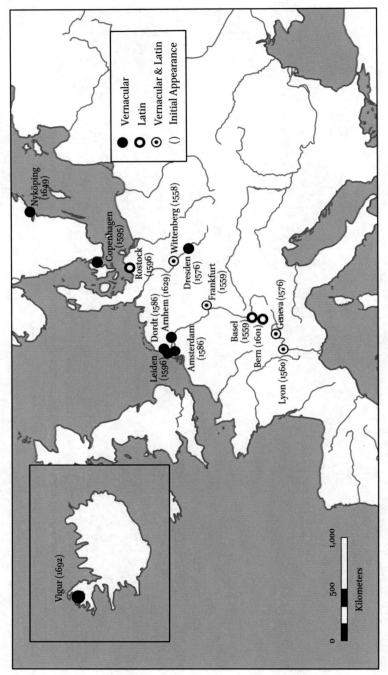

MAP 2 Melanchthon-Peucer *Chronicon Carionis* (1558–1565) Textual Transmission

APPENDIX D

Carion's Chronicle – Indices to the Editions

Carion-Melanchthon *Chronica* (1532):
I. Publisher
II. Language/Place of Publication

Melanchthon-Peucer *Chronicon Carionis* (1558–1565):
III. Publisher
IV. Place of Publication
V. Combined Publisher Index

I   Carion-Melanchthon *Chronica* (1532)

Publisher Index

1.1 *German (1532–1540)*
Rhau, Georg – 1532 [1], 1532 [2], 1532 [5], 1533 [6.A], 1533 [6], 1538 [13]
Rhode, Franz – 1532 [4]
Steiner, Heinrich – 1532 [3], 1533 [7], 1534 [8], 1540 [15]

1.2 *German – Funck/Frankfurt Edition (1546–1569)*
Feyerabend, Sigmund – *1566* [141], *1569* [148]
Hüter, Simon – *1566* [141]
Jacob, Cyriakus – 1546 [28]
Zöpfel, David – 1552 [53], 1555 [70], 1556 [75], 1558 [83]

1.3 *German – Wittenberg Edition (1546–1554)*
Berwald, Jacob – 1552 [55], 1553 [57.1], 1553 [57.2]
Rhau, Georg – 1546 [29]
Rhau, Georg (Heirs) – 1549 [41], 1550 [46], 1552 [54], 1554 [67]

1.4 *German – Beuther Edition (1564)*
Zöpfel, David – 1564 [122]

2.1 *Plattdeutsch (1534–1546)*
Lotter, Michael – 1534 [9], 1542 [18]

2.2 *Plattdeutsch – Funck/Frankfurt Edition (1547)*
Lotter, Michael – 1547 [34]

3.1 *Latin (1537–1546)*
Angelier, Arnold l' – 1543 [20.2]
Angelier, Charles l' – 1543 [20.1], 1543 [21], 1544 [25]
Brubach, Peter – 1537 [10], 1537 [11], 1539 [14], 1543 [19], 1546 [30]
Frellon, Jean & François – 1543 [22]
Gaultherot, Vivant – 1543 [20.3]
Preux, Poncet le – 1543 [20.4]
Steels, Jan – 1537 [12], 1540 [16]

3.2 *Latin – Paradin Supplement (1544–1548)*
Ad signum Spei – 1548 [37]
Boucher, Nicolas – 1544 [26.1]
Chaudière, Regnault – 1544 [26.2]
Frellon, Jean & François – 1546 [32]
Foucher, Jean – 1544 [27.3]
Gazeau, Jacques – 1544 [27.1]
Guillard, Charlotte – 1544 [27.2]
Kerver, Thielman – 1544 [26.3]
Pré, Galliot du – 1544 [26.4]
Ruelle, Jean – 1544 [26.5], 1546 [31]

3.3 *Latin – Morel Edition (1548–1554)*
Bogard, Jacques – 1548 [36.1]
Frellon, Jean – 1554 [68.1]
Guillard, Charlotte – 1548 [36.2]
Jeune, Martin le – 1550 [48.4]
Morel, Guillaume – 1548 [36.1], 1550 [48.1]
Petit, Oudin – 1550 [48.2]
Puys, Jacques du – 1550 [48.3]
Vincent, Antoine – 1554 [68.2]

3.4 *Latin – Wittenberg Edition (1550)*
Brubach, Peter – 1550 [47]

3.5 *Latin – du Puys Latin Text (1551–1564)*
Brachonier, Jean – 1557 [81.1], 1557 [81.2]
Calvarin, Simon – 1557 [81.3]

Cavellat, Guillaume – 1557 [81.4]
Corrozet, Gilles – 1557 [81.5]
Frellon, Jean – 1558 [84.1], 1560 [92.1]
Gourbin, Gilles – 1557 [81.6]
Harscher, Mathias – 1552 [56]
Isengrin, Michael – 1557 [80]
Jeune, Martin le – 1557 [81.7]
Julien, Guillaume – 1557 [81.8]
Julien, Michel – 1557 [81.9]
Macé, Jean – 1557 [81.10]
Nivelle, Sébastien – 1557 [81.11]
Oporinus, Johannes – 1564 [123]
Puys, Jacques du – 1551 [51], 1561 [103], 1563 [114]
Valgrisi, Vincenzo – 1553 [58], 1555 [72], 1556 [77]
Vincent, Antoine – 1558 [84.2], 1560 [92.2]

3.6 Latin – Funck/Frankfurt Edition (*1555*)
Zöpfel, David – 1555 [71]

4.1 Czech (*1541*)
Aujezdský, Alexander – 1541 [17]

4.2 Czech (*1584–1602*)
Veleslavina, Daniel Adam z – 1584 [176], 1602 [193]

5.1 Italian (*1543*)
Tramezzino, Michele – 1543 [23]

5.2 Italian – Paradin Supplement (*1548*)
Tramezzino, Michele – 1548 [40]

6 Dutch (*1543–1553*)
Grapheus, Jan – 1543 [24], 1553 [65]

7 French (*1546–1610*)
Angelier, Charles l' – 1546 [33], 1547 [35], 1548 [38], 1549 [43], 1553 [60.1]
Arnoullet, François – 1577 [161]
Bonfons, Nicolas – 1575 [158]
Boursette, Magdaleine – 1553 [60.4], 1555 [73.1]
Bret, Guillaume le (Widow) – 1553 [62]

Buon, Gabriel – 1562 [108]
Caveiller, Jean – 1553 [60.2], 1553 [63], 1555 [73.2], 1556 [78]
Cavellat, Guillaume – 1568 [145]
Corrozet, Gilles – 1548 [39.1]
Gazeau, Guillaume – 1549 [44], 1553 [64]
Groulleau, Estienne – 1548 [39.2], 1550 [49.1], 1553 [61], 1560 [93.1]
Haye, Jacques de La – 1609 [195]
Kerver, Jacques – 1562 [107], 1567 [142.1]
Longis, Jean – 1551 [52.1]
Marnef, Hiérosme de – 1568 [145]
Michel, Pierre – 1559 [87]
Prévost, Benoît – 1553 [60.3]
Puys, Mathurin du – 1553 [59]
Regnauld, François (Widow), see Magdaleine Boursette
Ruelle, Jean – 1548 [39.3], 1550 [49.2], 1551 [52.2], 1553 [60.5], 1556 [79], 1557 [82], 1560 [93.2], 1563 [115], 1567 [142.2]
Sertenas, Vincent – 1551 [52.3]
Tournes, Jean de – 1549 [44], 1553 [64]
Vincent, Barthélémy – 1610 [196]

8   *English – Funck/Frankfurt Edition (1550)*

Lynne, Walter – 1550 [50]

9   *Spanish (1553–1555)*

Nucio, Martin – 1553 [66], 1555 [74]

10   *Danish (1554)*

Rhau, Georg (Heirs) – 1554 [69]

11   *Turkish [Manuscript] (1654)*

Çelebi, Kâtip – 1654 [205]

II   Carion-Melanchthon *Chronica* (1532)

Language/Place of Publication

1532 – German (Wittenberg [1]), German (Wittenberg [2]), German (Augsburg [3]), German (Marburg [4]), German (Wittenberg [5])
1533 – German (Wittenberg [6.A]), German (Wittenberg [6]), German (Augsburg [7])

1534 – German (Augsburg [8]), Plattdeutsch (Magdeburg [9])
1537 – Latin (Schwäbish Hall [10]), Latin (Schwäbish Hall [11]), Latin (Antwerp [12])
1538 – German (Wittenberg [13])
1539 – Latin (Schwäbish Hall [14])
1540 – German (Augsburg [15]), Latin (Antwerp [16])
1541 – Czech (Litomyšl [17])
1542 – Plattdeutsch (Magdeburg [18])
1543 – Latin (Frankfurt [19]), Latin (Paris [20]), Latin (Paris [21]), Latin (Lyon [22]), Italian (Venice [23]), Dutch (Antwerp [24])
1544 – Latin (Paris [25]), Latin (Paris [26]), Latin (Paris [27])
1546 – German (Frankfurt [28]), German (Wittenberg [29]), Latin (Frankfurt [30]), Latin (Paris [31]), Latin (Lyon [32]), French (Paris [33])
1547 – Plattdeutsch (Magdeburg [34]), French (Paris [35])
1548 – Latin (Paris [36]), Latin (Venice [37]), French (Paris [38]), French (Paris [39]), Italian (Venice [40])
1549 – German (Wittenberg [41]), French (Paris [43]), French (Lyon [44])
1550 – German (Wittenberg [46]), Latin (Frankfurt [47]), Latin (Paris [48]), French (Paris [49]), English (London [50])
1551 – Latin (Paris [51]), French (Paris [52])
1552 – German (Frankfurt [53]), German (Wittenberg [54]), German (Leipzig [55]), Latin (Basel [56])
1553 – German (Leipzig [57]), Latin (Venice [58]), French (Paris [59]), French (Paris [60]), French (Paris [61]), French (Paris [62]), French (Paris [63]), French (Lyon [64]), Dutch (Antwerp [65]), Spanish (Antwerp [66])
1554 – German (Wittenberg [67]), Latin (Lyon [68]), Danish (Wittenberg [69])
1555 – German (Frankfurt [70]), Latin (Frankfurt [71]), Latin (Venice [72]), French (Paris [73]), Spanish (Antwerp [74])
1556 – German (Frankfurt [75]), Latin (Venice [77]), French (Paris [78]), French (Paris [79])
1557 – Latin (Basel [80]), Latin (Paris [81]), French (Paris [82])
1558 – German (Frankfurt [83]), Latin (Lyon [84])
1559 – French (Lyon [87])
1560 – Latin (Lyon [92]), French (Paris [93])
1561 – Latin (Paris [103])
1562 – French (Paris [107]), French (Paris [108])
1563 – Latin (Paris [114]), French (Paris [115])
1564 – German (Frankfurt [122]), Latin (Basel [123])
1566 – *German* (Frankfurt [141])
1567 – French (Paris [142])
1568 – French (Paris [145])

1569 – *German* (Frankfurt [148])
1575 – French (Paris [158])
1577 – French (Lyon [161])
1584 – Czech (Prague [176])
1602 – Czech (Prague [193])
1609 – French (Lyon [195])
1610 – French (Lyon [196])
1654 – Turkish Manuscript (Istanbul [205])

III Melanchthon-Peucer *Chronicon Carionis* (1558–1565)

Publisher Index
▶ Latin

1.1 *Pars Prima, Liber Primus & Liber Secundus (1558–1582)*

Crato, Johannes – 1566 [133], 1567 [143]
Frellon, Jean (?) – 1564 [125.1], 1564 [125.2]
Lufft, Hans – 1573 [155]
Perna, Peter – 1559 [90], 1563 [117]
Rhau, Georg (Heirs) – 1558 [85], 1558 [86], 1559 [88], 1559 [89], 1560 [94], 1561 [104], 1562 [109], 1564 [124]
Schleich, Clemens – 1570 [149], 1577 [162]
Schöne, Anton – 1570 [149], 1577 [162]
Tournes, Jean de – 1560 [102]
Welack, Matthäus – 1582 [172]
Zöpfel, David – 1559 [91]

1.2 *Pars Secunda, Liber Tertius (1560–1595)*

Crato, Johannes – 1566 [135], 1570 [150]
Frellon, Jean (?) – 1564 [127.1], 1564 [127.2]
Lehmann, Zarcharias – 1595 [185]
Lufft, Hans – 1573 [156]
Perna, Peter – 1560 [100], 1564 [126]
Rhau, Georg (Heirs) – 1560 [97], 1560 [98], 1560 [99], 1561 [105], 1562 [111.1], 1562 [111.2], 1563 [119], 1566 [134]
Schleich, Clemens – 1577 [163]
Schöne, Anton – 1577 [163]
Tournes, Jean de – 1560 [102]
Welack, Matthäus – 1582 [173]
Zöpfel, David – 1560 [101], 1561 [106]

1.3 *Pars Tertia, Liber Quartus (1562–1582)*

Crato, Johannes – 1569 [147]
Frellon, Jean (?) – 1564 [128]
Gazeau, Guillaume – 1564 [129]
Lufft, Hans – 1572 [152]
Perna, Peter – 1563 [121.1], 1563 [121.2]
Rhau, Georg (Heirs) – 1563 [120]
Schleich, Clemens – 1577 [164]
Schöne, Anton – 1577 [164]
Schwenck, Lorenz – 1566 [137]
Seitz, Peter – 1562 [113]
Tournes, Jean de – 1564 [129]
Welack, Matthäus – 1580 [167], 1582 [174]

1.4 *Pars Tertia (Pars Quarta), Liber Quintus (1565–1591)*

Feyerabend, Sigmund – 1566 [139]
Frellon, Jean (?) – 1566 [140], 1567 [144]
Hüter, Simon – 1566 [139]
Perna, Peter – 1568 [146]
Rühel, Johann – 1591 [179]
Rhau, Georg (Heirs) – 1565 [132]
Schleich, Clemens – 1570 [151], 1572 [153]
Schöne, Anton – 1570 [151], 1572 [153]
Schwertel, Johann – 1566 [138]
Welack, Matthäus – 1591 [179]

1.5 *Wittenberg Latin Edition (1572–1624)*

Crato, Johannes – 1572 [154]
Crato, Johannes (Heirs) – 1580 [168]
Feyerabend, Johann – 1594 [183]
Schmidt, Peter – 1581 [170]
Schürer, Zacharias – 1601 [191]
Tambach, Gottfried – 1624 [200]

1.6 *Geneva Latin Edition (1576–1625)*

Crespin, Samuel – 1617 [199], 1625 [201.1], 1625 [201.2]
Preux, Esaias le – 1610 [197]
Preux, Jean le – 1593 [181], 1593 [182], 1601 [190]
Saint André, Pierre de – 1576 [159.A], 1576 [159], 1581 [171], 1584 [175], 1592 [180]

▶ German

2.1   *Pars Prima, Liber Primus & Liber Secundus (1560–1563)*
Rhau, Georg (Heirs) – 1560 [95], 1560 [96], 1562 [110], 1563 [118]

2.2   *Pars Secunda, Liber Tertius (1562–1566)*
Rhau, Georg (Heirs) – 1562 [112.1], 1562 [112.2], 1566 [136]

2.3   *Pars Tertia, Liber Quartus (1564–1565)*
Rhau, Georg (Heirs) – 1564 [130], 1565 [131]

2.4   *Pars Tertia (Pars Quarta), Liber Quintus (None)*
None.

2.5   *Complete German Edition (1566/1573–1588)*
Bergen, Gimel – 1576 [160]
Feyerabend, Sigmund – *1566* [141], *1569* [148]
Hüter, Simon – *1566* [141]
Lehmann, Zacharias – 1588 [178]
Lufft, Hans – 1573 [157], 1578 [165]

3   *French (1579–1611)*
Berjon, Jacques – 1594 [184]
Berjon, Jean – 1579 [166], 1580 [169]
Chouet, Pierre & Jacques – 1611 [198.1]
Crespin, Samuel – 1611 [198.2]
Elzevier, Lowijs – 1596 [189]
Saint André, Pierre de – 1595 [186.1]
Stoer, Jacques – 1595 [186.2], 1611 [198.3]
Vignon, Jean – 1611 [198.4]

4.1   *Dutch (1586–1629)*
Canin, Jan – 1586 [177.1]
Claesz, Cornelis – 1586 [177.3]
Jacobsz, Laurens – 1586 [177.2]
Jansz, Jan – 1629 [202]

4.2   *Dutch Continuation (1629–1632)*
Colijn, Michael – 1632 [202]
Jansz, Jan – 1629 [203]

5   *Danish (1595)*
Benedicht, Laurentz – 1595 [187]

6   *Verse Compendium (1596–1606)*
Ferder, Augustin – 1596 [188]
Möllemann, Stephan – 1601 [192], 1604 [194.A], 1606 [194]

7   *Swedish (1649)*
Grefwe, Amund Nilszon – 1649 [204]

8   *Icelandic [Manuscript] (1692)*
Jónsson, Magnús – 1692 [206]

IV   Melanchthon-Peucer *Chronicon Carionis* (1558–1565)

Place of Publication
▶ Latin

1.1   *Pars Prima, Liber Primus & Liber Secundus (1558–1582)*
1558 – Wittenberg [85], Wittenberg [86]
1559 – Wittenberg [88], Wittenberg [89], Basel [90], Frankfurt [91]
1560 – Wittenberg [94], Lyon [102]
1561 – Wittenberg [104]
1562 – Wittenberg [109]
1563 – Basel [117]
1564 – Wittenberg [124], Lyon [125]
1566 – Wittenberg [133]
1567 – Wittenberg [143]
1570 – Wittenberg [149]
1573 – Wittenberg [155]
1577 – Wittenberg [162]
1582 – Wittenberg [172]

1.2   *Pars Secunda, Liber Tertius (1560–1595)*
1560 – Wittenberg [97], Wittenberg [98], Wittenberg [99], Basel [100], Frankfurt [101], Lyon [102]
1561 – Wittenberg [105], Frankfurt [106]
1562 – Wittenberg [111]
1563 – Wittenberg [119]

1564 – Basel [126], Lyon [127]
1566 – Wittenberg [134], Wittenberg [135]
1570 – Wittenberg [150]
1573 – Wittenberg [156]
1577 – Wittenberg [163]
1582 – Wittenberg [173]
1595 – Wittenberg [185]

1.3 *Pars Tertia, Liber Quartus (1562–1582)*
1562 – Wittenberg [113]
1562 – Wittenberg [120], Basel [121]
1564 – Lyon [128], Lyon [129]
1566 – Wittenberg [137]
1569 – Wittenberg [147]
1572 – Wittenberg [152]
1577 – Wittenberg [164]
1582 – Wittenberg [174]

1.4 *Pars Tertia (Pars Quarta), Liber Quintus (1565–1591)*
1565 – Wittenberg [132]
1566 – Wittenberg [138], Frankfurt [139], Lyon [140]
1567 – Lyon [144]
1568 – Basel [146]
1570 – Wittenberg [151]
1572 – Wittenberg [153]
1580 – Wittenberg [167]
1591 – Wittenberg [179]

1.5 *Wittenberg Latin Edition (1572–1624)*
1572 – Wittenberg [154]
1580 – Wittenberg [168]
1581 – Frankfurt [170]
1594 – Frankfurt [183]
1601 – Wittenberg [191]
1624 – Frankfurt [200]

1.6 *Geneva Latin Edition (1576–1625)*
1576 – Geneva [159.A], Lyon (Geneva) [159]
1581 – Geneva [171]
1584 – Geneva [175]

1592 – Geneva [180]
1593 – Geneva [181], Geneva [182]
1601 – Bern [190]
1610 – Geneva [197]
1617 – Geneva [199]
1625 – Geneva [201]

▶ German

2.1 *Pars Prima, Liber Primus & Liber Secundus (1560–1563)*
1560 – Wittenberg [95], Wittenberg [96]
1562 – Wittenberg [110]
1563 – Wittenberg [118]

2.2 *Pars Secunda, Liber Tertius (1562–1566)*
1562 – Wittenberg [112]
1566 – Wittenberg [136]

2.3 *Pars Tertia, Liber Quartus (1564–1565)*
1564 – Wittenberg [130]
1565 – Wittenberg [131]

2.4 *Pars Tertia (Pars Quarta), Liber Quintus (None)*
None.

2.5 *Complete German Edition (1566/1573–1588)*
1566 – *Frankfurt* [141]
1569 – *Frankfurt* [148]
1573 – Wittenberg [157]
1576 – Dresden [160]
1578 – Wittenberg [165]
1588 – Wittenberg [178]

3 *French (1579–1611)*
1579 – Geneva [166]
1580 – Geneva [169]
1594 – Geneva [184]
1595 – Geneva [186]
1596 – Leiden [189]
1611 – Geneva [198]

4.1 *Dutch (1586–1629)*
1586 – Dordt [177], Amsterdam [177]
1629 – Arnhem [202]

4.2 *Dutch Continuation (1629–1632)*
1629 – Arnhem [202]
1632 – Amsterdam [203]

5 *Danish (1595)*
1595 – Copenhagen [187]

6 *Verse Compendium (1596–1606)*
1596 – Rostock [188]
1601 – Rostock [192]
1604 – Rostock [194.A]
1606 – Rostock [194]

7 *Swedish (1649)*
1649 – Nyköping [204]

8 *Icelandic [Manuscript] (1692)*
1692 – Vigur [206]

V Combined Publisher Index

Ad signum Spei – 1548 [37]
Angelier, Arnold l' – 1543 [20.2]
Angelier, Charles l' – 1543 [20.1], 1543 [21], 1544 [25] 1546 [33], 1547 [35], 1548 [38], 1549 [43], 1553 [60.1]
Arnoullet, François – 1577 [161]
Aujezdský, Alexander – 1541 [17]

Benedicht, Laurentz – 1595 [187]
Bergen, Gimel – 1576 [160]
Berjon, Jacques – 1594 [184]
Berjon, Jean – 1579 [166], 1580 [169]
Berwald, Jacob – 1552 [55], 1553 [57.1], 1553 [57.2]
Bogard, Jacques – 1548 [36.1]
Bonfons, Nicolas – 1575 [158]

Boucher, Nicolas – 1544 [26.1]
Boursette, Magdaleine – 1553 [60.4], 1555 [73.1]
Brachonier, Jean – 1557 [81.1], 1557 [81.2]
Bret, Guillaume le (Widow) – 1553 [62]
Brubach, Peter – 1537 [10], 1537 [11], 1539 [14], 1543 [19], 1546 [30], 1550 [47]
Buon, Gabriel – 1562 [108]

Calvarin, Simon – 1557 [81.3]
Canin, Jan – 1586 [177.1]
Caveiller, Jean – 1553 [60.2], 1553 [63], 1555 [73.2], 1556 [78]
Cavellat, Guillaume – 1557 [81.4], 1568 [145]
Çelebi, Kâtip – 1654 [205]
Chaudière, Regnault – 1544 [26.2]
Chouet, Pierre & Jacques – 1611 [198.1]
Claesz, Cornelis – 1586 [177.3]
Colijn, Michael – 1632 [202]
Corrozet, Gilles – 1548 [39.1], 1557 [81.5]
Crato, Johannes – 1566 [133], 1566 [135], 1567 [143], 1569 [147], 1570 [150], 1572 [154]
Crato, Johannes (Heirs) – 1580 [168]
Crespin, Samuel – 1611 [198.2], 1617 [199], 1625 [201.1], 1625 [201.2]

Elzevier, Lowijs – 1596 [189]

Ferder, Augustin – 1596 [188]
Feyerabend, Johann – 1594 [183]
Feyerabend, Sigmund – 1566 [139], *1566* [141], *1569* [148]
Foucher, Jean – 1544 [27.3]
Frellon, Jean – 1554 [68.1], 1558 [84.1], 1560 [92.1]
Frellon, Jean (?) – 1564 [125.1], 1564 [125.2], 1564 [127.1], 1564 [127.2], 1564 [128], 1566 [140], 1567 [144]
Frellon, Jean & François – 1543 [22], 1546 [32]

Gaultherot, Vivant – 1543 [20.3]
Gazeau, Guillaume – 1549 [44], 1553 [64], 1564 [129]
Gazeau, Jacques – 1544 [27.1]
Gourbin, Gilles – 1557 [81.6]
Grapheus, Jan – 1543 [24], 1553 [65]
Grefwe, Amund Nilszon – 1649 [204]
Groulleau, Estienne – 1548 [39.2], 1550 [49.1], 1553 [61], 1560 [93.1]
Guillard, Charlotte – 1544 [27.2], 1548 [36.2]

Harscher, Mathias – 1552 [56]
Haye, Jacques de La – 1609 [195]
Hüter, Simon – 1566 [139], *1566* [141]

Isengrin, Michael – 1557 [80]

Jacob, Cyriakus – 1546 [28]
Jacobsz, Laurens – 1586 [177.2]
Jansz, Jan – 1629 [202], 1629 [203]
Jeune, Martin le – 1550 [48.4], 1557 [81.7]
Jónsson, Magnús – 1692 [206]
Julien, Guillaume – 1557 [81.8]
Julien, Michel – 1557 [81.9]

Kerver, Jacques – 1562 [107], 1567 [142.1]
Kerver, Thielman – 1544 [26.3]

Lehmann, Zacharias – 1588 [178], 1595 [185]
Longis, Jean – 1551 [52.1]
Lotter, Michael – 1534 [9], 1542 [18], 1547 [34]
Lufft, Hans – 1572 [152], 1573 [155], 1573 [156], 1573 [157], 1578 [165]
Lynne, Walter – 1550 [50]

Macé, Jean – 1557 [81.10]
Marnef, Hiérosme de – 1568 [145]
Michel, Pierre – 1559 [87]
Möllemann, Stephan – 1601 [192], 1604 [194.A], 1606 [194]
Morel, Guillaume – 1548 [36.1], 1550 [48.1]

Nivelle, Sébastien – 1557 [81.11]
Nucio, Martin – 1553 [66], 1555 [74]

Oporinus, Johannes – 1564 [123]

Perna, Peter – 1559 [90], 1560 [100], 1563 [117], 1563 [121.1], 1563 [121.2], 1564 [126], 1568 [146]
Petit, Oudin – 1550 [48.2]
Pré, Galliot du – 1544 [26.4]
Preux, Esaias le – 1610 [197]
Preux, Jean le – 1593 [181], 1593 [182], 1601 [190]
Preux, Poncet le – 1543 [20.4]
Prévost, Benoît – 1553 [60.3]

Puys, Jacques du – 1550 [48.3], 1551 [51], 1561 [103], 1563 [114]
Puys, Mathurin du – 1553 [59]

Regnauld, François (Widow), see Magdaleine Boursette
Rhau, Georg – 1532 [1], 1532 [2], 1532 [5], 1533 [6.A], 1533 [6], 1538 [13], 1546 [29]
Rhau, Georg (Heirs) – 1549 [41], 1550 [46], 1552 [54], 1554 [67], 1554 [69], 1558 [85], 1558 [86], 1559 [88], 1559 [89], 1560 [94], 1560 [95], 1560 [96], 1560 [97], 1560 [98], 1560 [99], 1561 [104], 1561 [105], 1562 [109], 1562 [110], 1562 [111.1], 1562 [111.2], 1562 [112.1], 1562 [112.2], 1563 [118], 1563 [119], 1563 [120], 1564 [124], 1564 [130], 1565 [131], 1565 [132], 1566 [134], 1566 [136]
Rhode, Franz – 1532 [4]
Ruelle, Jean – 1544 [26.5], 1546 [31], 1548 [39.3], 1550 [49.2], 1551 [52.2], 1553 [60.5], 1556 [79], 1557 [82], 1560 [93.2], 1563 [115], 1567 [142.2]
Rühel, Johann – 1591 [179]

Saint André, Pierre de – 1576 [159.A], 1576 [159], 1581 [171], 1584 [175], 1592 [180], 1595 [186.1]
Sertenas, Vincent – 1551 [52.3]
Schleich, Clemens – 1570 [149], 1570 [151], 1572 [153], 1577 [162], 1577 [163], 1577 [164]
Schmidt, Peter – 1581 [170]
Schöne, Anton – 1570 [149], 1570 [151], 1572 [153], 1577 [162], 1577 [163], 1577 [164]
Schürer, Zacharias – 1601 [191]
Schwenck, Lorenz – 1566 [137]
Schwertel, Johann – 1566 [138]
Seitz, Peter – 1562 [113]
Steels, Jan – 1537 [12], 1540 [16]
Steiner, Heinrich – 1532 [3], 1533 [7], 1534 [8], 1540 [15]
Stoer, Jacques – 1595 [186.2], 1611 [198.3]

Tambach, Gottfried – 1624 [200]
Tournes, Jean de – 1549 [44], 1553 [64], 1560 [102], 1560 [102], 1564 [129]
Tramezzino, Michele – 1543 [23], 1548 [40]

Valgrisi, Vincenzo – 1553 [58], 1555 [72], 1556 [77]
Veleslavina, Daniel Adam z – 1584 [176], 1602 [193]
Vincent, Antoine – 1554 [68.2], 1558 [84.2], 1560 [92.2]
Vincent, Barthélémy – 1610 [196]
Vignon, Jean – 1611 [198.4]
Welack, Matthäus – 1580 [167], 1582 [172], 1582 [173], 1582 [174], 1591 [179]

Zöpfel, David – 1552 [53], 1555 [70], 1555 [71], 1556 [75], 1558 [83], 1559 [91], 1560 [101], 1561 [106], 1564 [122]

APPENDIX E

Carion's Chronicle – Census of Editions

1532

1 Chronica || durch Magistru[m] || Johan Carion / vleis=||sig zusamen gezo=||gen / meniglich || nützlich zu || lesen.
Wittenberg : Georg Rhau, [1532]
[1], 170 [= 171] fol.; 4°
[Colophon: Gedruckt zu Wittem||berg durch Geor=||gen Ehaw.]
VD16 C 998
USTC 622327
[Erkennungslesart: sig. Aij v, line 28–29 "Datum || zu Berlin"; sig. [Aiiij] r, line 7–8, "also werden vns jnn Historien Exempel furge-||mahlet aller lahr von tugenden."]
Chicago, Newberry Library: Case F 09 .145
London, British Library: 9006.dd.5.
Wittenberg, Lutherhalle: Kn A 274/1882
Wolfenbüttel, Herzog August Bibliothek: M: Gb 56
Wolfenbüttel, Herzog August Bibliothek: H: T 1005.4° Helmst. (6)
Wolfenbüttel, Herzog August Bibliothek: A: 292.16 Hist. (1)

2 Chronica || durch Magistru[m] || Johan Carion / vleis=||sig zusamen gezo=||gen / meniglich || nützlich zu || lesen.
Wittenberg : Georg Rhau, [1532]
[1], 170 [= 171] fol.; 4°
[Colophon: Gedruckt zu Wittem||berg durch Geor=||gen Ehaw.]
VD16 C 995
USTC 622328
[Erkennungslesart: sig. Aij v, line 29, "Datum zu Berlin/||"; sig. [Aiiij] r, line 6–7, "also werden vns jnn Hi-||storien exempel furgemahlet aller lahr vnd tügenden."]
Jena, Thüringer Universitäts- und Landesbibliothek: 8 MS 27369
Wolfenbüttel, Herzog August Bibliothek: H: T 252.4° Helmst. (1)

3 Chronica || durch Magi||strum Johan Carion || fleissig zůsamen ge=||zoge[n] / menigklich || nützlich zů || lesen. || M.D.XXXII.
Augsburg : Heinrich Steiner, 1532
[6], CXXIX fol.; 4°
[Colophon: Gedruckt vnd säligklichen vollendt / in der Kayserlichen || Stat Augspurg / Durch Heynrichen Steyner || Am 16. tag Julij. M.D.XXXII.]

VD16 C 996

USTC 622322

[Erkennungslesart: sig. Aiij v, line 34–35, "also werden vns in Historien || Exempel fürgemalet aller ler von tugenden."]

Chicago, Newberry Library: Case F 09 .144

Wolfenbüttel, Herzog August Bibliothek: M: QuN 284 (1) [Incomplete]

4   Chronica durch || Magistrum Johan || Carion / vleissig zusamen gezogen / || meniglich nützlich zu lesen. || Sampt einem Register / darin Alle furnemisten || geschichten vnnd trefflichsten historien von || anfang der welt biß nu kürtzlich angezeigt sindt.

Marburg : Franz Rhode, 1532

[16], 272 fol.; 8°

[Colophon: Gedruckt zu Marpurg durch Franci=||scum Rhodum jm M.D || xxxij jar.]

VD16 ZV 20310

USTC 622369

[Erkennungslesart: sig. Aiij r, line 16–18, "also werden vns jn[n] || Historien Exempel furgemahlet aller lahr || von tugenden."]

Stuttgart, Württembergische Landesbibliothek: Allg.G.oct.390

5   Chronica || durch Magi=||strum Johan Carion / || vleissig zusamen ge=||zogen / menig=||lich nützlich || zu lesen. || Wittemberg. || M.D.XXXII.

Wittenberg : Georg Rhau, 1532

[238] fol.; 8°

[Colophon: Gedruckt zu Wittem=||berg durch Geor=||gen Rhaw.]

VD16 C 997

USTC 622324

[Erkennungslesart: sig. Aiiij v, line 28–29, "also werden vns jnn Historien Exempel || furgemahlet aller lahr von tügenden."]

London, Warburg Institute Library: NAH 6550

Wolfenbüttel, Herzog August Bibliothek: A: 527.3 Hist.

Wolfenbüttel, Herzog August Bibliothek: H: T 223.8° Helmst. (1)

1533

6.A   Chronica || durch Magi=||strum Johan Carion / || vleissig zusamen ge=||zogen / menig=||lich nützlich || zu lesen. || Wittemberg. || M.D.XXXIII.

Wittenberg : Georg Rhau, 1533

[238] fol.; 8°

[Colophon: Gedruckt zu Wittem=||berg durch Geor=||gen Rhaw.]

Tübingen, Universitätsbibliothek: Fn 81 t

6   Chronica || durch M. || Johan. Carion / || vleissig zusamen ge=||zogen / menig=||lich nützlich || zu lesen. || Wittemberg. || M.D.XXXIII.
Wittenberg : Georg Rhau, 1533
[1], 232 [= 236], [1] fol.; 8°
[Colophon: Gedruckt zu Wittem=||berg durch Geor=||gen Rhaw.]
VD16 ZV 2942
USTC 622320
München, Bayerische Staatsbibliothek: Chron. 200 v

7   Chronica || durch Magistru[m] || Johan Carion / fleissig zů=||samen gezogen / menig=||klich nutzlich zů || lesenn. || Gemert vnd gebessert. || M.D.XXXIII.
Augsburg : Heinrich Steiner, 1533
[6], CXLVIII fol.; 4°
[Colophon: Getruckt vnd volendet inn der Kayserlichen statt || Augspurg durch Heinrich Steiner / am VIII. || tag Marcij. M.D.XXXIII. Jar.]
VD16 C 999
USTC 622325
Moscow, Russian State Library: MK VI-3132
[Berlin, Staatsbibliothek zu Berlin Preußischer Kulturbesitz: Px 7932]
München, Bayerische Staatsbibliothek: Res/4 Chron. 10

1534

8[1] Chronica || durch Magistru[m] || Johan[n] Carion / fleissig zů=||samen gezogen / menig=||klich nutzlich zů || lesen. || Gemert vnd gebessert. || M.D.XXXIIII.
Augsburg : Heinrich Steiner, 1534
[6], CXLVIII fol.; 4°
[Colophon: Getruckt vnd volendet inn der Kaiserlichen statt || Augspurg durch Hainrich Stainer / am 30. || tag Marcij. M.D.XXXIIII. Jar.]
VD16 C 1000
USTC 622326
Berlin, Staatsbibliothek zu Berlin Preußischer Kulturbesitz:
Libri impr. cum notis mss. qu. 237 [Autographed by Luther]

---

1   Scherer listed VD16 C 1000 twice, as an Augsburg edition for 1533 and also for 1534: "Im folgenden Jahre erschienen wiederum drei Drucke, einer in Wittenberg 1533. 8°. 233 Bl. (Berlin), die beiden andern 'gemert vnd gebessert' in Augsburg; sie tragen am Ende den Druckvermerk: Getruckt vnd volendet inn der Kayserlichen statt Augsburg durch Heinrich Steiner am VIII. (bzw. 30.) tag Marcij M.D.XXXIII. Jar. 4°. 148 Bl. (Münch. St. B. bzw. Berlin). Weitere Auflagen: Augsburg 1534. 4°. 148 Bl. (Halle)..." Scherer, *Geschichte und Kirchengeschichte*, 468.

CARION'S CHRONICLE – CENSUS OF EDITIONS 377

Halle, Universitäts- und Landesbibliothek Sachsen-Anhalt: Pon Vg 4105 b
München, Bayerische Staatsbibliothek: 4 A.lat.b. 612

9   Chronica || dorch M. Jo=||han. Carion / vlitich || tosamende getagen / || men-||nichlick nüt=||lick tho le=||sen. || M.D.XXXIIII.
Magdeburg : Michael Lotter, 1534
[1], 203 fol.; 8°
[Colophon: Gedrückt tho Magde=||borg dorch Michael Lother. || Anno etc. 1534.]
VD16 C 1011
USTC 622310
Niederdeutsche Bibliographie: 1186
Rostock, Universitätsbibliothek: Rb-144
Wolfenbüttel, Herzog August Bibliothek: H: T 293.8° Helmst. (3) [Title page lost]

1537

10 CHRONICA || IOANNIS CARIONIS || conuersa ex Germanico in Lati-||num à doctissimo uiro Herma[n]||no Bono, & ab autore dili||genter recognita. || Halæ Sueuorum ex officina Petri Bru=||bachij, Anno M.D,XXXVII.
Schwäbish Hall : Peter Brubach, 1537
308 [= 296] fol.; 8°
VD16 ZV 2943
USTC 622333
London, British library: 9006.bb.7.
Wolfenbüttel, Herzog August Bibliothek: A: 513.1 Hist. (1)

11 CHRONICA || IOANNIS CARIONIS || conuersa ex Germanico in Lati-||num à doctissimo uiro Herman||no Bono, & ab autore dili-||genter recognita. || Halæ Sueuorum ex officina Petri Brubachij || Anno M.D.XXXVII. || Mense Septembri.
Schwäbish Hall : Peter Brubach, 1537
307 [= 295], [1] fol.; 8°
VD16 C 1014
USTC 622334
Bibliotheca Palatina: F2358/F2360
Wolfenbüttel, Herzog August Bibliothek: H: T 233.8° Helmst. (1)

12 CHRONICA || IOANNIS CARIONIS || conuersa ex Germanico in Latinu[m] || à doctissimo viro Hermanno || Bono, & ab autore di=||ligenter recog=||nita. || Accessit Catalogus omnium Regum, || Imperatorum, & Pontificum

Ro=||manorum, cum Appendice. || Antuerpiæ per Ioannem Steelsium || in scuto Burgundiæ, Anno || M.D.XXXVII.
Antwerp : Jan Steels [by Jan Grapheus], 1537
166 fol., [6] fol.; 8°
USTC 404828
Nederlandsche Bibliographie van 1500 tot 1540: 4205 [Incomplete]
Amsterdam, Universiteitsbibliotheek: Ned. Inc. 481 [Incomplete]
Gent, Universiteitsbibliotheek: BIB.HIST.007349
Köln, Universitäts- und Stadtbibliothek: GBXI269+B

1538

13   Chronica || durch Magi=||strum Johan Carion / || vleissig zusamen ge=||zogen / menig=||lich nützlich || zu lesen. || Wittemberg. || M.D.XXXVIII.
Wittenberg : Georg Rhau, 1538
238 fol.; 8°
[Colophon: Gedruckt zu Wittem=||berg durch Geor=||gen Rhaw.]
VD16 C 1001
USTC 622323
London, British Library: 1607/967
Wolfenbüttel, Herzog August Bibliothek: H: C 192b.8° Helmst. (2) [Incomplete]
Wolfenbüttel, Herzog August Bibliothek: A: 484.10 Hist.
Wolfenbüttel, Herzog August Bibliothek: S: Alv.: Ig 115 (1)

1539

14   CHRONI||CORVM LIBELLVS, MAXI=||mas quasq[ue] res gestas, ab initio mundi, apto ordi=||ne complectens, ita ut annorum ratio, ac præcipuæ || uicißitudines, quæ in regna, in religionem, & in || alias res magnas incidunt, quàm rectißi=||me cognosci ac obseruari || queant. || A IOANNE CARIONE || Mathematico conscriptus, ac per || Hermannum Bonnum in Lati||num conuersus. || HALAE SVEVORVM EX || officina Petri Brubachij, Anno || XXXIX.
Schwäbish Hall : Peter Brubach, 1539
[24], 255 fol.; 8°
VD16 C 1015
USTC 622269
Wolfenbüttel, Herzog August Bibliothek: H: T 234.8° Helmst.

1540

15   Chronica || durch Magistrum Jo||hann Carion / fleissig zůsa=||men gezogenn / menig=||klych nutzlich zů || lesen. || Gemert vnd gebessert. || M.D.XXXX.
Augsburg : Heinrich Steiner, 1540
[6], CXLVIII fol.; 4°
[Colophon: Getruckt vnnd volendet inn der Kaiserlichen statt || Augspurg / durch Hainrich Stainer / am 9. || tag Octobris / des M.D.XL. Jar.]
VD16 C 1002
USTC 622329
Einsiedeln, Stiftsbibliothek: He 2860
London, Warburg Institute Library: NAH 6550.C36 1540

16   CHRONICA || IOANNIS CARIONIS || MIRO ARTIFICIO AB OR=||bis conditi exordio res gestas continen=||tia, ex lingua Germanica in Latinam, || ab Hermanno Bono optima fi=||de transfusa, & ab authore di||ligentiss. recognita. || ACCESSIT CATALOGVS OM=||nium Regum, Imperatorum, & Pontificum Ro=||manorum, cum appendice quo ab Anno || XXXII. ad .XL. res memoria dig=||næ continentur. || ANTVERPIAE, || apud Ioan. Steelsium, In Scuto Burgun=||diæ, ANNO M.D. || XL.
Antwerp : Jan Steels [by Jan Grapheus], 1540
[3], 165, [8] fol.; 8°
USTC 438020
Nederlandsche Bibliographie van 1500 tot 1540: 522
Utrecht, Universiteitsbibliotheek: MAG: S OCT 895

1541

17   Knieha Kronyk owsselikych zna || menitych wěcech odpočatku swěta zbě || hľých mierně a pořádně wyprawugijcý / y kte||rých časuow a Let co se přihodiľo. gessto ztoho / || pměny kteréž w swětě buď p králowstwiech || a neb při náboženstwiech a neb přy w || sselikých znamenitých wěcech || se přiházegij. welmi do||bře spatřieny a || poznány bý||ti mo=||hau: || Od Jana Karyona Hwězdáře zname||nite° sepsána / a skrze pana Buryana z || Kornic z Latiny do Čžesstiny pľožena: || Letha paně M.D.XXXXI:
Litomyšl : Alexander Aujezdský, 1541
[4], [183], [11] fol.; 4°
[Colophon: Konec wykládanie / w Sobothu || před Swatým Bartoľoměgem / kteréhož || Počátek byľ / a se začaľo w Sobothu po=||Swatém Jakubě. Létha

páně Tisýcieho || Pětistého XXXIX w Oľomúcy. || Wytissteno a dokonáno w Lijthomyssli || Ten Cžtwrtek poSwátém Wijtu. || Létha Páně Tisýcieho Pětisté||ho XXXXI°: || Laus Deo Soli. || Allexander.]
USTC 568820
Knihopis českých a slovenských tisků: 1463
London, British Library: RB.23.a.25825

1542

18   Chronica || Dorch M. Johan || Carion / vlitich tho=||samende getagen / vnde || vppet nye gebetert / || mennichlick nüt=||lick tho lesen. || Magdeborch.
Magdeburg : Christian Rödinger d.Ä., [ca. 1542]
[198], [2] fol.; 8°
[Colophon: Gedrücket tho Magde||borch dorch Christian || Rödinger.]
VD16 C 1012
USTC 622311
Niederdeutsche Bibliographie: 1380
Wolfenbüttel, Herzog August Bibliothek: H: QuH 169.8
Wolfenbüttel, Herzog August Bibliothek: H: T 222.8° Helmst.
Wolfenbüttel, Herzog August Bibliothek: M: Gb 59 [Incomplete]
Wolfenbüttel, Herzog August Bibliothek: A: 527.58 Quod. (2)

1543

19   CHRONI||CORVM LIBELLVS, MAX-||IMAS QVASQVE RES || gestas, ab initio mundi, apto ordine complectens, ita || ut annorum ratio, ac præcipuæ vicißitudines, quæ in || Regna, in Religionem, & in alias res magnas || incidunt, quàm rectißime cognosci ac ob||seruari queant. || Avtore || Ioan. Car. || Anno XLIII.
Frankfurt a.M. : Peter Brubach, 1543
[16], 250, [2] fol.; 8°
VD16 C 1016
USTC 622268
London, British Library: 9005.aa.16.
Wolfenbüttel, Herzog August Bibliothek: H: T 235.8° Helmst.

20.1 Chronicorum || LIBELLVS, MAXIMAS QVAS-||QVE RES GESTAS, AB INITIO || mundi, apto ordine complectens : ita vt annorum || ratio, ac præcipuæ vicissitudines, quæ in regna, in || religionem, & in alias res magnas incidunt, quàm || rectissimè cognosci ac obseruari queant. || IOANNE CARIONE MATHE-

||MATICO AVCTORE. || Venundantur Parisiis, sub primo pilari palatij Regij || per Carolum Langelier. || 1543.
Paris : Charles l'Angelier, 1543
[12], 135, [1] fol.; 8°
Urbana, University of Illinois Library: IUA02382

20.2 Chronicorum || LIBELLVS, MAXIMAS QVAS-||QVE RES GESTAS, AB INITIO || mundi, apto ordine complectens : ita vt annorum || ratio, ac præcipuæ vicissitudines, quæ in regna, in || religionem, & in alias res magnas incidunt, quàm || rectissimè cognosci ac obseruari queant. || IOANNE CARIONE MATHE-||MATICO AVCTORE. || PARISIIS || Venundantur Parisiis, ad secundam columnam palatij || Regij, per Arnoldum Langelier. || 1543.
Paris : Arnold l'Angelier, 1543
[12], 135, [1] fol.; 8°
Dijon, Bibliothèque Municipale: 2989

20.3 Chronicorum || LIBELLVS, MAXIMAS QVAS-||QVE RES GESTAS, AB INITIO || mundi, apto ordine complectens : ita vt annorum || ratio, ac præcipuæ vicissitudines, quæ in regna, in || religionem, & in alias res magnas incidunt, quàm || rectissimè cognosci ac obseruari queant. || IOANNE CARIONE MATHE-||MATICO AVCTORE. || PARISIIS. || Venundantur, per Viuantium Gaultherot, sub intersi-||gnio sancti Martini, in via Iacobæa. || 1543.
Paris : Vivant Gaultherot, 1543
[12], 135, [1] fol.; 8°
Le Mans, Médiathèque Louis Aragon: H 8* 768

20.4 Chronicorum || LIBELLVS, MAXIMAS QVAS-||QVE RES GESTAS, AB INITIO || mundi, apto ordine complectens : ita vt annorum || ratio, ac præcipuæ vicissitudines, quæ in regna, in || religionem, & in alias res magnas incidunt, quàm || rectissimè cognosci ac obseruari queant. || IOANNE CARIONE MATHE-||MATICO AVCTORE. || PARISIIS. || Apud Poncetum le Preux, sub intersignio lupi, || in via Iacobæa. || 1543.
Paris : Poncet le Preux, 1543
[12], 135, [1] fol.; 8°
USTC 200343
USTC 196606
London, British Library: 580.c.2.
Aix-en-Provence, Bibliothèque Méjanes: G. 2306

21 Chronicorum || LIBELLVS, MAXIMAS QVAS-||QVE RES GESTAS, AB INITIO || mundi, apto ordine complectens : ita vt annorum || ratio, ac præcipuæ vicissitudines, quæ in regna, in || religionem, & in alias res magnas incidunt, quàm || rectissimè cognosci ac obseruari queant. || Iohanne Carione mathematico || Auctore. || Venundantur Parisiis, sub primo pilari palatii Regii per || Carolum Langelier. 1543.

Paris : Charles l'Angelier, 1543
[12], 135, [1] fol.; 8°
USTC 140798
Cuneo, Biblioteca civica: A 806

22 CHRONICO||RVM LIBELLVS, MAXI-||MAS QVASQVE RES GE=||stas, ab initio mundi, apto ordine comple-||ctens : ita ut annorum ratio, ac præcipuæ || uicißitudines, quæ in regna, in religionem, || & in alias res magnas incidunt, quàm re-||ctißimè cognosci ac obseruari queant. || IOANNE CARIONE MATHE||MATICO AVCTORE. || LVGD. sub scuto COLONIENSI, apud Ioan||nem & Franciscum Frellonios, fratres. || MDXLIII
Lyon : Jean & François Frellon, 1543
[16] fol., 366 p., [1] fol.; 8°
USTC 156865
Baudrier, Bibliographie Lyonnaise: V, 188
Halle, Universitäts- und Landesbibliothek Sachsen-Anhalt: Pon Vg 4113

23 CHRONICA DI GIOVANNI || Carione con mirabile artificio Composta, || nellaquale compre[n]desi il computo de || gli anni, i mutamenti ne i regni || e nella religione, et altri || gra[n]dißimi succeßi, || NVOVAMENTE TRA=||dotta in uolgare per Pietro || Lauro modonese. || In Venetia, Nel MDXXXXIII. || Con priuilegio del sommo Pontefice Paulo III. || & dello Illustriß. Senato Veneto, per anni X.
Venice : Michele Tramezzino, 1543
[16], 175, [1] fol.; 8°
[Colophon: IN VENETIA PER MICHELE || TRAMEZINO. LANNO || M.D.XLIII. || Del mese di settembre.]
USTC 818915
Le Edizioni italiane del XVI secolo: 1501
Braunschweig, Stadtbibliothek: I 110–760 [Title page lost]
Halle, Universitäts- und Landesbibliothek Sachsen-Anhalt: Pon Vg 4125

24 Een Chronijcke van al tghe=||ne datter gheschiet is vant begijinsel des weerelts totten iare || M.CCCC. ende xliij. met groote neersticheyt tot profijt van || allen menschen beschreuen doer den hoochgeleerden M. || Joannem Carionem Astronomijn des Kuer=||uorsten van Brandenborch. || Item een wonderlicke Prophecie gheduerende totten toecomen=||den iare van lx. ghemaeckt doer den seluen Carion / den ver=||standighen tot eenen spieghel ende den dwasen || tot een verachtinghe. || Ghedruckt Tantwerpen by my Jan Grapheus int iaer na || die gheboerte ons salichmakers Jesu Christi || M.CCCC. ende xliij.
Antwerp : Jan Grapheus, 1543
[6], 131, [3] fol.; 4°
USTC 407418

Belgica Typographica 1541–1600: 569
Amsterdam, Universiteitsbibliotheek: O 62-1738
Brussels, La Bibliothèque royale de Belgique: III 17.373 A
CRL, Books printed in the Low Countries before 1601: MF-5549 reel 176 item 1

1544

25 Chronicorum || LIBELLVS, MAXIMAS QVAS-||QVE RES GESTAS, AB INITIO || mundi, apto ordine complectens : ita vt annorum || ratio, ac præcipuæ vicissitudines, quæ in regna, in || religionem, & in alias res magnas incidunt, quàm || rectissimè cognosci ac obseruari queant. || Iohanne Carione mathematico || Auctore. || Venundantur Parisiis, sub primo pilari palatii Regii per || Carolum Langelier. 1544.
Paris : Charles l'Angelier, 1544
[12], 135, [1] fol.; 8°
USTC 195533
Blois, Bibliothèque Abbé Grégoire: I 263

26.1 Chronico||RVM LIBELLVS, MAXI-||mas quasque res gestas, ab initio mundi, || apto ordine complecte[n]s : ita vt annorum || ratio, ac præcipuæ vicissitudines, quæ in || regna, in religionem, & in alias res || magnas incidunt, quàm rectissimè || cognosci ac obseruari queant. || IOANNE CARIONE MA-||THEMATICO AVTHORE. || His accessit historia à Gulielmo Paradino || recens scripta, de rebus gestis in || Belgica anno 1543. || PARISIIS. || Apud Nicolaum Boucher, sub insigni Floris || è regione gymnasij Cameracensis. || 1544.
Paris : Nicolas Boucher, 1544
[16], 279 fol.; 16°
USTC 195532
Orléans, Bibliothèque municipale: E571

26.2 Chronico||RVM LIBELLVS, MAXI-||mas quasque res gestas, ab initio mundi, || apto ordine complecte[n]s : ita vt annorum || ratio, ac præcipuæ vicissitudines, quæ in || regna, in religionem, & in alias res || magnas incidunt, quàm rectissimè || cognosci ac obseruari queant. || IOANNE CARIONE MA-||THEMATICO AVTHORE. || His accessit historia à Gulielmo Paradino || recens scripta, de rebus gestis in || Belgica anno 1543. || PARISIIS. || Sub signo hominis siluestris, uia ad || diuum Iacobum. || 1544.
Paris : [Regnault Chaudière], 1544
[16], 279 fol.; 16°
Basel, Universitätsbibliothek: EA VI 10
Regensburg, Staatliche Bibliothek: 999/Hist.pol.1667

26.3 Chronico||RVM LIBELLVS, MAXI-||mas quasque res gestas, ab initio mundi, || apto ordine complecte[n]s : ita vt annorum || ratio, ac præcipuæ vicissitudines, quæ in || regna, in religionem, & in alias res || magnas incidunt, quàm rectissimè || cognosci ac obseruari queant. || IOANNE CARIONE MA-||THEMATICO AVTHORE. || His accessit historia à Gulielmo Paradino || recens scripta, de rebus gestis in || Belgica anno 1543. || PARISIIS. || Apud Thielmannum Keruer, sub insigni || cratis, Via ad diuum Iacobum. || 1544.
Paris : Thielman Kerver (Filius), 1544
[16], 279 fol.; 16°
London, British Library: 580.a.2.
Manchester, University of Manchester John Rylands Library: Deansgate R52091

26.4 Chronico||RVM LIBELLVS, MAXI-||mas quasque res gestas, ab initio mundi, || apto ordine complecte[n]s : ita vt annorum || ratio, ac præcipuæ vicissitudines, quæ in || regna, in religionem, & in alias res || magnas incidunt, quàm rectissimè || cognosci ac obseruari queant. || IOANNE CARIONE MA-||THEMATICO AVTHORE. || His accessit historia à Gulielmo Paradino || recens scripta, de rebus gestis in || Belgica anno 1543. || PARISIIS. || A Galeoto Pratensi aulo Regiæ co=|||lumna prima. || 1544.
Paris : Galeotus Pratensis [= Galliot du Pré], 1544
[16], 279 fol.; 16°
USTC 195531
Mâcon, Bibliothèque municipale: 190012

26.5 Chronico||RVM LIBELLVS, MAXI-||mas quasque res gestas, ab initio mundi, || apto ordine complecte[n]s : ita vt annorum || ratio, ac præcipuæ vicissitudines, quæ in || regna, in religionem, & in alias res || magnas incidunt, quàm rectissimè || cognosci ac obseruari queant. || IOANNE CARIONE MA-||THEMATICO AVTHORE. || His accessit historia à Gulielmo Paradino || recens scripta, de rebus gestis in || Belgica anno 1543. || PARISIIS. || Apud Ioannem Ruelliium, sub signo Caudæ || Vulpi, Via ad diuum Iacobum. || 1544.
Paris : Jean Ruelle, 1544
[16], 279 fol.; 16°
USTC 195534
Niort, Médiathèque de la communauté d'agglomération: 4544

27.1 Chronico||RVM LIBELLVS, MA-||ximas quasque res gestas, ab initio mun-||di, apto ordine complectens : ita vt anno-||rum ratio, ac præcipuæ vicissitudines, || quæ in regna, in religione[m], & in alias res || magnas incidunt, quàm rectissimè || cognosci ac obseruari queant, || IOANNE CARIONE MATHE-||MATICO AVTHORE. || His accessit historia à Gulielmo Paradino || recens scripta, de rebus gestis in || Belgica anno 1543. || PARISIIS. || Apud Iacobum Gazellu[m], sub insigni Inuidiæ, || è regione gymnasij Cameracensis. || 1544.

Paris : Jacobus Gazellus [= Jacques Gazeau], 1544
[16], 279 fol.; 16°
Dayton, Ohio State University Library: Rare D18 .C32 1544

27.2 Chronico||RVM LIBELLVS, MA-||ximas quasque res gestas, ab initio mun-||di, apto ordine complectens : ita vt anno-||rum ratio, ac præcipuæ vicissitudines, || quæ in regna, in religione[m], & in alias res || magnas incidunt, quàm rectissimè || cognosci ac obseruari queant, || IOANNE CARIONE MATHE-||MATICO AVTHORE. || His accessit historia à Gulielmo Paradino || recens scripta, de rebus gestis in || Belgica anno 1543. || PARISIIS. || Apud Carolam Guillard, sub Sole aureo, || uia ad Diuum Iacobum. || 1544.
Paris : Carola Guillard [= Charlotte Guillard], 1544
[16], 279 fol.; 16°
USTC 195535
Valognes, Bibliothèque municipale: C. 355
Halle, Universitäts- und Landesbibliothek Sachsen-Anhalt: Pon Vg 4114

27.3 Chronico||RVM LIBELLVS, MA-||ximas quasque res gestas, ab initio mun-||di, apto ordine complectens : ita vt anno-||rum ratio, ac præcipuæ vicissitudines, || quæ in regna, in religione[m], & in alias res || magnas incidunt, quàm rectissimè || cognosci ac obseruari queant, || IOANNE CARIONE MATHE-||MATICO AVTHORE. || His accessit historia à Gulielmo Paradino || recens scripta, de rebus gestis in || Belgica anno 1543. || PARISIIS. || Apud Ioannem Foucherium sub scuto Flo=||rentiæ, uia ad Diuum Iacobum. || 1544.
Paris : Jean Foucher, 1544
[16], 279 fol.; 16°
Chicago, Newberry Library: Wing ZP 539 .F823

1546

28 Chronica || Durch Magistrum Johan || Carion / fleissig zusamen ge-||zogen / meniglich nütz-||lich zulesen. || Sampt eynem Register / || darinn alle fürnemisten geschichten vnnd || trefflichsten Historien / von anfang der || Welt biß yetzt kürtzlich ange=||zeygt sindt. || Volstreckung dieser Chronica / || vom 32. Jar der mindern zal / biß in || 46. Durch M. Johan Fun=||cken zusamen getragen. || Cum Gratia & Priuilegio Imperiali.
[Frankfurt a.M.] : [Cyriakus Jakob], 1546
[28], 368, [1] fol.; 8°
[Colophon: Volendet am zwellfften Februarij 1546.]
VD16 C 1003
USTC 622330

[Erkennungslesart: sig. *5 v, line 29 – [*6] r, line 2, "also werden vns in || Historien Exempel fürgemahlet aller lahr vonn || tugenden."]
Bibliotheca Palatina: F91/F92
Hennef-Geistingen, Philosophisch Theologische Hochschule: 535+1 [Dispersed]
München, Bibliothek der Ludwig-Maximilians-Universität: 8° Hist. 1997
Nürnberg, Germanisches Nationalmuseum: 8° G.565 (Postinc.) [Incomplete]
Wolfenbüttel, Herzog August Bibliothek: H: T 226.8° Helmst.

29 Chronica || Durch M. Johan Ca=||rion / vleissig zusamen ge=||zogen / meniglich nütz=||lich zulesen. || Sampt einem Register / || darinn alle fürnemiste Ge=||schichte vnd trefflichste Histori=||en / von anfang der Welt bis || jtzt / kürtzlich angezeigt sind. || Volstreckung dieser Chroni=||ca / vom 32. Jar der min=||dern zal / bis ins 46. || Gedruckt zu Wittemberg / durch || Georgen Rhaw. 1546.
Wittenberg : Georg Rhau, 1546
244 [= 245], [17] fol.; 8°
[Colophon: Gedruckt zu Wittem=||berg / durch Geor=||gen Rhaw / || M.D.XLVI.]
VD16 C 1004
USTC 622315
München, Bayerische Staatsbibliothek: Chron. 200 z
Wolfenbüttel, Herzog August Bibliothek: H: Yt 47.8° Helmst.
Wolfenbüttel, Herzog August Bibliothek: H: Yv 233.8° Helmst. [Incomplete]
Wolfenbüttel, Herzog August Bibliothek: H: T 224.8° Helmst.

30 CHRONI||CON IOANNIS CA-||RIONIS CORRECTVM || & emendatum. || Complectitur hic libellus apto ordine || maximas quasq[ue] res gestas, ab initio Mun||di, usq[ue] ad nostra tempora, ut Annorum || ratio, ac præcipuæ uicissitudines, quæ in || Regna, in Religione[m], & in alias res || magnas incidunt, quàm rectissi-||mè cognosci & obserua-||ri queant. || VNA CVM INDICE RE-RVM MEMO=||rabilium copioso & diligenti. || FRANCOFORTI || IN OFFICINA PETRI || Brubachij, Anno M.||D.XLVI. MENSE || AVGVSTO.
Frankfurt a.M. : Peter Brubach, 1546
[16], 224 fol.; 8°
VD16 C 1017
USTC 622266
Chicago, Newberry Library: Case F 09 .1452
Wolfenbüttel, Herzog August Bibliothek: H: T 236.8° Helmst.

31 Chronicoru[m] || LIBELLVS, MAXIMAS || QVASQVE RES GESTAS, AB || initio mundi, apto ordine complecte[n]s: || ita vt annorum ratio, ac præcipuæ

vi-||cissitudines, quę in regna, in religione[m], || & in alias res magnas incidunt, || quàm rectissimé cognosci ac || obseruari queant. || IOANNE CARIONE MA-||THEMATICO AVTHORE. || His aceßit historia à Gulielmo Paradino || recens scripta, de rebus gestis in || Belgica anno 1543. || PARISIIS. || Apud Ioannem Ruellium, in via Iacobea, || sub signo caudæ Vulpinæ. || 1546.

Paris : Jean Ruelle, 1546

[16], 252 fol.; 16°

San Marino, Huntington Library: Rare Books 485176

32   CHRONICO-||rum Libellus, || MAXIMAS quasque res gestas, ab initio Mundi, || apto ordine complectens: ita vt annorum ratio, || ac præcipuæ vicissitudines, quæ in regna, in reli-||gionem, & in alias res magnas incidunt, quàm re-||ctissimè cognosci ac obseruari queant, || IOANNE CARIONE MA-||THEMATICO || AVTHORE. || His aceßit historia à Guilielmo Paradino || recens scripta, de rebus gestis in || Belgica, Anno 1543. || LVGDVNI, SVB SCVTO CO-||LONIENSI. || 1546

Lyon : Jean & François Frellon, 1546

[16] fol., 474 p., [3] fol.; 16°

[Colophon: Lugduni, || Excudebant Ioan||nes & Franci||scus Frellonii || Fratres. || 1546.]

USTC 157650

Baudrier, Bibliographie Lyonnaise: V, 204

Bibliotheca Palatina: G477/G479

Augsburg, Staats- und Stadtbibliothek: Gs 1522

Berlin, Staatsbibliothek zu Berlin Preußischer Kulturbesitz: 1 A 23162

33   Le Liure des || Chronicques du seigneur Iehan Ca-||rion philosophe, ou sont comprins tous haultz || actes & beaulx faictz en decent & co[n]uenable or-||dre, depuis le commencement du monde iusques || au regne du treschrestien Roy Fra[n]çoys premier || de ce nom, duquel mesmes les gestes sont conte-||nuz en la fin du present liure, & co[n]tinuez iusques || en l'an mil cinq centz quarante six: auquel ouura||ge on cognoistra le datte des ans estre tresiuste-||ment obserué, ensemble on voirra clerement les || principales mutations & changemens qui sont || aduenuz es Royaulmes, en la religion, & repu-||blicque du monde, || Tourné de Latin en Françoys par maistre || Iehan le Blond. || Auec preuilege. || Oii les uend à Paris par Charles l'Angelié, tenant sa bou||tique au premier pillier du Palais, deuant la cha=||pelle de meßieurs les Presidents: & en la rue || de la uielle drapperie, pres saincte Croix, || au logis dudict l'Angelié. || 1546.

Paris : Charles l'Angelier, 1546

[24], 235, [1], 60 fol.; 8°

USTC 11122
French Vernacular Books: 8887
Los Angeles, University of California Library: D18 .C19cF 1546
Jena, Thüringer Universitäts- und Landesbibliothek: 8 Hist.un.II,16

1547

34 Chronica dorch || Magistrum Johan Ca=||rion / Vlytich thosam=||men getagen / einem ye=||dermanne nütte || tho lesen. || Mit einem Register / dar=||ynne alle vörnemesten Geschich=||te vnde Dreplickste Historien / van || anfanck der Werlt beth tho || desser tydt / körtlick || angetöget sint. || Vormeringe desser Chro=||nica vam xxxij. Jar an / beth vp || dyth xlvij. Jar / Dorch M. Jo=||hann Funcken / thosa=||men gedregen.
Magdeburg : Michael Lotter, [1547]
CCCLXXVI fol.; 8°
[Colophon: Gedrücket tho Magdeborch / || dorch Michel Lotther.]
VD16 C 1013
USTC 622368
Niederdeutsche Bibliographie: 1480
Berlin, Staatsbibliothek zu Berlin Preußischer Kulturbesitz: Px 7964 [Lost]
Stuttgart, Württembergische Landesbibliothek: R 16 Car 3
Wolfenbüttel, Herzog August Bibliothek: H: T 225.8° Helmst. [Title page lost]

35 Le liure des || Chroniques du seigneur Iehan || Cario[n] Philosophe, co[n]tenant tous haultz || actes & gestes en conuenable ordre, de-||puis le co[m]mencement du monde iusques || au regne du Roy François premier de || ce nom, duquel mesme les gestes y sont || co[n]tenuz iusques à l'an mil cinq cens qua||rantesix. Par lequel liure sera congneu || le dacte des ans estre tresiusteme[n]t obser-||ué, ensemble les principales mutations || qui sont aduenuz es Royaumes, en la re-||ligion & Republique du monde. || Tourné de Latin en François par || Maistre Iehan le Blond, || Auec priuilege. || On les uend à Paris, en la grand' salle du Palais || en la boutique de Charles l'Angelié, deuant || la chappelle des Presidens. || 1547
Paris : Charles l'Angelier, 1547
[36], 364 fol.; 16°
USTC 8239
French Vernacular Books: 8888
Cambridge, Harvard University Houghton Library: *FC5 L4925 546lb
Versailles, Bibliothèque municipale: F.A. in-12 I 657 a

1548

36.1   IO. CARIO-||NIS MATHEMATICI BVE||tickheinensis Chronicorum libri tres || in Latinum sermonem conuersi, || Hermanno Bonno interprete. || APPENDIX DE REBVS AB || anno Christi 1532 gestis ad annum 1547, || ex optimis quibusque Historicis & Chro||nographis excerpta. || Catalogus Regum, Consulum, Cæsarum, & || Pontificum Romanorum. || Cum Priuilegio. || PARISIIS, || Apud Iacobum Bogardum, & Guliel-||mum Moreliu[m], sub insigni D. Christopho||ri, è regione gymnasii Cameracensium. || 1548.
Paris : Jacques Bogard & Guillaume Morel, 1548
[32], 280 [= 278], [4] fol.; 16°
Imprimeurs & Libraires Parisiens du XVIe siècle: Bogard (Jacques), 272
Troyes, Médiathèque de l'agglomération troyenne: ee.16.5766
Vienna, Österreichische Nationalbibliothek: 49.X.24.

36.2   IO. CARIO-||NIS MATHEMATICI BVE||tickheinensis Chronicorum libri tres || in Latinum sermonem conuersi, || Hermanno Bonno interprete. || APPENDIX DE REBVS AB || anno Christi 1532 gestis ad annum 1547, || ex optimis quibusque Historicis & Chro||nographis excerpta. || Catalogus Regum, Consulum, Cæsarum, & || Pontificum Romanorum. || Cum Priuilegio. || PARISIIS, || Apud Carolam Guillard, sub Sole || aureo, uia ad D. Iacobum. || 1548.
Paris : Carola Guillard [= Charlotte Guillard], 1548
[32], 280 [= 278], [4] fol.; 16°
USTC 116974
Imprimeurs & Libraires Parisiens du XVIe siècle: Bogard (Jacques), 272
College Park: University of Maryland Library: D18 .C22 1548

37 [2]   CHRONICORVM LIBELLVS, || Maximas quasq[ue] res gestas ab initio mundi ad || hæc usq[ue] tempora apto ordine co[m]plectens, || ita ut quibus annis & rerum uicis||ßitudines, et insigna quæq[ue] || acciderint qua[m] rectißi||me sciri poßit. || IO. CARIONE MATHE-||matico Authore. || His acceßit hictoria à Gulielmo Paradi-||no recens scripta de rebus gestis in || Belgica, Anno 1543. || Beatus uir, cuius est dominus || spes eius : & non respexit || in uanitates, & insanias falsas. || Venetijs ad signum spei. 1548.
Venice : ad signum spei, 1548
[32], 478 [= 480], [48] p.; 8°
USTC 818917
Le Edizioni italiane del XVI secolo: 1503
London, British Library: 1509/3595
Bloomington, University of Indiana Lilly Library: D21 .C2775 1548

---

2   "Beatus uir, cuius est dominus || spes eius : & non respexit || in uanitates, & insanias falsas. || Venetijs ad signum spei. 1548." – these four lines of text surround the four sides of the title page image, beginning from the lower left corner.

38 Le liure des || Chroniques du seigneur Iehan || Carion Philosophe, co[n]tenant tous haultz || actes & gestes en conuenable ordre, de-||puis le co[m]me[n]ceme[n]t du monde, Ensemble || les faictz & gestes du feu roy François, || iusque au regne du roy Henry deuxies-||me de ce nom, à present regna[n]t. Par lequel || liure sera congneu le dacte des ans estre || tresiustement obserué, ensemble les prin-||cipales mutationes qui sont aduenues es || Royaumes, en la religion & Republique || du monde. || Tourné de Latin en François par Maistre Ie-||han le Blond, & imprimé en ceste année. || 1548. || Auec priuilege. || On les uend à Paris en la grand' salle du pa-||lais, en la boutique de Charles l'Angelié, || deuant la chapelle des presidens.
Paris : Charles l'Angelier, 1548
[36], 368 fol.; 8°
USTC 57372
French Vernacular Books: 8889
Rennes, Bibliothèque Rennes Métropole Les Champs Libres: 84657

39.1 LE LIVRE DES || CHRONIQVES DV SEI||gneur Iehan Carion Philosophe, co[n]-||tenant en bel ordre tous haultz actes || & gestes dignes de memoire, depuis || le commencement du monde. Par || lequel le dacte des ans est tresiuste-||ment obserué, ensemble les princi-||pales mutations qui sont aduenues || es Royaumes, en la religion & Re-||publique du monde. || Auquel sont adioustez les faictz & ge-||stes du treschrestien roy Francois premier || de ce nom, ensemble les choses dignes de || memoire aduenues tant du regne dudict || roy Francois, que du roy Henry second de || ce nom à present regnant. || A PARIS, || Pour Gilles Corrozet, tenant sa boutique || en la grand' salle du palais. || 1548.
Paris : Gilles Corrozet, 1548
[36], 363 fol.; 8°
USTC 8266
French Vernacular Books: 8892
Montauban, Bibliothèque municipale Antonin Perbosc: Liv 70016 [Incomplete]

39.2 LE LIVRE DES || CHRONIQVES DV SEI||gneur Iehan Carion Philosophe, co[n]-||tenant en bel ordre tous haultz actes || & gestes dignes de memoire, depuis || le commencement du monde. Par || lequel le dacte des ans est tresiuste-||ment obserué, ensemble les princi-||pales mutations qui sont aduenues || es Royaumes, en la religion & Re-||publique du monde. || Auquel sont adioustez les faictz & ge-||stes du treschrestien roy Francois premier || de ce nom, ensemble les choses dignes de || memoire aduenues tant du regne dudict || roy Francois, que du roy Henry second de || ce nom à present regnant. || A PARIS, || Pour Estienne Groulleau, à l'image sainct || Ieha[n] baptiste, en le rue neuue nostre dame. || 1548.

Paris : Estienne Groulleau, 1548
[36], 363 fol.; 8°
USTC 30824
French Vernacular Books: 8891
Paris, Bibliothèque Sainte-Geneviève: 8 G 453 INV 3439 RES

39.3 LE LIVRE DES || CHRONIQVES DV SEI||gneur Iehan Carion Philosophe, co[n]-||tenant en bel ordre tous haultz actes || & gestes dignes de memoire, depuis || le commencement du monde. Par || lequel le dacte des ans est tresiuste-||ment obserué, ensemble les princi-||pales mutations qui sont aduenues || es Royaumes, en la religion & Re-||publique du monde. || Auquel sont adioustez les faictz & ge-||stes du treschrestien roy Francois premier || de ce nom, ensemble les choses dignes de || memoire aduenues tant du regne dudict || roy Francois, que du roy Henry second de || ce nom à present regnant. || A PARIS, || Chez Ieha[n] Ruelle en la rue sainct Iacques || à l'enseigne de la queue de Renard. || 1548.
Paris : Jean Ruelle, 1548¹
[36], 363 fol.; 8°
USTC 75650
French Vernacular Books: 8890
Nancy, Bibliothèque municipale: Res. 11 407

40 CHRONICA DI GIOVANNI || Carione, nella quale co[m]prendesi il computo de || gli anni, i mutamenti nei Regni e nella || Religione, et altri succeßi. Aggio[n]to || ui la guerra Belgica, et altre || cose à l'historia seque[n]ti. || NVOVAMENTE TRA=||dotta in uolgare per Pietro || Lauro Modonese. || In Venetia, Nel M D XXXXVIII. || Con priuilegio del sommo Pontefice Paolo. III. || & dello Illustriß. Senato Veneto, per anni X.
Venice : Michele Tramezzino, 1548
[16], 186, [2] fol.; 8°
[Colophon: IN VENETIA PER MICHELE || TRAMEZINO. LANNO || M.D.XXXXVIII. || Del mese di Giugno.]
USTC 818916
Le Edizioni italiane del XVI secolo: 1502
Chicago, Newberry Library: Case F 09 .152
London, British Library: 304.a.21.

1549

41 Chronica || Durch M. Johan Ca=||rion / vleissig zusamen ge=||zogen / meniglich nütz=||lich zulesen. || Sampt einem Register / || darin alle fürnemiste Geschichte || vnd trefflichste Historien / von an=||fang der Welt bis jtzt /

kürtz=|||lich angezeigt sind. || Volstreckung dieser Chroni=||ca / vom 32. Jar der min=||dern zal / bis ins 46. || Gedruckt zu Wittemberg / Durch Ge=||orgen Rhawen Erben. || 1549.

Wittenberg : Georg Rhau (Heirs), 1549

244 [= 245], [17] fol.; 8°

Rostock, Universitätsbibliothek: Rb-146.1

[42]³ *Chronicorum Libellvs, Maximas Qvasqve Res Gestas, Ab initio mundi, apto ordine complectens...*

Paris : ??, 1549

?? fol.

[Strobel, 175; see Scherer, 471]

43 *Le liure des Chroniques du seigneur Iehan Carion Philosophe...*

Paris : Charles l'Angelier, 1549

[36], 368 fol.; 8°

USTC 76761

French Vernacular Books: 8894

Carcassonne, Bibliothèque municipale: 8 22-2 [Title page lost]

Wrocław, Biblioteka Uniwersytecka: [Lost = Scherer, 471–472]

44 CRONIQVES || DE IEAN CARION || PHILOSOPHE. || Auec les faits et gestes du feu Roy Francois, || iusques au regne du Roy Henry || deuxieme de ce nom, à pre-||sent regnant. || Traduites en François par || maistre Iean le Blond. || A LYON, || Par Iean de Tournes, & Guil-||laume Gazeau. || 1549.

Lyon : Jean de Tournes & Guillaume Gazeau, 1549

[32] fol., 750 p., [1] fol.; 16°

USTC 24098

French Vernacular Books: 8893

Bibliographie des Livres Imprimés à Lyon au siezième siècle: IX, 153

Cartier, De Tournes: 131

München, Bibliothek der Ludwig-Maximilians-Universität: 0001/8 Hist. 1993

[45] *Chronicas compuest. por Juan Carion, traduzidas de Lengua Latina en Castellana per M.C.*

Anvers [Antwerp] : ??, 1549

?? fol.; 12°

[Moller, 22; see Strobel, 185; Scherer, 472]

---

3 "Ausgaben zu Paris. Diese sind sehr selten, und ich war nicht so glücklich, eine davon aufzutrieben. Ich führe daher blos die bey andern angezeigten Ausgaben an ohne für deren Richtigkeit und Gewißheit Bürge zu seyn. Paris. 1544, 1546, 1549, 1556. 1563. sämtlich in 12." Strobel, "Von Carions Leben und Schriften," 175.

1550

46   Chronica || Durch M. Johan Ca=||rion / vleissig zusamen ge=||zogen / meniglich nütz=||lich zulesen. || Sampt einem Register / || darin alle fürnemiste Geschichte || vnd trefflichste Historien / von an=||fang der Welt bis jtzt / kürtz=||lich angezeigt sind. || Volstreckung dieser Chroni=||ca / vom 32. Jar der min=||dern zal / bis ins 46. || Gedruckt zu Wittemberg / Durch Ge=||orgen Rhawen Erben. || 1550.
Wittenberg : Georg Rhau (Heirs), 1550
244 [= 245], [17] fol.; 8°
VD16 C 1005
USTC 622317
Wolfenbüttel, Herzog August Bibliothek: H: T 227.8° Helmst.

47   IO. CARIO-||ONIS MATHEMATICI || BVETICKHEINENSIS CHRONICO=||rum libri tres in Latinum sermonem || conuersi, || Hermanno Bonno interprete. || CONTINVATIO CHRONI||CORVM AB ANNO 1532. AD ANNVM || 1547. Vnà cum Catalogo Regum, Cæsarum, & || Pontificum Romanorum. || Complectitur hic libellus apto ordi-||ne maximas quasq[ue] res gestas, ab initio || Mundi, usq[ue] ad nostra tempora, ut anno||rum ratio, ac præcipuæ uicissitudines, || quæ in Regna, in Religionem, & in ali||as res magnas incidunt, quàm re-||ctissimè cognosci & obser-||uari queant. || Francoforti, M.D.L.
Frankfurt a.M. : Peter Brubach, 1550
[16], 232, [8] fol.; 8°
VD16 C 1018
USTC 667076
London, Warburg Institute Library: NAH 6550.C36b
Leipzig, Universitätsbibliothek: Allg.Gesch.240

48.1[4]   IO. CARIONIS || mathematici Buetickheime[n]-||sis Chronicorum libri tres in || Latinum sermonem conuersi || Hermanno Bonno interprete. || APPENDIX DE RE-||bus ab anno Christi 1532 gestis ad annu[m] || 1550, ex optimis quibusque Historicis & || Chronographis à G. Morelio excerpta. || Catalogus Regum, Consulum, Cæsarum, || & Pontificum Romanorum. || Cum Priuilegio. || PARISIIS, || Apud Guilielmum Morelium sub insigni || D. Stephani è regione gymnasij Reme[n]sium. || 1550.
Paris : Guillaume Morel, 1550
[24] fol., 568 p., [4] fol.; 8°

---

4 The *Belgian Index* includes a reference to a 1550 Morel edition by Jean Roigny that does not seem to have survived – "In Chronicon IOANNIS Carionis Mathematici excusum Parisiis apud Ioan. Roigny, anno 1550 in 16°." *Index Expvrgatorivs Librorvm* (Lyon: Mareschallus, 1586), 172–173.

USTC 150431
Berkeley, University of California Bancroft Library: t D17.C27 C4 1550
Amiens, Bibliothèque municipale: M 3671

48.2 IO. CARIONIS || mathematici Buetickheime[n]-||sis Chronicorum libri tres in || Latinum sermonem conuersi || Hermanno Bonno interprete. || APPENDIX DE RE-||bus ab anno Christi 1532 gestis ad annu[m] || 1550, ex optimis quibusque Historicis & || Chronographis à G. Morelio excerpta. || Catalogus Regum, Consulum, Cæsarum, || & Pontificum Romanorum. || Cum Priuilegio. || PARISIIS, || Apud Audoenum Paruum, via Iacobæa || sub insigni Lilij aurei. || 1550.
Paris : Audoenus Parvus [= Oudin Petit] [by Guillaume Morel], 1550.
[24] fol., 568 p., [4] fol.; 8°
USTC 196335
London, British Library: 9006.aa.4.

48.3 IO. CARIONIS || mathematici Buetickheime[n]-||sis Chronicorum libri tres in || Latinum sermonem conuersi || Hermanno Bonno interprete. || APPENDIX DE RE-||bus ab anno Christi 1532 gestis ad annu[m] || 1550, ex optimis quibusque Historicis & || Chronographis à G. Morelio excerpta. || Catalogus Regum, Consulum, Cæsarum, || & Pontificum Romanorum. || Cum Priuilegio. || PARISIIS, || Apud Iacobum Dupuys sub insigni Sama-||ritanæ in vico D. Ioannis Lateranensis. || 1550.
Paris : Jacques du Puys [by Guillaume Morel], 1550
[24] fol., 568 p., [4] fol.; 8°
USTC 158779
Chicago, Newberry Library: Case miniature F 09 .1453

48.4 IO. CARIONIS || mathematici Buetickheime[n]-||sis Chronicorum libri tres in || Latinum sermonem conuersi || Hermanno Bonno interprete. || APPENDIX DE RE-||bus ab anno Christi 1532 gestis ad annu[m] || 1550, ex optimis quibusque Historicis & || Chronographis à G. Morelio excerpta. || Catalogus Regum, Consulum, Cæsarum, || & Pontificum Romanorum. || Cum priuilegio. || PARISIIS, || Apud Martinum Iuuenem, sub insigni D. || Christophori, è regione collegij Camerace[n]siu[m]. || 1550.
Paris : Martin le Jeune [by Guillaume Morel], 1550
[24] fol., 568 p., [4] fol.; 8°
USTC 203709
Périgueux, Bibliothèque municipale: HI-II-2 6 203

49.1[5] CRONIQVES || DE IAN CARION || PHILOSOPHE. || Auec les faits & gestes du Roy François, || iusques au regne du Roy Henry || deuxiesme de ce nom,

---

5 "*Versio Gallica*, nempe (1) *La Chronique de Jean Carion*, traduicte de Latin par *Jean le Blond*, à Paris & à Lyon, 1550. in 16. item, à Lyon, 1549. in 12." Moller, *Dispvtationem*, 22(1); Strobel,

à pre-||sent regnant. || Traduites en François par || Maistre Ian le Blond. || A PARIS. || Par Estienne Groulleau, demorant à la rue || neuue nostre Dame à l'enseigne Saint || Ian Baptiste. || 1550.
Paris : Estienne Groulleau, 1550
[32], 367, [1] fol.; 16°
USTC 56649
French Vernacular Books: 8895
Orléans, Bibliothèque municipale: E573

49.2   CRONIQVES || DE IAN CARION || PHILOSOPHE. || Auec les faits & gestes du Roy François, || iusques au regne du Roy Henry || deuxiesme de ce nom, à pre-||sent regnant. || Traduites en François par || Maistre Ian le Blond. || A PARIS. || Pour Ian Ruelle en la rue saint Iacques à || l'enseigne de la queue de Regnard, || 1550.
Paris : Jean Ruelle, 1550
[32], 367, [1] fol.; 16°
USTC 83161
French Vernacular Books: 8896
Xanten, Stiftsbibliothek St. Viktor: 4167

50   The thre bokes of || Cronicles, whyche John Carion (a man || syngularly well sene in the Mathema=||tycall sciences) Gathered wyth great || diligence of the beste Authours || that haue written in He=||brue, Greke or || Latine. || Whervnto is added an Appendix, contey=||nyng all such notable thynges as be mentyoned || in Cronicles to haue chaunced in sundry par=||tes of the worlde from the yeare of || Christ .1532. To thys present || yeare of .1550. || Gathered by John Funcke of || Nurenborough. || Whyche was neuer afore prynted in Englysh. || Cum Priuilegio ad Imprimendum solum.
London : Gwalter Lynne [by Steven Mierdman], 1550
[8], cclxv, cclxvii-cclxxix, [13] fol.; 4°
[Colophon: Imprynted at Lon=||don for Gwalter Lynne, dwellynge on || Somers Keye, by Byl=||linges gate. || In the yeare of our Lord || M.D.L. || And they are to be solde in Paules || church yarde, nexte the great || Schole, at the sygne || of the sprede || Egle. || Cum Priuilegio ad Imprimendum solum.]
USTC 504410
STC (2nd ed.): 4626
London, British Library: G.5931.

"Von Carions Leben und Schriften," 184; Scherer, *Geschichte und Kirchengeschichte*, 472. The library in Nîmes has an additional copy from this year; the colophon matches the Xanten copy, but the title page is missing – Nîmes, Bibliothèque Carré d'art: 9959. (Colophon: "Fin des chroniques de Ian Carion & gestes || du feu Roy François premier de ce nom, || & de Henry deuxiesme iusques || à l'an présent. || 1550.")

London, British Library: 303.d.8. [Incomplete]
Chicago, Newberry Library: Case F 09 .151
Microform: Early English Books, 1475–1640, 30:01 [Incomplete]

1551

51   IOANNIS || CARIONIS MATHE-||matici Buticheimensis Chronicorum || libri tres, è Germanico in Latinu[m] ser-||monem conuersi, || Hermanno Bonno interprete. || Huic postremæ editioni accessere per-||multa scitu dignissima, suis locis pas-||sim inserta, cum accurata calculi reco-||gnitione, & eorum appendice quæ à || fine Carionis ad annu[m] || 1551. co[n]tigêre. || PRAETEREA || Catalogus Regum, Cæsarum, Pontificu[m] || Rom[anorum] ad hoc regu[m] Fra[n]c. Angl. & Sco. & || Index alphabeticus amplissimus. || Complectitur hic libellus apto ordine maximas || quasq[ue] res gestas ab initio mundi ad nostra || vsq[ue] tempora: vt annorum ratio, ac præcipuæ || vicißitudines quæ in regna, in religione[m], & || in alias res magnas incidunt, q[uam] rectißimè co-||gnosci & obseruari queant. || PARISIIS || Apud Iacobu[m] Dupuys sub Samaritana || in vico D. Ioannis Lateranensis. || M.D.LI. || CVM PRIVILEGIO.

Paris : Jacques du Puys, 1551
[128], 627, [45] p.; 16°
USTC 196356
London, British Library: 9006.a.7.
Oxford, Bodleian Library: Vet. E1 f.68

52.1   LES CHRO-||NIQVES DE IEAN || CARION PHILO-||SOPHE. || Auec les faicts & gestes du Roy Fran-||çois, iusques au regne du Roy || He[n]ry deuxiesme de ce nom, || à present regnant. || Traduictes en François par Maistre || Iean le Blond. || A PARIS. || Pour Iean Longis libraire tenant sa bou-||tique au Palais, en la galerie par ou lon va || à la chancellerie, || 1551.

Paris : Jean Longis, 1551
[32], 351, [1] fol.; 16°
USTC 76747
French Vernacular Books: 8897
Gotha, Forschungsbibliothek: Hist 8° 00302/02

52.2   LES CHRO-||NIQVES DE IEAN || CARION PHILO-||SOPHE. || Auec les faicts & gestes du Roy Fran-||çois, iusques au regne du Roy || He[n]ry deuxiesme de ce nom, || à present regnant. || Traduictes en François par Maistre || Iean le Blond. || A PARIS. || Pour Iean Ruelle demourant en la Rue || Sainct Iaques, à la queue de Regnard. || 1551.

Paris : Jean Ruelle, 1551

[32], 351, [1] fol.; 16°
USTC 7004
French Vernacular Books: 8898
Le Mans, Médiathèque Louis Aragon: H 8* 769

52.3 LES CHRO-||NIQVES DE IEAN || CARION PHILO-||SOPHE. || Auec les faicts & gestes du Roy Fran-||çois, iusques au regne du Roy || He[n]ry deuxiesme de ce nom, || à present regnant. || Traduictes en François par Maistre || Iean le Blond. || A PARIS. || Pour Vincent Sertenas libraire tenant sa || boutique au Palais, en la galerie par ou lon || va à la chancellerie, & au mont S. Hilaire à || l'hostel d'Albret. || 1551.
Paris : Vincent Sertenas, 1551
[32], 351, [1] fol.; 16°
USTC 12592
French Vernacular Books: 8899
Innerpeffray, Innerpeffray Library: E8

1552

53 Chronica || Durch M. Johann || Carion fleißig zusamen gezogen / || menniglich nützlich zu lesen. || Volstreckung diser Chronica vom || 32 Jar der mindern zal / biß inn das 52. || Sampt eym kurtzen außzug des grossen vn[d] || mechtigen kriegß / so Kei. Carolus V. mitt || den Protestierenden gefurt / im Jar 46. || Auch was sich in der schweren beläge=||rung der Stadt Magdeburg zu=||getragen hat. || Anno. M.D.L.II.
[Frankfurt a.M.] : [David Zöpfel], 1552
[1], 11, 424, [20] fol.; 8°
VD16 C 1006
USTC 622318
Wolfenbüttel, Herzog August Bibliothek: H: T 228.8° Helmst.

54 Chronica || Durch M. Johan Ca=||rion / vleissig zusamen ge=||zogen / menniglich nütz=||lich zu lesen. || Sampt einem Register / || darin alle fürnemiste Geschichte || vnd trefflichste Historien / von an=||fang der Welt bis jtzt / kürtz=||lich angezeigt sind. || Volstreckung dieser Chroni=||ca / vom 32. Jar der mindern || zal / bis ins 46. vnd etliche || jar hernach. || Gedruckt zu Wittemberg / Durch Ge=||orgen Rhawen Erben. || 1552.
Wittenberg : Georg Rhau (Heirs), 1552
244 [= 245], [17] fol.; 8°
VD16 ZV 22534
USTC 622313
München, Bayerische Staatsbibliothek: Chron. 201 d

55 Chronica || Durch M. Johan Ca=||rion / vleissig zusamen ge=||zogen / meniglich nütz=||lich zulesen. || Sampt einem Register / || darin alle fürnemeste Geschichte || vnd trefflichste Historien / von an=||fang der Welt bis jtzt / kürtz=||lich angezeigt sind. || Volstreckung dieser Chroni=||ca / vom 32. Jar der min=||dern zal / bis ins 46.
Leipzig : Jacob Berwald, 1552
244 [= 245], [17] fol.; 8°
[Colophon: Gedruckt zu Leipzig / || durch Jacobum || Berwald. || Anno M.D.LII.]
Arnstadt, Kirchenbibliothek: 750,2

56 IO. CARIONIS || MATHEMATICI BVTI=||cheimensis Chronicorum libri tres, è || Germanico in Latinum sermonem co[n]||uersi, HERMANNO Bonno in-||terprete. || HVIC postremæ editioni acceßere permul=||ta scitu dignißima, suis locis paßim inser-||ta, cum accurata calculi recognitione, & || eorum appendice quæ a fine Carionis ad || annum 1551. contigêre. || PRAETEREA || Catalogus, Regum, Cæsarum, Pontificum Ro. || ad hoc regum Franc. Angl. & Scot. & In=||dex alphabeticus amplißimus, multoq[ue] fide||lius, quàm hactenus unquam, restitutus. || BASILEAE, || Impensis Mathiæ Harscher, || M.D.LII.
Basel : Mathias Harscher, 1552
[Lyon : Godefroy & Marcellin Béringue, 1552]
[60] fol., 316 [= 613] p.; 16°
VD16 C 1019
USTC 115126
USTC 667019
Bibliographie des Livres Imprimés à Lyon au siezième siècle: X, 51
Wolfenbüttel, Herzog August Bibliothek: H: T 111.12° Helmst.

1553

57.1 Chronica || Durch M. Johan Ca=||rion / vleissig zusamen ge=||zogen / meniglich nütz=||lich zulesen. || Sampt einem Register / || darin alle fürnemeste Geschichte || vnd trefflichste Historien / von an=||fang der Welt bis jtzt / kürtz=||lich angezeigt sind. || Volstreckung dieser Chroni=||ca / vom 32. Jar der min=||dern zal / bis ins 46. || M.D.LIII.
Leipzig : Jacob Berwald, 1553 [1552]
244 [= 245], [17] fol.; 8°
[Colophon: Gedruckt zu Leipzig / || durch Jacobum || Berwald. || Anno M.D.LII.]
VD16 C 1007
USTC 622316
Wolfenbüttel, Herzog August Bibliothek: H: T 229.8° Helmst.

57.2 Chronica || Durch M. Johan Ca=||rion / vleissig zusamen ge=||zogen / meniglich nütz=||lich zulesen. || Sampt einem Register / || darin alle fürnemeste Geschichte || vnd trefflichste Historien / von an=||fang der Welt bis jtzt / kürtz=||lich angezeigt sind. || Volstreckung dieser Chroni=||ca / vom 32. Jar der min=||dern zal / bis ins 46. || M.D.LIII.
Leipzig : Jacob Berwald, 1553
244 [= 245], [17] fol.; 8°
[Colophon: Gedruckt zu Leipzig / || durch Jacobum || Berwald. || Anno M.D.LIII.]
Chicago, University of Chicago Crerar Library: D18.C37 1553
Bretten, Bibliothek des Melanchthonhauses: M 237

58 IO. CARIONIS || MATHEMATICI || CHRONICORVM || LIBRI TRES. || APPENDIX EORVM, || quæ à fine Carionis ad hæc || vsque tempora || contigêre. || CATALOGVS PONTIFICVM, || CAESARVM, REGVM, || & Ducum Venetorum, || cum Indice copiosißimo. || VENETIIS, || Ex Officina Erasmiana || Vincentij Valgrisij. || MDLIII.
Venice : Vincenzo Valgrisi, 1553
[108], 335 [= 535], [28] p.; 12°
USTC 818918
Le Edizioni italiane del XVI secolo: 1504
Chapel Hill, University of North Carolina Wilson Library: D18.C2 M3
Firenze, Biblioteca Nazionale Centrale: MAGL.4.8.8
Stuttgart, Württembergische Landesbibliothek: Allg.G.oct.392

59 LES CHRO-||NIQVES DE IEAN || CARION PHI-||LOSOPHE. || Auec les faicts & gestes du Roy || Fra[n]çois, iusques au regne du || Roy Henry deuxiesme || de ce nom, à présent || regnant. || Traduictes en François par Mai-||stre Iean le Blond. || A PARIS, || Chez Maturin dupuys Librarire iuré, de-||mourant en la rue sainct Iaques à l'en-||seigne de l'homme sauluaige & de l'E-||scu de Froben. || 1553.
Paris : Mathurin du Puys, 1553
[32], 351 fol.; 16°
Nürnberg, Stadtbibliothek: Strob. 521.8°

60.1 LES || CHRONI-||QVES DE IEAN || CARION PHI-||LOSOPHE. || Auec les faictz & gestes du Roy Fra[n]çois, || iusques au regne du Roy Henry || deuxiesme de ce nom, à || present regnant, || Traduict en François par maistre || Iean le Blond. || A PARIS, || Par Charles l'Angelier, en la grand salle || du Palais, au premíer pillier, deuant la || Chapelle de messieurs les Presidens. || 1553.
Paris : Charles l'Angelier, 1553
[32], 352 fol.; 16°
USTC 41005

French Vernacular Books: 8903

London, British Library: 9006.aa.5.

60.2 LES || CHRONI-||QVES DE IEAN || CARION PHI-||LOSOPHE. || Auec les faictz & gestes du Roy Fra[n]çois, || iusques au regne du Roy Henry || deuxiesme de ce nom, à || present regnant, || Traduict en François par maistre || Iean le Blond. || A PARIS, || Par Iehan Caueiller, demeurant en la rue || Frementel, pres le clos Bruneau, à || l'enseigne de l'Estoille d'or. || 1553.

Paris : Jean Caveiller, 1553

[32], 352 fol.; 16°

USTC 30721

French Vernacular Books: 8905

Paris, Bibliothèque Nationale: 8-H-1721, Arsenal - Magasin

60.3 LES || CHRONI-||QVES DE IEAN || CARION PHI-||LOSOPHE. || Auec les faictz & gestes du Roy Fra[n]çois, || iusques au regne du Roy Henry || deuxiesme de ce nom, à || present regnant, || Traduict en François par maistre || Iean le Blond. || A PARIS, || Par Benoist Preuost, demeurant en la rue || Frementel, pres le clos Bruneau, à || l'enseigne de l'Estoille d'or. || 1553.

Paris : Benoît Prévost, 1553

[32], 352 fol.; 16°

USTC 41050

French Vernacular Books: 8901

Avignon, Bibliothèque municipale: 8° 11496

Paris, Bibliothèque Nationale: RES-G-2920, Tolbiac - Rez de jardin - Magasin

60.4 LES || CHRONI-||QVES DE IEAN || CARION PHI-||LOSOPHE. || Auec les faictz & gestes du Roy Fra[n]çois, || iusques au regne du Roy Henry || deuxiesme de ce nom, à || present regnant, || Traduict en François par maistre || Iean le Blond. || A PARIS, || Par la vefue François Regnauld, en la rue || sainct Iaques, à l'enseigne de l'Elepha[n]t, || pres les Mathurins. || 1553.

Paris : François Regnauld (Widow) [= Magdaleine Boursette], 1553

[32], 352 fol.; 16°

USTC 20845

French Vernacular Books: 8908

Niort, Médiathèque de la communauté d'agglomération: 4545

60.5 LES || CHRONI-||QVES DE IEAN || CARION PHI-||LOSOPHE. || Auec les faictz & gestes du Roy Fra[n]çois, || iusques au regne du Roy Henry || deuxiesme de ce nom, à || present regnant, || Traduict en François par maistre || Iean le Blond. || A PARIS, || Par Iehan Ruelle, demeurant en la rue || sainct Iaques, à l'enseigne de la || queue de Regnard. || 1553.

Paris : Jean Ruelle, 1553

[32], 352 fol.; 16°
USTC 51160
USTC 42032
French Vernacular Books: 8906
French Vernacular Books: 8907
Paris, Bibliothèque Nationale: G-12267, Tolbiac - Rez de jardin - Magasin [Incomplete]
Spoleto, Biblioteca comunale Giosue' Carducci: XVI. L. 21

61   LES CHRO-||NIQVES DE IEAN || CARION PHILO-||SOPHE. || Auec les faicts & gestes du Roy || François, iusques au regne du || Roy Henry deuxiesme || de ce nom, à present || regnant. || Traduictes en François, par Mai-||stre Iean le Blond. || A PARIS, || Par Estienne Groulleau demourant en || la rue neuue nostre Dame, à l'en-||seigne sainct Ian baptiste. || 1553.
Paris : Estienne Groulleau [by Benoît Prévost], 1553
[Colophon: Imprimé à Paris, par Benoist Preuost, de-||meurant au Cloz Bruneau, rue || Frementel, à l'Estoille d'or. || 1553.]
[32], 336 fol.; 16°
USTC 13041
French Vernacular Books: 8904
Wolfenbüttel, Herzog August Bibliothek: A: 613.1 Hist.

62   LES CHRO-||NIQVES DE IEAN || CARION PHI-||LOSOPHE. || Auec les faicts & gestes du Roy || François, iusques au regne du || Roy Henry deuxiesme || de ce nom, à present || regnant. || Traduictes en François, par Mai-||stre Iean le Blond. || A PARIS, || Chez la veufue de Guillaume le Bret, de-||meurant au clos Bruneau, à l'en-||seigne de la corne de Cerf. || 1553.
Paris : Guillaume le Bret (Widow) [by Benoît Prévost], 1553
[Colophon: Imprimé à Paris, par Benoist Preuost, de-||meurant au Cloz Bruneau, rue || Frementel, à l'Estoille d'or. || 1553.]
[32], 336 fol.; 16°
USTC 47635
French Vernacular Books: 8902
Oxford, Queen's College Library: 11.a.250

63   LES || CHRONI-||QVES DE IEAN || CARION PHI-||LOSOPHE. || Auec les faicts & gestes du Roy François, || iusques au regne du Roy Henry || deuxiesme de ce nom, à || present regnant. || Traduict en François, par Maistre || Iean le Blond. || A PARIS, || Par Iean Caueiller, demeurant en la rue || Frementel, pres le cloz Bruneau, à || l'enseigne de l'Estoille d'Or. || 1553.
Paris : Jean Caveiller [by Benoît Prévost], 1553

[Colophon: Imprimé à Paris, par Benoist Preuost, de-||meurant au Cloz Bruneau, rue || Frementel, à l'Estoille d'or. || 1553.]
[32], 336 fol.; 16°
USTC 30721 [?]
French Vernacular Books: 8905 [?]
München, Bayerische Staatsbibliothek: Gall.g. 1019 u

64   CRONIQVES || DE IEAN CARION || PHILOSOPHE. || Auec les faits & gestes du feu Roy François, || iusques au regne du Roy Henri || deuxieme de ce nom, à pre-||sent regnant. || Traduites en François par || maistre Iean le Blond. || A LYON, || Par Iean de Tournes, & Guil-||laume Gazeau. || 1553.
Lyon : Jean de Tournes & Guillaume Gazeau, 1553
[64], 781, [3] p.; 16°
USTC 24100
French Vernacular Books: 8900
Bibliographie des Livres Imprimés à Lyon au siezième siècle: IX, 173
Cartier, De Tournes: 247
London, British Library: 1606/404.
München, Bibliothek der Ludwig-Maximilians-Universität: 0001/8 Hist. 1990

65   Een Chronijcke van || al tghene datter gheschiet is vant be=||ginsel des werelts totte[n] iare. M.CCCC. || ende xliij. met groote neersticheyt tot pro=||fijt van allen menschen / beschreuen doer || den hoochgeleerde[n] M. Joannem Ca=||rionem Astronomijn des Kueruor=||sten van Brandenborch. || Item een wonderlijcke Prophecie / || gheduerende totte[n] toecomende[n] iare van .lx. || ghemaeckt doer den seluen Carion / den || verstandighen tot eenen spiegel / || ende den dwasen tot een || verachtinghe. || Ghedruckt Tantwerpen by my Jan Gra||pheus int iaer na die gheboerte ons sa=||lichmakers Jesu Christi. M.||CCCCC. ende. Liij.
Antwerp : Jan Grapheus, 1553
246 fol.; 8°
USTC 400894
Belgica Typographica 1541–1600: 570
Brussels, La Bibliothèque royale de Belgique: VI 26613.A
CRL, Books printed in the Low Countries before 1601: MF-5549 reel 176 item 2

66[6]   Suma y com-||PENDIO DE TODAS LAS || Chronicas del mundo, || desde su principio || hasta el año presente, traduzida por el || Bachiller Francisco

---

6 Scherer (p. 472) lists a third Italian edition for 1553 (München, Bayerische Staatsbibliothek), but this seems to be a reference to the Spanish edition of 1553, which he does not list (München, Bayerische Staatsbibliothek: Chron. 108 m [Lost]).

Thamara || Cathedratico en || Cadiz. || Es la Chronica de Iuan Carion con dilige[n]cia || del Traductor quitado todo lo superfluo, y || añadidas muchas cosas notables de España. || En Anuers por Martin Nucio. || M.D.LIII. || Con priuilegio Imperial.
Antwerp : Martin Nucio, 1553
195, [13] fol.; 8°
USTC 440332
Peeters-Fontainas (1965): 188
Stuttgart, Württembergische Landesbibliothek: HBF 8085

1554

67   Chronica || Durch M. Johan Ca=||rion / vleissig zusamen ge=||zogen / meniglich nütz=||lich zu lesen. || Sampt einem Register / || darin alle fürnemeste Geschichte || vnd trefflichste Historien / von an=||fang der Welt bis jtzt / kürtz=||lich angezeigt sind. || Volstreckung dieser Chroni=||ca / vom 32. Jar der mindern zal / bis ins 46. vnd etliche || jar hernach. || Gedruckt zu Wittemberg / Durch Ge=||orgen Rhawen Erben. || 1554.
Wittenberg : Georg Rhau (Heirs), 1554
244 [= 245], [17] fol.; 8°
VD16 C 1008
USTC 622314
Wolfenbüttel, Herzog August Bibliothek: M: Gb 57

68.1 IOAN. || CARIONIS || MATHEMATICI || CHRONICORVM || LIBRI TRES. || APPENDIX EORVM, || quæ à fine Carionis ad hæc || vsque tempora || contigêre. || CATALOGVS PONTIFI-||cum, Cæsarum, Regum, & Ducum Vene-||torum, cum Indice copiosissimo. || LVGDVNI, || Apud Ioannem Frellonium. || 1554.
Lyon : Jean Frellon [by Michael Sylvius], 1554
[56] fol., 560 p., [16] fol.; 16°
[Colophon: LVGDVNI, ad confluentes. || Michaelis Sylvii || typis, 1554.]
USTC 158932 [?]
Baudrier, Bibliographie Lyonnaise: V, 228
Wolfenbüttel, Herzog August Bibliothek: M: Gb 50

68.2 IOAN. || CARIONIS || MATHEMATICI || CHRONICORVM || LIBRI TRES. || APPENDIX EORVM, || quæ à fine Carionis ad hæc || vsque tempora || contigêre. || CATALOGVS PONTIFI-||cum, Cæsarum, Regum, & Ducum Vene-||torum, cum Indice copiosissimo. || LVGDVNI, || Apud Antonium Vincentium. || 1554.
Lyon : Antoine Vincent, [by Michael Sylvius], 1554
[56] fol., 560 p., [16] fol.; 16°

69
[Colophon: LVGDVNI, ad confluentes. || Michaelis Sylvii || typis, 1554.]
USTC 151430 [?]
Halle, Universitäts- und Landesbibliothek Sachsen-Anhalt: AB 46541

Chronica || M. Johan Carion / paa || thet flitigste sammen dragen / || huer mand nytteligt att løese/ || oc er nu fordansket aff || M. Joenn Turszon || Canick i Lund. || Medt een skøn oc her=||lig Register som indholler al=||le fornemste handel oc Histo=||rier/ som seg fraa Verdens be=||gyndelse ind til Carolum || V. begiffuit haffue. || Met Kon. Ma. friihedt || paa fyre aar. || Prudens simplicitas & amor recti. || 1554.
Wittenberg : Georg Rhau (Heirs), 1554
264, [20] fol.; 8°
[Colophon: Prentet i || Wittenberg / hoff Jur=||gen Rhauues arff=||uinger / Aar effter || Guds Byrd. || 1554. || Oc findes til kiøbs hoff || Pauel Knufflock Bock=||binder i Lybeck.]
VD16 ZV 25443
USTC 302887
Nielson, Dansk Bibliografi 1551–1600: 481
Copenhagen, Det Kongelige Bibliotek: Hist. 6045 8°
Stockholm, Kungl. biblioteket: 125 A l c

1555

70
Chronica || Durch M. Johann || Carion fleißig zusammen gezogen / || menniglich nützlich zu lesen. || Volstreckung diser Chronica vom || 32. Jar der mindern zal / biß inn das 55. || Sampt eym kurtzen außzug des gros=||sen vnd mechtigen kriegs / so Keyser Carolus || V. mit den Protestierenden gefurt / im Jar || 46. Auch was sich in der schweren belä=||gerung der Stadt Magdeburg || vnd biß jtzt vffs lauffend 55. || Jar zugetragen hat. || Anno 1555.
Frankfurt a.M. : David Zöpfel, 1555
[1], 11, 431, [24] fol.; 8°
VD16 C 1009
USTC 622312
Wolfenbüttel, Herzog August Bibliothek: H: Yv 510.8° Helmst.
Wolfenbüttel, Herzog August Bibliothek: H: T 230.8° Helmst.

71[7]
IO. CARIO=||NIS MATHEMATI||CI BVETIKHEINENSIS CHRO=||NICORVM LIBRI TRES, IN LATINVM || Sermonem conuersi. || HERMANNO BONNO INTERPRETE. || CONTINVATIO CHRONICORVM AB AN=||no 1532. adiecta

---

7 "Nach Moller 17 soll diese Ausgabe 1581, 1584 und 1592 nochmals aufgelegt worden sein." Scherer, *Geschichte und Kirchengeschichte*, 470 n. 2.

breui narratione eorum, quæ in expeditio=||ne Protestantium contra Cæ-sarum Carol. v. anno 46. Quæq[ue] || post obsidionem Magdeburgensem usq[ue] in hunc præsen||tem 1555. annum contigerunt. || Complectitur hic Libellus apto ordine maximas quasq[ue] res ge||stas, ab initio Mundi, vsque ad nostra tempora, vt annorum ratio, || ac præcipuæ vicissitudines, quæ in Regna, in Religionem, & in ali||as res magnas incidunt, quàm rectissimè cogno-||sci & obseruari queat. || FRANCOFORTI, Dauid Zephelius excu=||debat, Anno 1555.
Frankfurt a.M. : David Zöpfel, 1555
317, [21] fol.; 8°
VD16 C 1020
USTC 667077
Wolfenbüttel, Herzog August Bibliothek: A: 466.3 Hist.
Wolfenbüttel, Herzog August Bibliothek: H: T 237.8° Helmst.

72   CARIONIS || CHRONICON, || Liber, cui, breuitate, perspicuitate, ordine, || vix quicquam est in hoc genere || comparandum. || APPENDIX RERVM || memorabilium, quæ ad hunc usque || annum contigerunt. || CATALOGVS PONTIFICVM, || CAESARVM, REGVM, || & Ducum Venetorum, || cum Indice copio-||sißimo. || VENETIIS, 1555. || Ex Officina Erasmiana Vincentij || Valgrisij.
Venice : Vincenzo Valgrisi, 1555
[108], 576 p.; 12°
USTC 818919
Le Edizioni italiane del XVI secolo: 1505
Padova, Biblioteca del Seminario Vescovile: 500.ROSSA.SUP.N.4X.-20

73.1 LES || CHRONI-||QVES DE IEAN || CARION PHILOSOPHE. || Auec les faictz & gestes du Roy Fran-||çois, iusques au regne du Roy Henry || deuxiesme de ce no[m], à present regnant. || Traduict en François par maistre || Iean le Blond. || A PARIS. || Par Magdaleine boursette à l'Elephant. || 1555.
Paris : Magdaleine Boursette [François Regnauld (Widow)], 1555
[32], 357, [2] fol.; 8°
USTC 75516
French Vernacular Books: 8910
Toronto, University of Toronto Thomas Fisher Library: smb RBSC

73.2 LES || CHRONI-||QVES DE IEAN || CARION PHILOSOPHE. || Auec les faictz & gestes du Roy Fran-||çois, iusques au regne du Roy Henry || deuxiesme de ce no[m], à present regnant. || Traduict en François par maistre || Iean le Blond. || A PARIS. || Par Iean Cauellier, demourant en la || rue Frementel à l'enseigne de || l'Estoille d'or, pres le || Cloz Bruneau. || [1555.]
Paris : Jean Caveiller, 1555
[32], 357, [2] fol.; 8°

74

USTC 74726
French Vernacular Books: 8909
Metz, Bibliothèque municipale: Q 1542 [Title page incomplete]
SVMA || Y COMPEN||DIO DE TODAS LAS || Chronicas del mundo, desde su || principio hasta el año presente, || traduzida por el Bachiller Fran-||cisco Thamara Cathedra-||tico en Cadiz. || Es la Chronica de Iuan Carion, qui-||tado todo lo superfluo, y aña-||didas muchas cosas notables de || España. || EN ANVERS. || En casa de Martin Nucio, a la ense-||ña de las dos Cigueñas. || 1555.
Antwerp : Martin Nucio, 1555
249, [12] fol.; 12°
USTC 440333
Peeters-Fontainas (1965): 189
Belgica Typographica 1541–1600: 572
Göttingen, Niedersächsische Staats- und Universitätsbibliothek: 8 H UN II, 139
Hamburg, Staats- und Universitätsbibliothek: A/200612
CRL, Books printed in the Low Countries before 1601: MF-5549 reel 23 item 2
CRL, Hispanic Culture Series: MF-7736 reel 262 item 3
CRL, Hispanic Culture Series: MF-7736 reel 153 item 2

1556

75

Chronica || Durch M. Johann || Carion fleißig zusamen gezogen / || menniglich nützlich zu lesen. || Volstreckung diser Chronica vom || 32. Jar der mindern zal / biß in das 56. || Sampt eym kurtzen außzug des gros=||sen vnd mechtigen kriegs / so Keyser Carolus || V. mit den Protestierenden gefurth / im Jar || 46. Auch was sich in der schweren belä=||gerung der Statt Magdeburg || vnd biß jtzt vffs lauffend 56. || Jar zugetragen hat. || Anno 1556.
[Frankfurt a.M.] : [David Zöpfel], 1556
[1], 11, 431, [24] fol.; 8°
VD16 C 1010
USTC 622319
Urbana, University of Illinois Library: 909 C19C1556
Wolfenbüttel, Herzog August Bibliothek: H: T 230*.8° Helmst. [Title page lost]

[76][8] *Chronicorum libellus, maximas quasque res gestas...*
Paris : ??, 1556

---

8 "Ausgaben zu Paris. Diese sind sehr selten, und ich war nicht so glücklich, eine davon aufzutrieben. Ich führe daher blos die bey andern angezeigten Ausgaben an ohne für deren Richtigkeit und Gewißheit Bürge zu seyn. Paris. 1544, 1546, 1549, 1556. 1563. sämtlich in 12." Strobel, "Von Carions Leben und Schriften," 175.

?? fol.

[Strobel, 175; see Scherer, 471]

77 CARIONIS || CHRONICON, || Liber, cui, breuitate, perspicuitate, ordine, || vix quicquam est in hoc genere || comparandum. || APPENDIX RERVM || memorabilium, quæ ad hunc usque || annum contigerunt. || CATALOGVS PONTIFICVM, || CAESARVM, REGVM, || & Ducum Venetorum, || cum Indice copio-||sißimo. || VENETIIS, 1556. || Ex Officina Erasmiana Vincentij || Valgrisij.

Venice : Vincenzo Valgrisi, 1556

[108], 576 p.; 12°

USTC 818920

Le Edizioni italiane del XVI secolo: 1506

Mannheim, Universitätsbibliothek: Sch 045/143

78 LES || CHRONI-||QVES DE IEAN || CARION PHILOSOPHE. || Auec les faictz & gestes du Roy || Françoys, iusques au regne du || Roy Henry deuxiesme || de ce nom, à pre-||sent regnant. || Traduict en Francois par maistre || Iean le Blond. || A PARIS. || Par Iean Cauelier, demourant en la || rue Frementel, à l'enseigne || de l'Estoille d'or. || 1556.

Paris : Jean Caveiller, 1556

[32], 358, [2] fol.; 16°

USTC 6621

French Vernacular Books: 8911

Lunel, Bibliothèque municipale: LUN 9

79 LES || CHRONI-||QVES DE IEAN || CARION PHILOSOPHE. || Auec les faictz & gestes du Roy Fran-||çois, iusques au regne du Roy Henry || deuxiesme de ce nom, à present regna[n]t. || Traduict en Francois par maistre || Iean le Blond. || A PARIS. || Par Iean Ruelle, demourant en la rue S. || Iacques, à l'enseigne sainct Nicolas. || 1556.

Paris : Jean Ruelle, 1556

[32], 374, [2] fol.; 16°

Paris, Librairie Le Feu Follet [Bookseller]: 13712

1557

80 IO. CARIO-||NIS MATHEMATICI || BVETIKHEIMENSIS CHRO-||nicorum libri tres, ut sunt in Lati-||num sermonem con-||uersi, || HERMANNO BONNO INTERP. || AD LECTOREM. || Continent hic prima gestas ab origine mundi || Historias nostrum tempus adusq[ue] liber. || Grandè sub exiguo co[m]prensum fasce volumen, || Exiguo ære tibi candide lector emè. || Basileae, 1557.

Basel : [Michael Isengrin], 1557
402 p., [11] fol.; 8°
VD16 ZV 25970
USTC 667017
Firenze, Biblioteca Nazionale Centrale: MAGL.9.7.316
Wiesbaden, Hessische Landesbibliothek: Wielb 404

81.1[9]   IOAN. || CARIONIS || MATHEMATICI || CHRONICORVM || LIBRI TRES. || AP-PENDIX EORVM, || quæ à fine Carionis ad hæc vsque || tempora contigêre. || CATALOGVS PONTI-||ficium, Cæsarum, Regum, & Ducum || Venetorum, cum Indice || copiosissimo. || PARISIIS, || Apud Ioannem Brachonier, ex aduerso || Diui Hylarij, in curia || Albretico. || 1557.
Paris : Jean Brachonier, 1557
[66] fol., 5–548 [lacks 549–619] p.; 16°
[Imprimeurs & Libraires Parisiens du XVIe siècle: Cavellat (Guillaume), 114]
Ebay Item Number: 290233500963 [Sold 1 June 2008]

81.2   IOAN. || CARIONIS || MATHEMATICI || CHRONICORVM || LIBRI TRES. || AP-PENDIX EORVM, || quæ à fine Carionis ad hæc vsque || tempora contigêre. || CATALOGVS PONTI-||ficium, Cæsarum, Regum, & Ducum || Venetorum, cum Indice || copiosissimo. || PARISIIS, || Apud Ioannem Brachonier, ex aduerso || Diui Hylarij, in curia || Albretico. || 1557.
Paris : Jean Brachonier, 1557
[66] fol., 5–619, [1 - blank] p., [16] fol.; 16°
USTC 152215
Imprimeurs & Libraires Parisiens du XVIe siècle: Cavellat (Guillaume), 114
Grenoble, Bibliothèque municipale d'étude et d'information: F.3523 CGA

81.3   IOAN. || CARIONIS || MATHEMATICI || CHRONICORVM || LIBRI TRES. || AP-PENDIX EORVM, || quæ à fine Carionis ad hæc vsque || tempora contigêre. || CATALOGVS PONTI-||ficium, Cæsarum, Regum, & Ducum || Venetorum, cum Indice || copiosissimo. || PARISIIS, || Apud Simônem Caluarinum, || in vico Bellouaco ad || Virtutis insigne. || 1557.
Paris : Simon Calvarin, 1557
[66] fol., 5–619, [1 - blank] p., [16] fol.; 16°
USTC 203710
Imprimeurs & Libraires Parisiens du XVIe siècle: Cavellat (Guillaume), 114
Wolfenbüttel, Herzog August Bibliothek: A: 617.6 Hist.

---

9   The Bibliothèque Nationale holds an incomplete edition consisting of pages 541–619 and [16] fol., handnumbered as 620–652. A handwritten colophon has been added on fol. [652] to mark the copy as a Brachonier edition – Paris, Bibliothèque Nationale: G-12258, Tolbiac - Rez de jardin - Magasin.

81.4 IOAN. || CARIONIS || MATHEMATICI || CHRONICORVM || LIBRI TRES. || APPENDIX EORVM, || quæ à fine Carionis ad hæc vsque || tempora contigêre. || CATALOGVS PONTI-||ficium, Cæsarum, Regum, & Ducum || Venetorum, cum Indice || copiosissimo. || PARISIIS, || Apud Gulielmum Cauellat, in pingui Galli-||na, è regione collegij Cameracensis. || 1557.
Paris : Guillaume Cavellat, 1557
[66] fol., 5–619, [1 - blank] p., [16] fol.; 16°
USTC 198049
Imprimeurs & Libraires Parisiens du XVIe siècle: Cavellat (Guillaume), 114
Wolfenbüttel, Herzog August Bibliothek: H: T 112.12° Helmst.

81.5 IOAN. || CARIONIS || MATHEMATICI || CHRONICORVM || LIBRI TRES. || APPENDIX EORVM, || quæ à fine Carionis ad hæc vsque || tempora contigêre. || CATALOGVS PONTI-||ficium, Cæsarum, Regum, & Ducum || Venetorum, cum Indice || copiosissimo. || PARISIIS, || Apud Aegidium Corrozet, || in Palatio Regis. || 1557.
Paris : Aegidius Corrozet [= Gilles Corrozet], 1557
[66] fol., 5–619, [1 - blank] p., [16] fol.; 16°
[Imprimeurs & Libraires Parisiens du XVIe siècle: Cavellat (Guillaume), 114]
Moscow, Russian State Library: Paris Corrozet 1557 8°
[Dresden, Sächsische Landesbibliothek: Hist.univ.A.669]

81.6 IOAN. || CARIONIS || MATHEMATICI || CHRONICORVM || LIBRI TRES. || APPENDIX EORVM, || quæ à fine Carionis ad hæc vsque || tempora contigêre. || CATALOGVS PONTI-||ficium, Cæsarum, Regum, & Ducum || Venetorum, cum Indice || copiosissimo. || PARISIIS, || Apud Aegidium Gourbinum, sub || insigni Spei, ad Colegium || Cameracense. || 1557.
Paris : Aegidius Gourbinus [= Gilles Gourbin], 1557
[66] fol., 5–619, [1 - blank] p., [16] fol.; 16°
[Imprimeurs & Libraires Parisiens du XVIe siècle: Cavellat (Guillaume), 114]
Aberdeen, Queen Mother Library: pi MN 20.315

81.7 IOAN. || CARIONIS || MATHEMATICI || CHRONICORVM || LIBRI TRES. || APPENDIX EORVM, || quæ à fine Carionis ad hæc vsque || tempora contigêre. || CATALOGVS PONTI-||ficium, Cæsarum, Regum, & Ducum || Indice || copiosissimo. || PARISIIS, || Apud Martinum Iuuenem, sub signo || Diui Christophori, è regione || collegij Cameracensis. || 1557.
Paris : Martin le Jeune, 1557
[66] fol., 5–619, [1 - blank] p., [16] fol.; 16°
USTC 198048
Imprimeurs & Libraires Parisiens du XVIe siècle: Cavellat (Guillaume), 114
Carcassonne, Bibliothèque municipale: 1033 21-1

81.8 IOAN. || CARIONIS || MATHEMATICI || CHRONICORVM || LIBRI TRES. || AP-
PENDIX EORVM, || quæ à fine Carionis ad hæc vsque || tempora contigêre. ||
CATALOGVS PONTI-||ficium, Cæsarum, Regum, & Ducum || Venetorum, cum
Indice || copiosissimo. || PARISIIS, || Apud Gulielmum Iulianum, sub signo ||
Amicitiæ, ad gymnasium || Cameracense. || 1557.
Paris : Guillaume Julien, 1557
[66] fol., 5–619, [1 - blank] p., [16] fol.; 16°
USTC 198047
[Imprimeurs & Libraires Parisiens du XVIe siècle: Cavellat (Guillaume), 114]
Oxford, All Souls College Library: SR.41.a.18
Niort, Médiathèque de la communauté d'agglomération: 110s
Poitiers, Médiathèque François Mitterrand: D 6473 [Title page incomplete]

[81.9] IOAN. || CARIONIS || MATHEMATICI || CHRONICORVM || LIBRI TRES. || AP-
PENDIX EORVM, || quæ à fine Carionis ad hæc vsque || tempora contigêre. ||
CATALOGVS PONTI-||ficium, Cæsarum, Regum, & Ducum || Venetorum, cum
Indice || copiosissimo. || PARISIIS, || ... || 1557.
Paris : Michael Julianus [= Michel Julien], 1557
[66] fol., 5–619, [1 - blank] p., [16] fol.; 16°
USTC 208028
Imprimeurs & Libraires Parisiens du XVIe siècle: Cavellat (Guillaume), 114
[Bordeaux, Bibliothèque municipale: ??]

[81.10] IOAN. || CARIONIS || MATHEMATICI || CHRONICORVM || LIBRI TRES. || AP-
PENDIX EORVM, || quæ à fine Carionis ad hæc vsque || tempora contigêre. ||
CATALOGVS PONTI-||ficium, Cæsarum, Regum, & Ducum || Venetorum, cum
Indice || copiosissimo. || PARISIIS, || ... || 1557.
Paris : Johannes Macaeus [= Jean Macé], 1557
[66] fol., 5–619, [1 - blank] p., [16] fol.; 16°
USTC 198050
Imprimeurs & Libraires Parisiens du XVIe siècle: Cavellat (Guillaume), 114
[Valognes, Bibliothèque municipale: C. 328 (Title page lost)]

81.11 IOAN. || CARIONIS || MATHEMATICI || CHRONICORVM || LIBRI TRES. || AP-
PENDIX EORVM, || quæ à fine Carionis ad hæc vsque || tempora contigêre. ||
CATALOGVS PONTI-||ficium, Cæsarum, Regum, & Ducum || Venetorum, cum
Indice || copiosissimo. || PARISIIS, || Apud Sebastianum Niuellium, || sub Ci-
coniis, in vico || Iacobeo. || 1557.
Paris : Sébastien Nivelle, 1557
[66] fol., 5–619, [1 - blank] p., [16] fol.; 16°
USTC 204746
[Imprimeurs & Libraires Parisiens du XVIe siècle: Cavellat (Guillaume), 114]
Copenhagen, Det Kongelige Bibliotek: 144, 73 00812
Köln, Erzbischöfliche Diözesan- und Dombibliothek: HP335 [= Aa 2242]

82   LES || CHRONI-||QVES DE IEAN || CARION PHILOSOPHE. || Auec les faictz & gestes du Roy Fran-||çois, iusques au regne du Roy Henry || deuxiesme de ce nom, à present regna[n]t. || Traduict en Francois par maistre || Iean le Blond. || A PARIS. || Par Iean Ruelle, demourant en la rue S. || Iacques, à l'enseigne sainct Nicolas. || 1557.
Paris : Jean Ruelle, 1557
[32], 358, [2] fol.; 16°
USTC 88138
French Vernacular Books: 8912
Jena, Thüringer Universitäts- und Landesbibliothek: 12 Hist.un.II,3

1558

83   Chronica || Durch M: Johann Carion || fleissig zusamen gezogen / me-||niglich nützlich zulesen. || Sampt einer newen volstreckung / || darinn kürtzlich begriffen / was sich von || dem 32. Jar der mindern zal / biß in das jetzig acht || vnd fünfftzigst / fürnemlichs hin vnd wi=||der zugetragen vnd ver=||lauffen hat. || Anno M.D.LVIII.
[Frankfurt a.M.] : [David Zöpfel], 1558
[8], 437, [19] fol.; 8°
VD16 ZV 2948
USTC 622321
Bibliotheca Palatina: F4243/F4245
London, Warburg Institute Library: NAH 6550.C36 1558
Wolfenbüttel, Herzog August Bibliothek: H: T 231.8° Helmst.
Wolfenbüttel, Herzog August Bibliothek: S: Alv.: Ig 116

84.1   IOAN. || CARIONIS || MATHEMATICI || CHRONICORVM || LIBRI III. || Appendix eorum, quæ à fine Ca-||rionis ad hæc vsque tempo-||ra contigere. || Catalogus Pontificum, Cæsarum, Re-||gum, & Ducum Venetorum, cum || Indice copiosissimo. || LVGDVNI, || Apud Ioannem Frellonium, || 1558
Lyon : Jean Frellon [by Symphorien Barbier], 1558
[56] fol., 572 p., [18] fol.; 16°
[Colophon: LVGDVNI, || Excudebat Symphorianus || Barbierus.]
USTC 154381
Baudrier, Bibliographie Lyonnaise: V, 245
Freiburg, Universitätsbibliothek: G 219,ct
München, Bayerische Staatsbibliothek: Chron. 28

84.2   IOAN. || CARIONIS || MATHEMATICI || CHRONICORVM || LIBRI III. || Appendix eorum, quæ à fine Ca-||rionis ad hæc vsque tempo-||ra contigere. ||

Catalogus Pontificum, Cæsarum, Re-||gum, & Ducum Venetorum, cum || Indice copiosissimo. || LVGDVNI, || Apud Antonium Vincentium, || 1558
Lyon : Antoine Vincent [by Symphorien Barbier], 1558
[56] fol., 572 p., [18] fol.; 16°
[Colophon: LVGDVNI, || Excudebat Symphorianus || Barbierus.]
USTC 158961
Stuttgart, Württembergische Landesbibliothek: Allg.G.oct.393

85   CHRONICON || CARIONIS LATI=||NE EXPOSITVM ET AV=||CTVM MVLTIS ET VETE=||RIBVS ET RECENTIBVS || Historijs, in narrationibus rerum Græ=||carum, Germanicarum & Ec=||clesiasticarum || A || PHILIPPO MELAN=||THONE. || VVITEBERGÆ || EXCVSVM IN OFFICINA || HÆREDVM GEORGII || RHAVV. || ANNO M.D.LVIII.
Wittenberg : Georg Rhau (Heirs), 1558
[8], [200] fol.; 8°
VD16 M 2698
USTC 622453
Atlanta, Emory University Pitts Theology Library: 1558 MELA A
[Includes Melanchthon's "De Monarchiis" in his own hand.]
Ithaca, Cornell University Library: Rare D18 C27 1558 v. 1
Erlangen, Universitätsbibliothek: H62/CIM.F 7[1
[Dedication Copy of Melanchthon to Elector Joachim II of Brandenburg]
Wolfenbüttel, Herzog August Bibliothek: H: Yt 39.8° Helmst.
Wolfenbüttel, Herzog August Bibliothek: H: T 238.8° Helmst. (1)

86   CHRONICON || CARIONIS LATI=||NE EXPOSITVM ET AV=||CTVM MVLTIS ET VETERI-||BVS ET RECENTIBVS HIS-||TORIIS, IN NARRATIONI-||BVS RERVM GRAECARVM, || GERMANICARVM ET || ECCLESIASTI-||CARVM. || A || PHILIPPO MELAN=||THONE. || CVM GRATIA ET PRIVILE-||gio Electoris Saxoniæ. || VVITEBERGÆ || EX OFFICINA HAERE-||DVM GEORGII RHAVV. || ANNO M.D.LVIII.
Wittenberg : Georg Rhau (Heirs), 1558
[8], 182 [= 200] fol.; 8°
VD16 M 2697
USTC 622454
Wolfenbüttel, Herzog August Bibliothek: S: Alv.: U 214 (1)

1559

87   LES || CHRONIQVES || DE IEAN CA=||RION PHILO-||SOPHE. || Auec les faictz & gestes du Roy Fran=||cois, iusques au regne du Roy Henry || deuziesme de

ce nom, à present regnant. || Nouuellement reueües & augmen||tees de plusieurs choses. || Traduict en François par mai-||stre Iean le Blond. || A LYON, || PAR PIERRE || MICHEL. || 1559.

Lyon : Pierre Michel, 1559

[32], 370, [2] fol.; 16°

München, Bayerische Staatsbibliothek: Chron. 52 [Lost]

Salzburg, Bibliothek des Franziskanerklosters: [Unpublished Shelfmark]

88   CHRONICON || CARIONIS LATI=||NE EXPOSITVM ET AV-||CTVM MVLTIS ET VETERI-||BVS ET RECENTIBVS HIS-||TORIIS, IN NARRATIONI-||BVS RERVM GRAECARVM, || GERMANICARVM ET || ECCLESIASTI-||CARVM. || A || PHILIPPO MELAN=||THONE. || CVM GRATIA ET PRIVILE-||gio Electoris Saxoniæ. || VVITEBERGÆ || EX OFFICINA HAERE-||DVM GEORGII RHAVV. || ANNO M.D.LIX.

Wittenberg : Georg Rhau (Heirs), 1559

[8], 182 [= 200] fol.; 8°

Hamburg, Staats- und Universitätsbibliothek Hamburg: Scrin 226b

[Includes Melanchthon's "De Monarchiis" in his own hand.]

89   CHRONICON || CARIONIS LATI=||NE EXPOSITVM ET AV-||CTVM MVLTIS ET VETERI-||BVS ET RECENTIBVS HIS-||TORIIS, IN NARRATIONI-||BVS RERVM GRAECARVM, || GERMANICARVM ET || ECCLESIASTI-||CARVM. || A || PHILIPPO MELAN=||THONE. || CVM GRATIA ET PRIVILE-||gio Electoris Saxoniæ. || VVITEBERGÆ || EX OFFICINA HAERE-||DVM GEORGII RHAVV. || ANNO M.D.LIX.

Wittenberg : Georg Rhau (Heirs), 1559

[8], 200 fol.; 8°

VD16 ZV 10739

USTC 622455

Freiburg, Universitätsbibliothek: G 219,da-1/2

Rostock, Universitätsbibliothek: Rb-131(1)

90[10]   CHRONI-||CON ABSOLVTIS||SIMVM AB ORBE CON||dito vsque ad Christum deductum, in quo non || Carionis solùm opus continetur, verùm || etiam alia multa eaq[ue] insignia expli-||cantur, adeo vt iustæ Histo-||riæ loco occupatis es-||se poßit. || PHILIPPO MELAN-||thone autore. || BASILEAE || M.D.LIX.

Basel : [Peter Perna ?], 1559

[7] fol., 355 p.; 8°

VD16 M 2699

USTC 622265

---

10   See Leandro Perini, *La vita e i tempi di Pietro Perna* (Roma: Edizioni di storia e letteratura, 2002). Sig. A2r has the "E" from Perini's Tavola 11; and sig. d4r has the "A" from his Tavola 9.

Bibliotheca Palatina: F5296
Chicago, Newberry Library: Case F 09 .1455
Wolfenbüttel, Herzog August Bibliothek: H: T 239.8° Helmst.

91   CHRO=||NICON CARIO-||NIS LATINE EX-||POSITVM ET AV-||ctum multis & veteri-||bus & recentibus Histo-||rijs, in narrationibus re-||rum Græcarum, Germa-||nicarum & Ecclesia-||sticarum. || A PHI. MEL. || FRANCOFOR||TI. || D.Z.
Frankfurt a.M. : David Zöpfel, 1559
495 p.; 12°
VD16 M 2700
USTC 622261
Wolfenbüttel, Herzog August Bibliothek: H: T 113.12° Helmst.

1560

92.1   IOAN. || CARIONIS || MATHEMATICI || CHRONICORVM || LIBRI III. || Appendix eorum, quæ à fine Ca-||rionis ad hæc vsque tempo-||ra contigere. || Catalogus Pontificum, Cæsarum, Re-||gum, & Ducum Venetorum, cum || Indice copiosissimo. || LVGDVNI, || Apud Ioannem Frellonium, || 1560
Lyon : Jean Frellon [by Symphorien Barbier], 1560
[56] fol., 572 p., [18] fol.; 16°
[Colophon: LVGDVNI, || Excudebat Symphorianus || Barbierus.]
USTC 152807
Stuttgart, Württembergische Landesbibliothek: Allg.G.oct.394

92.2   IOAN. || CARIONIS || MATHEMATICI || CHRONICORVM || LIBRI III. || Appendix eorum, quæ à fine Ca-||rionis ad hæc vsque tempo-||ra contigere. || Catalogus Pontificum, Cæsarum, Re-||gum, & Ducum Venetorum, cum || Indice copiosissimo. || LVGDVNI, || Apud Antonium Vincentium, || 1560
Lyon : Antoine Vincent [by Symphorien Barbier], 1560
[56] fol., 572 p., [18] fol.; 16°
[Colophon: LVGDVNI, || Excudebat Symphorianus || Barbierus.]
USTC 138930
Stuttgart, Württembergische Landesbibliothek: HB 394

93.1   LES || CHRONIQVES || DE IEAN CARION PHILOSO-||phe. La ou sont co[n]tenuz les choses me||morables depuis la creation du monde || iusques au regne du Roy François, deu||xiesme de ce nom, à present regnant. || Traduict en François, par Maistre || Iean le Blond, || A PARIS. || Par Estienne Groulleau, libraire iure de-||mourant en la rue neuue nostre Dame, || à l'enseigne sainct Iean Bapiste. || 1560
Paris : Estienne Groulleau, 1560

[32], 374, [2] fol.; 16°
USTC 41735
French Vernacular Books: 8914
Chicago, Newberry Library: Case miniature F 09 .1524

93.2 LES || CHRONIQVES || DE IEAN CARION PHILOSO-||phe. La ou sont co[n]tenuz les choses me-||morables depuis la creation du monde || iusques au regne du Roy François, deu-||xiesme de ce nom, à present regnant. || Traduict en François, par Maistre || Iean le Blond, || A PARIS. || Par Iean Ruelle, libraire demourant || en la Rue Sainct Iaques, à l'en-||seigne Sainct Nicolas. || 1560.
Paris : Jean Ruelle, 1560
[32], 374, [2] fol.; 16°
Paris, Bibliothèque Sainte-Geneviève: DELTA 72811 RES

94 CHRONICON || CARIONIS LATINE || EXPOSITVM ET AVCTVM || multis & ueteribus & recentibus Historijs, in || narrationibus rerum Græcarum, Germa=||nicarum & Ecclesiastica=||rum, à || PHILIPPO MELAN=||THONE. || Acceßit locupletißimus rerum ac uerbo=||rum memorabilium Index. || Cum Gratia & Priuilegio ad sexennium. || VVITEBERGÆ HÆREDES GE=||orgij Rhau excudebant, Anno 1560.
Wittenberg : Georg Rhau (Heirs), 1560
[12], 180, [20] fol.; 8°
VD16 ZV 16738
USTC 622456
Halle, Universitäts- und Landesbibliothek Sachsen-Anhalt: Pon Vg 4131 a (1)

95 Chronica || Carionis gantz new La||tine geschrieben. || Von || Dem Ehrwirdigen Herrn Philippo Me=||lanthone / Verdeutscht. || Durch || M. Eusebium Menium. || Aller Oberkeyt insonderheyt / auch allen Stenden || vnnd Vnterthanen nothwendig vnnd nützlich zulesen / || Dieweil diß Buch anleittung gibt zu Historien || Göttlicher Schrifft / vnnd allen andern. || Gedruckt zu Witteberg || Durch Georgen Rhawen Erben. || M.D.LX.
Wittenberg : Georg Rhau (Heirs), 1560
[6], 266 fol.; 4° [fol. 266r – 2 upside down]
VD16 ZV 26324
USTC 622279
Bibliotheca Palatina: E1740/E1741
München, Bayerische Staatsbibliothek: Res/4 Chron. 11 m

96 Chronica || Carionis gantz new || Latine geschrieben / von dem || Ehrwirdigen Herrn || PHILIPPO MELANTHONE. || Verdeudscht durch M. || Eusebium Menium. || Aller Oberkeit in sonderheit / auch allen || Stenden vnd Vnterthanen nothwendig vnd nützlich zulesen / || Dieweil dis Buch anleittung gibt

zu Historien || Göttlicher Schrifft / vnd allen andern. || Mit einer Vorrede D. Georgij Maioris. || CVM GRATIA ET PRIVILEGIO. || Witteberg / 1560.
Wittenberg : Georg Rhau (Heirs), 1560
[24], 266 fol.; 4° [fol. 266r – 2 upside down]
VD16 M 2723
USTC 622277
Wolfenbüttel, Herzog August Bibliothek: A: 127.30 Hist. (1)
Wolfenbüttel, Herzog August Bibliothek: S: Alv.: Li 192 (1)

97   SECVNDA PARS || CHRONICI || CARIONIS AB || AVGVSTO CÆSARE || VSQVE AD CARO=||LVM MAGNVM. || EXPOSITA ET AV=||CTA A PHILIPPO || MELANTHO=||NE. || VVITEBERGÆ || Cum Gratia & Priuilegio ad Sexennium. || ANNO M.D.LX.
Wittenberg : Georg Rhau (Heirs), 1560
[8], 190 fol.; 8°
VD16 M 2705
USTC 692895
Ithaca, Cornell University Library: Rare D18 C27 1558 v. 1
Wolfenbüttel, Herzog August Bibliothek: H: Yv 1166a.8° Helmst.
Wolfenbüttel, Herzog August Bibliothek: H: T 242.8° Helmst. (2)
Wolfenbüttel, Herzog August Bibliothek: S: Alv.: U 214 (2)

98   SECVNDA PARS || CHRONICI || CARIONIS AB AV=||GVSTO CAESARE VS=||QVE AD CAROLVM || MAGNVM. || EXPOSITA ET AV=||CTA A PHILIPPO ME=||LANTHONE. || Accesßit locupletiß. rerum ac uerborum || memorabilium Index. || VVITEBERGÆ || Cum Gratia & Priuilegio ad Sexennium. || ANNO M.D.LX.
Wittenberg : Georg Rhau (Heirs), 1560
[8], 182, [18] fol.; 8°
VD16 M 2703
USTC 692901
Coburg, Landesbibliothek: Cas A 4553(1)

99   SECVNDA PARS || CHRONICI || CARIONIS AB AV=||GVSTO CAESARE VS=||QVE AD CAROLVM || MAGNVM. || EXPOSITA ET AV=||CTA A PHILIPPO ME=||LANTHONE. || Accesßit locupletiß. rerum ac uerborum || memorabilium Index. || VVITEBERGÆ || Cum Gratia & Priuilegio ad Sexennium. || ANNO M.D.LX.
Wittenberg : Georg Rhau (Heirs), 1560
[8], 192, [16] fol.; 8°
VD16 M 2704
USTC 692902

Wolfenbüttel, Herzog August Bibliothek: H: T 243.8° Helmst. (2)

100 CHRONI-||CORVM AB OR-||BE CONDITO PARS SECVN-||da, historiam continens à CHRI-||STI natali Augustiq[ue] impe-||rio, vsq[ue] ad Carolum || Magnum. || PHILIPPO MELANTHONE || AVTORE. || BASILEÆ M.D.LX.
Basel : [Peter Perna ?], 1560
[8] fol., 347 p.; 8°
VD16 M 2701
USTC 622267
Bibliotheca Palatina: F5297
London, British Library: 580.c.7
Wolfenbüttel, Herzog August Bibliothek: H: T 239.8° Helmst. (2)

101 SECVNDA PARS || CHRONICI || CARIONIS AB || AVGVSTO CÆSARE VS-||QVE AD CAROLVM || MAGNVM. || EXPOSITA ET AVCTA || A PHILIPPO MELAN||THONE. || FRANCOFORTI DAVID || Zephelius excudebat.
Frankfurt a.M. : David Zöpfel, 1560
519, [1] p., [1] fol.; 12°
VD16 M 2702
USTC 692896
Wolfenbüttel, Herzog August Bibliothek: H: T 114.12° Helmst.

102 CHRONICON || ABSOLVTISSIMVM || AB ORBE CONDITO || vsque ad Christum || deductum, || In quo non Carionis solùm opus contine-||tur, verùm etiam alia multa eaq[ue] insi-||gnia explicantur, adeò vt iustæ Historiæ || loco occupatis esse poßit. || PHILIPPO MELANTHONE || AVTORE. || 1560.
[Lyon] : [Jean de Tournes], 1560
3–788 p., [3] fol.; 16° [Pts. 1–2]
USTC 124473
Bibliographie des Livres Imprimés à Lyon au siezième siècle: IX, 213
London, British Library: 800.a.28.
London, Warburg Institute Library: NAH 6550.C36 1560

1561

103 IO. CARIONIS || CHRONICORVM || AB ORBE CONDITO AD || hanc vsque nostram ætatem Libri III. || primùm ab ipso authore conscripti: || deinde multis accessionibus docto-||rum virorum aucti: postremò tandem || ad annum D. 1560 & veteribus & || recentibus historiis Pontificu[m] Rom[anorum] || atque Cæsaru[m] Regúmque insignium || Catalogis, & aliis nonnullis mirum in || modum locupletati. || Accessit prætereà huic editioni Index || alphabeticus

amplissimus. || Ad lectorem. || Continent hic prima gestas ab origine mundi || Historias nostrum tempus adusque liber. || Grande sub exiguo comprensum fasce volume[n], || Exiguo ære tibi candide lector eme. || PARISIIS, || Ex officina Puteana, || 1561. || CVM PRIVILEGIO.
Paris : Jacques du Puys, 1561
[8], 684, [188] p.; 16°
USTC 198469
Stuttgart, Württembergische Landesbibliothek: HBF 857

104   PRIMA PARS || CHRONICI || CARIONIS LATINE || EXPOSITI ET AVCTI || multis & veteribus & recentibus Historijs, || in narrationibus rerum Græcarum, || Germanicarum & Eccle-||siasticarum, à || PHILIPPO MELAN-||THONE. || Cui accessit locupletissimus rerum ac uer-||borum memorabilium Index. || Cum Gratia & Priuilegio. || VVITEBERGÆ HÆREDES || Georgij Rhau excudebant, || ANNO M.D.LXI.
Wittenberg : Georg Rhau (Heirs), 1561
[12], 190, [14] fol.; 8°
VD16 M 2706
USTC 686499
Wolfenbüttel, Herzog August Bibliothek: H: T 240.8° Helmst. (1)
Wolfenbüttel, Herzog August Bibliothek: H: T 255.8° Helmst. (1)
Wolfenbüttel, Herzog August Bibliothek: H: T 242.8° Helmst. (1)

105   SECVNDA PARS || CHRONICI || CARIONIS AB AV=||GVSTO CÆSARE VS-||QVE AD CAROLVM || MAGNVM. || EXPOSITA ET AV=||CTA A PHILIPPO ME-||LANTHONE. || Cum locupletißimo rerum ac verborum || memorabilium Indice. || VVITEBERGÆ || Cum Gratia & Priuilegio. || ANNO M.D.LXI.
Wittenberg : Georg Rhau (Heirs), 1561
[8], 192, [16] fol.; 8°
VD16 M 2706
USTC 686499
Wolfenbüttel, Herzog August Bibliothek: H: T 240.8° Helmst. (2)
Wolfenbüttel, Herzog August Bibliothek: H: T 255.8° Helmst. (2)

106   SECVNDA PARS || CHRONICI || CARIONIS AB || AVGVSTO CAESARE VS-||QVE AD CAROLVM || MAGNVM. || EXPOSITA ET AVCTA || A PHILIPPO MELAN-THONE. || FRANCOFORTI DAVID || Zephelius excudebat.
Frankfurt a.M. : David Zöpfel, 1561
[10], 519, [3] p.; 12°
VD16 ZV 16739
USTC 692897

Halle, Universitäts- und Landesbibliothek Sachsen-Anhalt: Pon Vg 4133 a (1/2)
Halle, Universitäts- und Landesbibliothek Sachsen-Anhalt: AB B 7330

1562

107 LES || CHRONIQVES || DE IEAN CARION PHILOSO-||phe. La ou sont co[n]-tenuz les choses me||morables depuis la creation du monde || iusques au regne du Roy François, deu||xiesme de ce nom, à present regnant. || Traduict en François, par Maistre || Iean le Blond. || A PARIS. || Par Iaques Keruer, de-mourant à la || Rue Sainct Iacques, à l'en-||seigne de la Licorne. || 1562.
Paris : Jacques Kerver, 1562
[32], 374, [29] fol.; 16°
USTC 845
French Vernacular Books: 8915
Angers, Bibliothèque municipale: SJ 1027

108 LES || CRONIQVES || DE IEAN CARION PHILOSO-||phe. La ou sont co[n]-tenuz les choses me-||morables depuis la creation du mo[n]de, || iusques au regne du roy Charles, neuf-||iesme de ce nom, à present regnant. || Traduict en François par Maistre || Iehan le Blond. || A PARIS. || Chez Gabriel Buon, libraire demou-||rant au cloz Bruneau, à l'ensei-||gne Sainct Claude. || 1562.
Paris : Gabriel Buon, 1562
[32], 374, [2] fol.; 16°
USTC 66981
French Vernacular Books: 8916
San Marino, Huntington Library: Rare Books 402048

109 PRIMA PARS || CHRONICI || CARIONIS LATINE || EXPOSITI ET AVCTI || mul-tis & veteribus & recentibus Historijs, || in narrationibus rerum Græcarum, || Germanicarum & Ecclesi-||asticarum, à || PHILIPPO MELAN-||THONE. || Cui accessit locupletissimus rerum ac uer-||borum memorabilium Index. || Cum Gratia & Priuilegio. || VVITEBERGÆ HÆREDES || Georgij Rhauu excudebant, || ANNO M.D.LXII.
Wittenberg : Georg Rhau (Heirs), 1562
[12], 190, [14] fol.; 8°
VD16 M 2707
USTC 686512
Bibliotheca Palatina: F2775/F2777
Wolfenbüttel, Herzog August Bibliothek: H: T 243.8° Helmst. (1)

110   Chronica || Carionis gantz new || Latine geschrieben / von dem || Ehrwirdigen Herrn || PHILIPPO MELANTHONE. || Verdeudscht durch M. || Eusebium Menium. || Aller Oberkeit inn sonderheit / auch allen || Stenden vnd Vnterthanen notwendig vnd nützlich zu lesen / || Dieweil dis Buch anleitung gibt zu Historien || Göttlicher Schrifft / vnd allen andern. || Mitt einer Vorrede D. Georgii Maioris. || CVM GRATIA ET PRIVILEGIO. || Witteberg / 1562.
Wittenberg : Georg Rhau (Heirs), 1562
[24], 170 fol.; 8°
Bibliotheca Palatina: E394/E395

111.1   SECVNDA PARS || CHRONICI || CARIONIS AB AV=||GVSTO CÆSARE VS-||QVE AD CAROLVM || MAGNVM. || EXPOSITA ET AV=||CTA A PHILIPPO ME-||LANTHONE. || Cum locupletißimo rerum ac verborum || memorabilium Indice. || VVITEBERGÆ || Cum Gratia & Privilegio. || ANNO M.D.LXII.
Wittenberg : Georg Rhau (Heirs), 1562
[8] fol., [1] p., 2 [= 192], [16] fol.; 8°
Bibliotheca Palatina: F2777/F2779

111.2   SECVNDA PARS || CHRONICI || CARIONIS AB AV=||GVSTO CÆSARE VS-||QVE AD CAROLVM || MAGNVM. || EXPOSITA ET AV=||CTA A PHILIPPO ME-||LANTHONE. || Cum locupletißimo rerum ac verborum || memorabilium Indice. || VVITEBERGÆ || Cum Gratia & Privilegio. || ANNO M.D.LXII.
Wittenberg : Georg Rhau (Heirs), 1562
[8], 192, [16] fol.; 8°
VD16 ZV 27394
USTC 692899
Urbana, University of Illinois Library: X 909 C19CLM1562
Augsburg, Staats- und Stadtbibliothek: Gs 1533-2
Rostock, Universitätsbibliothek: Rb-131.a(1)

112.1   Der Ander Teil || der || Chronica Cario=||nis / Vom Keiser Augusto bis || auff Carolum Magnum. || Geschrieben vnd vermehret vom || Herrn PHILIPPO ME-||LANTHONE. || Verdeudschet aus dem Latein durch || M. Eusebium Menium. || CVM GRATIA ET PRIVILEGIO. || Gedruckt zu Witteberg / durch Georgen || Rhawen Erben / 1562.
Wittenberg : Georg Rhau (Heirs), 1562
[8], 270 [= 272] fol.; 4°
VD16 M 2724
USTC 632757
Bibliotheca Palatina: E395/E396
Berlin, Staatsbibliothek zu Berlin Preußischer Kulturbesitz: Ebd 85-11B

[Dedication Copy of Menius to Archbishop Sigismund]
Wolfenbüttel, Herzog August Bibliothek: S: Alv.: Li 192 (2)

112.2[11] Der Ander Teil || der || Chronica Cario=||nis / Vom Keiser Augusto bis || auff Carolum Magnum. || Geschrieben vnd vermehret vom || Herrn PHILIPPO ME-||LANTHONE. || Verdeudschet aus dem Latein durch || M. Eusebium Menium. || CVM GRATIA ET PRIVILEGIO. || Gedruckt zu Witteberg / durch Georgen || Rhawen Erben / 1562.
Wittenberg : Georg Rhau (Heirs), 1562
[8], 271 [= 272] fol.; 4°
Augsburg, Staats- und Stadtbibliothek: 4 Gs 348-2
Wolfenbüttel, Herzog August Bibliothek: A: 127.30 Hist. (2)

113[12] TERTIA PARS || CHRONICI || CARIONIS, A CA=||ROLO MAGNO, VBI PHI=||lippus Melanthon desijt, usq[ue] ad || FRIDERICVM || Secundum. || EXPOSITA ET AV=||CTA A CASPARO || PEVCERO. || Accessit locupletiss. rerum ac uer=||borum memorabilium || Index. || VVITEBERGAE || EXCVDEBAT PETRVS || SEITZ. || ANNO M.D.LXII.
Wittenberg : Peter Seitz d.J., 1562
[8], 276, [35] fol.; 8°
VD16 P 1950
USTC 696135
Bibliotheca Palatina: F2779/F2782
Wolfenbüttel, Herzog August Bibliothek: S: Alv.: U 215 [Tabella lost]

1563

114 IO. CARIONIS || CHRONICORVM || AB ORBE CONDITO AD || hanc vsque nostram ætatem Libri III. || primùm ab ipso authore conscripti: || deinde multis accessionibus docto-||rum virorum aucti: postremò tandem || ad annum D. 1560 & veteribus & || recentibus historiis Pontificu[m] Rom[anorum] || atque Cæsaru[m] Regúmque insignium || Catalogis, & aliis nonnulis mirum in || modum locupletati. || Accessit præstereà huic editioni Index || alphabeticus

---

11 The cited Wolfenbüttel copy also includes, inserted after the title page, the prefaces of Melanchthon and Menius removed from a copy of VD16 M 2727.

12 An autograph dedication by Peucer to Archbishop Sigismund, possibly removed from a copy of this edition, survives as New York, Pierpont Morgan Library: 129486. In this edition, Peucer included, for the first time, his tabella on reading history: *Tabella Ostendens Qvo Ordine Legenda Et Cognoscenda Sit Series Historiarvm Mvndi. Dedicata Scholasticis Academiæ Witebergensis* (at end, opposite sig. [q 8 v]).

amplissimus. || Ad Lectorem. || Continent hic prima gestas ab origine mundi || Historias nostrum tempus adusque liber. || Grande sub exiguo comprensum fasce volume[n], || Exiguo ære tibi candide lector eme. || PARISIIS, || Ex officina Puteana, || 1563. || CVM PRIVILEGIO.
Paris : Jacques du Puys, 1563
[8], 684, [188] p.; 16°
USTC 153391
Wolfenbüttel, Herzog August Bibliothek: H: T 115.12° Helmst.

115   *Les Croniqves De Iean Carion Philosophe. La ou sont co[n]tenuz les choses memorables depuis la creation du mo[n]de, iusques au regne du roy Charles, neufiesme de ce nom, à present regnant. Traduict en François par Maistre Iehan le Blond ... 1563.*
Paris : Jean Ruelle, 1563
[32], 374, [2] fol.; 16°
Crissay-Sur-Manse, Librairie Ancienne J.-Marc Dechaud [Bookseller]: 5523

[116]   *Prima Pars Chronici Carionis Latine...*
Wittenberg : [Georg Rhau (Heirs) ?], 1563
?? fol.; 8°
München, Bayerische Staatsbibliothek: Chron. 39 [Lost]

117[13]   PRIMA PARS || CHRONI-||CI ABSOLVTISSI||MI AB ORBE CODDITO || vsque ad Christum deducti, in quo non || Carionis solùm opus continetur, verùm-||etiam alia multa, eaq[ue] insignia expli-||cantur, adeò vt iustæ Histo-||riæ loco occupatis es-||se possit. || Philippo Melanchthone || autore. || BASILEÆ || M.D.LXIII.
Basel : [Peter Perna], 1563
[8] fol., 346 p.; 8°
[VD16 M 2708 ?]
VD16 ZV 10756
[USTC 622478 ?]
USTC 686509
Augsburg, Staats- und Stadtbibliothek: Gs 1532 -1/2
Jena, Thüringer Universitäts- und Landesbibliothek: 8 Hist.un.II,10
[München, Bayerische Staatsbibliothek: Chron. 40 [Lost] ?]

118   Chronica || Carionis gantz new || Latine geschrieben / von dem || Ehrwirdigen Herrn || PHILIPPO MELANTHONE. || Verdeudscht durch M. || Eusebium Menium. || Aller Oberkeit inn sonderheit / auch allen || Stenden vnd Vnterthanen notwendig vnd nützlich zu lesen / || Dieweil dis Buch anleitung gibt

---

13   The record for VD16 M 2708 is based on a lost copy of *Carion's Chronicle* in Munich. VD16 gave a new set of entries to this Basel edition after copies were found in other libraries.

zu Historien || Göttlicher Schrifft / vnd allen andern. || Mitt einer Vorrede D. Georgij Maioris. || CVM GRATIA ET PRIVILEGIO. || Witteberg / 1563.
Wittenberg : Georg Rhau (Heirs), 1563
[24], 170 [= 172] fol.; 4°
VD16 M 2725
USTC 622278
Wrocław, Biblioteka Uniwersytecka: 459.323 [Title page incomplete]
Wolfenbüttel, Herzog August Bibliothek: A: 149.2 Hist. (1)

119 SECVNDA PARS || CHRONICI || CARIONIS AB AV=||GVSTO CÆSARE VS-||QVE AD CAROLVM || MAGNVM. || EXPOSITA ET AV=||CTA A PHILIPPO ME-||LANTHONE. || Cum locupletißimo rerum ac verborum || memorabilium Indice. || VVITEBERGÆ || Cum Gratia & Priuilegio. || ANNO M.D.LXIII.
Wittenberg : Georg Rhau (Heirs), 1563
[8], 192, [16] fol.; 8°
VD16 ZV 10757
USTC 692900
Halle, Universitäts- und Landesbibliothek Sachsen-Anhalt: AB B 6575 (2/3)
Halle, Universitäts- und Landesbibliothek Sachsen-Anhalt: Pon Vg 4131 b (2)
Köln, Universitäts- und Stadtbibliothek: WBI30+A

120 TERTIA PARS || CHRONICI || CARIONIS, A CAROLO || MAGNO, VBI PHILIP-PVS || Melanthon desijt, vsq[ue] ad || FRIDERICVM || Secundum. || EXPOSITA ET AV=||CTA A CASPARO || PEVCERO. || Acceßit locupletiß. rerum ac verborum me=||morabilium Index. || VVITEBERGÆ EXCV=||DEBANT HÆREDES GE-||ORGII RHAVV. || ANNO M.D.LXIII.
Wittenberg : Georg Rhau (Heirs), 1563
[8], 176 [= 276], [35] fol.; 8°
VD16 P 1951
USTC 696138
Urbana, University of Illinois Library: 909 C19CLM1562
Wolfenbüttel, Herzog August Bibliothek: H: T 241.8° Helmst.

121.1 TERTIA PARS || CHRONI-||CI CARIONIS, A || CAROLO MAGNO, VBI || Philippus Melanthon desijt, || vsque ad Fridericum || Secundum. || Exposita & aucta à Caspa-||ro Peucero. || Acceßit locupletiß. rerum ac uerborum || memorabilium INDEX. || BASILEAE || M.D.LXIII.
Basel : [Peter Perna], 1563
[8] fol., 547 [= 475] p., [29] fol.; 8°
[VD16 M 2708 ?]
[VD16 ZV 28332 ?]
[USTC 622478 ?]

Jena, Thüringer Universitäts- und Landesbibliothek: 8 Hist.un.11,10
[München, Bayerische Staatsbibliothek: Chron. 40 [Lost] ?]

121.2 TERTIA PARS || CHRONI-||CI CARIONIS, A || CAROLO MAGNO, VBI || Philippus Melanthon desijt, || vsque ad Fridericum || Secundum. || Exposita & aucta à Caspa-||ro Peucero. || Acceßit locupletiß. rerum ac uerborum || memorabilium INDEX. || BASILEAE || M.D.LXIII.
Basel : [Peter Perna], 1563
[8] fol., 475 p., [29] fol.; 8°
[VD16 ZV 28332]
Augsburg, Staats- und Stadtbibliothek: Gs 1532 -3

1564

122 Chronica || Johannis Carionis / Jetzt || von newem vbersehen / vnd an vilen or=||ten / da bißher durch mannicherley Truck / et=||wa mängel eingeschlichen / nach notturfft Corrigiert. || Darzu auch || Jm tritten Buch / souil die zeit nach Christi Ge=||burt belangt / mit vilen namhafften Historien / so bei eyner || kleynern Schriffte zuunterscheyden / erklärt || vnd gemehrt. || Deßgleichen || Eyne Verzeychniß allerley gedenckwirdiger Sachen vnd || Händel / so sich in etlichen vnd vierzig jaren bißher / vnder Key=||ser Carls des Füfften / vnd seines bruders Keyser Ferdinan=||des Regierungen / in vnd ausserhalb des heyligen Römi=||schen Reichs Teutscher Nation zugetragen || vnd verlauffen / jetz erstlich in || Truck gegeben. || Durch || Michaelem Beuther von Carlstatt / || der Rechten Doctorn. || M.D.LXIIII.
Frankfurt a.M. : David Zöpfel, 1564 [1563]
[12], 335, [1] fol.; 8°
[Colophon: Getruckt zu Franck=||furt am Mayn / durch || David Zöpffeln. || M.D.LXIII.]
VD16 ZV 2949
USTC 622335
Bibliotheca Palatina: F1444/F1447
Halle, Universitäts- und Landesbibliothek Sachsen-Anhalt: Pon Vg 4110
Wolfenbüttel, Herzog August Bibliothek: H: T 232.8° Helmst. [Incomplete]

123[14] IO. CARIONIS || CHRONICORVM || AB ORBE CONDITO AD || hanc usq[ue] nostram ætatem || Libri III. || Primùm ab ipso authore conscripti, || deinde multis

---

14 See Moller, *Dispvtationem*, 14; and especially the earlier remark by Pantaleon: "Illi primò 1538 Vuitebergæ Germanicè editi, hodie Latinè & Germanicè ab omnibus historiaru[m]

accessionibus docto-||rum uirorum aucti: postremò tande[m] || ad annum D. 1564. & ueteribus & || rece[n]tibus historijs Po[n]tificum Rom[anorum] || atq[ue] Cæsarum, Regumq[ue] insignium || Catalogis, & alijs nonnullis mi-||rum in modum locu-||pletati. || Accessit præterea huic editioni In-||dex alphabeticus amplissimus. || BASILEAE. || 1564.
Basel : [Johannes Oporinus], 1564
688 p., [96] fol.; 16°
VD16 ZV 2950
USTC 667018
Chicago, Newberry Library: Case F 09 .146 [Incomplete]
Köln, Erzbischöfliche Diözesan- und Dombibliothek: HP 197
Wolfenbüttel, Herzog August Bibliothek: H: T 116.12° Helmst. [Incomplete]

124   PRIMA PARS || CHRONICI || CARIONIS, LATINE || EXPOSITI ET AVCTI || multis & veteribus & recentibus Historijs, || in narrationibus rerum Græcarum, || Germanicarum & Ecclesia-||sticarum; à || PHILIPPO MELAN-||THONE. || Cui accessit locupletissimus rerum ac uer-||borum memorabilium Index. || Cum Gratia & Priuilegio. || VVITEBERGÆ HÆREDES || Georgij Rhauu excudebant. || ANNO M.D.LXIIII.
Wittenberg : Georg Rhau (Heirs), 1564
[12], 190, [14] fol.; 8°
VD16 ZV 10762
USTC 686513
Köln, Universitäts- und Stadtbibliothek: WB130+A [Title page lost]
Halle, Universitäts- und Landesbibliothek Sachsen-Anhalt: Pon Vg 4131 c (1)

studiosis magno applausu circumferuntur. Itaq[ue] ipse eos tandem per annos 20 continuaui, atq[ue] ut Basileæ 1564 per D. Oporinum ederentur, curaui." Heinrich Pantaleon, *Prosopographiae Herovm Atqve Illvstrivm Virorvm Totivs Germaniæ, Pars Tertia, Eaqve Primaria* (Basel: Nikolaus Brylinger (Heirs), 1566), 180. VD16 P 230. See also the contemporary catalog of Oporinus imprints: "Carionis Chronicon, cum Appendice usque ad annum LXVI. 16" ("LXVI" is a printer's error for LXIV [1564]). Johannes Oporinus, *Librorum per Ioannem Oporinvm partim excusorum hactenus, partim in eiusdem officina uenalium, Index: Singulis ad ordinem alphabeticum redactis, & adiecta impressionis forma. Basileae. 1567.* (Basel: Oporinus, 1567), 14. VD16 ZV 19007. See also the note in the catalog of Oporinus's works compiled at his death: "Carionis Chronicon, cum Appe[n]dice vsq[ue] ad annu[m] LXVI. 16." Andreas Jociscus, *Oratio De Ortv, Vita Et Obitv Ioannis Oporini Basiliensis, Typographicoru[m] Germaniæ Principis, recitata in Argentinensi Academia ab Ioanne Henrico Hainzelio Augustano. Avthore Andrea Iocisco Silesio, Ethicorum in eadem Academia professore. Adiunximus librorum per Ioannem Oporinum excusorum Catalogum.* (Strasbourg: Theodosius Rihelius, 1569), sig. Diij r. VD16 J 305. Again "LXVI" is a printer's error for LXIV [1564].

Halle, Universitäts- und Landesbibliothek Sachsen-Anhalt: AB B 6575
München, Monumenta Germaniae Historica Bibliothek: Bm 42104 Rara

125.1 PRIMA PARS || CHRONICI || CARIONIS LATINE || EXPOSITI ET AVCTI || multis & veteribus & recen-||tibus Historiis, in narra-||tionibus rerum Græ-||carum, Germanica-||rum & Ecclesia-||sticarum, à || PHILIPPO ME-||LANTHONE. || Cui acceßit locupletiß. rerum ac verbo-||rum memorabilium Index. || ANNO M.D.LXIIII.
[Lyon] : [Jean Frellon ?], 1564
203 fol., [43] p.; 8°
USTC 139347
Cambridge, University Library: M*.13.22-(G)
Madison, Drew University Library: McClintock 133 vol. 1
New Haven, Yale University Beinecke Library: Bf8 83i

125.2 PRIMA PARS || CHRONICI || CARIONIS LATINE || EXPOSITI ET AVCTI || multis & veteribus & recen-||tibus Historiis, in narra-||tionibus rerum Græ-||carum, Germanica-||rum & Ecclesia-||sticarum, à || PHILIPPO ME-||LANTHONE. || Cui acceßit locupletiß. rerum ac verbo-||rum memorabilium Index. || LVG-DVNI. || ANNO M.D.LXIIII.
Lyon : [Jean Frellon ?], 1564
203 fol., [43] p.; 8°
Wolfenbüttel, Herzog August Bibliothek: H: T 117.12° Helmst.

126 SECVNDA || CHRONI-||CORVM PARS || AB ORBE CONDITO HI-||storiam continens à CHRI-||STI natali Augustiq[ue] impe-||rio, vsq[ue] ad Carolum || Magnum. || PHILIPPO MELANTHONE || AVTORE. || BASILEAE. || M.D.LXIIII.
Basel : [Peter Perna], 1564
[8] fol., 347 p.; 8°
[VD16 M 2708 ?]
VD16 ZV 10763
USTC 692871
Jena, Thüringer Universitäts- und Landesbibliothek: 8 Hist.un.II,10
[München, Bayerische Staatsbibliothek: Chron. 40 [Lost] ?]

127.1 SECVNDA PARS. || CHRONICI || CARIONIS AB AV-||GVSTO CAESARE || vsque ad Carolum || magnum. || EXPOSITA ET AV-||CTA A PHILIPPO || Melanthone. || Cum locupletiß. rerum ac verborum || memorabilium Indice. || ANNO M.D.LXIIII.
[Lyon] : [Jean Frellon ?], 1564
209 fol., [44] p.; 8°
Cambridge, University Library: M*.13.22-(G)
Madison, Drew University Library: McClintock 133 vol. 2

127.2   SECVNDA PARS. || CHRONICI || CARIONIS AB AV-||GVSTO CAESARE || vsque ad Carolum || magnum. || EXPOSITA ET AV-||CTA A PHILIPPO || Melanthone. || Cum locupletiß. rerum ac verborum || memorabilium Indice. || LVGDVNI. || ANNO M.D.LXIIII.
Lyon : [Jean Frellon ?], 1564
209 fol., [44] p.; 8°
New Haven, Yale University Beinecke Library: Bf8 83i
Wolfenbüttel, Herzog August Bibliothek: H: T 117.12° Helmst. (2)

128   TERTIA PARS || CHRONICI || CARIONIS, A CAROLO || MAGNO, VBI PHILIPPVS || Melanthon desiit, vsque || ad FRIDERICVM || Secundum. || EXPOSITA ET AVCTA || A CASPARO PEVCERO. || Acceßit locupletiß. rerum ac verborum || memorabilium Index. || Anno M.D.LXIIII.
[Lyon] : [Jean Frellon ?], 1564
[8], 283, [37] fol.; 8°
USTC 158989
Cambridge, University Library: M*.13.23-(G)
New Haven, Yale University Beinecke Library: Bf8 83i
Montpellier, Médiathèque centrale d'agglomération Emile Zola: 44081 RES
Karlsruhe, Badische Landesbibliothek: 72 A 2184,R,3

129   TERTIA PARS || CHRONICI || CARIONIS, A CA-||rolo Magno, vbi Philippus || Melanthon desijt, vsque || ad Fridericum Se-||cundum. || Exposita & aucta à Casparo Peucero. || Acceßit locupletiß. rerum ac verborum || memorabilium Index. || LVGDVNI, || Apud Ioan. Tornæsium, & Gu-||lielmum Gazeium. || 1564.
Lyon : Jean de Tournes & Guillaume Gazeau, 1564
554 p., [35] fol.; 8°
USTC 124493
Cartier, De Tournes: 504
London, Warburg Institute Library: NAH 6550.C36 1560
Stuttgart, Württembergische Landesbibliothek: HBF 8176

130   Der Drit=||te Teil der Chronica || Carionis / || Von Keiser CARL dem grossen an / da || es der Herr Philippus Melanthon wenden || lassen / bis auff FRIDRICHEN den andern || Mit vleis erzelet vnd vermehret durch den Herrn || D. Casparum Peucerum. || Verdeudscht durch Eusebium || Menium M. || Wittemberg. 1564.
Wittenberg : Georg Rhau (Heirs), 1564
[14], 348 fol.; 4°
VD16 P 1966
USTC 633034

Bibliotheca Palatina: E1282/E1283
Wrocław, Biblioteka Uniwersytecka: 459.323
Wolfenbüttel, Herzog August Bibliothek: M: Gb 58
Wolfenbüttel, Herzog August Bibliothek: A: 105.18 Hist. (1)
Wolfenbüttel, Herzog August Bibliothek: S: Alv.: Li 193

1565

131   Der Drit=||te Teil der Chronica || Carionis / || Von Keiser CARL dem grossen an / da || es der Herr Philippus Melanthon wenden las=||sen / bis auff FRID-RICHEN den andern. || Mit vleis erzelet vnd vermehret durch den Herrn || D. Casparum Peucerum. || Verdeudscht durch Eusebium || Menium M. || Wittemberg. 1565.
Wittenberg : Georg Rhau (Heirs), 1565
[14], 271 [= 272] fol.; 4°
VD16 P 1967
USTC 633035
Wolfenbüttel, Herzog August Bibliothek: A: 149.2 Hist. (2)

132   LIBER QVINTVS || CHRONI=||CI CARIONIS || A FRIDERICO || secundo vsq[ue] ad Carolum || Quintum. || EXPOSITVS ET || AVCTVS à CASPA-||RO PEVCERO. || PERTINET HIC LI-||ber ad partem tertiam Chronici. || ACCESSIT LOCVPLE-||tißimus rerum & verborum me-||morabilium index. || VVITEBERGÆ || ANNO CHRISTI || 1565.
Wittenberg : [Georg Rhau (Heirs)], 1565
[16], 335, [64] fol.; 8°
VD16 P 1952
USTC 672866
Bibliotheca Palatina: F2782/F2786
Ithaca, Cornell University Library: Rare D18 C27 1558 v. 3
Wolfenbüttel, Herzog August Bibliothek: S: Alv.: U 216

1566

133   PRIMA PARS || CHRONICI || CARIONIS LATINE || EXPOSITI ET AVCTI MVL-TIS || & ueteribus & recentibus Historijs, narrationi-||bus rerum Græcarum, Germanicarum || & Ecclesiasticarum, à || PHILIPPO MELAN=||THONE. || Cui

accessit locupletissimus rerum ac uer-||borum memorabilium Index. || Cum Gratia & Priuilegio. || VVITEBERGÆ || ANNO 1566.
Wittenberg : [Johannes Crato = Johann Krafft d.Ä.], 1566
[12], 190, [14] fol.; 8°
VD16 M 2710
USTC 686514
Chicago, Newberry Library: Case F 09 .147
Halle, Universitäts- und Landesbibliothek Sachsen-Anhalt: Pon Vg 4138 (1/2)
Wolfenbüttel, Herzog August Bibliothek: H: T 245.8° Helmst. [Title page lost]

134   SECVNDA PARS || CHRONICI || CARIONIS AB AV=||GVSTO CÆSARE || vsq[ue] ad Carolum || Magnum. || EXPOSITA ET AV=||CTA A PHILIPPO || Melanthone. || Cum locupletißimo rerum ac verborum || memorabilium Indice. || VVITEBERGÆ || Cum Gratia & Priuilegio. || ANNO M.D.LXVI.
Wittenberg : [Georg Rhau (Heirs)], 1566
[8], 192, [16] fol.; 8°
VD16 M 2709
USTC 692898
Chicago, Newberry Library: Case F 09 .147
Wolfenbüttel, Herzog August Bibliothek: M: Gb 51 (2)

135   SECVNDA PARS || CHRONICI || CARIONIS AB AV=||GVSTO CÆSARE VSQVE AD || CAROLVM MAGNVM. || Exposita & aucta à || PHILIP. MELANTH. || Cum locupletissimo rerum ac verborum || memorabilium Indice. || Cum Gratia & Priuilegio Cæsareæ Maiesta-||tis & Ducis Saxoniæ Electoris &c. || VITEBERGAE || ANNO M.D.LXVI.
Wittenberg : [Johannes Crato = Johann Krafft d.Ä.], 1566
[7] fol., 370 p., [16] fol.; 8°
VD16 M 2711
USTC 692903
Wolfenbüttel, Herzog August Bibliothek: H: T 246.8° Helmst.

136[15]   Der Ander Teil || der || Chronica Cario=||nis / Vom Keiser Augusto bis || auff Carolum Magnum. || Geschrieben vnd vermehret vom || Herrn PHILIPPO ME=||LANTHONE. || Verdeudschet aus dem Latein durch || M. Eusebium Menium. || CVM GRATIA ET PRIVILEGIO. || Gedruckt zu Witteberg / || 1566.
Wittenberg : Georg Rhau (Heirs), 1566 [1565]
[8], 271 [= 272] fol.; 4°

---

15   The Wolfenbuettel copy (A: 127.30 Hist. (2a)) contains only the prefaces of Melanchthon and Menius, title page – sig. [ ](iiij) v., bound into A: 127.30 Hist. (2) after its own title page.

[Colophon: Gedruckt zu Wittemberg / durch Georgen Rhawen Erben. 1565]
[VD16 M 2727]
USTC 632756
Wrocław, Biblioteka Uniwersytecka: 459.323
[Wolfenbüttel, Herzog August Bibliothek: A: 127.30 Hist. (2a) [Incomplete]]

137   TERTIA PARS || CHRONICI || CARIONIS, A CAROLO || MAGNO, VBI PHILIP-PVS || MELANCHTHON desijt, usq[ue] ad || FRIDERICVM || Secundum: || EX-POSITA ET AV=||CTA A CASPARO || PEVCERO. || Acceßit locupletiß. rerum ac uerborum || memorabilium Index. || WITEBERGÆ EXCV=||DEBAT LAVRENTIVS || SCHVVENCK. || ANNO CHRISTI. || M.D.LXVI.
Wittenberg : Lorenz Schwenck, 1566
[8], 276, [35] fol.; 8°
VD16 P 1953
USTC 696137
Wolfenbüttel, Herzog August Bibliothek: H: T 247.8° Helmst.
Wolfenbüttel, Herzog August Bibliothek: A: 424.10 Hist.

138   LIBER QVINTVS || CHRONI=||CI CARIONIS || A FRIDERICO SE-||cundo vsque ad Carolum || Quintum. || EXPOSITVS ET AV-||CTVS A CASPARO || PEVCERO. || PERTINET HIC LI-||ber ad partem tertiam Chronici. || ACCESSIT LOCV-PLETIS-||simus rerum & verborum memora-||bilium index. || Cum gratia & priuilegio Cæsareo, & || Ducis Saxoniæ, Electoris. || VVITEBERGÆ || IOHAN. SCHWERTELIVS || EXCVDEBAT. || ANNO M.D.LXVI.
Wittenberg : Johann Schwertel, 1566
[16], 335, [63] fol.; 8°
VD16 P 1954
USTC 672867
Bibliotheca Palatina: I255/I258
Wolfenbüttel, Herzog August Bibliothek: H: Yv 1166c.8° Helmst.
Wolfenbüttel, Herzog August Bibliothek: H: T 248.8° Helmst.

139   LIBER QVINTVS || CHRONI=||CI CARIONIS || À FRIDERICO SECVN-||do usq[ue] ad Carolum || Quintum. || EXPOSITVS ET AVCTVS || À CASPARO PEV-CERO. || PERTINENT HIC LIBER || ad partem tertiam Chronici. || ACCESSIT IN HAC POSTREMA || æditione locupletissimus rerum & || verborum memorabi-||lium index. || FRANCOFVRTI ad Moenum, per Petrum || Fabricium, impensis Sigismundi Feyrabend || & Simonis Huteri. || 1566.
Frankfurt a.M. : Sigmund Feyerabend & Simon Hüter [by Peter Schmidt], 1566
[14], 246, [51] fol.; 8°
VD16 ZV 12368

140 USTC 672870
Mannheim, Universitätsbibliothek: Sch 045/011b
LIBER QVINTVS || CHRONICI || CARIONIS, A FRIDERI-||CO SECVNDO VSQVE || ad Carolum Quintum. || EXPOSITVS ET AVCTVS || A CASPARO PEVCERO. || Pertinet hic liber ad partem tertiam Chronici. || Cum indice copiosissimo. || ANNO M.D.LXVI.
[Lyon] : [Jean Frellon], 1566
[16] fol., 654 p., [56] fol.; 8°
VD16 ZV 12369
USTC 139733
USTC 672872
Zürich, Zentralbibliothek: Ochsn.1202-4
Augsburg, Staats- und Stadtbibliothek: S 263-5
Karlsruhe, Badische Landesbibliothek: 72 A 2184,R,4

141 Neuwe vollkommene Chronica || Philippi Melanthonis. || Zeytbuch Vnd || Warhafftige || Beschreibung / Was von anfang || der Welt biß auff diß gegenwertige Jar / nicht allein von || den Juden vnd Christen / sonder auch von allen Heiden / Türcken / vnd an=||dern Völckern so viel deren je gewesen / beide in Geistlichen vnd Weltlichen || sachen / rath vnd anschlägen / in fried vnd kriegßzeiten in der gantzen Welt / so viel von den Men=||schen hat erfaren vnd erkündiget mögen werden / sich zugetragen / fürgenommen / verhandelt / vnd || außgefürt ist worden / auß Biblischen vnd Heidnischen Historien / Darinnen auch / wie solche || Historien der zeit nach eigentlich zu vergleichen angezeigt vnd erkleret wirdt / || Vorhin in gleicher gestalt vnd Form nie außgangen. || Anfenglichs vnterm Namen Johan Carionis auffs kürtzest verfast / Nach=||mals durch Herrn Philippum Melanthonem vnd D. Casparum Peucerum auffs neuwe vberse=||hen / gemehrt / vnd jetzt auß dem Latein verdeutscht durch M. Eusebium Menium : Sampt || einem summarischen gründtlichen anhang dieses jetzt lauffende Tausent / || fünffhundert / sechs vnd sechtzigst Jar. || Mit einem ordentlichen neuwen Register. || Getruckt zu Franckfurt am Meyn / Anno M.D.LXVI.
Frankfurt a.M. : Sigmund Feyerabend & Simon Hüter [by Martin Lechler], 1566
[12], CX, [4], CXIIII, [12], CLXXXVIII, [8] fol.; 2°
[Colophon: Gedruckt zu Franckfurt am || Meyn / durch Martin Lechler in verle=||gung Sigmund Feirabends vnd || Simon Hüters. || M.D.LXVI.]
VD16 M 2726
VD16 P 1968
USTC 677049
Bibliotheca Palatina: C1530/C1538

London, British Library: 9005.g.12.
Stuttgart, Württembergische Landesbibliothek: Allg.G.fol.30
Wolfenbüttel, Herzog August Bibliothek: H: T 365.2° Helmst.

1567

142.1 LES || CHRONIQVES || DE IEAN CARION, PHILOSO-||phe. La ou sont co[n]tenuz les choses me-||morables depuis la creation du monde || iusques au regne du roy François, deu-||xiesme de ce nom, à present regnant. || Traduict en François, par maistre || Iean le Blond. || A PARIS. || Pour Iacques Keruer libraire, à la rue S. || Iacques, à l'enseigne de la Licorne. || 1567.
Paris : Jacques Kerver, 1567
[32], 377 [=374], [2] fol.; 16°
USTC 27794
French Vernacular Books: 8917
Aix-en-Provence, Bibliothèque Méjanes: D. 394

[142.2]   *Les Croniques de Iean Carion...*
Paris : Jean Ruelle, 1567
[32], 375 [=374?], [2] fol.; 16°
Brunet: vol. 1, pt. 2, col. 1579.

143 PRIMA PARS || CHRONICI || CARIONIS LATI=||NE EXPOSITI ET AVCTI || multis & veteribus & recentibus Histo-||rijs, in narrationibus rerum Græca-||rum, Germanicarum et Ec-||clesiasticarum, || A || PHILIPPO MELAN-||THONE, || Cui acceßit locupletißimus rerum ac verbo-||rum memorabilium Index. || Cum Gratia & Priuilegio Cæsareę Maiest. || & Electoris Saxoniæ. || VVITEBERGÆ 1567.
Wittenberg : [Johannes Crato = Johann Krafft d.Ä.], 1567
[12], 190, [14] fol.; 8°
VD16 M 2712
USTC 686510
Rostock, Universitätsbibliothek: Rb-133(1)
Wolfenbüttel, Herzog August Bibliothek: H: T 249.8° Helmst. (1)

144[16] LIBER QVINTVS || CHRONICI || CARIONIS, A FRIDERI-||CO SECVNDO VSQVE || ad Carolum Quintum. || EXPOSITVS ET AVCTVS || A CASPARO PEVCERO. ||

---

16   *Chronicon auct. a Ph. Melanchthon et Peucer.* 3 vols? (Lugdunum: ??, 1567). München, Bayerische Staatsbibliothek: Chron. 41 [Lost].

Pertinet hic liber ad partem || tertiam Chronici. || Cum indice copiosissimo. || ANNO M.D.LXVII.
[Lyon] : [Jean Frellon ?], 1567
[16] fol., 654 p., [56] fol.; 8°
Prague, Strahov Monastery Library [Strahovská knihovna]: HA IV 61
Hennef-Geistingen, Philosophisch Theologische Hochschule: 515+4 [Dispersed]

1568

145   LES || CHRONIQVES || DE IEAN CARION, PHILOSO-||phe. La ou sont co[n]tenuz les choses me-||morables depuis la creation du monde || iusques au regne du roy François, deu-||xiesme de ce nom, à present regnant. || Traduict en François, par maistre || Iean le Blond. || A PARIS, || Pour Hierosme de Marnef, & Guillau-||me Cauellat, au mont S. Hilaire, à || l'enseigne du Pelican. || 1568
Paris : Hiérosme de Marnef & Guillaume Cavellat, 1568
[32], 374, [2] fol.; 16°
USTC 66274
French Vernacular Books: 8918
Prague, Strahov Monastery Library [Strahovská knihovna]: AC XI 76

146   LIBER QVINTVS || CHRONI=||CI CARIONIS || À FRIDERICO SE-||CVNDO VSQVE AD || Carolum Quin-||tum: || EXPOSITVS ET AV-||CTVS A CASPARO || Peucero. || PERTINET HIC LIBER || ad partem tertiam Chronici. || ACCESSIT LOCVPLETIS-||simus rerum & verborum me-||morabilium INDEX. || BASILEAE, || PER PETRVM PERNAM. || Anno M.D.LXVIII.
Basel : Peter Perna, 1568
[11] fol., 554 p., [38] fol.; 8°
VD16 ZV 12370
USTC 672871
Jena, Thüringer Universitäts- und Landesbibliothek: 8 Hist.un.II,10

1569

147   TERTIA PARS || CHRONICI || CARIONIS, A CARO=||LO MAGNO, VBI PHILIPPVS || MELANTHON desijt, vsq[que] ad || FRIDERICVM || Secundum: || EXPOSITA ET AV=||CTA À CASPARO || PEVCERO. || Acceßit locupletißimus

rerum ac verborum || memorabilium Index. || VVITEBERGAE || EXCVDEBAT IOHANNES || CRATO. || ANNO M.D.LXIX.
Wittenberg : Johannes Crato [= Johann Krafft d.Ä.], 1569
[16], 485 [= 475], [67] p.; 8°
VD16 P 1955
USTC 696136
Wolfenbüttel, Herzog August Bibliothek: H: Yv 1166b.8° Helmst. (1)
Wolfenbüttel, Herzog August Bibliothek: H: T 252.8° Helmst.

148 Newe volkommene Chronica || Philippi Melanthonis. || Zeytbuch Vnd || Warhafftige || Beschreibung / Was von anfang || der Welt biß auff diß gegenwertige Jar / nicht allein von || den Juden vnd Christen / sonder auch von allen Heyden / Türcken / vnd an=||dern Völckern so viel deren je gewesen / beide in Geistlichen vnnd Weltlichen sachen / rath || vnd anschlegen / in fried vnd kriegßzeiten in der gantzen Welt / so viel von den Menschen hat er=||faren vnd erkündiget mögen werden / sich zugetragen / furgenomen / verhandelt / vnnd außgefürt || ist worden / auß Biblischen vnd Heydnischen Historien Darinnen auch / wie solche Histo=||rien der zeit nach eigentlich zu vergleichen angezeigt vnd erkleret wirdt / Vor=||hin in gleicher gestalt vnnd Form nie außgangen. || Anfenglichs vntrem Namen Johan Carionis auffs kürtzest verfast / Nachmals durch || Herrn Philippum Melanthonem vnnd D. Casparum Peucerum auffs neuwe vbersehen / ge=||mehrt / vnd jetzt auß dem Latein verdeutscht durch M. Eusebium Menium : Sampt einem || summarischen gründlichen anhang dieses jetzt lauffende Tausent / || fünffhundert / sechs vnd sechtzigst Jar. || Mit einem ordentlichen neuwen Register. || Getruckt zu Franckfurt am Mayn / Anno M.D.LXIX.
Frankfurt a.M. : Sigmund Feyerabend [by Martin Lechler], 1569
[12], CX, [4], CXIIII, [12], CLXXXVIII, [8] fol.; 2°
[Colophon: Getruckt zu Franckfurt am || Meyn / durch Martin Lechler / in verle=||gung Sigmund Feirabends. || M.D.LXVI.]
VD16 ZV 10777
[VD16 ZV 10778]
USTC 677297
[USTC 677296]
Göttingen, Niedersächsische Staats- und Universitätsbibliothek: 2 H UN II, 129
Halle, Universitäts- und Landesbibliothek Sachsen-Anhalt: AB 62237
Wolfenbüttel, Herzog August Bibliothek: H: T 366.2° Helmst.
Wolfenbüttel, Herzog August Bibliothek: M: Gb 4° 2 (1)

1570

149   PRIMA PARS || CHRONICI || CARIONIS LATINE || EXPOSITI ET AVCTI MVLTIS || & ueteribus & recentibus Historijs, in narratio=||nibus rerum Græcarum, Germanicarum & || Ecclesiasticarum, || A || PHILIP: MELANTH: || Cui acceßit locupletißimus rerum ac uerborum || memorabilium Index. || Cum Gratia & Priuilegio. || VVITEBERGÆ M.D.LXX.
Wittenberg : Clemens Schleich & Anton Schöne, 1570
[12] fol., 334 [= 336] p., [19] fol.; 8°
VD16 M 2714
USTC 686515
Berlin, Staatsbibliothek zu Berlin Preußischer Kulturbesitz: Px 8022 [Lost]
Wolfenbüttel, Herzog August Bibliothek: H: T 250.8° Helmst.
Wolfenbüttel, Herzog August Bibliothek: H: Yv 1166.8° Helmst. (1)
Wolfenbüttel, Herzog August Bibliothek: M: Gb 51 (1)

150   SECVNDA PARS || CHRONICI || CARIONIS AB AV=||GVSTO CÆSARE VSQVE AD || CAROLVM MAGNVM. || Exposita & aucta à || PHILIP. MELANTH. || Cum locupletißimo rerum ac verborum || memorabilium Indice. || Cum Gratia & Priuilegio Cæsareæ Maiesta-||tis & Ducis Saxoniæ Electoris &c. || VITEBERGAE || ANNO M.D.LXX.
Wittenberg : [Johannes Crato = Johann Krafft d.Ä.], 1570
[7] fol., 370 p., [16] fol.; 8°
VD16 M 2713
USTC 692904
Berlin, Staatsbibliothek zu Berlin Preußischer Kulturbesitz: Px 8022 [Lost]
Wolfenbüttel, Herzog August Bibliothek: H: Yv 1166.8° Helmst. (2)
Wolfenbüttel, Herzog August Bibliothek: H: T 249.8° Helmst. (2)
Wolfenbüttel, Herzog August Bibliothek: H: T 251.8° Helmst.

151   LIBER QVINTVS || CHRONI=||CI CARIONIS || A FRIDERICO SE-||cundo vsque ad Carolum || Quintum. || EXPOSITVS ET AV-||CTVS A CASPARO || PEVCERO. || PERTINET HIC LI-||ber ad partem tertiam Chronici. || ACCESSIT LOCVPLETISSIMVS || rerum & verborum memora=||bilium Index. || Cum gratia & priuilegio Cæsareo, & || Ducis Saxoniæ, Electoris. || VVITEBERGÆ M.D.LXX.
Wittenberg : Clemens Schleich & Anton Schöne, 1570
[16], 267, [52] fol.; 8°
VD16 P 1956

USTC 672868
Berlin, Staatsbibliothek zu Berlin Preußischer Kulturbesitz: Px 8026 [Lost]
Wolfenbüttel, Herzog August Bibliothek: Gb 52 11
Wolfenbüttel, Herzog August Bibliothek: H: T 253.8° Helmst.

1572

152 TERTIA PARS || CHRONICI || CARIONIS, A || CAROLO MAGNO, VBI || PHILIP-PVS MELANTHON || DESIIT, VSQVE AD || FRIDERICVM || Secundum: || EX-POSITA ET AV=||CTA A CASPARO || PEVCERO. || Accessit locupletiss. rerum ac ver-||borum memorabilium Index. || VVITEBERGÆ || EXCVDEBAT IOHANNES || LVFFT. || ANNO CHRISTI. || M.D.LXXII.
Wittenberg : Hans Lufft, 1572
[18] fol., 475, [1] p., [34] fol.; 8°
VD16 P 1958
USTC 696134
Ithaca, Cornell University Library: Rare D18 C27 1558 v. 2
Wolfenbüttel, Herzog August Bibliothek: H: T 254.8° Helmst.
Wolfenbüttel, Herzog August Bibliothek: A: 424.12 Hist.

153 LIBER QVINTVS || CHRONI=||CI CARIONIS || A FRIDERICO SE-||cundo vsque ad Carolum || Quintum. || EXPOSITVS ET AV-||CTVS A CASPARO || PEVCERO. || PERTINENT HIC LI-||ber ad partem tertiam Chronici. || ACCESSIT LOCVPLE-TISSIMVS || rerum & uerborum memora=||bilium Index. || Cum gratia & priuilegio Cæsareo, & || Ducis Saxoniæ, Electoris. || VVITEBERGÆ || M.D.LXXII.
Wittenberg : Clemens Schleich & Anton Schöne, 1572
[16], 267, [52] fol.; 8°
VD16 P 1959
USTC 672869
Jena, Thüringer Universitäts- und Landesbibliothek: 8 Hist.un.II,9

154 CHRONICON || CARIONIS || EXPOSITVM ET AVCTVM MVL=||TIS ET VET-ERIBVS ET RECENTIBVS HISTORIIS, || IN DESCRIPTIONIBVS REGNORVM ET GENTIVM AN=||tiquarum, & narrationibus rerum Ecclesiasticarum, & Politicarum, Græ=||carum, Romanarum, Germanicarum & aliarum, ab exordio || Mundi vsq[ue] ad CAROLVM QVIN=||TVM Imperatorem. || A PHILIPPO MELANTHONE ET || CASPARO PEVCERO. || Adiecta est narratio historica de electione & coronatione || CAROLI V. Imperatoris. || Cum Gratia & Priuilegio. || WITEBERGÆ || EXCVDEBAT IOHANNES CRATO, || ANNO M.D.LXXII.
Wittenberg : Johannes Crato [= Johann Krafft d.Ä.], 1572

[30] fol., 746 p., [28] fol.; 2°
VD16 M 2715
VD16 P 1957
USTC 622451
Bibliotheca Palatina: H1720/H1728
Chicago, Newberry Library: Case folio D18 .M42 1572
London, British Library: 1471.c.2.
Wolfenbüttel, Herzog August Bibliothek: M: Gb 2° 6
Wolfenbüttel, Herzog August Bibliothek: A: 75 Hist. 2°
Wolfenbüttel, Herzog August Bibliothek: S: Alv.: Lc 47 2°
Wolfenbüttel, Herzog August Bibliothek: A: 117.1 Hist. (2)

1573

155 PRIMA PARS || CHRONICI || CARIONIS LATINE || EXPOSITI ET AVCTI MVLTIS || & ueteribus & recentibus Historijs, in narratio-||nibus rerum Græcarum, Germanicarum & || Ecclesiasticarum, || A || PHILIP: MELANTH: || Cui acceßit locupletißimus rerum ac uerborum || memorabilium Index. || Cum Gratia & Priuilegio. || VVITEBERGÆ M.D.LXXIII.
Wittenberg : Hans Lufft, 1573
[11] fol., 334 [= 336] p., [19] fol.; 8°
VD16 M 2716
USTC 686500
Braunschweig, Stadtbibliothek: C 557(1).8°
Wolfenbüttel, Herzog August Bibliothek: M: Gb 52 I [Title page lost]

156 SECVNDA PARS || CHRONICI || CARIONIS, AB AV-||GVSTO CAESARE || vsq[ue] ad Carolum Ma-||gnum. || Exposita & aucta à || PHILIP. MELANTH. || Cum locupletißimo rerum ac uerborum || memorabilium Indice. || Cum Gratia & Priuilegio Cæsareæ Ma-||iestat. & Ducis Sax. Elect. &c. || VVITEBERGAE || ANNO M.D.LXXIII.
Wittenberg : Hans Lufft, 1573
[7] fol., 370 p., [16] fol.; 8°
VD16 M 2716
USTC 686500
Braunschweig, Stadtbibliothek: C 557(2).8°
Wolfenbüttel, Herzog August Bibliothek: M: Gb 52 I [Title page lost]

157 Chronica || CARIONIS. || Von anfang der Welt / bis || vff Keiser Carolum den Fünfften. || Auffs newe in Lateinischer || Sprach beschrieben / vnd mit vielen

alten vnd newen || Historien / Auch mit beschreibung vieler alten Königreich vnd Völ=||cker / Vnd mit erzelung etlicher furnemer Geschichten / so sich in der || Kirchen Gottes / vnd in Weltlichen Regimenten / sonderlich || in Griechenland / im Römischem Reich vnd Deud=||scher Nation / haben zugetragen / vermeh=||ret vnd gebessert || Durch Herrn PHILIPPVM MELAN=||THONEM, || vnd || Doctorem CASPARVM PEVCERVM. || Jtzund zum Ersten / aus dem Lateinischen || gantz vnd volkömlich in Deudsche Sprach || gebracht. || Am ende ist auch darzu gesetzt die Beschreibung || Herrn Philippi Melanthonis / von der Wahl vnd || krönung Keisers CAROLI des Fünfften / So || zu vor hin in Deudscher Sprach nie=||mals gedruckt worden. || Mit Römischer Keiserlicher Maiestet Freyheit. || M.D.LXXIII.
Wittenberg : Johann Krafft d.Ä. [= Johannes Crato], 1573
[88], 1187 [= 1185], [73] p.; 2°
VD16 M 2728
VD16 P 1969
USTC 622282
Bibliotheca Palatina: C578/C591
[Dedication Copy of Caspar Peucer to Elector August of Saxony]
London, British Library: 9005.h.1.
London, Warburg Institute Library: NAH 6550
Wolfenbüttel, Herzog August Bibliothek: A: 178 Hist. 2°

1575

158 HISTOIRE, OV || CRONIQVE || DES CHOSES PLVS MEMO-||RABLES DEPVIS LA CREATION || du monde, iusques au regne du Tres-chre-||stien Henry III. de ce nom, Roy de Fran-||ce & de Pologne. || Par Iean Carion Philosophe, traduict par M. Iean || le Blond, & depuis augmentée. || A PARIS, || Par Nicolas Bonfons, demeurant ruë neuue || nostre Dame, à l'enseigne S. Nicolas.
Paris : Nicolas Bonfons, [1575]
[32], 361 [= 341], [2] fol.; 16°
USTC 10539
French Vernacular Books: 8919
London, British Library: 1606/403.

1576

159.A CHRONICON || CARIONIS || EXPOSITVM ET AVCTVM MVL-||TIS ET VETERIBVS ET RECENTI-||bus historiis, in descriptionibus regnorum & gentium

|| antiquarum, & narrationibus rerum Ecclesiasticarum, || & Politicarum, Græcarum, Romanarum, Germanica-||rum & aliarum, ab exordio Mundi vsque ad Carolum || quintum imperatorem, || A PHILIPPO MELAN-||thone & Casparo Peucero. || GENEVÆ, || Apud Petrum Santandreanum, || M.D.LXXVI.

Geneva : Pierre de Saint André, 1576

[45] fol., 1080 p.; 8° [Pars 1–2 = 1–439; Pars 3 = 443–1080]

USTC 450714

[USTC 156197 ?]

Basel, Universitätsbibliothek: EA VI 19

159[17] CHRONICON || CARIONIS || EXPOSITVM ET AVCTVM MVL-||TIS ET VE-TERIBVS ET RECENTI-||bus historiis, in descriptionibus regnorum & gentium || antiquarum, & narrationibus rerum Ecclesiasticarum, || & Politicarum, Græcarum, Romanarum, Germanica-||rum & aliarum, ab exordio Mundi vsque ad Carolum || quintum imperatorem, || A PHILIPPO MELAN-||thone & Casparo Peucero. || LVGDVNI, || Apud Petrum Santandreanum, || M.D.LXXVI.

Lyon [Geneva] : Pierre de Saint André, 1576

[45] fol., 1080 p.; 8° [Pars 1–2 = 1–439; Pars 3 = 443–1080]

USTC 452036

[USTC 156197 ?]

Chicago, Newberry Library: Case F 09 .148 [Pars 3 only, title page lost]

Augsburg, Staats- und Stadtbibliothek: Gs 1536

Wiesbaden, Hessische Landesbibliothek: Ed 3028

160 CHRONICA CARIONIS. || Von Anfang der Welt / || bis auff Keyser Carolum den || Fünfften. || Auffs newe in Lateinischer Sprach || beschrieben / vnd mit vielen alten vnd newen Historien / Auch || mit beschreibung vieler alten Königreich vnd Völker / Vnd mit erzehlung etlicher || fürnemer Geschichten / so sich in der Kirchen Gottes / vnd in Weltlichen || Regimenten / sonderlich in Griechenland / im Römischen Reich || vnd Deudscher Nation / haben zugetragen / ver=||mehret vnd gebessert || Durch Herrn PHILIPPVM ME-||LANTHONEM. || vnd || Doctorem CASPARVM PEVCERVM. || Jtzund zum Ersten / aus dem Lateinischen gantz vnd || volkömlich in Deudsche Sprach gebracht. || Am Ende ist auch darzu gesetzt die || Beschreibung Herrn Philippi Melanthonis / von der Wahl || vnd Krönung Keysers CAROLI des Fünfften / So zuuor || hin in Deudscher Sprach niemals gedruckt worden. || Dreszden. || ANNO M.D.LXXVI.

Dresden : Gimel Bergen, 1576

Liber 1–3 = [58] fol., fol. 1–252; Liber 4 = fol. 2–208; Liber 5 = fol. 209–435, [1], [57] fol.; 2°

---

17 Moller's entry (p. 17) has occasionally lead to confusion concerning this edition, and Scherer thought that he was referring to a Lyon edition of the Bonnus translation (p. 471).

VD16 ZV 30762
Berlin, Staatsbibliothek zu Berlin Preußischer Kulturbesitz: 2" Ebd 97-4
Dresden, Sächsische Landesbibliothek: Hist.univ.A.73-1/3 [Lost]
Rostock, Universitätsbibliothek: Rb-156

160.L.4 Der Dritte Theil der Chro=||nica Carionis / von Carolo Magno (do Herr || Philippus Melanthon dieses Chronicon zu vorfertigen auffge=||hört) bis auff Keyser Friederich den Andern. || Geschrieben vnd auffs new vormehrt / durch Casparum || Peucerum der Philosophiæ vnd Artzney Doctorem, vnd Professorem || in der Vniuersitet Wittemberg. || Jtzund aber auffs new aus dem Lateinischen in das Deudsche || bracht / durch Doctorem Christophorum Pecelium. || Das vierdte Buch. || Dreszden. || ANNO M.D.LXXVI.
Dresden : Gimel Bergen, 1576
Liber 4 = fol. 2–208; 2°
[VD16 ZV 30762]
Berlin, Staatsbibliothek zu Berlin Preußischer Kulturbesitz: 2" Ebd 97-4
Dresden, Sächsische Landesbibliothek: Hist.univ.A.73-4 [Lost]
Rostock, Universitätsbibliothek: Rb-156

160.L.5 Das Fünffte Buch der || CHRONICA CARIO=||NIS, von Keiser FRIDERICO dem || Andern / anzufahen / bis auff CAROLVM || den Fünfften. || Beschrieben vnd vermehret / || Von || CASPARO PEVCERO, der Artzney vnd || Philosophiæ Doctorn. || Vnd gehöret auch dieses Buch / || wie die zwey vorgehenden zu dem Dritten teil der || Chroniken / welches sich mit der Römischen || Monarchi anfehet. || Dreszden: 1576.
Dresden : Gimel Bergen, 1576
Liber 5 = fol. 209–435, [1], [57] fol.; 2°
[VD16 ZV 30762]
Berlin, Staatsbibliothek zu Berlin Preußischer Kulturbesitz: 2" Ebd 97-4
Dresden, Sächsische Landesbibliothek: Hist.univ.A.73-5
Rostock, Universitätsbibliothek: Rb-156

1577

161 HISTOIRE, OV || CHRONIQVE || DES CHOSES PLVS ME-||MORABLES DEPVIS LA || creation du monde, iusques au regne du || Tres-chrestien Roy Henry III. de ce || nom, Roy de France & de Polongne. || Recueillie Par Iean Carion Philosophe, & || traduicte par M. Iean le Blond, & || depuis reueue & augmentée. || A LYON, || Par François Arnoullet. || 1577.
Lyon : François Arnoullet, 1577
[32] fol., 733 [= 731] p., [5] p.; 16°

USTC 13136
French Vernacular Books: 8920
Baudrier, Bibliographie Lyonnaise: X, 164
Crescentino, Biblioteca civica De Gregoriana: DEG 1731

162[18] PRIMA PARS || CHRONICI || CARIONIS LATINE || EXPOSITI ET AVCTI MVL-TIS || & veteribus & recentibus Historijs, in nar-||rationibus rerum Græcarum, Germani-||carum & Ecclesiasticarum, || A || Philippo Melanthone. || Cui accesßit locupletißimus rerum ac verborum || memorabilium Index. || Cum Gratia & Priuilegio. || VVitebergæ excudebant Clemens Schleich || & Antonius Schöne.
Wittenberg : Clemens Schleich & Anton Schöne, [1577]
[8], 160 fol.; 8°
VD16 M 2717
VD16 ZV 10651
USTC 686516
USTC 686517
Berlin, Staatsbibliothek zu Berlin Preußischer Kulturbesitz: Px 8049 [Lost]
Gotha, Forschungsbibliothek: H 8° 05015 (01)
Wolfenbüttel, Herzog August Bibliothek: A: 424.9 Hist. (1)

163 SECVNDA PARS || CHRONICI || CARIONIS, AB AV-||GVSTO CAESARE || vsq[ue] ad Carolum Ma-||gnum. || Exposita & aucta à || Philippo Melanthone. || Cum Gratia & Priuilegio Cæsareæ Ma-||iestat. & Ducis Sax. Elect. &c. || VVITEBERGAE || Excudebant Clemens Schleich & || Antonius Schöne. || ANNO M.D.LXXVII.
Wittenberg : Clemens Schleich & Anton Schöne, 1577
[1] fol., fol. 162–336; 8°
VD16 M 2717
USTC 686516
Berlin, Staatsbibliothek zu Berlin Preußischer Kulturbesitz: Px 8049 [Lost]
Wolfenbüttel, Herzog August Bibliothek: A: 424.9 Hist. (2)

164 TERTIA PARS || CHRONICI || CARIONIS, A CA-||ROLO MAGNO, VBI PHILIP=||PVS MELANTHON DESIIT. || vsque ad Fridericum Se=||cundum.

---

18 This edition was seen by Scherer in Berlin – "Nach Erscheinen des zweiten Bandes wurde dieser auch mit dem ersten zusammengedruckt, so z.B. Wittenberg (bei Schleich & Schöne) o. J. 336 Bl. (Berlin)." Scherer, *Geschichte und Kirchengeschichte*, 472.

|| Exposita & aucta || A || CASPARO PEVCERO. || VVITEBERGÆ || Apud Clementem Schleich & An=||tonium Schön. || Anno M.D.LXXVII.
Wittenberg : Clemens Schleich & Anton Schöne, 1577
fol. 331–575 [= 565]; 8°
VD16 M 2717
USTC 686516
Stuttgart, Württembergische Landesbibliothek: Allg.G.oct.408

1578[19]

165   Chronica || CARIONIS. || Von anfang der Welt / bis || vff Keiser Carolum den Fünfften. || Auffs newe in Lateinischer || Sprach beschrieben / vnd mit vielen alten vnd newen || Historien / Auch mit beschreibung vieler alten Königreich vnd Völ=||cker / Vnd mit erzelung etlicher furnemer Geschichten / so sich in der || Kirchen Gottes / vnd in Weltlichen Regimenten / sonderlich || in Griechenland / im Römischen Reich vnd Deudscher || Nation / haben zugetragen / vermehret || vnd gebessert || Durch Herrn PHILIPPVM MELAN=||THONEM, || vnd || Doctorem CASPARVM PEVCERVM. || Jtzund zum ersten / aus dem Lateinischen gantz || vnd volkömlich in Deudsche Sprach || gebracht. || Am ende ist auch darzu gesetzt die Beschreibung || Herrn Philippi Melanthonis / von der Wahl vnd || Krönung Keisers CAROLI des Fünfften / So || zuuor hin in Deudscher Sprach nie=||mals gedruckt worden. || Mit Römischer Keiserlicher Maiestet Freyheit. || Wittemberg / || Gedruckt durch Hans Lufft. || M.D.LXXVIII.
Wittemberg : Hans Lufft, 1578
[6] fol., 1142 [=1143], [1] p., [30] fol., [1] p.; 2°
VD16 M 2729
VD16 P 1970
USTC 622283
Bibliotheca Palatina: C75/C86
Syracuse, Syracuse University Library: Ranke 909 C27 f [Ranke's Copy]
Wolfenbüttel, Herzog August Bibliothek: A: 70.5 Hist. 2°

---

19   Scherer (p. 473) lists a complete revised Latin edition for this year – *Chronicon Carionis expositum et auctum...* (Lyon, 1578). He refers, however, to an edition from Paris, Bibliothèque Nationale, which seems to be the Lyon edition of 1576 (Paris, Bibliothèque Nationale: G-12257, Tolbiac - Rez-de-jardin - magasin).

1579

166.I[20] CHRONIQVE || ET HISTOIRE VNI-||VERSELLE, CONTENANT || les choses memorables auenues es qua-||tre souuerains Empires, Royaumes, Re-||publiques, & au gouuerneme[n]t de l'Eglise, || depuis le commencement du monde ius-||ques à l'Empereur Charles cinquiesme. || DRESSEE premierement par Iean CARION, puis augmen-||tee, amplement exposee & enrichie de diuerses histoires tant || Ecclesiastiques que Politiques, anciennes & modernes, par || Philippe MELANCTHON & Gaspar PEVCER, & re-||duite en cinq liures traduits de Latin en François. || PLVS, deux liures adioustez de nouueau aux cinq au-||tres, comprenans les choses notables auenues sous || l'empire de Charles cinquiesme, Ferdinand premier || & Maximilian second. || Tome premier. || PAR IEAN BERION. || CIƆ. IƆ. LXXIX.
[Geneva] : Jean Berjon, 1579
[32] fol., 858 p., [34] fol.; 8° [Contains Liber 1–4]
USTC 60842
[USTC 63093]
French Vernacular Books: 8922
[French Vernacular Books: 8923]
Dijon, Bibliothèque Municipale: 3185
Paris, Bibliothèque Nationale: 8-H-1725 (1), Arsenal - Magasin
München, Bayerische Staatsbibliothek: Chron. 200 l-1

166.II CHRONIQVE || ET HISTOIRE || VNIVERSELLE. || A ce volume est adioustee de nouueau vne qua-||triesme partie de Chroniques, comprinse en || deux liures, le premier desquels (qui est le sixies||me en ordre) comprend les choses notables aue-||nues sous l'Empire de Charles cinquiesme: & || le second (qui est le septiesme & dernier) pour-||suit l'histoire depuis Charles cinquiesme ius-||ques à la mort de Maximilian second. || Tome second. || PAR IEAN BERION. || CIƆ. IC. LXXIX.
[Geneva] : Jean Berjon, 1579
[16] fol., 1–366, [1]-665, [1] p., [28] fol.; 8° [Contains Liber 5 & Continuation]
[USTC 61998]
USTC 6697
[French Vernacular Books: 8921]

---

20 See Hans Joachim Bremme, *Buchdrucker und Buchhändler zur Zeit der Glaubenskämpfe: Studien zur Genfer Druckgeschichte, 1565–1580*. (Genève: Droz, 1969), 114 n. 18 – "Berjon druckte Jean Carion, Chronique et histoire... Claude Juge hatte das Buch am 5.XII 1578 zum Druck beantragt (vgl. Ms. fr. 3817, fol 189)."

French Vernacular Books: 8924
Paris, Bibliothèque Nationale: 8-H-1725 (2), Arsenal - Magasin
München, Bayerische Staatsbibliothek: Chron. 200 l-2
Wolfenbüttel, Herzog August Bibliothek: A: 327.3 Hist.
Wolfenbüttel, Herzog August Bibliothek: S: Alv.: Me 116

1580

167 QVARTA PARS || CHRONICI || CARIONIS A FRI-||DERICO SECVNDO || vsq[ue] ad Carolum Quintum. || EXPOSITVS ET AVCTVS || A CASPARO PEVCERO. || Pertinet hic liber ad partem || tertiam Chronici. || Index rerum & verborum memorabilium, || omnium Chronicorum PHILIPPI & || PEVCERI partium. || VVITEBERGÆ || Excudebat Matthæus VVelack. || Anno M.D.LXXX.
Wittenberg : Matthäus Welack, 1580
[12], 262, [75] fol.; 8°
VD16 P 1961
USTC 689372
Wolfenbüttel, Herzog August Bibliothek: H: Yv 1167a.8° Helmst. (2)
Wolfenbüttel, Herzog August Bibliothek: H: T 255.8° Helmst. (4)

168 CHRONICON || CARIONIS || EXPOSITVM ET AVCTVM MVL=||TIS ET VETERIBVS ET RECENTIBVS HISTORIIS, || IN DESCRIPTIONIBVS REGNORVM ET GENTIVM AN=||tiquarum, & narrationibus rerum Ecclesiasticarum, & Politicarum, || Græcarum, Romanarum, Germanicarum & aliarum, ab exor-||dio Mundi vsq[ue] ad CAROLVM QVIN-||TVM Imperatorem. || A PHILIPPO MELANTHONE ET || CASPARO PEVCERO. || Adiecta est narratio historica de electione & coronatione || CAROLI V. Imperatoris. || VVITEBERGÆ || Excudebant Hæredes Johannis Cratonis, Anno || M.D.LXXX.
Wittenberg : Johannes Crato [= Johann Krafft d.Ä] (Heirs), 1580
[30] fol., 746 p., [28] fol.; 2°
[Colophon: VVITEBERGÆ || Excudebant Hæredes Johannis Cratonis, Anno || M.D.LXXX.]
VD16 M 2718
VD16 P 1960
USTC 622452
Bibliotheca Palatina: B1347/B1354
London, British Library: C.75.g.4.
Wolfenbüttel, Herzog August Bibliothek: H: T 364.2° Helmst.
Wolfenbüttel, Herzog August Bibliothek: Schulenb. Gb 2° 1

169.I   CHRONIQVE || ET HISTOIRE VNI-||VERSELLE, CONTENANT || les choses memorables auenues es qua-||tre souuerains Empires, Royaumes, Re-||publiques, & au gouuerneme[n]t de l'Eglise, || depuis le commencement du monde ius-||ques à l'Empereur Charles cinquiesme. || DRESSEE premierement par Iean CARION, puis augmen-||tee, amplement exposee & enrichie de diuerses histoires tant || Ecclesiastiques que Politiques, anciennes & modernes, par || Philippe MELANCTHON & Gaspar PEVCER, & re-||duite en cinq liures traduits de Latin en François. || PLVS, deux liures adioustez de nouueau aux cinq au-||tres, comprenans les choses notables auenues sous || l'empire de Charles cinquiesme, Ferdinand premier || & Maximilian second. || Tome premier. || PAR IEAN BERION. || CIƆ. IƆ. LXXX.
[Geneva] : Jean Berjon, 1580
[32] fol., 858 p., [34] fol.; 8° [Contains Liber 1–4]
USTC 1843
French Vernacular Books: 8925
Wolfenbüttel, Herzog August Bibliothek: A: 327.2 Hist.

169.II   CHRONIQVE || ET HISTOIRE || VNIVERSELLE. || A ce volume est adioustee de nouueau vne qua-||triesme partie de Chroniques, comprinse en || deux liures, le premier desquels (qui est le sixies||me en ordre) comprend les choses notables aue-||nues sous l'Empire de Charles cinquiesme: & || le second (qui est le septiesme & dernier) pour-||suit l'histoire depuis Charles cinquiesme ius-||ques à la mort de Maximilian second. || Tome second. || PAR IEAN BERION. || CIƆ. IC. LXXX.
[Geneva] : Jean Berjon, 1580
[16] fol., 1–366, [1]-665, [1] p., [28] fol.; 8° [Contains Liber 5 & Continuation]
USTC 60843
French Vernacular Books: 8926
London, British Library: 901.e.2.

1581

170   CHRONICON || CARIONIS || EXPOSITVM ET || AVCTVM MVLTIS ET || VETERIBVS ET RECENTIBVS HI-||storijs, in descriptionibus regnorum & gentium anti-||quarum, & narrationibus rerum Ecclesiasticarum, & || Politicarum, Græcarum, Romanarum, Germa-||nicarum & aliarum, ab exordio Mundi || vsque ad CAROLVM V. Im-||peratorem. || A PHILIPPO MELANTHONE || & Casparo Peucero. || Recens vero summo studio adornatum, pristinæq[ue] in-||tegritati, exemplorum veterum ac recentium || collatione exquisita,

restitutum. || Quid præterea huic editioni accesserit versa osten-||det pagella. || FRANCOFVRTI M.D.LXXXI.
Frankfurt a.M.: Petrus Fabritius [= Peter Schmidt], 1581
[120] fol., 1189 p. [Pars 1 = p. 1–219; Pars 2 = p. 220–454; Pars 3 = p. 459–1189], [1] p.; 8°
VD16 M 2719
VD16 P 1962
USTC 622450
Wolfenbüttel, Herzog August Bibliothek: S: Alv.: Ii 164 [=Ji 164]

170.P.3   TERTIA PARS || CHRONICI || CARIONIS || A || CASPARO PEVCERO || expositi & aucti. || ANNO M.D.LXXXI.
Frankfurt a.M.: Petrus Fabritius [= Peter Schmidt], 1581
[1] fol., p. 459–1189; 8° [Pars 3]
[VD16 M 2719]
VD16 P 1962
USTC
[Wolfenbüttel, Herzog August Bibliothek: S: Alv.: Ii 164 [=Ji 164]]

171[21]   CHRONICON || CARIONIS || EXPOSITVM ET AVCTVM MVL-||TIS ET VE-TERIBVS ET RECENTI-||bus historiis, in descriptionibus regnorum & gentium || antiquarum, & narrationibus rerum Ecclesiasticaru[m], || & Politicarum, Græcarum, Romanarum, Germani-||carum & aliarum, ab exordio Mundi vsque ad Caro-||lum quintum imperatorem, || A PHILIPPO MELAN-||thone & Casparo Peucero. || Apud Petrum Santadreanum, || M.D.LXXXI.
[Geneva] : Pierre de Saint André, 1581
[44] fol., 1080 [Pars 1–2 = 1–439; Pars 3 = 443–1080] p.; 8°
USTC 450886
[USTC 156376 ?]
London, British Library: 580.c.3.
Wolfenbüttel, Herzog August Bibliothek: H: T 256.8° Helmst.

1582

172   PRIMA PARS || CHRONICI || CARIONIS LATINE || expositi & aucti multis & veteribus & || recentibus Historijs, in narrationibus || rerum Græcarum,

---

21   Scherer (p. 473) lists this edition by Santandreanus (Berlin, Staatsbibliothek zu Berlin Preußischer Kulturbesitz), but also additional Latin editions from Lyon (Paris, Bibliothèque Nationale) and Paris (London, British Library). These entries seem to refer to this edition.

Germanicarum || & Ecclesiasticarum, || A || Philippo Melanthone. || Cui acceßit locupletißimus rerum ac verbo-||rum memorabilium Index. || Cum Gratia & Priuilegio. || VVITEBERGÆ || Excudebat Matthæus VVelack. || Anno M.D.LXXXII.
Wittenberg : Matthäus Welack, 1582
[8], 160 fol.; 8°
VD16 M 2720
USTC 686511
Wolfenbüttel, Herzog August Bibliothek: H: Yv 1167.8° Helmst.
Wolfenbüttel, Herzog August Bibliothek: H: Yv 1213.8° Helmst.
Wolfenbüttel, Herzog August Bibliothek: A: 424.11 Hist. (1)

173   SECVNDA PARS || CHRONICI || CARIONIS, AB AV-||GVSTO CÆSARE || vsq[ue] ad Carolum Magnum. || Exposita & aucta à || Philippo Melanthone. || Cum Gratia & Priuilegio Cæsareæ Maiestat. || & Ducis Sax. Elect. &c. || VVITEBERGÆ || Excudebat Matthæus VVelack. || Anno M.D.LXXXII.
Wittenberg : Matthäus Welack, 1582
[1] fol., fol. 162–336; 8°
VD16 M 2720
USTC 686511
Wolfenbüttel, Herzog August Bibliothek: H: Yv 1167.8° Helmst.
Wolfenbüttel, Herzog August Bibliothek: H: Yv 1213.8° Helmst.

174   TERTIA PARS || CHRONICI || CARIONIS, A || CAROLO MAGNO, VBI || PHILIPPVS MELANTHON desijt, || vsque ad Fridericum Se=||cundum. || Exposita & aucta || A || CASPARO PEVCERO. || WITEBERGÆ || Excudebat Matthæus Welack. || Anno M.D.LXXXII.
Wittenberg : Matthäus Welack, 1582
[1] fol., fol. 331–575 [= 564]; 8°
[VD16 M 2720]
VD16 P 1963
[USTC 686511]
Wolfenbüttel, Herzog August Bibliothek: H: Yv 1167a.8° Helmst. (1)
Wolfenbüttel, Herzog August Bibliothek: H: T 255.8° Helmst. (3) [Title page incomplete]

1584

175   CHRONICON || CARIONIS || EXPOSITVM ET AVCTVM || MVLTIS ET VETERIBVS ET || recentibus historiis, in descriptionibus re-||gnorum & gentium

antiquarum, & narra-||tionibus rerum Ecclesiasticarum & Politi-||carum, Græcarum, Romanarum, Germani-||carum & aliarum, ab exordio Mundi vsque || ad Carolum Quintum Imperatorem, || A PHILIPPO MELAN-||thone & Casparo Peucero. || Apud Petrum Santandreanum. || M.D.LXXXIIII.
[Geneva] : Pierre de Saint André, 1584
[78], 1080 p.; 8°
[Pars 1 = [40] fol., p. 1–212; Pars 2 = p. [213]-439; Pars 3 = p. [441]-1080]
USTC 450986
Berlin, Staatsbibliothek zu Berlin Preußischer Kulturbesitz: Px 8054.
Halle, Universitäts- und Landesbibliothek Sachsen-Anhalt: Pon Vg 4143 a

176[22] Kronyka Swěta || O znamenitěgssých wěcech a proměnách / || kteréž se kde a kdy hned odpočátku w Swětě / buďto || při nábožestwij a Cýrkwi / aneb při Krá=||lowstwijch Zemských přicházely || a zbijhaly. || Od Jana Karyona krátce sebraná a ney=||prwé w Yazyku Latinském a Německém wyda=||ná: Potom w Yazyk Čzeský před lety XLIII. od || BurJana z Kornic přeložená / a w Li-||tomyssli wytisstěná. || Nynij pak znowu přehlednutá / w Čzessti=||ně poopravená / a s poznamenánijm některých || předněgssých wěcý / až do smrti slawné a swaté || paměti Cýsaře Maxmiliána II. dow-||edená / od || M. Danyele Adama z Weleslawijna. || W Starém Městě Pražském || Léta Páně || M.D.XXCIV.
Prague : Daniel Adam z Veleslavina, 1584
[8], 480, [23] p.; 4°
USTC 568821
Knihopis českých a slovenských tisků: 1464
Prague, Strahov Monastery Library [Strahovská knihovna]: AP XV 30
Prague, Strahov Monastery Library [Strahovská knihovna]: BC VI 86
Vienna, Österreichische Nationalbibliothek: 241468-B. Alt Mag

1586

177.1 Chronica || Carionis: || VAN DEN BEGHIN=||ne der Werelt aen tot op Keyser Carolum, || den vijfden van dien Name. || Op een nieu in de Latijnsche Sprake beschreuen / ende || met menigerleye oude ende nieuwe Historien / oock met beschrijuinge || von vele oude Coniucrijcken eñ Volcken / ende met vertellinge von eenige der voor=||naemste dingen / die in de Kercke Gods /

---

22 The catalogue entry presents the date as "M.D.XXCIIII" (Knihopis českých a slovenských tisků: 1464); however, the copies I have consulted present the date as "M.D.XXCIV."

ende inde Wereltlicke Regimenten / || maer sonderlinge in Grieckerlant / int Roomsche Rijcke eñ de Duyt=||sche Natie gheschiet zijn / seer vermeerdert ende gebetert / || Door Philippum Melanthonem ende || D. Casparum Peucerum. || Wt de Hooch-Duytsche Sprake getrouwelicken ouer=||ghesett in de Neder-Duytsche Tale, door || W. V. N. || Tot Dordrecht. || Ghedruckt by Jan Canin / woonende in de || Wijnstrate. Jnt Jaer. 1586. || Met gratie ende Priuilegie voor 10. Iaren.
Dordrecht : Jan Canin, 1586
[4], 784, [53] p.; 2°
USTC 422415
Amsterdam, Universiteitsbibliotheek: OTM OF 63–282
Amsterdam, Bibliotheek van de Vrije Universiteit: XE.05049
Leiden, Universiteitsbibliotheek: 1195 A 12

177.2 Chronica || Carionis: || VAN DEN BEGHIN=||ne der Werelt aen tot op Keyser Carolum, || den vijfden van dien Name. || Op een nieu in de Latijnsche Sprake beschreuen / ende || met menigerleye oude ende nieuwe Historien / oock met beschrijuinge || von vele oude Coniucrijcken eñ Volcken / ende met vertellinge von eenige der voor=||naemste dingen / die in de Kercke Gods / ende inde Wereltlicke Regimenten / || maer sonderlinge in Grieckerlant / int Roomsche Rijcke eñ de Duyt=||sche Natie gheschiet zijn / seer vermeerdert ende gebetert / || Door Philippum Melanthonem ende || D. Casparum Peucerum. || Wt de Hooch-Duytsche Sprake getrouwelicken ouer=||ghesett in de Neder-Duytsche Tale, door || W. V. N. || Tot Dordrecht. || Ghedruckt by Jan Canin / woonende in de || Wijnstrate. Jnt Jaer. 1586. || Met gratie ende Priuilegie voor 10. Iaren. || Men vintse te coope by Lauwerens Iacobz. woonen-||de inden vergulden Bybel, opt water, tot || Amstelredam.
Amsterdam [Dordrecht] : Laurens Jacobsz [by Jan Canin], 1586
[4], 784, [53] p.; 2°
USTC 422416
Amsterdam, Universiteitsbibliotheek: OTM OF 63–973

177.3 Chronica || Carionis: || VAN DEN BEGHIN=||ne der Werelt aen tot op Keyser Carolum, || den vijfden van dien Name. || Op een nieu in de Latijnsche Sprake beschreuen / ende || met menigerleye oude ende nieuwe Historien / oock met beschrijuinge || von vele oude Coniucrijcken eñ Volcken / ende met vertellinge von eenige der voor=||naemste dingen / die in de Kercke Gods / ende inde Wereltlicke Regimenten / || maer sonderlinge in Grieckerlant / int Roomsche Rijcke eñ de Duyt=||sche Natie gheschiet zijn / seer vermeerdert ende gebetert / || Door Philippum Melanthonem ende || D. Casparum Peucerum. || Wt de Hooch-Duytsche Sprake getrouwelicken ouer=||ghesett in de Neder-Duytsche Tale, door || W. V. N. || Tot Dordrecht. || Ghedruckt by Jan Canin / woonende in de || Wijnstrate. Jnt Jaer. 1586. || Met gratie ende

Priuilegie voor 10. Iaren. || Men vintse te coope, by Cornelis Claesz. woonen-||de int Reckenboeck, opt water, tot || Amstelredam.
Amsterdam [Dordrecht] : Cornelis Claesz [by Jan Canin], 1586
[4], 784, [53] p.; 2°
USTC 422438
Den Haag, Koninklijke Bibliotheek: 1707 A 5
London, British Library: 9005.g.16.(1.) [Incomplete, title page from Den Haag.]

1588

178   Chronica || CARIONIS. || Von anfang der Welt / bis || vff Keiser Carolum den Fünfften. || Auffs newe in Lateinischer || Sprach beschrieben / vnd mit vielen alten vnd newen || Historien / Auch mit beschreibung vieler alten Königreich vnd Völ-||cker / Vnd mit erzelung etlicher furnemer Geschichten / so sich in der Kirchen || Gottes / vnd in Weltlichen Regimenten / sonderlich in Griechen-land / im Römischen || Reich vnd Deudscher Nation / haben zugetragen / vermeh-||ret vnd gebessert || Durch Herrn PHILIPPVM MELAN=||THONEM. || vnd || Doctorem CASPARVM PEVCERVM. || Jtzund zum ersten / aus dem Lateinischen gantz vnd || volkömlich in Deudsche Sprach gebracht. || Am ende ist auch darzu gesetzt die Beschreibung Herrn Philippi || Melanthonis / von der Wahl vnd Krönung Keisers CAROLI || des Fünfften / So zuuorhin in Deudscher Sprach || niemals gedruckt worden. || Cum Gratia & Privilegio. || Wittemberg / || Gedruckt durch Zachar: Lehman. || Anno, M.D.L.XXXVIII.
Wittenberg : Zacharias Lehmann, 1588
[6] fol., 1142 [= 1143], [1] p., [30] fol.; 2°
VD16 M 2730
VD16 P 1971
VD16 ZV 10805
USTC 622281
USTC 622280
Chicago, Newberry Library: Case F 09 .15
Braunschweig, Stadtbibliothek: C 111 2°
Wolfenbüttel, Herzog August Bibliothek: M: Gb 4° 3

1591

179   QVARTA PARS || CHRONICI || CARIONIS A FRI-||DERICO SECVNDO || usq[ue] ad Carolum Quintum. || EXPOSITVS ET AVCTVS || A CASPARO PEVCERO. ||

Pertinet hic liber ad partem ter-||tiam Chronici. || Index rerum & verborum memorabilium, || omnium Chronicorum PHILIPPI || & PEVCERI partium. || CVM PRIVILEGIO. || Sumptibus M. Iohannis Rhuelij. || ANNO M.D.XCI.
Wittenberg : Johann Rühel [by Matthäus Welack], 1591
[12], 262, [75] fol.; 8°
[Colophon: VVITEBERGÆ || Excudebat Matthæus VVelack. || Anno M.D. LXXXXI.]
VD16 P 1964
USTC 689371
Wolfenbüttel, Herzog August Bibliothek: A: 424.13 Hist.

1592

180[23]   CHRONICON || CARIONIS || EXPOSITVM ET AVCTVM MVL-||TIS ET VE-TERIBVS ET RECENTI-||bus historiis, in descriptionibus regnorum & gen-||tium antiquarum, & narrationibus rerum Ecclesiasti||carum, & Politicarum, Græcarum, Romanarum, Ger-||manicarum & aliarum, ab exordio Mundi vsque ad || Carolum quintum imperatorem, || A PHILIPPO MELANCH-||thone & Casparo Peucero. || Apud Petrum Santandreanum. || M.D.XCII.
[Geneva] : Pierre de Saint André, 1592
[88], 1080 p.; 8°
USTC 451311
Wolfenbüttel, Herzog August Bibliothek: H: T 257.8° Helmst.

1593

181   CHRONICON || CARIONIS || EXPOSITVM ET AVCTVM MVL-||TIS ET VETERIBVS ET RECENTI-||bus historiis, in descriptionibus regnorum & || gentium antiquarum, & narrationibus re-||rum Ecclesiasticarum, & Politicarum, Græca-||rum, Romanarum, Germanicarum & alia-||rum, ab exordio Mundi vsque ad Carolum || quintum imperatorem, || A Philippo Melanchthone & Caspa-||ro Peucero. || Postrema editio, cui accesserunt Capitum & || Rerum Indices. || Apud Ioannem le Preux. || M.D.XCIII.
[Geneva] : Jean le Preux, 1593
[64], 1418 [Pars 1–2 = p. 1–573, Pars 3 = p. 579–1418], [78] p.; 16°

---

23   Moller's entry (p. 17) has occasionally lead to confusion concerning this edition, and Scherer thought that he was referring to a Lyon edition of the Bonnus translation (p. 471).

USTC 452031
Wolfenbüttel, Herzog August Bibliothek: H: T 118.12° Helmst.
Wolfenbüttel, Herzog August Bibliothek: H: T 119.12° Helmst.
Wolfenbüttel, Herzog August Bibliothek: M: Gb 53 [Pars 3 only]

182[24]   CHRONICON || CARIONIS || EXPOSITVM ET AVCTVM MVLTIS ET || VETERI-BVS ET RECENTIBVS HISTORIIS, || in descriptionibus regnorum & gentium antiquarum, || & narrationibus rerum Ecclesiasticarum, & Politica-||rum, Græcarum, Romanarum, Germanicarum & alia-||rum, ab exordio Mundi vsque ad Carolum quintum || imperatorem, || A || Philippo Melanchthone & || Casparo Peucero. || Postrema editio, cui acceßerunt Capitum & || Rerum Indices. || Apud Ioannem le Preux. || M.D.XCIII.
[Geneva] : Jean le Preux, 1593
[48], 957 [Pars 1–2 = p. 1–392, Pars 3 = p. 395–957], [51] p.; 8°
USTC 451367
London, British Library: 9006.b.2.

1594

183   CHRONICON || CARIONIS || EXPOSITVM || ET AVCTVM MVL-||TIS ET VE-TERIBVS ET || RECENTIBVS HISTORIIS, IN || descriptionibus regnorum & gentium antiquarum, || & narrationibus rerum Ecclesiasticarum, & Politica-||rum, Græcarum, Romanarum, Germani-||carum & aliarum, ab exordio Mundi || vsque ad CAROLVM V. || Imperatorem. || A || PHILIPPO MELAN-THONE || & Casparo Peucero. || RECENS VERO SVMMO STVDIO || adornatum, pristinæq[ue] integritati, exemplorum || veterum ac recentium collatione ex-||quisita, restitutum. || QVID PRAETEREA HVIC EDITIONI || accesserit, versa ostendet pagella. || FRANCOFVRTI AD MOENVM, || apud Ioannem Feyrabendt. || M.D.XCIIII.
Frankfurt a.M. : Johann Feyerabend, 1594
1377, [123] p.; 8°
VD16 M 2721
VD16 P 1965
USTC 622449
Chicago, Newberry Library: Case F 09 .149
Wolfenbüttel, Herzog August Bibliothek: H: T 258a.8° Helmst.

---

24   Scherer (p. 473) does not list any editions from Geneva for this year, but he refers to an edition from Paris (London, British Library), which seems to be this le Preux edition.

183.P.3 TERTIA PARS || CHRONICI || CARIONIS || A || CASPARO PEVCERO || expositi & aucti. || FRANCOFVRTI AD MOENVM. || M.D.XCIIII.
Frankfurt a.M. : Johann Feyerabend, 1594
p. 599–1377, [123] p.; 8°
[VD16 M 2721]
VD16 P 1965
USTC 622449
Wolfenbüttel, Herzog August Bibliothek: H: T 258b.8° Helmst.

184.I CHRONIQVE || ET HISTOIRE VNI-||VERSELLE, CONTENANT || LES CHOSES MEMORABLES ADVE-||nues és quatre souuerains Empires, Royau-||mes, Republiques, & au gouuernement de || l'Eglise, depuis le cómencement du monde || iusques à l'Empereur Charles cinquiesme. || Dressee premierement par IEAN CARION, puis au-||gmentee, amplement exposee & enrichie de diuerses hi-||stoires, tant Ecclesiastiques que Politiques, anciennes || & modernes, par PHILIPPE MELANCTHON, || & GASPAR PEVCER, & reduite en cinq liures, || traduits de Latin en François. || Ensemble deux liures adioustez de nouueau aux cinq || precedens, comprenans les choses notables aduenues || sous Charles cinquiesme, Ferdinand || premier, & Maximilian second. || Tome premier. || PAR IAQVES BERION. || CIƆ. IƆ. XCIIII.
[Geneva] : Jacques Berjon, 1594
[32] fol., 858 p., [34] fol.; 8° [Contains Liber 1–4]
Dresden, Sächsische Landesbibliothek: Hist.univ.A.684

184.II CHRONIQVE || ET HISTOIRE || VNIVERSELLE. || A ce volume est adioustee de nouueau vne qua-||triesme partie de Chroniques, comprinse en || deux liures, le premier desquels (qui est le sixies||me en ordre) comprend les choses notables ad-||uenues sous l'Empire de Charles cinquiesme: || & le second (qui est le septiesme & dernier) || poursuit l'histoire depuis Charles cinquiesme, || iusques à la mort de Maximilian second. || Tome second. || PAR IAQVES BERION. || CIƆ. IƆ. XCIIII.
[Geneva] : Jacques Berjon, 1594
[16] fol., 1–366, [1]-665, [1] p., [28] fol.; 8° [Contains Liber 5 & Continuation]
Dijon, Bibliothèque Municipale: 3185

1595

185 SECVNDA PARS || CHRONICI || CARIONIS, AB AV-||GVSTO CAESARE VSQVE || ad Carolum Magnum. || Exposita & aucta à || PHILIPPO MELANTHONE. || Cum Gratia & Priuilegio Cæsareæ Maiestat. || & Ducis Sax. Elect. &c. || VVITEBERGAE, || Excudebat Zacharias Lehman, || ANNO M.D.XCV.

Wittenberg : Zacharias Lehmann, 1595
[1] fol., fol. 162–336, [63] fol.; 8°
VD16 M 2722
USTC 692905
Wolfenbüttel, Herzog August Bibliothek: A: 424.11 Hist. (2)

186.1.I CHRONIQVE || ET HISTOIRE || VNIVERSELLE, || CONTENANT LES CHOSES PLVS || memorables auenues es quatre souuerains Em-||pires, Royaumes, Republiques, & au gouuerne-||ment de l'Eglise, depuis le commencement du || monde iusques à l'Empereur Charles cinquiesme. || Dressee premiere-ment par Iean CARION, puis augmen-||tee, amplement exposee & enrichie de diuerses histoires || tant Ecclesiastiques que Politiques, anciennes & mo-||dernes, par Ph. MELANCHTHON & Gaspar || PEVCER, & reduite en cinq li-ures, traduits de || Latin en François. || Plus deux Liures adioustez de nouueau aux cinq autres, compre-||nans les choses notables auenues en l'Europe sous l'Em-||pire de Charles cinquiesme, Ferdinand premier, || Maximilian se-cond, & Rodolphe || second. || Tome Premier. || Pour Pierre de Sainct André. || M.D.XCV.
[Geneva] : Pierre de Saint André, 1595
[8] fol., 1071 p.; 8° [Contains Liber 1–5]
USTC 3164
French Vernacular Books: 8928
Bibliotheca Palatina: H1742/H1747
Bibliotheca Palatina: I259/I264
London, British Library: C.75.a.15.
Wolfenbüttel, Herzog August Bibliothek: M: Gb 60

186.1.II CHRONIQVE || ET HISTOIRE || VNIVERSELLE, || OU || RECVEIL DES CHOSES || MEMORABLES DE NOSTRE || temps en diuerses parties du || monde, sous l'Em-||pire de || CHARLES V. || FERDINAND I. || MAXIMILIAN II. || RODOLPHE II. || Depuis l'an M.D.XVII. iusques à l'an M.D.XCV. || seruant de suite & supplement à la Chro-||nique de CARION. || Tome Second. || Pour Pierre de Sainct André. || M.D.XCV.
[Geneva] : Pierre de Saint André, 1595
[8] fol., 690 p., [70] fol., [1] p.; 8° [Contains Continuation]
USTC 66011
French Vernacular Books: 8929
Bibliotheca Palatina: H1747/H1751
Bibliotheca Palatina: I264/I268
London, British Library: C.75.a.15.

186.2.I CHRONIQVE || ET HISTOIRE || VNIVERSELLE, || CONTENANT LES CHOSES PLVS || memorables auenues es quatre souuerains Em-||pires, Royaumes,

Republiques, & au gouuerne-||ment de l'Eglise, depuis le commencement du || monde iusques à l'Empereur Charles cinquiesme. || Dressee premiere-ment par Iean CARION, puis augmen-||tee, amplement exposee & enrichie de diuerses histoires || tant Ecclesiastiques que Politiques, anciennes & mo-||dernes, par Ph. MELANCHTHON & Gaspar || PEVCER, & reduite en cinq li-ures, traduits de || Latin en François. || Plus deux Liures adioustez de nouueau aux cinq autres, compre-||nans les choses notables auenues en l'Europe sous l'Em-||pire de Charles cinquiesme, Ferdinand premier, || Maximilian se-cond, & Rodolphe || second. || Tome Premier. || Imprimé pour Iacob Stœr. || M.D.XCV.
[Geneva] : Jacques Stoer, 1595
[8] fol., 1071 p.; 8° [Contains Liber 1–5]
USTC 65689
French Vernacular Books: 8927
Basel, Universitätsbibliothek: EA VI 26
Stuttgart, Württembergische Landesbibliothek: Allg.G.oct.414

186.2.II CHRONIQVE || ET HISTOIRE || VNIVERSELLE, || OU || RECVEIL DES CHOSES || MEMORABLES DE NOSTRE || temps en diuerses parties du || monde, sous l'Em-||pire de || CHARLES V. || FERDINAND I. || MAXIMILIAN II. || RODOLPHE II. || Depuis l'an M.D.XVII. iusques à l'an M.D.XCV. || seruant de suite & supplement à la Chro-||nique de CARION. || Tome Second. || Imprimé pour Iacob Stœr. || M.D.XCV.
[Geneva] : Jacques Stoer, 1595
[8] fol., 690 p., [70] fol., [1] p.; 8° [Contains Continuation]
USTC 65689
Basel, Universitätsbibliothek: EA VI 26a

187 CHRONICA || IOHANNIS || Carionis. || Hvor vdi findis bescreff=||uen Tiden oc Aarene / oc huad der vdi skeet || er fra Verdsens begyndelse: Det er / fra Adam oc indtil || Abraham, &c. Disligeste om de fire Monarchiers Opreiselse || oc Nederfald: Met mange andre skøne oc merckelige || Historier oc Exempler / baade Geistlig || oc Verdslig. || forbedret aff PHILIPPO || Melanthone. || Oc nu nyligen vdset paa Danske / oc forbe=||dret aff PHILIPPI Scriffter || Aff || Christen Lauritzøn Linued / Guds Ords Tienere || vdi Vig i Sogn vdi Bergen-huss || Stict i Norge. || Igennemloest / Corrigerit oc Prentet i Kiøben=||haffn / aff Laurentz Benedicht. Vic. Ros. || 1595. || Cum gratia & Priuilegio Regiæ || Maiestatis.
Copenhagen : Laurentz Benedicht, 1595
[24], 191 fol.; 4°
USTC 302888
Nielson, Dansk Bibliografi 1551–1600: 482
Copenhagen, Det Kongelige Bibliotek: Hist. 6049 4°

1596

188[25] Chronicon || CARIONIS PHI-||LIPPICVM IN ENCHIRI=||DII FORMAM RE-DACTVM, || & juuandæ memoriæ causa, versibus Heroi-||cis comprehensum. || DEDVCTA CONTINVA SERIE || ab initio mundi vsq[ue] ad CHRistum || natum || In gratiam & vsum juuentutis historiarum || studiosæ, bono studio contextum || à || M. HALVARDO GVNARIO || Norvego, S.S. Theologiæ lectore in Gymnasio || Asloiensi. || Sunt Regum specula historiæ, quibus omnia, paßim || Quæ fugienda sibi, quæ facienda, vident. || Rostochij typis Ferberi junioris, Anno || M.D.XCVI.
Rostock : Augustin Ferber d.J., 1596
[56] p.; 4°
VD16 ZV 7166
USTC 622457
Nielson, Dansk Bibliografi 1551–1600: 693
London, British Library: 154.e.7.(3.)

189.I CHRONIQVE || ET HISTOIRE || VNIVERSELLE, || Contenant les choses plus memorables || auenues es quatre souuerains Empires, || Royaumes, Reipubliques, & au gouuernement de || l'Eglise, depuis le commencement du monde ius-||ques à l'Empereur Charles cinquiesme. || Dressee premierement par Iean CARION, puis aug-||mentee, amplement exposee & enrichie de diuerses hi-||stoires tant Ecclesiastiques que Politiques, anciennes || & modernes, par Ph. MELANCHTHON & Gaspar || PEVCER, & reduite en cinq liures, traduits de La-||tin en François. || Ensemble deux liures adioustez de nouueau aux cinq prece-||dens, comprenans les choses notables auenues en l'Euro-||pe sous l'Empire de Charles cinquiesme, Ferdinand || premier, Maximilian second, & Ro-||dolphe second. || Tome Premier. || Pour Louys Elzeuier. || M.D.XCVI.
[Leiden] : Lowijs Elzevier, 1596
[32] fol., 858 p., [34] fol.; 8° [Contains Liber 1–4]
USTC 4314
French Vernacular Books: 8930
Willems, Les Elzevier: 30
Den Haag, Koninklijke Bibliotheek: 1707 D 3

189.II CHRONIQVE || ET HISTOIRE || VNIVERSELLE, || ou || RECVEIL DES CHOSES || MEMORABLES DE NOSTRE || temps en diuerses parties || du

---

25 On this verse adaptation, see Inger Ekrem, *Historieskrivning og -undervisning på latin i Oslo omkring år 1600: Halvard Gunnarssøns Philippiske Carionkrønike, Rostock 1596. Med innledning, oversettelse og kommentar* (Oslo: Scandinavian University Press, 1998).

monde, sous l'Em-||pire de || CHARLES V. || FERDINAND I. || MAXIMILIAN II. || RODOLPHE II. || Depuis l'an M.D.XVII. iusques à l'an M.D.XCV. || seruant de suite & supplement à la Chro-||nique de CARION. || [Tome Second.] || Pour Louys Elzeuier. || M.D.XCVI.
[Leiden] : Lowijs Elzevier, 1596
[16] fol., 366 p. [Liber 5], 665 p. [Liber 6–7], 103 p. [Continuation]; 8°
USTC 4314
[French Vernacular Books: 8930]
Willems, Les Elzevier: 30
St. Petersburg, National Library of Russia: 8.15.9 [Title page incomplete]

1601[26]

190   CHRONICON || CARIONIS, || EXPOSITVM, ET AVCTVM MVLTIS, || ET VE-TERIBVS, ET RECENTIBVS HISTORIIS, || in descriptionibus regnorum, & gentium antiquarum, || & narrationibus rerum Ecclesiasticarum, & Politica-||rum, Græcarum, Romanarum, Germanicarum, & alia-||rum, ab exordio Mundi, vsque ad Carolum Quintum || Imperatorem: || A || Philippo Melanchthone, & || Casparo Peucero. || Postrema editio, prioribus omnibus longè castigatior: || cui accesserunt Capitum, & Rerum || Indices. || BERNÆ, || Excudebat Iohannes le Preux Illustriss. || DD. Bern. Typographus. || M.D.CI.
Bern : Jean le Preux, 1601
[24] fol., 957 p., [24] fol.; 8°
VD17 12:133763G
Kiel, Universitätsbibliothek: K 3320
München, Bayerische Staatsbibliothek: Chron. 49

191   Operum || REVERENDI VIRI || PHILIPPI MELANCHTHONIS. || PARS QVINTA. || CONTINENS ENARRATIONEM CHRONICI CA-||RIONIS; expositi & aucti multis & veteribus & recentibus historiis, in || descriptionibus regnorum & gentium antiquarum, & narrationibus || rerum Ecclesiasticarum, & Politicarum, Græcarum, Romana-||rum, Germanicarum, & aliarum, ab exordio mundi vsque || ad Carolum Quintum Imperatorem; ab ipso Auto-||re, & CASPARO PEVCERO. || Adiecta est narratio historica de electione & corona-||tione

---

26   Scherer (p. 474) lists a complete French translation of the revised *Chronicle* from Geneva for 1601, but this seems to be a reference to the 1611 edition (Kiel, Universitätsbibliothek: K 3314-1, K 3314-2). Kiel also has the Latin edition of the revised *Chronicle* from 1601 (Kiel, Universitätsbibliothek: K 3320).

CAROLI V. Imperatoris. || Cum Gratia & Priuilegio ad annos quindecim. || VVITEBERGAE || Typis Simonis Gronenbergij; sumptum impendente || Zacharia Schürerio, & eius socijs. || M.DCI.
Wittenberg : Zacharias Schürer [by Simon Gronenberg], 1601
[30] fol., 746 p., [28] fol.; 2°
[Colophon: VVITEBERGÆ || Excudebant Hæredes Johannis Cratonis, Anno || M.D.LXXX.]
VD17 3:610324H
London, British Library: 478.g.2.
Halle, Universitäts- und Landesbibliothek Sachsen-Anhalt: Ib 4242 b, 4° (5)

192   CHRONICI || CARIONIS PHILIP-||PICI IN COMPENDIVM || redacti, & juvandæ memoriæ gra-||tiâ elegiaco carmine redditi, partes duæ po-||steriores de Cæsaribus Romanis, By-||zantinis, & Germanicis. || Deductâ continuâ serie à C. Iulio Cæsare || usq[ue] ad Rudolphum II. Imperatorem. || In usum studiosæ juventutis concinnati || Curâ & industriâ || M. HALVARDI GVNARII, || NORVEGI in Gymnasio Aslojensi S.S. || Theologiæ lectoris. || Sunt regum specula historiæ, quibus omnia paßim, || Quæ fugienda sibi, quæ facienda, vident. || ROSTOCHII || Typis Myliandrinis, Anno M.D.CI.
Rostock : Stephan Möllemann, 1601
[92] p.; 4°
Oslo, Nasjonalbiblioteket: NA/A a 4816/si
Oslo, Nasjonalbiblioteket: NA/A f 5909/si

1602

193   Kronyka Swěta || O znamenitěgssjch wěcech a proměnách / || kteréž se kde a kdy hned odpočátku w Swětě / buďto || při náboženstwij a Cýrkwi / aneb při Krá=||lowstwjch Zemských přicházeľy || a zbjhaľy. || Od Jana Karyona krátce sebraná / a ney=||prwé w Gazyku Latinském a Německém wyda=||ná: Potom w Gazyk Cžeský před lety XLIII. od || Bur Jana z Kornic přeľožená / a w Li-||tomyssli wytisstěná. || Nynij pak znowu přehlednutá / w Cžessti=||ně pooprawená / a s poznamenánjm některých || přednějssjch wěcý, až do smrti sľawné a swaté || paměti Cýsaře Maxmiliana II. do-||wedená / od || M. Danyele Adama z Weleslawjna || W Starém Městě Pražském. || A nynj znowu Wytľačená v Dědicůw geho. || Léta Páně: || M.DC.II
Prague : Daniel Adam z Veleslavina, 1602
[8], 480, [23] p.; 4°
Knihopis českých a slovenských tisků: 1465
Prague, Strahov Monastery Library [Strahovská knihovna]: BC VI 103

1604

194.A CHRONICI || CARIONIS PHILIP- || PICI IN COMPENDIVM || redacti, & juvandæ memoriæ gra- || tiâ elegiaco carmine redditi, partes duæ po- || steriores de Cæsaribus Romanis, By- || zantinis, & Germanicis. || Deductâ continuâ serie à C. Julio Cæsare || usq[ue] ad Rudolphum II. Imperatorem. || In usum studiosæ juventutis concinnati, || Curâ & industriâ || M. HALVARDI GVNARII, || NORVEGI, in Gymnasio Aslojensi S.S. || Theologiæ lectoris. || Sunt regum specula historiæ, quibus omnia paßim || Quæ fugienda sibi, quæ facienda, vident. || ROSTOCHII || Typis Stephani Myliandri. Anno 1604.
Rostock : Stephan Möllemann, 1604
[92] p.; 4°
Uppsala, Universitetsbibliotek: Danica vet. 199 (2)

1606

194 CHRONICI || CARIONIS PHILIPPICI || in Compendium redacti, & juvan-||dæ memoriæ gratiâ elegiaco carmine red-||diti, partes duæ posteriores de Cæ-||saribus Romanis, Bizantinis, || & Germanicis. || Deductâ continuâ serie à C. Iulio Cæ-||sare usq[ue] ad Rudolphum II. Imperatorem. || In usum studiosæ juventutis concinnati, || Curâ & industriâ || M. HALVARDI GVNARII, || NORVEGI, in Gymnasio Aslojensi S.S. || Theologiæ lectoris. || Sunt regum specula historiæ, quibus omnia paßim || Quæ fugienda sibi, quæ facienda, vident. || ROSTOCHII || Ex Typographia Stephani Myliandri, || Anno M.DC.VI.
Rostock : Stephan Möllemann, 1606
[92] p.; 4°
VD17 7:693501X
London, British Library: 154.e.7.(3.)
Göttingen, Niedersächsische Staats- und Universitätsbibliothek: 8NORV 2050 (3)

1609

195 HISTOIRE, || OV CHRONIQVE || DES CHOSES PLVS || MEMORABLES, || Aduenuës dés le commencement du monde, || iusques au regne du tres-Chrestien || Roy de France & de Nauarre || HENRY IIII. || Recueillie Premierement par IEAN CARION, || & depuis suyuie, traduicte & augmentée par || IEAN LE BLOND. || A LYON, || Par IAQVES DE LA HAYE. || M.DC.IX.
Lyon : Jacques de La Haye, 1609

[32] fol., 733, [4] p.; 16°
Répertoire bibliographique des livres imprimés en France au XVIIe siècle: XXVI, 37
London, British Library: 1606/405.
Göttingen, Niedersächsische Staats- und Universitätsbibliothek: 8 H UN II, 137

1610

[196] *Histoire, ou Chronique des choses plus memorables...*
Lyon : Barthélémy Vincent, 1610
?? fol.; 8°
Brunet, Supplément: vol. 1, col. 206
[Moller, 22 (2); see Strobel, 184; Scherer, 472]

197 CHRONICON || CARIONIS, || EXPOSITVM, ET AVCTVM MVLTIS, || & veteribus & recentibus historiis, in descriptionibus re-||gnorum & gentium antiquarum, & narrationibus rerum || Ecclesiasticarum, & Politicarum, Gręcarum, Romanarum, || Germanicarum, & aliarum, ab exordio Mundi, vsque ad || Carolum V. Ferdinandum I. Maximilianum II. Rudol-||phum II. Imperatores. || A Philippo Melanchthone, & || Casparo Peucero. || Postrema editio, prioribus omnibus longè castigatior: cui accesse-||runt Capitum & Rerum Indices locupletissimi. || Aureliæ Allobrogum, || EXCVDEBAT ESAIAS LE PREVX. || CIƆ IƆCX.
Geneva : Esaias le Preux, 1610
[20] fol., 1000, [46] p.; 8°
London, British Library: 9004.e.3.
Wolfenbüttel, Herzog August Bibliothek: M: Gb 54

1611

198.1.I CHRONIQVE || ET HISTOIRE || VNIVERSELLE, || CONTENANT LES CHO-||SES PLVS MEMORABLES AVE-||nues es quatre souuerains Empires, Royaumes, Repu-||bliques, & au gouuernement de l'Eglise, depuis le || commencement du monde, iusques à l'Empereur || Charles cinquiesme. || Dressee premierement par Iean CARION, puis augmentee, ample-||ment exposee, & enrichie de diuerses histoires, tant Ecclesiastiques || que Politiques, anciennes & modernes, par PH. MELANCH-||THON & GASPAR PEVCER, & reduite en cinq || liures traduits de Latin en François. || Plus deux liures adioustez de nouueau aux cinq autres, || comprenans les choses notables auenues en l'Europe || sous l'Empire de Charles cinquiesme, Ferdinand pre-||mier, Maximilian second, & Rodolphe second, iusques à || la fin de l'an Mil six cens & dix. || Tome premier. || Pour PIERRE & IAQVES CHOVET. || M.DC.XI.

Geneva : Pierre & Jacques Chouet, 1611

[8] fol., 1071 p.; 8° [Contains Liber 1–5]

Metz, Bibliothèque municipale: P 1133

Oxford, Bodleian Library: 8° C 135 Art.

198.1.II CHRONIQVE || ET HISTOIRE || VNIVERSELLE, || OU || RECVEIL DES CHOSES || memorables de nostre temps en diuerses || parties du monde, sous l'Em-||pire de || CHARLES V. || FERDINAND I. || MAXIMILIAN II. || RODOLPHE II. || Depuis l'an M.D.XVII. iusques à la fin de l'an MDCX. ser-||uant de suite & supplement à la Chronique || de CARION. || Tome Second. || Pour PIERRE & IACQVES CHOVET. || M.DC.XI.

Geneva : Pierre & Jacques Chouet, 1611

[8] fol., 736 p., [72] fol.; 8° [Contains Continuation]

Metz, Bibliothèque municipale: P 1134

Oxford, Bodleian Library: 8° C 136 Art.

198.2.I CHRONIQVE || ET HISTOIRE || VNIVERSELLE, || CONTENANT LES CHO-||SES PLVS MEMORABLES AVE-||nues es quatre souuerains Empires, Royaumes, Repu-||bliques, & au gouuernement de l'Eglise, depuis le || commencement du monde, iusques à l'Empereur || Charles cinquiesme. || Dressee premierement par Iean CARION, puis augmentee, ample-||ment exposee, & enrichie de diuerses histoires, tant Ecclesiastiques || que Politiques, anciennes & modernes, par PH. MELANCH-||THON & GASPAR PEVCER, & reduite en cinq || liures traduits de Latin en François. || Plus deux liures adioustez de nouueau aux cinq autres, || comprenans les choses notables auenues en l'Europe || sous l'Empire de Charles cinquiesme, Ferdinand pre-||mier, Maximilian second, & Rodolphe second, iusques à || la fin de l'an Mil six cens & dix. || Tome premier. || GENEVÆ || Pour SAMVEL CRESPIN. || M.DC.XI.

Geneva : Samuel Crespin, 1611

[8] fol., 1071 p.; 8° [Contains Liber 1–5]

Boston, Tufts University Library: D18 .C2 1611 v.1 c.1

198.2.II CHRONIQVE || ET HISTOIRE || VNIVERSELLE, || OU || RECVEIL DES CHOSES || memorables de nostre temps en diuerses || parties du monde, sous l'Em-||pire de || CHARLES V. || FERDINAND I. || MAXIMILIAN II. || RODOLPHE II. || Depuis l'an M.D.XVII. iusques à la fin de l'an MDCX. ser-||uant de suite & supplement à la Chronique || de CARION. || Tome Second. || GENEVÆ || POVR SAMVEL CRESPIN. || M.DC.XI.

Geneva : Samuel Crespin, 1611

[8] fol., 736 p., [72] fol.; 8° [Contains Continuation]
Boston, Tufts University Library: D18 .C2 1611 v.2 c.1
Oxford, Taylor Institution Library: VET.FR.I.A.447

198.3.I CHRONIQVE || ET HISTOIRE || VNIVERSELLE, || CONTENANT LES CHO-||SES PLVS MEMORABLES AVE-||nues es quatre souuerains Empires, Royaumes, Repu-||bliques, & au gouuernement de l'Eglise, depuis le || commencement du monde, iusques à l'Empereur || Charles cinquiesme. || Dressee premiere-ment par Iean CARION, puis augmentee, ample-||ment exposee, & enrichie de diuerses histoires, tant Ecclesiastiques || que Politiques, anciennes & mo-dernes, par PH. MELANCH-||THON & GASPAR PEVCER, & reduite en cinq || liures traduits de Latin en François. || Plus deux liures adioustez de nouueau aux cinq autres, || comprenans les choses notables auenues en l'Europe || sous l'Empire de Charles cinquiesme, Ferdinand pre-||mier, Maximilian se-cond, & Rodolphe second, iusques à || la fin de l'an Mil six cens & dix. || Tome premier. || A GENEVE || De l'Imprimerie de IACOB STOER. || M.DC.XI
Geneva : Jacques Stoer, 1611
[8] fol., 1071 p.; 8° [Contains Liber 1–5]
Kiel, Universitätsbibliothek: K 3314-1

198.3.II CHRONIQVE || ET HISTOIRE || VNIVERSELLE, || OU || RECVEIL DES CHOSES || memorables de nostre temps en diuerses || parties du monde, sous l'Em-||pire de || CHARLES V. || FERDINAND I. || MAXIMILIAN II. || RODOLPHE II. || Depuis l'an M.D.XVII. iusques à la fin de l'an MDCX. ser-||uant de suite & supplement à la Chronique || de CARION. || Tome Second. || A GENEVE || De l'Imprimerie de Iacob Stoer. || M.DC.XI
Geneva : Jacques Stoer, 1611
[8] fol., 736 p., [72] fol.; 8° [Contains Continuation]
Kiel, Universitätsbibliothek: K 3314-2

198.4.I CHRONIQVE || ET HISTOIRE || VNIVERSELLE, || CONTENANT LES CHO-||SES PLVS MEMORABLES AVE-||nues es quatre souuerains Empires, Royaumes, Repu-||bliques, & au gouuernement de l'Eglise, depuis le || commencement du monde, iusques à l'Empereur || Charles cinquiesme. || Dressee premiere-ment par Iean CARION, puis augmentee, ample-||ment exposee, & enrichie de diuerses histoires, tant Ecclesiastiques || que Politiques, anciennes & mo-dernes, par PH. MELANCH-||THON & GASPAR PEVCER, & reduite en cinq || liures traduits de Latin en François. || Plus deux liures adioustez de nouueau aux cinq autres, || comprenans les choses notables auenues en l'Europe || sous l'Empire de Charles cinquiesme, Ferdinand pre-||mier, Maximilian se-cond, & Rodolphe second, iusques à || la fin de l'an Mil six cens & dix. || Tome premier. || Pour IEAN VIGNON. || M.DC.XI
Geneva : Jean Vignon, 1611

CARION'S CHRONICLE – CENSUS OF EDITIONS 463

[8] fol., 1071 p.; 8° [Contains Liber 1–5]
Paris, Bibliothèque Nationale: G-12269, Tolbiac - Rez de jardin - Magasin [Lost]
St. Petersburg, National Library of Russia: 32.1a.5.21

198.4.II CHRONIQVE || ET HISTOIRE || VNIVERSELLE, || ou || RECVEIL DES CHOSES || memorables de nostre temps en diuerses || parties du monde, sous l'Em-||pire de || CHARLES V. || FERDINAND I. || MAXIMILIAN II. || RODOLPHE II. || Depuis l'an M.D.XVII. iusques à la fin de l'an MDCX. ser-||uant de suite & supplement à la Chronique || de CARION. || Tome Second. || POVR IEAN VIGNON. || M.DC.XI.
[Geneva] : Jean Vignon, 1611
[8] fol., 736 p., [72] fol.; 8° [Contains Continuation]
Paris, Bibliothèque Nationale: G-12270, Tolbiac - Rez de jardin - Magasin
Stuttgart, Württembergische Landesbibliothek: Allg.G.oct.416

1617

199 CHRONICON || CARIONIS. || EXPOSITVM ET AVCTVM, || multis & veteribus, & recentibus historiis, in || descriptionibus regnorum & gentium anti-||quarum, & narrationibus rerum Ecclesiasti-||carum & Politicarum, Græcarum, Romana-||rum, Germnicarum, & aliarum, ab exordio || Mundi, vsque ad annum Salutis per Christum || partæ 1612. nempe Rudolphi II. excessum. || A PHILIPPO MELANCTHONE, & || CASPARO PEVCERO. || Postrema editio, prioribus omnibus longè castigator: cui || accesserunt Capitum & Rerum INDICES || locupletissimi. || Sumptibus SAMVELIS CRISPINI. || M.DC.XVII.
[Geneva] : Samuel Crespin, 1617
[20] fol., 1015 p., [27] fol.; 8°
London, Warburg Institute Library: NAH 6550.C36 1617
Wolfenbüttel, Herzog August Bibliothek: H: T 259.8° Helmst.

1624

200 CHRONICON || CARIONIS || EXPOSITVM ET || AVCTVM MVLTIS ET || VETERIBVS ET RECENTIBVS HISTORIIS, || in descriptionibus regnorum & gentium antiquarum, || & narrationibus rerum Ecclesiasticarum, & Politicarum, || Græcarum, Romanarum, Germanicarum & aliarum, || ab exordio Mundi vsque ad CAROLVM V. || Imperatorem. || A || PHILIPPO MELANTHONE || & Casparo Peucero. || RECENS VERO SVMMO STVDIO || adornatum, pristinæque integritati, exemplorum || veterum ac recentium collatione exquisita, ||

restitutum. || QVID PRÆTEREA HVIC EDITIONI || accesserit, versa ostendet pagella. || FRANCOFVRTI AD MOENVM, || Impensis GODEFRIDI TAMPACHII, || M.DC.XXIV.
Frankfurt a.M. : Gottfried Tambach, 1624
1377 p., [55] fol.; 8°
VD17 23:299941N
Halle, Universitäts- und Landesbibliothek Sachsen-Anhalt: Pon Vg 4152
Wolfenbüttel, Herzog August Bibliothek: M: Gb 55

200.P.3   TERTIA PARS || CHRONICI || CARIONIS || A || CASPARO PEVCERO || expositi & aucti. || FRANCOFVRTI AD MOENVM, || impensis GODEFRIDI TAMPACHII. || M.DC.XXIV.
Frankfurt a.M. : Gottfried Tambach, 1624
p. [597]-1377, [55] fol.; 8°
VD17 23:299941N
[Wolfenbüttel, Herzog August Bibliothek: M: Gb 55]

1625

201.1   CHRONICON || CARIONIS, || EXPOSITVM ET AVCTVM, || multis & veteribus, & recentibus historiis, || in descriptionibus regnorum & gentium || antiquarum, & narrationibus rerum Eccle-||siasticarum & Politicarum, Græcarum, Ro-||manarum, Germnicarum, & aliarum, ab || exordio Mundi, vsque ad annum Salutis || per Christum partæ 1612. nempe Rudolphi || II. excessum. || A PHILIPPO MELANCTHONE, & || CASPARO PEVCERO. || Postrema editio, prioribus omnibus longè castigatior: cui || accesserunt Capitum & Rerum INDICES || locupletissimi. || Sumptibus SAMVELIS CRISPINI. || M.DC.XXV.
[Geneva] : Samuel Crespin, 1625
[20] fol., 1015 p., [27] fol.; 8°
London, British Library: 9004.e.1.

201.2   CHRONICON || CARIONIS, || EXPOSITVM ET AVCTVM, || multis & veteribus, & recentibus historiis, || in descriptionibus regnorum & gentium || antiquarum, & narrationibus rerum Eccle-||siasticarum & Politicarum, Græcarum, Ro-||manarum, Germnicarum, & aliarum, ab || exordio Mundi, vsque ad annum Salutis || per Christum partæ 1612. nempe Rudolphi || II. excessum. || A PHILIPPO MELANCTHONE, & || CASPARO PEVCERO. || Postrema editio, prioribus omnibus longè castigatior: cui || accesserunt Capitum & Rerum INDICES || locupletissimi. || Geneuæ, || Sumptibus SAMVELIS CRISPINI. || M.DC.XXV.
Geneva : Samuel Crespin, 1625

[20] fol., 1015 p., [27] fol.; 8°
London, British Library: 580.c.8.
London, British Library: 9006.b.3.
Cambridge, Trinity College Library: NQ.8.124 [Isaac Newton's copy]

1629

202   PHILIPPUS MELANTHON || CHRONICA || CARIONIS || Vanden Beginne des werelts aen || tot op den Keyser Carolum den || vyfden van dien name. || In't Latyn beschreven door de geleerde en||de wel vermaerde Mannen || D. PHIL. MELANTHONEM en[de] D. CASPAR. PEUCERUM. || Uijt de Hooch-duytsche spraeke inde Neder-lantsche || getrouwelyck overgeset, door den wel Edelen Joncker || Wilhem van Zuylen van Nyvelt. || Heere van Heer-aerts-berge. || Daer by op nieus ge-voecht ende Noyt voor desen in Ne=||derlands gedruckt syn de Vervolgende geschiedenißen || onder de Regeringe der Keyseren Caerle de V.^{de} voornoint || Ferdinand de eerste ende Maximiliaen de Tweede || tot op Rodolphum de Tweede. || Uijt den Françoysche overgeset Door den voor-noemden || Heere W.V.Z.V.N. || Inde welcke des Werelts Loop. Handel, Aert ende Werck, || Doen ende Laten, merckelycke Veranderingen von Geluck || ende Ongeluck, Straffen der Quaden, opkomen eñ beloo=||ninge der Vromen ende beproevinge der selver eñ veel || wonderlycke geschiedenissen verhaelt werden alles || Dienstelyck tot verlustinge, ende vermakinge || profyt, voor-deel ende oock waerschouwinge || van eenen yegelyck. || TOT || AERNHEM || By Ian Ianß. Boeck-verkooper. || Anno 1629.
Arnhem : Jan Jansz, 1629
[16], 770 [= 786], [5] p. [= Liber 1–5]; [4], 324, [4] p. [= Continuation]; 2°
London, British Library: RB.23.b.4680
Amsterdam, Universiteitsbibliotheek: OTM OM 63–367
Amsterdam, Bibliotheek van de Vrije Universiteit: XL.05108

202.II   HET VYFDE DEEL || der Chronijcke || CARIONIS. || Wt den Francoyschen in Nederduytsch vertaelt door den || Edelen ende seer verstandighen Heere / S. Ged. || W. V. N. || Inhoudende de Waerachtighe ende Ghedenck-vverdichste sa-||ken ende geschiedenissen, gebeurt in de voornaemste deelen der geheel-er || vverelt, daer inne te lesen zijn veel wonderlijcke saken: veranderinghe van || Rijcken, straffe der quaden, opcomen ende belooninge der vromen, vvesende niet || alleen lustich, maer oock voorderlick, nut ende profijtelick om lesen || voor allen staten ende soorten van menschen. || Handelende van alles dat gheschiet is / gheduerende de Regieringhe || van Carolus de V.^{de}, Ferdinandus den eersten, ende Maximilianus || den tweeden, Roomsche

Keyseren. || Noyt voor desen in de Nederduytsche tale ghesien. || TOT || ARNHEM, || By Ian Iansz: Boeck-verkooper. ANNO 1629.
Arnhem : Jan Jansz, 1629
[4], 324, [4] p. [= Continuation]; 2°
[Amsterdam, Bibliotheek van de Vrije Universiteit: XL.05108]

1632

203.II   Het Seste Deel, || DER || CHRONYCKE || CARIONIS: || Inhoudende de Voornaemste ende Ghe-||denck-weerdighste saken ende Gheschiedenissen, || in Geestelicke ende Wereltlicke saken, de welcke beyde in tijde van || Vrede ende Oorloge, te VVater ende te Lande geschiet zijn, in de || voornaemste deelen des gheheelen Aertbodems, zedert den aen-||vanck van de Regieringe des Groot-machtigen Rodolphi de II. de || welcke den 27. Octobris 1567. gecroont is, tot den overlyden van Mat-||thias den I. des voorsz. Rodolphi Broeder, beyde Roomsche Keyseren, || die den 20. Martij 1619. overleden is, begrijpende over sulcx den tijdt van twee-en-||veertigh Iaren ende vier Maenden. || Vervolght ende beschreven || Door Pieter Bor Christiaensz. || Waer inne veel wonderlicke saken verhaelt ende te bemercken staen / sonderlinghe den || loop / ydelheyt / veranderlicheyt / ende ongestadigheyt van alle menschelicke saken / de || verwisselinghe van gheluck in ongheluck / den opganck ende den onderganck van Regieringen der || Rijcken ende Republijquen; de boosheyt / archlistigheyt ende verkeertheyt van de meeste menschen; || de plagen ende schrickelicke straffen / die Godt Landen ende menschen / om de grouwelicke sonden / || dickwils in dit leven is toe-sendende. || Nut ende voorderlick voor allen Lief-hebberen der Historien ende Chronijcken, || ende allen Staten ende soorten der Menschen. || Esther 6. 1. 2. || In de selve nacht conde de Coninck niet vele slapen, ende hiet de Chronijcken ende Hi-||storien voort brengen: Doe die voor den Coninck ghelesen werden, treftemen de plaetse || daer gheschreven was, hoe dat Mardachai hadde aengheseyt, &c. || Esra 4. 15. || Datmen late soecken in de Chronijcke uwer Vaderen, soo sult ghy vinden in de selve || Chronijcken, ende bevinden, &c. || t'AMSTERDAM, || By Michiel Colijn, Boeck-vercooper / woonende op't Water aen de Cooren-Marckt / || by de Oude Brugghe / in't Huys-Boeck / ANNO DOMINI 1632.
Amsterdam : Michael Colijn, 1632
[10], 128, 140, 104, 104, 158, [1], 192, [60] p.; 2° [Continuation Only]
Den Haag, Koninklijke Bibliotheek: 37 G 19
Leiden, Universiteitsbibliotheek: 1195 A 13

1649

204 Chrönika || CARIONIS, || Jfrån werldennes begynnelse / in til || Keyser Carl then femte. || Vppå thet Latiniske Språket författat / och || medh månge sköne Historier / theolijkes medh månge gamle || Konungarijkens / Nationers och Folks / såsom och förnemlige Bedriffters || Beskrifwelse / enkannerligen / hwad sigh vthi Gudz Försambling och the werldzlinge Regementen i || Grekeland / Romerske Rijket och then Tydske Nation / sigh tildragit hafwa / förmerat och || förbättrat / först aff || Herrn PHILIPPO MELANTHONE, || Och sedan aff || Doctore CASPARO PEUCERO. || Men nu aff thet Tydske / in på wårt Swenske Tungomål vthtolkat || genom || ERICUM SCHRODERUM, || Translatorem Regium. || År och så här tilökt the syra förnemlige och berömelige Keysares / Nemligen / || Caroli V. Ferdinandi I. Maximiliani II. och Rudophi II. Handlingar och Bedriffter / ||| aff thet Latiniske Spraket förswenskade. || Cum Gratia || Et Privilegio. || Nyköping / || Tryckt hoos Amund Nilszon Grefwe / på hans egen || Typographia, Åhr 1649.
Nyköping : Amund Nilszon Grefwe, 1649
[46], 1148, [32] p.; 2°
Sveriges bibliografi, 1600-talet: I, 147
Stockholm, Kungl. biblioteket: F1700 Fol.164
Stockholm, Kungl. biblioteket: MfCollijn R.197, R.198
CRL, Scandinavian culture series: MF-1680 reel 206 item 6-reel 207 item 1

1654

205[27] Târîh-i Firengî Tercümesi. [Manuscript]
Istanbul : Kâtip Çelebi, 1654
Konya, Izzet Koyunoglu Library: Nr. 14031

1692

206[28] Vr Chronicu Johannis Carjonis. Nockud med fæstum ordum saman skrifad wr dønsku. [Manuscript]

---

27 On this translation, see Gottfried Hagen, *Ein osmanischer Geograph bei der Arbeit: Entstehung und Gedankenwelt von Katib Celebis Gihannüma* (Berlin: Klaus Schwarz Verlag, 2003), 67.
28 On this manuscript, see Robert Cook, "The Chronica Carionis in Iceland," *Bibliotheca Arnamagnæana* 38 (1985): 226–263.

Vigur [Iceland] : Magnús Jónsson, 1692
London, British Library: MS Add 11153

1843

207   CORPUS || REFORMATORUM. || Edidit || Carolus Gottlieb Bretschneider. || VOLUMEN IX. || HALIS SAXONUM || APUD C. A. SCHWETSCHKE ET FILIUM. || 1843.
Halis Saxonum : Apud C. A. Schwetschke Et Filium, 1843
Col. 531–538; [Dedicatory Epistle to Archbishop Sigismund (April 1558)]
Col. 1073–1077; [Dedicatory Epistle to Archbishop Sigismund (25 March 1560)]
Wolfenbüttel, Herzog August Bibliothek: TH 17-3703

1844

208   CORPUS || REFORMATORUM. || Edidit || Carolus Gottlieb Bretschneider. || VOLUMEN XII. || HALIS SAXONUM || APUD C. A. SCHWETSCHKE ET FILIUM. || 1844.
Halis Saxonum : Apud C. A. Schwetschke Et Filium, 1844
Col. [705] – 1094; [Privilegium (12 February 1558) = 711; Prima Pars = 712–902; Secunda Pars = 901–1094]
Wolfenbüttel, Herzog August Bibliothek: TH 17-3703

1847

209   EXTRAIT || DE || IEAN CARION || SUR LE || SIÈGE DE METZ || EN 1552. || METZ, || SE VEND CHEZ LECOUTEUX, LIBRAIRE, || Rue des Clercs, 24. || 1847.
Metz : Se Vend Chez LeCouteux Libraire, Rue des Clercs, 24., 1847
24 p.
London, British Library: 9004.bb.4.(3.)

1963

210   CORPUS || REFORMATORUM. || Edidit || Carolus Gottlieb Bretschneider. || VOLUMEN IX. || HALIS SAXONUM || APUD C. A. SCHWETSCHKE ET FILIUM. || 1843.

CARION'S CHRONICLE – CENSUS OF EDITIONS   469

Halis Saxonum : Apud C. A. Schwetschke Et Filium, 1843
[New York : Johnson Reprint Corporation, 1963]
Col. 531–538; [Dedicatory Epistle to Archbishop Sigismund (April 1558)]
Col. 1073–1077; [Dedicatory Epistle to Archbishop Sigismund (25 March 1560)]
Melbourne, University of Melbourne Library: 270.6 MELA

211   CORPUS || REFORMATORUM. || Edidit || Carolus Gottlieb Bretschneider. || VOLUMEN XII. || HALIS SAXONUM || APUD C. A. SCHWETSCHKE ET FILIUM. || 1844.
Halis Saxonum : Apud C. A. Schwetschke Et Filium, 1844
[New York : Johnson Reprint Corporation, 1963]
Col. [705] – 1094; [Privilegium (12 February 1558) = 711; Prima Pars = 712–902; Secunda Pars = 901–1094]
Melbourne, University of Melbourne Library: 270.6 MELA

1966

212   Texte zur Kirchen- und Theologiegeschichte || Herausgegeben von Gerhard Ruhbach unter Mitarbeit || von Gustav Adolf Benrath, Heinz Scheible und Kurt-Victor Selge || Heft 2 || Die Anfänge der reformatorischen Geschichtsschreibung || Melanchthon, Sleidan, Flacius und || die Magdeburger Zenturien. || Herausgegeben von Heinz Scheible || Gütersloher Verlagshaus Gerd Mohn
Gütersloh : Gerd Mohn, 1966
p. 14–18; [Introduction to Chronica (1532)]
p. 26–33; [Dedicatory Epistle to Archbishop Sigismund (April 1558)]
p. 33–41; [Introduction to Chronicon (1558)]
Wolfenbüttel, Herzog August Bibliothek: 21.667

20XX

213   [MBW 8600] = Dedicatory Epistle to Archbishop Sigismund (April 1558)

20XX

214   [MBW 9269] = Dedicatory Epistle to Archbishop Sigismund (25 March 1560)

Bibliography

Notes to Bibliography

In studying the history of sixteenth century Europe, I have gained a profound respect for the scholars who have preceded me in the field. Reformation history and theology are fields with particularly long and distinguished traditions, and the labours of earlier scholars have provided a foundation on which I have often relied in carrying out my research. In the text itself and here in the bibliography, I have made reference to the primary sources and secondary literature I have used in preparing this monograph, and any error or omission is unintentional. My study of "Wittenberg Historiography" has been a silent conversation with generations past and present, and with the works of scholars such as Georg Theodor Strobel, Karl Gottlieb Bretschneider, Karl Hartfelder, Paul Joachimsen, Aby Warburg, Heinz Scheible, and especially Emil Clemens Scherer. Although I have not always agreed with these intellectual forebears, the medieval adage still holds true: "We stand on the shoulders of giants...."

With regard to secondary literature, I have often turned to the major reference works in the field for general background, especially *Allgemeine Deutsche Biographie* (ADB), and the *Realencyklopädie für Protestantische Theologie und Kirche* (RE), as well as the *Theologische Realenzyklopädie* (TRE), the *Oxford Encyclopedia of the Reformation*, and various articles in the Cambridge Histories series. Over the years, I have relied on these works for areas of "general knowledge," as well as specific factual background, and they have provided default resources to inform my understanding and presentation of those matters. Similarly, some of the secondary literature that has contributed to my thinking is listed here in the bibliography but is not repeated in the footnotes.

With regard to the primary source material, I used many different editions and copies of early printed works as I traveled back and forth between North America and Europe. Thus, in some cases, I relied initially on copies in the British Library or in the Herzog August Bibliothek, but later I turned to resources in Ithaca or Minnesota to recheck the transcriptions, whether printed books or digital copies and microform collections (such as *Flugschriften des frühen 16. Jahrhunderts*). Eventually, as digital scans increasingly became available, I turned to those while working in Milwaukee. In the bibliography and the footnotes, I have indicated the appropriate reference number in *Verzeichnis der im deutschen Sprachbereich erschienenen Drucke des XVI. Jahrhunderts* (VD16) for sixteenth century German imprints rather than providing the specific shelfmarks to the copies I have used, and I have followed the same approach for *Das*

Verzeichnis der im deutschen Sprachraum erschienenen Drucke des 17. Jahrhunderts (VD17). Furthermore, I have not included in the bibliography an expanded reference to all the editions cited above by VD16 or VD17 number. For reference purposes this seemed preferable, even though VD16 and VD17 remain works-in-progress, because the standardized entries provide a convenient way of accessing the bibliographical information and locating a corresponding copy. In those instances where I refer to a particular copy for specific reasons, such as handwritten annotations, I have provided the shelfmark in the footnotes.

With regard to *Carion's Chronicle*, I have used many copies over the years, but I relied on the following for the transcriptions from the two key editions: for the 1532 Rhau edition, I used a digital scan from the Lutherhalle in Wittenberg (Kn A 274/1882), which corresponds to VD16 C 998; and for the 1572 Crato edition, I used a personal copy of the 1580 reprint, which corresponds to VD16 M 2718 and VD16 P 1960. Since the editions of *Carion's Chronicle* are listed in the "Census of Editions" Appendix, they are not repeated here in the bibliography.

Primary Sources

Adam, Melchior. *Vitae Germanorum philosophorum*. Heidelberg: Jonas Rosa, 1615.

Adelung, Johann Christoph. *Geschichte der menschlichen Narrheit, oder Lebensbeschreibungen berühmter Schwarzkünstler, Goldmacher, Teufelsbanner, Zeichen- und Liniendeuter, Schwärmer, Wahrsager, und anderer philosophischer Unholden*, vol. 3. Leipzig: in der Weygandschen Buchhandlung, 1787.

Althamer, Andreas. *Commentaria Germaniae In P. Cornelij Taciti Equitis Rom. libellum de situ, moribus, & populis Germanorvm*. Nuremberg: Petreius, 1536. VD16 ZV 14839.

Annius of Viterbo. *Berosvs Babilonicvs De His Quæ præcesserunt inundationem terrarum. Item. Myrsilus de origine Turrhenorum. Cato in fragmentis. Archilochus in Epitheto de temporibus. Metasthenes de iudicio temporum. Philo in breuiario temporum. Xenophon de equiuocis temporum. Sempronius de diuisione Italiæ. Q. Fab. Pictor de aureo sæculo & origine vrbis Rhomæ. Fragmentum Itinerarij Antonini Pij. Altercatio Adriani Augusti & Epictici. Cornelij Taciti de origine & situ Germanorum opusculum. C.C. de situ & moribus Germanorum*. [Strasbourg]: [Grüninger], 1511. VD16 B 1649 [VD16 C 1902].

Anonymous. *Chronica Von vil Namhafftigen geschichten die geschehen seynd seid man zalt nach Christ geburt neün hundert vnd dreü iar in Ungern Behem Osterreich Steürmackt Bayern Schwab[e]n Francken Wälsch vnnd Teütsch landen biß auf das M.CCCC.XV*. [Augsburg]: [Erhard Oeglin], 1515. VD16 C 2478.

Anonymous. *Chronica New: Manicherlay Historien / vnnd besondere geschichten / Kürtzlich begreyffend / Von dem Jar der geburt vnsers seligmachers Jesu Christi / biß in das M.D.vnd. xxviij. Erlengeret.* Augsburg: Ulhart, 1528. VD16 C 2471.

Anonymous. *Chronica Darinn auff das kurtzest werden begriffen / die Namhafftigsten geschichten / so sich vnder allen Kaysern / von der geburt Christi / biß auff das M.D.vñ. xxxj. Jar / verlaffen haben.* Augsburg: Ulhart, 1531. VD16 C 2457.

Anonymous. *Chronica Darynn auffs kürtzest werden begriffen / die namhafftigsten geschichten / so sich vnter allen Keisern / von der gepurt Christi / biß auff das Tausent Fünffhundert ein vnd dreyssigst Jar verlauffen haben. Auch findestu hinden jnn diesem Büchlein die Meissnische Chronica.* Wittenberg: Rhau, 1532. VD16 C 2461.

Anonymous. *Chronica Darin auffs kürtzest werden begriffen / die namhafftigsten Geschichten / so sich vnter allen Keisern / von der geburt Christi / bis auff das Tausent Fünffhundert ein vnd dreissigst jar verlauffen haben. Auch findestu hinden in diesem Büchlein die Meissnische Chronica.* Wittenberg: Seitz, 1553. VD16 C 2463.

Augustine, Saint. *The City of God Against the Pagans*. Translated by R.W. Dyson. Cambridge: Cambridge University Press, 1998.

Baronio, Cesare. *Annales ecclesiastici denuo excusi et ad nostra usque tempora perducti ab Augustino Theiner....* 37 vols. Paris: Barri-Ducis, 1864–1883.

Batízi, András. "Meglött és megleendő dolgoknak teremtéstül fogva mind az ítéletig való história." In *XVI. századbeli magyar költők művei*, vol. 1 (1527–1546), 95–113. Edited by Áron Szilády. Budapest: Magyar Tudományos Akadémia, 1880.

Bayle, Pierre. *Dictionaire historique et critique*. Amsterdam: Brunel, 1740.

Becmann, Johann Christoph and Bernhard Ludwig Beckmann. *Historische Beschreibung der Chur und Mark Brandenburg.... Erster Theil.* Berlin: Christian Friedrich Voß, 1751.

Bede. *The Reckoning of Time*. Translated by Faith Wallis. Liverpool: Liverpool University Press, 1999.

Die Bekenntnisschriften der evangelisch-lutherischen Kirche. Göttingen: Vandenhoeck & Ruprecht, 1998.

Bellarmine, Robert. *De Translatione Imperii Romani A Graecis Ad Francos, Adversvs Matthiam Flaccivm Illyricvm, Libri Tres.* Antwerp: Plantin, 1589.

Bodin, Jean. *Methodus, Ad Facilem Historiarum Cognitionem*. Paris: Martin le Jeune, 1566.

Bodin, Jean. *Apologie de Rene Herpin Pour la Republique de I. Bodin*. Paris: Jacques du Puys, 1581.

Bodin, Jean. *De Republica Libri Sex*. Paris: Jacques du Puys, 1586.

Bodin, Jean. *Method for the Easy Comprehension of History*. Translated by Beatrice Reynolds. New York: Columbia University Press, 1945.

Bodin, Jean. *The six bookes of a commonweale. A facsimile reprint of the English translation of 1606, corrected and supplemented in the light of a new comparison with the*

French and Latin texts. Edited by Kenneth Douglas McRae. Cambridge, M.A.: Harvard University Press, 1962.

The Book of Concord: The Confessions of the Evangelical Lutheran Church. Edited by Robert Kolb and Timothy J. Wengert. Minneapolis: Fortress Press, 2000.

Bossuet, Jacques-Bénigne. *Discourse on Universal History*. Translated by Elborg Forster. Edited with an Introduction by Orest Ranum. Chicago: University of Chicago Press, 1976.

Brahe, Tycho. *Opera omnia*, VII, *Epistolae astronomicae*. Edited by I.L.E. Dreyer. Copenhagen: Libraria Gyldendaliana, 1924.

Brenz, Johann. *Wie sich Prediger vnd Leyen halten sollen / so der Turck das deutsche land vberfalle[n] würde / Christliche vnd notturfftige vnterricht / Johannis Brentij Predigers zu Hall in Swaben*. Wittenberg: Rhau, 1531. VD16 B 7985.

Bujanda, Jesús Martínez de, ed. *Index des livres interdits*, vol. VIII, *Index De Rome 1557, 1559, 1564*. Sherbrooke: Centre d'Études de la Renaissance, 1990.

Bujanda, Jesús Martínez de, ed. *Index des livres interdits*, vol. VII, *Index d'Anvers 1569, 1570, 1571*. Sherbrooke: Centre d'Études de la Renaissance, 1988.

Burchard of Ursberg. *Chronicvm Abbatis Vrspergensis*. Strasbourg: Mylius, 1537. VD16 B 9801.

Calov, Abraham. *Biblia Testam. Veteris Illustrata*, vol. 2. Frankfurt a.M.: Wustius, 1672.

Calov, Abraham. *Das Andere VOLUMEN Der Göttlichen Schrifften Alten Testaments*. Wittenberg: Schrödter, 1682.

Canisius, Peter. *Beati Petri Canisii,Societatis Iesu, epistulae et acta collegit et adnotationibus illustravit Otto Braunsberger*, vol. 6, *1567–1571*. Freiburg i.B.: Herder, 1913.

Carion, Johann. *Practica M. Joa[n]nis Nägelin von Bütighaim auff das 15.19. iar. Des durchleüchtigsten Fürsten vn[d] herren herr Joachim Margraue[n] zů Brandenburg &c. Astronomus*. [Augsburg]: [Johann Miller], [1518]. VD16 ZV 24181.

Carion, Johann. *Prognosticatio vnd erklerung der grossen wesserung / Auch anderer erschrockenlichenn würckungen. So sich begeben nach Christi vnsers lieben hern geburt / Funfftzehen hundert vn[d] xxiiij. Jar. Durch mich Magistru[m] Joha[n]nem Carion vo[n] Buetikaym Churfürstlicher gnaden tzu Brandenburg Astronomu[m] mit fleyssiger arbeit tzusame[n] gebracht. Gantz erberlich tzulesen / in nutz vn[d] warnung aller Christglaubigen menschen &c*. [Leipzig]: [Martin Landsberg], [1521]. VD16 C 1030.

Carion, Johann. *Bedeütnusz vnnd Offenbarung / warer Hymlischer Jnfluxion / des Hocherfarnen Magistri Johannis Carionis Buetikaimensis / Churfürstlicher gnaden vo[n] Brandenburg &c. Mathematici / von Jarn zů Jaren werende / biß man schreybt. M.D.vn[d] xxxx. jar. Alle Landtschafft / Stende vnd einflüß clarlich betreffend*. [Augsburg]: [Philipp Ulhart d.Ä.], 1526. VD16 C 962.

Carion, Johann. *Bedeutnus vnd Offenbarung warer hymlischer jnfluentz des hocherfarnen Magistri Johannis Carionis Bütickheymensis C.F.G. von Brandenburg Mathematici / von jaren zů jarn werende / Biß man schreibt. 1550. Jar / alle Landschafft*

Stände vnnd einfluß / klerlich betreffendt. Gebessert vnnd verlengt mit anhang einer verborgnen Prophecey / auch Johannis Carionis. [Augsburg]: [Heinrich Steiner], 1531. VD16 C 972.

Carion, Johann. *Ivdicivm Magistri Iohannis Carionis de Anno M.D.XXXIII. Cum purgatione in qua respondet Perlachio.* [Wittenberg]: [Hans Weiß], 1532. VD16 C 1021.

Carion, Johann. *Vom Cometen den man newlich jm M.D.XXXII. jar gesehen hat / iudicium gestellet durch Magistrum Johan. Carion.* Wittenberg: Rhau, 1533. VD16 C 1036.

Carion, Johann. *Außlegung der verborgenen Weissagung / Doctor Johannis Carionis / von verenderung vnd zůfelligem glück / der höchsten Potentaten des Römischen Reichs.* [Augsburg]: [Otmar], 1546. VD16 C 952.

Chytraeus, David. *Dauidis Chytraei Chronicon Saxoniae & vicinarum aliquot Gentium: Ab Anno Christi 1500. vsque ad M.D.XCIII. Appendix Scriptorvm Certis Chronici Locis Inserendorum. Additus est Jndex Personarum & Rerum maximè insignium copiosiß.* Leipzig: Grosius [Lantzenberger], 1593. VD16 C 2554.

Chytraeus, David. *De Lectione Historiarvm Recte Institvenda. Et Historicorvm Fere Omnivm Series Et Argumenta, breviter et perspicue exposita A Davide Chytrœo. Addita Est Chronologia Historiœ Herodoti, Thucydidis, Xenophontis, Diodori Siculi, Cornelij Taciti, Procopij &c.* Wittenberg: Crato, 1563. VD16 C 2644.

Clemen, Otto, ed. *Supplementa Melanchthoniana: Werke Philipp Melanchthons die im Corpus Refomatorum vermisst werden.* 6 Parts. Leipzig: Haupt, 1910–1929.

Conring, Hermann. *New Discourse on the Roman-German Emperor.* Edited by Constantin Fasolt. Tempe: Arizona Center for Medieval and Renaissance Studies, 2005.

Concordia Self-Study Bible. St. Louis: Concordia Publishing House, 1986.

Cusa, Nicolas of. *The Catholic Concordance.* Translated by Paul E. Sigmund. Cambridge: Cambridge University Press, 1991.

Dante. *Monarchy.* Translated by Prue Shaw. Cambridge: Cambridge University Press, 1996.

Dommerich, Johann Christoph. *De M. Ioannis Carionis Chronico Epistola Ad Virvm Svmme Venerabilem Eberhardvm Davidem Havbervm S.S. Theol. Doctor. Et Ad D. Petri Aedem Qvae Hafniae Est Pastorem Scripta A Joan. Christoph. Dommerich.* Wolfenbüttel: Bartschivs, 1750.

Dresser, Matthaeus. *Oratio De Qvatvor Monarchiis, Sive Svmmis Imperiis, A Daniele Propheta Expressis. Contra Veterem Ivdaeorum errorem, hoc tempore à Ioanne Bodino Gallo, in methodo historica renouatum.* Leipzig: Beyer, 1581. VD16 D 2737.

Dresser, Matthaeus. *Oratio De Monarchia Qvarta Romano Germanica, quam Ioannes Bodinus, cum Iudaeis, conuellere nondum desistit. Separatim, & cum millenario isagoges historicae quinto coniuncte edita.* Leipzig: Defner, 1587. VD16 D 2713.

Dresser, Matthaeus. *Isagoges Historicae Pars prima.* Leipzig: Lantzenberger, 1598. VD16 D 2721.

Dresser, Matthaeus. *Isagoges Historicae Millenarius Quintus*. Leipzig: Lantzenberger, 1599. VD16 ZV 4777.

Egenolff, Christian. *Chronic von an vn[d] abgang aller Weltwesenn. Auß den glawbwirdigsten Historien / On alle Gloß vnnd Zůsatz / Nach Historischer warheyt beschriben. Künig / Keyser / vnnd fürneme Personen / nach warer fürbildung Controfeit*. Frankfurt a.M.: Egenolff, 1533. VD16 E 573.

Einhard. *The Life of Charlemagne*. With a foreword by Sidney Painter. Ann Arbor: University of Michigan Press, 1960.

Einhard and Notker the Stammerer. *Two Lives of Charlemagne*. Translated by Lewis Thorpe. New York: Penguin Books, 1969.

Erasmus, Desiderius. *Opus epistolarum des Erasmi Roterdami*. 12 vols. Edited by P.S. Allen. Oxford: Oxford University Press, 1992 [Reprint].

Faust, Lorenz. *Anatomia Statuae Danielis. Kurtze und eigentliche erklerung der grossen Bildnis des Propheten Danielis*. Leipzig: Steinman, 1586 [1585]. VD16 F 660.

Felwinger, Johann Paul. *Declaratio Colossi, In Qua Recitatur Ordine, Ex Sacris Et Profanis Scriptoribus Desumta Monarcharum Series, Ad Nostra Usque Tempora, Et Historiae Quaedam Obiter Annotatae Sunt*. Altdorf: Schönnerstaedt, 1667. VD17 23:675074R.

Flacius, Matthias. *De Translatione Imperii Romani Ad Germanos*. Basel: Perna, 1566. VD16 F 1502.

Flacius, Matthias, et al. *Ecclesiastica Historia, Integram Ecclesiae Christi Ideam, Qvantvm Ad Locum, Propagationem, Persecutionem, Tranquillitatem, Doctrinam, Haereses, Ceremonias, Gubernationem, Schismata, Synodos, Personas, Miracula, Martyria, Religiones extra Ecclesiam, & statum Imperii politicum attinet, secundum singulas Centurias, perspicuo ordine complectens: singulari diligentia & fide ex vetustissimis & optimis historicis, patribus et aliis scriptoribus congesta: Per aliquot studiosos & pios uiros in urbe Magdeburgica. Quo opere nullum aliud ab Orbe condito, eiusdem quidem argumenti, Reipub. Christianae & utilius & magis necessarium, in lucem esse editum, aequus atq[ue] sinceri iudicij Lector uel ex Praefatione, qua etiam contexendi huius causae exponuntur, adiectaq[ue] in primis historici operis Methodo ac singulorum capitum metis generarlibus, facile deprehendet. Accessit etiam cum Rerum uerborum[que] in singulis Centurijs praecipue memorabilium, tum Locorum Scripturae explicatorum copiosus ac geminus Index*. 13 vols. Basel: Oporinus, 1559–1574. VD16 E 218-238.

Förstemann, Karl Eduard, ed. *Album academiae Vitebergensis ab a. Ch. 1502 usque ad a. 1560*. Leipzig: Tauchnitz, 1841.

Fontaine, Jacques. *De Bello Rhodio, Libri Tres, Clementi Vii. Pont. Max. dedicati, Iacobo Fontano Brugensi autore. Ad Reuerdendiss. Principem ac Dominum D. Albertum S. Romanae Ecclesiae Cardinalem, Moguntinumque Archiepscopam &c. ut deliberet, non modo de bello Turcico, sed etiam de sanandis Ecclesiasticis dissensionibus, Philippi Melanchthonis Exhortatoria Epistola*. Hagenau: Johann Setzer, 1527. VD16 F 1843.

Foxe, John. *Actes and monuments of these latter and perillous dayes, touching matters of the church: wherein ar comprehended and described the great persecutions & horrible troubles that have been wrought and practised by the Romishe prelates, speciallye in this realme of England and Scotlande, from the yeare of Our Lorde a thousande, vnto the tyme nowe present*.... London: Iohn Day, 1563.

Franck, Sebastian. *Chronica, Zeytbůch vnd geschycht bibel von anbegyn biß inn diß gegenwertig M. D. xxxj. jar*.... Strasbourg: Beck, 1531. VD16 F 2064.

Franck, Sebastian. *Germaniae Chronicon*.... Augsburg: Westermair, 1538. VD16 F 2088.

Franckenberger, Andreas. *De Amplitvdine Et Excellenti Historiæ Propheticae Dignitate : De Cavsis Ad Lectionem illius nos impellentibus : & adminiculis in meditatione : in quibus pleraq[ue] in hoc genere accuratè excutiuntur, quæ studiosis sacræ antiquitatis & historiarum scitu necessaria sunt : Authore M. Andrea Franckenbergero, Profeß. publico in Acad: VVitebergensi. Inserta est pagina 172, quòd res ita postularet, refutatio sententiæ Iohannis Bodini, Galli Andegaui, qui celebritate nominis multorum regnorum aures & animos compleuit, de monarchijs quatuor, pro Daniele Propheta : pro Imperio Romanorum Germanico : Doctore Luthero & Domino Philippo Melanthone, quibus iniuria facta est. Index ordinis & rerum memorabilium sequitur dedicationem*. Wittenberg: Simon Gronenberg, [ca. 1585]. VD16 F 2196.

Franckenberger, Andreas. *Institvtionvm Antiqvitatis Et Historiarvm Pars Prima, In Libros Sex Distribvta, Qvorvm Priores Tres Agunt de iudicio ac delectu Authorum, in Chronico Carionis Philippico, & in omni Antiquitate adhibendo : Posteriores idem Chronicon cum fontibus sacris, atq[ue] ethnicis græcis & latinis, ad vsum vitę humanæ transferunt, in cultu numinis diuini, consilijs, praedictionibus, morum emendatione, & consolationibus : Scripta Et Pvblice Proposita in Academia Witebergensi A M. Andrea Franckenbergero ibidem Professore. Ἀξίωμα : Nobilissima & difficilima pars est Historici Operis iudicare, non tantùm de Authorum elocutione & charactere, sed multò magis de rebus ipsis, & qua quisque fide dignus sit*. Wittenberg: Crato, 1586. VD16 F 2198.

Franckenberger, Andreas. *Oratio In Honorem Domini Philippi Melanthonis De Magnitvdine rerum diuinarum & politicarum, quae in Chronico eius continentur, Scripta et publicè habita VVitebergae A M. Andrea Franckenbergero, Antiquitatis & Historiarum Professore*. Wittenberg: Crato, 1589. VD16 ZV 6023.

Franckenberger, Reinhold. *Chronologiae Scaligero-Petauianae Breve Compendium*. Wittenberg: Henckel, 1661. VD17 23:299944L.

Frechulf of Lisieux. *Opera Omnia*. 2 vols. Edited by Michael I. Allen. Turnhout: Brepols, 2002.

Friedensburg, Walter, ed. *Urkundenbuch der Universität Wittenberg*. 2 vols. Magdeburg: Selbstverlag der Historischen Kommission, 1926–1927.

Funck, Johann. *Chronologia hoc est omnium temporum et annorum ab initio mundi, usque ad hunc praesentem a nato Christo annum M.D.LII. computatio*. Königsberg: Lufft, 1552. VD16 F 3382.

Georgi, Theophil. *Allgemeines Europäisches Bücher-Lexicon.* Leipzig: Theophil Georgi, 1742.

Gerhard, Johann. *Locorum Theologicorum Cum Pro Adstrenda Veritate, Tum Pro Destruenda quorumvis contradicentium falsitate Tomus In quo continentur haec Capita: 26. De Ministerio Ecclesiastico. 27. De Magistratu Politico.* Jena: Steinmann, 1619. VD17 3:608870U.

Gesner, Conrad. *Appendix Bibliothecae Conradi Gesneri.* Zürich: Froschauer, 1555. VD16 G 1702.

Gesner, Conrad. *Bibliotheca Vniuersalis.* Zürich: Froschauer, 1545. VD16 G 1698.

Goethe, Johann Wolfgang von. *Faust Part One.* Translated by David Luke. New York: Oxford University Press, 1998.

Grundig, Christoph G. *De optima historiae providentiam divinam feliciter pervestigandi ac eruendi methodo, itemque de Chronico Melanchthonis, quod Carionis vulgo audit, ob eandem maxime commedando, nonnulla disserit, qui viro nobilissimo atque doctissimo Johanni Henrico Blumbacho Lipsiensi, singulari s. theol. ejusdemque hist. cultori ac phil. baccal. summos in philosophia honores amice congratulatur Christophorus Gottlob Grundigius Dorffhaeyna Misnicus s. theol. cult. et philosoph. baccal.* Leipzig: Saalbach, 1731.

Hardt, Hermann von der. *Danielis Quatuor Animalia, non Quatuor Monarchiarum fabula, sed Quatuor Regvm Babylonis Nebucadnezaris, Evilmerodachi, Belsazaris & Cyri, historia, demonstrata.* Helmstedt: Hamm, 1715.

Harms, Wolfgang. *Deutsche Illustrierte Flugblätter des 16. Und 17. Jahrhunderts*, Band II, Wolfenbüttel Band 2: Historica. München: Kraus International Publications, 1980.

Hoch, Erhard Ernst. *Disquisitio de chronici, quod extat sub nomine Ioannis Carionis, vera et genuina origine.* Wolfenbüttel: Meisner, 1755.

Index Expvrgatorivs Librorvm Qvi Hoc Secvlo Prodiervnt, vel doctrinæ non sanæ erroribus inspersis, vel inutilis & offensiuæ maledicentiæ fellibus permixtis, iuxta sacri Concilij Tridentini decretum: Philippi II Regis Catholici iussu & auctoritate, atque Albani Ducis consilio ac ministerio in Belgia concinnatus; anno M D LXXI. Lyon: Mareschallus, 1586.

Irenicus, Franciscus. *Germaniae Exegeseos Volvmina Dvodecim.* Hagenau: Koberger [Anshelm], 1518. VD16 F 2815.

Isidore of Seville. *The Etymologies of Isidore of Seville.* Translated by Stephen A. Barney et al. Cambridge: Cambridge University Press, 2006.

Jahn, Johann Wilhelm. *Dissertatio Historico-Politica De Qvatvor Monarchiis : Qva Recentiorvm Qvorvndam, Nominatim I.C. Becmanni, H. Hardtii, Et Observ. Halensis Sententiae Modeste Excvtivntvr.* Wittenberg: Kreusig, 1712.

Jahn, Johann Wilhelm. *Antiqvae Et Pervulgatae De Qvatvor Monarchiis Sententiae Contra Recentiorvm Qvorvndam Obiectiones Plenior Et Vberior Assertio.* Frankfurt a.M. and Leipzig: Knoch, 1728.

Jahn, Johann Wilhelm. "Antiquae et pervulgatae De Quatvor Monarchiis sententiae Contra Recentiorum Quorundam Objectiones Plenior et Uberior Assertio." In *Historisches Magazin*, ed. C.W.F. Breyer, vol. 1, 114–220. Jena: Cröcker, 1805.

Jerome, Saint. *The Chronicle of St. Jerome* (2005). Translated by Roger Pearse. http://www.ccel.org/ccel/pearse/morefathers/files/jerome_chronicle_00_eintro.htm.

Jociscus, Andreas. *Oratio De Ortv, Vita Et Obitv Ioannis Oporini Basiliensis, Typographicoru[m] Germaniae Principis, recitata in Argentinensi Academia ab Ioanne Henrico Hainzelio Augustano. Avthore Andrea Iocisco Silesio, Ethicorum in eadem Academia professore. Adiunximus librorum per Ioannem Oporinum excusorum Catalogum. Vel Invitis Piratis: Qvod Per Piratas Liceat.* Strasbourg, Theodosius Rihelius, 1569. VD16 J 305.

Jonas, Justus. *Das siebend Capitel Danielis / von des Türcken Gottes lesterung vnd schrecklicher morderey / mit vnterricht Justi Jonae.* Wittemberg: Lufft, [1529]. VD16 J 897.

Julius Africanus. *Chronographiae: The Extant Fragments.* Edited by Martin Wallraff et al. Berlin: Walter de Gruyter, 2007.

Justin. *Ivstini Ex Trogo Pompeio Historia, Diligentissime recognita, & ab omnibus, quibus scatebat mendis, collatis ad authorem Graecis & Latinis Historicis repurgata. Cui praeterea non parum lucis, ex iisdem transcriptis sententiis, & indicato historiae ordine, adcessit.* Hagenau: Johann Setzer, 1526. VD16 T 2051.

Justin. *Ivstini Ex Trogo Pompeio Historia iam denuo diligenter recognita, ac plurimis aucta scholiis, quibus quo quaeq[ue] res tempore gesta sit indicatur. Adiecta est breuis legendae historiae ratio, multum historiae studiosis profutura. Per Georgium Maiorem.* Magdeburg: Michael Lotther, 1537. VD16 T 2055.

Justin. *Epitome of the Philippic History of Pompeius Trogus.* Translated by J.C. Yardley. Atlanta: Scholar's Press, 1994.

Keckermann, Bartholomäus. *Operum omnium quae extant.* Geneva: Aubert, 1614.

Lactantius. *The Divine Institutes.* Translated by William Fletcher. In *The Ante-Nicene Fathers*, vol. VII, ed. Alexander Roberts and James Donaldson. Grand Rapids: Eerdmans Publishing Co., 1989 [Reprint].

Lambert of Hersfeld. *The Annals of Lampert of Hersfeld.* Translated by I.S. Robinson. Manchester: Manchester University Press, 2015.

Lanquet, Thomas and Thomas Cooper. *An Epitome Of Chronicles Conteining the whole discourse of the histories as well of this realme of England, as all other countreis, with the succession of their kynges, the tyme of their reigne, & what notable actes thei did : much profitable to be redde namely of magistrates and suche as haue auctoritee in co[m]men weales : gathered out of most p[ro]bable auctors, fyrst, by Thomas Lanquet, from the beginnyng of the world to the incarnacion of Christ, and now finished and continued to the reigne of our soueraine lorde kynge Edwarde the sixt by Thomas Cooper. Anno. M.D.LXIX.* London: Thomas Berthelet, 1549.

Lanquet, Thomas and Thomas Cooper. *Coopers Chronicle*. London: Thomas Berthelette (Heirs), 1560.

Lanquet, Thomas, Thomas Cooper, and Robert Crowley. *An Epitome of Cronicles*. London: Thomas Marshe, 1559.

Liudprand of Cremona. *The Complete Works of Liudprand of Cremona*. Translated by Paolo Squatriti. Washington, D.C.: The Catholic University of America Press, 2007.

Livy. *Titi Livi Ab vrbe condita libri XLI–XLV*. Edited by John Briscoe. Stuttgart: Teubner, 1986.

Livy. *Livius: Codex Vindobonensis Lat. 15 / Praefatus est Carolus Wessely*. Leiden: Sijthof, 1907.

The Lutheran Study Bible. St. Louis: Concordia Publishing House, 2008.

Marsilius of Padua. *Defensor minor and De translatione Imperii*. Translated by Cary J. Nederman. Cambridge: Cambridge University Press, 1993.

Márton, Tarnóc and Varjas Béla, eds. *Hoffgreff-énekeskönyv. Kolozsvár, 1554–1555. A kísérő tanulmányt írta Tarnóc Márton. A fakszimile svővegét gondozta Varjas Béla*. Biblioteca Hungarica Antiqua VII. Budapest: Akadémiai Kiadó, 1966.

Melanchthon, Philipp. *Die Histori Thome Muntzers / des anfengers der Döringischen vffrur / seer nutzlich zulesen. Ermanung des Durchleuchtigen Fursten vnnd Herren / Herrn Philippsen Landtgraue zu Hessen &c. an die Ritterschafft / die Bauren (vnder dem scheyn des Euangelions sich wider alle oberkeit / durch falsch Predicanten verfurt / setzende) trostlich anzugreyffen*. Hagenau: Setzer, [1525]. VD16 M 3431.

Melanchthon, Philipp. *Georgii Sabini Brandeburgensis, de Electione & Coronatione Caroli V Caesario Historia : Ecloga eiusdem Sabini, de Gallo ad Ticinum capto*. Mainz: J. Schöffer, 1544. VD16 M 3089

Melanchthon, Philipp. *Wie newlich zu Newburg jn Beiern einer genant Alphonsus Diasius seinen bruder Johanem, grausamlich ermort hatt, alleine aus has Wider die Einige Ewige Christliche lahr, wie Cain den Abel ermordet*. [Wittenberg]: [Klug], 1546. VD16 M 4415.

Melanchthon, Philipp. *Historia necis Petri Loisij Farnesij. Honestissimae sententiae Gonzagae narratio, quae conuenit cum veteribus exemplis, quorum alterum ab Augustino describitur, alterum recitatur in historijs ducis Burgund*. [Wittenberg]: [Rhau], 1548. VD16 H 3902.

Melanchthon, Philipp. *Orations on Philosophy and Education*. Edited by Sachiko Kusukawa. Cambridge: Cambridge University Press, 1999.

Meusel, Johann Georg. *Bibliotheca Historica*. Leipzig: Weidmannus & Reichius, 1784.

Moller, Daniel Wilhelm. *Disputationem Circularem De Joh. Carione, Sub Praesidio Dan. Guil. Molleri, Com. Palat. Caesar. & Prof. Publ. Facult. Philosoph. h.t. Decani, Iuventuti Karinophilus P.P. Joh. Leonhardus Kulmichius, Norimb. Altdorf. d. 13. Febr. A. MDCXCVII. H.L.Q.C.* [Altdorf]: Meyerus, 1697. VD17 12:136858G

Moller, Daniel Wilhelm. *Dissertationes academicae: De vitis quinquaginta historicorum*. Nuremberg & Altdorf: Tauber, 1726.

Müntzer, Thomas. *Schriften und Briefe: Kritische Gesamtausgabe.* Edited by Günther Franz. Gütersloh: Verlaghaus Gerd Mohn, 1968.

Müntzer, Thomas. *The Collected Works of Thomas Müntzer.* Translated by Peter Matheson. Edinburgh: T & T Clark, 1988.

Mylius, Martin. *Chronologia scriptorum Philippi Melanchthonis.* Görlitz: Fritschius, 1582. VD16 M 7406.

Nanni, Giovanni. See Annius of Viterbo.

Nauclerus, Johannes. *Memorabilivm omnis aetatis et omnivm gentivm chronici commentarii A Ioanne Navclero I. V. Doctore Tubing. Praeposito, & Vniuersitatis Cancellario, digesti an annum Salutis M.D. Adiecta Germanorum rebus Historia de Svevorvm ortu, institutis ac Imperio. Compleuit opus F. Nicolavs Basellivs Hirsaugiensis annis XIIII. ad M.D. additis.* Tübingen: Anshelm, 1516. VD16 N 167.

Oporinus, Johannes. *Librorum per Ioannem Oporinvm partim excusorum hactenus, partim in eiusdem officina uenalium, Index: Singulis ad ordinem alphabeticum redactis, & adiecta impressionis forma. Basileae. 1567.* Basel: Oporinus, 1567. VD16 ZV 19007.

Orosius, Paulus. *The Seven Books of History Against the Pagans.* Translated by Roy J. Deferrari. Washington, D.C.: The Catholic University of America Press, 1964.

Otto of Freising. *The Two Cities.* Translated by Charles Mierow. New York: Columbia University Press, 2002.

Pantaleon, Heinrich. *Prosopographiae Herovm Atqve Illvstrivm Virorvm Totivs Germaniæ, Pars Tertia, Eaqve Primaria.* Basel: Nikolaus Brylinger (Heirs), 1566. VD16 P 230.

Paradin, Guillaume. *Gulielmvs Paradinus de rebus in Belgica gestis ad Philippum Gayanum.* [Paris]: Vivant Gaultherot, 1544.

Perlach, Andreas. *Des Cometen vn[d] ander erscheinung in den lüfften / Jm XXXI. Jar gesehenn bedütung Durch Andreen Perlach von Witschein / der sibenn freyen / vnd natürlichen kunst maister / Diser zeyt auff der löbliche[n] hohen schůl zů Wien / in der Astronomey / was die himlische[n] leüff würckung vnd jre einflüß betreffen ist / verordenter Läser. Darbey auch ein anzaigung / das Charion seine Judicia nicht auß der natürliche[n] kunst Astrologia gemacht hat.* [Nuremberg]: [Johann Stuchs], [1531]. VD16 P 1448.

Peucer, Caspar, ed. *Orationes Ex Historia Thvcydidis, Et Insigniores Aliqvot Demosthenis & aliorum Oratorum Græcorum, conversæ in latinum sermonem à Philippo Melanchthone. Editæ a Casparo Pevcero. Cum Præfatione Ad amplissimum uirum Doctorem Georgium Sigismundum Seldium, sacræ Cæsareæ Maiestatis Procancellarium &c.* Wittenberg: Rhau, 1562. VD16 P 2017.

Peucer, Caspar. *Commentarivs De Præcipvis Divinationvm Generibvs, In Qvo, A Prophetiis, Avtoritate diuina traditis, & à Physicis coniecturis, discernuntur artes & imposturæ Diabolicæ, atq[ue] obseruationes natæ ex superstitione, & cum hac coniunctæ : Et monstrantur fontes ac causæ Physicarum prædictionum : Diabolicæ verò ac superstitiosæ confutatæ damnantur, ea serie, quam tabella præfixa ostendit. Recognitus vltimo, & auctus Ab Avtore Ipso Casparo Pevcero D. Cvm Interpretatione Græcorum.* Zerbst: Faber, 1591. VD16 P 1977.

Peucer, Caspar. *Historia Carcerum et liberationis diuinae....* Zürich: [s.n.], 1605. VD17 12:116322H.

Piccolomini, Aeneas Silvius. *Germania und Jakob Wimpfeling: "Responsa et Replicae ad Eneam Silvium."* Edited by Adolf Schmidt. Cologne: Böhlau Verlag, 1962.

Pölitz, Karl Heinrich Ludwig. *Symbolae ad historiam Academiae Vitebergensis illustrandam.* Wittenberg: C.H. Grässlerus, 1811.

Postel, Guillaume. *Apologies et Rétractions Manuscrits inédits publiés avec une introduction et des notes par François Secret.* Nieuwkoop: De Graaf, 1972.

Pufendorf, Samuel. *An Introduction to the History of the Principal Kingdoms and States of Europe.* Edited By Michael J. Seidler. Indianapolis: Liberty Fund, 2013.

Pufendorf, Samuel. *The Present State of Germany.* Edited By Michael J. Seidler. Indianapolis: Liberty Fund, 2007.

Quenstedt, Johann Andreas. *Dialogus De Patriis Illustrium Doctrina et Scriptis Virorum.* Wittenberg: Wendt, 1654.

Ralegh, Walter. *The History of the World.* London: Walter Burre, 1614 [1617].

Regino of Prüm. *History and Politics in Late Carolingian and Ottonian Europe: The Chronicle of Regino of Prüm and Adalbert of Magdeburg.* Translated by Simon MacLean. New York: Manchester University Press, 2009.

Reineccius, Reiner. *Methodvs Legendi Cognoscendiqve Historiam Tam sacram quam profanam....* Helmstedt: Lucius, 1583. VD16 R 890.

Reineccius, Reiner. *Historia Iulia.* Helmstedt: Lucius, 1594. VD16 R 886.

Reinkingk, Theodor. *Tractatus De Regimine Seculari Et Ecclesiastico: Exhibens Brevem Et Methodicam Iuris Publici Delineationem, Ac Praecipuarum Controversiarum, circa hodiernum Sacri Imperii Romani Statum ac Gubernationem, tam secularem, quam in genere Ecclesiasticam vertentium resolutionem.* Marburg: Hampel, 1632. VD17 1:018724B.

Reynmann, Leonhard. *Practica vber die grossen vnd manigfeltigen Coniunction der Planeten / die ĩm jar M.D.XXiiij. erscheinen / vn[d] vngezweiffelt vil vnderparlicher ding geperen werden.* Nürnberg: Hieronymus Höltzel, 1523. VD16 R 1620.

Robinson, I.S., trans. *Eleventh-Century Germany: The Swabian Chronicles.* New York: Manchester University Press, 2008.

Rolevinck, Werner. *Fasciculus Temporum: Compendio Cronológico.* León: Universidad de León, 1993. [Facsimile of 1481 Venetian Edition].

Sabinus, Georg. *Descriptio reditus illustris Principis ac Domini D. Ioachimi II. Marchionis Brandenburgensis etc. depulsis Turcis anno MDXXXII.* Wittenberg: Rhau, 1533. VD16 S 104.

Sabinus, Georg. *Poëmata.* Leipzig: Hans Steinmann (Heirs), 1589. VD16 S 139.

Schardius, Simon. *Historicvm Opvs*. 4 vols. Basel: Heinrich Petri, 1574. VD16 S 2278.

Scheible, Heinz, ed. *Die Anfänge der reformatorischen Geschichtsschreibung: Melanchthon, Sleidan, Flacius und die Magdeburger Zenturien*. Gütersloh: Mohn, 1966.

Schelhorn, Johann Georg. *Amoenitates Historiæ Ecclesiasticæ Et Literariæ Quibus Variæ observationes, Scripta item quædam anecdota & rariora Opuscula, diversis utriusque historiæ capitibus elucidandis inservientia, exhibentur. Tomus Secvndvs*. Frankfurt & Leipzig: Daniel Bartholomaeus & Sons, 1738.

Schroeckh, Matthias. *Christliche Kirchengeschichte*, 43 vols. Leipzig: Schwickert, 1768–1808.

Schroeckh, Matthias. *Lehrbuch der allgemeinen Weltgeschichte zum Gebrauche bey dem ersten Unterrichte der Jugend*. Berlin: Nicolai, 1774.

Schroeckh, Matthias. *Allgemeine Weltgeschichte für Kinder*. 4 vols. Leipzig: Weidmann und Reich, 1779–1784.

Schurzfleisch, Konrad. *Solida Ac Necessaria Disquisitio, De Forma Imperii Romano-Germananici, Ad Severini De Monzambano Caput VI. Diss. De Statu Imp. Germ.* [Leipzig]: [s.n.], 1668. VD17 1:019283L.

Schurzfleisch, Konrad. *Divisionem Imperii Karolini*. Wittenberg: Fincelius, 1682.

Seitz, Alexander. *Ain Warnung des Sündtfluss oder erschrockenlichen wassers Des XXIIII. jars auß natürlicher art des hymels zu besorgen mit sambt außlegung der grossen Wunderzaichen zu Wien in Osterreych erschinen, des xx iars*. [Augsburg]: [Erhard Oeglin (Heirs)], [1520]. VD16 S 5396.

Seitz, Alexander. *Sämtliche Schriften*, vol. 2. Edited by Peter Ukena. Berlin: Walter de Gruyter, 1975.

Simler, Josias. *Epitome Bibliothecæ Conradi Gesneri*. Zürich: Froschauer, 1555. VD16 G 1703.

Sleidanus, Johann. *Ioan. Sleidani, De Statv Religionis Et Reipvblicae, Carolo Qvinto, Caesare, Commentarij. Cvm indice luculentißimo*. Strasbourg: Rihel, 1555. VD16 S 6668.

Sleidanus, Johann. *Ioan. Sleidani, De Qvatvor Svmmis Imperiis, Libri Tres, In gratiam iuuentutis confecti. Cum gratia & priuilegio Cæsareo ad annos octo*. Strasbourg: Josias and Theodosius Rihel, 1556. VD16 S 6657.

Sleidanus, Johann. *Iohannis Sleidanus, De Statv Religionis Et Reipvblicae, Carolo Qvinto Caesare, Commentarii Varia Ac Mvltiplici Rervm Vtilissimarvm Cognitione Referti, Nvnc Recens Accvrata Diligentia, Svmmaqve Fide Recogniti, Et Novis Svmmariis Singvlorvm Librorvm, Pro Faciliori Rervm Cognitione, Et Inventione, Avcti, Et Illvstrati. Auctor Iohannes Sleidanus ad Lectorem. Mvlti queruntur multa per hos libros,... Adiecta Est Etiam Appendix, Sev Continuatio eorundem Commentariorum, Ab Anno Christ M. D. LVI. quo Autor e Vita excessit, vsq[ue] ad præsentem M. D. LXVIII. Annum, ex fide dignissimis historijs ad publicam vtilitatem collecta. Auctore Viro Clarissimo D. Iustino Goblero, Goarino, V. I. Doctore. Cum Indice Rerum omnium locupletissimo*. Frankfurt a.M.: Peter Schmidt, 1568. VD16 S 6686.

Spangenberg, Cyriacus. *Mansfeldische Chronica Der Erste Theil. Von Erschaffung vnd Austheilung der Welt/ vnd insonderheit von der Graueschafft Mansfelt/ vnd den alten vnd ersten Deutschen Königen vnd Fürsten/ der Schwaben vnd Marckmannen/ Cherusken/ Francken vnd Sachsen. Vnd von gemeinen Polittischen vnd Weltlichen hendeln/ so sich in Friede Oder Kriegsleufften in dieser Landart/ Sachsen/ Thüringen vnd am Hartz/ auch etwan anderswo zugetragen/ dabey dieser Landart/ Oberkeiten oder Vnterthanen mit gewesen. Durch M. Cyriacum Spangenberg*. Eisleben: Andreas Petri, 1572. VD16 S 7635.

Spangenberg, Cyriacus. *Sächssische Chronica....* Frankfurt a.M.: Feyerabend, 1585. VD16 S 7636.

Starke, Johann Georg. *Synopsis Bibliothecae Exegeticae in Vetus Testamentum.... Fünfter Theil*. Leipzig: Breitkopf, 1747.

Stöffler, Johannes. *Almanach nova plurimis annis venturis inservientia*. Venice: Liechtensteyn, 1504.

Stöffler, Johannes. *Elucidatio Fabricae ususque astrolabii*. Oppenheim: Köbel, 1513. VD16 S 9191.

Stöffler, Johannes. *Tabulae astronomicae*. Tübingen: Anshelm, 1514. VD16 S 9204.

Stöffler, Johannes. *Calendarium Romanum Magnum*. Oppenheim: Köbel, 1518. VD16 S 9188.

Strigel, Victor. *Reverendae Et Clarissimae memoriae D. Victorini Strigelii. Scholae Historicae Quibus in Academia Heidelbergensi Chronicon viri incomparabilis D. Philippi Melanchthonis illustravit : proposita continua serie historiarum à condito mundo vsque ad Christum natum. Nunc primùm in lucem editae. Opera et studio Christophori Pezelii D*. Neustadt an der Haardt: Harnisch, 1586. VD16 S 9645.

Sulpitius Severus. *The Sacred History*. Translated by Alexander Roberts. In *A Select Library of Nicene and Post-Nicene Fathers of the Christian Church*, vol. XI, ed. Philip Schaff and Henry Wace. Grand Rapids: Eerdmans Publishing Co., 1986 [Reprint].

Székely, István. *Chronica Ez Vilagnac Yeles Dolgairol. Szekel Estvan. Craccoba Niomtatot. Striykouiai Lazar Altal, Christvs ßweletesenec M.D.L.LIX. eßtendeibe*. Kraków: Lazar, 1559.

Teuteburg, Christian A. see Schurzfleisch, Konrad.

Torsellini, Orzaio. *Horatii Tvrsellini E Societate Iesv Epitome Historiarvm libri X. Editio Secvnda Diligenter Recognita collatione manuscriptorum, multis mendis, quae etiam in historiam irrepserant, sublatis*. Cologne: Gualterus, 1621. VD17 23:256455W.

University of Wittenberg. *De Ecclesiastica Historia: Qvae Magdebvrgi Contexitvr, Narratio, Contra Menivm, Et Scholasticorvm Wittebergensivm Epistolas. A Gvbernatoribvs*

Et Operariis Eivs Historiae Edita Magdebvrgi. Cvm Responsione Scholasticorvm Witebergensivm Ad Eandem. Edita Witebergæ Anno M.D.LVIII. Wittenberg: [Georg Rhau (Heirs)], 1558. VD16 E 242.

University of Wittenberg. *Rector Et Consilium Academiae Wittebergensis Publ.* Wittenberg: Rothe, 1634. VD17 547:637629Z.

Valla, Lorenzo. *On the Donation of Constantine.* Translated by G.W. Bowersock. Cambridge, M.A.: Harvard University Press, 2007.

Valla, Lorenzo. *The Treatise of Lorenzo Valla on the Donation of Constantine.* Translated by Christopher B. Coleman. Toronto: University of Toronto Press, 2000 [Reprint].

Vandiver, Elizabeth, Ralph Keen, and Thomas Frazel, eds. *Luther's Lives: Two Contemporary Accounts of Martin Luther.* Manchester: Manchester University Press, 2002.

Wolf, Johann, ed. *Io. Bodoni Methodvs Historica, Dvodecim eiusdem argumenti Scriptorum, tam veterum quàm recentiorum, Commentariis adaucta: quorum elenchum Præfationi subiecimus.* Basel: Perna, 1576. VD16 B 6274.

Wolf, Johann, ed. *Artis Historicae Penvs Octodecim Scriptorum tam veterum quàm recentiorum monumentis & inter eos Io. præcipuè Bodini libris Methodi historicæ sex instructa.* Basel: Perna, 1579. VD16 W 4208.

Secondary Literature

Agnoletto, Attilio. "Storia e non storia in Filippo Melantone." *Nuova rivista storica* 48 (1964): 491–528.

Albrecht, O. and P. Flemming. "Das sogenannte Manuscriptum Thomasianum. V. Aus Knaakes Abschrift veröffentlicht von O. Albrecht und P. Flemming. Dritter Teil. Nr. 94–126. Briefe Besolds an Dietrich aus den Jahren 1541–1546. Zweiter Abschnitt: Nr. 111–126." *Archiv für Reformationsgeschichte* 13 (1916): 161–199.

Alexander, Paul J. "The Medieval Legend of the Last Roman Emperor and Its Messianic Origin." *Journal of the Warburg and Courtauld Institutes* 41 (1978): 1–15.

Allen, Don Cameron. *The Legend of Noah: Renaissance Rationalism in Art, Science, and Letters.* Urbana: University of Illinois Press, 1949.

Allen, Don Cameron. "Milton's Busiris." *Modern Language Notes* 65 (February 1950): 115–116.

Allen, Michael I. "Universal History 300–1000: Origins and Western Developments." In *Historiography in the Middle Ages*, ed. Deborah Mauskopf Deliyannis, 17–42. Leiden: Brill, 2003.

Althaus, Paul. *The Ethics of Martin Luther.* Translated by Robert C. Schultz. Philadelphia: Fortress Press, 1972.

Althaus, Paul. *The Theology of Martin Luther.* Translated by Robert C. Schultz. Philadelphia: Fortress Press, 1966.

American Book-Prices Current: A Record of Books, Manuscripts and Autographs Sold at Auction in New York, Boston, and Philadelphia, from September, 1918, to July, 1919 Being the Season 1918–1919, Compiled from the Auctioneers' Catalogues. New York: E.P. Dutton & Co., 1919.

Andermann, Ulrich. "Geschichtsdeutung und Prophetie: Krisenerfahrung und bewältigung am Beispiel der osmanischen Expansion im Spätmittelalter und in der Reformationszeit." In *Europa und die Türken in der Renaissance,* ed. Bodo Guthmüller and Wilhelm Kühlmann, 29–54. Tübingen: Niemeyer, 2000.

Anderson, Andrew Runni. *Alexander's Gate, Gog and Magog, and the Inclosed Nations.* Cambridge, MA: The Mediaeval Academy of America, 1932.

Andersson, Bo. "Melanchthons Polemik gegen Thomas Müntzer: Die Histori Thome Muntzers / des anfengers des Döringischen uffrur." In *Philipp Melanchthon und seine Rezeption in Skandinavien,* ed. Birgit Stolt, 25–50. Stockholm: Distributed by Almqvist & Wiksell International, 1998.

Andersson, Christiane. "Die Spalatin-Chronik und ihre Illustrationen aus der Cranach-Werkstatt." In *Lucas Cranach: Ein Maler-Unternehmer aus Franken,* ed. Claus Grimm et al., 208–217. Regensburg: Verlag Friedrich Pustet, 1994.

Ankwicz-Kleehoven, Hans. *Der Wiener Humanist Johannes Cuspinian: Gelehrter und Diplomat zur Zeit Kaiser Maximilians I.* Graz and Köln: Böhlau, 1959.

Archambault, Paul. "The Ages of Man and the Ages of the World: A Study of two Traditions." *Revue des études augustiniennes* 12 (1966): 193–228.

Armitage, David, ed. *Theories of Empire, 1450–1800.* Brookfield, VT: Ashgate, 1998.

Armstrong, Elizabeth. *Before Copyright: The French Book-Privilege System 1498–1526.* Cambridge: Cambridge University Press, 1990.

Arnold, Benjamin. "The Western Empire, 1125–1197." In *The New Cambridge Medieval History,* vol. 4, Part 1 c. 1024 - c. 1198, ed. David Luscombe and Jonathan Riley-Smith, 384–421. Cambridge: Cambridge University Press, 2004.

Arnold, Klaus. *Johannes Trithemius (1462–1516).* Würzburg: Kommissionsverlag F. Schöningh, 1991.

Aston, Margaret. "John Wycliffe's Reformation Reputation." *Past & Present* 30 (April 1965): 23–51.

Augustijn, Cornelis. "Melanchthons Editionen der Akten von Worms und Regensburg 1540 und 1541." In *Dona Melanchthoniana: Festgabe für Heinz Scheible zum 70. Geburtstag,* ed. Johanna Loehr, 24–39. Stuttgart-Bad Cannstatt: Frommann-Holzboog, 2001.

Augustijn, Cornelis. "Melanchthon und die Religionsgespräche." In *Der Theologe Melanchthon,* ed. Günter Frank, 213–226. Stuttgart: Thorbecke, 2000.

Augustijn, Cornelis. "The Quest of *Reformatio*: The Diet of Regensburg 1541 as a Turning-Point." In *Die Reformation in Deutschland und Europa: Interpretationen und*

Debatten, ed. Hans R. Guggisberg and Gottfried G. Krodel, 64–80. Gütersloh: Mohn, 1993.

Backus, Irena. *Historical Method and Confessional Identity in the Era of the Reformation (1378–1615)*. Leiden: Brill, 2003.

Backus, Irena. "The Beast: Interpretations of Daniel 7.2-9 and Apocalypse 13.1-4, 11–12 in Lutheran, Zwinglian and Calvinist Circles in the Late Sixteenth Century." *Reformation and Renaissance Review* 3 (2000): 59–77.

Bagchi, D.V.N. "'Teutschlandt uber alle Welt:' Nationalism and Catholicism in Early Reformation Germany." *Archiv für Reformationsgeschichte* 82 (1991): 39–58.

Barnes, Robin B. "Alexander Seitz and the Medical Calling: Physic, Faith and Reform." In *Ideas and Cultural Margins in Early Modern Germany: Essays in Honor of H.C. Erik Midelfort*, ed. Majorie Elizabeth Plummer and Robin B. Barnes, 183–199. Burlington, VT: Ashgate, 2009.

Barnes, Robin B. "Astrology and the Confessions in the Empire, c. 1550–1620." In *Confessionalization in Europe, 1555–1570: Essays in Honor and Memory of Bodo Nischan*, ed. John Headley et al., 131–153. Burlington, VT: Ashgate, 2004.

Barnes, Robin B. "Hope and Despair in Sixteenth-Century German Almanacs." In *Die Reformation in Deutschland und Europa: Interpretationen und Debatten*, ed. Hans R. Guggisberg and Gottfried G. Krodel, 440–461. Gütersloh: Gütersloher Verlagshaus Mohn, 1993.

Barnes, Robin B. *Prophecy and Gnosis: Apocalypticism in the Wake of the Lutheran Reformation*. Stanford: Stanford University Press, 1988.

Bartmuß, Alexander. "Melanchthon erzählt: Ein Beitrag zu den 'Dicta und Exempla' Melanchthons." *Luther* 79, no. 1 (2008): 26–40.

Bäumel, Jutta. *The Dresden Armory: Guide to the Permanent Collection in the Semper Building*. Translated by Daniel Kletke. Munich & Berlin: Deutscher Kunstverlag, 2004.

Bäumer, Remigius. *Johannes Cochlaeus (1479–1552): Leben und Werk im Dienst der Katholischen Reform*. Münster: Aschendorff, 1980.

Bauer, Barbara. "Die *Chronica Carionis* von 1532, Melanchthons und Peucers Bearbeitung und ihre Wirkungsgeschichte." In *Himmelszeichen und Erdenwege: Johannes Carion (1499–1537) und Sebastian Hornmold (1500–1581) in ihrer Zeit*, ed. Elke Osterloh, 203–246. Ubstadt-Weiher: Verlag Regionalkultur, 1999.

Bauer, Barbara. "Caspar Peucer: De praecipuis divinationvm generibvs. Frankfurt a. M. 1593." In *Melanchthon und die Marburger Professoren (1527–1627)*, ed. Barbara Bauer, 382–388. Marburg: [Universitätsbibliothek Marburg], 1999.

Bauer, Barbara. "Die göttliche Ordnung in der Natur und Gesellschaft: Die Geschichtsauffassung im Chronicon Carionis." In *Melanchthon und das Lehrbuch des 16. Jahrhunderts*, ed. Jürgen Leonhardt, 217–229. Rostock: Universität Rostock, 1997.

Beer, Barrett L. "Robert Crowley and Cooper's Chronicle: The Unauthorized Edition of 1559." *Notes and Queries* 55, no. 2 (June 2008): 148–152.

Beer, Barrett L. "John Stow and Tudor Rebellions, 1549–1569." *The Journal of British Studies* 27, no. 4 (October 1988): 352–374.

Beller, E.A. "The Thirty Years War." In *The New Cambridge Modern History*, vol. IV, *The Decline of Spain and the Thirty Years War 1609–48/59*, ed. J.P. Cooper, 306–358. Cambridge: Cambridge University Press, 1970.

Benario, Herbert W. "Arminius into Hermann: History into Legend." *Greece & Rome* 51, no. 1 (April 2004): 83–94.

Benert, R.R. "Lutheran Resistance Theory and the Imperial Constitution." *Pensiero politico* 6, no. 1 (1973): 17–36.

Benning, Stefan. "Johannes Carion aus Bietigheim: Eine biographische Skizze." In *Himmelszeichen und Erdenwege: Johannes Carion (1499–1537) und Sebastian Hornmold (1500–1581) in ihrer Zeit*, ed. Elke Osterloh, 193–202. Ubstadt-Weiher: Verlag Regionalkultur, 1999.

Benrath, Gustav Adolf. "Das Verständnis der Kirchengeschichte in der Reformationszeit." In *Literatur und Laienbildung im Spätmittelalter und in der Reformationszeit: Symposion Wolfenbüttel 1981*, ed. Ludger Grenzmann and Karl Stackmann, 97–113. Stuttgart: J.B. Metzlersche Verlagsbuchhandlung, 1984.

Ben-Tov, Asaph. *Lutheran Humanists and Greek Antiquity: Melanchthonian Scholarship between Universal History and Pedagogy*. Leiden: Brill, 2009.

Benz, Ernst. "Der Traum Kurfürst Friedrichs des Weisen." In *Humanitas-Christianitas*, ed. Karlmann Beyschlag, Gottfried Maron and Eberhard Wölfel, 134–149. Witten: Luther Verlag, 1968.

Benz, Stefan. *Zwischen Tradition und Kritik: Katholische Geschichtsschreibung im barocken Heiligen Römischen Reich*. Husum: Matthiesen Verlag, 2003.

Benzing, Josef. *Die Buchdrucker des 16. und 17. Jahrhunderts im deutschen Sprachgebiet*. Wiesbaden: Harrassowitz, 1982.

Benzing, Josef. "Der Drucker Cyriacus Jacob zu Frankfurt a. M. 1533 (1539)–1551." *Archiv für Geschichte des Buchwesens* 3 (1961): 1–18.

Berger, Samuel. "Melanchthons Vorlesungen über Weltgeschichte." *Theologische Studien und Kritiken: Beiträge zur Theologie und Religionswissenschaft* 70 (1897): 781–790.

Beyer, Michael. "Georg Major als Übersetzer." In *Georg Major (1502–1574): Ein Theologe der Wittenberger Reformation*, ed. Irene Dingel and Günther Wartenberg, 123–158. Leipzig: Evangelische Verlagsanstalt, 2005.

Binder, Gerhard. "Der Praeceptor Germaniae und die 'Germania' des Tacitus: Über eine Tacitus-Ausgabe Philipp Melanchthons." In *Philipp Melanchthon: Exemplarische Aspekte seines Humanismus*, ed. Gerhard Binder, 103–140. Trier: WFT Wissenschaftlicher Verlag, 1998.

Black, Anthony. "Popes and Councils." In *The New Cambridge Medieval History*, vol. VII, c. 1415 - c. 1500, ed. Christopher Allmand, 65–86. Cambridge: Cambridge University Press, 1998.

Black, Robert. "The New Laws of History." *Renaissance Studes* 1 (1987): 126–156.

Black, Robert. "Benedetto Accolti and the Beginnings of Humanist Historiography." *English Historical Review* 96 (1981): 36–58.

Blair, Ann. "Reading Strategies for Coping With Information Overload ca. 1550–1700." *Journal of the History of Ideas* 64 (January 2003): 11–28.

Bobzin, Hartmut. *Der Koran im Zeitalter der Reformation*. Stuttgart: Steiner, 1995.

Bobzin, Hartmut. "Zur Anzahl der Drucke von Biblianders Koranausgabe im Jahr 1543." *Basler Zeitschrift für Geschichte und Altertumskunde* 85 (1985): 213–219.

Bödeker, Hans Erich et al., ed. *Aufklärung und Geschichte: Studien zur deutschen Geschichtswissenschaft im 18. Jahrhundert*. Göttingen: Vandenhoeck & Ruprecht, 1992.

Bönnen, Gerold and Burkard Keilmann, eds. *Der Wormser Bischof Johann von Dalberg (1482–1503) und seine Zeit*. Trier: Gesellschaft für Mittelrheinische Kirchengeschichte, 2005.

Boettcher, Susan. "German Orientalism in the Age of Confessional Consolidation: Jacob Andreae's *Thirteen Sermons on the Turk*, 1568." *Comparative Studies of South Asia, Africa and the Middle East* 24, no. 2 (2004): 101–115.

Bohnstedt, John. "The Infidel Scourge of God: The Turkish Menace as Seen by German Pamphleteers of the Reformation Era." *Transactions of the American Philosophical Society* New Ser. 58, no. 9 (1968): 1–58.

Bollbuck, Harald. *Wahrheitszeugnis, Gottes Auftrag und Zeitkritik: Die Kirchengeschichte der Magdeburger Zenturien und ihre Arbeitstechniken*. Wiesbaden: Harrassowitz, 2014.

Bollbuck, Harald. "Universalgeschichte, Kirchengeschichte und die Ordnung der Schöpfung. Philipp Melanchthon und die Anfänge der protestantischen Geschichtsschreibung." In *Fragmenta Melanchthoniana: Humanismus und Europäische Identität*, vol. 4, ed. Günter Frank, 125–152. Ubstadt-Weiher: Verlag Regionalkultur, 2009.

Bonacker, Wilhelm and Hans Volz. "Eine Wittenberger Weltkarte aus dem Jahr 1529." *Die Erde* 8, no. 2 (1956): 154–170.

Bond, John J. *Handy-Book of Rules and Tables for Verifying Dates with the Christian Era*. New York: Russell & Russell, 1966 [Reprint].

Borchardt, Frank. *German Antiquity in Renaissance Myth*. Baltimore: The Johns Hopkins University Press, 1971.

Borda, Lajos. "Ein unbekannter Hamburger Druck. Der Almanach von Johannes Carion (1537)." *Gutenberg Jahrbuch* 79 (2004): 183–186.

Borst, Arno. *Der Turmbau von Babel: Geschichte der Meinungen über Ursprung und Vielfalt der Sprachen und Völker*. 4 vols. Stuttgart: Anton Hiersemann, 1957–1963.

Bosbach, Franz. "The European Debate on Universal Monarchy." In *Theories of Empire, 1450–1800*, ed. David Armitage, 81–98. Brookfield, VT: Ashgate, 1998.

Brady, Thomas, Heiko A. Oberman and James D. Tracy. *Handbook of European History, 1400–1600: Late Middle Ages, Renaissance, and Reformation*. 2 vols. Leiden: Brill, 1994.

Brandis, C.G. "Luther und Melanchthon als Benützer der Wittenberg Bibliothek." *Theologische Studien und Kritiken* 90 (1917): 206–217.

Brann, Noel. "Pre-Reformation humanism in Germany and the papal monarchy: a study in ambivalence." *Journal of Medieval and Renaissance Studies* 14, no. 2 (Fall 1984): 159–185.

Brann, Noel. *The Abbot Trithemius (1462–1516): The Renaissance of Monastic Humanism*. Leiden: Brill, 1981.

Bräuer, Siegfried. "Cyriakus Spangenberg als mansfeldisch-sächsischer Reformationshistoriker." In *Reformatoren im Mansfelder Land: Erasmus Sarcerius und Cyriakus Spangenberg*, ed. Stefan Rhein, 171–189. Leipzig: Evangelische Verlagsanstalt, 2006.

Bräuer, Siegfried. "Die Überlieferung von Melanchthons Leichenrede auf Luther." In *Humanismus und Wittenberger Reformation: Festgabe anläßlich des 500. Geburtstages des Praeceptor Germaniae Philipp Melanchthon am 16. Februar 1997*, ed. Michael Beyer, 185–252. Leipzig: Evangelische Verlagsanstalt, 1996.

Braude, Benjamin. "The Sons of Noah and the Construction of Ethnic and Geographical Identities in the Medieval and Early Modern Periods." *The William and Mary Quarterly* 3rd Ser. 54, no. 1 (January 1997): 103–142.

Brecht, Martin. "'Die Historie ist nichts anderes denn eine Anzeigung göttlicher Werke.' Martin Luther und das Ende der Geschichte." In *"Wach auf, wach auf, du deutsches Land!" Martin Luther Angst und Zuversicht in der Zeitenwende*, ed. Peter Freybe, 10–24. Wittenberg: Drei Kastanien, 2000.

Brecht, Martin. "Luther und die Türken." In *Europa und die Türken in der Renaissance*, ed. Bodo Guthmüller and Wilhelm Kühlmann, 9–28. Tübingen: Niemeyer, 2000.

Breen, Quirinus. "Melanchthon's Sources for a Life of Agricola: The Heidelberg Memories and the Writings." *Archiv für Reformationsgeschichte* 52 (1961): 49–74.

Breisach, Ernst. *Historiography: Ancient, Medieval, and Modern*, 2nd ed. Chicago: University of Chicago Press, 1994.

Bremme, Hans Joachim. *Buchdrucker und Buchhändler zur Zeit der Glaubenskämpfe: Studien zur Genfer Druckgeschichte, 1565–1580*. Genève: Droz, 1969.

Brendecke, Arndt. "Tabellenwerke in der Praxis der frühneuzeitlichen Geschichtsvermittlung." In *Wissenssicherung, Wissensordnung und Wissensverarbeitung: Das Europäische Modell der Enzyklopädien*, ed. Theo Stammen and Wolfgang Weber, 157–185. Berlin: Akademie Verlag, 2004.

Brendle, Franz et al., eds. *Deutsche Landesgeschichtsschreibung im Zeichen des Humanismus*. Stuttgart: Franz Steiner Verlag, 2001.

Brettschneider, Harry. *Melanchthon als Historiker: Ein Beitrag zur Kenntnis der deutschen Historiographie im Zeitalter des Humanismus.* Insterburg: Wilhelmi, 1880.

Brincken, Anna-Dorothee von den. "Studien zur Überlieferung der Chronik des Martin von Troppau: Zweiter Teil." *Deutsches Archiv für Erforschung des Mittelalters* 45 (1989): 551–591.

Brincken, Anna-Dorothee von den. "Martin von Troppau." In *Geschichtsschreibung und Geschichtsbewusstsein im späten Mittelalter,* ed. Hans Patze, 155–193. Sigmaringen: Jan Thorbecke Verlag, 1987.

Brincken, Anna-Dorothee von den. "Anniversaristische und chronikalische Geschichtsschreibung in den 'Flores Temporum' (um 1292)." In *Geschichtsschreibung und Geschichtsbewusstsein im späten Mittelalter,* ed. Hans Patze, 195–214. Sigmaringen: Jan Thorbecke Verlag, 1987.

Brincken, Anna-Dorothee von den. "Die Rezeption mittelalterlicher Historiographie durch den Inkunabeldruck." In *Geschichtsschreibung und Geschichtsbewusstsein im späten Mittelalter,* ed. Hans Patze, 195–214. Sigmaringen: Jan Thorbecke Verlag, 1987.

Brincken, Anna-Dorothee von den. "Studien zur Überlieferung der Chronik des Martin von Troppau." *Deutsches Archiv für Erforschung des Mittelalters* 41 (1985): 460–531.

Brincken, Anna-Dorothee von den. "Die lateinische Weltchronistik." In *Mensch und Weltgeschichte: Zur Geschichte der Universalgeschichtsschreibung,* ed. Alexander Randa, 43–86. Salzburg and Munich: Pustet, 1969.

Brockman, Eric. *The Two Sieges of Rhodes, 1480–1522.* London: J. Murray, 1969.

Brown, John. *The Methodus ad facilem historiarum cognitionem of Jean Bodin: A Critical Study.* Washington, D.C.: The Catholic University of America Press, 1939.

Brosseder, Claudia. "The Writing in the Wittenberg Sky: Astrology in Sixteenth-Century Germany." *Journal of the History of Ideas* 66 (October 2005): 557–576.

Brosseder, Claudia. *Im Bann der Sterne: Caspar Peucer, Philipp Melanchthon und andere Wittenberger Astrologen.* Berlin: Akademie Verlag, 2004.

Bruning, Jens. "Caspar Peucer und Kurfürst August: Grundlinien kursächsischer Reichs- und Konfessionspolitik nach dem Augsburger Religionsfrieden (1555–1586)." In *Caspar Peucer (1525–1602): Wissenschaft, Glaube und Politik im konfessionellen Zeitalter,* ed. Hans-Peter Hasse and Günther Wartenberg, 157–174. Leipzig: Evangelische Verlagsanstalt, 2004.

Buchanan, Harvey. "Luther and the Turks 1519–1529." *Archiv für Reformationsgeschichte* 47 (1956): 145–160.

Buchholz, Ingeborg. "Die Varusschlacht im Urteil der Humanisten." *Lippische Mitteilungen aus Geschichte und Landeskunde* 28 (1959): 5–57.

Büttner, M. "The Significance of the Reformation for the Reorientation of Geography in Lutheran Germany." *History of Science* 17, no. 3 (September 1979): 151–169.

Bundschuh, Benno von. *Das Wormser Religionsgespräch von 1557 unter besonderer Berücksichtigung der kaiserlichen Religionspolitik.* Münster: Aschendorff, 1988.

Burmeister, Karl Heinz. *Sebastian Münster: Versuch eines biographischen Gesamtbildes.* Basel and Stuttgart: Helbing & Lichtenhahn, 1963.

Calinich, Robert. *Kampf und Untergang des Melanchthonismus in Kursachsen in den Jahren 1570 bis 1574 und die Schicksale seiner vornehmsten Häupter: Aus den Quellen des königlichen Hauptstaatsarchivs zu Dresden.* Leipzig: Brockhaus, 1866.

Cameron, Euan. "The Bible and the early modern sense of history." In *The New Cambridge History of the Bible: Volume III, From 1450 to 1750*, ed. Euan Cameron, 657–685. Cambridge: Cambridge University Press, 2016.

Cameron, Euan. "Cosmic Time and the Theological View of World History." *Irish Theological Quarterly* 77:4 (2012): 349–364.

Cameron, Euan. *Interpreting Christian History: The Challenge of the Churches' Past.* Oxford: Blackwell Publishing, 2005.

Cameron, Euan. "The possibilities and limits of conciliation: Philipp Melanchthon and inter-confessional dialogue in the sixteenth century." In *Conciliation and Confession: The struggle for unity in the age of reform, 1415 - 1648*, ed. Howard Louthan, 73–88. Notre Dame: University of Notre Dame Press, 2004.

Cantimori, Delio. "Umanesimo e luteranesimo di fronte alla scolastica." In *Umanesimo e religione nel Rinascimanento*, 88–111. Turin: Piccola Biblioteca Einaudi, 1975. [First published as "Umanesimo e luteranesimo di fronte alla scolastica: Caspar Peucer." *Rivista di studi germanici* 2 (1937): 417–438.]

Caroti, Stefano. "Melanchthon's Astrology." In *"Astrologi hallucinati": Stars and the End of the World in Luther's Time*, ed. Paola Zambelli, 109–121. Berlin: de Gruyter, 1986.

Carsten, F.L., ed. *The New Cambridge Modern History*, vol. V, *The Ascendancy of France 1648–88*. Cambridge: Cambridge University Press, 1961.

Castan, Joachim. "Caspar Peucers letzte Lebensperiode in Anhalt – eine Wiederentdeckung." In *Caspar Peucer (1525–1602): Wissenschaft, Glaube und Politik im konfessionellen Zeitalter*, ed. Hans-Peter Hasse and Günther Wartenberg, 283–297. Leipzig: Evangelische Verlagsanstalt, 2004.

Chaix, Gérald. "Laurentius Surius (1523–1578)." In *Rheinische Lebensbilder*, vol. 11, ed. Wilhelm Janssen, 77–100. Köln: Rheinland Verlag, 1988.

Chaix, Paul et al. *Les livres imprimés à Genève de 1550 à 1600.* Geneve: Droz, 1966.

Christensen, Carl C. *Princes and Propaganda: Electoral Saxon Art of the Reformation.* Kirksville, Mo.: Sixteenth Century Journal, 1992.

Christensen, Carl C. *Art and the Reformation in Germany.* Athens, Ohio: Ohio University Press, 1979.

Christmann, Curt. *Melanchthons Haltung im schmalkaldischen Kriege.* Berlin: E. Ebering, 1902.

Clark, Harry. "The Publication of the Koran in Latin: A Reformation Dilemma." *Sixteenth Century Journal* 15, no. 1 (Spring 1984): 3–12.

Clasen, Claus Peter. *The Palatinate in European History 1555–1618*. Oxford: Blackwell, 1966.

Claus, Helmut. *Melanchthon-Bibliographie 1510–1560*. 4 vols. [Gütersloh]: Gütersloher Verlagshaus, 2014.

Clavuot, Ottavio. *Biondos "Italia Illustrata" – Summa oder Neuschöpfung? Über die Arbeitsmethoden eines Humanisten*. Tübingen: Niemeyer, 1990.

Clemen, Otto. *Unbekannte Drucke, Briefe und Akten aus der Reformationszeit*. Leipzig: Harrassowitz, 1942.

Clemen, Otto. "Vier Briefe des Buchdruckers Johann Oporin an Kaspar Peucer." *Gutenberg Jahrbuch* (1936): 146–149.

Clemen, Otto. "Schriften und Lebensaugang des Eisenacher Franziskaners Johann Hilten." *Zeitschrift für Kirchengeschichte* 47 (1928): 402–412.

Clemen, Otto. "Der Prozeß des Johannes Pollicarius." *Archiv für Reformationsgeschichte* 18 (1921): 63–74.

Cochrane, Eric. *Historians and Historiography in the Italian Renaissance*. Chicago: University of Chicago Press, 1981.

Cochrane, Eric. "The Profession of the Historian in the Italian Renaissance." *Journal of Social History* 15, no. 1 (Autumn 1981): 51–72.

Cohn, Henry J. "Did Bribes Induce the German Electors to Choose Charles V as Emperor in 1519?" *German History* 19, no. 1 (January 2001): 1–27.

Cole, Richard. "Pamphlet Woodcuts in the Communication Process of Reformation Germany." In *Pietas et Societas: New Trends in Reformation Social History*, ed. Kyle C. Sessions and Phillip N. Bebb, 103–121. Kirksville, Mo.: Sixteenth Century Journal, 1985.

Cole, Richard. "Reformation Printers: Unsung Heroes." *Sixteenth Century Journal* 15, no. 3 (Autumn 1984): 327–339.

Cole, Richard. "The Reformation Pamphlet and Communication Processes." In *Flugschriften als Massenmedium der Reformationzeit*, ed. Hans-Joachim Köhler, 139–161. Stuttgart: Ernst Klett Verlag, 1981.

Cook, Robert. "The Chronica Carionis in Iceland." *Bibliotheca Arnamagnæana* 38 (1985): 226–263.

Cordes, Günter. "Franciscus Irenicus von Ettlingen. Aus dem Leben eines Humanisten und Reformators." In *Oberrheinische Studien* III, *Festschrift für Günther Haselier aus Anlaß seines 60. Geburtstages*, ed. Alfons Schäfer, 353–371. Bretten: Druckerei Esser, 1975.

Courtenay, William J. and Jürgen Miethke, eds. *Universities and Schooling in Medieval Society*. Leiden: Brill, 2000.

D'Amico, John. "Ulrich von Hutten and Beatus Rhenanus as Medieval Historians and Religious Propagandists in the Early Reformation." In *Roman and German Humanism, 1450–1550*, ed. Paul F. Grendler, XII:1–33. Brookfield, VT: Variorum, 1993.

D'Amico, John. *Theory and Practice in Renaissance Textual Criticism: Beatus Rhenanus between Conjecture and History.* Berkeley: University of California Press, 1988.

D'Amico, John. *Renaissance Humanism in Papal Rome: Humanists and Churchmen on the Eve of the Reformation.* Baltimore: Johns Hopkins University Press, 1983.

Daniel, Norman. *Islam and the West: The Making of an Image.* Oxford: Oneworld, 1997 [Reprint].

Dauber, Noah. "Civil Authority and Aristotelian Argument in Philip Melanchthon's Commentary on Aristotle's Politics." In *Politischer Aristotelismus: Untersuchungen zur Rezeption der aristotelischen Politik von der Antike bis zum 19. Jahrhundert*, ed. Christoph Horn and Ada Neschke-Hentschke, 173–191. Basel: Schwabe Verlag, 2008.

Dauber, Noah. "The Invention of Political Science." Ph.D. diss., Harvard University, 2006.

Decot, Rolf. "Die Entstehung des Papsttums: Martin Luthers historische Sicht in seiner Schrift 'Wider das Papsttum zu Rom, vom Teufel gestiftet' (1545)." In *Deutschland und Europa in der Neuzeit: Festschrift für Karl Otmar Frhr. von Aretin zum 65. Geburtstag*, ed. Ralph Melville, 133–154. Stuttgart: F. Steiner Verlag Wiesbaden, 1988.

Deflers, Isabelle. "Aristotelismus in Melanchthons Rechtsauffassung." In *Politischer Aristotelismus und Religion in Mittelalter und Früher Neuzeit*, ed. Alexander Fidora et al., 119–130. Berlin: Akademie Verlag, 2007.

Deflers, Isabelle. *Lex und Ordo: Eine rechtshistorische Untersuchung der Rechtsauffassung Melanchthons.* Berlin: Duncker & Humblot, 2005.

Deflers, Isabelle. "Orationes de legibus: Zwei Reden über das Gesetz verfasst durch Philipp Melanchthon." In *Studien zur Rechts- und Zeitgeschichte: Liber discipulorum Professor Dr. Wulf Eckart Voß zum 60. Geburtstag*, ed. Andreas Bauer, 51–69. Göttingen: V&R Unipress, 2005.

Deflers, Isabelle. "Melanchthon und die Rezeption des römischen Rechts in Sachsen und im Alten Reich." In *Sachsen im Spiegel des Rechts: Ius Commune Propriumque*, ed. Adrian Schmidt-Recla, 185–203. Köln: Böhlau, 2001.

Dejung, Christoph. "Geschichte lehrt Gelassenheit." In *Beiträge zum 500. Geburtstag von Sebastian Franck (1499–1542)*, ed. Siegried Wollgast, 89–126. Berlin: Weidler Buchverlag, 1999.

Dejung, Christoph. *Wahrheit und Häresie: Eine Untersuchung zur Geschichtsphilosphie bei Sebastian Franck.* Zurich: Samisdat, 1980.

Delgado, Mariano et al., eds. *Europa, Tausendjähriges Reich und Neue Welt: Zwei Jahrtausende Geschichte und Utopie in der Rezeption des Danielbuches.* Stuttgart: Kohlhammer, 2003.

Dellsperger, Yvonne. *Lebendige Historien und Erfahrungen: Studien zu Sebastian Francks "Chronica Zeitbuoch vnnd Geschichtbibell" (1531/1536).* Berlin: E. Schmidt, 2008.

Deppermann, Klaus. "Sebastian Francks Straßburger Aufenhalt." In *Sebastian Franck (1499–1542)*, ed. Jan Dirk Müller, 103–129. Wiesbaden: Harrassowitz, 1993.

Dickens, A.G. "Johannes Sleidan and Reformation History." In *Reformation, Conformity and Dissent: Essays in honour of Geoffrey Nuttall*, ed. R. Buick Knox, 17–43. London: Epworth Press, 1977.

Dickens, A.G. and John Tonkin. *The Reformation in Historical Thought*. Cambridge, MA.: Harvard University Press, 1985.

Diefenbacher, Michael et al. *"Auserlesene und allerneueste Landkarten": der Verlag Homann in Nürnberg 1702–1848*. Nürnberg: Tümmels, 2002.

Diener, Ronald. "The Magdeburg Centuries: A Bibliothecal and Historiographical Analysis." Ph.D. diss., Harvard Divinity School, 1978.

Dinan, Desmond, ed. *Origins and Evolution of the European Union*. Oxford: Oxford University Press, 2006.

Dingel, Irene. "Melanchthon und die Normierung des Bekenntnisses." In *Der Theologe Melanchthon*, ed. Günter Frank, 195–211. Stuttgart: Thorbecke, 2000.

Dingel, Irene. *Concordia Controversa: Die öffentlichen Diskussionen um das lutherische Konkordienwerk am Ende des 16. Jahrhunderts*. Gütersloh: Gütersloher Verlagshaus Mohn, 1996.

Dingel, Irene and Günther Wartenberg, eds. *Georg Major (1502–1574): Ein Theologe der Wittenberger Reformation*. Leipzig: Evangelische Verlagsanstalt, 2005.

Dixon, C. Scott. "The Sense of the Past in Reformation Germany: Part 2." *German History* 30:2 (2012), 175–198.

Dixon, C. Scott. "The Sense of the Past in Reformation Germany: Part 1." *German History* 30:1 (2012), 1–21.

Dixon, C. Scott. "The Politics of Law and Gospel: The Protestant Prince and the Holy Roman Empire." In *The Impact of the Reformation: Princes, Clergy and People*, ed. Bridget Heal and Ole Peter Grell, 37–62. Burlington, VT: Ashgate, 2008.

Dixon, C. Scott. "Popular Astrology and Lutheran Propaganda in Reformation Germany." *History* 84, no. 3 (1999): 403–418.

Dozo, Björn-Olav. "Jean Le Blond, premier traducteur français de l'*Utopie*." *Lettres Romanes* 49 (2005): 187–210.

Dreitzel, Horst. *Absolutismus und ständische Verfassung in Deutschland: Ein Beitrag zu Kontinuität und Diskontinuität der politischen Theorie in der frühen Neuzeit*. Mainz: Verlag Philipp von Zabern, 1992.

Dreyer, J.L.E. *Tycho Brahe: A Picture of Scientific Life and Work in the Sixteenth Century*. Edinburgh: Adam and Charles Black, 1890.

Du Boulay, F.R.H. *Germany in the Later Middle Ages*. London: Athlone Press, 1983.

Du Boulay, F.R.H. "The German town chroniclers." In *The Writing of History in the Middle Ages: Essays Presented to Richard William Southern*, ed. R.H.C. Davis and J.M. Wallace-Hadrill, 445–469. Oxford: Clarendon Press, 1981.

Duchhardt, Heinz. *Protestantisches Kaisertum und Altes Reich: Die Diskussion über die Konfession des Kaisers in Politik, Publizistik und Staatsrecht*. Wiesbaden: Franz Steiner Verlag, 1977.

Dupèbe, Jean. "L'écriture chez l'ermite Pelagius: Un cas de théurgie chrétienne au xve siècle." In *Le Texte et son inscription*, ed. R. Laufer, 113–153. Paris: Editions du C.N.R.S., 1989.

Edington, Carol. *Court and Culture in Renaissance Scotland: Sir David Lindsay of the Mount*. Amherst: University of Massachusetts Press, 1994.

Edwards, Mark U. *Printing, Propaganda, and Martin Luther*. Berkeley: University of California Press, 1994.

Edwards, Mark U. *Luther's Last Battles: Politics and Polemics, 1531–46*. Ithaca: Cornell University Press, 1983.

Edwards, Mark U. *Luther and the False Brethren*. Stanford: Stanford University Press, 1975.

Ehmer, Hermann. "Reformatorische Geschichtsschreibung am Oberrhein: Franciscus Irenicus, Kaspar Hedio, Johannes Sleidanus." In *Historiographie am Oberrhein im Späten Mittelalter und in der Frühen Neuzeit*, ed. Kurt Andermann, 227–245. Sigmaringen: Jan Thorbecke Verlag, 1988.

Ehmer, Hermann. "Andreas Althamer und die gescheiterte Reformation in Schwäbisch Gmünd." *Blätter für württembergische Kirchengeschichte* 78 (1978): 46–72.

Eire, Carlos. *Reformations: The Early Modern World, 1450–1650*. New Haven: Yale University Press, 2016.

Eisenstein, Elizabeth L. *The Printing Revolution in Early Modern Europe*. Cambridge: Cambridge University Press, 1993.

Eisenstein, Elizabeth L. "Clio and Chronos an Essay on the Making and Breaking of History-Book Time." *History and Theory* 6, no. 6 (1966): 36–64.

Ekrem, Inger. *Historieskrivning og -undervisning på latin i Oslo omkring år 1600: Halvard Gunnarssøns Philippiske Carionkrønike, Rostock 1596. Med innledning, oversettelse og kommentar*. Oslo: Scandinavian University Press, 1998.

Ekrem, Inger. "Drei Versionen von Carions Chronica in Dänemark-Norwegen 1554–1606." *Symbolae Osloenses* 73 (1998): 168–187.

Ekrem, Inger. "Melanchthon – Chytraeus – Gunarius: Der Einfluss des Geschichtsunterrichts und der Geschichtsschreibung in den deutschen Ländern und in Dänemark-Norwegen auf einen norwegischen Lektor (ca. 1550–1608)." In *Reformation and Latin Literature in Northern Europe*, ed. Inger Ekrem et al., 207–225. Oslo: Scandinavian University Press, 1996.

Ekrem, Inger. "Historiography in Norway c. 1523–1614." In *A History of Nordic Neo-Latin Literature*, ed. Minna Skafte Jensen, 240–250. Odense: Odense University Press, 1995.

Estes, James. *Peace, Order and the Glory of God: Secular Authority and the Church in the Thought of Luther and Melanchthon, 1518–1559*. Leiden: Brill, 2005.

Estes, James. "The role of godly magistrates in the church: Melanchthon as Luther's interpreter and collaborator." *Church history* 67 (1998): 463–483.

Evans, James. *History and Practice of Ancient Astronomy*. Oxford: Oxford University Press, 1998.

Fabisch, Peter. *Iulius exclusus e coelis: Motive und Tendenzen gallikanischer und bibelhumanistischer Papstkritik im Umfeld des Erasmus.* Münster: Aschendorff, 2008.

Fasolt, Constantin. "Hermann Conring and the European History of Law." In *Politics and Reformations: Histories and Reformations. Essays in Honor of Thomas A. Brady, Jr.*, ed. Christopher Ocker et al., 113–34. Leiden: Brill, 2007.

Fasolt, Constantin. *The Limits of History.* Chicago: University of Chicago Press, 2004.

Fasolt, Constantin. "Sovereignty and Heresy." In *Infinite Boundaries: Order, Disorder, and Reorder in Early Modern German Culture*, ed. Max Reinhart, 381–391. Kirksville: Sixteenth Century Journal Publishers, 1998.

Fasolt, Constantin. "A Question of Right: Hermann Conring's New Discourse on the Roman-German Emperor." *Sixteenth Century Journal* 28, no. 3 (Autumn 1997): 739–758.

Fasolt, Constantin. "Conring on History." In *Supplementum Festivum: Studies in Honor of Paul Oskar Kristeller*, ed. James Hankins et al., 563–87. Binghamton, NY: Medieval and Renaissance Texts and Studies, 1987.

Feil, Ernst. *Religio: Die Geschichte eines neuzeitlichen Grundbegriffs vom Frühchristentum bis zur Reformation.* Göttingen: Vandenhoeck & Ruprecht, 1986.

Ferguson, Wallace K. *The Renaissance in Historical Thought: Five Centuries of Interpretation.* Boston: Houghton Mifflin, 1948.

Fester, Richard. "Sleidan, Sabinus, Melanchthon." *Historische Zeitschrift* 89 (1902): 1–16.

Fichtner, Paula Sutter. *Emperor Maximilian II.* New Haven: Yale University Press, 2001.

Fink, Hans-Peter. "Hildebrand Grathus, Philipp Melanchthon und Lippe als Schauplatz der Varusschlacht." *Lippische Mitteilungen aus Geschichte und Landeskunde* 58 (1989): 65–71.

Fiori, Giorgio. "Il Governo di Pier Luigi Farnese (1545–1547)." In *Storia di Piacenza*, vol. 4, *Dai Farnese ai Borbone (1545–1802)*, pt. 1, 13–26. Piacenza: Cassa di Risparmio di Piacenza e Vigevano, 1999.

Firth, Katharine. *The Apocalyptic Tradition in Reformation Britain, 1530–1645.* Oxford: Oxford University Press, 1979.

Fischer-Galati, Stephen A. *Ottoman Imperialism and German Protestantism, 1521–1555.* Cambridge, M.A.: Harvard University Press, 1959.

Fischer-Galati, Stephen A. "Ottoman Imperialism and the Religious Peace of Nürnberg (1532)." *Archiv für Reformationsgeschichte* 47 (1956): 160–180.

Fleischer, Manfred. "Melanchthon as Praeceptor of Late-Humanist Poetry." *Sixteenth Century Journal* 20, no. 4 (Winter 1989): 559–580.

Fodor, Pál. "The View of the Turk in Hungary: The Apocalyptic Tradition and the Legend of the Red Apple in Ottoman-Hungarian Context." In *In Quest of the Golden Apple: Imperial Ideology, Politics, and Military Administration in the Ottoman Empire*, 71–103. Istanbul: Isis Press, 2000.

Foncke, Robert. *Duitse vlugschriften van de tijd over het proces en de terechtstelling van de protestanten Frans en Nikolaas Thys te Mechelen (1555) met inleiding en aantekeningen opnieuw uitgegeven.* Antwerpen: De Sikkel, 1937.

Fontaine, P.F.M. "'Praeceptor historiae': Philippus Melanchthon als geschiedenis leraar." *Tijdschrift voor geschiedenis* 88 (1975): 313–332.

Fraenkel, Pierre. *Testimonia Patrum: The Function of the Patristic Argument in the Theology of Philip Melanchthon*. Geneva: Librairie E. Droz, 1961.

Frank, Günter. "Philipp Melanchthon und die europäische Kulturgeschichte." In *Fragmenta Melanchthoniana*, ed. Günter Frank, 133–146. Heidelberg: Verlag Regionalkultur, 2003.

Frank, Günter, ed. *Melanchthon und die Naturwissenschaften seiner Zeit*. Sigmaringen: Thorbecke, 1998.

Franklin, Julian. *Jean Bodin and the Sixteenth-Century Revolution in the Methodology of Law and History*. New York: Columbia University Press, 1963.

Franz, Günther. *Der deutsche Bauernkrieg*, 10th ed. Darmstadt: Wissenschaftliche Buchgesellschaft, 1975.

Freedman, Joseph. "Philipp Melanchthon's views concerning Petrus Ramus as expressed in a private letter written in 1543: A brief assessment." In *Melanchthon und die Marburger Professoren (1527–1627)*, ed. Barbara Bauer, 841–848. Marburg: [Universitätsbibliothek Marburg], 1999.

Freedman, Joseph. "The Career and Writings of Bartholomew Keckermann (d. 1609)." *Proceedings of the American Philosophical Society* 141, no. 3 (September 1997): 305–364.

Freeman, Arthur. "Editions of Fontanus, *De bello Rhodio*." *The Library* 5th series, 24 (1969): 336–339.

Fricke-Hilgers, Almut. "Die Sintflutprognose des Johannes Carion für 1524 mit einer Vorhersage für das Jahr 1789." In *Himmelszeichen und Erdenwege: Johannes Carion (1499–1537) und Sebastian Hornmold (1500–1581) in ihrer Zeit*, ed. Elke Osterloh, 277–302. Ubstadt-Weiher: Verlag Regionalkultur, 1999.

Fricke-Hilgers, Almut. "'...das der historiographus auch sei ein erfarner der gschicht des himels.' Die Sintflutprognose des Johannes Carion für 1524 mit einer Vorhersage für das Jahr 1789." *Pirckheimer Jahrbuch* 5 (1989/1990): 33–68.

Friedeberg, Max. "Das Bildnis des Philosophen Johannes Carion von Crispin Herranth. Hofmaler des Herzogs Albrecht von Preußen." *Zeitschrift für Bildende Kunst, Neue Folge* XXX, 54 (1919): 309–316.

Friedeburg, Robert von. *Luther's Legacy: The Thirty Years War and the Modern Notion of 'State' in the Empire, 1530s to 1790s*. Cambridge: Cambridge University Press, 2016.

Friedeburg, Robert von. "The Making of Patriots: Love of Fatherland and Negotiating Monarchy in Seventeenth Century Germany." *The Journal of Modern History* 77 (December 2005): 881–916.

Friedeburg, Robert von. "The Problem of Passions and of Love of the Fatherland in Protestant Thought: Melanchthon to Althusius, 1520s to 1620s." *Cultural and Social History* 2 (2005): 81–98.

Friedeburg, Robert von. "In Defense of Patria: Resisting Magistrates and the Duties of Patriots in the Empire from the 1530s to the 1640s." *Sixteenth Century Journal* 32, no. 2 (Summer 2001): 357–382.

Friedeburg, Robert von and Michael Seidler. "The Holy Roman Empire of the German Nation." In *European Political Thought 1450–1700*, ed. Howell A. Lloyd et al., 102–172. New Haven: Yale University Press, 2007.

Friedensburg, Walter. *Geschichte der Universität Wittenberg*. Halle a.S.: Niemeyer, 1917.

Friesen, Abraham. "Philipp Melanchthon (1497–1560), Wilhelm Zimmermann (1807–1878) and the Dilemma of Muntzer Historiography." *Church History* 43, no. 2 (June 1974): 164–182.

Fuchs, Thomas. "Wittenberger historiographische Drucke." In *Buchdruck und Buchkultur im Wittenberg der Reformationszeit*, ed. Stefan Oehmig, 231–244. Leipzig: Evangelische Verlagsanstalt, 2015.

Fürst, Dietmar and Jürgen Hamel, eds. *Johann Carion (1499–1537): Der erste Berliner Astronom mit einem Reprint der Schrift Carions "Bedeutnuss und Offenbarung" (1527)*. Berlin-Treptow: Archenhold-Sternwarte, 1988.

Fueter, Eduard. *Geschichte der neueren Historiographie*. Munich & Berlin: R. Oldenbourg, 1936.

Gallner, Ernst. "Daniel's Dream Map: The Wittenberg World Map 1529–1661." *International Map Collector's Society Journal* 114, no. 3 (Autumn 2008): 49–53.

Garcia Archilla, Aurelio. *The Theology of History and Apologetic Historiography in Heinrich Bullinger: Truth in History*. San Francisco: Mellen Research University Press, 1992.

Gellinek, Christian. "Daniel's Vision of Four Beasts in Twelfth-Century German Literature." *Germanic Review* 41, no. 1 (January 1966): 5–26.

Gemeinhardt, Peter. "Das Chronicon Carionis und seine Überarbeitung durch Philipp Melanchthon." In *Welt-Zeit: Christliche Weltchronistik aus zwei Jahrtausenden in Beständen der Thüringer Universitäts- und Landesbibliothek Jena*, ed. Martin Wallraff, 115–125. Berlin: De Gruyter, 2005.

Gieseke, Ludwig. *Vom Privileg zum Urheberrecht: Die Entwicklung des Urheberrechts in Deutschland bis 1845*. Baden-Baden: Nomos Verlagsgesellschaft, 1995.

Gilbert, Felix. "Biondo, Sabellico, and the beginnings of Venetian official historiography." In *Florilegium Historiale*, ed. J.G. Rowe and W.H. Stockdale, 275–293. Toronto: University of Toronto Press, 1971.

Goerlitz, Uta. "The Chronicle in the Age of Humanism: Chronological Structures and the Reckoning of Time between Tradition and Innovation." In *The Medieval Chronicle: Proceedings of the 1st International Conference on the Medieval Chronicle*, ed. Erik Kooper, 133–143. Amsterdam and Atlanta: Rodopi, 1999.

Goertz, Hans Jürgen. *Thomas Müntzer: Apocalyptic, Mystic and Revolutionary*. Translated by Jocelyn Jaquiery and edited by Peter Matheson. Edinburgh: T & T Clark, 1993.

Goertz, Hans Jürgen. *Thomas Müntzer: Mystiker, Apokalyptiker, Revolutionär*. Munich: Verlag C.H. Beck, 1989.

Goez, Werner. *Translatio imperii: Ein Beitrag zur Geschichte des Geschichtsdenkens und der politischen Theorien im Mittelalter und in der frühen Neuzeit*. Tübingen: Mohr, 1958.

Goffman, Daniel. *The Ottoman Empire and Early Modern Europe*. Cambridge: Cambridge University Press, 2002.

Goldbrunner, Hermann. "Humanismus im Dienste der Reformation: Kaspar Hedio und seine Übersetzung der Papstgeschichte des Platina." *Quellen und Forschungen aus italienischen Archiven und Bibliotheken* 63 (1983): 125–142.

Gordon, Bruce, ed. *Protestant History and Identity in sixteenth-century Europe*. 2 vols. Brookfield, Vt.: Ashgate, 1996.

Gow, Andrew. *The Red Jews: Antisemitism in an Apocalyptic Age 1200–1600*. Leiden: Brill, 1995.

Graf, Klaus. "Heinrich Bebel (1472–1518) Wider ein barbarisches Latein." In *Humanismus im deutschen Südwesten: Biographische Profile*, ed. Paul Gerhard Schmidt, 179–194. Sigmaringen: Thorbecke, 1993.

Grafton, Anthony. *What was History? The Art of History in Early Modern Europe*. Cambridge: Cambridge University Press, 2007.

Grafton, Anthony. "Johannes Trithemius: Magie, Geschichte und Phantasie." In *Erzählende Vernunft*, ed. Günter Frank, 77–89. Berlin: Akademie Verlag, 2006.

Grafton, Anthony. "The Identities of History in Early Modern Europe: Prelude to a Study of the *Artes Historicae*." In *Historia: Empiricism and Erudition in Early Modern Europe*, ed. Gianna Pomata and Nancy Siraisi, 41–74. Cambridge, MA: MIT Press, 2005.

Grafton, Anthony. "Some Uses of Eclipses in Early Modern Chronology." *Journal of the History of Ideas* 64 (April 2003): 213–229.

Grafton, Anthony. "Where was Salomon's House? Ecclesiastical History and the Intellectual Origins of Bacon's *New Atlantis*." In *Die europäische Gelehrtenrepublik im Zeitalter des Konfessionalismus*, ed. Herbert Jaumann, 21–38. Wiesbaden: Harrassowitz, 2001.

Grafton, Anthony. *Bring out Your Dead: The Past as Revelation*. Cambridge, MA: Harvard University Press, 2001.

Grafton, Anthony. *Cardano's Cosmos: The Worlds and Works of a Renaissance Astrologer*. Cambridge, MA: Harvard University Press, 1999.

Grafton, Anthony. "Jean Hardouin: The Antiquary as Pariah." *Journal of the Warburg and Courtauld Institutes* 62 (1999): 241–267.

Grafton, Anthony. *The Footnote: A Curious History*. Cambridge, MA: Harvard University Press, 1997.

Grafton, Anthony. "Chronology and its Discontents in Renaissance Europe: The Vicissitudes of a Tradition." In *Time: Histories and Ethnologies*, ed. Diane Owen Hughes and Thomas R. Trautmann, 139–166. Ann Arbor: University of Michigan Press, 1995.

Grafton, Anthony. "Tradition and Technique in Historical Chronology." In *Ancient History and the Antiquarian: Essays in Memory of Arnaldo Momigliano*, ed. Michael Crawford and C.R. Ligota, 15–31. London, 1995.

Grafton, Anthony. *Defenders of the Text: The Traditions of Scholarship in an Age of Science, 1450–1800*. Cambridge, MA: Harvard University Press, 1991.

Grafton, Anthony. *Forgers and Critics: Creativity and Duplicity in Western Scholarship*. Princeton: Princeton University Press, 1990.

Grafton, Anthony. "The World of the Polyhistors: Humanism and Encyclopedism." *Central European History* 18:1 (March 1985): 31–47.

Grafton, Anthony. *Joseph Scaliger: A Study in the History of Classical Scholarship*. 2 vols. Oxford: Clarendon Press, 1983–1993.

Grafton, Anthony. "The Importance of Being Printed." *Journal of Interdisciplinary History* 11, no. 2 (Autumn 1980): 265–286.

Grafton, Anthony, April Shelford, and Nancy Siraisi. *New Worlds, Ancient Texts: The Power of Tradition and the Shock of Discovery*. Cambridge, MA: Harvard University Press, 1992.

Grafton, Anthony and Lisa Jardine. *From Humanism to the Humanities: Education and the Liberal Arts in Fifteenth- and Sixteenth-Century Europe*. Cambridge, MA: Harvard University Press, 1986.

Graus, František. "Funktionen der spätmittelalterlichen Geschichtsschreibung." In *Geschichtsschreibung und Geschichtsbewusstsein im späten Mittelalter*, ed. Hans Patze, 11–55. Sigmaringen: Jan Thorbecke Verlag, 1987.

Green, Lowell. "Unpublished autographs of Melanchthon and of the Grynaeus family in the University of Chicago Library." *Archiv für Reformationsgeschichte* 65 (1974): 161–171.

Gregory, Brad. *Salvation at Stake: Christian Martyrdom in Early Modern Europe*. Cambridge, MA: Harvard University Press, 1999.

Grendler, Paul. *The Universities of the Italian Renaissance*. Baltimore: Johns Hopkins University Press, 2002.

Grendler, Paul. "Form and Function in Italian Renaissance Popular Books." *Renaissance Quarterly* 46, no. 3 (Autumn 1993): 451–485.

Grendler, Paul. "Printing and Censorship." In *The Cambridge History of Renaissance Philosophy*, ed. Charles B. Schmitt et al., 25–53. Cambridge: Cambridge University Press, 1991.

Grendler, Paul. *Schooling in Renaissance Italy: Literacy and Learning, 1300–1600*. Baltimore: Johns Hopkins University Press, 1989.

Grieco, Allen J., Michael Rocke, and Fiorella Gioffredi Superbi, eds. *The Italian Renaissance in the Twentieth Century*. Florence: L.S. Olschki, 2002.

Gross, Hanns. *Empire and Sovereignty: A History of the Public Law Literature in the Holy Roman Empire, 1599–1804*. Chicago: University of Chicago Press, 1973.

Groß, Reiner. "Ernestinisches Kurfürstentum und albertinisches Herzogtum Sachsen zur Reformationszeit: Grundzüge außen- und innenpolitscher Entwicklung." In *Glaube & Macht: Sachsen im Europa der Reformationszeit*, ed. Harald Marx and Eckhard Kluth, vol. 2, 52–60. Dresden: Sandstein, 2004.

Grossmann, Maria. *Humanism in Wittenberg, 1485–1517*. Nieuwkoop: De Graaf, 1975.

Grossmann, Maria. "Wittenberg Printing, Early Sixteenth Century." *Sixteenth Century Essays and Studies* 1 (January 1970): 53–74.

Guggisberg, Hans Rudolf et al., eds. *Ketzerverfolgung im 16. und frühen 17. Jahrhundert*. Wiesbaden: Harrassowitz, 1992.

Gulick, E.V. "The Final Coalition and the Congress of Vienna, 1813–15." In *The New Cambridge Modern History*, vol. IX, *War and Peace in an Age of Upheaval 1793–1830*, ed. C.W. Crawley, 639–667. Cambridge: Cambridge University Press, 1965.

Guthmüller, Bodo and Wilhelm Kühlmann, eds., *Europa und die Türken in der Renaissance*. Tübingen: Niemeyer, 2000.

Gutschera, Herbert. *Reformation und Gegenreformation innerhalb der Kirchengeschichtsschreibung von Johann Matthias Schröckh*. Göppingen: Kümmerle, 1973.

Haering, Hermann. "Johannes Vergenhans, gennant Nauclerus: Erster Rektor der Universität Tübingen und ihr langjahriger Kanzler, Verfasser einer Weltchronik 1425–1510." In *Schwäbische Lebensbilder*, vol. 5, 1–25. Stuttgart: Kohlhammer Verlag, 1950.

Hagen, Gottfried. *Ein osmanischer Geograph bei der Arbeit: Entstehung und Gedankenwelt von Katib Celebis Gihannüma*. Berlin: Klaus Schwarz Verlag, 2003.

Hallman, Barbara. "Italian 'Natural Superiority' and the Lutheran Question: 1517–1546." *Archiv für Reformationsgeschichte* 71 (1980): 134–148.

Hallowell, Robert E. "Ronsard and the Gallic Hercules Myth." *Studies in the Renaissance* 9 (1962): 242–255.

Hamel, Jürgen. "Johann Carion – Entdecker der Kometen Gegenschweife?" In *Beiträge zur Astronomiegeschichte*, Bd. 3, ed. Wolfgang R. Dick and Jürgen Hamel, 201–202. Frankfurt a.M.: H. Deutsch, 2000.

Hammerstein, Helga Robinson. "The Battle of the Booklets: Prognostic Tradition and Proclamation of the Word in early sixteenth-century Germany." In *"Astrologi hallucinati": Stars and the End of the World in Luther's Time*, ed. Paola Zambelli, 129–151. Berlin: de Gruyter, 1986.

Hammerstein, Notker. "Universitäten und Landeschronistik im Zeichen des Humanismus." In *Deutsche Landesgeschichtsschreibung im Zeichen des Humanismus*, ed. Franz Brendle et al., 33–47. Stuttgart: Franz Steiner Verlag, 2001.

Hammerstein, Notker. "Samuel Pufendorf." In *Staatsdenker in der Frühen Neuzeit*, 3d ed., ed. Michael Stolleis, 172–196. München: C.H. Beck, 1995.

Hammerstein, Notker. "Geschichte als Arsenal: Geschichtsschreibung im Umfeld deutscher Humanisten." In *Geschichtsbewusstsein und Geschichtsschreibung in der Renaissance*, ed. August Buck et al., 19–32. Budapest: Akadèmiai Kiadó, 1989.

Hammerstein, Notker. "'Imperium Romanum cum omnibus suis qualitatibus ad Germanos est translatum' : Das vierte Weltreich in der Lehre der Reichsjuristen." *Zeitschrift für Historische Forschung* Beiheft 3 (1987): 187–202.

Hammerstein, Notker. "Das Römische am Heiligen Römischen Reich Deutscher Nation in der Lehre der Reichs-Publicisten." *Zeitschrift der Savigny-Stiftung für Rechtsgeschichte. Germanistische Abtheilung* 100:1 (1983): 119–144.

Hammerstein, Notker. "Humanismus und Universitäten." In *Die Rezeption der Antike: Zum Problem der Kontinuität zwischen Mittelalter und Renaissance*, ed. August Buck, 23–39. Hamburg: Hauswedell, 1981.

Hammerstein, Notker and Gerrit Walther, eds. *Späthumanismus: Studien über das Ende einer kulturhistorischen Epoche*. Göttingen: Wallstein Verlag, 2000.

Harder, Hans-Bernd, ed. *Landesbeschreibungen Mitteleuropas vom 15. bis 17 Jahrhundert*. Köln: Böhlau Verlag, 1983.

Hartfelder, Karl. *Philipp Melanchthon als Praeceptor Germaniae*. Berlin: A. Hofmann & comp., 1889.

Hartmann, Martina. *Humanismus und Kirchenkritik: Matthias Flacius Illyricus als Erforscher des Mittelalters*. Stuttgart: Jan Thorbecke Verlag, 2001.

Hase, Karl Alfred von. *Herzog Albrecht von Preussen und sein Hofprediger: Eine Königsberger Tragödie aus dem Zeitalter der Reformation*. Leipzig: Breitkopf und Härtel, 1879.

Hasse, Hans-Peter. "Peucers Prozeß und die 'Historia carcerum.'" In *Caspar Peucer (1525–1602): Wissenschaft, Glaube und Politik im konfessionellen Zeitalter*, ed. Hans-Peter Hasse and Günther Wartenberg, 135–155. Leipzig: Evangelische Verlagsanstalt, 2004.

Hasse, Hans-Peter. "Konfessionelle Identität und Philippismus in Kursachsen: Die identitätsstiftende Funktion des 'Corpus doctrinae Philippicum': Am Beispiel der 'Christlichen nützlichen Fragen' (1590) des Liebenwerdaer Superintendenten Paul Franz." In *Dona Melanchthoniana: Festgabe für Heinz Scheible zum 70. Geburtstag*, ed. Johanna Loehr, 119–146. Stuttgart-Bad Cannstatt: Frommann-Holzboog, 2001.

Hasse, Hans-Peter. *Zensur theologischer Bücher in Kursachsen im konfessionellen Zeitalter: Studien zur kursächsischen Literatur- und Religionspolitik in den Jahren 1569 bis 1575*. Leipzig: Evangelische Verlagsanstalt, 2000.

Hasse, Hans-Peter and Günther Wartenberg, eds. *Caspar Peucer (1525–1602): Wissenschaft, Glaube und Politik im konfessionellen Zeitalter*. Leipzig: Evangelische Verlagsanstalt, 2004.

Hay, Denys. *Annalists and Historians: Western Historiography from the VIIIth to the XVIIIth Century*. London: Meuthen & Co., 1977.
Hayton, Darin. "Astrology as Political Propaganda: Humanist Responses to the Turkish Threat in Early Sixteenth-Century Vienna." *Austrian History Yearbook* 38 (2007): 61–91.
Haug, Karl Hubert. "Luthers Bedeutung in der Geschichte des Urheberrechts." *Archiv für Urheber-, Film-, Funk- Und Theaterrecht* 135 (1997): 145–241.
Headley, John. "The Reformation in historical thought." *Journal of the History of Ideas* 48 (1987): 521–532.
Headley, John. "The Reformation as Crisis in the Understanding of Tradition." *Archiv für Reformationsgeschichte* 78 (1987): 5–23.
Headley, John. "'Ehe Türckisch als Bäpstisch': Lutheran Reflections on the Problem of Empire, 1623–28." *Central European History* 20, no. 1 (March 1987): 3–28.
Headley, John. *Luther's View of Church History*. New Haven: Yale University Press, 1963.
Headley, John et al., eds. *Confessionalization in Europe, 1555–1570: Essays in Honor and Memory of Bodo Nischan*. Burlington, VT: Ashgate, 2004.
Hebenstreit-Wilfert, Hildegard. "Märtyrerflugschriften der Reformationszeit." In *Flugschriften als Massenmedium der Reformationszeit*, ed. Hans-Joachim Köhler, 397–427. Stuttgart: Ernst Klett Verlag, 1981.
Heiliges Römisches Reich Deutscher Nation 962–1806. 4 vols. Dresden: Sandstein Verlag, 2006.
Helmrath, Johannes. "Probleme und Formen nationaler und regionaler Historiographie des deutschen und europäischen Humanismus um 1500." In *Spätmittelalterliches Landesbewusstsein in Deutschland*, ed. Matthias Werner, 333–392. Ostfildern: Jan Thorbecke Verlag, 2005.
Helmrath, Johannes et al., eds. *Diffusion des Humanismus: Studien zur nationalen Geschichtsschreibung europäischer Humanisten*. Göttingen: Wallstein Verlag, 2002.
Henke, Ernst Ludwig Theodor. *Caspar Peucer und Nicolaus Krell: Zur Geschichte des Lutherthums und der Union am Ende des 16. Jahrhunderts*. Marburg: Elwert, 1865.
Herde, Peter. "From Adolf of Nassau to Lewis of Bavaria, 1292–1347." In *The New Cambridge Medieval History*, vol. VI, *c. 1300 - c. 1415*, ed. Michael Jones, 515–550. Cambridge: Cambridge University Press, 2000.
Herding, Otto. "Heinrich Meibom (1555–1625) und Reiner Reineccius (1541–1595) Eine Studie zur Historiographie in Westfalen und Niedersachsen." *Westfälische Forschungen* 18 (1965): 5–22.
Hermelink, Heinrich, ed. *Die Matrikeln der Universität Tübingen, Bd. 1: Die Matrikeln von 1477–1600*. Stuttgart: Kohlhammer, 1906.

Hieronymus, Frank. "Habent sua fata libelli: Ein Widmungsgedicht Johannes Cratos und ein Lutherbild in der Bibliothek eines Jesuiten." *Gutenberg Jahrbuch* 66 (1991): 230–245.

Hildebrant, E. "Die kurfürstlichen Schlosz und Universitätsbibliothek zu Wittenberg 1512–47." *Zeitschrift für Buchkunde* 2 (1925): 34–42, 109–129, 157–158.

Hille, Martin. *Providentia Dei, Reich und Kirche: Weltbild und Stimmungsprofil altgläubiger Chronisten 1517-1618*. Göttingen: Vandenhoeck & Ruprecht, 2010.

Himmighöfer, Traudel. "'De Monarchiis' - Ein Melanchthon-Autograph in der Bibliothek der Evangelischen Kirche der Pfalz in Speyer." *Ebernburg-Hefte* 29 (1995): 105–122.

Hirstein, James S. *Tacitus' Germania and Beatus Rhenanus (1485–1547): A Study of the Editorial and Exegetical Contribution of a Sixteenth Century Scholar*. Frankfurt a.M.: Peter Lang, 1995.

Hodgen, Margaret T. "Sebastian Muenster (1489–1552): A Sixteenth-Century Ethnographer." *Osiris* 11 (1954): 504–529.

Höfert, Almut. *Den Feind beschreiben: "Türkengefahr" und europäisches Wissen über das Osmanische Reich 1450–1600*. Frankfurt a.M.: Campus Verlag, 2003.

Holborn, Hajo. *A History of Modern Germany*. 3 vols. New York: Knopf, 1967 [Reprint].

Holstein, H. "Das altstädtische gymnasium zu Magdeburg." *Neue Jahrbücher Für Philologie Und Pädagogik* 130 (1884): 16–25.

Honemann, Volker. "Theologen, Philosophe, Geschichtsscreiber, Dichter und Gelehrte im 'Fasciculus temporum' des Werner Rolevinck: Ein Beitrag zur mittelalterlichen Literaturgeschichtsschreibung." In *Der weite Blick des Historikers: Einsichten in Kultur-, Landes- und Stadtgeschichte: Peter Johanek zum 65. Geburtstag*, ed. Wilfried Ehbrecht, 337–356. Köln: Böhlau, 2002.

Horbank, Fritz. "Laurentius Faustus – Pfarrer und Geschichtsschreiber." *Mitteilungen des Vereins für Geschichte der Stadt Meißen* 1:2 (2010): 134–145.

Höss, Irmgard. *Georg Spalatin, 1484–1545: Ein Leben in der Zeit des Humanismus und der Reformation*. Weimar: Böhlau, 1989.

Hsia, R. Po-Chia. *The World of Catholic Renewal 1540–1770*. Cambridge: Cambridge University Press, 2005.

Hug, Wolfgang. "Melanchthon und der oberrheinische Humanismus." In *Philipp Melanchthon 1497–1997: Die bunte Seite der Reformation*, ed. Wilhelm Schwendemann, 170–180. Münster: Lit Verlag, 1997.

Humphries, Mark. "Rufinus's Eusebius: Translation, Continuation, and Edition in the Latin Ecclesiastical History." *Journal of Early Christian Studies* 16, no. 2 (Summer 2008): 143–164.

Hund, Johannes. "Die Debatte um die Wittenberger Christologie und die konsequentphilippistische Abendmahlslehre Caspar Peucers." In *Gottes Wort in der Zeit: Verstehen, verkündigen, verbreiten; Festschrift für Volker Stolle*, ed. Christoph Barnbrock, 85–109. Münster: Lit, 2005.

Huppert, George. "The Trojan Franks and their Critics." *Studies in the Renaissance* 12 (1965): 227–241.

Huschke, Rolf Bernhard. *Melanchthons Lehre vom Ordo politicus : Ein Beitrag zum Verhältnis von Glauben und politischem Handeln bei Melanchthon*. Gütersloh: Mohn, 1968.

Hutter, Peter. *Germanische Stammväter und römisch-deutsches Kaisertum*. Hildesheim: Georg Olms Verlag, 2000.

Ianziti, Gary. *Humanistic Historiography under the Sforzas: Politics and Propaganda in Fifteenth-Century Milan*. New York: Oxford University Press, 1988.

Ikas, Wolfgang-Valentin. "Martinus Polonus' Chronicle of the Popes and Emperors: A Medieval Best-Seller and Its Neglected Influence on Medieval English Chroniclers." *The English Historical Review* 116, no. 466 (April 2001): 327–341.

Imber, Colin. *The Ottoman Empire, 1300–1650: The Structure of Power*. New York: Palgrave MacMillan, 2002.

Immenkötter, Herbert. "Von Engeln und Teufeln: Über Luther-Biographien des 16. Jahrhunderts." In *Biographie und Autobiographie in der Renaissance*, ed. August Buck, 91–102. Wiesbaden: Harrassowitz, 1983.

Irmscher, Günter. "Metalle als Symbole der Historiographie – zu den Statuae Danielis resp. Nabuchodonosoris von Lorenz Faust und Giovanni Maria Nosseni." *Anzeiger des Germanischen Nationalmuseums Nürnberg* (1995): 93–106.

Jardine, Lisa. *Erasmus, Man of Letters: The Construction of Charisma in Print*. Princeton: Princeton University Press, 1993.

Jardine, Lisa and Anthony Grafton. "'Studied for Action': How Gabriel Harvey Read His Livy." *Past and Present* 129 (November 1990): 30–78.

Jedin, Hubert. *Kardinal Caesar Baronius: Der Anfang der katholischen Kirchengeschichtsschreibung im 16. Jahrhundert*. Münster: Aschendorff, 1978.

Jensen, De Lamar. "The Ottoman Turks in Sixteenth Century French Diplomacy." *Sixteenth Century Journal* 16, no. 4 (Winter 1985): 451–470.

Joachimsen, Paul. *Gesammelte Aufsätze: Beiträge zu Renaissance, Humanismus und Reformation*. 2 vols. Edited by Notker Hammerstein. Aalen: Scientia Verlag, 1983.

Joachimsen, Paul. "Humanism and the Development of the German Mind." In *Pre-Reformation Germany*, ed. Gerald Strauss, 162–224. New York: The MacMillan Press, 1972.

Joachimsen, Paul. *Geschichtsauffassung und Geschichtsschreibung in Deutschland unter dem Einfluß des Humanismus. Erster Teil*. Leipzig und Berlin: Teubner, 1910.

Johanek, Peter. "Historiographie und Buchdruck im ausgehenden 15. Jahrhundert." In *Historiographie am Oberrhein im Späten Mittelalter und in der Frühen Neuzeit*, ed. Kurt Andermann, 89–120. Sigmaringen: Jan Thorbecke Verlag, 1988.

Johanek, Peter. "Weltchronistik und regionale Geschichtsschreibung im Spätmittelalter." In *Geschichtsschreibung und Geschichtsbewusstsein im späten Mittelalter*, ed. Hans Patze, 287–330. Sigmaringen: Jan Thorbecke Verlag, 1987.

Johansen, Paul. "Johann von Hilten in Livland: Ein franziskanischer Schwarmgeist am Vorabend der Reformation." *Archiv für Reformationsgeschichte* 36 (1939): 24–50.

Johns, Adrian. *The Nature of the Book: Print and Knowledge in the Making*. Chicago: University of Chicago Press, 1998.

Jones, Norman L. "Matthew Parker, John Bale, and the Magdeburg Centuriators." *Sixteenth Century Journal* 12, no. 3 (Autumn 1981): 35–49.

Jung, Martin. "Evangelisches Historien- und Heiligengedenken bei Melanchthon und seinen Schülern: Zum Sitz im Leben und zur Geschichte der protestantischen Namenkalender." In *Melanchthonbild und Melanchthonrezeption in der Lutherischen Orthodoxie und im Pietismus*, ed. Udo Sträter, 49–80. Wittenberg: Edition Hans Lufft, 1999.

Jung, Otto. *Dr. Michael Beuther aus Karlstadt: Ein Geschichtschreiber des XVI Jahrhunderts (1522–1587)*. Würzburg: Freunde mainfränkischer Kunst und Geschichte E.V., 1957.

Kaminsky, Howard. "The Great Schism." In *The New Cambridge Medieval History*, vol. VI, c. 1300 - c. 1415, ed. Michael Jones, 674–696. Cambridge: Cambridge University Press, 2000.

Kampers, Franz. *Die deutsche Kaiseridee in Prophetie und Sage*. München: Lüneburg, 1896.

Kathe, Heinz. *Die Wittenberger Philosophische Fakultät 1502–1817*. Köln: Böhlau, 2002.

Kedar, Benjamin Z. *Crusade and Mission: European approaches toward the Muslims*. Princeton: Princeton University Press, 1984.

Keen, Ralph. *Divine and Human Authority in Reformation Thought: German Theologians on Political Order 1520–1555*. Nieuwkoop: De Graaf Publishers, 1997.

Keen, Ralph. "Political Authority and Ecclesiology in Melanchthon's 'De Ecclesiae Autoritate.'" *Church History* 65 (March 1996): 1–14.

Keen, Ralph. "Melanchthon's Two Lives of Aristotle." *Wolfenbütteler Renaissance Mitteilungen* 8 (1984): 7–11.

Keller, Rudolf. "David Chytraeus (1530–1600). Melanchthons Geist in Luthertum." In *Melanchthon in Seinen Schülern*, ed. Heinz Scheible, 361–371. Wiesbaden: Harrassowitz, 1997.

Kelley, Donald. "Tacitus Noster: The *Germania* in the Renaissance and Reformation." In *Tacitus and the Tacitean Tradition*, ed. T.J. Luce and A.J. Woodman, 152–167. Princeton: Princeton University Press, 1993.

Kelley, Donald. "Johann Sleidan and the Origins of History as a Profession." *The Journal of Modern History* 52, no. 4 (December 1980): 573–598.

Kelley, Donald. *Foundations of Modern Historical Scholarship: Language, Law, and History in the French Renaissance.* New York: Columbia University Press, 1970.
Kess, Alexandra. *Johann Sleidan and the Protestant Vision of History.* Burlington, VT: Ashgate, 2008.
Kestenbaum & Company. *Fine Judaica: Printed Books, Manuscripts, Autograph Letters & Graphic Arts.* New York: Auction held on December 8, 2011.
Keute, Hartwig. *Reformation und Geschichte: Kaspar Hedio als Historiograph.* Göttingen: Vandenhoeck & Ruprecht, 1980.
King, John. *Foxe's Book of Martyrs and Early Modern Print Culture.* Cambridge: Cambridge University Press, 2006.
Kintzinger, Marion. *Chronos und Historia: Studien zur Titelblattikonographie historiographischer Werke vom 16. bis zum 18. Jahrhundert.* Wiesbaden: Harrassowitz Verlag, 1995.
Kirchner, Hubert. "Der deutsche Bauernkrieg im Urteil der frühen reformatorischen Geschichtsschreibung." *Zeitschrift für Kirchengeschichte* 85 (1974): 239–269.
Kisch, Guido. *Melanchthons Rechts- und Soziallehre.* Berlin: de Gruyter, 1967.
Klatt, Detloff. "Chyträus als Geschichtslehrer und Geschichtschreiber." *Beiträge zur Geschichte der Stadt Rostock* 5 (1909): 1–202.
Klee, Udo. *Beiträge zur Thukydides-Rezeption während des 15. und 16. Jahrhunderts in Italien und Deutschland.* Frankfurt a.M.: Lang, 1990.
Klein, Thomas. *Der Kampf um die zweite Reformation in Kursachsen: 1586–1591.* Köln: Böhlau, 1962.
Klempt, Adalbert. *Die Säkularisierung der universalhistorischen Auffassung: zum Wandel des Geschichtsdenkens im 16. und 17. Jahrhundert.* Göttingen: Musterschmidt, 1960.
Kliger, Samuel. "The Gothic Revival and the German *Translatio*." *Modern Philology* 45, no. 2 (November 1947): 73–103.
Kloft, Hans. "Die Germania des Tacitus und das Problem eines deutschen Nationalbewußtseins." *Archiv für Kulturgeschichte* 72 (1990): 93–114.
Knape, Joachim. "Melanchthon und die Historien." *Archiv für Reformationsgeschichte* 91 (2000): 111–126.
Knape, Joachim. "Geohistoriographie und Geoskopie bei Sebastian Franck und Sebastian Münster." In *Sebastian Franck (1499–1542)*, ed. Jan Dirk Müller, 239–271. Wiesbaden: Harrassowitz, 1993.
Knape, Joachim. *Historie in Mittelalter und früher Neuzeit: Begriffs- und gattungsgeschichtliche Untersuchungen im interdisziplinären Kontext.* Baden-Baden: Verlag Valentin Koerner, 1984.
Knobloch, Eberhard. "Melanchthon und Mercator: Kosmographie im 16. Jahrhundert." In *Melanchthon und die Naturwissenschaften seiner Zeit*, ed. Günter Frank, 253–272. Sigmaringen: Thorbecke, 1998.

Koch, Ernst. "Victorin Strigel (1524–1569). Von Jena nach Heidelberg." In *Melanchthon in Seinen Schülern*, ed. Heinz Scheible, 391–404. Wiesbaden: Harrassowitz, 1997.

Koch, Ernst. "Auseinandersetzungen um die Autorität von Philipp Melanchthon und Martin Luther im Kursachsen im Vorfeld der Konkordienformel von 1577." *Lutherjahrbuch* 59 (1992): 128–159.

Koch, Ernst. "Der kursächsische Philippismus und seine Krise in den 1560er und 1570er Jahren." In *Die reformierte Konfessionalisierung in Deutschland – Das Problem der »Zweiten Reformation«: Wissenschaftliches Symposion des Vereins für Reformationsgeschichte 1985*, ed. Heinz Schilling, 60–77. Gütersloh: Gütersloher Verlagshaus G. Mohn, 1986.

Koch, Klaus. "Daniel in der Ikonographie des Reformationszeitalters." In *Die Geschichte der Daniel-Auslegung in Judentum, Christentum und Islam: Studien zur Kommentierung des Danielbuches in Literatur und Kunst*, ed. Katharina Bracht and David S. du Toit, 269–291. Berlin: Walter de Gruyter, 2007.

Koch, Klaus. *Europa, Rom und der Kaiser vor dem Hintergrund von zwei Jahrtausenden Rezeption des Buches Daniel*. Göttingen: Vandenhoeck & Ruprecht, 1997.

Koch, Uwe et al. *Zwischen Katheder, Thron und Kerker: Leben und Werk des Humanisten Caspar Peucer, 1525–1602*. Bautzen: Domowina-Verlag [Stadtmuseum Bautzen], 2002.

Köhler, Joachim. "Gescheiterte Reformationen: Andreas Althamer in Schwäbisch Gmünd, Konrad Stücklin in Rottweil und Theobald Billican in Weil der Stadt." In *Reformationsgeschichte Württembergs in Porträts*, ed. Siegfried Hermle, 396–415. Holzgerlingen: Hänssler, 1999.

Köhler, Manfred. *Melanchthon und der Islam: ein Beitrag zur Klärung des Verhältnisses zwischen Christentum und Fremdreligion in der Reformationszeit*. Leipzig: Klotz, 1938.

Koehn, Horst. "Philipp Melanchthons Reden." *Archiv für Geschichte des Buchwesens* 25 (1984): 1277–1486.

Koehn, Horst. "Philipp Melanchthons 24 Thesen zum Bauernkrieg." *Luther Jahrbuch* 50 (1983): 25–35.

Koepplin, Dieter and Tilman Falk. *Lukas Cranach: Gemälde, Zeichungen, Druckgraphik*. 2 vols. Basel: Birkhäuser Verlag, 1976.

Kohfeldt, Gustav. "Der akademische Geschichtsunterricht im Reformationszeitalter, mit besonderer Rücksicht auf David Chytraeus in Rostock." *Mitteilungen der Gesellschaft für deutsche Erziehungs- und Schulgeschichte* 13 (1902): 201–228.

Kolb, Robert. *Martin Luther as Prophet, Teacher, Hero: Images of the Reformer, 1520–1620*. Grand Rapids: Baker Books, 1999.

Kolb, Robert. "Philipp's Foes, but Followers Nonetheless: Late Humanism among the Gnesio-Lutherans." In *The Harvest of Humanism in Central Europe: Essays in Honor of Lewis W. Spitz*, ed. Manfred P. Fleischer, 159–176. St Louis: Concordia Publishing House, 1992.

Kolb, Robert. *For All the Saints: Changing Perceptions of Martyrdom and Sainthood in the Lutheran Reformation*. Macon, GA: Mercer University Press, 1987.

Kolb, Robert. "The Theologians and the Peasants: Conservative Evangelical Reactions to the German Peasants' Revolt." *Archiv für Reformationsgeschichte* 69 (1978): 103–131.

Kolb, Robert. "Dynamics of Party Conflict in the Saxon Late Reformation: Gnesio-Lutherans vs. Philippists." *The Journal of Modern History* 49 (1977): On Demand Supplement, D1289-D1305.

Kolb, Robert. *Caspar Peucer's Library: Portrait of a Wittenberg Professor of the Mid-Sixteenth Century*. St. Louis: Center for Reformation Research, 1976.

Kolb, Robert. "Georg Major as Controversialist: Polemics in the Late Reformation." *Church History* 45, no. 4. (December 1976): 455–468.

König, H. "Zur Quellenkritik des Nauclerus." *Forschungen zur deutschen Geschichte* 18 (1878): 47–88.

Köstlin, Julius. "Ein Beitrag zur Eschatologie der Reformatoren." *Theologische Studien und Kritiken* 51 (1878): 125–135.

Koon, Sam and Jamie Wood. "The Chronica Maiora of Isidore of Seville." *e-Spania* 6 (December 2008): 1–44. http://e-spania.revues.org/index15552.html.

Kramer, Ernst. "Die Vier Monarchien: Der Traum Nebucadnezars als Thema keramischer Werke." *Keramos* 28 (1965): 3–27.

Krebs, Christopher. *Negotiatio Germaniae: Tacitus' Germania und Enea Silvio Piccolomini, Giannantonio Campano, Conrad Celtis und Heinrich Bebel*. Göttingen: Vandenhoeck & Ruprecht, 2005.

Kretzmann, Paul. *Popular Commentary of the Bible: Old Testament*. 2 vols. St. Louis: Concordia Publishing House, 1922–1924.

Krewson, Margrit B., ed. *Dresden: Treasures from the Saxon State Library*. Washington, D.C.: Library of Congress, 1996.

Kriechbaum, Maximiliane. "Römisches Recht und Heiliges Römisches Reich Deutscher Nation: Die Entdeckung einer ideologischen Linie von Melanchthon zu Savigny?" *Ius commune* 19 (1992): 237–253.

Krueger, Ingeborg. "Ein Prunkbecken des Barock: Zur Ikonographie der Vier Weltreiche nach Daniels Visionen." *Kunst & Antiquitäten* (1984): Heft 2, 36–45, Heft 3, 37–45.

Krüger, Karl Heinrich. *Die Universalchroniken*. Turnhout: Brepols, 1976.

Kühlmann, Wilhelm. "Der Poet und das Reich – Politische kontextuelle und ästhetische Dimension der humanistischen Türkenlyrik in Deutschland." In *Europa und die Türken in der Renaissance*, ed. Bodo Guthmüller and Wilhelm Kühlmann, 191–248. Tübingen: Niemeyer, 2000.

Kuehnemund, Richard. *Arminius or the Rise of a National Symbol in Literature (From Hutten to Grabbe)*. Chapel Hill: University of North Carolina Press, 1953.

Kuhlow, Hermann. "Johannes Carion (1499–1537): Ein Wittenberger am Hofe Joachim I." *Jahrbuch für Berlin-Brandenburgische Kirchengeschichte* 54 (1983): 53–66.

Kühne, Heinrich. "Kaspar Peuker, Leben und Werk eines großen Gelehrten an der Wittenberger Universität im 16. Jahrhundert." *Lětopis. Reihe B, Geschichte: Jahresschrift des Instituts für Sorbische Volksforschung* 30, no. 2 (1983): 151–161.

Kuntz, Marion Leathers. "The Myth of Venice in the thought of Guillaume Postel." In *Svpplementvm Festivvm Studies in Honor of Paul Oskar Kristeller*, ed. James Hankins et al., 505–523. Binghamton, NY: Medieval & Renaissance Texts & Studies, 1987.

Kunz, Armin. "Cranach as Cartographer: The Rediscovered *Map of the Holy Land*." *Print Quarterly* 12, no. 2 (June 1995): 123–144.

Kuropka, Nicole. "Caspar Peucer und Philipp Melanchthon: Biographische Einblicke in eine reformatorische Gelehrtenfreundschaft." In *Caspar Peucer (1525–1602): Wissenschaft, Glaube und Politik im konfessionellen Zeitalter*, ed. Hans-Peter Hasse and Günther Wartenberg, 237–257. Leipzig: Evangelische Verlagsanstalt, 2004.

Kuropka, Nicole. *Philipp Melanchthon: Wissenschaft und Gesellschaft*. Tübingen: Mohr Siebeck, 2002.

Kusukawa, Sachiko. "Melanchthon's life of Erasmus (1557)." *Erasmus of Rotterdam Society Yearbook* 23 (2003): 1–24.

Kusukawa, Sachiko. "Vinculum Concordiae: Lutheran Method by Philip Melanchthon." In *Method and Order in Renaissance Philosophy of Nature: The Aristotle Commentary Tradition*, ed. Daniel A. Di Liscia et al., 337–354. Brookfield, VT: Ashgate, 1997.

Kusukawa, Sachiko. *A Wittenberg University Library Catalogue of 1536*. Binghamton, N.Y.: Medieval & Renaissance Texts & Studies, 1995.

Kusukawa, Sachiko. *The Transformation of Natural Philosophy: The Case of Philip Melanchthon*. Cambridge: Cambridge University Press, 1995.

Kusukawa, Sachiko. "*Aspectio divinorum operum:* Melanchthon and astrology for Lutheran medics." In *Medicine and the Reformation*, ed. Ole Peter Grell and Andrew Cunningham, 33–56. London: Routledge, 1993.

Lalla, Sebastian. "Über den Nutzen der Astrologie: Melanchthons Vorwort zum 'Liber de sphaera.'" In *Fragmenta Melanchthoniana*, ed. Günter Frank, 147–160. Heidelberg: Verlag Regionalkultur, 2003.

Landfester, Rüdiger. *Historia Magistra Vitae: Undersuchungen zur humanistischen Geschichtstheorie des 14. bis 16. Jahrhunderts*. Geneva: Librairie Droz, 1972.

Lange, Albrecht. "Lyndesay's Monarche und die Chronica Carionis." *Anglia* 28, no. 1 (January 1905): 81–126.

Laub, Peter, ed. *Ulrich von Hutten: Ritter, Humanist, Publizist, 1488–1523, Katalog zur Ausstellung des Landes Hessen anläßlich des 500. Geburtstages*. Kassel: Hessischer Museumsverband, 1988.

Laubach, Ernst. "Wahlpropaganda im Wahlkampf um die deutsche Königswürde 1519." *Archiv für Kulturgeschichte* 53 (1971): 207–248.

Laube, Stefan. *Das Lutherhaus Wittenberg: eine Museumsgeschichte*. Leipzig: Evangelische Verlagsanstalt, 2003.

Latendorf, Friedrich. "Melanchthoniana: Aufzeichnungen eines Wittenberger Studenten aus den Jahren 1558 bis 1560." *Zentralblatt für Bibliothekswesen* 10 (1893): 483–486.

Lehmann-Brauns, Sicco. "Die Sintflut als Zäsur der politischen Institutionsgeschichte." In *Sintflut und Gedächtnis: Erinnern und Vergessen des Ursprungs*, ed. Martin Mulsow and Jan Assmann, 265–289. München: Fink, 2006.

Lemmens, Leonhard. "Der Franziskaner Johannes Hilten († um 1500)." *Römische Quartalschrift* 37 (1929): 315–347.

Leonhardt, Jürgen, ed. *Melanchthon und das Lehrbuch des 16. Jahrhunderts*. Rostock: Universität Rostock, 1997.

Leppin, Volker. "Humanistische Gelehrsamkeit und Zukunftsansage: Philipp Melanchthon und das 'Chronicon Carionis.'" In *Zukunftsvoraussagen in der Renaissance*, ed. Klaus Bergdolt, 131–142. Wiesbaden: Harrassowitz, 2005.

Leppin, Volker. *Antichrist und Jüngster Tag: Das Profil apokalyptischer Flugschriftenpublizistik im deutschen Luthertum 1548–1618*. Gütersloh: Gütersloher Verlagshaus Mohn, 1999.

Lerner, Robert. *The Powers of Prophecy: The Cedar of Lebanon vision from the Mongol Onslaught to the Dawn of the Enlightenment*. Berkeley: University of California Press, 1983.

Levy, F.J. *Tudor Historical Thought*. San Marino, CA: The Huntington Library, 1967.

Liebers, Andrea. "Johannes Carions Arbeiten zur Horoskopie im Vergleich zum heutigen Stand der Astrologie." In *Himmelszeichen und Erdenwege: Johannes Carion (1499–1537) und Sebastian Hornmold (1500–1581) in ihrer Zeit*, ed. Elke Osterloh, 303–332. Ubstadt-Weiher: Verlag Regionalkultur, 1999.

Lietzmann, Hilda. "Der kaiserliche Antiquar Jacopo Strada und Kurfürst August von Sachsen." *Zeitschrift für Kunstgeschichte* 60 (1997): 377–399.

Ligota, Christopher. "Annius of Viterbo and Historical Method." *Journal of the Warburg and Courtauld Institutes* 50 (1987): 44–56.

Lindgren, Uta. "Philipp Melanchthon und die Geographie." In *Melanchthon und die Naturwissenschaften seiner Zeit*, ed. Günter Frank, 239–252. Sigmaringen: Thorbecke, 1998.

Link, Christoph. "Dietrich Reinkingk." In *Staatsdenker in der Frühen Neuzeit*, 3rd ed., ed. Michael Stolleis, 78–99. München: C.H. Beck, 1995.

Loewenstein, Joseph. *The Author's Due: Printing and the Prehistory of Copyright*. Chicago: University of Chicago Press, 2002.

Löwith, Karl. *Meaning in History*. Chicago: University of Chicago Press, 1949.

Ludwig, Ulrike. "Caspar Peucer als Professor an der Artistenfakultät der Universität Wittenberg." In *Caspar Peucer (1525–1602): Wissenschaft, Glaube und Politik im konfessionellen Zeitalter*, ed. Hans-Peter Hasse and Günther Wartenberg, 33–49. Leipzig: Evangelische Verlagsanstalt, 2004.

Ludwig, Walter. "Johannes Vergenhans über Eberhard im Bart und Heinrich Bebel über Johannes Vergenhans." *Zeitschrift für Württembergische Landesgeschichte* 59 (2000): 29–41.

Lübbe-Wolff, Gertrude. "Die Bedeutung der Lehre von den Vier Weltreichen für das Staatsrecht des Römisch-Deutschen Reichs." *Der Staat* 23:3 (1984): 369–389.

Lyon, Gregory. "Baudouin, Flacius, and the Plan for the Magdeburg Centuries." *Journal of the History of Ideas* 64 (April 2003): 253–272.

MacDonald, Michael. "The Fearefull Estate of Francis Spira: Narrative, Identity, and Emotion in Early Modern England." *The Journal of British Studies* 31, no. 1 (January 1992): 32–61.

Maclean, Ian. "Melanchthon at the book fairs, 1560–1601: Editors, markets and religious strife." In *Melanchthon und Europa*, ed. Günter Frank, vol. 2, 211–232. Stuttgart: Thorbecke, 2002.

MacPhail, Eric. "The Plot of History from Antiquity to the Renaissance." *Journal of the History of Ideas* 62, no. 1 (January 2001): 1–16.

Magyar Tudományos Akadémia Országos Széchényi Könyvtár. *Régi Magyarországi Nyomtatványok (1473–1600)*. Budapest: Akadémiai Kiadó, 1971.

Mahlmann, Theodor. "Melanchthon als Vorläufer des Wittenberger Kryptocalvinismus." In *Melanchthon und der Calvinismus*, ed. Günter Frank, 173–230. Stuttgart-Bad Cannstatt: Frommann-Holzboog, 2005.

Manschreck, Clyde. *Melanchthon: The Quiet Reformer*. New York: Abingdon Press, 1958.

Markus, R.A. *Saeculum: History and Society in the Theology of St. Augustine*. Cambridge: Cambridge University Press, 1988.

Marsch, Edgar. *Biblische Prophetie und chronographische Dichtung: Stoff- und Wirkungsgeschichte der Vision des Propheten Daniel nach Dan. VII*. Berlin: Erich Schmidt Verlag, 1972.

Martens, Johan. "The 'Fasciculus Temporum' printed by Nicolaus Götz (Cologne, 1473)." *Gutenberg Jahrbuch* 74 (1999): 89–105.

Martens, Johan. "Arnold ther Hoernen and his Cologne competitors: of sheets, corrections, and variants." *Quaerendo* 24:1 (1994): 30–38.

Martens, Johan. "The *Fasciculus Temporum* of 1474: On form and content of the incunable." *Quaerendo* 22:3 (1992): 197–204.

Marx, Harald and Eckhard Kluth, eds. *Glaube & Macht: Sachsen im Europa der Reformationszeit*. Dresden: Sandstein, 2004.

Mau, Rudolf. "Luthers Stellung zu den Türken." In *Leben und Werk Martin Luthers von 1526–1546*, ed. Helmar Junghans, vol. 1, 647–662. Berlin: Evangelische Verlaganstalt, 1983.

Maurer, Wilhelm. *Der junge Melanchthon*. 2 vols. Göttingen: Vandenhoeck & Ruprecht, 1967–1969.

McLean, Matthew. *The Cosmographia of Sebastian Münster: Describing the World in the Reformation*. Burlington, VT: Ashgate, 2007.

Meckelnborg, Christina and Anne-Beate Riecke. "Die 'Chronik der Sachsen und Thüringer' von Georg Spalatin." In *Fata Libellorum: Festschrift für Franzjosef Pensel zum 70. Geburtstag*, ed. Rudolf Bentzinger und Ulrich-Dieter Oppitz, 131–162. Göppingen: Kümmerle Verlag, 1999.

Menke-Glückert, Emil. *Die Geschichtsschreibung der Reformation und Gegenreformation: Bodin und die Begründung der Geschichtsmethodologie durch Bartholomäus Keckermann*. Leipzig: J.C. Hinrichs, 1912.

Mennecke-Haustein, Ute. *Conversio ad ecclesiam: der Weg des Friedrich Staphylus zurück zur vortridentinischen katholischen Kirche*. Gütersloh: Gütersloher Verlagshaus Mohn, 2003.

Mentzel-Reuters, Arno and Martina Hartmann, eds. *Catalogus und Centurien: Interdisziplinäre Studien zu Matthias Flacius und den Magdeburger Centurien*. Tübingen: Mohr Siebeck, 2008.

Mertens, Dieter. "Bischof Johan von Dalberg (1455–1503) und der deutsche Humanismus." In *Ritteradel im Alten Reich: Die Kämmerer von Worms genannt von Dalberg*, ed. Kurt Andermann, 35–50. Darmstadt: Hessische Historische Kommission, 2009.

Mertens, Dieter. "Die Instrumentalisierung der 'Germania' des Tacitus durch die deutschen Humanisten." In *Zur Geschichte der Gleichung "germanisch – deutsch" : Sprache und Namen, Geschichte und Institutionen*, ed. Heinrich Beck, 37–101. Berlin: De Gruyter, 2004.

Mertens, Dieter. "Landeschronistik im Zeitalter des Humanismus und ihre spätmittelalterlichen Wurzeln." In *Deutsche Landesgeschichtsschreibung im Zeichen des Humanismus*, ed. Franz Brendle et al., 19–31. Stuttgart: Franz Steiner Verlag, 2001.

Mertens, Dieter. "Jakob Wimpfeling (1450–1528) Pädagogischer Humanismus." In *Humanismus im deutschen Südwesten: Biographische Profile*, ed. Paul Gerhard Schmidt, 35–57. Sigmaringen: Thorbecke, 1993.

Mertens, Dieter. "Mittelalterbilder in der Frühen Neuzeit." In *Die Deutschen und Ihr Mittelalter: Themen und Funktionen moderner Geschichtsbilder vom Mittelalter*, ed. Gerd Althoff, 29–54. Darmstadt: Wissenschaftliche Buchgesellschaft, 1992.

Meserve, Margaret. *Empires of Islam in Renaissance Historical Thought*. Cambridge, MA: Harvard University Press, 2008.

Meserve, Margaret. "Medieval Sources for the Renaissance Theories on the Origins of the Ottoman Turks." In *Europa und die Türken in der Renaissance*, ed. Bodo Guthmüller and Wilhelm Kühlmann, 409–436. Tübingen: Niemeyer, 2000.

Methuen, Charlotte. "*Lex Naturae* and *Ordo Naturae* in the Thought of Philip Melanchthon." *Reformation and Renaissance Review* 3 (June 2000): 110–125.

Methuen, Charlotte. "Zur Bedeutung der Mathematik für die Theologie Philipp Melanchthons." In *Melanchthon und die Naturwissenschaften seiner Zeit*, ed. Günter Frank, 85–103. Sigmaringen: Thorbecke, 1998.

Methuen, Charlotte. "The Role of the Heavens in the Thought of Philip Melanchthon." *Journal of the History of Ideas* 57 (July 1996): 385–403.

Metzger, Marcia Lee. "Controversy and 'Correctness': English Chronicles and the Chroniclers, 1553–1568." *Sixteenth Century Journal* 27, no. 2 (Summer 1996): 437–451.

Meuthen, Erich. "Humanismus und Geschichtsunterricht." In *Humanismus und Historiographie*, ed. August Buck, 5–50. Weinheim: VCH Acta Humaniora, 1991.

Mierau, Heike Johanna. "Das Reich, Politische Theorien und Die Heilsgeschichte: Zur Ausbildung eines Reichsbewußtseins durch die Papst-Kaiser-Chroniken des Spätmittelalters." *Zeitschrift für Historische Forschung* 32, no. 4 (2005): 543–573.

Mierau, Heike Johanna, Antje Sander-Berke, and Birgit Stunt. *Studien zur Überlieferung der Flores Temporum*. Hannover: Hahnsche Buchhandlung, 1996.

Miller, Gregory J. "Holy War and Holy Terror: Views of Islam in German Pamphlet Literature, 1520–1545." Ph.D. diss., Boston University, 1994.

Miller, Peter. *Peiresc's Europe: Learning and Virtue in the Seventeenth Century*. New Haven: Yale University Press, 2000.

Moeller, Bernd. "Karl der Große im 16. Jahrhundert." In *Die Präsenz der Antike im Übergang vom Mittelalter zur Frühen Neuzeit: Bericht über Kolloquien der Kommission zur Erforschung der Kultur des Spätmittelalters 1999 bis 2002*, ed. Ludger Grenzmann et al., 109–124. Göttingen: Vandenhoeck & Ruprecht, 2004.

Moltmann, Jürgen. *Christoph Pezel (1539–1604) und der Calvinismus in Bremen*. Bremen: Verlag Einkehr, 1958.

Momigliano, Arnaldo. "The Origins of Universal History." In *On Pagans, Jews, and Christians*, 31–57. Middleton, CT: Wesleyan University Press, 1987.

Momigliano, Arnaldo. "The Introduction of the Teaching of History as an Academic Subject and its Implications." *Minerva* 21, no. 1 (March 1983): 1–15.

Momigliano, Arnaldo. "Pagan and Christian Historiography in the Fourth Century A.D." In *The Conflict Between Paganism and Christianity in the Fourth Century*, ed. Arnaldo Momigliano, 79–99. Oxford: Oxford University Press, 1963.

Mommsen, Theodor E. "Orosius and Augustine." In *Medieval and Renaissance Studies*, ed. Eugene F. Rice, Jr., 325–348. Ithaca: Cornell University Press, 1959.

Monfasani, John. *Fernando of Cordova: A Biographical and Intellectual Profile*. Philadelphia: American Philosophical Society, 1992.

Moore, Cornelia. *Patterned Lives: The Lutheran Funeral Biography in Early Modern Germany*. Wiesbaden: Harrassowitz, 2006.

Moran, Bruce. "German Prince-Practitioners: Aspects in the Development of Courtly Science, Technology, and Procedures in the Renaissance." *Technology and Culture* 22, no. 2 (April 1981): 253–274.

Moxey, Keith. *Peasants, Warriors and Wives: Popular Imagery in the Reformation*. Chicago: University of Chicago Press, 1989.

Muhlack, Ulrich. "German Enlightenment Historiography and the Rise of Historicism." In *A Companion to Enlightenment Historiography*, ed. Sophie Bourgault and Robert Sparling, 249–305. Leiden: Brill, 2013.

Muhlack, Ulrich. "Das Projekt der 'Germania illustrata:' Ein Paradigma der Diffusion des Humanismus?" In *Diffusion des Humanismus: Studien zur nationalen Geschichtsschreibung europäischer Humanisten*, ed. Johannes Helmrath, 142–158. Göttingen: Wallstein-Verlag, 2002.

Muhlack, Ulrich. "Die humanistische Historiographie. Umfang, Bedeutung, Probleme." In *Deutsche Landesgeschichtsschreibung im Zeichen des Humanismus*, ed. Franz Brendle et al., 3–18. Stuttgart: Franz Steiner Verlag, 2001.

Muhlack, Ulrich. "Der Tacitismus – ein späthumanistisches Phänomen." In *Späthumanismus: Studien über das Ende einer kulturhistorischen Epoche*, ed. Notker Hammerstein and Gerrit Walther, 160–182. Göttingen: Wallstein Verlag, 2000.

Muhlack, Ulrich. *Geschichtswissenschaft im Humanismus und in der Aufklärung: Die Vorgeschichte des Historismus*. Munich: C.H. Beck, 1991.

Müller, Gernot. *Die "Germania generalis" des Conrad Celtis: Studien mit Edition, Übersetzung und Kommentar*. Tübingen: Niemeyer, 2001.

Müller, Hermann. "Nicht Melanchthon, sondern Nikolaus Basellius Urheber der Interpolationen in der Chronographie des Nauklerus." *Forschungen zur deutschen Geschichte* 23 (1882): 595–600.

Müller, Jan-Dirk. "Zur Einführung. Sebastian Franck: der Schreiber als Kompilator." In *Sebastian Franck (1499–1542)*, ed. Jan Dirk Müller, 13–38. Wiesbaden: Harrassowitz, 1993.

Müller, Jan-Dirk, ed. *Sebastian Franck (1499–1542)*. Wiesbaden: Harrassowitz, 1993.

Müller, Manfred. "Geschichte und allgemeine Bildungstheorie: Eine Untersuchung über die Auffassung des Geschichtsunterrichts bei Johann Ludwig Vives und Philipp Melanchthon." *Geschichte in Wissenschaft und Unterricht: Zeitschrift des Verbandes der Geschichtslehrer Deutschlands* 14 (1963): 418–428.

Müller, Nikolaus. "Die Funde in den Turmknäufen der Stadtkirche zu Wittenberg." *Zeitschrift des Vereins für Kirchengeschichte in der Provinz Sachsen* 8 (1911): 94–118, 129–180.

Müller-Jahncke, Wolf-Dieter. "Kaspar Peucers Stellung zur Magie." In *Die Okkulten Wissenschaften in der Renaissance*, ed. August Buck, 91–102. Wiesbaden: Harrassowitz, 1992.

Münch, Gotthard. "Das Chronicon Carionis Philippicum: ein Beitrag zur Würdigung Melanchthons als Historiker." *Sachsen und Anhalt* 1 (1925): 199–283.

Neddermeyer, Uwe. "'Darümb sollen die historien billich fürsten bücher sein und genennet werden': Universalhistorische Werke als Ratgeber der Fürsten im Mittelalter und in der frühen Neuzeit." In *Les princes et l'histoire du xive au xviiie siècle :*

Actes du colloque organisé par l'université de Versailles-Saint Quentin et l'Institut Historique Allemand, Paris/Versailles, 13–16 mars 1996, ed. Chantal Grell, 67–102. Bonn: Bouvier, 1998.

Neddermeyer, Uwe. "Kaspar Peucer (1525–1602). Melanchthons Universalgeschichtsschreibung." In *Melanchthon in Seinen Schülern*, ed. Heinz Scheible, 69–101. Wiesbaden: Harrassowitz, 1997.

Neddermeyer, Uwe. "'Was hat man von solchen confusionibus [...] recht und vollkömmlichen berichten können?' Der Zusammenbruch des einheitlichen europäischen Geschichtsbildes nach der Reformation." *Archiv für Kulturgeschichte* 76 (1994): 77–109.

Neddermeyer, Uwe. "Das katholische Geschichtslehrbuch des 17. Jahrhunderts: Orazio Torsellinis *Epitome Historiarum*." *Historisches Jahrbuch* 108 (1988): 469–483.

Neddermeyer, Uwe. *Das Mittelalter in der deutschen Historiographie vom 15. bis zum 18. Jahrhundert: Geschichtsgliederung und Epochenverständnis in der frühen Neuzeit.* Köln: Böhlau, 1988.

Nellen, Henk. "Bible Commentaries as a Platform for Polemical Debate: Abraham Calovius versus Hugo Grotius." In *Neo-Latin Commentaries and the Management of Knowledge in the Late Middle Ages and the Early Modern Period (1400–1700)*, ed. Karl Enenkel and Henk Nellen, 445–472. Leuven: Leuven University Press, 2013.

Newsom Carol A., with Brennan W. Breed. *Daniel: A Commentary*. Louisville: Westminster John Knox Press, 2014.

Nicholson, Oliver. "Broadening the Roman Mind: Foreign Prophets in the Apologetic of Lactantius." In *Studia Patristica*, vol. XXXVI, ed. M.F. Wiles and E.J. Yarnold, 364–374. Leuven: Peeters, 2001.

Nischan, Bodo. "Germany after 1550." In *The Reformation World*, ed. Andrew Pettegree, 387–409. London: Routledge, 2000.

Nischan, Bodo. *Prince, People, and Confession: The Second Reformation in Brandenburg.* Philadelphia: University of Pennsylvania Press, 1994.

Nonn, Ulrich. "Heiliges Römisches Reich Deutscher Nation: Zum Nationen-Begriff im 15. Jahrhundert." *Zeitschrift für Historische Forschung* 9 (1982): 129–142.

Nordman, Viljo Adolf. *Victorinus Strigelius als Geschichtslehrer*. Abo Turku: Aura, 1930.

Norelli, Enrico. "The Authority Attributed to the Early Church in the *Centuries of Magdeburg* and the *Ecclesiastical Annals* of Caesar Baronius." In *The Reception of the Church Fathers in the West*, ed. Irena Backus, vol. 2, 745–774. Leiden: Brill, 1997.

Oakley, Francis. "Christian obedience and authority, 1520–1550." In *The Cambridge History of Political Thought 1450–1700*, ed. J.H. Burns and Mark Goldie, 159–192. Cambridge: Cambridge University Press, 1991.

Oberman, Heiko. *The Two Reformations*. New Haven: Yale University Press, 2003.

Oberman, Heiko. *Masters of the Reformation: The Emergence of a New Intellectual Climate in Europe*. Cambridge: Cambridge University Press, 1981.

Oberman, Heiko. *The Harvest of Medieval Theology: Gabriel Biel and Late Medieval Nominalism*. Cambridge, M.A.: Harvard University Press, 1963.

Oestmann, Günther. "Johannes Stoeffler, Melanchthons Lehrer in Tübingen." In *Philipp Melanchthon in Südwestdeutschland: Bildungsstationen eines Reformators*, ed. Stefan Rhein, 75–86. Karlsruhe: Badische Landesbibliothek, 1997.

Oestmann, Günther. *Schicksalsdeutung und Astronomie: der Himmelsglobus des Johannes Stoeffler von 1493*. Stuttgart: Württembergisches Landesmuseum, 1993.

Ohr, Kirsti. "Historiographie." In *Melanchthon und die Marburger Professoren (1527–1627)*, ed. Barbara Bauer, vol. 1, 197–261. Marburg: [Universitätsbibliothek Marburg], 1999.

Olson, Oliver. *Matthias Flacius and the Survival of Luther's Reform*. Wiesbaden: Harrassowitz Verlag, 2002.

O'Malley, John. *The First Jesuits*. Cambridge, M.A.: Harvard University Press, 1993.

Osterloh, Elke, ed. *Himmelszeichen und Erdenwege: Johannes Carion (1499–1537) und Sebastian Hornmold (1500–1581) in ihrer Zeit*. Ubstadt-Weiher: Verlag Regionalkultur, 1999.

Ott, Joachim and Martin Treu, eds. *Luthers Thesenanschlag – Faktum oder Fiktion*. Leipzig: Evangelische Verlagsanstalt, 2008.

Overell, M.A. "The Exploitation of Francesco Spiera." *Sixteenth Century Journal* 26, no. 3 (Autumn 1995): 619–637.

Overfield, James. *Humanism and Scholasticism in Late Medieval Germany*. Princeton: Princeton University Press, 1984.

Ozment, Steven. *The Age of Reform: 1250–1550, An Intellectual and Religious History of Late Medieval and Reformation Europe*. New Haven: Yale University Press, 1980.

Pade, Marianne. "Thucydides." In *Catalogus Translationum et Commentariorum*, ed. Virginia Brown, 103–182. Washington, D.C.: The Catholic University of America Press, 2003.

Pade, Marianne. "A Melanchthonian Commentary to the First Three Books of Thucydides? Cod. Philol. 166, Staats- und Universitätsbiliothek Hamburg." In *Reformation and Latin Literature in Northern Europe*, ed. Inger Ekrem et al., 193–206. Oslo: Scandinavian University Press, 1996.

Pallmann, Heinrich. *Sigmund Feyerabend, sein Leben und seine geschäftlichen Verbindungen: ein Beitrag zur Geschichte des Frankfurter Buchhandels im sechzehnten Jahrhunert*. Frankfurt a.M.: Völcker, 1881.

Parks, George B. "The Pier Luigi Farnese Scandal: An English Report." *Renaissance News* 15, no. 3 (Autumn 1962): 193–200.

Parry, G.J.R. *A Protestant Vision: William Harrison and the Reformation of Elizabethan England*. Cambridge: Cambridge University Press, 1987.

Patrides, C.A. *The Grand Design of God: The literary form of the Christian view of History*. London: Routledge & Kegan Paul, 1972.

Patrides, C.A. "Renaissance Estimates of the Year of Creation." *The Huntington Library Quarterly* 26, no. 4 (August 1963): 315–322.

Patterson, Lyman Ray. *Copyright in Historical Perspective*. Nashville: Vanderbilt University Press, 1968.

Plathow, Michael. "Philipp Melanchthons Stellung zu den 'Türken': Ein Teil im Ganzen des reformatorischen Gedächtnisses." *Luther* 73 (2002): 140–153.

Perini, Leandro. *La vita e i tempi di Pietro Perna*. Roma: Edizioni di storia e letteratura, 2002.

Peters, Eckhart W. and Günther Korbel, eds. *Die Magdeburger Centurien*. 2 vols. Dößel: Stekovics, 2007.

Petersen, Kathi. "Melanchthon als Lehrer der Geschichte." In *Politik, Religion, Kunst: Beiträge zur Geschichte Schweinfurts, Festschrift Horst Ritzmann*, ed. Uwe Müller, 361–370. Schweinfurt: Historischer Verein, 1998.

Pohlig, Matthias. *Zwischen Gelehrsamkeit und konfessioneller Identitätsstiftung Lutherische Kirchen- und Universalgeschichtsschreibung 1546–1617*. Tübingen: Mohr Siebeck, 2007.

Pohlmann, Hansjörg. "Der Urheberrechtsstreit des Wittenberger Professors Dr. Med. Peuker mit dem Frankfurter Verleger Sigismund Feyerabend (1568 bis 1570): Ein Quellenbeitrag der Wirksamkeit des kaiserlichen und kursächsischen Autorenschutzes." *Archiv für Geschichte des Buchwesens* 6 (1965): 593–640.

Polman, Pontien. *L'Élément Historique dans la Controverse religieuse du XVIe Siècle*. Gembloux: J. Duculot, 1932.

Posselt, Bernd. *Konzeption und Kompilation der Schedelschen Weltchronik*. Wiesbaden: Harrassowitz Verlag, 2015.

Preus, Robert D. *The Theology of Post-Reformation Lutheranism*. 2 vols. St. Louis: Concordia Publishing House, 1970–1972.

Prietz, Frank. *Das Mittelalter im Dienst der Reformation: Die* Chronica *Carions und Melanchthons von 1532. Zur Vermittlung mittelalterlicher Geschichtskonzeptionen in die protestantische Historiographie*. Stuttgart: W. Kohlhammer Verlag, 2014.

Prietz, Frank. "Geschichte und Reformation. Die deutsche Chronica des Johannes Carion als Erziehungsbuch und Fürstenspiegel." In *Universitas: Die mittelalterliche und frühneuzeitliche Universität im Schnittpunkt wissenschaftlicher Disziplinen. Festschrift für Georg Wieland zum 70. Geburtstag*, ed. Oliver Auge and Cora Dietl, 153–165. Tübingen: Francke, 2007.

Probst, Veit. "Melanchthons Studienjahre in Heidelberg." In *Philipp Melanchthon in Südwestdeutschland: Bildungsstationen eines Reformators*, ed. Stefan Rhein, 19–38. Karlsruhe: Badische Landesbibliothek, 1997.

Pullapilly, Cyriac. *Caesar Baronius: Counter-Reformation Historian*. Notre Dame: University of Notre Dame Press, 1975.

Putter, Jasper van. *Networked Nation: Mapping German Cities in Sebastian Münster's 'Cosmographia.'* Leiden: Brill, 2018.

Rädle, Fidel. "Biographie als 'Declamatio': Zu Melanchthons 'Vita Hieronymi.'" In *Scripturus vitam: Lateinische Biographie von der Antike bis in die Gegenwart, Festgabe für Walter Berschin zum 65. Geburtstag*, ed. Dorothea Walz, 273–285. Heidelberg: Mattes, 2002.

Rädle, Herbert. "Briefe / Simon Grynaeus (1493–1541)." *Basler Zeitschrift für Geschichte und Altertumskunde* 90 (1990): 35–118.

Rahn, Thomas. "Geschichtsgedächtnis am Körper – Fürstliche Merk- und Meditationsbilder nach der Weltreiche-Prophetie des 2. Buches Daniel." In *Seelenmaschinen – Gattungstraditionen, Funktionenund Leistungsgrenzen der Mnemotechniken bis zum Beginn der Moderne*, ed. Jörg-Jochen Berns and Wolfgang Neuber, 521–561. Vienna: Böhlau Verlag, 2000.

Rambeau, Eugen. "Über die Geschichtswissenschaft an der Universität Wittenberg." In *450 Jahre Martin-Luther-Universität Halle-Wittenberg*, vol. 1, 255–270. Halle: [s.n.], 1953.

Ranke, Leopold von. *Deutsche Geschichte im Zeitalter der Reformation*. 2 vols. Berlin: Duncker und Humblot, 1839.

Ranke, Leopold von. *Zur Kritik neuerer Geschichtschreiber: Eine Beylage zu desselben romanischen und germanischen Geschichten*. Leipzig: Reimer, 1824.

Rau, Susanne. *Geschichte und Konfession: Städtische Geschichtsschreibung und Erinnerungskultur im Zeitalter von Reformation und Konfessionalisierung in Bremen, Breslau, Hamburg und Köln*. Hamburg: Dölling und Galitz Verlag, 2002.

Rau, Susanne. "Stadthistoriographie und Erinnerungskultur in Hamburg, Köln und Breslau." In *Deutsche Landesgeschichtsschreibung im Zeichen des Humanismus*, ed. Franz Brendle et al., 227–257. Stuttgart: Franz Steiner Verlag, 2001.

Rein, Nathan. *The Chancery of God: Protestant Print, Polemic and Propaganda against the Empire, Magdeburg 1546–1551*. Burlington, VT: Ashgate, 2008.

Reinhard, Wolfgang. "Pressures toward Confessionalization? Prolegomena to a Theory of the Confessional Age." In *The German Reformation: The Essential Readings*, ed. C. Scott Dixon, 169–192. Oxford: Blackwell Publishing, 1999.

Reinhard, Wolfgang. "Martin Luther und der Ursprung der historischen Geschichtswissenschaft in Deutschland." In *Die Reformation in Deutschland und Europa: Interpretationen und Debatten*, ed. Hans R. Guggisberg, 371–409. Gütersloh: G. Mohn, 1993.

Reisinger, Reiner. *Historische Horoskopie: Das iudicium magnum des Johannes Carion für Albrecht Dürers Patenkind*. Wiesbaden: Harrassowitz, 1997.

Reske, Christoph. *Die Buchdrucker des 16. und 17. Jahrhunderts im deutschen Sprachgebiet: Auf der Grundlage des gleichnamigen Werkes von Josef Benzing*. Wiesbaden: Harrassowitz, 2007.

Reynolds, L.D. *Texts and Transmission: A Survey of the Latin Classics*. Oxford: Clarendon Press, 1983.

Rhein, Stefan. "Buchdruck und Humanismus: Melanchthon als Korrektor in der Druckerei des Thomas Anshelm." In *Philipp Melanchthon in Südwestdeutschland: Bildungsstationen eines Reformators*, ed. Stefan Rhein, 63–74. Karlsruhe: Badische Landesbibliothek, 1997.

Rhein, Stefan. "Nationalbewußtsein bei Philipp Melanchthon." In *Philipp Melanchthon 1497–1997: Die bunte Seite der Reformation*, ed. Wilhelm Schwendemann, 181–193. Münster: Lit Verlag, 1997.

Rhein, Stefan. "Melanchthon und der italienische Humanismus." In *Humanismus und Wittenberger Reformation: Festgabe anläßlich des 500. Geburtstages des Praeceptor Germaniae Philipp Melanchthon am 16. Februar 1997*, ed. Michael Beyer, 367–388. Leipzig: Evangelische Verlagsanstalt, 1996.

Riché, Pierre. *The Carolingians: A Family who Forged Europe*. Translated by Michael I. Allen. Philadelphia: University of Pennsylvania Press, 1993.

Ricklefs, Jürgen. "Oratio de Ernesto duce Brunsvicensi." *Jahrbuch der Gesellschaft für niedersächsische Kirchengeschichte* 78 (1980): 97–114.

Ridé, Jacques. "Arminius in der Sicht der deutschen Reformatoren." In *Arminius und die Varusschlacht: Geschichte, Mythos, Literatur*, ed. Rainer Wiegels, 239–248. Paderborn: Schöningh, 2003.

Ridé, Jacques. *L'Image du Germain dans la pensée et la littérature allemandes: de la redécouverte de Tacite à la fin du XVIème siècle: contribution à l'étude de la genèse d'un mythe*. 3 vols. Lille: Atelier Reproduction des thèses, Université de Lille III [Paris: diffusion H. Champion], 1977.

Ritter, Michael. "Seutter, Probst und Lotter: An Eighteenth-Century Map Publishing House in Germany." *Imago Mundi* 53 (2001): 130–135.

Ritter, Michael et al. *Die Welt aus Augsburg: Landkarten von Tobias Conrad Lotter (1717–1777) und seinen Nachfolgern*. Berlin: Deutscher Kunstverlag, 2014.

Robert, Jörg. *Konrad Celtis und das Projekt der deutschen Dichtung: Studien zur humanistischen Konstitution von Poetik, Philosophie, Nation und Ich*. Tübingen: Niemeyer, 2003.

Robinson, I.S. "Reform and the Church, 1073–1122." In *The New Cambridge Medieval History*, vol. 4, *Part 1 c. 1024 - c. 1198*, ed. David Luscombe and Jonathan Riley-Smith, 268–334. Cambridge: Cambridge University Press, 2004.

Roebel, Martin. "Humanistische Medizin und Kryptocalvinismus: Leben und medizinisches Werk des Wittenberger Medizinprofessors Caspar Peucer (1525–1602)." Ph.D. diss., Ruprecht-Karls-Universität Heidelberg, 2004.

Roebel, Martin. "Caspar Peucer als Humanist und Mediziner." In *Caspar Peucer (1525–1602): Wissenschaft, Glaube und Politik im konfessionellen Zeitalter*, ed. Hans-Peter Hasse and Günther Wartenberg, 51–73. Leipzig: Evangelische Verlagsanstalt, 2004.

Roloff, Hans-Gert. "Der 'Arminius' des Ulrich von Hutten." In *Arminius und die Varusschlacht: Geschichte, Mythos, Literatur*, ed. Rainer Wiegels, 211–238. Paderborn: Schöningh, 2003.

Rosenberg, Daniel and Anthony Grafton. *Cartographies of Time: A History of the Timeline*. New York: Princeton Architectural Press, 2010.

Rowley, Harold Henry. *Darius the Mede and the Four World Empires in the Book of Daniel: A Historical Study of Contemporary Theories*. Cardiff: University of Wales Press Board, 1959 [Reprint].

Rummel, Erika. "Humanists, Jews, and Judaism." In *Jews, Judaism and the Reformation in sixteenth-century Germany*, ed. Dean Phillip Bell, 3–31. Leiden: Brill, 2006.

Rummel, Erika. *The Case against Johann Reuchlin: Religious and Social Controversy in sixteenth-century Germany*. Toronto: University of Toronto Press, 2002.

Rummel, Erika. *The Confessionalization of Humanism in Reformation Germany*. Oxford: Oxford University Press, 2000.

Rummel, Erika. *The Humanist-Scholastic Debate in the Renaissance & Reformation*. Cambridge, MA: Harvard University Press, 1995.

Salmon, J.H.M. "The Legacy of Jean Bodin: Absolutism, Populism or Constitutionalism." *History of Political Thought* 17, no. 4 (Winter 1996): 500–522.

Salmon, J.H.M. "Bodin and the Monarchomachs." In *Jean Bodin*, ed. Horst Denzer, 359–378. Munich: Verlag C.H. Beck, 1973.

Sandler, Christian. *Johann Baptista Homann, Matthäus Seutter und ihre Landkarten: Ein Beitrag zur Geschichte der Kartographie*. Amsterdam: Meridian, 1963.

Sandow, Erich. "Das Hermannsdenkmal in New Ulm, Minnesota U.S.A." *Lippische Mitteilungen aus Geschichte und Landeskunde* 25 (1956): 61–93.

Savigny, Friedrich Karl von. *Geschichte des Römischen Rechts im Mittelalter*, Vierter Band, *Das zwölfte Jahrhundert*. Heidelberg: J.C.B. Mohr, 1850.

Savvidis, Petra. *Hermann Bonnus, Superintendent von Lübeck (1504–1548): Sein kirchenpolitisch-organisatorisches Wirken und sein praktisch-theologisches Schrifttum*. Lübeck: Schmidt-Römhild, 1992.

Schäfer, Ernst. *Luther als Kirchenhistoriker: Ein Beitrag zur Geschichte der Wissenschaft*. Gütersloh: C. Bertelsmann, 1897.

Schaeffer, Peter. "The Emergence of the Concept '*Medieval*' in Central European Humanism." *Sixteenth Century Journal* 7, no. 2 (October 1976): 21–30.

Schäufele, Wolf-Friedrich. "Kirche Christi und Teufelskirche: Verfall und Kontinuität der Kirche bei Nikolaus von Amsdorf." In *Nikolaus von Amsdorf (1483–1565) zwischen Reformation und Politik*, ed. Irene Dingel, 57–90. Leipzig: Evangelische Verlagsanstalt, 2008.

Scheible, Heinz. "Melanchthons Verhältnis zu Johannes Setzer." In *Buchwesen in Spätmittelalter und Früher Neuzeit: Festschrift für Helmut Claus zum 75. Geburtstag*, ed. Ulman Weiß, 313–321. Ependorf/Neckar: Bibliotheca Academica Verlag, 2008.

Scheible, Heinz. "Melanchthons Verständnis des Danielbuchs." In *Die Geschichte der Daniel-Auslegung in Judentum, Christentum und Islam: Studien zur Kommentierung des Danielbuches in Literatur und Kunst*, ed. Katharina Bracht and David S. du Toit, 293–321. Berlin: Walter de Gruyter, 2007.

Scheible, Heinz. "Die Verfasserfrage der 'Histori Thome Muntzers.'" In *Flugschriften der Reformationszeit: Colloquium im Erfurter Augustinerkloster 1999*, ed. Ulman Weiß, 201–213. Tübingen: Bibliotheca Academica Verlag, 2001.

Scheible, Heinz. "Melanchthon und die oberrheinischen Humanisten." *Zeitschrift für die Geschichte des Oberrheins* 149 (2001): 111–129.

Scheible, Heinz. "Die Reform von Schule und Universität in der Reformationszeit." *Lutherjahrbuch* 66 (1999): 237–262.

Scheible, Heinz. *Melanchthon: Eine Biographie*. München: Verlag C.H. Beck, 1997.

Scheible, Heinz. "Melanchthon als akademischer Lehrer." In *Melanchthon in Seinen Schülern*, ed. Heinz Scheible, 13–29. Wiesbaden: Harrassowitz, 1997.

Scheible, Heinz. "Der Catalogus testium veritatis: Flacius als Schüler Melanchthons." *Ebernburg-Hefte* 30 (1996): 91–105.

Scheible, Heinz. *Melanchthon und die Reformation: Forschungsbeiträge*, ed. Gerhard May and Rolf Decot. Mainz: von Zabern, 1996.

Scheible, Heinz. "Melanchthons biographische Reden: Literarische Form und akademischer Unterricht." In *Biographie zwischen Renaissance und Barock: Zwölf Studien*, ed. Walter Berschin, 73–96. Heidelberg: Matthes Verlag, 1993.

Scheible, Heinz. "Reuchlins Einfluß auf Melanchthon." In *Reuchlin und die Juden*, ed. Arno Herzig, 123–149. Sigmaringen: Thorbecke, 1993.

Scheible, Heinz. "Melanchthons Werdegang." In *Humanismus im deutschen Südwesten: Biographische Profile*, ed. Paul Gerhard Schmidt, 221–238. Sigmaringen: Thorbecke, 1993.

Scheible, Heinz. "Melanchthons Pforzheimer Schulzeit: Studien zur humanistischen Bildungselite." In *Pforzheim in der frühen Neuzeit: Beiträge zur Stadtgeschichte des 16. bis 18. Jahrhunderts*, ed. Hans-Peter Becht, 9–50. Sigmaringen: Thorbecke, 1989.

Scheible, Heinz. "Melanchthons Bildungsprogramm." In *Lebenslehren und Weltentwürfe im Übergang vom Mittelalter zur Neuzeit: Politik, Bildung, Naturkunde, Theologie*, ed. Hartmut Boockmann, 233–248. Göttingen: Vandenhoeck & Ruprecht, 1989.

Scheible, Heinz. *Die Entstehung der Magdeburger Zenturien: Ein Beitrag zur Geschichte der historiographischen Methode*. [Gütersloh]: Gerd Mohn, 1966.

Scheible, Heinz, ed. *Melanchthon in Seinen Schülern*. Wiesbaden: Harrassowitz, 1997.

Schellhase, Kenneth C. *Tacitus in Renaissance Political Thought*. Chicago: University of Chicago Press, 1976.

Scherer, Emil Clemens. *Geschichte und Kirchengeschichte an den deutschen Universitäten: Ihre Anfänge im Zeitalter des Humanismus und ihre Ausbildung zu selbständigen Disziplinen*. Freiburg i. B.: Herder, 1927.

Scherer, Emil Clemens. "Die letzten Vorlesungen Melanchthons über Universalgeschichte." *Historisches Jahrbuch* 47 (1927): 359–366.
Schilling, Heinz. "Confessional Europe." In *Handbook of European History 1400–1600*, ed. Thomas A Brady, Jr., Heiko Oberman and James D. Tracy, vol. 2, 639–681. Leiden: E.J. Brill, 1994.
Schilling, Heinz. "Confessionalization in the Empire: Religious and Societal Change in Germany Between 1555 and 1620." In his *Religion, Political Culture and the Emergence of Early Modern Society: Essays in German and Dutch History*, 205–245. Leiden: E.J. Brill, 1992.
Schilling, Johannes. "Die Wiederentdeckung des Evangeliums: Wie die Wittenberger Reformatoren ihre Geschichte rekonstruierten." In *Die Präsenz der Antike im Übergang vom Mittelalter zur Frühen Neuzeit: Bericht über Kolloquien der Kommission zur Erforschung der Kultur des Spätmittelalters 1999 bis 2002*, ed. Ludger Grenzmann et al., 125–142. Göttingen: Vandenhoeck & Ruprecht, 2004.
Schmeling, Timothy. "Abraham Calov (1612–86): The Prussian on the *Cathedra Lutheri*." In *Lives & Writings of the Great Fathers of the Lutheran Church*, ed. Timothy Schmeling, 243–262. St. Louis: Concordia Publishing House, 2016.
Schmeling, Timothy, ed. *Lives & Writings of the Great Fathers of the Lutheran Church*. St. Louis: Concordia Publishing House, 2016.
Schmidt, Friedrich. *Geschichte der Erziehung der Pfälzischen Wittelsbacher: Urkunden nebst geschichtlichem Überblick und Register*. Berlin: A. Hofmann & Comp., 1899.
Schmidt, Peter. *Unbekannter Jakob-Krause-Einband zum Chronicon Carionis in Freiberg*. Freiberg i.B.: Informationszentrum der Bergakademie, 1981.
Schmidt, Roderich. "Aetates mundi: Die Weltalter als Gliederungsprinzip der Geschichte." *Zeitschrift für Kirchengeschichte* LXVII (Vierte Folge V) (1955/56): 288–317.
Schmidt, Roderich. "Die Pomerania als Typ territorialer Geschichtsdarstellung und Landesbeschreibung des 16. und beginnenden 17. Jahrhunderts (Bugenhagen - Kantzow - Lubinus)." In *Landesbeschreibungen Mitteleuropas vom 15. bis 17 Jahrhundert*, ed. Hans-Bernd Harder, 49–78. Cologne: Böhlau Verlag, 1983.
Schmidt-Biggemann, Wilhelm. "Heilsgeschichtliche Inventionen. Annius von Viterbos 'Berosus' und die Geschichte der Sintflut." In *Sintflut und Gedächtnis: Erinnern und Vergessen des Ursprungs*, ed. Martin Mulsow and Jan Assmann, 85–111. München: Fink, 2006.
Schmidt-Biggemann, Wilhelm. *Philosophia perennis: Historical Outlines of Western Spirituality in Ancient, Medieval and Early Modern Thought*. Dordrecht: Springer, 2004.
Schmit von Tavera, Carl. *Bibliographie zur Geschichte des Österreichischen Kaiserstaats*. Vienna: L.W. Seidel, 1858.
Schneider, Bernd Christian. "Andreas Althammer und sein Vierfrontenkrieg." *Zeitschrift für bayerische Kirchengeschichte* 71 (2002): 48–68.

Schneider, John. *Philip Melanchthon's Rhetorical Construal of Biblical Authority – Oratio Sacra.* Lewiston: E. Mellen Press, 1990.

Schottenloher, Karl. "Johann Sleidanus und Markgraf Albrecht Alcibiades." *Archiv für Reformationsgeschichte* 35 (1938): 193–202.

Schrader, Franz. "Anhalt." In *Die Territorien des Reichs im Zeitalter der Reformation und Konfessionalisierung: Land und Konfession 1500–1650*, vol. II, *Der Nordosten*, 88–101. Münster: Aschendorff, 1993.

Schreyer-Mühlpfordt, Brigitta. "Die Karolingerzeit im Blickfeld deutscher Humanisten: unter Berücksichtigung der Chronica Carionis des Philipp Melanchthon." In *Philipp Melanchthon 1497–1560*, vol. 1, 74–82. Berlin: Akademie-Verlag, 1963.

Schubert, Friedrich Hermann. *Die deutschen Reichstage in der Staatslehre der frühen Neuzeit.* Göttingen: Vandenhoeck & Ruprecht, 1966.

Schulze, Winfried. *Reich und Türkengefahr im späten 16. Jahrhundert: Studien zu den politischen und gesellschaftlichen Auswirkungen einer äußeren Bedrohung.* München: Beck, 1978.

Schuster, Georg and Friedrich Wagner. *Die Jugend und Erziehung der Kürfursten von Brandenburg und Könige von Preußen*, Erster Band, *Die Kürfursten Friedrich I. und II., Albrecht, Johann, Joachim I. und II.* Berlin: A. Hofmann & Comp., 1906.

Schutte, Anne Jacobson. *Pier Paolo Vergerio: The Making of an Italian Reformer.* Geneva: Droz, 1977.

Schwarz, Reinhard. "Die Wahrheit der Geschichte im Verständnis der Wittenberger Reformation." *Zeitschrift für Theologie und Kirche* 76 (1979): 159–190.

Schwiebert, Ernest. *The Reformation*, vol. 2, *The Reformation as a University Movement.* Minneapolis: Fortress Press, 1996.

Schwiebert, Ernest. "Remnants of a Reformation Library." *The Library Quarterly* 10 (1940): 494–531.

Scott, Tom. "Germany and the Empire." In *The New Cambridge Medieval History*, vol. 7, *c.1415 - c.1500*, ed. Christopher Allmand, 337–366. Cambridge: Cambridge University Press, 1998.

Scott, Tom. *Thomas Müntzer: Theology and Revolution in the German Reformation.* London: Macmillan, 1989.

Scott, Tom. "From Polemic to Sobriety: Thomas Müntzer in Recent Research." *Journal of Ecclesiastical History* 39 (1988): 557–572.

Scott, Tom. "The Peasants' War: A Historiographical Review: Part II." *The Historical Journal* 22, no. 4 (December 1979): 953–974.

Scott, Tom. "The Peasants' War: A Historiographical Review: Part I." *The Historical Journal* 22, no. 3 (September 1979): 693–720.

Scott, Tom and Bob Scribner, eds. *The German Peasants' War: A History in Documents.* New Jersey: Humanities Press, 1991.

Scribner, Robert. *For the Sake of Simple Folk: Popular Propaganda for the German Reformation.* New York: Oxford University Press, 1994.

Scribner, Robert. "Politics and the Institutionalisation of Reform in Germany." In *The New Cambridge Modern History*, vol. II, *The Reformation 1520–1559*, ed. G.R. Elton, 172–197. Cambridge: Cambridge University Press, 1990.

Scribner, Robert. "Luther Myth: A Popular Historiography of the Reformer." In *Popular Culture and Popular Movements in Reformation Germany*, 301–322. London: Hambledon Press, 1987.

Scribner, Robert. "Incombustible Luther: The Image of the Reformer in Early Modern Germany." In *Popular Culture and Popular Movements in Reformation Germany*, 323–353. London: Hambledon Press, 1987.

Scribner, Robert. "Luther-Legenden des 16. Jahrhunderts." In *Martin Luther: Leben, Werk, Wirkung*, ed. Günter Vogler, 377–390. Berlin: Akademie Verlag, 1986.

Secret, François. "Notes Sur Guillaume Postel XV. L'Appendice De Postel Aux *Chronicorum libri tres* De Carion." *Bibliothèque d'Humanisme et Renaissance Travaux et Documents* XXII, no. 3 (Septemter 1960): 552–555.

Secret, François. "L'Emithologie de Guillaume Postel." *Archivio di Filosofia* (1960) [*Umanesimo e Esoterismo*]: 381–437.

Seifert, Arno. *Der Rückzug der biblischen Prophetie von der neueren Geschichte: Studien zur Geschichte der Reichstheologie des frühneuzeitlichen deutschen Protestantismus*. Cologne: Böhlau Verlag, 1990.

Setton, Kenneth M. "Lutheranism and the Turkish Peril." *Balkan Studies* 3 (1962): 133–168.

Shirley, R.W. *Maps in the Atlases of The British Library: A Descriptive Catalogue*. 2 vols. London: British Library, 2004.

Silver, Larry. *Marketing Maximilian: The Visual Ideology of a Holy Roman Emperor*. Princeton: Princeton University Press, 2008.

Silver, Larry. "Germanic Patriotism in the Age of Dürer." In *Dürer and His Culture*, ed. Dagmar Eichberger and Charles Zika, 38–68. Cambridge: Cambridge University Press, 1998.

Skinner, Quentin. *The Foundations of Modern Political Thought*, vol. 2, *The Age of Reformation*. Cambridge: Cambridge University Press, 1978.

Skovgaard-Petersen, Karen. *Historiography at the Court of Christian IV, 1588–1648*. Copenhagen: Museum Tusculanum Press, 2002.

Skovgaard-Petersen, Karen. "Carion's Chronicle in Sixteenth-Century Danish Historiography." *Symbolae Osloenses* 73 (1998): 158–167.

Smith, W. Bradford. "Germanic Pagan Antiquity in Lutheran Historical Thought." *The Journal of the Historical Society* IV, no. 3 (Fall 2004): 351–374.

Sparn, Walter. "Die Welt als Natur und als Geschichte: Zur wissenschaftsgeschichtlichen Bedeutung Melanchthons." In *Melanchthon: Zehn Vorträge*, ed. Hanns Christof Brennecke, 33–54. Erlangen: Universitätsbund Erlangen-Nürnberg, 1998.

Spitz, Lewis. *The Renaissance and Reformation Movements*. 2 vols. St. Louis: Concordia Publishing House, 1987.

Spitz, Lewis. *The Religious Renaissance of the German Humanists*. Cambridge, M.A.: Harvard University Press, 1963.

Spitz, Lewis. *Conrad Celtis: The German Arch-Humanist*. Cambridge, M.A.: Harvard University Press, 1957.

Sprandel, Rolf. "World Historiography in the Late Middle Ages." In *Historiography in the Middle Ages*, ed. Deborah Mauskopf Deliyannis, 157–179. Leiden: Brill, 2003.

Springer, Carl P.E. *Cicero in Heaven: The Roman Rhetor and Luther's Reformation*. Leiden: Brill, 2018.

Staats, Reinhart. "Orosius und das Ende der Christlich-Römischen Universalgeschichte im Zeitalter der Reformation." In *Auctoritas Patrum: Zur Rezeption der Kirchenväter im 15. und 16. Jahrhundert*, ed. Leif Grane, vol. 2, 201–221. Mainz: Philipp von Zabern, 1998.

Staats, Reinhart. "Luthers Geburtstag 1484 und das Geburtsjahr der evangelischen Kirche 1519." *Bibliothek und Wissenschaft* 18 (1984): 61–84.

Stadtwald, Kurt. *Roman Popes and German Patriots: Antipapalism in the Politics of the German Humanist Movement from Gregor Heimburg to Martin Luther*. Geneva: Librairie Droz, 1996.

Stadtwald, Kurt. "Patriotism and Antipapalism in the Politics of Conrad Celtis's 'Vienna Circle.'" *Archiv für Reformationsgeschichte* 84 (1993): 83–102.

Stadtwald, Kurt. "Pope Alexander III's Humiliation of Emperor Frederick Barbarossa as an Episode in Sixteenth-Century German History." *Sixteenth Century Journal* 23, no. 4 (Winter 1992): 755–768.

Stahl, Andreas. "Cyriakus Spangenberg als Chronist: Zur Authentizität des Sterbehauses von Martin Luther." In *Reformatoren im Mansfelder Land: Erasmus Sarcerius und Cyriakus Spangenberg*, ed. Stefan Rhein, 191–216. Leipzig: Evangelische Verlagsanstalt, 2006.

Staubach, Nikolaus. "*Christiana Tempora*: Augustin und das Ende der alten Geschichte in der Weltchronik Frechulfs von Lisieux." *Frühmittelalterliche Studien* 29 (1995): 167–206.

Stauber, Reinhard. "Hartmann Schedel, der Nürnberger Humanistenkreis und die 'Erweiterung der deutschen Nation.'" In *Diffusion des Humanismus: Studien zur nationalen Geschichtsschreibung europäischer Humanisten*, ed. Johannes Helmrath, 159–185. Göttingen: Wallstein, 2002.

Stayer, James M. "Thomas Muntzer in 1989: A Review Article." *Sixteenth Century Journal* 21, no. 4 (Winter 1990): 655–670.

Steadman, John M. "Busiris, the Exodus, and Renaissance Chronography." *Revue belge de Philologie et d'Histoire* 39-3 (1961): 794-803.

Stegbauer, Kathrin. "Perspektivierungen des Mordfalles Diaz (1546) im Streit der Konfessionen : Publizistische Möglichkeiten im Spannungsfeld zwischen reichspolitischer

Argumentation und heilsgeschichtlicher Einordnung." In *Wahrnehmungsgeschichte und Wissensdiskurs im illustrierten Flugblatt der Frühen Neuzeit (1450–1700)*, ed. Wolfgang Harms, 371–414. Basel: Schwabe, 2002.

Steiff, Karl. *Der erste Buchdruck in Tübingen (1498–1545): ein Beitrag zur Geschichte der Universität*. Tübingen: Laupp, 1881.

Steinmann, Andrew. *Daniel*. St. Louis: Concordia Publishing House, 2008.

Steinmetz, Max. *Das Müntzerbild von Martin Luther bis Friedrich Engels*. Berlin: VEB Deutscher Verlag der Wissenschaften, 1971.

Steinmetz, Max. "Philipp Melancthon über Thomas Müntzer und Nikolaus Storch." In *Philipp Melanchthon 1497–1560*, vol. 1, 138–173. Berlin: Akademie-Verlag, 1963.

Stewart, Alasdair M. "Carion, Wedderburn, Lindsay." *Aberdeen University Review* XLIV, no. 147 (1972): 271–274.

Stillman, Robert E. *Philip Sydney and the Poetics of Renaissance Cosmopolitanism*. Burlington, VT: Ashgate, 2008.

Stolleis, Michael. *Public Law in Germany: A Historical Introduction from the 16th to the 21st Century*. Translated by Thomas Dunlap. Oxford: Oxford University Press, 2017.

Stolleis, Michael. *Geschichte des öffentlichen Rechts in Deutschland: Erster Band 1600–1800*, 2nd ed. München: C.H. Beck Verlag, 2012.

Stolleis, Michael. "Public Law and Patriotism in the Holy Roman Empire." In *Infinite Boundaries: Order, Disorder, and Reorder in Early Modern German Culture*, ed. Max Reinhart, 11–33. Kirksville: Sixteenth Century Journal Publishers, 1998.

Stolleis, Michael, ed. *Hermann Conring (1606–1681): Beiträge zu Leben und Werk*. Berlin: Duncker & Humblot, 1983.

Stopp, F.J. "Verbum Domini Manet in Aeternum: The Dissemination of a Reformation Slogan, 1522–1904." In *Essays in German Language, Culture and Society*, ed. Siegbert S. Prawer, R. Hinton Thomas and Leonard Forster, 123–135. London: University of London, 1969.

Strauss, Gerald. *Law, Resistance, and the State: The opposition to Roman law in Reformation Germany*. Princeton, N.J.: Princeton University Press, 1986.

Strauss, Gerald. "The Course of German History: The Lutheran Interpretation." In *Renaissance Studies in Honor of Hans Baron*, ed. Anthony Molho and John A. Tedeschi, 663–686. Dekalb, IL: Northern Illinois University Press, 1971.

Strauss, Gerald. "A Sixteenth-Century Encyclopedia: Sebastian Münster's *Cosmography* and Its Editions." In *From the Renaissance to the Counter-Reformation: Essays in Honor of Garrett Mattingly*, ed. Charles H. Carter, 145–163. New York: Random House, 1965.

Strauss, Gerald. *Historian in an Age of Crisis: The Life and Work of Johannes Aventinus 1477–1534*. Cambridge: Cambridge University Press, 1963.

Strauss, Gerald. "The Image of Germany in the Sixteenth Century." *Germanic Review* 34, no. 3 (October 1959): 223–234.

Strauss, Gerald. *Sixteenth Century Germany: Its Topography and Topographers*. Madison: University of Wisconsin Press, 1959.

Strauss, Gerald. "Topographical-Historical Method in Sixteenth-Century German Scholarship." *Studies in the Renaissance* 5 (1958): 87–101.

Strauss, Gerald, ed. *Manifestations of Discontent in Germany on the Eve of the Reformation: A Collections of Documents Selected, Translated, and Introduced by Gerald Strauss*. Bloomington: Indiana University Press, 1971.

Strobel, Georg Theodor. *Leben, Schriften und Lehren Thomas Müntzers, des Urhebers des Bauernaufruhrs in Thüringen*. Nürnberg & Altdorf: Monath & Kussler, 1795.

Strobel, Georg Theodor. "Von Carions Leben und Schriften." *Miscellaneen literarischen Innhalts, Sechste Sammlung* (Nürnberg, 1782): [139]–206.

Stupperich, Robert. *Der unbekannte Melanchthon*. Stuttgart: W. Kohlhammer Verlag, [1961].

Swain, Joseph. "The Theory of the Four Monarchies: Opposition History under the Roman Empire." *Classical Philology* 35 (1940): 1–21.

Szabó, András. "Die Türkenfrage in der Geschichtsauffassung der ungarischen Reformation." In *Europa und die Türken in der Renaissance*, ed. Bodo Guthmüller and Wilhelm Kühlmann, 275–281. Tübingen: Niemeyer, 2000.

Talkenberg, Heike. "Die Sintflutprophetie 1524: Prophetie und Zeitgeschehen in astrologischen Flugschriften des frühen 16. Jahrhunderts." In *Himmelszeichen und Erdenwege: Johannes Carion (1499–1537) und Sebastian Hornmold (1500–1581) in ihrer Zeit*, 203–246. Ubstadt-Weiher: Verlag Regionalkultur, 1999.

Talkenberg, Heike. *Sintflut: Prophetie und Zeitgeschehen in Texten und Holzschnitten astrologischer Flugschriften 1488–1528*. Tübingen: Niemeyer, 1990.

Tanaka, Julie K. "Historical writing and German identity: Jacob Wimpheling and Sebastian Franck." In *Politics and Reformations: Essays in honor of Thomas A. Brady, Jr.*, ed. Christopher Ocker, 155–175. Leiden: Brill, 2007.

Tanner, Marie. *The Last Descendant of Aeneas: The Mythic Image of the Emperor*. New Haven: Yale University Press, 1993.

Tentler, Thomas N. *Sin and Confession on the Eve of the Reformation*. Princeton: Princeton University Press, 1977.

Theuerkauf, Gerhard. "Soziale Bedingungen humanistischer Weltchronistik: Systemtheoretische Skizzen zur Chronik Nauclerus." In *Landesgeschichte und Geistesgeschichte: Festschrift für Otto Herding zum 65. Geburtstag*, ed. Kaspar Elm, Eberhard Gönner and Eugen Hillenbrand, 315–340. Stuttgart: W. Kohlhammer Verlag, 1977.

Thomaidis, Speros Thomas. "The Political Theory of Philip Melanchthon." Ph.D. diss., Columbia University, 1965.

Thorndike, Lynn. *A History of Magic and Experimental Science*, vol. 5, *The Sixteenth Century*. New York: Columbia University Press, 1941.
Tode, Sven. "Melanchthon und der Bauernkrieg von 1524/25." In *Fragmenta Melanchthoniana*, ed. Günter Frank, vol. 1, 87–103. Heidelberg: Verlag Regionalkultur, 2003.
Töppen, Max. *Die Gründung der Universität zu Königsberg und das Leben ihres ersten Rectors Georg Sabinus: Nach gedruckten und ungedruckten Quellen dargestellt und bei Gelegenheit der dritten Säcularfeier der Universität mitgetheilt*. Königsberg: Verlag der Universitäts-Buchhandlung, 1844.
Tonkin, John. "Luther's Writings on the Turks." *Luther-Jahrbuch* 71 (2004): 268–270.
Trapp, Joseph. "The image of Livy in the Middle Ages and the Renaissance." *Lecturas de Historia del Arte* 3 (1992): 211–238.
Trauner, Karl-Reinhart. "Carion, Johann(es)." In *Biographisch-Bibliographischen Kirchenlexikons*, vol. 28, 287–300. Hamm: Traugott Bautz, 2007.
Traut, Hermann. *Kurfürst Joachim II. von Brandenburg und der Türkenfeldzug vom Jahre 1542*. Gummersbach: Luyken, 1892.
Treu, Martin. "Hutten, Melanchthon und der nationale Humanismus." In *Humanismus und Wittenberger Reformation: Festgabe anläßlich des 500. Geburtstages des Praeceptor Germaniae Philipp Melanchthon am 16. Februar 1997*, ed. Michael Beyer, 353–366. Leipzig: Evangelische Verlagsanstalt, 1996.
Tschirch, Otto. "Johannes Carion, Kurbrandenburgischer Hofastrolog." *Jahresbericht des Historischen Vereins zu Brandenburg* 36/37 (1906): 54–62.
Tutino, Stefania. *Empire of Souls: Robert Bellarmine and the Christian Commonwealth*. Oxford: Oxford University Press, 2010.
Ullman, B.L. "The Post-Mortem Adventures of Livy." In his *Studies in the Italian Renaissance*, 53–77. Rome: Edizioni storia e letteratura, 1973.
Uppenkamp, Barbara. "Representation of History: The Four Empires snd the Statua Danielis in the Castle of Güstrow." In *Beyond Scylla and Charybdis. European Courts and Court Residences outside Habsburg and Valois/Bourbon Territories 1500–1700*, ed. Birgitte Bøggild Jahannsen and Konrad Ottenheym, 253–264. Copenhagen: University Press of Southern Denmark, 2016.
Van der Vekene, Emile. *Johann Sleidan (Johann Philippson): Bibliographie seiner gedruckten Werke und der von ihm übersetzten Schriften von Philippe de Comines, Jean Froissart und Claude de Seyssel, mit einem bibliographischen Anhang zur Sleidan Forschung*. Stuttgart: Hiersemann, 1996.
Van Liere, Katherine et al., eds. *Sacred History: Uses of the Christian Past in the Renaissance World*. Oxford: Oxford University Press, 2012.
Völkel, Markus. "German Historical Writing from the Reformation to the Enlightenment." In *The Oxford History of Historical Writing*, vol. 3, *1400–1800*, ed. José Rabasa et al., 324–346. Oxford: Oxford University Press, 2012.

Völkel, Markus. "Aufstieg und Fall der Protestantischen Universalgeschichte." *Storia della Storiografia* 39 (2001): 67–73.

Völkel, Markus. "Theologische Heilanstalt und Erfahrungswissen: David Chytraeus' Auslegung der Universalhistorie zwischen Prophetie und Modernisierung (UB-Rostock, MSS. hist. 5)." In *David Chytraeus (1530–1600) Norddeutscher Humanismus in Europa: Beiträge zum Wirken des Kraichgauer Gelehrten*, ed. Karl-Heiz Glaser and Steffen Stuth, 121–141. Ubstadt-Weiher: Verlag Regionalkultur, 2000.

Vogel, Klaus A. "Hartmann Schedel als Kompilator. Notizen zu einem derzeit kaum bestellten Foschungsfeld." *Pirckheimer Jahrbuch* 9 (1994): 73–97.

Vogler, Günther. "Luthers Geschichtsauffassung im Spiegel seines Türkenbildes." In *450 Jahre Reformation*, ed. Leo Stern and Max Steinmetz, 118–127. Berlin: VEB Deutscher Verlag der Wissenschaften, 1967.

Voigt, Georg. "Über den Ramismus an der Universität Leipzig." *Berichte über die Verhandlungen der könglichen sächsischen Gesellschaft der Wissenschaften zu Leipzig, Philologisch-historische Classe* 40 (1888): 31–61.

Voigt, Johannes. *Briefwechsel der berühmtesten Gelehrten des Zeitalters der Reformation mit Herzog Albrecht von Preußen*. Königsberg: Bornträger, 1844.

Volz, Hans. "Zu der Wittenberger Landkarte aus dem Jahr 1529." *Die Erde* 89, no. 2 (1958): 136–139.

Volz, Hans. "Beiträge zu Melanchthons and Calvins Ausgelungen des Propheten Daniel." *Zeitschrift für Kirchengeschichte* 67 (1955/56): 93–118.

Volz, Hans. "Neue Beiträge zu Luthers Bibelübersetzung: Luthers Arbeiten am Propheten Daniel." *Beiträge zur Geschichte der deutschen Sprache und Literatur* 77 (1955): 393–423.

Volz, Hans. "Melanchthons Anteil an der Lutherbibel." *Archiv für Reformationsgeschichte* 45 (1954): 196–233.

Vredeveld, Harry. "'Lend a Voice': The Humanistic Portrait Epigraph in the Age of Erasmus and Dürer." *Renaissance Quarterly* 66, no. 2 (Summer 2013): 509–567.

Warburg, Aby. "Pagan-Antique Prophecy in Words and Images in the Age of Luther (1920)." In *The Renewal of Pagan Antiquity: Contributions to the Cultural History of the European Renaissance*, trans. David Britt, 597–697. Los Angeles: Getty Research Institute for the History of Art and the Humanities, 1999.

Ward, Laviece C. "A Carthusian View of the Holy Roman Empire: Werner Rolevinck's *Fasciculus Temporum*." In *Die Kartäuser und das Heilige Römische Reich*, 23–44. Salzburg: Institut für Anglistik und Amerikanistik, 1999.

Wartenberg, Günther. "Melanchthon als Politiker." In *Der Theologe Melanchthon*, Günter Frank, 153–168. Stuttgart: Thorbecke, 2000.

Wartenberg, Günther. "Philipp Melanchthon und die kurfürstlich-sächsische Politik zwischen 1520 und 1560." In *Philipp Melanchthon und seine Rezeption in Skandinavien*, ed. Birgit Stolt, 13–23. Stockholm: Distributed by Almqvist & Wiksell International, 1998.

Watt, J.A. "Spiritual and Temporal Powers." In *The Cambridge History of Medieval Political Thought, c. 450 - c. 1450*, ed. J.H. Burns, 367–423. Cambridge: Cambridge University Press, 1988.

Watt, J.A. "The Papacy." In *The New Cambridge Medieval History*, vol. 5, *c.1198-c.1300*, ed. David Abulafia, 107–163. Cambridge: Cambridge University Press, 1999.

Wegele, Franz Xaver von. *Geschichte der deutschen Historiographie seit dem Auftreten des Humanismus*. Munich & Leipzig: R. Oldenbourg, 1885.

Weichenhan, Michael. "Astrologie und natürliche Mantik bei Caspar Peucer." In *700 Jahre Wittenberg: Stadt, Universität, Reformation im Auftrag der Lutherstadt Wittenberg*, ed. Stefan Oehmig, 213–224. Weimar: H. Böhlaus Nachfolger, 1995.

Weiss, James Michael. "The Harvest of German Humanism: Melchior Adam's Collective Biographies as Cultural History." In *The Harvest of Humanism in Central Europe: Essays in Honor of Lewis W. Spitz*, ed. Manfred P. Fleischer, 341–350. St Louis: Concordia Publishing House, 1992.

Weiss, James Michael. "Erasmus at Luther's Funeral: Melanchthon's Commemorations of Luther in 1546." *Sixteenth Century Journal* 16 (Spring 1985): 91–114.

Weiss, James Michael. "The Six Lives of Rudolph Agricola: Forms and Functions of the Humanist Biography." *Humanistica Lovaniensia* 30 (1981): 19–39.

Weissenborn, Johann Christian. *Hierana: Beiträge zur Geschichte des Erfurtischen Gelehrtenschulwesens, I Abteilung*. Erfurt: [s.n.], 1862.

Welti, Manfred. "Das Gräzist Simon Grynaeus und England: ein Beitrag zur Geschichte der baslerischen Renaissance." *Archiv für Kulturgeschichte* 45 (1963): 232–242.

Wengert, Timothy. "Philip Melanchthon and the Jews: A reappraisal." In *Jews, Judaism and the Reformation in sixteenth-century Germany*, ed. Dean Phillip Bell, 105–135. Leiden: Brill, 2006.

Wengert, Timothy. "The Scope and Contents of Philip Melanchthon's *Opera Omnia*, Wittenberg, 1562–1564." *Archiv für Reformationsgeschichte* 88 (1997): 57–76.

Wengert, Timothy. "Georg Major (1502–1574): Defender of Wittenberg's faith an Melanchthonian exegete." In *Melanchthon in Seinen Schülern*, ed. Heinz Scheible, 129–156. Wiesbaden: Harrassowitz, 1997.

Wetzel, Richard. "Christoph Pezel (1539–1604). Die Vorreden zu seinen Melanchthon-Editionen als Propagandatexte der Zweiten Reformation." In *Melanchthon in Seinen Schülern*, ed. Heinz Scheible, 465–566. Wiesbaden: Harrassowitz, 1997.

Whaley, Joachim. *The Holy Roman Empire: A Very Short Introduction*. Oxford: Oxford University Press, 2018.

Whaley, Joachim. *Germany and the Holy Roman Empire*. 2 vols. Oxford: Oxford University Press, 2012.

Whitman, James Q. *The Legacy of Roman Law in the German Romantic Era: Historical Vision and Legal Change*. Princeton: Princeton University Press, 1990.

Wieden, Helge bei der. "Dietmar Blefken, Island und Philipp Melanchthon." In *Melanchthon und Europa*, ed. Günter Frank, 101–116. Stuttgart: Thorbecke, 2001.

Wiemers, Michael. "1533 in Halle: Johannes Carion zu Gast bei Albrecht von Brandenburg." In *Ein "höchst stattliches Bauwerk:" Die Moritzburg in der hallischen Stadtgeschichte 1503–2003*, ed. Michael Rockmann, 95–106. Halle a.S.: Mitteldeutscher Verlag, 2004.

Wilks, Michael. *The Problem of Sovereignty in the Later Middle Ages: The Papal Monarchy with Augustinus Triumphus and the Publicists*. Cambridge: Cambridge University Press, 1964.

Wilson, Peter. *Heart of Europe: A History of the Holy Roman Empire*. Cambridge, M.A.: Harvard University Press, 2016.

Winkler, Eberhard. "Lob des friedlischen Regenten. Melanchthons lateinische Leichenrede auf Kurfürst Friedrich den Weisen." *Zeitschrift für Religions- und Geistesgeschichte* 18 (1966): 33–42.

Winter, Christian. "Die Außenpolitik des Kurfürsten Moritz von Sachsen." In *Glaube & Macht: Sachsen im Europa der Reformationszeit*, ed. Harald Marx and Eckhard Kluth, vol. 2, 124–136. Dresden: Sandstein, 2004.

Wirth, Gisela. *Die Entwicklung der alten Geschichte an der Philipps-Universität Marburg: Eine Untersuchung zu Entstehung, Inhalten und Funktion einer historischen Disziplin*. Marburg: N.G. Elwert Verlag, 1977.

Witcombe, Christopher L.C.E. *Copyright in the Renaissance: Prints and the* Privilegio *in Sixteenth-Century Venice And Rome*. Leiden: Brill, 2004.

Wolgast, Eike. "Thomas Müntzer's 'Fürstenpredigt' 1524." In *Recht, Kultur, Finanzen: Festschrift für Reinhard Mußgnug zum 70. Geburtstag am 26. Oktober 2005*, ed. Klaus Grupp, 543–554. Heidelberg: Müller, 2005.

Wolgast, Eike. "Melanchthons Beziehungen zu Südwestdeutschland." *Lutherjahrbuch* 66 (1999): 89–106.

Wolgast, Eike. "Melanchthon als politischer Berater." In *Melanchthon: Zehn Vorträge*, ed. Hanns Christof Brennecke, 179–208. Erlangen: Universitätsbund Erlangen-Nürnberg, 1998.

Wolgast, Eike. "Melanchthons Fürstenwidmungen in der Wittenberger Lutherausgabe." In *Humanismus und Wittenberger Reformation: Festgabe anläßlich des 500. Geburtstages des Praeceptor Germaniae Philipp Melanchthon am 16. Februar 1997*, ed. Michael Beyer, 253–265. Leipzig: Evangelische Verlagsanstalt, 1996.

Wolgast, Eike. "Biographie als Autoritätsstiftung: Die ersten evangelischen Lutherbiographien." In *Biographie zwischen Renaissance und Barock: Zwölf Studien*, ed. Walter Berschin, 73–96. Heidelberg: Matthes Verlag, 1993.

Wolgast, Eike. "Die Wittenberger Luther-Ausgabe." *Archiv für Geschichte des Buchwesens* 11 (1970/1971): 1–336.

Wolgast, Eike. "Der Streit um die Werke Luthers im 16. Jahrhundert." *Archiv für Reformationsgeschichte* 59 (1968): 177–202.

Wood, Christopher S. *Forgery Replica Fiction: Temporalities of German Renaissance Art*. Chicago: University of Chicago Press, 2008.

Woolf, Daniel R. *Reading History in early modern England*. Cambridge: Cambridge University Press, 2000.

Woolfson, Jonathan, ed. *Palgrave Advances in Renaissance Historiography*. New York: Palgrave Macmillan, 2005.

Wriedt, Markus. "Luther's concept of history and the formation of an evangelical identity." In *Protestant History and Identity in sixteenth-century Europe*, ed. Bruce Gordon, vol. 1, 31–45. Brookfield, Vt.: Ashgate, 1996.

Wüthrich, Lucas Heinrich. *Matthaeus Merian d.Ä.: Eine Biographie*. Hamburg: Hoffmann und Campe Verlag, 2007.

Wüthrich, Lucas Heinrich. "Der Chronist Johann Ludwig Gottfried (ca. 1584–1633)." *Archiv für Kulturgeschichte* 43 (1961): 188–216.

Wuttke, Dieter. "Humanismus als integrative Kraft. Die Philosophia des deutschen 'Erzhumanisten' Conrad Celtis. Eine ikonologische Studie zu programmatischer Graphik Dürers und Burgkmairs." *Artibus et Historiae* (1985): 65–99.

Zakai, Avihu. *Exile and Kingdom: History and Apocalypse in the Puritan Migration to America*. Cambridge: Cambridge University Press, 1992.

Zakai, Avihu. "Reformation, History, and Eschatology in English Protestantism." *History and Theory* 26, no. 3 (October 1987): 300–318.

Zambelli, Paola. *White Magic, Black Magic in the European Renaissance: From Ficino, Pico, Della Porta to Trithemius, Agrippa, Bruno*. Leiden: Brill, 2007.

Zambelli, Paola. "Der Himmel über Wittenberg: Luther, Melanchthon und andere Beobachter von Kometen." *Annali dell'Istituto storico italo-germanico in Trento* 20 (1994 [1995]): 39–62.

Zambelli, Paola. "Astrologi consiglieri del principe a Wittenberg." *Annali dell'Istituto Storico Italo-Germanico in Trento* 18 (1992): 497–542.

Zambelli, Paola, ed. *"Astrologi hallucinati": Stars and the End of the World in Luther's Time*. Berlin: de Gruyter, 1986.

Zeeden, Ernst Walter. "'...denn Daniel lügt nicht.' Daniels Prophetie über den Gang der Geschichte in der Exegese des Kirchenvaters Hieronymus und Martin Luthers. Von der Dominanz der Tradition über das Bibelwort." In *Recht und Reich im Zeitalter der Reformation: Festschrift für Horst Rabe*, ed. Christine Roll, 357–385. Frankfurt a.M.: Peter Lang, 1997.

Zeeden, Ernst Walter. *The Legacy of Luther: Martin Luther and the Reformation in the estimation of the German Lutherans from Luther's death to the beginning of the age of Goethe*. Translated by Ruth Mary Bethell. London: Hollis & Carter, 1954.

Ziebell, Thomas I. "Establishing an Educational Subculture: The 19th Century German Gymnasium Arrangement of Northwestern College in Watertown, Wisconsin to 1915." Ph.D. diss., University of Wisconsin (Madison), 1994.

Ziegler, Hildegard. *Chronicon Carionis: ein Beitrag zur Geschichtsschreibung des 16. Jahrhunderts*. Halle a.S.: Niemeyer, 1898.

Zimmermann, T.C. Price. *Paolo Giovio: The Historian and the Crisis of Sixteenth-Century Italy*. Princeton: Princeton University Press, 1995.

Zimmermann, Wilhelm. *Allgemeine Geschichte des großen Bauernkrieges. Nach Handschiften und gedruckten Quellen*. 3 vols. Stuttgart: Franz Heinrich Köhler, 1841–1843.

Zöllner, Walter. "Geschichte und Geschichtswissenschaft an der Universität Wittenberg." In *Recht – Idee – Geschichte: Beiträge zur Rechts- und Ideengeschichte für Rolf Lieberwirth anläßlich seines 80. Geburtstages*, ed. Heiner Lück and Bernd Schildt, 373–401. Köln: Böhlau, 2000.

Zöllner, Walter. "Melanchthons Stellung zum Bauernkrieg." In *Philipp Melanchthon 1497–1560*, vol. 1, 174–189. Berlin: Akademie-Verlag, 1963.

Zutschi, P.N.R. "The Avignon Papacy." In *The New Cambridge Medieval History*, vol. VI, *c. 1300 - c. 1415*, ed. Michael Jones, 653–673. Cambridge: Cambridge University Press, 2000.

Index

Abel   237
Abraham   45, 47, 65, 147, 148, 169, 172
Accursius   160
Adam   45, 47, 75, 131 n. 188, 174, 328
Adam, Melchior   89, 139 n. 229, 275 n. 245, 337
Adelung, Johann Christoph   99
Adolf, Prince of Saxony   254
Agathocles   232
Agnes Hedwig of Anhalt, Electress of Saxony   275
Agricola, Rudolph   20, 185 n. 143
Alba, Duke of *See* Alva, Duke of
Albinus, Petrus   331
Albrecht Alcibiades, Margrave of Brandenburg-Kulmbach   234 n. 115
Albrecht of Mainz, Archbishop   136, 138
Albrecht, Duke of Prussia   110–112, 136, 138–139, 240
Alexander Severus, Emperor   129
Alexander the Great   69, 128–129, 173, 305, 328, 334 n. 2
Alfonso, King of Aragon   131 n. 188
Althamer, Andreas   72, 117, 119 n. 144, 213
Alva, Duke of (Fernando Álvarez de Toledo)   224
Ambrose of Milan, Saint   176
Amel-Marduk, King of Babylon *See* Evilmerodach, King of Babylon
Amman, Jost   258
Amsdorf, Nicolaus von   5
Anna, Electress of Saxony   269, 275
Anne of Brittany   82
Annius of Viterbo   77–78, 117–121, 125
Anshelm, Thomas   214
Antoninus Pius, Emperor   130
Apelles   255
Apian, Peter   169
Apology of the Augsburg Confession   114, 121, 203, 297
Appian   36
Arianism   132 n. 194, 171, 176–177, 241 n. 133
Aristophanes   87
Aristotle   22 n. 81, 177
Arminius   24, 153 n. 36

Artaxerxes Longimanus, King of Persia   128–129
Augsburg Confession   11, 114, 121, 203, 297
Augsburg Interim   106, 239
August I, Elector of Saxony   124, 247, 252, 254–256, 261, 265–267, 269, 271–277, 289, 292, 296, 309, 319
Augustine of Hippo, Saint   16, 42, 44–47, 50, 75, 147, 176, 199, 206, 333
Augustus, Emperor   36, 43, 55–56, 64, 70, 118, 129, 153.n 36, 175, 248, 251

Bach, Johann Sebastian   300
Baronio, Cesare   27, 244, 299
Basellius, Nicolaus   73–74, 79
Batizi, András   350
Baumgartner, Hieronymus   231, 242
Bayle, Pierre   337, 343–344
Beatus Rhenanus   16 n. 47, 71 n. 159, 114, 143 n. 2, 213
Bebel, Heinrich   72, 117
Becmann, Johann Christoph   315
Bede, Venerable   46–47
Bellarmine, Robert   297, 299
Belshazzar   150, 315
Benedict VIII, Pope   225
Berengar of Tours   182
Bergen, Gimel   274
Berthold of Reichenau   49
Besinger, Johann   226
Besold, Hieronymus   232
Beuther, Michael   242
Bindseil, Heinrich   25
Biondo, Flavio   72
Blond, Jean le   218–219, 224, 282
Bodin, Jean   30, 282, 285–296, 300, 310, 314, 334
Boniface III, Pope   178, 319 n. 136
Boniface VIII, Pope   297
Boniface, Saint   184
Bonincontri, Lorenzo   133
Bonnus, Hermann   136, 213–216, 249, 341
Book of Concord   297
Bora, Katharina von   231
Brahe, Tycho   275 n. 247

Brenz, Johann   164n71
Bretschneider, Karl Gottlieb   25, 339, 345, 348 n. 40, 470
Brosamer, Hans   342
Brubach, Peter   214, 237
Brutus, King of England   219
Bugenhagen, Johannes   110 n. 95
Burchard of Ursberg
    See also Ursberger Chronicle   49, 207

Caesar, Julius   131 n. 188, 220, 346
Cain   237
Calliope   85
Calov, Abraham   299–300, 302, 314
Cambyses II, King of Persia   150
Camerarius, Joachim   115–117, 122, 127, 139, 344
Canisius, Peter   228
Carion, Johann *passim*
Carion's Chronicle passim
Cassiodorus   86 n. 13
Catiline   186
Čelebi, Kātib   353
Cellarius, Christoph   34, 313
Celtis, Conrad   8–9, 24, 71–72, 84
Cerinthus   176
Charlemagne, Emperor   1–2, 26, 29–31, 48, 51–53, 56, 58, 62, 65, 68, 70, 79–81, 116, 125, 130, 131 n. 188, 132 n. 194, 133–134, 145, 150–151, 153, 154 n. 38, 155, 156 n. 43, 165, 180, 192–194, 197, 201, 205, 251, 255, 287, 297, 298, 301, 305, 313, 315, 320 n. 138, 323, 328, 333, 342
Charles II (the Bald), Emperor   1, 70, 80, 151
Charles III (the Simple), King of France   51
Charles IV, Emperor   60, 196, 212
Charles V, Emperor   6, 13, 15, 19, 21, 79, 106, 114, 127, 133–134, 144–145, 183, 192, 205, 235, 237–240, 258, 267, 273, 284, 287–288, 299, 311
Charon   137
Christ   17, 37, 43–45, 47, 54, 56, 64–65, 75, 99, 128–130, 147, 169, 175–176, 182, 188, 201, 211, 219, 291, 293, 297–298, 300, 317, 319, 320, 328
Christian I, Elector of Saxony   276–277, 295–296
Christian II, Elector of Saxony   276
Chytraeus, David   12 n. 38, 250, 274

Cicero   186
Claudian   36
Claudius, Emperor   132 n. 194
Clio   85 n. 4
Clovis I, King of the Franks   184
Colloquy of Worms (1557)   6, 246, 254
Complaynt of Scotland, The   222
Congress of Vienna   3
Conrad III, Emperor   50
Conring, Hermann   152, 304–307, 313–314
Constantine I, Emperor   41–42, 52–56, 60–61, 66, 78–79, 133, 143, 155, 180, 189, 193, 305, 323
Constantine VI, Emperor   155
Constantius II, Emperor   241 n. 133
Cooper, Thomas   219–222, 351
Corvinus, Antonius   123–124, 131
Council of Constance   3, 61, 179, 181, 203–204
Cracow, Georg   271, 273
Cranach, Lucas (the Elder)   5 n. 12, 24, 112–114, 167 n. 80
Crato, Johannes   348
Cronberg, Walter von   111–112
Crowley, Robert   220–221
Cyrus the Great, King of Persia   125, 150, 223, 315, 328, 334 n. 2

d'Ailly, Pierre   98
Dalberg, Bishop Johann von   22 n. 84, 185
Daniel, Prophet   16–17, 24, 37–40, 42–44, 46–50, 53–54, 62, 71, 76, 127–129, 149–150, 161–174, 188–189, 205–206, 256 n. 184, 282–283, 285–324
Dante Alighieri   59–60
Darius III, King of Persia   128–129
David, King of Israel   45
de' Medici, Lorenzo   148 n. 17, 183
Decius, Emperor   150
Diaz, Alfonso   19, 25, 236–237
Diaz, Juan   19, 25, 236–237
Diet of Augsburg (1530)   18, 112, 114, 183
Dietrich, Veit   232, 240
Dionysius Exiguus   46
Dommerich, Johann Christoph   338
Dresser, Matthias   291–296, 310, 314
du Puys, Jacques   215–216, 347
Dudley, John (Duke of Northumberland)   220
Dürer, Albrecht   248

INDEX 537

Eber, Paul 331
Eberhard II, Count of Württemberg 212
Eberhard im Bart, Duke of Württemberg 73
Edward VI, King of England 221
Egenolff, Christoph 68, 210–211
Einhard 1
Elizabeth, Princess of Saxony 255 n. 179
Elizabeth of Denmark, Electress of Brandenburg 100
Erasmus, Desiderius 6, 22 n. 84, 24, 73, 161, 234 n. 112
Eudoxus 131 n. 188
Eusebius of Caesarea 39–40, 42, 46–48, 50, 63–64, 77, 86 n. 13, 149
Eve 174
Evilmerdoch, King of Babylon 315
Ezekiel, Prophet 172–173, 320 n. 137

Faber, Basil 243
Farnese, Pier Luigi 19, 25
Faust, Lorenz 316–320
Felwinger, Johann Paul 320
Ferdinand I, Emperor 104, 127, 145, 192, 205, 258
Ferdinand, King of Aragon 134
Fernando of Cordova 108 n. 90
Feyerabend, Johann 266 n. 218
Feyerabend, Sigmund 258–266, 341, 349
Flacius Illyricus, Matthias
    See also Magdeburg Centuries 16, 27, 60, 243, 244 n. 143, 254, 279, 297, 299
Flores Temporum 57–58, 63
Fontaine, Jacques 18, 163 n. 67
Formula of Concord 272, 277
Foxe, John 27
Francis I, King of France 52, 79, 218
Francis II, Emperor 4, 330
Franck, Sebastian 212–213, 234, 245 n. 146
Franckenberger, Andreas 274, 289–296, 310, 314, 331, 338
Franckenberger, Reinhold 310–311, 331, 342 n. 20
Franz, Wolfgang 331
Frechulf of Lisieux, Bishop 47, 52, 63
Frederick II, Emperor 131 n. 188, 255, 256, 261
Frederick III, Elector of Brandenburg 313
Frederick III, Elector Palatine 263, 255 n. 179, 266

Frederick III, Emperor 61, 287
Frederick the Great, King of Prussia 329
Frederick the Wise, Elector of Saxony 86
Frederick Wilhelm I, Duke of Saxony-Weimar-Altenburg 276–277
Friedrich III, King of Denmark 303
Frutolf-Ekkehard 49–50, 63, 207
Funck, Johann 188, 221–222, 228–236, 239–242, 247, 261, 263–265, 279–280, 285, 341, 349

Gall, Saint 184
Gansfort, Wessel 203
Georg Augustus, Elector of Hanover 313
Gerhard, Johann 300
Gesner, Conrad 337, 342–343
Glossa Ordinaria 40
Göbler, Justinus 265
Goethe, Johann Wolfgang von 308 n. 98
Gog 172–174, 189
Golden Legend 58
Gordian III, Emperor 132
Gottfried, Johan Ludwig 307–308, 315, 334 n. 1
Goulart, Simon 219, 277
Grafton, Richard 222
Gratian 53, 59, 65
Green, Georg 312, 331
Gregory the Great, Pope 98, 176, 184, 197, 200, 205
Gregory V, Pope 66, 81, 157, 178
Gregory VII, Pope 52, 75, 95, 158, 225, 328
Grotius, Hugo 298, 300, 314
Grundig, Christoph G. 339 n. 12
Gruterus, Janus 331
Gunnarssøn, Halvard (Halvardus Gunarius) 350

Habakkuk, Prophet 102, 112
Hadrian, Emperor 130, 131 n. 188
Hafftiz, Peter 100
Hagar 172
Halley's Comet 107, 122, 132–133
Hardt, Hermann von der 315
Harrison, William 223
Hedio, Caspar 207
Hedwig Jagiellon, Electress of Brandenburg 138
Helen of Troy 150

Henry IV, Emperor   75, 95, 159, 201
Henry the Fowler, Duke of Saxony   51–52, 66, 151, 165
Henry VII, Emperor   179
Heraclius, Emperor   170
Hercules   116, 119
Heresbach, Konrad   250
Herodotus   116 n. 123, 185 n. 143, 251 n. 164
Herpin, René *See* Bodin, Jean
Higden, Ranulf   13 n. 39
Hildebrand *See* Gregory VII, Pope
Hildegard of Bingen   98
Hilten, Johann   174, 203 n. 213
Hippolytus of Rome, Saint   39
Hoch, Erhard Ernst   339 n. 13
Hoffmann, Johann Wilhelm   332
Homeric Oracle   135
Hus, Jan   180–181, 202–204
Hutten, Ulrich von   16 n. 47, 24, 62, 71 n. 159, 143, 161
Hütter, Simon   261, 265–266
Hystaspes   41

Innocent III, Pope   53–54
Irencius, Franciscus   21, 73, 117
Irene, Empress   155, 191
Irnerius   160
Isidore of Seville, Saint   46–47, 58, 63

Jacob, Cyriakus   228–230, 236, 240, 261, 263–265
Jahn, Johann Wilhelm   314–315, 324, 331
Japheth   119, 212
Jeremiah, Prophet   55
Jerome of Prague   181, 203
Jerome, Saint   22 n. 81, 39–40, 42–50, 54, 63–64, 68, 77, 149, 164, 206
Joachim Ernst, Prince of Anhalt   275
Joachim I, Elector of Brandenburg   87–89, 91, 100, 106, 108, 110, 112, 136, 138, 345
Joachim II, Elector of Brandenburg   88, 91, 104, 123–125, 126 n. 169, 131 n. 187, 133, 137–139, 174, 232–233, 235, 237, 248–249, 261, 263–264, 279, 341–342, 344–345, 349
Joachim of Fiore   98, 134
Joan, Pope   57, 178
Johann Casimir, Palsgrave   255 n. 179

Johann, Margrave of Brandenburg-Küstrin   106
John Frederick, Elector of Saxony   6, 238, 251 n. 162
John George II, Elector of Saxony   314 n. 123
John XII, Pope   302
John XXII, Pope   59–60
John, Evangelist   172, 176
Jonah   93
Jonas, Justus   24, 110 n. 95, 164 n. 71, 166 n. 77, 167
Jordanes   49
Josephus, Flavius   42
Judah, Patriarch   319
Judex, Matthaeus   243
Judith, Empress   1
Julius Africanus   40
Julius Excluded from Heaven   24
Julius II, Pope   180, 183
Julius III, Pope   249
Julius, Duke of Braunschweig-Lüneburg   309
Justin   35–37, 118, 163, 211, 351
Justinian I, Emperor   132 n. 194, 133, 155 n. 41

Karlstadt, Andreas Bodenstein von   182
Keckermann, Bartholomaus   256 n. 183, 290
Khunrath, Heinrich   110
Kilian, Wolfgang   320–323
Krause, Johann Gottlieb   331
Krell, Nicolaus   277
Kretzmann, Paul   301–302

Lactantius   41
Lambert of Hersfeld   22
Landolfo Colonna   60–61
Languet, Hubert   252, 258
Lanquet, Thomas   219–221, 351 n. 48
Laski, Johannes   138
Lechler, Martin   265
Leipzig Debate   18
Leipzig Interim   239
Leo III, Pope   1, 81, 154 n. 38, 156 n. 43
Leo VIII, Pope   51
Leo X, Pope   148 n. 17, 183
Levi, Patriarch   65
Libanius Gallus   108
Lipsius, Justus   292
Liudprand of Cremona   48
Livy   22, 85, 116, 251 n. 164

INDEX

Lothar I, Emperor 1
Lothar III, Emperor 159–160, 212, 305
Lotter, Melchior (the Elder) 86
Lotter, Michael 211, 239 n. 126
Lotter, Tobias 322–323, 328
Louis the Pious, Emperor 1, 194
Louis XIV, King of France 2 n. 4
Lucian 21, 87
Lucidus (Johannes Lucidus Samotheus) 285
Lucretia 150
Ludwig IV of Bavaria, Emperor 59–60, 143
Ludwig the German, Emperor 1
Luke, Evangelist 55
Luther, Martin 4–6, 10, 18, 20–21, 25, 27, 32, 86, 110–112, 114–115, 119, 123, 137–139, 142–143, 145, 148, 162, 164 n. 72, 165 n. 73, 166 n. 76–77, 168, 169, 173 n. 92, 182–183, 197 n. 195, 199–200, 202, 203 n. 211, 204–206, 208–209, 215, 220, 225, 229–231, 236, 238–239, 246 n. 147, 248, 252, 256, 258–259, 272 n. 227, 285, 291, 296–298, 300, 302, 314, 328, 334, 342
Lyndsay, Sir David 222
Lynne, Walter 27 n. 94, 221–222

Magdeburg Centuries 9, 16, 27, 243–245, 299
Magog 119 n. 142, 172–174, 189
Major, Georg 211, 259, 351
Manichaeism 176–177, 182
Marcus Aurelius, Emperor 130
Mark Anthony 186
Marsilius of Padua 60–62
Martin of Troppau 55–60, 62–64, 66, 68, 76, 81, 146, 156, 207, 279
Martinus Polonus *See* Martin of Troppau
Matilda of Tuscany 160
Maximilian I, Emperor 61, 71, 81–82, 95, 144, 154, 161, 185, 205, 267, 287, 348
Maximilian II, Emperor 252, 254, 272
Maximinus I, Emperor 130
Meibom, Heinrich 309–310
Melanchthon, Philipp *passim*
Menius, Eusebius 198 n. 197, 258–260, 265, 272, 349
Menius, Justus 258–259
Meusel, Johann Georg 337
Michaelis, Johann David 326
Mierdman, Steven 27 n. 94, 221
Milichius, Jakob 139

Milton, John 223
Mohammed *See* Muhammad
Moller, Daniel Wilhelm 338–339, 343–344
Monogrammist AW 167 n. 80
Mordeisen, Ulrich 247
Morel, Guillaume 215–216, 347
Moritz, Elector of Saxony 223 n. 110, 238–239, 254
Moses 45, 47, 328
Mosheim, Johann Lorenz von 326
Muhammad 133, 170–173, 177, 190–191, 328
Münster, Sebastian 8–9, 72, 213
Müntzer, Thomas 19, 21, 24, 162, 182–183
Mylius, Martin 337, 344

Naegelin, Johannes 89
Nanni, Giovanni *See* Annius of Viterbo
Nauclerus, Johannes 21, 71–82, 118, 120, 132, 151, 156 n. 45, 158, 190, 212, 225, 245 n. 146
Nebuchadnezzar II, King of Babylon 38, 76, 164–165, 305, 315–316, 319
Nero, Emperor 132 n. 194, 176
Newton, Sir Isaac 223
Nicolas II, Pope 178
Nicolas V, Pope 179
Nicolas of Cusa 61–62, 78–79, 155
Ninus, King of Assyria 56
Noah 45, 78, 95, 97–98, 119, 212, 269, 328, 341
Notker Balbus 48
Novatianism 177
Nuremberg Chronicle
    See also Schedel, Hartmann 8–9, 66–68, 70–71, 74–75, 81, 146, 211, 279

Odoacer, King of Italy 52
Oecolampadius, Johann 182
Oertel, Veit 86 n. 9
Oldenborch, Niclaes von *See* Mierdman, Steven
Oporinus, Johannes 216, 244, 338, 348
Origen 177, 199
Orosius, Paulus 42–50, 54, 56, 58, 63, 68, 76, 149, 206, 333
Osiander, Andreas 111, 240
Osman, Sultan 172
Otto I, Emperor 51–52, 57, 68, 70, 81
Otto III, Emperor 58, 66, 81, 156–157, 178, 184, 195–196, 302

Otto of Freising, Bishop 50–53, 63

Panvinio, Onofrio 228, 285
Paradin, Guillaume 214, 347
Paris, Prince of Troy 150
Paul IV, Pope 192, 223
Paul of Burgos 146
Paul of Samosata 189–190
Paul, Saint 176, 184
Peace of Augsburg (1555) 4, 6, 145, 299, 302, 304
Peace of Westphalia (1648) 3, 299, 303, 306, 330
Pelagianism 177
Pelagius 177 n. 107, 224, 341
Pelagius of Majorca 107–109
Perlach, Andreas 104–110, 115, 127, 136
Peter Lombard 65
Peter, Saint 3, 44, 176, 184
Peucer, Caspar *passim*
Peucer, Magdalena 122, 253, 272
Peutinger, Conrad 213
Pezel, Christoph 267, 269, 272, 277, 285, 349
Pflaum, Jacob 92 n. 36
Philip I, Landgrave of Hesse 238
Philip the Arabian, Emperor 130
Philip the Upright, Elector Palatine 185
Philip II, King of Spain 224
Phocas, Emperor 47, 178, 319 n. 136
Piccolomini, Aeneas Silvius *See* Pius II, Pope
Pippin the Short, King of the Franks 155, 194
Piscator, Hermann 243 n. 138
Pius II, Pope 8, 70–73, 142
Pius IV, Pope 223
Pölitz, Karl Heinrich Ludwig 330–332
Pollicarius, Johannes 272 n. 227
Polybius 35–36
Pompeius Trogus 35–36
Pontius Pilate 65
Postel, Guillaume 215
Prätorius, Abdias 250
pseudo-Berosus 118–119, 212
pseudo-Metasthenes 118, 120–121, 128–129
pseudo-Methodius 98, 172–173, 189
pseudo-Philo 120, 125
Ptolemy, Claudius 37 n. 18, 95, 107, 131 n. 188
Pufendorf, Samuel von 306–309, 312

Quenstedt, Johann Andreas 300

Ralegh, Sir Walter 223
Ranke, Leopold von 335
Regino of Prüm 48
Regiomantanus (Johannes Müller von Königsberg) 92 n. 36
Rehm, Margaretha 138–139
Reineccius, Reiner 274, 289, 296 n. 58, 309
Reinhold, Erasmus 110, 253
Reinking, Theodor von 303–305
Reuchlin, Johann 72–73, 185
Reynmann, Leonhard 93
Rhau Press
  See also Rhau, Georg 247, 259–260, 264, 348
Rhau, Georg 125–126, 140, 210, 235, 247, 340–342, 344–346
Rhode, Francis 125, 210 n. 14
Rhodoman, Laurentius 331
Rigler, Christoph 101
Ritter, Johann Daniel 332
Rolevinck, Werner 63–70, 77, 146, 151
Romulus, King of Rome 328
Romulus Augustulus, Emperor 193
Rudolf of Rheinfelden 159
Rudolph of Hapsburg, Emperor 57
Rufinus 86 n. 13

Sabinus, Anna (Melanchthon) 139
Sabinus, Anna 259
Sabinus, Georg 114, 122, 137–139, 235 n. 115
Sahl ibn Bishr *See* Zebel the Arab
Sallust 21
Sarah, Matriarch 172
Savigny, Friedrich Carl von 307
Schedel, Hartmann
  See also Nuremberg Chronicle 8, 66–70, 75–78, 81–82, 132, 146, 211, 279
Scheurl, Christoph 85, 331
Schirlentz, Nicolaus 345
Schosser, Johannes 248 n. 155
Schroeckh, Johann Matthias 325–330, 332
Schurzfleisch, Heinrich Leonhard 331
Schurzfleisch, Konrad Samuel 312–314, 331
Schütz, Christian 271
Schwertel, Johann 264, 348 n. 40
Seitz, Alexander 93–97, 132

INDEX 541

Seitz, Peter 347–348
Seld, Georg Sigismund 195, 258
Sergius II, Pope 178
Sergius III, Pope 178 n. 116
Servetus, Michael 190
Seth 131 n. 188
Setzer, Johann 214
Seutter, Matthias 322–327
Seymour, Edward (Duke of Somerset) 220
Sigebert of Gembloux 16, 50, 158, 159 n. 54, 225
Sigismud, Emperor 179–180
Sigismund I, King of Poland 111, 138
Sigismund, Archbishop of Magdeburg 248, 251, 255, 259
Simler, Josias 342–343
Sleidanus, Johann 9, 21, 234–235, 273, 278, 283, 307, 309, 311–316, 351
Solis, Vergil 258
Solomon, King of Israel 47
Spalatin, Georg 5, 251 n. 162
Spangenberg, Cyriakus 152
Spener, Jakob Karl 331
Stabius, Johann 154
Staphylus, Friedrich 246
Starke, Christoph 301 n. 81
Starke, Johann Georg 301
Steiner, Heinrich 125, 210 n. 14, 210 n. 17, 341
Stephen II, Pope 80
Stöffler, Johannes 89, 92
Stoll, Michael 266
Stössel, Johann 271
Stow, John 222
Strabo 116, 118 n. 132
Strauch, Aegidius 311–314, 331
Strigel, Victorin 12 n. 38, 338, 353
Strobel, Georg Theodor 19 n. 63, 339, 344–345, 348 n. 40
Strupp, Johann Ulrich 265
Suetonius 85
Suleyman the Magnificent, Sultan 144, 161, 232
Sulpitius Severus 40
Surius, Laurentius 74, 245 n. 146
Sydney, Sir Philip 222
Sylvester I, Pope 54
Sylvester II, Pope 178

Székely, István 350–351

Tacitus 24, 71, 78, 84, 119, 213, 267, 348
Tambach, Gottfried 266 n. 218
Tarquinius Superbus 56
Tauler, Johannes 203
Tetzel, Johann 21 n. 72
Thales 131 n. 188
Theodoret of Cyrus 292
Theodosius I, Emperor 155, 328
Thiessen, Francis 19 n. 64
Thiessen, Nicolaus 19 n. 64
Thucydides 22, 86–87, 251 n. 164
Tiberius, Emperor 175, 219
Tilemann, Friedrich 331
Timaeus 232
Todaeus, Nikolaus 331
Torsellini, Orazio 228, 278
Treatise on the Power and Primacy of the Pope 297–298
Treaty of Verdun (843) 2
Trithemius, Johannes 108, 110
Trozendorf, Valentin Friedland 253
Tuisco 78, 119, 212

Ulhart, Philip 346
Ulrich of Augsburg, Saint 346
Ursberger Chronicle 22, 50, 63 n. 131, 160, 207

Valens, Emperor 42
Valentinian III, Emperor 155
Valgrisi, Vincenzo 224
Valla, Lorenzo 61–62, 78–79, 143, 155
Vergenhans, Johannes *See* Nauclerus, Johannes
Vergil 36
Virdung, Johann 95
Vives, Juan 12 n. 37
Volkmar, Johann Georg 331

Waldseemüller, Martin 169
Wanckel, Johannes 331
Warburg, Aby 10–11, 92, 121, 340
Webster, Noah 216 n. 43
Wenceslaus, Emperor 70, 181 n. 126
Wigand, Johann 243
Wilhelm IV, Landgrave of Hesse-Kassel 274
William of Ockham 60

Wimpfeling, Jacob   71–72, 78, 155, 212
Winsemius, Vitus *See* Oertel, Veit
Wittenberg Annals   20, 24
Wolch, Nicolas   265
Wolf, Johann   284–285, 292
Wyclif, John   203–204

Xenophon   22, 185 n. 143, 251
Xerxes I, King of Persia   132

Zachary, Pope   184
Zebel the Arab   110
Ziska, Jan *See* Zizka, Jan
Zizka, Jan   181
Zöpfel, David   240–243, 248, 258, 261, 264 n. 203, 341
Zwingli, Ulrich   126 n. 169, 132 n. 194, 133, 182–183